CLASSICAL MYTHOLOGY IN ENGLISH LITERATURE

From the Middle Ages to the beginning of the twentieth century, writers in English have continually returned to the stories of Greek and Roman mythology. In the process, those stories have often been transformed out of all recognition. *Classical Mythology in English Literature* brings together a range of English versions of three classical myths, allowing students for the first time to explore the ways in which they have been reinterpreted and reinvented by writers throughout history.

Beginning with a concise introduction to the main classical sources and principal Greco-Roman gods and heroes, the anthology then focuses on three stories: Orpheus and Eurydice, Venice and Adonis, and Pygmalion. Each section begins with the classical sources and ends with contemporary versions, and in the intervening centuries we see the ancient tales successively transformed by Christian allegorists and chivalric romancers, philosophers and pornographers, Victorian mystics, twentieth-century Freudians and feminists. The spelling has been modernised throughout, and Geoffrey Miles supplies helpful introductions and comprehensive notes and glossaries.

Geoffrey Miles is at the School of English, Film and Theatre, Victoria University of Wellington, New Zealand. He is the author of *Shakespeare and the Constant Romans*.

CLASSICAL MYTHOLOGY IN ENGLISH LITERATURE

A critical anthology

Edited by Geoffrey Miles

London and New York

First published 1999
by Routledge
11 New Fetter Lane, London EC4P 4EE

Simultaneously published in the USA and Canada
by Routledge
29 West 35th Street, New York, NY 10001

Routledge is an imprint of the Taylor & Francis Group

Typeset in Baskerville by RefineCatch Limited, Bungay, Suffolk
Printed and bound in Great Britain by
TJ International Ltd, Padstow, Cornwall

British Library Cataloguing in Publication Data
A catalogue record for this book is available from the British Library

Library of Congress Cataloging in Publication Data
Classical mythology in English literature: a critical anthology / edited by Geoffrey Miles.
p. cm.
Includes bibliographical references and indexes.
1. English literature. 2. Mythology, Classical – Literary collections. 3. Pygmalion (Greek mythology) – Literary collections. 4. Orpheus (Greek mythology) – Literary collections. 5. Adonis (Greek deity) – Literary collections. 6. English literature – Classical influences. 7. Mythology, Classical, in literature.
I. Miles, Geoffrey.
PR1111.M95C58 1999
820.8′.015 – dc21 98–43914
CIP

ISBN 0–415–14754–9 (hbk)
ISBN 0–415–14755–7 (pbk)

To my mother

CONTENTS

CONTENTS

TEXTS

PREFACE

This book has grown out of an undergraduate course on 'Classical Traditions in English Literature' which I have taught for several years at Victoria University of Wellington. One of the aims of the course was to take a handful of classical myths and trace the ways in which they had been reworked and reinterpreted by writers in English from the Middle Ages to the 1990s. I quickly discovered that, though there were many texts on classical mythology and some excellent studies of the reception of particular myths, there was no anthology which brought together the kind of material I wished to teach. So, with scissors and paste, I started assembling my own anthology, which has evolved into this volume.

The enormous number and diversity of English rewritings of classical myth has meant that the volume has swelled in size and narrowed in range, until it now covers just three myths: those of Orpheus, Venus and Adonis, and Pygmalion. Needless to say, these three do not adequately represent the whole of Greek mythology – but then no selection could. They do, however, have sufficient thematic links (as I have suggested in chapter 1) to make interesting comparisons possible, while their popularity with English writers and readers has allowed the inclusion of a wide range of texts, both famous and obscure. I hope, if this volume finds a market among teachers and students, to follow it up with further volumes covering other myths – the great heroic sagas, for instance, or the Trojan War, or the women of Greek mythology.

In selecting texts, my main principle has been to represent as fully as possible the variety of different interpretations and treatments, together with their chronological span and geographical range (Scottish, Irish, American, Canadian, Australian, and New Zealand writers are represented). Most of the great canonical writers of English literature find a place here, but mingled with the minor, the unknown, and the positively bizarre. Indeed, I have regretfully abridged some of the more famous (but easily accessible) texts in order to make space for lesser texts that provide interesting comparisons and contexts: Shakespeare's *Venus and Adonis* is familiar, but readers are less likely to stumble across (say) Bartholomew Griffin, Richard Barnfield, William Browne, or Thomas Heywood. However, nothing has been included that I did not think worth reading in its own right (even if occasionally for its entertaining badness), rather than as mere historical background. The introductions to each chapter sketch a context for the texts and glance at other texts not included (bibliographical information is supplied in the list of 'Other Versions' at the end of each chapter).

Wherever possible the texts have been newly edited from the original editions. My aim has been to minimise artificial obstacles between students and the texts. To that end, spelling has been consistently modernised in all post-medieval texts (including Spenser – it seems pedantic to maintain Spenser's deliberately archaic spellings when his work is already so genuinely archaic to present-day students). Punctuation has also been freely modernised in texts before 1800; after that date I have retained the original punctuation apart from altering some obsolete forms (such as the comma–dash combination). To the same end I have provided fairly detailed footnotes, as well as marginal glosses (marked >) for Middle English or Scots texts. From experience in teaching many of these texts, I have erred on the side of over- rather than under-annotation; I hope those who do not need the assistance will bear with the irritation of being told what they already know.

I am grateful to Victoria University of Wellington for a year's leave in 1996 to work on this book, and for a subvention grant towards the cost of permissions to use copyright material; and to the librarians of Victoria University, the Bodleian Library, and the Library of Congress, for help in locating material.

I owe a great debt to my colleagues who have contributed over the last six years to the 'Classical Traditions' course: Robert Easting, Vincent O'Sullivan, Harry Ricketts, Kathryn Walls, and especially Kim Walker, who with characteristic generosity allowed me to use her lecture material on the Pygmalion legend, and Heidi Thomson, whose energy and enthusiasm kick-started this book into life. I am grateful to Paul Millar, David Norton and Peter Whiteford for frequent advice and support, and to John Davidson for helping to set me straight on Adonis. Thanks too to my students on the course for many helpful discussions of the material. My editors at Routledge, Talia Rodgers, Kate Chenevix Trench, Sophie Powell, and Jason Arthur, have been helpful and patient. Finally, once again, thanks to Deborah, Jennifer, David, Celia, Barry, Marjan, and Marian, for friendship, distraction, and sanity maintenance.

Sources of copyright material are acknowledged in the footnotes to the relevant texts. It has not been possible to trace all copyright holders before this book went to press. The editor and publishers will gladly insert further acknowledgements in subsequent editions.

Geoffrey Miles
Wellington, July 1998

Part 1

1

THE MYTH-KITTY

> As a guiding principle I believe that every poem must be its own sole freshly created universe, and therefore have no belief in 'tradition' or a common myth-kitty . . . To me the whole of the ancient world, the whole of classical and biblical mythology, means very little, and I think that using them today not only fills poems full of dead spots but dodges the poet's duty to be original.
>
> (Larkin 1983: 69)

Philip Larkin's dismissal of the notion of a 'myth-kitty' raises a real question. Why, at the start of the twenty-first century, should writers, readers, or students of English literature still be taking an interest in the fantastic tales told by Greek peasants three millennia ago? Why should I, at a university on the Pacific rim twelve thousand miles from Mount Olympus, be compiling yet another volume about the classical myths and their influence?

The shortest answer is that, despite Larkin's disbelief, a classical 'tradition' does exist: a continuous line of inheritance and influence connects ancient Greece and Rome with the modern 'western' world, shaping our arts, our instutitions, our values and philosophies. One small aspect of that tradition has been the use of classical mythology in English literature. For many centuries writers in English have been able to draw upon a common stock of mythological stories, characters, and images – a 'myth-kitty', to use Larkin's derisive term – in the confidence that their readers will recognise and understand their allusions. In the words of the critic George Steiner,

> From Chaucer to [Eliot's] *Sweeney among the Nightingales* much of English poetry has relied on a code of instantaneous recognition. Where the code lapses . . . a good deal of the poetry may lapse too.
>
> (Quoted in Radice 1973: 13)

For educated readers from the fourteenth to the early twentieth century, a reference to (say) Hercules, or Venus, or Helen, or the sack of Troy, could be relied on to produce 'instantaneous recognition' – not an anxious search of school memories for a vaguely familiar name, but the involuntary and subliminal flash of images and associations that a modern reader would have on encountering the name of (say) Superman, or Sherlock Holmes, or Marilyn Monroe. Hence mythological references can work as a language, a 'code', to communicate instant and vivid meaning. When Hamlet describes his mother at his father's funeral as 'like Niobe, all tears', or says that his hated uncle is 'no more like my father / Than I to Hercules' (*Hamlet*, 1. 2. 149, 152–3), he is invoking mythical archetypes: Hercules, the strongest and bravest of men; Niobe, who wept for her children's deaths until she turned to stone, the ultimate in grief and misery. The mythic allusions, set against the realities of Hamlet's own situation, convey his disillusionment and self-loathing with extraordinary vividness and economy – so long as the audience understands the code.

The language or code of mythology, however, is not a fixed one. The mythic images may remain stable and simple, but the interpretation of the stories shifts from period to period and from writer to writer. For instance, the image of Orpheus the musician has remained more or less stable over the centuries (though his lyre may change to a lute, a violin, or an electric guitar), but the meaning of his story shifts radically. For the Greeks, he was a religious teacher and mystic; for the Romans, a tragically bereaved lover. In the Middle Ages he may be a symbol of sinful man trying to save his soul from hell, or of Christ successfully saving human souls. In the Renaissance he is a symbol of cosmic order and harmony. In the eighteenth century he is the great civiliser, bringing order and culture to society. In the nineteenth century he is again primarily the tragic lover. In the twentieth century he may be a fearless explorer of the darkness of the soul, a symbol of the limitations of human art, a revolutionary liberator, or an arrogant male chauvinist. To study the evolution of a single myth over time reveals not only the richness and adaptability of the myths, but also the characteristic themes and preoccupations of successive literary periods.

Moroever, these changing interpretations do not simply displace each other, but rather build up on top of one another, creating increasingly complex layers of meaning. A myth is in a sense a palimpsest – a document that has been repeatedly written over, so that traces of earlier texts can be faintly read beneath the surface text. For instance, a feminist text like Elaine Feinstein's 'The Feast of Eurydice' in a sense depends on the earlier, more heroic views of Orpheus which the reader brings to the poem, and which partly emerge between the lines of the poem itself. The significance of Orpheus, in a twentieth-century text, is potentially a compound of all the various significances he has acquired in earlier texts.

It is, I believe, this combination of simple 'instantaneous recognition' and complex and multiple meanings which makes classical mythology a continuingly popular resource for writers. Even if it were possible for a writer to be, as Larkin demands, totally original, and to create, like God, a 'sole freshly created universe' in every work, such a work would lack the richness and complexity attainable by drawing on the centuries of tradition accumulated around the figures in the 'myth-kitty'.

The main purpose of this anthology is to bring together versions and rewritings of three major classical myths, starting with the ancient sources and then moving through English literature from the Middle Ages to the present day. The stories are those of Orpheus the musician, Pygmalion the sculptor, and the lovers Venus and Adonis. These are not necessarily 'typical' or 'representative' myths; many typical concerns of Greek mythology – war, heroic quests, hubris and nemesis, the family feud – are barely touched on in them. Nevertheless they are linked by a knot of common concerns which make them interesting to compare: art, and love, and death, and the borderlines between life and death and immortality, and the relationship between the human and the divine. Perhaps more important, each has been treated by a number of major writers across the centuries, making it possible to see how the treatment of each myth shifts with changing literary fashions, moral values, and intellectual concerns.

First, however, the book aims to provide a basic introduction to Greek mythology, a kind of primer to the 'code'. The remainder of this chapter will introduce the principal ancient sources of the myths, and sketch the history of classical mythology in English literature. Chapter 2 will briefly introduce the classical gods, goddesses, and demigods; and chapter 3 is a rapid survey of the whole story of Greek myth, from the creation of the universe down to the foundation of Rome.

The ancient sources of the myths

The ultimate 'source' of the Greek myths is, of course, the people who originally made them up, told them as stories, and passed them on to later generations. That source is inaccessible, though we can speculate about it. Scholars have propounded many views of the origins of myths: that they were pre-scientific attempts to explain the world and its phenomena; that they were aetiological stories, explaining the origins of things; that they acted as 'charters', explaining and justifying social institutions; that they were records of religious rituals, garbled over time into narratives of real events; that they were political propaganda; that they taught moral lessons; that they were historical facts distorted and fantasticated over time into legends of gods and superheroes (this theory is known as Euhemerism after its ancient inventor).

The most sensible view (argued by Kirk 1974) is that myths can be any or all of these things; no single theory can explain all the great variety of traditional stories told by the Greeks or any other people. For example, the figure of Zeus the sky god, gathering clouds and hurling thunderbolts, is clearly a primitive attempt to explain weather. The story of how Zeus was tricked by Prometheus is an aetiological or charter-myth, explaining why the Greeks ate the meat of their sacrificed animals and sent the gods only the smoke and bones. On a higher level, the figure of Zeus as archetypal king, giver of laws, protector of guests and strangers, functions as a kind of moral charter-myth, justifying the importance of law and custom. On the other hand, the stories of Zeus's adulteries with assorted women and nymphs seem to be told primarily for entertainment – though they may serve both a political purpose (in tracing a historical family back to an ancestor casually begotten by Zeus) and a social purpose (in embodying conventional assumptions about male/female roles and power relationships). No single view of myth will explain all the ways in which the myths about Zeus work.

To take another example: the three myths dealt with in this anthology seem to be of quite different types. The story of Venus and Adonis seems to be an ancient 'explanatory' myth, which traces the fertility of the world to the sexual union of the goddess and her consort, and the cycle of the seasons to the repeated ritual death and rebirth of the young god. The story of Orpheus may be explained in Euhemerist terms: it is possible that he was originally a real person, revered by the Greeks as a poet and religious teacher, who came to be an archetype of the poet-musician and a symbol of the powers and limitations of human art. The story of Pygmalion may have had a ritual origin, in the sacred marriage of a king to the goddess's statue; but it has been thoroughly remade by the poet Ovid into a humorous literary fantasy about art and love. The interesting thing is that all three legends, as retold in classical and English texts, cover almost exactly the same range from profound seriousness to sheer frivolity. The origins of a myth seem to have little to do with how it is treated by later writers.

The primary concern of this book is with the literary uses of myth, and by the time the myths were written down by classical writers they were already generations or centuries removed from the people who had originally created them. For this reason I will spend no more time on the origins of the myths, but turn instead to the literary texts in which they were handed down.

First in age and authority are **Homer**'s two epic poems, the *Iliad* and the *Odyssey*. Almost everything about Homer is debatable, including whether or not he existed; scholars agree that the Homeric poems derive from a tradition of orally improvised poetry, but disagree whether a single author (or two authors) put the poems into their present form. The orthodox current view seems to be that there was a 'Homer' around the end of the eighth century BC. What is indisputable is that the Homeric poems became the basis of Greek literature and education, carrying the combined cultural prestige of Shakespeare, Chaucer, and the Bible for English readers. Both poems deal with the stories of the Trojan War; the *Iliad* focuses on the destructive anger of the Greek warrior Achilles, his quarrel with his commander Agamemnon, and his eventual duel to the death with the Trojan Hector; the *Odyssey* follows a different kind of hero, the patient and resourceful Odysseus, on his journey home after the war. Homer created the classic picture of the Greek heroic age, and also of the very human, quarrelsome and meddling Olympian gods. Other poets completed the '**epic cycle**' by filling in the gaps around the Homeric epics, but these later and lesser poems are now almost entirely lost.

Contemporary with Homer, or a little later, is **Hesiod**. His *Theogony* ('Origin of the Gods') gives the fullest account of the earliest Greek myths, dealing with the creation of the world and the early battles of gods, Titans, and Giants leading up to the establishment of Zeus as ruler of the universe. His *Works and Days*, a didactic poem about farming life, also includes the myths of Prometheus and Pandora and the Four Ages.

In the so-called 'lyric age' (mid-seventh to mid-fifth centuries), the dominant literary form was song: poems to be publicly sung, either by an individual or by a choir. From the earlier part of this period probably come the **Homeric Hymns** (which, despite their traditional name, have no connection with Homer): choral hymns to various deities, sometimes including vivid retellings of stories about them. The five longest hymns are those to Demeter (telling the story of her search for her lost daughter Persephone), to Apollo (about his birth and the founding of his temple at Delphi), to Hermes (about his mischievous childhood thefts), to Aphrodite (about her love for Anchises), and to Dionysus (about his transformation of a band of pirates into dolphins). Other lyric poets also take their subjects from myth, but the treatment becomes gradually less narrative and more allusive. An early poet like **Stesichorus** writes miniature epics (his lost song about Hercules' battle with Geryon ran to over 1,800 lines); later poets like **Simonides**, **Sappho**, and **Bacchylides** focus on brief, vivid vignettes of mythic scenes and characters. Most subtly, **Pindar** (early fifth century), in his odes in honour of victors at the athletic games, makes an art of quick, glancing allusion to a variety of myths. His audiences were clearly expected to know the stories well enough to pick up the allusions and understand their often oblique and unstated relevance to the subject of the ode.

Myth is also central to classical Athenian drama. The tragic playwrights **Aeschylus** (late sixth to early fifth century), **Sophocles** (fifth century), and **Euripides** (fifth century) took their plots from the age of heroes and the Trojan War, and many of the great tragic stories – Agamemnon and his children, Oedipus, Pentheus, Jason and Medea, Phaedra and Hippolytus – took on their classic form in their plays. The dramatists took stories which were already familiar to their audience, and reinterpreted them in the light of contemporary issues and shifting ethical debates; Euripides' plays about the Trojan War, for instance, clearly offer a commentary on Athens's involvement in the Peloponnesian War. In at least one case – the plays of Aeschylus, Sophocles, and Euripides about the revenge of Orestes and Electra – we can see all three dramatists successively reworking a single myth, casting a progressively more 'realistic' and disillusioned eye on the heroic story. The comic playwright **Aristophanes** (fifth to early fourth century) also on occasion plays irreverently with myth, as in *Birds* (in which an Athenian entrepreneur founds a kingdom of the birds and blockades Mount Olympus) or *Frogs* (in which the god Dionysus disguises himself rather unconvincingly as Heracles for a trip to the underworld).

While Greek poets and dramatists were reworking the myths, Greek philosophers were beginning to criticise them. **Plato** (early fourth century), for instance, though he was happy to create his own allegorical myths (such as the vision of Er in the *Republic*), attacked the traditional tales of the gods' tricks and thefts and adulteries as immoral, objected to their central role in literature and education, and proposed to ban them from his ideal state. Plato's attitude is the sign of a growing gap between the traditional myths and the beliefs of the educated Greek citizen.

That gap widened in the Hellenistic age (late fourth and third centuries), the period after the conquests of Alexander the Great, in which Greek culture becomes a world culture and the cultural centre shifts eastward from Athens to Alexandria. With the collapse of the Greek city states, the old religion lost much of its power, and the old connection between the myths and the civic life of the state, when Homer's epics or Pindar's odes or Aeschylus's tragedies would be performed before people to whom these stories were vital cultural treasures, was broken. For the Hellenistic writers the myths are essentially good stories, and their treatment is both more romantic and more realistic than that of the classical Greeks: **Apollonius of Rhodes**'s short epic *Argonautica*, about the voyage of the Argo, is as full of magic and marvels as a medieval romance, but also focuses closely on the psychology of a young woman in love; **Theocritus**'s *Idylls* juxtapose mythic stories with down-to-earth domestic detail. At the same time myth becomes a subject of scholarly study: **Callimachus** in his *Aetia* ('Origins') takes pride in his learning, searching out rare stories and arcane allusions to test and tease his sophisticated readers.

For related reasons, this period also sees the first handbooks of mythography: pocket guides to the myths for those who wish to appear better educated than they are. Later works like **Apollodorus**'s *Library*, **Eratosthenes**' *Catasterisms* ('Star Legends'), **Antoninus Liberalis**'s *Metamorphoses*, and the Roman **Hyginus**'s *Fables* (all dating from the first or second centuries AD) are invaluable resources for modern scholars, often giving the only connected account of myths that would otherwise only exist in scattered poetic allusions.

The Romans, who took over so many Greek literary forms – epic, lyric, comedy, tragedy, pastoral, and so on – also took over Greek mythology as a central poetic subject. The first work of Latin literature, appropriately, was a translation of Homer's *Odyssey*. Two Roman writers made especially vital contributions to the transmission of classical mythology, and both of them belong to the Augustan period – the time of the first Roman emperor Augustus, from around 40 BC to AD 14, traditionally considered the high point of Latin literature.

Virgil began by writing pastoral poems, the *Eclogues*, and a didactic poem about farming life, the *Georgics*; both include mythological elements, notably the story of Orpheus and Eurydice at the end of the *Georgics*. But his masterpiece was the *Aeneid*, an epic poem about the escape of the Trojan prince Aeneas after the fall of Troy, and his long wanderings and wars before he founded a settlement in Italy that was to be the origin of Rome. In this work Virgil is both challenging Homer's supremacy as a writer of epic, and also attempting to tie Rome in to the great design of Greek mythology – though, as a gesture of independence, he derives Rome's ancestry not from the Greeks but from their ancient rivals the Trojans. The *Aeneid* is a great feat, the construction almost from scratch of a new national myth.

Ovid, a generation younger than Virgil, is a very different poet. He made his name as the author of light-hearted, cynical love poems, the *Amores*, and a witty self-help manual for lovers, the *Ars Amatoria* ('Art of Love'). Later he turned to mythology, in the *Heroides*, letters from mythological heroines to their lovers; the *Metamorphoses*; and the unfinished *Fasti* ('Holidays'), an account of the Roman calendar, apparently cut short when Augustus exiled Ovid to the Black Sea (partly for his immoral poetry and partly for a mysterious 'error' that may have been connected with a sex scandal in the imperial family). Ovid's masterpiece is the *Metamorphoses*: a collection of mythological tales from the creation of the world to the deification of Julius Caesar, woven together in 'one continuous song' by the unifying theme of metamorphosis or change of shape. The poem itself is metamorphic, slipping from story to story on what seems like a continuous stream of free association, while continually changing moods – ironic humour, romance, pathos, moral earnestness, violence and horror, and then back to comedy again . . . The *Metamorphoses* was for many centuries one of the most popular books in Europe, and it is by far the most important text in transmitting the myths to later writers.

Some later Latin works contributed in a smaller way to the mythological tradition, such as **Seneca**'s bloody and horrific tragedies (loved by the Elizabethans), or **Statius**'s *Thebaid*, an epic on the war of the Seven Against Thebes (much respected in the Middle Ages). Perhaps the last classical writer to give a distinctive turn to the myths was the Syrian Greek satirist **Lucian** (second century AD), whose 'Dialogues of the Gods' and 'Dialogues of the Dead' show up the absurdity of the traditional tales by treating them with poker-faced literal-mindedness.

Finally, Christian writers like **St Clement of Alexandria** (second century AD), **St Jerome**, and **St Augustine of Hippo** (both fourth to fifth century AD), in their polemics against pagan religion, not only contributed to a continuing debate about the meaning and value of the myths, but also (unintentionally) preserved accounts of myths that would otherwise have been forgotten. One author on the borderline between pagan and Christian is particularly important: **Boethius** (fifth to sixth century AD), whose enormously popular *Consolation of Philosophy* set an example for the use of classical myth as moral and spiritual allegory.

The myths in English literature

The fall of the Roman Empire in western Europe – a long, slow collapse over the course of two centuries, but symbolically marked by the deposition of the last Roman emperor by a Gothic chieftain in AD 476 – was the end of Rome's political power, but not its literature and culture. Throughout the 'Dark Ages' (fifth to tenth centuries), and the 'Middle Ages' that followed, it was the Christian Church which preserved classical literature. In this context 'classical' effectively means 'Latin': hardly anyone in the west knew Greek, and Greek literature fell virtually into oblivion (with the exception of a few authors such as the philosopher Aristotle, who survived in Latin and – later – Arabic translations). Latin works, on the other hand, were repeatedly copied and recopied, ensuring not only that they survived but that they continued to be a living cultural influence.

To preserve Latin literature inevitably meant preserving classical mythology. This posed a serious problem for the Church and Christian readers: the myths were an integral part of the literature they loved and revered (especially the poetry of Virgil and Ovid), but also part of a false, pagan belief system. The most popular medieval solution to this dilemma was to treat the myths allegorically. This was a strategy already tried out by pagan critics, who had suggested that (for example) the voyages of Odysseus or Aeneas could be seen as allegorical of the human journey through life, or that the disturbing story of Cronus eating his children could be rationalised as a symbol of devouring Time; it was also one familiar to Christian interpreters of the Bible, who were accustomed to read the biblical narratives on both a literal and an allegorical level. By allegorical interpretation any myth could be given a Christian meaning. For instance, in the anonymous thirteenth-century *Ovide Moralisé*, a 70,000-line moral commentary on the *Metamorphoses*, the story of Apollo's attempted rape of Daphne becomes a symbol of the Incarnation: Daphne is the Virgin Mary, and Apollo crowning himself with the laurel is Christ entering the womb of his mortal mother.

At the same time, intermingled with this earnest allegorical tradition, there is an enjoyment of the mythical stories for their own sake – especially in the so-called 'Ovidian age' of the eleventh to fifteenth centuries. In fourteenth-century English poets like Chaucer and Gower, it is hard to draw a line between where the stories are being told as moral *exempla* and where they are simply being told as good stories. Medieval writers easily assimilated the ancient stories to the story-telling conventions of medieval romance; with little sense of historical distance or anachronism, they unselfconsciously imagined the ancient characters in the dress and behaviour of their own times. So the anonymous author of 'Sir Orfeo' imagines Orpheus as a troubadour-king rescuing his 'dame Heurodis' from the fairy king who has stolen her away to fairyland. In medieval hands 'the Matter of Troy' becomes a romance of chivalric combat and love, and in Chaucer's *Troilus and Criseyde* and Henryson's *Testament of Criseyde* the war of Greeks and Trojans becomes merely backdrop to the tragic love story of prince Troilus and his faithless Cressida.[1]

The Renaissance was given that name ('rebirth') by those who lived through it, because they saw it as the rediscovery of a lost classical world, the reawakening of civilisation after the long darkness of the Middle Ages.[2] Obviously this is an emotive and value-laden term, and some modern scholars prefer the more neutral label 'the early modern period' (which perhaps raises just as many questions about how one defines 'modernity'); but in a discussion of the classical tradition it is hard to avoid talking about 'the Renaissance', and I shall continue to do so. Whether or not one sees it as a rebirth, it certainly was a period of rediscovery of the classics. The lead was taken by the scholars who called themselves 'humanists', because they were interested in human rather than theological studies, and because they believed in the ideal of 'humane' learning which creates a well-rounded human being. They searched out manuscripts of forgotten Latin texts, and re-edited and published them using the recently invented printing press; they also rediscovered Greek texts long unknown in the west, and began to learn and teach Greek, helped by Greek scholars who had fled to the west after the fall of Constantinople to the Turks in 1453.

Out of this rediscovery came a new set of attitudes to the classical world. There was a new sense of historical perspective – a realisation that Greece and Rome were alien worlds, separated from us by the gulf of the Middle Ages, requiring to be studied and understood on their own terms rather than merely assimiliated to our world in the medieval manner. There was a new kind of respect for classical literature as a model for imitation: writers now strove, not only to grasp the wisdom of the ancient texts, but also to imitate their generic forms, their style and conventions. And – perhaps most important in the long run – there was a new ideal of education: the secular 'grammar school' or (later) 'public school', whose curriculum was centred on Latin and (to a lesser extent) Greek, and where gentlemen's sons were raised on knowledge of the classics. Such an education was for boys only; girls did not attend school and (with a few notable exceptions) were not taught Latin or Greek. This is one of the reasons why women generally, before the nineteenth century, did not write in the classical genres or on mythological subjects, and why their first major incursions into the English canon came with the rise of that non-classical form, the novel.

Despite these new developments, the treatment of myth in the Renaissance shows clear continuities with the Middle Ages. The tradition of allegorical interpretation continued. A successsion of Renaissance mythographers – Lilius Geraldus in 1548, Natale Conti (or Natalis Comes) in 1551, Vincenzo Cartari in 1556 – produced illustrated handbooks of mythology, describing the gods and interpreting the myths; and they were followed in English by writers such as Abraham Fraunce (1592), Francis Bacon (1609), George Sandys (1632), or Alexander Ross (1647). The main difference is that the Renaissance allegorisers were more ambitious. With a heightened respect for the wisdom and subtlety of the Greeks and Romans, they sought in the myths not only simple moral lessons, but profound secrets of nature, philosophy, politics, and society, cunningly veiled under the appearance of simple stories. So the philosopher-scientist Bacon, in *The Wisdom of the Ancients*, reads the myths as symbolically teaching doctrines similar to his own about the nature of the universe and the proper conduct of scientific research. Others are ready to accept whatever meanings may emerge: George Sandys's commentary on his translation of Ovid's *Metamorphoses* is a fascinatingly ecletic jumble of moral, psychological, scientific, political, philosophical, and historical interpretations.

In Renaissance literature, too, we can see the blurry medieval distinction between myth-as-allegory and myth-as-romance continuing in the contrast between (to use Douglas Bush's terms) the 'sensuously symbolic or allegorical' and the 'merely sensuous' treatment of myth (Bush 1937/1969: xxii). Major writers like Edmund Spenser, George Chapman, and John Milton draw upon the tradition of allegorical interpretation, interweaving classical myths with Christian doctrine. In Spenser's vast allegorical romance *The Faerie Queene*, for instance, the goddesses Venus and Diana appear as the complex embodiments of sexuality and of chastity; in Milton's *Comus* the heroine's chastity is threatened by an enchanter who is the son of Bacchus and Circe, and defended by a Spirit who is at once a Christian guardian angel and an inhabitant of a pagan paradise presided over by Venus and Cupid. This serious blend of the pagan and the Christian, of course, is an unstable compound. We see this particularly in Milton, who embodies pagan myth in unforgettable poetry, and yet is capable, in the opening book of *Paradise Lost*, of dismissing the classical gods as devils. Here, for instance, he describes the fall of Vulcan:

> . . . and how he fell
> From heaven they fabled, thrown by angry Jove
> Sheer o'er the crystal battlements; from morn
> To noon he fell, from noon to dewy eve,
> A summer's day; and with the setting sun
> Dropped from the zenith like a falling star
> On Lemnos the Aegean isle . . .

and then abruptly undercuts the tale by reminding us of Vulcan's real nature as one of Satan's fallen angels:

> thus they relate,
> Erring; for he with this rebellious rout
> Fell long before . . .
>
> (*Paradise Lost*, 1. 740–8)

This dash-of-cold-water effect recurs repeatedly in Milton, suggesting the difficulty of at once imaginatively embracing and intellectually rejecting the myths.

An alternative approach to myth is what Bush calls the 'merely sensuous': to approach the myths in an Ovidian spirit as pure stories, full of beauty and humour and horror and eroticism and opportunities for gorgeous scene-painting and rhetorical fireworks. It is best exemplified in poems such as Shakespeare's *Venus and Adonis* and Marlowe's *Hero and Leander*, which scholars label 'erotic epyllions' – mini-epics about mythological lovers, set in pastoral landscapes, and fantastically embroidered with descriptions, digressions, and rhetorical debates until the simple story almost disappears from view. Such poems create an idealised mythic world, without allegory or Christianising (though *Venus and Adonis*, with its serious debate about love and chastity, shows how easily moral concerns can creep back into such a 'merely sensuous' world). Lesser Elizabethan poems and songs swarm with nymphs and shepherds, Venuses and Cupids, golden

Phoebuses and silver Dians; just as Elizabethan tragedy is haunted by allusions to classical crimes and punishments and the lurid scenery of Hades.

The problem with the 'merely sensuous' treatment of myth is that it can become merely conventional and decorative, and so, by degrees, merely boring. Already in the early seventeenth century the 'metaphysical' poets like Donne, Herbert, and Carew were beginning to dismiss 'the goodly exiled train / Of gods and goddesses' in favour of more original and challenging subjects and imagery (see **O18**). At the same time a new scientific rationalism began to undercut the claims of myth to serious treatment; as Renaissance reverence for 'the wisdom of the ancients' gave way to an Enlightenment belief in progress, the classical myths ceased to be seen as vehicle of moral and philosophical truth, and became instead mere fictions from the primitive childhood of mankind. So Joseph Addison in 1712 rejects as childish the whole notion of mythology in literature:

> When we are at school it is necessary for us to be acquainted with the system of pagan theology, and may be allowed to enliven a theme or point an epigram with an heathen god; but when we would write a manly panegyric that should carry in it all the colours of truth, nothing can be more ridiculous than to have recourse to our Jupiters and Junos . . . Virgil and Homer might compliment their heroes by interweaving the actions of deities with their achievements; but for a Christian author to write in the pagan creed . . . would be downright puerility, and unpardonable in a poet that is past sixteen.
>
> (*The Spectator*, no. 523, 30 October 1712)

The result of these changing attitudes is paradoxical. The period from 1660 to the 1780s is the heyday of English classicism – especially the earlier eighteenth century, often called 'Augustan' for its conscious emulation of the Augustan age of ancient Rome; yet this period also saw the lowest decline of myth in English literature. The eighteenth century produced magnificent translations (Dryden's Virgil and Ovid, Pope's Homer), and brilliant satires and travesties, but hardly a single treatment of myth that was both serious, original, and memorable. Unfortunately, at the same time that myth had become impossible to take seriously, the principles of neoclassical imitation meant that it remained a compulsory part of the language of poetry. Hence eighteenth-century poetry is cluttered with conventional, fossilised allusions to 'Jupiters and Junos'. As Lord Chesterfield wrote to his son: 'in prose, you would say very properly, "it is twelve of the clock at noon" . . . but that would be too plain and flat in poetry, and you would rather say, "the Chariot of the Sun had already finished half its course" . . . This is what is called poetic diction' (*Letters*, no. 641, 1739, quoted in Bush 1937/1969: 20). Such conventional uses of myth, of course, only made it seem all the more tedious and irrelevant.

By a further paradox, the same spirit of scientific inquiry which had almost killed myth in the seventeenth century also contributed to its revival at the end of the eighteenth century. It was eighteenth-century scholars who inaugurated the scientific study of religion and mythology, studying the classical myths simply as cultural phenomena rather than as sources of ancient wisdom or of pagan corruption. New popular handbooks of mythology, like Lemprière's *Dictionary* (1788), *Bell's New Pantheon* (1790), and Godwin's *Pantheon* (1806), simply recounted the ancient stories and beliefs without medieval allegories or Christian tub-thumping. Such new developments made it possible to take myth seriously again.

The writers of the Romantic movement, arising in the last decades of the eighteenth century, were predisposed to do so. With their exaltation of imagination over mere reason, their worship of nature, their love of fantasy and romance, they were prepared to see myth not as a childish and outmoded habit of thought but as a perennially valid vehicle of insight; for them, to see the landscape as inhabited by the presences of gods, nymphs, and satyrs was not a primitive superstition or a conventional image but a vivid metaphor for the divine power which pervades the natural world. For the first generation of Romantics, however, classical myth was still tainted with the fustiness of eighteenth-century convention; the Wordsworth and Coleridge of *Lyrical Ballads* turned more readily to medieval ballads and folk-tales. It was the second generation who found a new inspiration in Greek myth. Keats embodied his concerns with love and beauty and human suffering in *Endymion* and the unfinished *Hyperion* poems; Shelley more radically transformed myths in *Adonais* and *Prometheus Unbound*. Whereas Keats largely taught himself mythology out of texts such as Lemprière, Shelley was a scholar who loved and translated much of Plato and the Greek poets and dramatists. In the preface to his play *Hellas* (1822) he declared:

> We are all Greeks. Our laws, our literature, our religion, our arts have their roots in Greece . . . The human form and the human mind attained to a perfection in Greece which has impressed its image on those faultless productions, whose very fragments are the despair of modern art, and has propagated impulses which cannot cease . . . to ennoble and delight mankind until the extinction of the race.

Shelley's panegyric reflects a new sense that the art and literature and mythology of Greece, even in 'fragments', were the real thing, and superior to their Roman imitations. Homer and Plato, rather than Virgil and Horace and Ovid, are the great classical figures of the nineteenth century (see Jenkyns 1980; Turner 1981). The long dominance of the *Metamorphoses* now began to wane; Ovid began to seem a little frivolous and superficial beside the antique grandeur of Homer and Aeschylus and Sophocles. Even the names of the gods and heroes begin to change, the original Greek names replacing the Roman ones (Jupiter becomes Zeus), and, for some enthusiastic Hellenists, the long-familiar Latinised spellings giving way to spiky, alien-looking Greek ones (Circe becomes Kirkê, Aeschylus becomes Aischulos).

Even in the Romantic exaltation of Greek myth, however, there are undertones of doubt. Keats in the preface to *Endymion* (1818) hoped that he had not 'in too late a day touched the beautiful mythology of Greece, and dulled its brightness'. This fear that it was too late for Greek mythology was echoed jokingly by Peacock when he said that there are no dryads in Hyde Park nor naiads in the Regent's Canal (*The Four Ages of Poetry*, 1820), and more seriously by Wordsworth in a famous sonnet in which, lamenting his age's preoccupation with materialistic 'getting and spending', he declared:

Great God! I'd rather be
A pagan suckled in a creed outworn;
So might I, standing on this pleasant lea,
Have glimpses that would make me less forlorn;
Have sight of Proteus rising from the sea;
Or hear old Triton blow his wreathèd horn.
('The World Is Too Much With Us', 1807)

Wordsworth wishes he could recapture that innocence, and yet he knows that he is not going to see Proteus; the world has changed, and Greek paganism is a 'creed outworn'.

In the course of the nineteenth century this sense of belatedness grew stronger. The Victorian period (1837–1901) produced a huge volume of poetry on mythological themes (see Bush 1937/1969), and among the mass some genuinely major works: Tennyson's 'Ulysses' (1842) and other dramatic monologues, Arnold's 'The Strayed Reveller' (1849), perhaps Robert Browning's rewriting of Euripides' *Alcestis* in *Balaustion's Adventure* (1871). Nevertheless, as the century goes on, mythology comes to seem increasingly marginal. On the one side the 'creed outworn' was once again being challenged by Christianity: Elizabeth Barrett Browning, for instance, dismisses the 'vain false gods of Hellas' as subjects of worship or art:

Earth outgrows the mythic fancies
Sung beside her in her youth,
And those debonair romances
Sound but dull beside the truth.
('The Dead Pan', 1844, 232–5)

On the other hand, the modern world of 'getting and spending', industrialism, commerce, science, political reform, and empire, made the old myths seem increasingly remote and irrelevant, while the creative energies of the period thrived in the novel and discursive prose rather than in mythological poetry. In the latter half of the century the irrelevance of myth becomes its positive attraction. Pre-Raphaelites like D. G. Rossetti and William Morris (who hark back beyond the Renaissance to the Middle Ages and the ancient world), and aesthetes like Swinburne and Wilde and De Tabley, use it to create an idealised dream-world, a vanished time which can be contemplated with wistful nostalgia. Where the Middle Ages simply assimilated classical myth to their own world, and the Renaissance and the Romantics used it to deal with contemporary concerns, the late Victorians, aware of looking back at it over a vast abyss of time and change, see it as a refuge from drab contemporary reality.

The early twentieth century brought myth back to startling life and relevance precisely by shattering that nineteenth-century image of idealised beauty and serenity. Once again the impetus came from new scholarly developments, in anthropology and psychology. Sir James Frazer in his massive study *The Golden Bough*, and his followers in the 'Cambridge School' such as Jane Harrison and Gilbert Murray, applied the techniques of modern anthropology to ancient myth and religion, finding startling similarities between classical myths and the beliefs of present-day 'primitive' peoples. Behind the statuesque dignity of Greek myths, they suggested, there often lay barbaric and bloody rites, such as the sacrifice of a sacred god-king to ensure the fertility of the soil. At the same time Sigmund Freud and Carl Jung argued the vital psychological importance of myths. For Freud, they embody primal human drives of sexuality and violence, which may emerge in dreams or fantasies when the rational mind represses them: for instance, the story of Oedipus, who (unwittingly) killed his father and married his mother, reflects the instinctive desire of every young male child to do precisely that (the 'Oedipus complex'). For Jung, they are 'archetypes', powerful images from the 'collective unconscious' of the entire human race, embodying our deepest desires and needs; understanding them can help us to achieve psychic integration and health. Once again, as in the Renaissance, myths are seen as symbolic representations of profound truth. Their irrationality is no longer a barrier to taking them seriously – in fact, in an irrational and chaotic modern world, it guarantees their significance and value.

T. S. Eliot, in a 1923 review of James Joyce's *Ulysses* (1922), wrote:

> Psychology . . ., ethnology, and *The Golden Bough* have concurred to make possible what was impossible only a few years ago. Instead of narrative method, we may now use the mythical method. It is, I seriously believe, a step toward making the modern world possible for art.
>
> (*The Dial*, 75 (1923), 483; quoted in Feder 1971: 26)

The 'modernist' writers of the earlier twentieth century embraced myth as a way of imposing significance (if sometimes by ironic contrast) on a chaotic or shabby modern world. Joyce's *Ulysses* overlays a day in Dublin in 1904 on top of the epic plot of Homer's *Odyssey*, at once mocking the littleness of modern life and suggesting the persistence of archetypal, age-old concerns from archaic Greece to modern Ireland. Eliot's *Waste Land* (1922) draws on Frazer's discussion of ancient fertility myths, creating a waste land which images both the chaos of post-war Europe and the arid psyche of contemporary western man. W. B. Yeats, interweaving Celtic, classical, and his own occult mythology; Ezra Pound, using the figure of Odysseus as his persona; D. H. Lawrence, fascinated with the Etruscans and the mysteries of the underworld; H.D. (Hilda Doolittle), repeatedly returning to a mythic Greece of hot sun and terrifyingly present divinities; Robert Graves, creating his own interpretations of Greek myth (half scholarly, half crackpot) and his own poetic religion of the White Goddess – almost all the modernist writers use Eliot's 'mythical method'. Each of them, moreover, in a sense creates his or her own private mythology, as if it is no longer enough to draw upon a common stock of familiar stories and images.

The later twentieth century might seem a period inimical to myth, with the enormous explosion of science and technology, the proliferation of non-classical literary forms and media (journalism, cinema, television), the decline of the 'classical education' and of knowledge of the classical languages, the rising protests against literary elitism and the dominance of Dead White European Males . . . Nevertheless, as the contents of this anthology demonstrate, myth has remained throughout the century a powerful force in twentieth-century literature. The field of its influence has also widened out, in at least two significant ways.

Firstly, 'classical myth in English literature' in the twentieth century embraces not only the literature of England, but also that of the United States, Canada, Australia, New Zealand, and English-speaking parts of Africa, the Caribbean, and the Pacific. Classical myth has arguably been part of American literature since George Sandys translated the *Metamorphoses* as a colonial official in seventeenth-century Virginia, but up to the end of the nineteenth century the field was mostly left to minor and conventional versifiers; the major American writers (with some notable exceptions – Emerson, Poe, Hawthorne) seemed to agree with Walt Whitman's impatient demand:

> Come Muse, migrate from Greece and Ionia,
> Cross out please those immensely overpaid accounts,
> That matter of Troy and Achilles' wrath, and Aeneas', Odysseus' wanderings,
> Placard REMOVED and TO LET on the rocks of your snowy Parnassus . . .
> For know a better, fresher, busier sphere, a wide untried domain awaits, demands you.
>
> ('Song of the Exposition', 1876)

In the twentieth century, however, the old accounts have been reopened. As this anthology demonstrates, American poets and dramatists such as Ashbery, Duncan, Jarrell, Jeffers, Levertov, Lowell, MacLeish, O'Neill, Rexroth, Rich, Rukeyser, Tennessee Williams (a brief alphabetical sample) have found the mythology of the Old World a powerful vehicle for New World themes. The same is true of other countries and literatures even more remote from the Old World. To take my own country as an example, New Zealand literature is haunted by the figure of Odysseus – from A. R. D. Fairburn's romantic vision of the wanderer making landfall in New Zealand (1930), to James K. Baxter's war veteran coming home to 'the gully farm' (1950), to Alistair Paterson's globetrotting 'Odysseus Rex' (1986). Baxter, who declared that 'What happens is either meaningless to me, or else it is mythology' (Baxter 1967: 122), draws with equal conviction on classical, Christian, and Maori images; and Alastair Te Ariki Campbell, in the very act of rejecting the classical Greek myths in favour of those of Polynesia, evokes an unforgettable image of the death of the old gods:

> Face downward
> And in a small creek mouth all unperceived,
> The drowned Dionysus, sand in his eyes and mouth,
> In the dim tide lolling – beautiful, and with the last harsh
>
> Glare of divinity from lip and broad brow ebbing . . .
> ('The Return')

So too writers from parts of the 'Third World' who might be expected to draw on their own indigenous mythical traditions have found use for the myths of Greece and Rome. The Nigerian Wole Soyinka's version of Euripides' *Bacchae* (1973), or the St Lucian Derek Walcott's revision of the Homeric characters in *Omeros* (1990), have shown that the ancient stories can gain a new vividness when naturalised in a completely alien setting.

The second widening-out of the myths is in terms of gender. Occasional women had written on mythological themes in the eighteenth century, and more in the nineteenth century (a few of them appear in this anthology). But it was not until the twentieth century that women writers really began to focus on the ancient myths, taking the stories traditionally told by and about men, reimagining and reinterpreting them from a female point of view, and allowing the women characters of the myths to speak for the first time. Some of the most original and challenging mythological writing of this century has come from such feminist revisions: H.D. or Margaret Atwood giving Eurydice a voice, Sandra Gilbert allowing the Bacchantes to justify their murder of Orpheus, Atwood presenting the Odysseus–Circe relationship from Circe's point of view, Angela Carter merging the Pygmalion myth with those of Frankenstein and Dracula to give the statue a bloody revenge . . .

At the beginning of the twenty-first century, classical mythology shows no signs of going away. If knowledge of Greek and Latin has declined, translations of classical works and popular accounts of the myths proliferate. Ovid, in particular, seems to be undergoing a boom in the 1990s, with the appearance of several new translations of the *Metamorphoses*, at least three novels based on his life and exile, and two volumes of poetic revisions of his tales – the anthology *After Ovid: New Metamorphoses* (1994), and Ted Hughes's prizewinning *Tales from Ovid* (1997). In the age of postmodernism and magical realism, Ovid, with his mixture of wit and fantasy and violence, his artful fragmentariness and his hints of serious meaning under a kaleidoscopically frivolous surface, once again seems a very modern writer. (With the development of cinematic 'morphing' effects, surely *Metamorphoses: The Movie* cannot be far off?) At any rate, it seems a safe bet that, so long as our civilisation lasts through the new millennium, the classical myths will survive as well.

Notes

1 Troilus appears in Homer, and Cressida is distantly derived from Homer's Briseis and Chryseis (in *Iliad*, book 1), but the love story is a medieval invention (by the twelfth-century French poet Benoît de Saint-Maure). The medieval writers, of course, had no access to Homer; their main authorities were two late classical prose works, claiming to be eyewitness accounts of the war, by 'Dares the Phrygian' and 'Dictys the Cretan'.

2 In Italy the 'Renaissance' is the period from the late fourteenth century to the mid-sixteenth century. In England it comes a century later, stretching from the end of the fifteenth century (1485, the accession of the first Tudor king Henry VII, is a conventional marker) to the mid-seventeenth century (conventional dates are 1642, the beginning of the Civil War, or 1660, the Restoration of Charles II). Of course, any such dates are arbitrary markers for processes of gradual cultural change.

2

A ROUGH GUIDE TO THE GODS

The most essential item in the classical myth-kitty is a knowledge of the classical gods and goddesses – their names, attributes, personalities, areas of power, and the complex web of relationships which sometimes makes classical mythology seem like a vast divine soap opera. This chapter aims to provide a brief guide to the gods as they appear in classical and European literature and art (rather than as the objects of ancient Greek and Roman worship and ritual, a quite different matter).

Simply knowing the names of the gods is more complex than it might appear, since almost all of them go by two names, one Greek, one Roman. It was the Greeks (sometimes borrowing from older Middle Eastern traditions) who created the personalities, stories, and relationships of the gods. The Romans, on the other hand, originally worshipped mostly impersonal, faceless spirits of place and personifications. When the Romans came in contact with Greek culture they borrowed the whole colourful apparatus of Greek mythology and applied it to their own pantheon, identifying each Greek god with his or her nearest Roman equivalent. So, for instance, Hephaestus, the Greek master-craftsman and smith who has his forge under a volcano, became identified with Vulcan, a Roman god of volcanic fire. Over time – although classical scholars, naturally, maintain the distinctions between them – the Greek and Roman gods effectively fused into a single personality. It was the Roman names of the gods which were passed down through the Middle Ages, and became standard in English: eighteenth-century writers, even translating Homer or Sophocles, would speak of 'Jupiter' and 'Mars' and 'Venus'. In the later nineteenth and twentieth centuries the original Greek names have gradually come back. Anyone following the history of the myths needs to be familiar with both. I considered consistently using the Roman names (which are the most familiar in English literature), but this sounds absurd in relating the more archaic Greek myths; instead I have introduced each god by giving both names (first Greek, then Roman: **Hera/Juno**), and thereafter used either or both as seems appropriate. For quick reference the following table may be useful.

Greek name	*Roman name*	*Principal function*
Zeus	Jupiter, Jove	king, god of the sky
Hera	Juno	queen, goddess of marriage
Poseidon	Neptune	god of the sea
Hades	Pluto, Dis	god of the underworld
Demeter	Ceres	goddess of agriculture
Hestia	Vesta	goddess of home and hearth
Athena	Minerva, Pallas	goddess of war and wisdom
Apollo	Apollo	god of light, music, healing, the sun
Artemis	Diana	goddess of the wild, virgin huntress, the moon
Aphrodite	Venus	goddess of love and beauty
Ares	Mars	god of war
Hephaestus	Vulcan	god of fire, blacksmith and craftsman
Hermes	Mercury	messenger, god of travel and communication
Dionysus	Bacchus	god of wine and madness
Persephone	Proserpina	goddess of underworld and of spring
Eros	Cupid	god of love
Cronus/Kronos	Saturn	father of the gods
Rhea	Ops	mother of the gods

The Olympian gods

The most important Greek gods lived on the summit of Mount Olympus, the highest mountain in Greece (nearly 10,000 feet high), or in the clouds above it. The Greeks conceived Olympus like an ancient Greek city, with the citadel of the king (Zeus) on the highest peak and the homes of the other nobles/gods clustered round. Ovid re-envisages it in terms of Rome's palatial Palatine Hill (*Metamorphoses*, 1. 168–76), and a seventeenth-century translator in turn 'Englishes' it as 'Heaven's Whitehall' (Sandys, *Ovid's Metamorphoses Englished*).

The principal gods were categorised by the Greeks as 'the Twelve Olympians', though there was some disagreement about the composition of the list; the following discussion includes thirteen major gods as well as some of their more important hangers-on. They fall into two generations: the older generation of Zeus/Jupiter and his siblings, and the younger generation who are his children by various mothers. The underworld god Hades/Pluto, who seldom sets foot on Olympus, is not counted among the Olympians; he, his consort, and his kingdom are separately dealt with later.

Zeus/Jupiter/Jove

King of the gods and ruler of the universe from his throne on Mount Olympus. Originally a god of the sky and storm, thunder and lightning, he also becomes patron of kingship and government, law and custom, the patriarchal lord of the status quo. He is depicted as a powerfully built bearded man of middle age, often grasping a thunderbolt or lightning flash, attended by his messenger the eagle and his sacred tree the oak. Homer depicts Zeus impressively as the cloud-gatherer, 'father of gods and men', whose nod shakes heaven:

> He bent his ponderous black brows down, and locks
> ambrosial of his immortal head
> swung over them, as all Olympos trembled.
> (*Iliad*, 1. 528–30; trans. Robert Fitzgerald)

And Virgil gives a similarly powerful picture of Jupiter:

> the Almighty Father then,
> Chief power of the world, began to speak,
> And as he spoke the great hall of the gods
> Fell silent, and earth quaked . . .
> (*Aeneid*, 10. 100–2; trans. Robert Fitzgerald)

This 'Almighty Father' has a striking resemblance to the Christian God, and English writers have often taken advantage of the accidental similarity between Latin 'Jove' and Hebrew 'Jehovah' to create a composite pagan/Christian image of the supreme being.

Zeus/Jupiter has a less exalted aspect, however. He is also an insatiable lecher, pursuing nymphs and mortal women and boys, and seducing or raping them in various forms, thus fathering many heroes and heroines and founding many of the great royal and noble families of mythology (for more details, see 'Tales of love' in chapter 3, pp. 38–40). His sexual exploits have provided endless material for artists and poets, who (being mostly male) have tended to treat them in a light-hearted spirit. Ovid, observing the spectacle of the lord of the universe transformed into a bull and mooing his love for Europa, comments wryly that 'majesty and love go ill together' (*Metamorphoses*, 2. 846–7).

Hera/Juno

Queen of the gods, sister and wife of Zeus/Jupiter, goddess of marriage and childbirth, and the pre-eminent women's deity. Some scholars conjecture that she was once the mother goddess of a matriarchal society, later forcibly married and subjected to Zeus – which might explain something of their rather rocky marital relationship. She is depicted as a beautiful and stately queen, with a full 'Junoesque' figure and large liquid 'ox-eyes' (in Homer's phrase); her attendant is the proud peacock, and **Iris**, the shining rainbow goddess, is her messenger. Less majestically, Hera is the archetypal jealous wife, forever quarrelling with her husband, suspicious (with reason) of his infidelities, and vengefully pursuing his mistresses and his bastard children. Her malice in this regard means that she is often cast in a villainous role: as Hercules' wicked stepmother, for instance, or as 'baleful Juno' whose 'sleepless rage' against Aeneas and his Trojans prompts Virgil's question, 'Can anger / Black as this prey on the minds of heaven?' (*Aeneid*, 1. 4–11).

Poseidon/Neptune

God of the sea, who won that realm by lot from his brothers Zeus and Hades; called 'Earthshaker', he is also the god of earthquakes and of horses. He appears as a bearded middle-aged man, very similar to Zeus, but holding the three-pointed spear or trident with which he rules the waves; he rides in a shell-shaped chariot drawn by sea-horses, attended by his wife **Amphitrite**, by his herald **Triton** (a merman, half man and half fish, who blows on a conch shell – sometimes turned into a multitude of tritons), and by sea-nymphs. Like the element he rules, he can be fierce of temper and a dangerous enemy (as he is to Odysseus in Homer's *Odyssey*), and as ruthless as his brother in his sexual affairs. As 'King Neptune' he is still a familar icon, and used to turn up (perhaps still does) to initiate passengers on ships crossing the Equator.

Among his followers are **Proteus**, the Old Man of the Sea, prophet and shape-changer, and **Thetis**, the beautiful sea-nymph who becomes the father of Achilles. Like other sea gods they can change shape, flowing like water into various forms, to evade capture or questioning by mortals.

Demeter/Ceres

Goddess of grain and crops, agriculture and fertility. An earth-mother goddess, she is depicted as a matronly figure, sometimes rising out of the earth, with ears of grain in her hands. The only important myth connected with Demeter is that of her search for her stolen daughter **Persephone/Proserpina** (see below). Otherwise she is a rather colourless figure, and when her name appears in literature it is often a mere metaphor for grain or food (Ceres is the origin of the word 'cereal'): so Pope writes of the time when an aristocratic garden will revert to farmland 'And laughing Ceres reassume the land' ('Epistle to Burlington', 186).

Hestia/Vesta

Goddess of the hearth-fire, home, family, and community. Eldest of the Olympian family, the one who stayed home to look after the fire, Hestia is the most respectable and dullest of the gods, important in religion but almost entirely devoid of myth. Some say she later stepped down to make room among the Twelve for the more exciting Dionysus. She appears in literature only as patroness of the Vestal Virgins, the Roman priestesses who guarded the sacred flame and were sworn to lifelong virginity on pain of being buried alive.

Athena/Minerva

Goddess of war, of arts, crafts, and skills (especially spinning and weaving), of intelligence and wisdom. Her birth is the subject of a strange archaic myth: Zeus swallowed her mother, the titaness Metis ('wisdom'), in the traditional family fear that her child would be stronger than himself, and so Athena was born from his head – his brainchild, one might say, born directly from the father without feminine intervention. Hence she is the most 'masculine' of goddesses, an asexual virgin and an incarnation of militant intelligence. She is depicted as a tall, sternly beautiful young woman, 'grey-eyed' or 'flashing-eyed', dressed in full armour with helmet and spear, and often wearing the head of the Gorgon Medusa (see the story of Perseus in chapter 3) on her breastplate; her attributes include the owl (symbol of wisdom), the snake, and the olive tree – the gift with which she won the honour of being patron goddess of Athens. In Homer's *Odyssey* she is the loyal friend of Odysseus, for whose tricky intelligence she has an almost sisterly regard.

Apollo

Apollo, whose name is the same in Latin and Greek, is also sometimes called **Phoebus** (bright), and this is perhaps his key attribute. He is the god of light and enlightenment in all its senses, of reason and perception, music and poetry, prophecy, medicine, and of the sun. (This last is a later development – the original sun god was Helius – but in English literature 'Phoebus' often refers to the sun.) He describes himself in Shelley's 'Hymn of Apollo':

> I am the eye with which the Universe
>   Beholds itself, and knows itself divine;
> All harmony of instrument or verse,
>   All prophecy, all medicine are mine,
> All light of art or nature . . .

He is depicted as a beardless young man of perfect classical beauty, often surrounded by a halo of light, carrying a bow and arrows and a lyre. As a hunter he is often linked with his twin sister Artemis/Diana (they are the children of Zeus and the titaness Leto); together they kill monsters and send disease and death on evildoers. Apollo also heals disease, and his son **Asclepius/Aesculapius** is the god of medicine. As prophet he speaks from his shrines such as the great Oracle at Delphi, the centre of the earth, where the Pythia-priestess utters her riddling oracles in his name. As god of music and poetry he is associated with the mountains of Parnassus and Helicon, where he is attended by the nine **Muses** (see below). Apollo was often seen by the Greeks as the epitome of Greek civilisation; so he takes a central place in the frieze on the Parthenon in Athens, calmly wrestling a centaur into submission, the symbol of reason overcoming barbarism.

It may be added, to qualify his almost insufferable perfection, that he inherits his father's sexual appetite, and that his love affairs with women or boys nearly always have unhappy endings (see 'Tales of love' in chapter 3, pp. 38–40).

The Muses are the nine daughters of Zeus and the titaness Mnemosyne ('memory'), who live on Mount Helicon beside the spring of Hippocrene; they are the patronesses of the creative arts and the givers of inspiration. Later writers give each of them responsibility for a particular art, though the assignments vary; this is one traditional version.

Calliope	epic poetry
Clio	history
Erato	lyric poetry
Euterpe	music
Melpomene	tragedy
Polyhymnia	sacred music and poetry
Terpsichore	dance
Thalia	comedy, pastoral poetry
Urania	astronomy

Artemis / Diana

The virgin huntress, goddess of wild places and wild creatures, of chastity, and of the moon. (Like her brother Apollo's association with the sun, this is a later development, by which she displaced the original moon goddess Selene; in this role she is often called **Phoebe**, the feminine counterpart of Phoebus, or **Cynthia**.) She is depicted as a beautiful, athletic young woman, dressed as a huntress with bow and arrows, often wearing a small crescent moon in her hair or on her breast, and often accompanied by a deer or other wild creatures. She is a virgin, like Athena, but unlike her sister avoids courts and cities, preferring to run free in the forests and groves with her band of huntress-nymphs, and fiercely punishing male intruders (like the hunter Actaeon), as well as females (like the nymph Callisto) who fall below her standards of chastity. The 'Queen and huntress, chaste and fair . . . Goddess excellently bright' (Ben Jonson) is a particularly potent figure in Elizabethan literature, when Elizabeth, the Virgin Queen, liked to be associated with her. On a more sinister level, she is sometimes identified with **Hecate**, goddess of witchcraft and black magic – the trinity of huntress, moon goddess, and witch-goddess making her 'Diana of the three faces'.

Aphrodite / Venus

Goddess of love and sexuality. She is depicted as a beautiful woman (in whatever style of beauty is currently in fashion), usually naked, often accompanied by her son **Eros/Cupid** (see below), or by a whole flock of small winged Loves or

Cupids; her attributes include doves, sparrows, roses, and mirrors. It is the mirror which is represented in her astrological symbol (♀), which has become the conventional symbol for women or femaleness. Homer calls her the daughter of Zeus and Dione, but Hesiod tells a more striking story of her origins: when Cronus/Saturn castrated his father Uranus, the sky god's genitals fell into the sea and gathered sea-foam (Gk. *aphros*) around them, and Aphrodite arose from the sea.

Plato, in the *Symposium* (180), declared that there are two Aphrodites: 'Common Aphrodite', goddess of ordinary love and sex, and 'Heavenly Aphrodite', *Aphrodite Urania*, a potent spiritual force. This is a philosopher's concept rather than a genuine myth, but it does suggest the goddess's range of personalities. At one extreme is the goddess of the universal cycle of life, magnificently invoked by the Roman philosopher-poet Lucretius (in Dryden's translation):

All nature is thy gift; earth, air, and sea;
Of all that breathes, the various progeny,
Stung with delight, is goaded on by thee.
O'er barren mountains, o'er the flowery plain,
The leafy forest, and the liquid main,
Extends thy uncontrolled and boundless reign . . .
(*De rerum natura*, 1. 17–20)

Common Aphrodite, on the other hand, is the embodiment of human love, and can be regarded in as many ways as love can be: as something rapturous, or kind and caring, or wantonly lustful, or elegantly frivolous, or cruel – 'Venus with her claws fixed deep in her prey' (Racine, *Phèdre*, 1.3). She is married to Hephaestus/Vulcan, but continually unfaithful to him; her principal lover is Ares/Mars, but she also has human lovers, of whom Adonis is the most famous. The opposite in most ways of chaste Artemis/Diana, she is like her in her harsh punishment of those who offend against her and her values; the most famous example is the tragedy of Hippolytus and Phaedra.

Eros/Cupid, the personification of love or desire (Gk. *eros*, Lat. *cupido*), is a god who has come down in the world. According to Hesiod, Eros was there at the very beginning of things, emerging out of Chaos along with Earth and Tartarus, and so is older than Aphrodite. Later, and more commonly, he is called the son of Aphrodite and Ares. At first depicted by the Greeks as a beautiful winged youth, he has shrunk by Roman times into the familiar figure of a pudgy little winged boy, often blind or blindfolded, with a little bow from which he shoots at random his arrows of desire. Shakespeare spells out the allegory:

Love looks not with the eyes, but with the mind,
And therefore is winged Cupid painted blind.
Nor hath love's mind of any judgement taste;
Wings and no eyes figure unheedy haste.

And therefore is love said to be a child
Because in choice he is so oft beguiled.
(*A Midsummer Night's Dream*, 1. 1. 234–9)

Ares / Mars

The god of war. He is depicted as a warrior, with armour, sword, spear, and shield (or the contemporary equivalents, in later art); his astrological symbol (♂) represents the phallically raised spear, and has become the symbol of the male, as Venus's mirror is of the female (a rather depressing comment on traditional gender roles). Ares and Mars are rather different figures, reflecting different cultural attitudes to war: Ares was a minor Greek god, and Homer portrays him as a nasty and ineffectual bully; Mars, on the other hand, is one of the principal Roman gods, embodiment of the military virtues, and patron and defender of Rome. Mars and Venus, as archetypes of man and woman, are appropriately lovers, and the disarming of Mars by Venus is a common theme in art.

Hephaestus / Vulcan

The smith, god of metalworking and of fire. Son of Zeus and Hera (or, in some versions, of Hera alone), he is ugly and lame – either because he was born so, or because his mother or father threw him out of heaven and he was crippled by the fall to earth. (The lame blacksmith is a traditional figure in many cultures, perhaps because it was a craft open to those who could not fight or farm.) He makes houses and furniture, weapons and armour, and other treasured possessions for the gods, as well as arms for heroes like Achilles and Aeneas. His forge is located underneath a volcano, usually Mount Etna in Sicily, where he is assisted by the **Cyclopes** (one-eyed giants). The other gods laugh at him for his clumsy appearance, and also for being a cuckold – husband of the most spectacularly unfaithful wife in all mythology. On one occasion, however, described by Homer, he had the last laugh on his wife Aphrodite/Venus and her lover Ares/Mars: he booby-trapped the marital bed with an invisible and unbreakable net, caught the lovers there, and invited the other deities in to enjoy their discomfiture.

Hermes / Mercury

The messenger of the gods. The son of Zeus and Maia, he carries messages and aid to mortals on behalf of his father. He is depicted as a handsome, beardless youth, wearing a winged cap and sandals, and carrying the *caduceus* – a herald's staff with two snakes entwined around it. (For some reason the caduceus has become the symbol of medicine, which was never one of Hermes' functions.) He is the god of language and communication, of orators, diplomats, writers, and scholars; his medium is prose, 'the words of Mercury' rather than 'the songs of

Apollo' (Shakespeare, *Love's Labour's Lost*, 5. 2. 912–13). He is also the patron of travellers, traders, and thieves (categories the Greeks obviously regarded as closely related). According to the 'Homeric Hymn to Hermes', he demonstrated his precocious abilities when he was only one day old by stealing a herd of cattle from his brother Apollo, then pacifying Apollo with some fast talk and the gift of the lyre (which he had just invented) in exchange. Quick-witted, agile of foot, tongue, and brain, his 'mercurial' qualities are reflected in the metal named after him – mercury, or quicksilver. He also has a more sombre function as *psychopomp* or spirit guide, guiding the spirits of the dead down to the underworld.

Dionysus / Bacchus

The god of wine, intoxication and ecstasy. A latecomer to Olympus, he is the son of Zeus and a mortal, Semele, daughter of King Cadmus of Thebes. Semele was already pregnant with the god when (on Hera's malicious advice) she unwisely asked Zeus to appear to her in his full heavenly glory, and was burnt to cinders; but Zeus rescued the unborn child and sewed him into his thigh, from which he was subsequently born. (Dionysus and Athena are thus both the children of Zeus as solo parent, so to speak; the parts of his body from which they were born suggest the contrast between Athena's pure intellect and Dionysus' 'lower', more sensual nature.) Tutored by the wise old drunkard **Silenus**, he set off on a tour of the East as far as India, spreading the knowledge of wine and his worship, before returning in triumph to claim his place on Olympus. Only his home city, Thebes, refused to acknowledge him; the tragic story of King Pentheus's defiance of Dionysus is told in Euripides' *Bacchae*.

Dionysus is depicted as a handsome young man (bearded in early Greek art, more androgynous-looking in later versions), crowned with ivy and vine-leaves, holding a wine-cup, and carrying the *thyrsus*, an ivy-wreathed staff tipped with a pine-cone; he is followed by leopards and panthers, satyrs, and fauns, old Silenus riding on a donkey, and a rout of wild (mainly female) worshippers, the *bacchantes* or *maenads*. This image reflects the actual Bacchic rites (or 'orgies'), in which women would go up into the mountains and work themselves up with wine and music and dancing into a frenzied ecstasy, culminating in the ceremonial tearing to pieces of a sacrificial animal. In later times Bacchus may become merely a personification of wine or a comic drunkard; but for the ancient Greeks he represented something more serious – the emotional and irrational, inspiration and ecstasy, whatever lifts human beings out of their normal selves and beyond rational control. He has his own kinds of poetry and music, and acting and the theatre are his special province. The German philosopher Friedrich Nietzsche, in *The Birth of Tragedy* (1872), proposed an influential distinction between Apollonian and Dionysian forms of art – the former rational, orderly, harmonious, 'classic'; the latter emotional, instinctive, mysterious, 'romantic'. Dionysus is the least 'classical' of classical deities.

The gods of the underworld

Hades / Pluto / Dis

King of the underworld and god of the dead, who gained that realm when he cast lots with his brothers Zeus/Jupiter and Poseidon/Neptune. He is a shadowy figure. On the principle of 'speak of the devil. . .', he was seldom depicted and his name seldom spoken. In fact, his various names are all euphemisms: Hades and Aidoneus mean 'the unseen one' (Hades is also the name of his realm); Pluto and Dis mean 'the rich one' (since wealth comes from underground). It is worth stressing that he is *not* the devil, not evil or malevolent, merely a cold, grim, inflexible enforcer of the necessity of death for all mortal creatures. He has little mythology, apart from the story of his abduction of Persephone (see below), and his dealings with the heroes who from time to time invade his realm.

Persephone / Proserpina

Queen of the underworld, and goddess of spring. Also known as **Cora** or **Kore**, 'the maiden', she is the daughter of Zeus/Jupiter and Demeter/Ceres. Her uncle Hades/Pluto fell in love with her, and, with the connivance of Zeus, seized her and carried her off in his black chariot as she was picking flowers; in Milton's words,

> Proserpine, gathering flowers,
> Herself a fairer flower, by gloomy Dis
> Was gathered, which cost Ceres all that pain
> To seek her through the world.
> (*Paradise Lost*, 4. 269–72)

Demeter searched the earth for her lost daughter. In her grief, or her rage at finding how her brothers had conspired against her, she withdrew the blessings of fertility from the world; crops died, the world turned barren, human life was threatened. Zeus had to ask Hades to return Persephone. But Hades, knowing that those who had eaten the food of the underworld could not return to earth, had persuaded Persephone to take a bite of a pomegranate, and she had swallowed some seeds. As a compromise, Zeus decreed that she should spend half the year in the underworld, half with the other gods. This is, of course, a seasonal myth: while Persephone is underground in winter the earth is cold and barren, but she returns with new life in the spring. The Eleusinian Mysteries – the famous, secret rites held yearly at Eleusis, near Athens – apparently acted out the story of Demeter and Persephone, and seem to have promised not only the cyclic renewal of life, but also life after death to their initiates. In literature, apart from versions of the story of her abduction, Persephone/Proserpina almost always appears as the queen of the underworld – sometimes cold and stern, sometimes a kindlier influence on her husband.

The underworld

The underworld, the land of the dead, was originally 'the realm of Hades'; by extension it comes to be called simply 'Hades' (other names are Orcus and Erebus). Thanks to the visits of various heroes – Odysseus, Aeneas, Hercules, Theseus, Orpheus – its geography and inhabitants are fairly familiar, though the terrain can shift disconcertingly. For Homer it is a land somewhere in the far west, beyond the encircling Ocean (Odysseus is able to get there by ship), and it consists simply of an endless, featureless plain, on which only asphodel (a kind of white lily) grows, and on which the ghosts of the dead wander mindlessly and aimlessly. This simple and depressing picture becomes more complex, and more interesting, in later accounts.

Later writers usually place the underworld underneath the earth, where it can be reached by various passages: Orpheus descends through a cave at Taenarus in southernmost Greece, Aeneas through the Sibyl's cavern near Lake Avernus in Italy. Its boundary is marked by the river Styx, the 'hateful river', by whose black and poisonous water the gods swear their most unbreakable oaths. (Virgil makes the river Acheron the border, but later tradition has agreed on the Styx.) The spirits of the newly dead wait on its bank to be ferried across by **Charon**, the filthy and churlish old boatman. The fare is an *obolus*, a small coin (hence the ancient custom of putting a coin in a dead person's mouth, and perhaps the later custom of putting pennies on a dead person's eyes); those who lack the coin, or have not been properly buried, are doomed to wait in limbo on the banks of the Styx. On the other side, the boundaries of the underworld are marked out by five rivers: Styx, Acheron ('sorrowful'), Cocytus ('wailing'), Phlegethon ('fiery'), and Lethe ('forgetful'); those who drink from Lethe forget their former lives and identities. The entrance to the underworld, or the gate of Hades' palace, is guarded by the fearsome three-headed (or, more extravagantly, fifty-headed) hell-hound **Cerberus**.

Whereas the essential feature of Homer's underworld is the levelling of all souls without distinction, later versions show more interest in posthumous rewards and punishments. There are three judges, **Minos**, **Rhadamanthys**, and **Aeacus**, who decide the fates of the dead. There are also equivalents of heaven and hell, though they are reserved for the exceptionally good or the exceptionally wicked. On one side there is **Elysium**, or the **Elysian Fields**: a paradisal place where blessed souls take their ease with conversation, music, and games amid flowering meadows. Originally reserved for heroes of divine ancestry, Elysium is later open to anyone of exceptional virtue or distinction.

On the other side is **Tartarus**, a deep gulf in which the wickedest sinners are tormented. The Titans and Giants are imprisoned here, along with other famous sinners who appear in almost every description of the underworld. Some receive straightforward torments: **Ixion**, who tried to rape Hera, is tied to a turning wheel of fire; the giant **Tityus**, who tried to rape Leto, is tied to the ground while vultures feed on his liver. Other punishments are more subtle, relying on frustration rather than pain. **Tantalus**, who tried to trick the gods into eating human flesh, is 'tantalised' by hunger and thirst in the midst of plenty: he stands in water which drains away when he tries to drink, under hanging fruit which swings out of his reach when he tries to eat. The **Danaids**, the husband-killing daughters of King Danaus, spend their time pouring water into a leaky jar. And the trickster **Sisyphus** – in an image that the Existentialist philosopher Albert Camus took as symbolic of the absurdity of human life – pushes a huge stone up a steep hill, and, every time he nears the top, sees it roll back down again. Presiding over the torments are the **Furies**, repulsive snake-haired female demons armed with whips and torches; originally responsible for hunting down and punishing murderers (as in Aeschylus's *Oresteia*), they later become generalised tormentors of the wicked; their names are **Alecto**, **Megaera**, and **Tisiphone**.

Other Greek monsters sometimes encountered in the underworld include the **Harpies** (bird-like creatures with the faces of women, of filthy habits, whose talons snatch food and other possessions); the **Gorgons** (snake-haired women, so hideous that the mere sight of them turns you to stone); and the **Chimaera** (a grotesque fire-breathing creature, part lion, part goat, and part snake, whose name has become a synonym for the completely unbelievable).

Just as Hades (the god) is not the devil, so Hades (the underworld) is not hell. This distinction, however, tends to be blurred by English writers, who from the Middle Ages onwards equate the two, speaking (for instance) of Orpheus's journey to hell. Elizabethan dramatists in particular loved to describe the afterlife in pagan terms, with lurid blood-and-thunder evocations of the horrors of Hades; and an eighteenth-century writer noted wryly that 'The poet generally sits down wholly undetermined whether Furies or Devils are to be the executioners he will make use of, and brings in either the one or the other, just as the humour takes or as the verse demands. If two syllables are wanting, it is Satan; but if four, you are sure of meeting with Tisiphone' (Joseph Spence, *Polymetis*, p. 300, quoted in Zwerdling 1964: 452).

Other gods

Some lesser gods, godlings, and creatures, mainly associated more closely with the earth than with Olympus or Hades.

Sun, Moon, Dawn, and Winds

The gods of Sun, Moon, and Dawn are rather insubstantial personifications. They are siblings, children of the Titans Hyperion and Thea. **Helius**, the sun god – sometimes confused with his father Hyperion, and sometimes simply called 'Titan' – drives the four-horse chariot of the sun across the sky each day, and returns each night in a golden cup across the Ocean. **Selene**, the moon goddess, rides across the night sky. In later mythology, they tend to get identified with Apollo and Artemis, who also take over the few legends associated with them (such as Helius's ill-fated loan of the sun-chariot to his son Phaethon, or Selene's love for the beautiful shepherd Endymion). **Eos/Aurora**, the dawn goddess (Homer's 'rosy-fingered Dawn'), accompanies the sun god; she is mainly a personification, but also known for her affairs with mortals such as Orion and Tithonous. (For all these legends, see chapter 3.)

The Winds in Homer are under the command of **Aeolus**, who keeps them locked up in a cave on his island in the Mediterranean. In later mythology some of them become substantial gods in their own right, particularly **Boreas**, the boisterous north wind, and **Zephyrus**, the gentle west wind – Chaucer's 'Zephirus . . . with his sweete breeth' (*Canterbury Tales*, General Prologue, 5).

Cronus / Saturn

Father of the Olympian gods, and one of the most ambiguous figures in the pantheon. In Greek myth, Cronus is the father of Zeus and his siblings, a savage figure who castrated his own father Uranus with a sickle, devoured his children, and was finally overthrown by Zeus. Another tradition, however, painted his rule as a Golden Age. The Romans identified him with the agricultural god Saturn (his sickle becoming a farmer's implement), and explained that the deposed god went into exile in Italy and there ruled over a golden age of peace, plenty, and justice; his December festival, the Saturnalia, was a time of anarchic merrymaking whose traditions contributed to those of Christmas. The combination of ogre and Father Christmas is hard to reconcile. To compound the confusion, some scholars identified Cronus with the Greek *chronos*, 'time', rationalising his cannibalism as a symbol of the devouring effects of time; hence he develops into the traditional figure of Old Father Time, the old man with his scythe (rather than sickle) and hourglass. In astrology the planet Saturn is associated with old age, disease, death, and misfortune, and those born under it are of 'saturnine' or gloomy temperament.

Rhea / Ops / Cybele

Rhea (Ops to the Romans), wife of Cronus and mother of the gods, tended to merge with her own mother Gaea (Earth) into a composite figure of the great earth mother. In later classical times she became identified with **Cybele**, a powerful Asian mother goddess, whose worship was formally introduced into Rome in 204 BC. Cybele rode in a chariot drawn by lions, wearing a turreted crown and followed by eunuch priests playing tambourines, flutes, and castanets. Her most famous myth concerned her young lover **Attis**, who betrayed her, was driven mad by the goddess, castrated himself and died. In Cybele's orgiastic rites her followers sometimes followed Attis's example and castrated themselves, an excess of religious enthusiasm regarded with astonishment and horror by the Greeks and Romans.

Pan

God of shepherds and wild nature, Pan is sometimes identified with the Roman **Faunus**. The son of Hermes/Mercury and a nymph, he is represented as a goat-man, with horns, hairy legs, hooves and a tail, and often playing on the pan-pipes (see the story of Syrinx in chapter 3). He haunts the mountains and forests of Arcadia in northern Greece, and is the friend of shepherds and goatherds; he is wild, mischievous, and lecherous, and his shout can induce irrational 'panic' fear. Pan would be only a minor rustic deity except for the coincidence that his name in Greek means 'all', and hence some ancient philosophers interpreted him as the god of everything, the personification of Nature. Moreover, the Greek essayist Plutarch (*Moralia*, 419) tells a strange story of a voice which was heard, during the reign of the emperor Tiberius, crying out 'Great Pan is dead' – a story which Christian writers associated with the death of Christ. Some, however, identified Pan with Christ, the Good Shepherd and all-ruler; others saw the horned and hooved god as a devilish figure, embodying the pagan gods giving way before the new age of Christ.

Some related Roman gods, often encountered in pastoral poetry, are **Silvanus** the god of forests, **Pomona** the goddess of fruits, **Flora** the goddess of flowers, and **Priapus** the garden god, whose statues, as a kind of gnome with a huge phallus, were used as garden scarecrows.

Nymphs, satyrs, and others

For the Greeks, all nature was alive with divine or semi-divine presences. Each river has its own **river god**, who may appear as a man with blue-green skin and hair streaming with water. Lesser features of the landscape are inhabited by female spirits called **nymphs**. They are of various kinds: **oceanids** and **nereids** are spirits of the sea, **oreads** of the mountains, **naiads** of lakes, streams, and fountains, **dryads** of trees. They are long-lived but not immortal, tied to the place that they inhabit, and dying if that place is destroyed. In mythology nymphs are often the object of love or lust by gods, and are treated almost as if they were human women.

If nymphs are halfway between humans and gods, **satyrs**, **fauns**, and **centaurs** are halfway between humans and beasts. Satyrs and fauns are both half man, half goat, like the god Pan, but fauns tend to be shy woodland creatures; satyrs are more boisterous, drunken, and lecherous, followers of Dionysus and chasers of nymphs. They were the heroes of the farcical 'satyr plays' that followed and mocked Greek tragedies.

The **centaurs** are creatures with a horse's body and a human torso. They are said to be the descendants of Ixion, who tried to rape Hera but was deceived with a cloud shaped to resemble her; the product of that unnatural union was the first centaur. In Greek mythology they are, for the most part, savage and violent, embodiments of the animal side of human nature. They are most famous for their savage battle with the Lapiths, a hill-country Greek tribe, which broke out when the centaurs became drunk at a Lapith wedding feast and tried to carry off the bride. An exception is Chiron, the wise and gentle old centaur who was tutor to a number of Greek heroes including Jason and Achilles.

The Fates

Last comes a group of deities who may be the most powerful of all: the three Fates. Sometimes called the daughters of Night, sometimes of Zeus and Themis, they oversee or control human destinies. They are usually portrayed as old women spinning: **Clotho** spins the thread, **Lachesis** measures it, and **Atropos** – 'the blind fury with the abhorrèd shears', in Milton's phrase (*Lycidas*, 75) – cuts it off. They embody the implacability of fate, whereas the related Roman and medieval goddess **Fortuna**, with her blindfold, turning wheel, and 'rolling restless stone' (Shakespeare, *Henry V*, 3. 6. 27), embodies the blind arbitrariness of chance.

3

A MYTHICAL HISTORY OF THE WORLD IN ONE CHAPTER

The myths of some cultures seem to occur in a timeless limbo, like the Australian Aboriginal Dreamtime – a period which is at once then, now, and always, in which normal laws of succession and causation are suspended. Classical mythology is very different. The Greeks saw their myths in a historical context, stretching from the ancient myths of the creation down to the Trojan War and the borders of recorded history, and held together by an elaborate (if at times contradictory) web of chronology and genealogy.[1] Ancient summaries of mythology, like Apollodorus's *Library*, are organised around the genealogies of heroic families and the histories of the great city-states that they ruled. For modern readers interested in the myths as they appear in English literature, such a framework is less relevant; and I have tried in this summary to focus on the stories that are interesting for their own sake, and to keep catalogues of kings and lists of 'X begat Y' to a minimum. Nevertheless, my account naturally falls into the framework of a mythological history of the world, in four broad periods:

- *Myths of origin*: stories of the origins of the world, the gods, and the human race.
- *Gods and mortals*: stories of the early interactions between gods, demigods, and mortals, in both love and enmity.
- *The age of heroes*: the sagas of great heroes and their families in the generations preceding the Trojan War – especially the stories of Perseus, Hercules, Jason, Theseus, and Oedipus.
- *The Trojan War and after*: the last and greatest of the heroic sagas.

Inevitably such a one-chapter summary is skeletal and oversimplified, skipping over significant details and omitting most of the variant versions which proliferate around every story. For fuller and more complex accounts, readers should turn to the works listed in the Bibliography, or, even better, to the classical sources noted in the course of the chapter.

Myths of origin

The origins of the gods

The most widely accepted account of beginning of things (as reported by Hesiod's *Theogony*) starts with Chaos, a yawning nothingness. Out of the void emerged **Ge** or **Gaea**, the Earth, and other primeval figures – including **Eros** or Love. Without male assistance Gaea gave birth to **Uranus**, the Sky, and **Pontus**, the Sea. Father Sky lay with Mother Earth and fertilised her. From that union were born, first, the next generation of gods, the **Titans**, six male and six female (**Cronus** and **Rhea**, **Oceanus** and **Tethys**, **Hyperion** and **Thea**, **Coeus** and **Phoebe**, **Iapetus**, **Crius**, **Themis**, and **Mnemosyne**); then more monstrous offspring, the one-eyed **Cyclopes** and the many-limbed **Hundred-Handers**.[2]

Uranus, understandably alarmed at his terrible children and fearing that they would try to overthrow him, refused to let them see the light of day and buried them back within the body of their mother, Earth. Gaea, in pain and grief, encouraged them to break out and rebel. The youngest and boldest of the Titans, 'crooked-minded' Cronus, took up the challenge. He lay in wait and, when Uranus came to make love to Gaea, castrated him with a jagged sickle. Uranus in his agony retreated up into the sky where he remains; his blood falling on the earth gave birth to the Giants and the Furies, and where his genitals were flung into the sea, sea-foam gathered and **Aphrodite**, goddess of love and desire, rose from the waters.

Cronus now took his father's place as ruler of the gods, with his sister-wife Rhea as his consort and the other Titans as his court. But the story of father/son conflict was repeated in the next generation: Cronus feared that his children would treat him as he had treated Uranus, and so disposed of each of them by swallowing them as soon as they were born. At last Rhea, like Gaea, took her children's side against her husband. When the sixth and youngest child, Zeus, was born, she tricked Cronus into swallowing a stone wrapped in swaddling clothes, while she spirited the child away to the pastoral island of Crete. There Zeus was brought up in a cave by nymphs, fed on honey and suckled by a she-goat. When he was grown he returned to confront Cronus, force him to vomit up his other children (**Hestia**, **Demeter**, **Hera**, **Hades**, and **Poseidon**), and challenge him to war for the kingship of the gods.

There followed ten years of literally titanic battles in which thunderbolts and lightning and whole mountaintops were tossed back and forth. At last, with the help of the Cyclopes, Zeus and his siblings were victorious, and Cronus and the other Titans were hurled down to imprisonment in Tartarus, the bottommost part of the underworld. (Some say, however, that Cronus went into exile on earth, and some of the other Titans, like Rhea, Oceanus, and Hyperion, continue to have a shadowy presence in later myths.) This was not the end of the wars in heaven: Zeus had to defend his throne against further rebellions – by the earth-born Giants, the Hundred-Handers, the great serpent-tailed man-dragon

Typhon, and other monstrous opponents who supplied material for thundering epic verse by later poets.[3]

At last, however, Zeus was established as ruler on Mount Olympus, with Hera as his sister-wife. He cast lots with his brothers for their areas of power, Zeus taking the sky, Poseidon the sea, and Hades the underworld; and he proceeded to father, on Hera and other goddesses, a fourth generation of gods (the legends of whose birth and early life have mostly been related in chapter 2). In Greek myth, Zeus remains the undisputed ruler of gods and men. Nevertheless, the bickering of the Olympian family and the fraught marital relationship of Zeus and Hera suggest that tensions still exist, and Zeus shares his father and grandfather's anxiety about being overthrown by one of his children. When warned that **Metis**, one of his wives, would bear a child wiser than its father, he swallowed Metis and her unborn child, thus ensuring that **Athena** was born (from his forehead) as his sole child, with no mother to encourage her to rebel; and a similar warning about the sea-nymph **Thetis** caused him to abandon his pursuit of her and marry her off instead to the mortal king **Peleus**, who became the father of Achilles.

The origins of humankind

The origins of humankind in Greek myth are obscure. Some versions say that men simply sprang up from the earth; others that they were created by Zeus or by some other deity; others that **Prometheus** ('forethought'), a second-generation Titan, son of Iapetus, made the first men out of clay. (I say 'men' advisedly, for, as we shall see, women had a separate origin.) In any case, whether or not Prometheus was the creator of men, he quickly became their protector and benefactor. Among other gifts of knowledge and practical skills, he stole fire from heaven so they could keep warm and cook their food, and he cunningly tricked Zeus into agreeing that they could keep the meat of the animals they sacrificed to the gods, while the gods got only the smoke and bones. Enraged by these thefts and tricks, Zeus had Prometheus nailed to a cliff in the Caucasus mountains, where an eagle or vulture daily pecked at his liver. Some say that he is still there, others that **Hercules** eventually freed him; in one story, he bought his release by telling Zeus the vital secret that Thetis's son was destined to be greater than his father.

Zeus also punished mankind, by creating the first woman. Constructed by Hephaestus and endowed with gifts of beauty, skill, and charm by the gods, she was named **Pandora** ('all gifts'). Zeus sent her down as a gift to mankind, bearing a sealed jar (in later versions it becomes 'Pandora's box') as her dowry. Prometheus's foolish brother **Epimetheus** ('afterthought', that is, he who acts first and thinks later) accepted the gift. When the curious Pandora opened the jar, out flew all the evils – old age, poverty, disease, hard work – which ever since have afflicted humanity; only hope remained hidden inside. Thus, according to the misogynistic Hesiod, it is woman who is responsible for all the miseries of human life. (The stories of Prometheus and Pandora are told by Hesiod in *Theogony*,

507–616, and *Works and Days*, 47–105; Prometheus is also the hero of Aeschylus's tragedy *Prometheus Bound*.)

As time passed, Zeus became increasingly disgusted with the wickedness of the human race, and eventually, like the biblical God, he resolved to wipe it out in a great **Flood** and start again. The Greek equivalent of Noah and his family, the virtuous humans who were spared from the calamity, were **Deucalion**, son of Prometheus, and his wife **Pyrrha**, daughter of Epimetheus. After the waters receded and their little boat touched dry land, they consulted an oracle for advice, and were shocked to be told to 'throw your mother's bones behind your back'. Then they realised that their mother was Mother Earth, and her bones were stones. They walked along throwing stones behind their backs; those thrown by Deucalion turned into men, those thrown by Pyrrha into women. So the world was repopulated and the survival of humankind assured. (The best account of the Flood is that of Ovid in *Metamorphoses*, 1. 244–437.)

Any account of the mythical history of the world should mention the concept of **the Four Ages**. According to Hesiod (*Works and Days*, 106–200) and Ovid (*Met.*, 1. 89–162), human history has passed through four periods, each worse than the last. First came the Golden Age, an age of primitive innocence and perpetual summer, in which people lived on wild fruits and milk and honey, without government, laws, or warfare (this is sometimes identified with the rule of Cronus/Saturn). Then came the Silver Age, in which the seasons began and agriculture and work were invented; then the Bronze (or Brazen) Age, in which warfare began; and finally the Iron Age, in which we now live, a time of violence, cruelty, corruption, and misery. It is hard to reconcile this pattern with the rest of Greek mythology, and in fact Hesiod inserts an 'Age of Heroes' between the Bronze and Iron Ages to order to make room for most of the great mythological sagas. Nevertheless, the Golden Age is a potent myth, and the whole pattern is a useful reminder that the Greeks and Romans, on the whole, saw history as a matter not of progress but of decline from original perfection.

Gods and mortals

This section contains a collection of legends about relationships between gods, demigods (such as nymphs and river-spirits), and mortals, in the early days of the world when the groups mingled more freely than they did later. Most of these tales are most famously told in Ovid's *Metamorphoses* (and therefore I have used the Roman names of the gods in this section). These are mainly isolated stories, not linked to any major family or national saga. It seems most useful to divide them into two thematic groups: tales of love, and tales of punishment.

Tales of love

'Tales of love' is perhaps an over-romantic term, for many of the stories show gods 'committing heady riots, incest, rapes' (in Marlowe's phrase, *Hero and*

Leander, l. 144) upon unwilling women or nymphs; and even consenting relationships rarely have happy endings. The stories generally suggest that relationships between gods and mortals are something to avoid.

Jupiter was the most insatiable divine lover, seducing, raping, or abducting nymphs and women (and occasional boys) in a variety of disguises. He approached **Antiopa** in the shape of a satyr; **Danae** as a shower of gold; **Leda** as a swan; **Europa** as a bull; **Alcmena** in the form of her husband; the Trojan prince **Ganymede** as an eagle, which carried him up to Olympus to be his cupbearer. Several unfortunate women found themselves caught between Jupiter's advances and Juno's jealous rage. **Io**, for instance, was turned by Jupiter into a cow to conceal her from Juno's inquiring eye, but Juno demanded the cow as a gift, and proceeded to torment her, driving her from place to place by the stinging of a monstrous gadfly; she finally found shelter in Egypt, where, in some accounts, she became the Egyptian cow-goddess Isis (*Met.*, 1). **Callisto**, a huntress-nymph in Diana's train, was raped by Jupiter (disguised as Diana), cast out by Diana when her pregnancy became obvious, and, after the birth of her child, transformed by the jealous Juno into a bear. Years later her son, out hunting, encountered her in bear form and was about to kill her – but Jupiter averted this final tragedy by turning them both into the constellations of the Great and Little Bear (*Met.*, 2). **Semele** was tricked by Juno into making Jupiter promise to appear to her in his full divine glory, and was consequently blasted to ashes, though her child Dionysus/Bacchus was saved (*Met.*, 3).

Apollo was also a keen, and usually unlucky, lover. **Coronis** betrayed him with a mortal lover and died of an arrow from Apollo's deadly bow, though he saved her unborn child Aesculapius (Pindar, Pythian Ode 3; *Met.*, 2). **Daphne**, fleeing his advances, prayed for escape and was transformed into a laurel tree, which Apollo adopted as his sacred emblem (*Met.*, 1). His male lovers were equally unfortunate: **Hyacinthus** died when Apollo accidentally hit him with a misthrown discus, and was turned into the flower that bears his name; **Cyparissus** pined away after accidentally killing his own pet stag, and was turned into a cypress tree (*Met.*, 10). Apollo could be vindictive to those who refused his advances. He granted the Trojan princess **Cassandra** powers of prophesy but, when she refused to submit to him, added the rider that no one would ever believe her. To another great prophetess who resisted him, the **Sibyl of Cumae**, he granted as many years of life as there were grains in a handful of sand, but refused to add the gift of youth; the Sibyl lived a thousand years, and was described by the Roman novelist Petronius as hanging in a wicker bottle and telling visitors, 'I want to die' (*Met.*, 14; Petronius, *Satyricon*, 48).

A similar tale was told of **Tithonus**, lover of the dawn goddess Aurora: she asked Jupiter to grant him immortality but forgot to ask for agelessness as well, and he gradually shrivelled away until she transformed him into a cicada, a small bony creature with a creaking voice. The shepherd-prince **Endymion**, lover of the moon goddess Selene, had a perhaps happier fate: she cast him into a perpetual sleep, so that she could always come and look at his beauty. Venus, the love goddess, has surprisingly few recorded lovers; the most famous was **Adonis**, who was killed by a wild boar, and whose story is dealt with in detail in chapter 5. Another was the Trojan prince **Anchises**, to whom she bore the hero **Aeneas**; Anchises made the error of boasting about the relationship and was crippled by a lightning bolt from the irritated goddess (see the 'Homeric Hymn to Aphrodite'). The story of Pan and **Syrinx** resembles that of Apollo and Daphne: Syrinx, pursued by the goat-god, turned herself into a bunch of reeds, out of which Pan fashioned his famous pan-pipes (*Met.*, 1).

A rare story with a happy ending is that of **Cupid and Psyche**, told (and perhaps invented) by Lucius Apuleius in his romance *The Golden Ass* (books 4–6). Venus had ordered Cupid to punish Psyche because her beauty was attracting worshippers away from the goddess, but Cupid fell in love with her instead. He visited her every night in the dark, only forbidding her to look on him. Tempted by curiosity and fear, she lit a lamp one night to see him sleeping; a falling drop of oil woke him, and he vanished. Psyche searched the world for her lost lover, and fell into the hands of the vengeful Venus, who imposed on her a series of cruel tasks. At last, however, Cupid returned to claim his bride, Venus was pacified, and Psyche became a goddess. The name 'Pysche' means 'soul', and the story can easily be read as an allegory of a spiritual quest.

Other Ovidian tales involve unnatural or hopeless love. The handsome **Narcissus** fell in love with his own reflection in a pool, and pined away and died of frustrated love, to become a flower and a psychological term ('narcissism'); while his rejected lover **Echo**, condemned only to repeat the words spoken to her, pined away into a mere wandering voice (*Met.*, 3). The water-nymph **Salmacis** fell in love with **Hermaphroditus** when he came to bathe in her pool and, seizing him in her embrace, prayed that they might never be parted; the gods over-literally turned the two into the first hermaphrodite (*Met.*, 4). In other cases Venus intervened more benevolently, bringing the sculptor **Pygmalion**'s statue to life so he could marry it (see chapter 6 below), or transforming the girl **Iphis** into a boy so she could marry her beloved **Ianthe** (*Met.*, 9).

The most tragic Greek myths of love, however, do not necessarily involve gods or magic, just human beings in the grip of sexual obsession, like **Medea** (see 'Jason') or **Phaedra** (see 'Theseus'). Perhaps the most terrible is that of the Thracian king **Tereus**, who married **Procne** but became obsessed with her sister **Philomela**. He raped Philomela, cut out her tongue to prevent her revealing the story, and locked her in a cabin in the woods; but Philomela sewed a picture of the scene into a tapestry and sent it to Procne, who released her. The women avenged themselves by killing **Itys**, Tereus' and Procne's little boy, and serving his flesh up to his father at dinner. When he discovered the truth Tereus tried to kill the women, but the gods turned them all into birds – Tereus a hoopoe, Procne a swallow, Philomela a nightingale (*Met.*, 6).[4] For the Greeks, as these stories suggest, sexual desire was a powerful, dangerous, and often destructive force.

Tales of punishment

The other great theme of stories is the gods' punishment of mortals who offended or defied them. A central Greek concept was *hubris*: the sin of over-reaching pride, which attempts to achieve more than is permitted to humans, and invites *nemesis*, divine punishment. This theme runs through many of the great Greek myths, perhaps because the striving to achieve heroic fame almost inevitably leads to hubris and hence to nemesis.

The worst punishments were reserved for those who directly challenged the gods' power. Into this category fell some of the great sinners in Tartarus (see 'The underworld' in chapter 2), like **Tantalus**, who tested the gods' omniscience by serving up the cooked flesh of his own son to them at a banquet; or **Salmoneus**, who (whether in impiety or insanity) claimed to be Zeus, and rode around in a chariot flinging torches for thunderbolts. The most tragic case is that of **Pentheus**, king of Thebes, who tried to ban the orgiastic rites of Dionysus from his city; Dionysus lured him into disguising himself as a woman to go and spy on the rites, where he was caught and torn to pieces by the maddened women led by his own mother **Agave**. (The story is told in Euripides' tragedy *The Bacchae*.)

Some mortals invite divine punishment by boasting. The Lydian queen **Niobe** boasted that her twelve sons and daughters were superior to Leto's children, Apollo and Diana; all her children were killed by the arrows of the angry god and goddess, and the bereaved Niobe wept and wept until she turned to stone (*Met.*, 6). Andromeda (see 'Perseus' below) and Myrrha (see chapter 5) were similarly punished for the boasting of their over-fond parents. Others challenged the gods by claiming superior skills. **Arachne** claimed to be a better weaver than Athena; the goddess turned her into a spider, to continue spinning and weaving webs in that form (*Met.*, 6). The satyr **Marsyas** claimed to be a better musician with his flute than Apollo with his lyre; Apollo defeated him in a contest, and celebrated the victory by skinning him alive (*Met.*, 6). In another musical contest it was the judge who suffered: King **Midas** of Phrygia gave Pan's pipes the victory over Apollo's lyre, and was rewarded by the ungracious loser with a pair of donkey's ears. Midas was proverbially foolish; he was also the king who, offered a wish by Bacchus, asked that everything he touched should turn to gold – a gift he was happy to relinquish after a few days of luxurious starvation (*Met.*, 11).

Others offended the gods more or less accidentally. **Actaeon**, for instance, while hunting accidentally stumbled into a glade where Diana and her nymphs were bathing; the offended goddess turned him into a stag, and he was hunted down and torn to pieces by his own hounds (*Met.*, 3). Another whose only sin was tactlessness was the great Theban seer **Tiresias**, who appears in many stories and haunts Greek tragedy with his usually unheeded warnings. Tiresias had been both a man and a woman in the course of his life, and so was called on by Jupiter and Juno to settle an argument about which sex got the greater pleasure from the sexual act; he replied 'women', and was promptly struck blind by Juno, though Jupiter gave him the gift of prophesy as compensation (*Met.*, 3).

A few attempted more literally to rise above their place. One such was **Bellerophon** of Corinth, who rode the winged horse **Pegasus** and achieved many heroic deeds, including the killing of the monstrous Chimaera. At last, in his overweening pride, he attempted to fly to Olympus on Pegasus's back; but Jupiter sent a gadfly to sting the horse, which bucked and threw him to earth, leaving him a crippled outcast. **Icarus** also suffered for flying too high (see 'Theseus' below). So did **Phaethon**, the young son of the sun god (Helius or Apollo), who, when his father offered him anything he wanted, demanded to be allowed to drive the sun-chariot for a day. Bound by his rash promise, the god had to agree. But Phaethon could not control the wild horses of the sun; he careered off course, scorching the earth, and Jupiter had to strike him down with a thunderbolt to save the world from destruction (*Met.*, 1–2). Such myths of heroic flights and falls epitomise the Greek conviction that human beings should keep their feet on the ground and avoid challenging the gods.

The age of heroes

The 'age of heroes' in Greek mythology is fairly well defined. It is the generation or two leading up to the Trojan War, during which most of the greatest Greek heroes were active, and from which the Greek tragedians took most of the material for their plays. This section will deal with four major figures from this period (Hercules, Jason, Theseus, Oedipus), and one (Perseus) from a slightly earlier period.[5]

It will be obvious that these tales share many repeated themes and motifs: the hero's mysterious birth and his quest to regain his inheritance; the father or grandfather who tries to kill the hero out of fear; the impossible quest or set of tasks, imposed by a rival who seeks to dispose of the hero; the love-struck enemy princess who helps him; the descent into the underworld; the fated disaster and the attempt (inevitably unsuccessful) to evade it; most of all, perhaps, the contrast between the heroes' public achievements and their tragic private lives. In the ultimately bleak world of the Greek sagas, it sometimes seems that the most dangerous thing a hero can do – far worse than confronting Hydras or Minotaurs or Gorgons – is to marry or have children.

Perseus

Perseus belongs to an earlier generation than the other heroes; he is, in fact, Hercules' great-grandfather. (The only complete account of his career is given by the mythographer Apollodorus, 2. 4, but Ovid tells much of it in *Metamorphoses*, 4–5.)

Perseus was the son of Zeus and **Danae**, daughter of King **Acrisius** of Argos. Acrisius had been warned by an oracle that Danae's child would kill him, and so he locked her up in a tower of brass which no man was permitted to approach. But Zeus entered the tower in the form of a shower of gold (a scene beloved of artists and moralists), and soon Danae gave birth to Perseus. Acrisius did not dare to incur the blood-guilt of directly killing his daughter and grandson, but he sealed the two of them up in a wooden chest and floated it out to sea. With Zeus's help, it washed up on the island of Seriphos, where Danae and Perseus were taken in by a kindly fisherman.

The king of Seriphos, **Polydectes**, became interested in the beautiful castaway, and as Perseus grew up he had to protect his mother from the king's unwelcome attentions. Deciding to rid himself of the interfering youth, Polydectes lured him into a rash boast that he would give the king the head of the Gorgon **Medusa** – and sent him off on the impossible quest. The **Gorgons** were three female monsters with living snakes for hair and faces so hideous that the mere sight of them would turn you to stone. Two of them were immortal, but Medusa was once a mortal woman whom Athena had changed into this horrible shape as a punishment, either for boasting that she was more beautiful than the goddess, or for making love to Poseidon in one of her shrines.

Whether from friendship for Perseus or hostility to Medusa, it was Athena who now decided to help the hero in his task (in some versions, Hermes also helped). By her guidance, Perseus gathered the magical tools he needed to kill the Gorgon: a pair of winged sandals, a cap of invisibility, a leather bag, and an adamantine sword. Using the winged sandals he flew to the far edge of the world, where he found the Gorgons sleeping. Looking (by Athena's advice) not at Medusa's deadly face but only at her reflection in his shield, he cut off her head. From her body sprang the winged horse **Pegasus**, Poseidon's child.

By flight and invisibility Perseus escaped the rage of the other Gorgons. Flying home, with Medusa's head in his leather bag, he passed over the coast of Libya, where he saw a beautiful princess, **Andromeda**, chained to a rock and menaced by a sea-monster. Her mother **Cassiopeia** had foolishly boasted that Andromeda was more beautiful than the sea-nymphs, and the offended Poseidon had sent a flood and a sea-monster to ravage the shores; the king and queen were forced to offer her up as a sacrifice to appease the sea god. Perseus flew down and – after a rapid negotiation with the king about marriage terms – slew the monster and rescued the princess. Perseus and Andromeda were married – though the ceremony was interrupted by a rival suitor, Andromeda's uncle **Phineus**, and Perseus had to use Medusa's head to turn him and his followers to stone.

Perseus returned to Seriphos, where he found King Polydectes on the point of forcibly marrying Danae. Perseus triumphantly announced that, as promised, he had brought back the Gorgon's head, and as he drew it from his bag the dismayed king and his lords turned to stone. Leaving the good fisherman as the new king of Seriphos, Perseus returned to Argos with his mother and wife, hoping for a reconciliation with his grandfather Acrisius. Stopping by the way to take part in an athletics contest, he accidentally struck another contestant with a discus and killed him. It was, of course, Acrisius, and so the oracle was at last fulfilled. Having accidentally incurred this blood-guilt, Perseus refused the throne of Argos, and instead, by an exchange of kingdoms, took the throne of neighbouring Tiryns. He ruled well, founded the great city of Mycenae, and – almost uniquely among Greek heroes – lived happily with his wife for the rest of his long life. After their deaths both Perseus and Andromeda were placed in the sky as constellations, along with Andromeda's parents Cepheus and Casssiopeia and the sea-monster (Cetus); all of them can still be seen in the northern sky. As for the Gorgon's head, Athena took it and wore it thereafter on her shield.

Hercules

Heracles, or Hercules, to use his more familiar Latin name,[6] is unquestionably the greatest and most famous of the Greek heroes. Even today the brawny man with his great club, his lion-skin cloak, and his 'herculean' strength is still a recognisable figure, and his fame has recently been perpetuated in a popular TV series and a Disney cartoon. Such modern versions, however, tend to simplify and sanitise the original hero, who is a benefactor of humankind but also violent, unpredictable, and destructive. (Despite Hercules' fame, there is no surviving literary work that tells his story at length; the fullest account is in Apollodorus, 2. 4–7, and Ovid, *Met.*, 9, tells the stories of his birth and death.)

Hercules was the son of Zeus by a mortal woman, **Alcmena**. Alcmena and her husband **Amphitryon** were both grandchildren of Perseus, and Amphitryon would have succeeded Alcmena's father as king of Mycenae, if only he had not accidentally killed the king in the confusion of a battle, and been exiled to Thebes. While Amphitryon was away on a long military campaign, Zeus disguised himself as Amphitryon, visited Thebes, and spent a long night with Alcmena. When the real Amphitryon returned later that night he was somewhat confused to find he had already been home; but he accepted the god's intervention and spent the rest of the night with his wife. So were begotten Hercules and his mortal twin **Iphicles**. (The possibilities for bedroom farce in this situation were exploited by the Roman playwright Plautus in his *Amphitryon*, and by later dramatists including Molière, Dryden, and Giraudoux.)

Zeus's intention was that Hercules should become king of Mycenae and the greatest of Greek rulers: 'a child of my blood born today,' he prophesied, 'will rule over all who dwell round him.' But Hera, always bitterly jealous of her husband's bastard children, determined to frustrate his plans. Using her powers as goddess of childbirth, she delayed Hercules' birth, and speeded up the birth of his cousin **Eurystheus** in Mycenae. So the feeble, cowardly Eurystheus (also a descendant of Perseus and hence of Zeus) got the benefit of the prophesy: he would be king, and Hercules his vassal. Not content with this, Hera sent a pair of snakes to kill Hercules in his cradle; but the newborn hero happily strangled them (see Pindar, Nemean Ode 1, and Theocritus, Idyll 24).

Hercules grew up immensely strong, utterly fearless, with an ungovernable temper (he killed his music teacher **Linus** by hitting him with his lyre) and a huge appetite for food, drink, and sex (he slept with the fifty daughters of a local king, either on successive nights or, in the more heroic version, in a single night). As a reward for his services in battle he married the Theban princess **Megara**, and they had three children. But Hera was still plotting revenge. She sent a fit of madness on Hercules, in which he killed Megara and the children, taking them for monsters. (This madness is the subject of Euripides' *Heracles* and Seneca's *Hercules Furens* – though both tragedies place it after, not before, the Twelve Labours.) Having recovered his sanity, he asked Apollo's oracle at Delphi how he could purify himself of blood-guilt, and the oracle ordered him to serve his cousin King Eurystheus for twelve years and carry out twelve tasks that he would impose.

This was the start of the famous **Twelve Labours of Hercules**, which began with local quests around Mycenae but gradually extended – as Eurystheus became more desperate to get rid of Hercules – to all parts of the known world and beyond. The Labours were as follows:

1 To kill the **Nemean Lion**. Hercules killed it either with his club or with his bare hands, skinned it, and thereafter wore the lion-skin.
2 To kill the **Lernaean Hydra**, a poisonous, many-headed monster, which grew two new heads whenever one was destroyed. Hercules killed it with the help of his nephew **Iolaus**, who cauterised the stumps with a burning torch to prevent them regenerating. He used the Hydra's blood as poison for his arrows.
3 To capture the **Golden Hind of Cerynea**, a swift-footed deer with golden horns, sacred to Artemis.
4 To capture the **Erymanthian Boar**. When Hercules returned with this monstrous beast casually slung over his shoulders, Eurystheus was so terrified that he hid inside a large bronze jar, which he kept ready for Hercules' subsequent visits.
5 To clean up the **Augean Stables**. The stables of King Augeas of Elis held vast herds of cattle, and the accumulated dung of decades had never been cleared. Hercules cleaned them out in a day by diverting two rivers through them. ('Cleansing the Augean stables' is still a cliché for dealing with a mess of monstrous proportions.)
6 To kill the **Stymphalian Birds**, a vast flock infesting Lake Stymphalus; Hercules either scared them off with brass castanets, or shot them.
7 To capture the **Cretan Bull** – the bull which had fathered the Minotaur (see under **Theseus** below), and which had escaped to ravage Crete. Hercules brought it back to Greece and rather thoughtlessly released it, where it created more havoc until Theseus killed it.
8 To capture the **Thracian Horses**, a flock of savage mares kept by the wicked Thracian king Diomedes and fed by him on human flesh; Hercules fed Diomedes himself to his horses before bringing them home.
9 To bring back the **Belt of the Amazon Queen**. The **Amazons** were a tribe of warrior women who lived in the north of Asia and fought fiercely with bows and arrows, cutting off one breast (*amazon* means 'breastless') to

give them more free play with the bow. Hercules (accompanied in some versions by Theseus) fought the Amazons, killed their queen, **Hippolyta**, and took her gold-studded belt.

10 To steal the **Cattle of Geryon**. Geryon, a monstrous being described sometimes as three-headed, sometimes as three-bodied, tended a flock of cattle on an island in the far west. Hercules borrowed the golden cup of the sun god Helius to sail across the Ocean to the island, where he killed Geryon, along with his giant herdsman and his two-headed dog, and brought back the cattle. On his return he set up the **Pillars of Hercules** on either side of the strait of Gibraltar, marking the furthest limit of the known world; he also had many adventures as he drove the cattle back across Europe, including killing the fire-breathing giant **Cacus** on the site of the future city of Rome.

11 To steal the **Apples of the Hesperides**. The Hesperides, daughters of Night, lived in a paradisal garden somewhere in the far west, singing and dancing round a grove of trees which grew golden apples, and was guarded by an immortal hundred-headed dragon. According to some, Hercules himself killed the dragon and stole some apples. A more common version says that Hercules persuaded **Atlas**, the gigantic Titan (brother of Prometheus) who holds up the sky on his shoulders, to go and fetch the apples while Hercules took his place holding up the sky. (Hence the famous image of Hercules holding the sky, or in some versions the globe of the world, on his shoulders.) Then, after tricking the reluctant Atlas into shouldering his load again, he returned home with the apples.

12 To kidnap **Cerberus**, the monstrous three-headed guard dog of the underworld. Hades agreed that Hercules could take the hound if he could overcome it with his bare hands; Hercules did so, and carried the snarling beast back to Mycenae to show it to the terrified Eurystheus, before returning it to the underworld. So the Labours were completed.

The other deeds which Hercules carried out, in the course of his Labours or afterwards, are far too many to list. He briefly sailed with the Argonauts (see 'Jason' below). He is said to have released Prometheus from his chains on Mount Caucasus, and Theseus from his imprisonment in the underworld (see 'Theseus' below). He successfully wrestled with Death for the soul of **Alcestis**, who had willingly agreed to die in the place of her husband **Admetus** (see Euripides' tragicomedy *Alcestis*). He killed innumerable giants, monsters, and brigands, most notably the giant **Antaeus**, a child of Gaea who drew his strength from the earth; Hercules hoisted him up in the air and strangled him. He waged a number of wars, some just, some less so, against cities and kings who offended him: for instance, when king **Laomedon** of Troy refused him the promised reward for rescuing his daughter **Hesione** from a sea-monster, Hercules came back with an army, sacked Troy, killed Laomedon, and put his son **Priam** on the throne.

After the Labours were over Hercules took a second wife: **Deianira**, a princess of Calydon, whom he won by defeating his rival, the river god **Achelous**, in a wrestling contest. Returning home, they came to a river where the centaur **Nessus** offered to carry Deianira across; but on the way he tried to rape her, and Hercules, from the river bank, shot him with a poisoned arrow. The dying Nessus pretended remorse, and told Deianira to take some of the blood from his wound: if she ever lost Hercules' affection, it would act as an infallible love potion.

Later Hercules fell in love with another woman, **Iole**, princess of Oechalia. He pursued her with some vigour, in the process murdering her brother (for which crime he did penance by being made a slave to queen **Omphale** of Libya, who dressed him in women's clothes and set him to spin wool), and making war on her city. In an attempt to reclaim his love, Deianira soaked a tunic in the centaur's blood and sent it by a servant to Hercules. When he put it on the Hydra's poison began to burn him, and when he tried to tear it off it tore away his flesh. Raging in intolerable pain, he flung the messenger into the sea (while Deianira, hearing the news, hanged herself in remorse); then he built a funeral pyre on Mount Oeta and burned himself to death. But, although his mortal body died, his divine part ascended to heaven, where his father Zeus welcomed him as a god and married him to Hebe, the goddess of youth. (The death of Hercules is the subject of Sophocles' *Women of Trachis* and the Roman tragedy *Hercules on Oeta*, attributed to Seneca; see also Ovid, *Met.*, 9.)

Jason

Jason is perhaps one of the less heroic of the Greek heroes – fully human, and dependent in most of his adventures on the help of his companions and his wife. His story falls into two distinct parts: the romantic adventure of the Argonauts and the quest for the Golden Fleece, and the tragedy of the marriage of Jason and Medea. (The story of Jason and the Argonauts is told in Apollonius of Rhodes' *Argonautica*, and more briefly in Pindar's Fourth Pythian Ode; Ovid, *Met.*, 7, tells much of the story, focusing on Medea's magic.)

Jason was the son of **Aeson**, the rightful king of Iolcos (a small kingdom in Thessaly), whose throne had been usurped by his half-brother **Pelias**. Jason was brought up in secret in the hills, and tutored by the wise old centaur **Chiron**. When he reached manhood he set off for Iolcos to claim his father's kingdom. On the way, he helped an old woman across a river, losing one of his sandals in the process. The old woman was in fact the goddess Hera, who had her own reasons for hating Pelias (who had refused to sacrifice to her), and who decided to help Jason. When the youth arrived in Iolcos, Pelias was alarmed: an oracle had warned him to beware of a man with only one sandal. Like Polydectes in the Perseus legend, he decided that the best way to get rid of this inconvenient young hero was to send him off on a dangerous quest, and so he promised Jason that he would surrender the throne if Jason could bring him back the **Golden Fleece**.

The Golden Fleece was a treasure famous in Jason's family. A generation or two earlier, a young Thessalian prince and princess had been about to be sacrificed, by the machinations of their wicked stepmother, when a magnificent golden ram with wings flew down and carried them off to the east. The girl, **Helle**, fell off and drowned in what was thereafter known as the Hellespont, but the boy, **Phrixus**, arrived safely in **Colchis**, a rich and eerily magical barbarian land on the far shore of the Black Sea, where king **Aeetes**, son of the sun god, welcomed him and gave him his daughter in marriage. The ram was sacrificed, and its golden fleece hung up in a sacred grove guarded by a dragon.

Jason had a great ship built, the **Argo** ('swift') – according to some, the first ship, or the first ocean-going ship, ever built. He assembled a crew of fifty **Argonauts** that included most of the heroes of the age: Hercules, **Orpheus** the musician, the brothers **Castor** and **Polydeuces/Pollux**, **Meleager**, **Atalanta**, **Peleus**, **Telamon**, the seer **Mopsus**, the keen-eyed **Lynceus**, **Zetes** and **Calais** the winged sons of the north wind, and others. They had many adventures on the journey: the loss of young **Hylas**, stolen by amorous water-nymphs (and of his lover Hercules, who left the ship to search for him); Pollux's boxing match to the death with the brutal king **Amycus**; a pleasant if slightly nervous interlude with the women of Lemnos, who had killed their husbands, and whose queen **Hypsipyle** fell in love with Jason; a battle with the Harpies which tormented the blind king **Phineas**; an encounter with the bronze giant **Talus** (whom they killed by shooting out the bronze nail in his ankle and letting the ichor that animated him drain out); the deadly passage between the **Clashing Rocks**, which would crush any ship that passed between them. At last they arrived at Colchis.[7]

King Aeetes did not welcome them. He told Jason that to win the Golden Fleece he must carry out a series of impossible tasks: to yoke a pair of fire-breathing bulls and plough a field with them, to sow it with dragon's teeth, and then to kill the warriors who would grow from the teeth. However, the king's daughter **Medea**, herself a powerful sorceress, fell in love with Jason. She helped Jason to carry out the tasks, giving him a magic ointment that made him invulnerable to fire or sword, showing him how to trick the earth-born warriors into killing one another, and charming the dragon guardian to sleep so that Jason could kill it and steal the fleece. And as the Argo escaped from Colchis, with Medea on board, she aided their escape by a ruthless strategem – killing her little brother and throwing the pieces of his body overboard to distract the pursuing Colchian ships.

After many more adventures – including Jason's marriage to Medea along the way – the Argonauts returned to Iolcos and delivered the Golden Fleece to Pelias. Pelias, however, refused to surrender the throne. Once again, Medea took bold steps to solve the problem. Having already magically restored the youth of Aeson, Jason's father, she persuaded Pelias's daughters that they could do the same for their father, by chopping him up into pieces and boiling him in a cauldron of magical herbs. They did so – but (Medea having left out the vital ingredient) Pelias failed to survive the treatment. However, Jason and Medea did not profit by this murder, for they were banished from Iolcos.

They went into exile in Corinth, where Medea bore Jason two children.

However, Jason was clearly beginning to regret his marriage to a barbarian witch, and at last decided to divorce her in order to marry **Glauce**, the king of Corinth's daughter. Euripides' tragedy *Medea* deals with the enraged Medea's revenge for this betrayal: she sent the bride a poisoned robe and crown, which burned both her and her father to death; then murdered her own children by Jason, and flew away in a chariot drawn by dragons towards Athens (where she reappears in the story of Theseus).[8] Jason was left to mourn, until at last he met a sad and ironic end: as he sat brooding under the rotting hulk of the Argo, a piece of its stern fell and killed him.

Theseus

Theseus is the national hero of Athens, later the greatest of Greek cities, and his saga seems to have been built up by the Athenians in conscious imitation of the exploits of Hercules. Like that of Jason, his story moves from romantic and heroic youth to a painful and tragic old age. (The best connected account of Theseus's story is the biographer Plutarch's 'Life of Theseus', though he tends to rationalise the mythical elements. Mary Renault's novels *The King Must Die* and *The Bull from the Sea* are excellent modern retellings.)

Theseus was the son of **Aegeus**, king of Athens, and **Aethra**, a princess of Troezen, with whom Aegeus spent one night when he passed through her father's kingdom. (It is also said, however, that Aethra was visited on the same night by Poseidon, and that the sea god was Theseus's true father.) Before Aegeus left, he placed a sword underneath a great rock, and ordered Aethra not to tell their child of his parentage until he was able to lift the rock. When Theseus grew to manhood he took the sword from under the stone, learned his true identity, and set out for Athens to claim his inheritance. On the coastal road from Troezen to Athens he killed a number of monsters and brigands, including **Procrustes**, who forced his victims to lie in his notorious bed and cut or stretched them to length if they did not fit (hence the adjective 'Procrustean' for those who doggedly attempt to force square pegs into round holes).

In Athens, King Aegeus had fallen under the malign spell of the witch Medea, who had taken refuge there after her escape from Corinth (see 'Jason' above). When Theseus arrived, Medea persuaded Aegeus that this young monster-slayer was a dangerous threat, and Aegeus agreed to let her poison him. At the last moment he recognised the sword Theseus was wearing and dashed the poisoned cup from his lips. He embraced his son and publicly proclaimed him his heir, while Medea was banished, to return to her native Colchis.

At this time Athens was bound to send every year a tribute of seven youths and seven girls to Crete, to be fed to the **Minotaur**. The story behind this is a dark and tragic one. **Minos**, king of Crete, though a son of Zeus and renowned for his stern justice, had offended Poseidon by failing to sacrifice a magnificent bull which the sea god had sent him for that purpose, but keeping it for his own herd. As punishment, Poseidon caused Minos's queen, **Pasiphae**, to conceive an unnatural lust for the bull. With the help of the great Athenian craftsman and inventor **Daedalus**, who constructed a wooden model of a cow for her to hide inside, Pasiphae consummated her lust, and subsequently gave birth to the Minotaur – a savage monster with a human body and a bull's head. Minos had Daedalus build a **Labyrinth**, a massive maze of incomprehensibly twisting passages, and hid his shameful secret at the heart of it, feeding the monster on human prisoners. He also imprisoned Daedalus and his son **Icarus** inside the Labyrinth, so they could not reveal the secret of the maze. But the inventor constructed wings for himself and his son out of feathers fastened with wax, and so flew away from Crete. Daedalus made it to Sicily, but young Icarus in his exhilaration flew too high, the sun melted the wax of his wings, and he plunged into the sea – becoming a classic example of hubris (*Met.*, 8).

To return to Theseus: when he learned of the tribute to Crete, he volunteered to be one of the fourteen sacrifices, and Aegeus reluctantly let him go – asking only that, if he returned safely, he should hoist a white sail on his ship instead of the usual black one. When he arrived in Crete, Minos's daughter **Ariadne** (repeating the story of Jason and Medea) fell in love with the handsome prisoner. She gave him a ball of thread, with which he was able to find his way into the heart of the Labyrinth, kill the Minotaur, find his way out, and escape from Crete with the other prisoners and Ariadne. However, Theseus's triumphant homecoming was marred by two episodes. First, he left Ariadne behind on the island of Naxos – an act which some writers condemn as a cynical betrayal, others excuse as obedience to a divine command, for the god Dionysus later descended on Naxos to make Ariadne his wife. (Her story is told by Catullus, poem 64, and no less than three times by Ovid: in *Heroides*, 10, *Ars Amatoria*, 1, and *Met.*, 8.) Secondly, Theseus forgot to change his sail as he approached Athens, and Aegeus, seeing the black sail and assuming his son was dead, threw himself from a cliff into what was thereafter called the Aegean Sea.

Theseus was now king of Athens. He was remembered as a good king, establishing new codes of laws and fairer social institutions, and always sympathetic to the underdog: for instance, he sheltered the exiled **Oedipus**, and later intervened to put down the tyranny of **Creon** at Thebes (see 'Oedipus' below). He also embarked on many adventures overseas, often accompanied by his close friend **Pirithous**, king of the Lapiths (a wild tribe of Thessaly); together they fought in the famous battle of the Lapiths and the centaurs. One of his most famous adventures, though also the most tangled in contradictory versions, is the story of the Amazon queen. Theseus went on an expedition against the Amazons (some say along with Hercules, others say on an expedition of his own), and carried off and married an Amazon queen, named by some as **Antiopa**, by others as **Hippolyta**, who bore him a son, **Hippolytus**. Her fate is also obscure: it is said that the Amazons made war on Athens to recover her, and that she was killed, either fighting for her freedom, or else fighting alongside Theseus against her own people; others say that Theseus abandoned her for **Phaedra**, and she died in an angry attempt to prevent the wedding. (From this period in the legend come the figures of the good Duke Theseus and his wife Hippolyta in Chaucer's 'Knight's Tale' and Shakespeare's *Midsummer Night's Dream* and *Two Noble Kinsmen*.)

In any case, Theseus subsequently married the Cretan princess Phaedra, Ariadne's younger sister. Predictably, given Theseus's earlier dealings with the Cretan royal family, the marriage ended in tragedy. Phaedra fell hopelessly in love with her stepson Hippolytus; but he, a devotee of the chaste huntress Artemis, rejected her advances in horror. Phaedra killed herself, leaving a message accusing Hippolytus of attempting to rape her. The enraged Theseus called on Poseidon for revenge, and was answered: as Hippolytus drove his chariot along the shore, a bull emerged from the sea, the horses bolted in fear, and Hippolytus was dragged to death. Theseus learned the truth too late. (This tragedy is the subject of Euripides' *Hippolytus* and Seneca's *Phaedra*.)

Again a widower, Theseus made a rash bargain with Pirithous that each would help the other obtain a daughter of Zeus for his wife. Theseus chose **Helen** of Sparta, as yet a child but already famously beautiful, and they carried her off to Athens. Pirithous, more ambitious, chose to try and win the goddess Persephone. They descended into the underworld, where Hades smoothly welcomed them and invited them to sit in magical chairs – from which they were unable to rise. There they remained for a long time, until Hercules (visiting the underworld on his twelfth Labour) was able to tear Theseus free, but had to leave Pirithous behind. Limping back to Athens, Theseus found that Helen's brothers Castor and Pollux had made war on Athens to rescue her, and installed a new king. Cursing the city, the old king departed into exile. He subsequently died on the island of Scyros, where he fell – or was pushed by his treacherous host – from a cliff.

Oedipus

The legend of Oedipus and his family differs from the others in this section in that it contains virtually no elements of heroic adventure, but focuses entirely on tragically entangled human relationships and insoluble moral dilemmas. Hence its appeal to the ancient tragedians (most notably Sophocles in his *Oedipus the King* and *Oedipus at Colonus*) – and to Sigmund Freud, who saw the myth as embodying one of our most fundamental psychological drives, the 'Oedipus complex'.

Oedipus was born the son of King **Laius** and Queen **Jocasta** of Thebes. His story begins with that now familiar motif: a father's prophetic fear of his son. Laius was warned by an oracle that his son would grow up to kill his father and marry his mother. To avert this destiny, Laius thrust a spike through the baby's feet to cripple him (hence his name Oedipus, 'swollen-foot') and had him left out on a mountainside to die. However, a Corinthian shepherd rescued the child and took him to the king and queen of Corinth, who adopted him and brought him up as their own.

When he grew up, Oedipus was taunted one day about his uncertain parentage. He consulted the oracle at Delphi, and was appalled to receive the same message as his father had received: that he would kill his father and marry his mother. Believing that the king and queen of Corinth were his parents, he resolved to avoid the fated disaster by leaving Corinth – and heading for Thebes. On the road, he met a man in a chariot going the opposite way; they quarrelled about the right of way, blows were exchanged, and the other man died. So Oedipus unwittingly killed his father Laius, who, warned by omens that his son was on his way, had been hurrying to leave the city to avoid meeting him.

When Oedipus arrived at Thebes, he found the rulerless city plagued by a monster: the **Sphinx**, a creature with a lion's body, a woman's head, and wings, which killed and devoured all comers who could not answer its riddle: what goes on four legs in the morning, two legs at noon, and three legs in the evening? Oedipus correctly answered: a man – who crawls as a baby, walks upright as an adult, and hobbles with a stick in old age. The Sphinx in chagrin threw itself off a cliff, and the grateful Thebans rewarded Oedipus with the kingship – and marriage to the widowed Queen Jocasta. So the second part of the oracle was fulfilled.

Oedipus and Jocasta lived together for many years and had four children. Then Thebes was struck by a terrible plague, which the priests said was caused by the pollution of some great and undisclosed crime. Oedipus set himself to solve the mystery, and by a gradual and painful process (brilliantly dramatised in *Oedipus the King*) uncovered the truth about his own crime. Jocasta hanged herself; Oedipus blinded himself and went into exile. He wandered Greece for many years, an object of pity and fear, accompanied only by his daughter **Antigone**; at last he was given shelter by King Theseus at Colonus, near Athens, and died there (see *Oedipus at Colonus*).

This did not end the troubles of the Theban royal family. When Oedipus's two sons **Eteocles** and **Polynices** came of age, they quarrelled over the kingship, and agreed to rule in alternate years; but Eteocles refused to hand over the throne when his year was up. Polynices gathered up six allies among the neighbouring princes, and the **'Seven Against Thebes'** led their armies in an assault on the city, in which nearly all the main combatants died, and Eteocles and Polynices killed each other in single combat. (The war is the subject of Aeschylus's *Seven Against Thebes*, Euripides' *The Theban Women*, and Statius's epic *Thebaid*.) After the battle the regent **Creon**, Jocasta's brother, ordered that the bodies of the rebellious Seven should be left unburied, on pain of death. Antigone, knowing that a spirit could not rest in the underworld until its body was properly buried, disobeyed the order by burying her brother Polynices, and was condemned to death (see Sophocles' *Antigone*). The wives of the other princes appealed to Theseus, who put down Creon's tyrannical regime and saw to the burial of the dead (see Euripides' *Suppliants*). Ten years later the sons of the original Seven came back for revenge on Thebes, and, it seems, finally destroyed the unfortunate city.

The Trojan War and after

The story of the Trojan War – the seige and sack of the great city of Troy, on the coast of Asia Minor, by a Greek alliance, and the adventures of the Greek leaders on their return home from the war – is the last and most famous of the Greek heroic sagas, partly because it was the subject of Homer's two epic poems, the *Iliad* and *Odyssey*. Historians believe that it has some basis in historical fact, though the war was more likely to have been about trade routes than about the love of a Greek princess.

The origins of the war

According to the Greeks, it all began with an apple. The gods were at a banquet to celebrate the wedding of King **Peleus** and the sea-nymph **Thetis**, when **Eris**, goddess of strife and discord, who had not been invited, turned up and threw on to the table a golden apple labelled 'For the Most Beautiful'. Three goddesses, Hera, Athena, and Aphrodite, immediately laid claim to it. Zeus prudently declined to settle the dispute, and referred it instead to a mortal judge: the young Trojan prince **Paris**, known for his handsomeness and charm with women. The three goddesses paraded before Paris as he herded sheep on Mount Ida, and in addition to their beauty they each offered him a bribe: Hera offered kingly power, Athena success in war, and Aphrodite the love of the most beautiful woman in the world. Paris awarded the apple to Aphrodite.

The most beautiful woman in the world was **Helen** – officially the daughter of King **Tyndareus** of Sparta and his queen **Leda**, but in fact the daughter of Leda by Zeus, who had seduced her in the form of a swan.[9] Helen's beauty had already led to her abduction by Theseus, and when Tyndareus invited suitors to offer for her hand, most of the kings and princes in Greece took part in the bidding. The successful suitor was **Menelaus**, who married Helen and took over the throne of Sparta; and all the unsuccessful suitors, at Tyndareus's request, swore to defend Menelaus' right to her against any challengers. However, Helen's marriage did not deter Paris. He visited Menelaus and Helen at Sparta, seduced Helen (helped by the irresistible power of Aphrodite), and carried her off with him to Troy.

Menelaus appealed to his fellow Greek kings to honour their oath and help him recover his wife. His brother **Agamemnon**, the powerful king of Mycenae, took the leadership of the expedition, and other kings rallied to him: the aged elder statesman, **Nestor** of Pylos; the sturdy **Diomedes** of Argos; **Aias/Ajax**, son of Telamon, called 'Great Ajax', strong and brave and stubborn as an ox, and his friend **Aias/Ajax**, son of Oileus, called 'Little Ajax'; the cunning **Palamedes**; the great archer **Philoctetes**, who bore Hercules' bow; and many others. Two of the greatest Greek heroes were harder to recruit. **Odysseus** (or **Ulysses**), the clever and resourceful king of Ithaca, newly married with a new-born son, tried to dodge the draft by pretending to be mad. When the Greek generals called at Ithaca they found him ploughing a field and sowing it with salt; but Palamedes placed his infant son in the path of the plough, and Odysseus was forced to reveal his sanity by rescuing the boy. And young **Achilles**, the son of Peleus and Thetis – destined to be the bravest, handsomest, swiftest, and most formidable of the Greek warriors – was kept back by his goddess mother. She had already dipped him as a baby in the River Styx to make him invulnerable (except for the heel by which she was holding him), but she still wished to prevent him going to war, because it was prophesied that he would live either a long peaceful life or a short but glorious one. She therefore dressed him up as a girl and concealed him among the princesses at the court of Scyros. It was Odysseus who exposed him, visiting the court disguised as a trader; while the other girls exclaimed over the clothes and jewellery, Achilles betrayed his manhood by instantly seizing on the sword which was concealed among them. So Achilles went off to glory and death, leaving the princess **Deidamia** pregnant with his child.

The Greek army and fleet assembled at Aulis, but were delayed for a long time by contrary winds. The Greek seer **Calchas** told Agamemnon that he could only change the weather by sacrificing his own daughter, **Iphigenia**. Reluctantly Agamemnon did so – sealing his own fate in the process – and the fleet was able to sail. Some say, however, that Artemis saved Iphigenia from death by substituting a deer on the altar, and carried the girl off to a barbarian kingdom in the east, where her brother **Orestes** later found and rescued her. (Euripides' *Iphigenia in Aulis* is about the sacrifice; his *Iphigenia in Tauris* about the rescue.) The expedition suffered one more loss on its way: Philoctetes was bitten by a snake, his wound would not heal, and the Greeks, unable to stand the stench and the cries of pain, left him behind on the island of Lemnos, while they sailed on to Troy.

The war at Troy

The city of Troy (also called **Ilium**, after its royal palace) was ruled by the aged King **Priam**, supported by his queen **Hecuba** and his fifty sons (by various mothers), of whom the the eldest, the brave and noble **Hector**, was the city's greatest warrior. When the Greeks landed they sent a delegation to demand the return of Helen, but the Trojans refused – despite the warnings of Priam's prophetess daughter **Cassandra**, ignored as usual, that Troy was doomed to destruction. So the seige began.

The first years of the war were comparatively uneventful: the Trojans remained barricaded in their well-supplied and fortified city, while the Greeks raided the neighbouring towns and countryside, trying to cut off Troy's support, and the two sides met only in occasional skirmishes. Meanwhile the gods took sides in the conflict: Hera and Athena (resentful of Paris's judgement) and Poseidon supported the Greeks; Aphrodite, Apollo, Ares, and Artemis took the Trojan side; Zeus remained a neutral umpire.

The dramatic events of the war begin in the ninth year, at the start of Homer's

Iliad, when Achilles was mortally angered by the commander Agamemnon's demand that he hand back a Trojan woman captive granted to him as a slave. Seeing this as an insult to his honour, Achilles refused to fight and withdrew to his tent. Encouraged by the Greeks' loss of their greatest champion, Hector led a Trojan assault which cut a swathe through the Greek army and threatened to burn their ships. At this crisis Achilles' closest friend **Patroclus** begged him to return; Achilles refused, but agreed to let Patroclus borrow his armour and go into battle in his name. Patroclus did so, performed great deeds, but was finally killed by Hector. In rage and grief at his friend's death, Achilles returned to the battle, wearing magnificent new armour and arms made for him by Hephaestus. He killed Hector, and vindictively dragged his body three times round the walls of Troy. The old King Priam came to Achilles' tent to beg for the return of his son's body, and Achilles, touched by a sense of their common mortality, agreed. So the *Iliad* ends with the funeral of Hector.

Achilles defeated and killed two more of Troy's allies, the Amazon queen **Penthesilea** and the Ethopian king **Memnon**, before he met his own fated death, shot by Paris in his vulnerable heel (hence the proverbial 'Achilles' heel'). After his funeral, Odysseus and Great Ajax contested to inherit his divinely made armour. The Greek generals awarded the armour to Odysseus; Ajax went mad with anger and humiliation, and (in his mind) slaughtered his ungrateful comrades; when he recovered his sanity and discovered he had only slaughtered a herd of sheep, he killed himself. On Odysseus's generous advice, he too received a hero's funeral. (See Sophocles' *Ajax*, and Ovid's account of the Ajax/Odysseus debate in *Met.*, 13, which wittily summarises almost every major event of the war.)

As the war dragged on into its tenth year, the Greeks became increasingly desperate to get an edge over the Trojans. A prophet declared that Troy would fall if the **Palladium**, the sacred image of Pallas Athena, was stolen from her temple; Odysseus sneaked into the city and stole the image, but Troy still stood. Another prophet said that the Greeks needed the bow of Philoctetes. Odysseus went back to Lemnos, accompanied by a new young warrior, **Neoptolemus** (also called **Pyrrhus**), son of Achilles and Deidamia; they persuaded the understandably resentful Philoctetes to return to Troy with them. He was cured of his wound, and used the bow to shoot and kill Paris (see Sophocles' *Philoctetes*). However, even this did not end the war: the Trojans simply handed Helen on to Paris's brother **Deiphobus**, and the seige continued.

At last Odysseus proposed a new plan. The Greeks constructed a gigantic **Wooden Horse**, and stationed a party of their best warriors in its hollow belly; they left it outside the gates of Troy and sailed away. Convinced by the lies of the Greek agent **Sinon** that the Greeks had left this offering to the gods when they sailed for home, and ignoring the warnings of Cassandra and the priest **Laocoon**, the Trojans dragged it inside the city. That night the warriors inside the horse emerged and opened the gate to the returned Greek army. Troy was taken, sacked, and burned; King Priam was murdered at the altar by Neoptolemus;

Cassandra was raped by Little Ajax; the men of Troy were slaughtered, the women taken into slavery, and Hector's little son was thrown from the walls to ensure the end of the Trojan royal family. Menelaus found Helen, but could not bring himself to kill her; he forgave her and took her back as the victorious Greeks sailed for home. (The most vivid account of the fall of Troy is in Virgil's *Aeneid*, 2; Euripides' *Trojan Women* and *Hecuba* deal memorably with the plight of the defeated.)

After the war: Agamemnon

A number of the Greek leaders encountered further adventures and disasters on their return from the Trojan War. The bloodiest homecoming was that of Agamemnon. His wife **Clytemnestra** (Helen's sister) had never forgiven him for the sacrifice of their daughter Iphigenia, and during his absence she had become the lover of his cousin **Aegisthus**, who had his own bitter hereditary grudge. (Agamemnon's father **Atreus** and Aegisthus's father **Thyestes** had fought a long and vicious battle for the throne of Mycenae, in the course of which each had successively driven the other into exile, Thyestes had seduced Atreus's wife, and Atreus had tricked Thyestes into eating a cannibal feast of the bodies of his murdered children – a story bloodily dramatised in Seneca's *Thyestes*.) Clytemnestra and Aegisthus joined their grievances to plot Agamemnon's murder, and when he returned home they entangled him in a net as he bathed and Clytemnestra hacked him to death with an axe.

Agamemnon's son **Orestes**, when he was grown to manhood, returned to Mycenae with a command from Apollo to avenge his father's death. Helped by his sister **Electra**, he killed Aegisthus and Clytemnestra. But to kill one's mother incurred a terrible blood-guilt, and Orestes was pursued and driven to madness by the Furies. At last (according to Aeschylus's *Oresteia*) he came to Athens, where an Athenian court heard his case argued by Apollo (for the defence) and Athena (for the prosecution), and pronounced the murder justified; Orestes was purified of guilt, and the Furies soothingly renamed the **Eumenides** ('Kindly Ones'). (Aeschylus's *Oresteia* trilogy is the classic version of the story, the three plays dealing in turn with Agamemnon's murder, Orestes' revenge, and the trial; Sophocles' *Electra* and Euripides' *Electra* dramatise the same story from different points of view.)

After the war: Odysseus

The longest homecoming was that of Odysseus, as related in Homer's *Odyssey*. Odysseus spent ten years getting home, pursued by the anger of Poseidon, but helped by Athena, who admired his cleverness and resilience and his skill at talking or lying his way out of sticky situations. On the way he encountered and avoided many perils. He escaped the cave of the **Cyclops Polyphemus**, a one-eyed ogre who tried to eat his men, by getting him drunk and blinding him – and so incurred the anger of Poseidon, the Cyclops's father. He resisted the spells of the witch **Circe**, who had turned his men (temporarily) into pigs, and became her lover for a year. He passed the **Sirens**, seductively musical bird-women whose song enticed sailors on to their murderous rocks, by plugging his crew's ears with wax and having them tie him to the mast, so he safely could hear the wonderful song. He passed almost unscathed through the narrow passage between the monster **Scylla** and the whirlpool **Charybdis**. But in the end all his ships were wrecked, and Odysseus alone was cast up on the island of the nymph **Calypso**, who kept him as her lover and prisoner for seven years. Released at last through Athena's help, he came to the land of the Phaeacians, who welcomed him, listened to his story, and gave him passage home to Ithaca at last.

In Ithaca all was not well. After twenty years Odysseus was presumed dead, and his faithful wife **Penelope** was beseiged with suitors, arrogant young lords who had occupied his palace while they competed to marry Penelope and take over the kingdom. His young son **Telemachus** could not withstand them; Penelope had held them off for several years by promising to marry when she had finished weaving her father-in-law's funeral shroud, which she wove by day and unravelled by night; but the suitors had finally discovered the trick and were pressing her for an answer. Helped by Telemachus and some faithful old servants, Odysseus came to the palace disguised as a beggar, and persuaded Penelope to set up an archery contest for her hand; Odysseus was the only one who could string his great bow, and, having won the contest, he turned his arrows on the suitors and killed them all. He revealed himself to Penelope, and they lived happily (and without adventures) for the rest of their lives.

After the war: Aeneas and Rome

The final 'homecoming' of this post-war era is that of a Trojan: the Trojan prince **Aeneas**, as related by the Roman poet Virgil in his *Aeneid*. According to Virgil, Aeneas, son of Anchises and Venus, was commanded by the gods to escape the fall of Troy and establish a new kingdom. Carrying his crippled father, his little son, and his household gods out of the burning city, he set sail with a few followers in search of the promised land. They had a hard journey, pursued by the malevolent hatred of Juno; Aeneas's love affair with Queen **Dido** of Carthage ended tragically in Aeneas's departure and Dido's embittered suicide; and on arrival in Italy they were embroiled in an accidental war with the local people under the leadership of the fiery **Turnus**. But in the end Aeneas won the war, killed Turnus, married the local princess **Lavinia**, and established a Trojan city in Italy.

Three hundred years later (the Romans say) a descendant of Aeneas founded Rome. The virgin priestess **Rea Silvia** was seduced by the god Mars, and gave birth to twin sons, **Romulus** and **Remus**, who were cast out by their wicked uncle and suckled by a friendly she-wolf. Grown to manhood, they set out to found a new city; they quarrelled over its rulership, and Romulus killed Remus, becoming the first king of the city he called 'Rome' after himself. At this point, however, the mythical history of the world starts to merge into the real history of Rome.

Notes

1 A wallchart compiled by Robert A. Brooks (1991) sets out a gigantic family tree which includes every significant figure from Gaea and Uranus down to Telemachus and Neoptolemus.

2 This is a rather simplified version of the account given by Hesiod in the *Theogony*. The pairing of the Titans reflects the marriages between brother and sister.

3 The chronology of these wars is confused: some say Zeus was helped against the Giants by Dionysus and Hercules, who were not born until many generations after the Flood.

4 Originally Philomela was the mute swallow, but the other version has become standard, and 'Philomel' is still a poetic name for the nightingale.

5 Technically, in Greek religion, a 'hero' is defined as a demigod, the son of one divine and one mortal parent. However, I use the word in a looser sense; Jason and Oedipus, both fully human, do not fit the strict definition.

6 An alternative name for him, often used by Shakespeare, is **Alcides**, after his grandfather Alcaeus.

7 Accounts of the Argonauts' journey vary, and some of these adventures may have taken place on the return trip.

8 Some other versions clear Medea of the murder of her children, saying that they died accidentally when she tried to make them immortal, or that they were killed by the angry people of Corinth.

9 Leda produced four children at a birth (some say in an egg, or a pair of eggs): Helen, her sister **Clytemnestra**, and her brothers **Castor** and **Polydeuces/Pollux**. It is usually said that Helen and Pollux were the half-divine children of Zeus, and Clytemnestra and Castor the mortal children of Tyndareus. However, the brothers were so devoted to each other that when they both died, Pollux gave up half his immortality to Castor, and they each spent alternate days on Olympus and in the underworld. They are sometimes called the **Dioscuri** (sons of Zeus) or the Heavenly Twins.

Part 2

4
ORPHEUS

INTRODUCTION

The ancient Orpheus

For obvious reasons, the legend of Orpheus has always had a particular appeal for writers. Orpheus is the archetypal poet and the archetypal musician; beyond that, he can be seen as the embodiment of 'art' in its widest sense, of all kinds of creative activity, all human attempts to find or create harmony and order in the world, through literature, music, art, philosophy, science, politics, or religion. In his unsuccessful attempt to reclaim his wife Eurydice from death, and his own death at the hands of an angry mob, he embodies the limitations of art in the face of mortality and human irrationality. On a less abstract level, the Orpheus legend is a wonderful story. Dramatically structured, movingly tragic and ironic, it invites constant retelling and constant reinterpretation of the motives and feelings of the two principal characters.[1]

The legend in its classic form can be quickly summarised. Orpheus came from Thrace, the wild region to the north of classical Greece. His mother was Calliope, one of the nine Muses; his father was either Oeagrus, an otherwise obscure Thracian king, or the god Apollo. Orpheus sang and played on the lyre with such beauty and skill that he enchanted not only humans but even wild nature: animals and birds flocked to hear him, rivers paused in their courses, even trees and stones uprooted themselves and lumbered to follow his voice. He sailed with the Argonauts on the quest for the Golden Fleece, where he caused fish to leap out of the water to hear his music, and outsang the seductive songs of the Sirens.

He married the nymph Eurydice, but lost her on the very day of their wedding when she was bitten by a snake and died. The grieving Orpheus descended to the underworld and played before Hades and Persephone, begging to be allowed to take his wife back to life. They agreed, on one condition: that he should go on ahead, and not look back to see if she was following. Orpheus had reached the very verge of the upper world when, overcome by love or fear, he looked back, and Eurydice was lost again, this time irretrievably. Inconsolable, Orpheus retreated into the wilderness to sing his songs to animals and trees, abandoning human company and rejecting the love of women (according to Ovid, he turned to homosexuality). Enraged at his misogyny, or his scorn of their love, or his allegiance to Apollo, or simply the insufferable harmony of his music, the Thracian Bacchantes (wild women followers of Dionysus) turned on him and tore him to pieces. His head and his lyre were thrown into the River Hebrus, floated out to sea, and landed on the island of Lesbos, which became a centre of poetry; some say that his severed head continued to give oracles until Apollo silenced it.

This is the classic form of the story, as set in place by the Roman poets Virgil and Ovid in the decades around the birth of Christ. The original Greek conception of Orpheus may have been rather different.

The Greeks believed Orpheus was a real person, an ancient poet (perhaps the inventor of poetry) and religious teacher. They attributed to him an unorthodox version of the creation of the world and the nature and destiny of the human soul. At the heart of this theology was a myth which strangely parallels the story of the death of Orpheus himself: how the young god Dionysus was torn to pieces and devoured by the Titans, who were then killed by a thunderbolt, and how human beings arose from their ashes, thus partaking both of the divine nature of the god and the evil of the Titans. Orpheus (it is said) taught that men could purify themselves of this taint of original sin by proper ritual practices and an ascetic lifestyle, including vegetarianism, celibacy, and avoidance of women (there seems to have been a misogynistic strain in his teaching which may be reflected in the myth of his death at women's hands). 'Orphic' poems expounding such doctrines still survive, though those that survive are clearly not pre-Homeric but of much later date.

Scholars still fiercely debate whether 'Orphism' was in fact a coherent religious tradition, or merely a conveniently antique label pinned on any kind of mystical otherworldly doctrine – and, even more unanswerably, whether there ever existed a real Orpheus. One suggestion is that behind the legend and the tradition lies the primitive figure of a Thracian shaman. Shamans (the word is Russian, but the concept exists in many cultures) are magicians who claim power over nature, the ability to talk with birds and animals, and in particular the ability to travel out of the body to the lands of the dead, and to guide the souls of the sick and dying there and back again. Such a magical traveller beyond death, it is suggested, may have subsequently been rationalised into the religious teacher who saves the souls of his disciples, and mythologised into the legendary bard who descends into the underworld to reclaim his wife.

In any case, the Greek figure of Orpheus as shaman/poet/teacher gives rise to two important conceptions of Orpheus in later tradition. One is that of the Orphic poet: the divinely inspired bard with profound insight into life and death and the nature of things – a figure epitomised in Apollonius's acccount of Orpheus's song to the Argonauts (**O1**).[2] The other is that of Orpheus the civiliser, teacher of arts and morals, whose melodious wisdom draws people together into an ordered and humane society – a figure classically depicted by the Roman poet Horace (**O3**). Both these conceptions can be metaphorically expressed in the image of Orpheus's power over nature – whether that power is conceived in terms of taming and subduing the wildness of nature, or of sympathetic oneness with the natural order.

All these Orpheuses – the shaman, the religious guru, the inspired poet, the civiliser – have one thing in common: they are essentially public figures, whose efforts are directed towards the welfare of their community or their disciples. The idea of the Orpheus legend as essentially a love story, and Orpheus as a hero driven by personal love and grief, is a later development. Eurydice is barely referred to by Greek writers, and it is hard to say at what point she entered the tradition. Her name ('wide-ruling' or 'wide-judging') has suggested to some scholars that she was originally an underworld goddess, an aspect of Persephone (in modern times Renault, **O42**, and Hoban, **O46**, play interestingly with this notion). Even when she was accepted as Orpheus's wife, there is some evidence that the story may once have had a happy ending; ambiguous references in Euripides, Plato, and Moschus seem to imply that in the accepted Greek version of the story Orpheus succeeded in bringing back Eurydice from the underworld. It may have been some unknown Hellenistic poet, or possibly even Virgil, who invented the now canonical tragic ending of the story.

Virgil (**O2**) is the first to tell the story in its current form. It comes in the unexpected, even bizarre context of a didactic poem on farming. The *Georgics*, ostensibly a practical guide to the farmer, are in fact a poetic evocation of the beauty of the Italian countryside and the moral values of country life. The story of Orpheus comes at the end of the last book, which deals with bees, and is enclosed within the story of the demigod Aristaeus, inventor of beekeeping (and, as son of Apollo, Orpheus's half-brother). Aristaeus's bees have died of a mysterious plague; questioning the prophetic sea god Proteus, he learns that he is being punished for the deaths of Eurydice, who was snake-bitten while fleeing his advances, and of Orpheus; having heard the story, he is able to do penance and magically create a new hive of bees. The relevance of this story to the *Georgics* as a whole, and the relationship between the stories of Aristaeus and Orpheus, have been endlessly debated. Clearly Aristaeus's successful quest to recover his bees parallels Orpheus's failed quest to recover his wife. Aristaeus, the briskly unsentimental farmer, seems to be offered as a role model to the practical Roman, as his bees are a miniature model of the efficient Roman state. By contrast, Orpheus, the poet not as public teacher but as private singer of his own love and grief, seems to be offered as a moral warning against the dangers of excessive emotion. But Virgil is rarely so one-sided, and readers have always found the failed Orpheus by far the more memorable and sympathetic figure.

Ovid (**O4**), writing some forty years after Virgil, is very conscious of the need to do the story differently. In the *Metamorphoses* it becomes merely one of hundreds of mythological stories, and the intensity, starkness, and jagged abruptness of Virgil are replaced by smoothly flowing narrative, romance, quiet pathos, and subtly subversive humour. At the same time, with characteristic delight in the complex interweaving of his stories, Ovid makes Orpheus the narrator of a whole series of other stories. Ovid's Orpheus, in fact, is as much the master storyteller as the lover; at the point where Virgil's broken hero is wandering off into the snowy wastes to die, Ovid's is just getting into his stride as narrator of a series of cautionary tales of unhappy love and wicked women. Revelling like his Orpheus in the sheer pleasure of storytelling, Ovid imposes no obvious moral; perhaps for that very reason, his text invites, and has received, the widest range of interpretations.

The medieval Orpheus: allegory and romance

Of the three myths dealt with in this book, that of Orpheus was by far the most popular in the Middle Ages, and provides a fascinating case study in Christian strategies for dealing with a pagan story. The basic medieval strategy was allegorisation, making the story a metaphor for an acceptable moral or natural truth. This strategy was already in use in classical times (Horace, for instance, explains Orpheus's taming of savage beasts as a metaphor for his influence over uncivilised human beings), but it became much more popular in the Middle Ages.

There are three main strands to the allegorising of Orpheus. The first – appropriately enough, given his origins as shaman and religious teacher – is to treat him as a 'type' or symbol of Christ. This approach perhaps begins in art, as early Christian artists conflate the figure of Orpheus playing to the animals with those of Christ the good shepherd and David the shepherd-psalmist-king. The theologian Clement of Alexandria (late second century) associates Orpheus with Christ, the incarnate Word of God, whose 'new song' harmonises the world and makes 'men out of stones, men out of beasts'; later writers see Orpheus's descent into the underworld to save Eurydice as a type of Christ's descent to earth, and later to hell, to redeem human souls from original sin – with more or less emphasis on the fact that Orpheus, unlike Christ, failed in his quest.

A second strand derives from the enormously popular and influential *Consolation of Philosophy* of the sixth-century writer Boethius (**O5**). In one of the poems in that work, the lady Philosophy retells the story of Orpheus and the fatal backward glance by which he 'saw, lost, and killed his Eurydice'. Orpheus here represents the human soul, seeking to rise out of darkness to (philosophical) enlightenment or (Christian) salvation, but in danger of backsliding if it is tempted to look back at the worldly things it is leaving behind. In later developments of this approach, Orpheus becomes specifically 'reason', the rational part of the soul, and Eurydice becomes its emotional and 'sensual' part, corrupted by temptation and led to hell by the bite of the serpent-devil; reason must bring the soul back out of hell while turning its back on sensual temptation.

A third strand takes the legend as an allegory of music. Fulgentius, a fifth-century mythographer with a taste for far-fetched etymologies, explained Orpheus as meaning 'best voice' (*oraia-phonos*) and Eurydice as 'profound judgement': the good musician must have not only Orpheus's technical skill but also the deeper understanding of musical theory represented by Eurydice. Later writers broaden this approach to equate Orpheus with eloquence and Eurydice with wisdom: the true practitioner of any art, literary or rhetorical as well as musical, must be wise as well as skilful with words and notes.

It is clear that these interpretations are potentially contradictory. Orpheus may be God incarnate, or the sinful human soul, or an aspiring musician; Eurydice may embody sensuality, which Orpheus must turn his back on, or wisdom, which he must seek out. They may also seem wildly inappropriate to the literal story: in one version Aristaeus, the would-be rapist, becomes an allegory of 'virtue'. Medieval commentators were untroubled by such problems: all that mattered was how many useful meanings could be spun out of a story, and commentators like Bersuire (**O6a**) move with a casual 'Or . . .' from one reading to another.

In the later Middle Ages a very different treatment of the story emerges. From the eleventh century onwards, in popular songs, ballads, and chivalric romances, Orpheus and Eurydice appear as ideal courtly lovers, the perfect minstrel-knight and his lady-love. The first important English (or Scottish) treatments of the story are in this tradition: *Sir Orfeo* (**O7**), a Middle English romance of the early fourteenth century, and the *Orpheus and Eurydice* of the fifteenth-century Scots poet Robert Henryson (**O8**). *Sir Orfeo* blends the classical myth with Celtic fairy tale: Orfeo, minstrel-king of Traciens (the old name for Winchester, the poet helpfully explains), successfully rescues his wife from fairyland after she is stolen away by the king of the fairies. Henryson reunites romance with allegory and musical learning, and restores the tragic ending: his Orpheus journeys through the heavens in search of Eurydice, learning the secrets of the music of the spheres, before descending into hell to reclaim her; but he loses her by a backward glance, and a long concluding *moralitas* imposes the Boethian moral.

Orphic harmony in the Renaissance

In Renaissance England Orpheus remains a central myth, but Eurydice and the love story fade from prominence. The Renaissance Orpheus is primarily the musician and poet, whose powerful art reflects the harmony of the cosmos and creates harmony on earth and in the human soul.

The classic Renaissance account of Orpheus is in Shakespeare's *Merchant of Venice* (**O13b**), where Lorenzo expounds to Jessica the idea of the music of the spheres. According to this ancient cosmological concept, which goes back to the fifth-century BC mathematician-philosopher Pythagoras, the planets are mounted upon crystal spheres which, as they turn around the earth, each give out a musical tone and combine to create a heavenly harmony. Here on earth, trapped inside our imperfect human bodies, we cannot hear this harmony, but we retain a buried memory of it; and that is why we instinctively respond to music:

> Therefore the poet
> Did feign that Orpheus drew trees, stones, and floods,
> Since naught so stockish, hard, and full of rage
> But music for the time doth change his nature.

Music is thus at the very heart of God's creation, and the musician, by tapping our innate sensitivity to it, can draw us closer to heavenly perfection on earth. Similarly Chapman's Ovid (in *Ovid's Banquet of Sense*, **O12**), listening to his mistress singing, wishes the 'Orphean' music could permeate the whole dull earth 'that she like heaven might move / In ceaseless music and be filled with love'; and Milton in 'L'Allegro' (**O20a**) prays for heavenly verse and music, 'Untwisting all the chains that tie / The hidden soul of harmony', capable of 'quite' – rather than only half – releasing Eurydice from death. In each case, Orpheus's music stands for a principle capable of transforming our limited, dull, chained human condition into something nearer the divine.

Others portray Orpheus's power in social rather than cosmic terms. Critics like Puttenham (**O10**) and Sidney (*Apology for Poetry*) reiterate the Horatian theme of the poet as the architect of a civilised society; for Puttenham poets like Orpheus are, among other things, the world's first priests, prophets, legislators, politicians, and philosophers. For Spenser (**O9b**), Orpheus is the wise statesman whose harmony calms 'wicked discord', the 'firebrand of hell'; in Chapman's *Shadow of Night*, he is the Promethean poet who draws men from savagery to 'civil love of art'. Bacon (**O14**) identifies Orpheus with 'philosophy' (which includes what we would now call science): his descent into hell is the scientific attempt to prolong or make immortal human life; his charming of the animals is the political attempt to create a civilised and humane society.

It would be misleading to suggest that these lofty Renaissance views of Orpheus are blindly optimistic. Bacon acknowledges that his philosopher-Orpheus fails in both his projects, and ends with an apocalyptic vision of the collapse of civilisation in the face of ineradicable human barbarism. Shakespeare's praise of the transforming power of Orpheus's music is qualified by the recognition that its effect lasts only 'for a time', and that there are those upon whom it does not work at all; the memory of Shylock, 'the man who hath no music in himself', and the harsh treatment meted out to him, remains a discordant note in the harmony of the play's ending. For Spenser (**O9a**), the heroic achievements of Orpheus also suggest a sad contrast with the poverty and neglect of poets today; and Milton, more powerfully, in *Lycidas* (**O20c**) and *Paradise Lost* (**O20d**), takes the death of Orpheus at the hands of the Bacchantes as a symbol of the dangers which threaten the poet in a world inherently hostile to poetry.

Not all Renaissance versions of Orpheus, of course, are at this level of seriousness; many are trivial or conventional. Praises of a poet or composer, for instance, called almost compulsorily for a comparison with Orpheus: so Michael Drayton advises the composer Thomas Morley, in 1595, not to worry about Orpheus's competition ('Draw thou the shepherds still, and bonny lasses, / And envy him not stocks, stones, oxen, asses'), and Thomas Jordan, in 1665, assures a fellow writer that 'Thy poetry would make great Orpheus lese / His lyre, and dance a part with his own trees.' To compare a lady's singing or playing to that of Orpheus is similarly a cliché of love poetry and courtly compliment, as in Sidney (**O11**) or Barnabe Barnes ('Thy sweet enchanting voice did Orpheus raise . . .');

Edmund Waller further trivialises the theme when he commends a lady's skill in cutting trees out of paper ('Orpheus could make the forest dance, but you / Can make the motion and the forest too'). Lyric poets and song-writers exploit the legend for songs either sad (like William Byrd's 'Come woeful Orpheus') or merry (like William Strode's delightful 'When Orpheus sweetly did complain', **O16**). Humorists use it for comic squibs, like Everard Guilpin's on the musician who has married a young wife and now 'plays continually both day and night', or John Davies of Hereford's 'Of Maurus his Orpheus-like Melody', in which the stones which come flying after the musician are thrown by his unappreciative mistress. Orpheus, in fact, crops up everywhere in Elizabethan and Stuart literature, in the most varied contexts – perhaps the most bizarre being when Sir Robert Chester cites him as an authority on the aphrodisiac qualities of the carrot ('The Thracian Orpheus . . . / By his example oftentimes did prove / This root procured in maids a perfect love').

Despite the popularity of Orpheus, occasional voices are raised to remind us that he is a pagan fiction. Giles Fletcher (**O15**) insists that Christ, rescuing human souls from hell, 'Another Orpheus was than dreaming poets feign'; and Milton (**O20d**), after an unforgettable vision of the death of Orpheus, turns away from the pagan Muse Calliope to his personal muse the Holy Spirit – 'For thou art heavenly, she an empty dream.' Both Fletcher and Milton, however, are deeply imaginatively involved with the myth and fascinated by its relationship to Christian truth. A much more damaging rejection is that of Thomas Carew (**O18**), who in 1633 praises his mentor John Donne for abandoning the stale apparatus of mythological poetry such as 'good old Orpheus'. His dismissive attitude prefigures the decline of the Orpheus myth in the Restoration and eighteenth century.

Orpheus in the eighteenth century: translations and travesties

In the 'Augustan' period the Orpheus myth, like myth in general, loses much of its power. Though translations of Virgil, Ovid, and Boethius abound, there are few original treatments of the myth, and those few treat it decoratively rather than as a vehicle for the profound meanings that medieval and Renaissance writers saw in it. Poets like Dryden (**O21**) and Pope (**O22**) continue to use Orpheus to celebrate the power of music. But Dryden's vision of Orpheus/Purcell establishing harmony in hell is a witty conceit, not a serious claim; and Pope, after celebrating Orpheus for over a hundred lines, abandons him for St Cecilia with a flippant ease very different from Milton's gravity in making a similar rejection. On a more trivial level, Orpheus is continually invoked in poems of social compliment with titles such as 'To Lucia Playing on Her Lute', 'Impromptu to a Young Lady Singing' (**O26**), or 'To the Elegant Seraphina, Performing on the Piano Forte at a Private Concert'.

The image of Orpheus the civiliser continues to have some serious resonance.

Interestingly, however, later eighteenth-century and early nineteenth-century versions place more emphasis on the domestic rather than the political virtues. William Collins (**O28**), around 1750, celebrates Orpheus in Horatian terms as the founder of 'Society, and law, and sacred order', but also of 'dear domestic life . . . / And all the charities that softened man'. Anna Seward (**O29**), in 1780, compares Captain Cook to Orpheus, driven by Benevolence to reform the domestic manners of the savages: 'See! chastened love in softer glances flows – / See! with new fires parental duty glows.' John Galt's opera *Orpheus* (published 1814–15) presents Orpheus as establishing 'primitive society' by separating out 'the most obvious and appropriate duties' of men and women: men must hunt, women must stay at home. Orpheus has become the archetype of bourgeois domestic virtue.

By far the greatest imaginative vitality in the period, however, goes into comic and ironic treatments of the myth. Much of this humour is misogynistic in tone, turning on the outrageousness of the notion that a man fortunate enough to lose his wife should actually want to get her back: this simple joke is the point of short squibs by R.M. (**O24**), Matthew Coppiner, Mary Monck, and the American Nathaniel Evans, and underlies William King's intermittently amusing travesty, in which Orpheus is a gipsy fiddler in quest of his nagging wife 'Dice'. Against these may be set Anne Finch's clever and unsettling feminist version (**O23**), in which the Bacchantes become 'resenting heroines' punishing the complacent male satirist Orpheus. Two dramatic versions parody operatic treatments of the myth: in Fielding's *Eurydice* (**O27**) a sophisticated Eurydice, very much at home in hell, cunningly evades the duty of going home with her wimpish *castrato* husband; in Garrick's less subtle *Peep Behind the Curtain* Orpheus has to extricate himself from his mistress's clutches in order to go and get his wife. Gay's fable of the educated monkey (**O25**) casts a disenchanted eye on the figure of Orpheus the civiliser and the whole notion of 'civilisation'. Treating the myth frankly as a joke allowed free play to the eighteenth-century love of satire and irony, when the myths taken straight seemed merely a bore.

Romantics and Victorians: from Orphic song to the melancholy lyre

The Romantic movement, with its renewed interest in myth and its lofty conception of poetry and art, might have been expected to bring Orpheus into new prominence. Surprisingly, this is not entirely true. A survey of the major Romantic poets reveals only two poems specifically about the legend: Shelley's (discussed below) and, perhaps, a rather weak Wordsworth poem which hails a blind street musician as 'An Orpheus! An Orpheus!' Moreover, the central critical texts of the movement – the Preface to *Lyrical Ballads*, Shelley's *Defence of Poetry*, Coleridge's *Biographia Literaria* – noticeably omit the traditional homage to Orpheus as arch-poet, and Byron (**O31**) and Peacock (**O32**) irreverently send up the motif – as if the Horatian notion of Orpheus the poet-civiliser had become too hackneyed, or too associated with a pompously public type of poetry, to be taken seriously.

Nevertheless, the Romantics were drawn to the image of the 'Orphic poet', associated with the figure of the ancient poet-teacher, whose supposed hymns were re-edited with a commentary by Thomas Taylor in 1787. Wordsworth invokes this ideal of the poet as mystic philosopher at the start of *The Prelude* (**O30**): hesitating over his poetic vocation, he aspires to write 'immortal verse / Thoughtfully fitted to the Orphean lyre', but then, with a significant half-pun, recoils from that 'awful burden'. Later Coleridge acclaims the finished poem as 'an Orphic song indeed, / A song divine of high and passionate thoughts / To their own music chanted' ('To William Wordsworth', 45–7). And in Shelley's *Prometheus Unbound*,

> Language is a perpetual Orphic song,
> Which rules with Daedal harmony a throng
> Of thoughts and words, which else senseless and shapeless were.

Orpheus the poet fuses with Daedalus the craftsman in an image of the power of the creative imagination to remake reality.

Shelley embodies this remaking of reality in the one sustained Romantic treatment of the legend, his dramatic fragment 'Orpheus' (**O33**). Perhaps taking off from Ovid's tongue-in-cheek remark (10. 104–6) about Orpheus's convenient ability to create shade wherever he went, he places the poet in a bleak purgatorial landscape which, by the end of the poem, is miraculously transformed into an earthly paradise. Shelley's Orpheus is not a public teacher or civiliser but a tormented individual, isolated from society, singing his pain in the wilderness. Nevertheless the power of his song is enough to – literally or metaphorically – transform the world. The extremity of Shelley's claim for the power of art is perhaps exceeded only by a Victorian poet writing in the Romantic tradition, R. W. Dixon (**O36**), whose Prospero-like poet-mage commands thunder and lightning and comes to the very brink of apotheosis, before he declines it in order to pursue his earthly love. Such 'art', however, Dixon insists, depends on a pantheistic understanding of 'the sources of eternal law' which is now lost to us; his Orpheus is not a model of the modern artist but a superhuman figure from a lost age.

Other Victorian versions return to the more earthbound figure of Orpheus the civiliser and moral teacher. Coventry Patmore and R. C. Trench both take his victory over the Sirens as an allegory of the poet's duty and power to lead people away from sensual temptation and towards virtue. R. W. Buchanan is more sceptical: his Orpheus, singing to the spirits of wild nature, can raise their moral consciousness – 'as they listened, satyrs, nymphs, and fauns / Conceived their immortality' – but (like Shakespeare's Orpheus) only 'for the time'; when the song ceases, 'the satyr-crew / Rushed back to riot and carouse', and Silenus 'bawled for wine'.

In some minor poets (Mackay, Gosse, Ward) this scepticism rises to a sense of the irrelevance or impotence of poetry: Orpheus, the true poet, has no place in the vulgar, corrupt, prosaic modern world. These moralised readings often have an implicitly or explicitly Christian tenor. Isaac Williams, in *The Christian Scholar*, adapts Boethius's moral to Victorian family values: the Orpheus-figure not only seeks his own salvation but also 'with him draws to realms above / The objects of his earthly love'; but if he looks back, 'He loses both himself and them.' On the other hand, Charles Tennyson Turner (the laureate's brother) raises a stern Miltonic objection to the old identification of Christ with Orpheus: 'What means this vain ideal of Our Lord, / With "Orpheus" underwritten?' The pagan story has its own beauty and pathos, but Christians should not 'match Messias with a shade' or attempt to 'fuse / Redemption into harp-notes'.

Others, especially in the later nineteenth and early twentieth centuries, avoided such didacticism and instead exploited the story for its human pathos. Andrew Lang offers a poem about Orpheus and Eurydice as a tongue-in-cheek example of how 'When first we heard Rossetti sing, / We twanged the melancholy lyre.' In this tradition of autumnal melancholy are poems by De Tabley (**O38**), Gosse, Binyon, and William Morris, whose massive 1,386-line 'Story of Orpheus and Eurydice' plays on the Gothic horror of the haunted wood in which Orpheus tries to summon up his dead wife's spirit, and the conflicting emotions at work in his soul.

In this late Victorian humanising and psychologising of the myth we see the first attempts to take Eurydice as a subject in her own right and explore her feelings. Robert Browning shows her pleading with Orpheus to look at her (**O35**), and Bourdillon makes her the one who foolishly looks back, whereas Dowden's formidable Eurydice regrets that she had not taken the task of leading the way out of hell (**O37**). In some versions she is less than eager to be resurrected. Gosse's Eurydice begs Orpheus to 'forbear and leave me painless'; in T. Sturge Moore's play she baulks at the last moment from returning to the 'hideous hunger' of mortal life. These hints would be taken up by twentieth-century writers.

Alongside such serious versions the comic tradition continues, especially in popular stage entertainments like Planché's extravaganzas and Brough's Christmas pantomimes. I have included a little of Brough's piece (**O34**), with its knockabout farce and appalling puns, as a slight corrective to the rather overpowering earnestness of most Victorian Orpheuses.

The twentieth century: Eurydice sings her own song and Orpheus remembers himself

In the twentieth century Orpheus remains an immensely powerful figure. It sometimes seems that every poet has written at least one poem on the theme – to say nothing of plays, novels, films, operas, and comic strips. The twentieth-century treatment of Orpheus, however, has been largely bleak. Orpheus the lover is subject to unprecedentedly harsh criticism; Orpheus the poet is seen most vividly in terms of his failure and death, and his power, if he has any, is gained painfully through suffering and loss.

Orpheus the lover, of course, is often depicted with great sympathy. Many male poets, and some female ones, have movingly identified with him as they use the legend to express personal experiences of loss and grief – among them Peter Davison, Denis Devlin, Lauris Edmond (**O47**), Edwin Honig, D. G. James, Louis Simpson. Others, however, have taken a more critical view of Orpheus's conduct towards Eurydice, seeing him as careless, weak, or self-indulgent. Sydney Goodsir Smith (**O41**) presents an Orpheus bitterly guilty for letting his wife die while he was lecherously 'daffan . . . wi the water-lassies'. Thomas Blackburn criticises his self-absorbed slide into despair, James Merill the 'opulence of grief' which has turned into a theatrical performance.

The most radical of such revisions of the story are the feminist versions which attempt to see the story from Eurydice's point of view. In the words of the American poet Alta:

> all the male poets write of orpheus
> as if they look back & expect
> to find me walking patiently
> behind them. they claim i fell into hell.
> damn them, i say.
> i stand in my own pain
> & sing my own song.

The first and fiercest of these feminist Eurydices is H.D.'s in 1917 (**O39**), who bitterly condemns Orpheus for the 'arrogance' and 'ruthlessness' which have prevented her escape from hell, yet claims a kind of victory in her self-assertion: 'Against the black / I have more fervour / than you in all the splendour of that place'. Similarly Sandra Gilbert's Bacchante – rather in the spirit of Anne Finch's 'resenting heroines' – justifies her sisters' punishment of Orpheus for his callous betrayal of Eurydice (**O50**). The 'swaggering bastard', armed with his phallic flute, tried to silence the voices of nature and of women: 'Without his manly anthems, / everything . . . would sing, would sing.'

Others more subtly criticise Orpheus not for his failure to save Eurydice but for his attempt to do so in the first place: who says Eurydice *wanted* to return to life? Rachel Blau du Plessis's Eurydice deliberately retreats into dark labyrinthine caves to escape male control, transforming herself into a primeval fertility goddess. Elaine Feinstein's Eurydice (**O48**) loves Orpheus, and the music they make together is genuinely life-enhancing; nevertheless, they represent opposed and incompatible principles – the harsh male Apollonian sun of reason, order, control, language-as-power, versus the still shadowy waters of female intuition, emotion, acceptance, silence. His possessiveness is destructive, and his attempt to drag her out of the grave a horrible violation of nature. Margaret Atwood (**O49**) similarly presents an Orpheus who cannot accept Eurydice's acceptance of death, and tries to recreate her in the shape of what he wants her to be. He ultimately fails because the Eurydice he loves is the reflection of his own needs and desires, not the real woman: 'You could not believe I was more than your echo.' For all these feminist writers Orpheus's sin is his desire for control – of Eurydice, of the natural world, of mortality. We may recall Bacon's claim that the conquest of death would be the noblest achievement of 'philosophy'; for a writer like Feinstein such an Orphean quest to control and defeat nature epitomises destructive masculine hubris.

This feminist view of Orpheus's music as a controlling and repressive force is a radical reinterpretation of the myth; most twentieth-century versions more traditionally see Orpheus the poet-musician as a positive figure. A few are simply celebratory, especially those which deal with Orpheus's union with wild nature: for instance, Denise Levertov's imaginative recreation of his playing to the trees from a tree's point of view, or Donald Davie's exuberant vision of the stones dancing in an expression of 'his holy joy . . . that stones should be'. Feinstein, rather unexpectedly, also evokes this joyously life-enhancing and consciousness-raising quality in Orpheus's music: as he and Eurydice pass, spring breaks out, the city traffic comes to a stop, and men and women look up from their mechanical work with a new awareness of their own humanity.

More often, though, there is a wary scepticism about the effect to which art can actually change the world. Orpheus's music is often presented as impotent: Horace Gregory's Orpheus waits helplessly as the Bacchantes approach and his birds desert him as 'deathless music flies like hope to heaven'; John Hollander's finds that since Eurydice's death his songs have no effect on the natural world, and wryly waits for his 'cracked lyre to crawl away / In silent tortoise-hood some day'. W. H. Auden's challenging question 'What does the song hope for?' (**O40**), Yvor Winters's image of the 'immortal tongue' singing 'unmeaning down the stream', John Ashbery's quiet insistence on the transience of all things including poets and poetry, Paul Breslin's vision of the mortal poet who cannot break 'Death's mortise-bond in all created things' – all use the Orpheus myth to raise disquieting questions about the value, effect, or permanence of art.

Such scepticism can be especially acute and ironic when Orpheus is brought anachronistically into juxtaposition with the modern world. In Michael Hamburger's 'Orpheus Street, SE5' (**O45**) he is a drug-popping protest poet, 'well paid' for singing of love and peace and freedom, in a seedy commercialised London. 'Orpheus transfigures, Orpheus transmutes all things' – but can he transfigure this world? The image of park benches taking off and flying, 'narrowly missing the sparrows', captures both the exhilaration and the improbability of the prospect. There is even less hope of redemption in the bored and cynical poet of Donald Justice's 'Orpheus Opens his Morning Mail' or the rock musician of John Heath-Stubbs's 'Story of Orph' (**O51**), whose death at the hands of a obsessed fan merely results in increased album and t-shirt sales; in this modern world, music and martyrdom are trivialised. More grimly, Stanley

Kunitz presents Orpheus as a Holocaust survivor, traumatised and silenced by the horrors he has seen.

On the other hand, an Orpheus who is vulnerable and doomed can acquire a new kind of tragic heroism – David Gascoyne's shaman-like figure, for instance, returning with his 'shattered lyre' to try to tell in 'bewildered words' of his experiences, or William Jay Smith's, descending like Childe Roland into the darkness of the underworld 'Bearing his flaming shield, his lyre'. Such portrayals suggest a psychological reading: the poet who risks his own sanity to explore the darkness of the human psyche on our behalf. Often there is a sense that the power and value of Orpheus's music comes precisely from his confrontation with suffering and death. For A. D. Hope (**O52**) it is only after the loss of Eurydice that Orpheus's music acquires its 'deathless harmony'; Iain Crichton Smith's Pluto tells Orpheus that he can play so movingly only because he has experienced loss, and sends him back without Eurydice to play his vision of 'the human / invincible spirit' in twentieth-century slums. Paul Goodman (in a short story) and Rolfe Humphries (**O44**) go further to suggest that Orpheus deliberately sacrifices Eurydice. Aware that he must choose between happiness and artistic greatness, Humphries's Orpheus looks back and consigns Eurydice 'with everlasting love, to Hell' – a necessary sacrifice (though feminist writers might see it rather differently) to achieve the 'immortal voice' that in 'The Thracian Women' triumphs over the Bacchantes' malice. Ted Hughes, by contrast, allows suffering to achieve both love and art. In his short musical play, Orpheus's cheerful pop music jangles into discord when Eurydice dies, and then, in hell, is reborn as 'solemn Bach, Handel, Vivaldi'; with this he wins her back, though as a spiritual presence that he alone can recognise – the nearest to a happy ending in any twentieth-century version.

Sometimes the power of Orpheus's music is explicitly political. In Atwood's 'Orpheus (2)' (**O49c**), Orpheus in the stadium, 'trying to sing / love into existence again', takes on unmistakable overtones of the poet writing in the face of political tyranny: 'Praise is defiance.' One of the most bizarrely powerful images in Neil Gaiman's *Sandman* graphic novels (in which Orpheus is woven into Gaiman's complex mythology as the son of Morpheus/Dream/Sandman) is in the French Revolution story 'Thermidor': the head of Orpheus leads a chorus of guillotined heads in a song of liberty, silencing the despot Robespierre. In such versions, Orpheus the civiliser takes on a new life as Orpheus the rebel, defending civilised and humane values against tyranny.

Perhaps the most extreme vision of Orpheus achieving power through suffering is Muriel Rukeyser's (**O43**), which consciously re-enacts the Orphic myth of Dionysus: the dismembered parts of Orpheus's body, torn apart and scattered by the Bacchantes, come together again in a miraculous rebirth: 'He has died the death of the god . . . He has opened the door of pain. / It is a door and a window and a lens / opening on another land . . .' Russell Hoban (**O46**), describing the same process, sums it up in a brilliant pun: 'He's found his members, said Kleinzeit. He's remembered himself.' Hoban's version, however, one of the most complex as well as the wittiest of twentieth-century rewritings of the myth, goes further than that. His Orpheus is trapped in an endless cycle of death and rebirth. In what looks like a conscious reminiscence of the Fulgentian allegory of the quest of 'best voice' for 'profound judgement', he needs to be reunited with Eurydice, 'the female element complementary to himself', who dwells in 'the inside of things, the place under the places. Underworld, if you like to call it that.' But, as in Feinstein, Orpheus with his masculine desire for power and control cannot accept the nirvana-like peace of Eurydice's underworld, insists on pursuing worldly fame, and so loses Eurydice, dies, and is reborn to enact the cycle again. If only the cycle could be broken, Hoban implies, harmony could return to the world. The nonsense phrases that echo through the novel ('barrow full of rocks', 'harrow full of crocks', etc.) turn out absurdly to stand for Milton's 'The hidden soul of harmony' (**O20a**). As things are, harmony can only emerge into the world in a nonsensically garbled form, and we have to be content with what can be achieved by Kleinzeit, a 'small-time' Orpheus.

Notes

1 The popularity of the Orpheus myth means that there are far more literary treatments of it than of Adonis or Pygmalion; however, it also tends (perhaps because of its familiarity) to be treated more briefly. That is why the present chapter contains almost twice as many texts as chapters 5 and 6, but is approximately the same length.

2 Reference codes in **bold** refer to texts in the anthology: **O1** is the first text in the 'Orpheus' section. Bibliographical details for these texts can be found in the footnote attached to the title of each text. For texts which are referred to but not included in the anthology, brief bibliographical details are given in 'Other Versions of Orpheus', below.

TEXTS

O1 Apollonius of Rhodes, from *Argonautica*, *c*.250 BC. Trans. Richard Hunter, 1993°

Apollonius of Rhodes, third century BC, Hellenistic Greek poet and scholar, head of the famous Library of Alexandria in Egypt. His *Argonautica* is a short epic in four books about Jason's quest for the Golden Fleece; Orpheus is a minor but important character. He is introduced as the first of the Argonauts:

First let us recall Orpheus to whom Kalliope herself is said to have given birth near the Pimpleian height,° after she had shared the bed of Thracian Oiagros. Men say that the sound of his songs bewitched the hard rocks on the mountains and the streams of rivers. As signs of his music, the wild oak trees which flourish on the Thracian coast at Zone stand to this day in close-set ranks; he brought them all the way down from Pieria by the bewitching music of his lyre.

Later in book 1 Orpheus calms a quarrel among the Argonauts with his song. His song of the origins of the world includes some unorthodox details (for instance, Eurynome and Ophion rather than Gaea and Uranus as the primal parents) which may derive from 'Orphic' doctrines.

. . . So [Idas] attacked [Idmon] angrily, and the quarrel would have gone further, had not their companions and the son of Aison° himself restrained their dispute with words of rebuke. Moreover Orpheus took up his lyre in his left hand and began to sing.

He sang of how the earth, the heavens, and the sea – once upon a time united with each other in a single form – were sundered apart by deadly strife; and how a position fixed for eternity in the sky is held by the stars and the paths of the moon and the sun; how the mountains rose up, and the origin of sounding rivers with their own nymphs, and all creatures upon the ground. He sang how first Ophion and Eurynome, daughter of Ocean, held power over snowy Olympos, and how a violent struggle caused them to yield their positions of honour, he to Kronos and she to Rheia, and to fall into the waves of Ocean. Kronos and Rheia then ruled over the blessed Titan gods, while Zeus was still a young boy, still with the thoughts of an infant, and lived in the Diktaian cave;° the earth-born

° from *The Voyage of Argo*, trans. Richard Hunter, Oxford: Oxford University Press, 1993, book 1, pp. 3, 15. Reproduced by permission of Oxford University Press.

° **the Pimpleian height**: in the mountain range of Pieria, in northern Greece, sacred to the Muses.

° **son of Aison**: i.e. Jason.

° **Diktaian cave**: on Mount Dicte in Crete, where Rhea (Rheia) hid the baby Zeus from Cronus (Kronos).

Kyklopes had not yet armed him with his blazing bolts, his thunder, and his lightning – the weapons which guarantee Zeus his glory.

This was his song. He checked his lyre and his divine voice, but though he had finished, the others all still leaned forwards, ears straining under the peaceful spell; such was the bewitching power of the music which lingered amongst them.

O2 Virgil, from the *Georgics*, *c.*29 BC. Trans. C. Day Lewis, 1940°

Virgil (Publius Vergilius Maro), 70–19 BC, Roman poet of the Augustan period, author of the *Eclogues*, *Georgics*, and *Aeneid*. The story of Orpheus and Eurydice comes from the end of the *Georgics*; the problems of its relevance to the rest of the poem and the relationship between Orpheus and Aristaeus are discussed in the introduction to this chapter. The extract begins as Aristaeus prepares to catch and question the sea god Proteus, who (as his mother Cyrene has warned him) will change into various forms to try to evade questioning.

Virgil wrote in hexameters, the lines of six metrical feet that are the standard form for serious long poems in Greek and Latin. C. Day Lewis's translation uses an English line of similar length with a loose six-beat pattern.

Now Proteus came to his customed
Den from the water: around him the dripping tribes of the deep
Frolicked, flinging the bitter spray far and wide about them.
All over the beach the seals were sprawled for their siesta.
The wizard himself, just like a herdsman might on the mountains,
When evening herds the calves homeward out of their pasture
And wolves prick up their ears hearing the lambs bleating,
Sat in the midst of them on a rock and took their tally.
Aristaeus saw his chance:
Scarcely letting the old man lay down his weary limbs,
He rushed him with a great shout and shackled him where he lay.
The wizard for his part remembered well his magic
And turned himself into all kinds of uncanny things –
Became a fire, a fearful wild beast, a flowing river.
But, seeing that no deception could spirit him away, beaten
He returned to himself and spoke at last in human tones.
'Boldest of youths, who bade you

° from *The Georgics of Virgil*, trans. C. Day Lewis, London: Jonathan Cape, 1940, book 4 (line numbers are the same in the Latin and the English translation). Reproduced by permission of Jonathan Cape and the Executors of the Estate of C. Day Lewis and Peteis Fraser v Dunlop. 503/4 The Chambers, Chelsea Harbour, London SW10 0XF.

Approach my house? What do you want with me?' The other,
'You know, Proteus, you know very well: for nothing escapes you.
Stop being stubborn. Obeying the gods' commands we are come
To ask the oracle how to revive my drooping fortunes.'
So much he said. At last now the seer convulsively
Rolled his glaring eyes so they shone with a glassy light,
Harshly ground his teeth, and thus gave tongue to Fate. –

'Not without sanction divine is the anger that hunts you down.
Great is the crime you pay for. Piteous Orpheus calls
This punishment on you. Well you deserve it. If destiny
So wills it. Bitter his anguish for the wife was taken from him.
Headlong beside that river she fled you. She never saw,
Poor girl, her death there, deep in the grass before her feet –
The watcher on the river-bank, the savage watersnake.
The band of wood-nymphs, her companions, filled with their crying
The hilltops: wailed the peaks of Rhodope: high Pangaea,
The warlike land of Rhesus,
The Getae lamented, and Hebrus, and Attic Orithyia.°
Orpheus, sick to the heart, sought comfort of his hollow lyre:
You, sweet wife, he sang alone on the lonely shore,
You at the dawn of day he sang, at day's decline you.
The gorge of Taenarus° even, deep gate of the Underworld,
He entered, and that grove where fear hangs like a black fog:
Approached the ghostly people, approached the King of Terrors°
And the hearts that know not how to be touched by human prayer.
But, by his song aroused from Hell's nethermost basements,
Flocked out the flimsy shades, the phantoms lost to light,
In number like to the millions of birds that hide in the leaves
When evening or winter rain from the hills has driven them –
Mothers and men, the dead
Bodies of great-heart heroes, boys and unmarried maidens,
Young men laid on the pyre before their parents' eyes –
And about them lay the black ooze, the crooked reeds of Cocytus,
Bleak the marsh that barred them in with its stagnant water,

° **Rhodope . . . Orithyia**: all these names are associated with Thrace, Orpheus's homeland: **Rhodope** and **Pangaea** are mountains, **Hebrus** a river, the **Getae** a Thracian tribe; **Rhesus** was a Thracian king who fought in the Trojan war; **Orithyia** was an Athenian (**Attic**) princess who was abducted by Boreas, the god of the north wind, to his home in Thrace.

° **Taenarus**: the southermost point of mainland Greece, in legend containing an entrance to the underworld.

° **King of Terrors**: i.e. Pluto.

And the Styx coiling nine times around corralled them there.°
Why, Death's very home and holy of holies was shaken
To hear that song, and the Furies with steel-blue snakes entwined
In their tresses; the watch-dog Cerberus gaped open his triple mouth;
Ixion's wheel stopped dead from whirling in the wind.
And now he's avoided every pitfall of the homeward path,
And Eurydice, regained, is nearing the upper air
Close behind him (for this condition has Proserpine made),
When a moment's madness catches her lover off his guard –
Pardonable, you'd say, but Death can never pardon.
He halts. Eurydice, his own, is now on the lip of
Daylight. Alas! he forgot. His purpose broke. He looked back.
His labour was lost, the pact he had made with the merciless king
Annulled. Three times did thunder peal over the pools of Avernus.°
"Who," she cried, "has doomed me to misery, who has doomed us?
What madness beyond measure? Once more a cruel fate
Drags me away, and my swimming eyes are drowned in darkness.
Good-bye. I am borne away. A limitless night is about me
And over the strengthless hands I stretch to you, yours no longer."
Thus she spoke: and at once from his sight, like a wisp of smoke
Thinned into air, was gone.
Wildly he grasped at shadows, wanting to say much more,
But she did not see him; nor would the ferryman of the Inferno°
Let him again cross the fen that lay between them.

What could he do, where go, his wife twice taken from him?
What lament would move Death now? What deities hear his song?
Cold she was voyaging now over the Stygian stream.
Month after month, they say, for seven months alone
He wept beneath a crag high up by the lonely waters
Of Strymon,° and under the ice-cold stars poured out his dirge
That charmed the tigers and made the oak trees follow him.
As a nightingale he sang that sorrowing under a poplar's
Shade laments the young she has lost, whom a heartless ploughman
Has noticed and dragged from the nest unfledged; and the nightingale
Weeps all night, on a branch repeating the piteous song,
Loading the acres around with the burden of her lament.
No love, no marriage could turn his mind away from grief:

° **Cocytus . . . Styx**: two of the four rivers of the underworld; for these and other features and inhabitants of Virgil's underworld, see 'The gods of the underworld' in ch. 2, pp. 30–1 above.

° **Avernus**: a lake near Naples, near which was supposed to be an entrance to the underworld.

° **ferryman of the Inferno**: Charon (see ch. 2).

° **Strymon**: a Thracian river.

Alone through Arctic ice, through the snows of Tanais, over
Frost-bound Riphaean plateaux°
He ranged, bewailing his lost Eurydice and the wasted
Bounty of Death. In the end Thracian Bacchantes, flouted
By his neglect, one night in the midst of their Master's revels
Tore him limb from limb and scattered him over the land.
But even then that head, plucked from the marble-pale
Neck, and rolling down mid-stream on the river Hebrus –
That voice, that cold, cold tongue cried out "Eurydice!"
Cried "Poor Eurydice!" as the soul of the singer fled,
And the banks of the river echoed, echoed "Eurydice!"'
Thus Proteus spake, and dived into the sea's depths,
And where he dived the water, foaming, spun in a funnel.

Cyrene waited and spoke a word to her frightened son:
'You may cast your cares away,'
She said, 'for here is the whole truth of your bees' sickness
And the death they were dealt by the nymphs with whom Eurydice
Danced in the deep woods. So offer them gifts and make your
Peace with them, and pray to the Gracious Ones of the grove.°
They will answer your prayers with forgiveness, they will forget their anger.
But first let me tell you the form your orisons° must take.
Choose four bulls of excellent body that now on the heights of
Green Lycaeus are grazing,
And as many heifers whose necks have never felt the yoke.
Build for these four altars beside the lofty shrines
Of the goddesses, and let the sacred blood from their throats,
Then leave the oxen's bodies alone in a leafy thicket.
When the ninth day has dawned
You shall send oblivion's poppies as a funeral gift to Orpheus,
Slay a calf in honour of Eurydice placated,
Slaughter a black ewe and go to the thicket again.'

Without delay he acts at once on his mother's advice:
He comes to the shrine, erects – as she told him – altars, and brings
Four bulls of excellent body
With as many heifers whose necks have never felt the yoke:
When the ninth day has dawned,
Sends funeral gifts to Orpheus and goes to the thicket again.
Here, to be sure, a miracle sudden and strange to tell of

° The **Tanais** (or Don river) and the **Riphaean** mountains are in Scythia, the region to the north of the Black Sea.

° **Gracious Ones of the grove**: the wood-nymphs.

° **orisons**: prayers.

They behold: from the oxen's bellies all over their rotting flesh
Creatures are humming, swarming through the wreckage of their ribs –
Huge and trailing clouds of bees, that now in the treetops
Unite and hang like a bunch of grapes from the pliant branches.°

O3 Horace, from *The Art of Poetry*, *c*.10 BC. Trans. Wentworth Dillon, Earl of Roscommon, 1680°

Horace (Quintus Horatius Flaccus), 65 BC–AD 8, Roman poet of the Augustan period, contemporary of Virgil, wrote with great virtuosity in two very different styles: compactly lyrical in his *Odes*, humorously conversational in his *Satires* and *Epistles*. The epistle on *The Art of Poetry* is an informal letter of advice to the two sons of his friend Piso, aspiring poets. Here he presents Orpheus – along with another mythical bard, Amphion, whose music caused stones to rise and build the walls of the city of Thebes – as symbols of the civilising power of poetry. The 1680 translation comes from a period when Horace's urbane and civilised view of poetry was especially influential.

Orpheus, inspired by more than human power,
Did not (as poets feign) tame savage beasts,
But men as lawless and as wild as they,
And first dissuaded them from rage and blood.
Thus, when Amphion built the Theban wall,
They feigned the stones obeyed his magic lute.
Poets, the first instructors of mankind,
Brought all things to their proper, native use:
Some they appropriated to the gods,
And some to public, some to private ends.
Promiscuous love by marriage was restrained,
Cities were built, and useful laws were made.
So ancient is the pedigree of verse,
And so divine a poet's function.
Then Homer's and Tyrtaeus'° martial muse
Wakened the world and sounded loud alarms.
To verse we owe the sacred oracles
And our best precepts of morality.

° **clouds of bees**: that bees and other insects could be spontaneously generated from rotting flesh was a popular superstition, but almost certainly not one that Virgil literally believed.

° from *Horace's Art of Poetry. Made English by the Right Honourable the Earl of Roscommon*, London, 1680, pp. 27–8.

° **Tyrtaeus**: a Spartan soldier-poet of the seventh century BC.

Some have by verse obtained the love of kings
(Who with the Muses ease their wearied minds).
460 Then blush not, noble Piso, to protect
What gods inspire and kings delight to hear.

O4 Ovid, from the *Metamorphoses*, *c.* AD 10. Trans. A. D. Melville, 1986°

Ovid (Publius Ovidius Naso), 43 BC–AD 17, Roman poet of the Augustan period, a generation younger than Virgil and Horace; for an account of his life, and his masterpiece the *Metamorphoses*, see chapter 1. The story of Orpheus, which spans books 10–11 of the *Metamorphoses*, is only casually related to the poem's supposed theme of changes of shape by the final transformation of the Bacchantes into trees. But Ovid, with characteristic delight in interweaving his stories or enclosing them within one another (Chinese-box fashion), uses Orpheus as the frame and narrator for a whole series of other tragic love stories, supposedly sung by the grieving bard to his audience of trees, rocks, and animals.

Ovid's poem, like Virgil's, is written in hexameters. A. D. Melville translates it into blank verse, 'the tried and tested measure of English tradition' (xxxi), varied with occasional rhyming couplets for special emphasis.

Thence Hymen° came, in saffron mantle clad,
At Orpheus' summons through the boundless sky
To Thessaly, but vain the summons proved.
True he was present, but no hallowed words
He brought nor happy smiles nor lucky sign;
Even the torch he held sputtered throughout
With smarting smoke, and caught no living flame
For all his brandishing. The ill-starred rite
Led to a grimmer end. The new-wed bride,
Roaming with her gay Naiads through the grass,
Fell dying when a serpent struck her heel.
And when at last the bard of Rhodope
Had mourned his fill in the wide world above,
He dared descend through Taenarus' dark gate

° from *Metamorphoses*, trans. A. D. Melville, Oxford: Oxford University Press, 1986, books 10 (1–154) and 11 (1–84). Reprinted by permission of Oxford University Press. Line numbers in the text are those of the English translation, which runs to more lines than the Latin.

° **Hymen**: Roman god of marriage, depicted wearing a yellow robe and bearing a torch. **Thence**: from Crete, where at the end of Book 9 he was presiding over the wedding of Iphis and Ianthe; Ovid moves from a wedding which ends a comic story to one which begins a tragic story.

To Hades to make trial of the shades;
And through the thronging wraiths and grave-spent ghosts
He came to pale Persephone and him,
Lord of the shades, who rules the unlovely realm,
And as he struck his lyre's sad chords he said:
'Ye deities who rule the world below,
Whither we mortal creatures all return,
If simple truth, direct and genuine,
May by your leave be told, I have come down
Not with intent to see the glooms of Hell,
Nor to enchain the triple snake-haired necks
Of Cerberus, but for my dear wife's sake,
In whom a trodden viper poured his venom
And stole her budding years. My heart has sought
Strength to endure; the attempt I'll not deny;
But love has won, a god whose fame is fair
In the world above; but here I doubt, though here
Too, I surmise; and if that ancient tale
Of ravishment is true, you too were joined
In love.° Now by these regions filled with fear,
By this huge chaos, these vast silent realms,
Reweave, I implore, the fate unwound too fast
Of my Eurydice. To you are owed
Ourselves and all creation; a brief while
We linger; then we hasten, late or soon,
To one abode; here one road leads us all;
Here in the end is home; over humankind
Your kingdom keeps the longest sovereignty.
She too, when ripening years reach their due term,
Shall own° your rule. The favour that I ask
Is but to enjoy her love; and, if the Fates
Will not reprieve her, my resolve is clear
Not to return: may two deaths give you cheer.'

So to the music of his strings he sang,
And all the bloodless spirits wept to hear;
And Tantalus forgot the fleeing water,
Ixion's wheel was tranced; the Danaids
Laid down their urns; the vultures left their feast,

° **if that ancient tale . . . joined in love**: a tactful allusion to the story of Pluto's rape of Proserpina.

° **own**: acknowledge.

And Sisyphus sat rapt upon his stone.°
Then first by that sad singing overwhelmed,
The Furies' cheeks, it's said, were wet with tears;
And Hades' queen and he whose sceptre rules
The Underworld could not deny the prayer,
And called Eurydice. She was among
The recent ghosts and, limping from her wound,
Came slowly forth; and Orpheus took his bride
And with her this compact that, till he reach
The world above and leave Avernus' vale,
He look not back or else the gift would fail.

The track climbed upwards, steep and indistinct,
Through the hushed silence and the murky gloom;
And now they neared the edge of the bright world,
And, fearing lest she faint, longing to look,
He turned his eyes – and straight she slipped away.
He stretched his arms to hold her – to be held –
And clasped, poor soul, naught but the yielding air.
And she, dying again, made no complaint
(For what complaint had she save she was loved?)
And breathed a faint farewell, and turned again
Back to the land of spirits whence she came.

The double death of his Eurydice
Stole Orpheus' wits away; (like him who saw
In dread the three-necked hound of Hell with chains
Fast round his middle neck, and never lost
His terror till he lost his nature too
And turned to stone; or Olenos, who took
Upon himself the charge and claimed the guilt
When his ill-starred Lethaea trusted to
Her beauty, hearts once linked so close, and now
Two rocks on runnelled Ida's mountainside).°
He longed, he begged, in vain to be allowed
To cross the stream of Styx a second time.
The ferryman repulsed him. Even so
For seven days he sat upon the bank,

° **And Tantalus . . . upon his stone**: see 'The underworld' in ch. 2, pp. 30–1 for these famous inmates of Tartarus.

° **like him . . . mountainside**: nothing else is known of these two metamorphoses: the man who turned to stone in terror at seeing Cerberus is probably part of the story of Hercules' twelfth labour (see ch. 3); the story of Lethaea and her husband Olenos looks like a familiar kind of punishment-for-hubris legend, similar to that of Niobe.

Unkempt and fasting, anguish, grief and tears
His nourishment, and cursed Hell's cruelty.
Then he withdrew to soaring Rhodope
And Haemus° battered by the northern gales.

Three times the sun had reached the watery Fish
That close the year,° while Orpheus held himself
Aloof from love of women, hurt perhaps
By ill-success or bound by plighted troth.
Yet many a woman burned with passion for
The bard, and many grieved at their repulse.
It was his lead that taught the folk of Thrace
The love for tender boys, to pluck the buds,
The brief springtime, with manhood still to come.

There was a hill, and on the hill a wide
Level of open ground, all green with grass.
The place lacked any shade. But when the bard,
The heaven-born bard, sat there and touched his strings,
Shade came in plenty. Every tree was there:
Dodona's holy durmast,° poplars once
The Sun's sad daughters,° oaks with lofty leaves,
Soft limes, the virgin laurel and the beech;
The ash, choice wood for spearshafts, brittle hazels,
The knotless fir, the ilex curving down
With weight of acorns, many-coloured maples,
The social plane,° the river-loving willow,
The water-lotus, box for ever green,
Thin tamarisks and myrtles double-hued,
Viburnums bearing berries of rich blue.
Twist-footed ivy came and tendrilled vines,
And vine-clad elms, pitch-pines and mountain-ash,
Arbutus laden with its blushing fruit,
Lithe lofty palms, the prize of victory,
And pines, high-girdled, in a leafy crest,
The favourite of Cybele, the gods'

° **Haemus**: a mountain in Thrace.
° **the watery Fish . . . close the year**: Pisces, the last sign of the zodiac, marks the end of the (northern) winter.
° **durmast**: a type of oak, associated with the temple of Zeus at Dodona.
° **The Sun's sad daughters**: in book 2 Ovid related how the Sun's daughters were turned to poplar trees in grief for their brother Phaethon.
° **social plane**: the plane tree, with its broad spreading branches, was a traditional shade tree.

Great mother, since in this tree Attis doffed
His human shape and stiffened in its trunk.°
Amid the throng the cone-shaped cypress stood,
A tree now, but in days gone by a boy . . .

Ovid briefly tells the story of Cyparissus, a boy whom Apollo loved, who pined away with grief after accidentally killing his pet stag, and was metamorphosed into a cypress tree.

Such was the grove the bard assembled. There
He sat amid a company of beasts,
A flock of birds, and when he'd tried his strings
And, as he tuned, was satisfied the notes,
Though different, agreed in harmony,
He sang this song: 'From Jove, great Mother Muse,
Inspire my song: to Jove all creatures bow;
Jove's might I've often hymned in days gone by.
I sang the giants in a graver theme
And bolts victorious in Phlegra's plains.°
But now I need a lighter strain, to sing
Of boys beloved of gods and girls bewitched
By lawless fires who paid the price of lust . . .'

The remainder of book 10 is taken up with the tales told by Orpheus, including those of Hyacinthus, Pygmalion, Myrrha, Adonis, and Atalanta. Orpheus's own story resumes at the beginning of the next book.

Book 11

While Orpheus sang his minstrel's songs and charmed
The rocks and woods and creatures of the wild
To follow, suddenly, as he swept his strings
In concord with his song, a frenzied band
Of Thracian women, wearing skins of beasts,
From some high ridge of ground caught sight of him.
'Look!' shouted one of them, tossing her hair
That floated in the breeze, 'Look, there he is,
The man who scorns us!' and she threw her lance
Full in Apollo's minstrel's face, but, tipped

° **pines . . . in its trunk**: Attis, lover of the goddess Cybele, castrated himself; his transformation into a pine tree (sacred to Cybele) may be Ovid's invention.

° **Phlegra's plains**: the volcanic region around Mount Vesuvius, traditionally the site of the war between the gods and giants.

With leaves, it left a bruise but drew no blood.
Another hurled a stone; that, in mid air,
Was vanquished by the strains of voice and lyre
And grovelled at his feet, as if to ask
Pardon for frenzy's daring. Even so
The reckless onslaught swelled; their fury knew
No bounds; stark madness reigned. And still his singing
Would have charmed every weapon, but the huge
Clamour, the drums, the curving Phrygian fifes,
Hand-clapping, Bacchic screaming drowned the lyre.
And then at last, his song unheard, his blood
Reddened the stones. The Maenads first pounced on
The countless birds still spellbound by his song,
The snakes, the host of creatures of the wild,
His glory and his triumph. Next they turned
Their bloody hands on Orpheus, flocking like
Birds that have seen a midnight owl abroad
By day, or in the amphitheatre
Upon the morning sand a pack of hounds
Round a doomed stag. They rushed upon the bard,
Hurling their leaf dressed lances, never meant
For work like that; and some slung clods, some flints,
Some branches torn from trees. And, lest they lack
Good weapons for their fury, as it chanced,
Oxen were toiling there to plough the land
And brawny farmhands digging their hard fields
Not far away, and sweating for their crop.
Seeing the horde of women, they fled and left
Their labour's armoury, and all across
The empty acres lay their heavy rakes,
Hoes and long-handled mattocks. Seizing these,
Those frantic women tore apart the oxen
That threatened with their horns, and streamed to slay
The bard. He pleaded then with hands outstretched
And in that hour for the first time his words
Were useless and his voice of no avail.
In sacrilege they slew him. Through those lips
(Great Lord of Heaven!) that held the rocks entranced,
That wild beasts understood, he breathed his last,
And forth into the winds his spirit passed.

The sorrowing birds, the creatures of the wild,
The woods that often followed as he sang,
The flinty rocks and stones, all wept and mourned

For Orpheus; forest trees cast down their leaves,
Tonsured in grief, and rivers too, men say,
Were swollen with their tears, and Naiads wore,
And Dryads too, their mourning robes of black
And hair dishevelled. All around his limbs
Lay scattered. Hebrus' stream received his head
And lyre, and floating by (so wonderful!)
His lyre sent sounds of sorrow and his tongue,
Lifeless, still murmured sorrow, and the banks
Gave sorrowing reply. And then they left
Their native river, carried out to sea,
And gained Methymna's shore on Lesbos' isle.
There, as his head lay on that foreign sand,
Its tumbled tresses dripping, a fierce snake
Threatened, until at last Apollo came
To thwart it as it struck and froze to stone
That serpent's open mouth and petrified,
Just as they were, its jaws that gaped so wide.

The ghost of Orpheus passed to the Underworld,
And all the places that he'd seen before
He recognized again and, searching through
The Elysian fields, he found Eurydice
And took her in his arms with leaping heart.
There hand in hand they stroll, the two together;
Sometimes he follows as she walks in front,
Sometimes he goes ahead and gazes back –
No danger now – at his Eurydice.

Bacchus did not permit this crime to pass
Unpunished, unavenged. Distressed to lose
The minstrel of his mysteries, at once
He fastened in the woods by twisting roots
All the women who had seen that wickedness,
Each at the place of her pursuit, their toes
Drawn down to points forced deep in the firm soil.
And as a bird, its foot held in a snare
Hidden by a clever fowler, feels it's caught
And flaps its wings and by its flutterings
Tightens the trap, so each of them was stuck
Fast in the soil and struggled, terrified,
In vain, to escape and as she jerked away,
The lithe root held her shackled. When she asked
Where were her toes, her nails, her feet, she saw
The bark creep up her shapely calves. She tried,

Distraught, to beat her thighs and what she struck
Was oak, her breast was oak, her shoulders oak;
Her arms likewise you'd think were changed to long
Branches and, thinking so, you'd not be wrong.°

O5 Boethius, from *The Consolation of Philosophy*, *c.* AD 520. Trans. J.T., 1609°

Anicius Manlius Severinus Boethius, *c.* AD 480–524, late Roman writer on philosophy, theology, music, and mathematics; he held high office under the Gothic king Theodoric, but was accused of treason, imprisoned, tortured, and executed. In *The Consolation of Philosophy*, written during his imprisonment, he presents himself as visited in prison by the lady Philosophy, who teaches him to bear his misfortunes courageously by instructing him in the nature of good and evil and the way in which the world is governed by divine providence. The prose dialogue is interspersed with short poems and songs. At the end of book 3, which deals with the nature of the Good, Philosophy 'with a soft and sweet voice, observing due dignity and gravity in her countenance and gesture' sings the story of Orpheus, which becomes a parable of the search for spiritual enlightenment.

The *Consolation* was enormously popular and influential in the Middle Ages and the Renaissance, and was translated by, among others, Alfred the Great, Chaucer, and Elizabeth I. This passage is from an early seventeenth-century translation published under the initials 'J.T.'.

Happy is he that can behold
The well-spring whence all good doth rise;
Happy is he that can unfold
The bands with which the earth him ties.

The Thracian poet, whose sweet song
Performed his wife's sad obsequies,°
And forced the woods to run along
When his mournful tunes did play,
Whose powerful music was so strong

° **you'd not be wrong**: the transformation of the Bacchantes into trees neatly mirrors Orpheus's earlier summoning of the trees: where Orpheus's music brought motionless wood to life, the murderers who silenced his music are transformed into motionless wood.

° from *The Consolation of Philosophy*, with the English translation of 'I.T.' (i.e. J.T., 1609), revised by H. F. Stewart, in *Boethius*, Loeb Classical Library, Cambridge, MA: Harvard University Press, 1918, book 3, metre 12.

° **obsequies**: funeral rites.

That it could make the rivers stay;°
The fearful hinds not daunted were,
But with the lions took their way,
Nor did the hare behold with fear
The dog whom these sweet notes appease –
When force of grief drew yet more near
And on his heart did burning seize,
Nor tunes which all in quiet bound°
Could any jot their master ease,
The gods above too hard he found,
And Pluto's palace visiting,
He mixed sweet verses with the sound
Of his loud harp's delightful string,
All that he drank with thirsty draught
From his high mother's chiefest spring,°
All that his restless grief him taught,
And love, which gives grief double aid.
With this even hell itself was caught,
Whither he went and pardon prayed
For his dear spouse (unheard request).
The three-head porter was dismayed,
Ravished with his unwonted guest;
The Furies, which in tortures keep
The guilty souls with pains opprest,
Moved with his song, began to weep;
Ixion's wheel now standing still
Turns not his head with motions steep;
Though Tantalus might drink at will,
To quench his thirst he would forbear;
The vulture full with music shrill
Doth not poor Tityus' liver tear.
'We by his verses conquered are,'
Saith the great King whom spirits fear.
'Let us not then from him debar
His wife whom he with songs doth gain.
Yet lest our gift should stretch too far,
We will it with this law restrain,
That when from hell he takes his flight,

° **stay**: stand still.

° **which all in quiet bound**: which subdue everything (else) to calmness.

° **All . . . spring**: i.e. all his poetic inspiration, gained by drinking from the fountain of the Muses on Mount Helicon.

He shall from looking back refrain.'
Who can for lovers laws indite?
Love hath no law but her own will.
Orpheus, seeing on the verge of night
Eurydice, doth lose and kill
Her and himself with foolish love.°

But you this feignèd tale fulfil
Who think unto the day above
To bring with speed your darksome mind.°
For if, your eye conquered, you move
Backward to Pluto left behind,
All the rich prey which thence you took
You lose while back to hell you look.

O6 Medieval mythographers

Two samples of medieval allegorisation of the Orpheus story. Pierre Bersuire, a fourteenth-century French Benedictine monk and scholar, author of a moral commentary on Ovid, gives two alternative interpretations (Orpheus as Christ, Orpheus as sinful man). Thomas of Walsingham, an English Benedictine, in the early fifteenth century, presents the Fulgentian interpretation (Orpheus the musician in search of Eurydice/wisdom) rather more lucidly than Fulgentius himself presented it.

(a) Pierre Bersuire
from **Metamorphosis Ovidiana,** *c. 1330*°

Say allegorically that Orpheus, son of the sun, is Christ, son of God the Father, who from the beginning, through love and desire, took Eurydice (i.e. the human soul) for his wife and united her with himself in marriage by his special prerogative. But the serpent (the devil) came upon the new (i.e. newly created) bride as she was gathering flowers (i.e. reaching for the forbidden apple), and bit her (by temptation) and killed her (by sin) and finally dispatched her to hell. Seeing this, Orpheus (Christ) resolved to descend in person into hell and so recovered his wife

° **Orpheus . . . foolish love**: In the Latin *Orpheus Eurydicen suam / Vidit, perdidit, occidit* can mean 'Orpheus saw, lost, and killed his Eurydice', or (more probably) 'Orpheus saw his Eurydice, lost her, and died'. J.T.'s translation combines both possible meanings.

° **But you . . . darksome mind**: i.e. this fictional (**feignèd**) story is a metaphor for your (Boethius's, and the reader's) real experience in attempting to climb from spiritual darkness to enlightenment.

° Latin texts from John Block Friedman, ***Orpheus in the Middle Ages***, Cambridge, MA: Harvard University Press, 1970, pp. 127–9, 133–4; my translations.

(i.e. humankind), wrested her away from the kingdom of darkness, and led her with him back to the upper world, saying these words from the Song of Solomon [2: 10]: 'Rise up, my love, my fair one, and come away.'

Or say that Orpheus is a sinner who by the bite of a serpent (i.e. by the temptation of the devil) lost his wife (i.e. his soul) while she carelessly gave her attention to gathering flowers (i.e. accumulating the transitory things of this world). But he recovered her spiritually when he descended to hell (by means of meditation) and sang sweetly (by means of prayer). For fear alone of hell's torments made him repent his sins, and so he was able to regain his wife by means of grace . . . But there are many who, through love of worldly things, look backwards and mentally return as a dog returns to its vomit. They love their recovered wife (i.e. soul) so excessively that they give way to her fleshly desires, and turn back the eyes of the mind upon her, and so lose her once again, and hell takes her back. 'He that loveth his life shall lose it' [John 12: 25].

(b) Thomas of Walsingham
from **Arcana Deorum**, *c. 1405*

Orpheus . . . should be interpreted as 'best voice', and Eurydice as 'profound judgement'. Orpheus (that is, anyone who devotes himself to music) wished to be united with her in marriage; he allured her with his lyre and took her as his wife. For a student of music cannot become a musician until he has understood the hidden depths of that art; but at length he attained her by the repeated and skilful melody of his voice. But in truth the pinnacle of this skill, though it is loved by the best, as it was by Aristaeus (for Aristaeus means 'best' in Greek), nevertheless shuns the company of men. And so [Eurydice] died by the bite of a serpent, because the secret of her extreme subtlety had not been perceived, and (as it were) transmigrated to the underworld. But he descended to seek out and bring back this art, and he was forbidden to look back, and when he saw her he lost her.

O7 From *Sir Orfeo, c.* 1330°

An anonymous Middle English romance, probably translated from a French source around 1330. In it Eurydice is not killed but stolen by the king of fairies, and Orpheus has to journey not to the underworld but to Faerie to rescue her.

Orfeo was a king
In Inglond, an high lording,
A stalworth man and hardi bo,> *bold as well*
Large> and curteys he was also. *generous*

° text edited by the English Department, Victoria University of Wellington.

His father was comen of King Pluto
And his mother of King Juno,
That sum-time were as godes y-hold> *held to be gods*
For aventours that they did and told.
This King sojourned in Traciens,
That was a city of noble defens> *nobly fortified*
(For Winchester was cleped tho> *called then*
Traciens, withouten no>). *denial*
The King had a queen of pris> *of price = 'excellent'*
That was y-cleped Dame Heurodis,
The fairest leuedi,> for the nones,° *lady*
That might go on body and bones°
Full of love and of goodenesse
Ac no man may> tell her fairnesse.> *can / beauty*

Heurodis tells Orfeo of a strange dream that she has had.

'. . . As I lay this under-tide> *morning*
And slepe under our orchard-side
There came to me two fair knightes
Well y-armed all to rightes,> *properly*
And bad me comen an heighing> *in haste*
And speke with their lord the king.
And I answered [in] wordes bold –
I no durst nought. No, I nold!°
They priked again as they might drive.°
Then cam their king, also blive,> *as quickly*
With an hundred knightes and mo> *more*
And damisels an hundred also,
All on snowe-white steedes,
As white as milke were their weedes.> *clothes*
I no seighe never yet before> *had never seen before*
So fair creatours y-core.> *excellent*
The king had a crown on hed –
It nas of silver, nor of gold red
Ac it was of a precious stone –
As bright as the sunne it shone.
And as soon as he to me cam,

° **for the nones**: a rhyming tag, with no particular meaning.
° **that might go on body and bones**: who could walk in the flesh.
° **I no durst . . . nold!**: I dared not. No, I would not!
° **They pricked . . . drive**: They rode back as fast as they could gallop.

Wold I, nold I, he me nam,°
And made me with him ride
Upon a palfray by his side;
And brought me to his palays
Well atired in ich ways,> *equipped in every way*
And shewed me castels and towers,
Rivers, forestes, frith> with flowers *woodland*
And his riche> stedes> ichon;> *noble / estates, or steeds / each one*
And sethen> me brought again hom> *then / back home*
Into our owhen orchard
And said to me thus afterward:
"Loke, dame, to-morwe thatow be> *that you*
Right here under this ympe-tree> *grafted tree*
And then thou shalt with us go
And live with us ever mo.
And if thou makest us y-let> *resistance*
Whar> thou be, thou worst y-fet,> *wherever / you shall be fetched*
And to-tore> thine limes> all *torn to pieces / limbs*
That nothing help thee no shall.> *So that nothing can (ever) help you*
And though thou be so to-torn
Yet thou worst with us y-born." '°

The next day the dream is fulfilled: in spite of all the efforts of Orfeo and his knights to protect her, Heurodis is seized and taken away by the fairy king. The grief-stricken Orfeo hands over his kingdom to a steward and goes out into the wilderness, where he spends ten years mourning and playing his harp to the birds and beasts. From time to time he sees the fairy court riding by, and one day he recognises Heurodis among a group of fairy ladies. He follows them through a rock into their land.

When he was in the rocke y-go> *gone*
Welle three mile, other mo,> *or more*
He came into a fair countray,
As bright so> sonne on somers day, *as*
Smooth and plain> and all grene, *level*
Hille no dale nas ther non y-sene.°
Amidde the lond a castel he sighe,> *saw*
Riche and real> and wonder highe. *splendid and royal*
All the utmast> wall *outermost*

° **Wold I, nold I, he me nam**: Whether I wanted to or not, he took me.
° **Yet thou worst with us y-born**: You'll still be carried off by (literally 'with') us.
° **Hille no dale . . . y-sene**: There was no hill nor dale visible there.

Was clear and sheen> as crystal. *bright*
An hundred towers ther were about,
Degiselich> and bataild stout.> *strange / with sturdy battlements*
The buttress came out of the diche> *moat*
Of rede gold y-arched riche;> *splendidly*
The vousour> was avowed> all *vaulting / adorned*
Of ich maner divers aumal.> *with all kinds of different enamel*
Within ther wer wide wones> *halls*
All of precious stones;
The worst> pillar on to bihold> *meanest / to be seen*
Was all of burnished gold.
All that lond was ever> light, *always*
For when it should be therk> and night *dark*
The riche stones light gonne> *began to shine*
As bright as doth at noone the sonne.
No man may telle, no thenche in thought,> *nor imagine*
The riche werk that there was wrought.
By all things him think that> it is *it seems to him*
The proude> court of Paradis. *magnificent*
In this castle the leuedis alight> – *dismounted*
He wold> in after, if he might. *wanted to (go)*

Orfeo knocketh at the gate –
The porter was ready there-at
And asked what he would have y-do.> *wanted done*
'Parfay!' quoth he, 'Icham> a minstrel, lo! *I am*
To solas> thy lord with my glee> *delight / music*
If his sweete wille be.'
The porter undide the gate anon> *at once*
And let him into the castle gon.
Then he gan behold about all> *look all about*
And sawe lying within the wall
Of folk that were thither y-brought,
And thought dead, and nere> nought. *were not*
Sum stoode withouten hade,> *head*
And sum non armes nade,> *had no arms*
And sum through the body hadde wounde,
And sum lay wode,> y-bounde, *mad*
And sum armed on hors sete,> *sat*
And sum astrangled> as they ete,> *choked / ate*
And sum were in water adreynt,> *drowned*
And sum with fire all for-schreynt.> *shrivelled up*
Wives ther lay on child-bedde,> *in childbirth*
Sum ded and sum awedde.> *gone mad*

And wonder fele> ther lay bisides *very many (more)*
Right as> they slepe> their under-tides. *just as / slept*
Eche was thus in this world y-nome,> *seized*
With fairy> thither y-come.> *by magic / brought*
Ther he saw his owhen wif,
Dame Heurodis, his lef> lif, *beloved*
Slepe under an ympe-tree. *sleeping*
By her clothes he knewe that it was she.

Orfeo enters the king's hall, introducing himself as a poor minstrel.

Befor the king he sat adoun
And tok his harp so merry of sound,
And tempreth> his harp as he well can, *tunes*
And blisseful notes he ther gan,> *began (to play)*
That all that in the palays were
Come to him for to hear
And lie adoun to his feete –
Them thenketh his melody so sweete.°
The king herkneth> and sitt full stille; *listens*
To hear his glee he hath goode wille.
Good bourde> he hadde of his glee,> *enjoyment / music*
The riche queen also hadde she.
When he hadde stint> his harping *stopped*
Then said to him the king:
'Minstrel, me liketh well> thy glee. *pleases me greatly*
Now aske of me, what> it be, *whatever*
Largelich ichil> thee pay. *Generously I will*
Now speak, and thou might assay.'> *can test it*
'Sir,' he said, 'Ich beseeche thee
Thatow> woldest give me *That you*
That ich> leuedi bright on blee> *very / fair of face*
That sleepeth under the ympe-tree.'
'Nay!' quoth the king, 'That nought nere!> *cannot be*
A sorry couple of you it were,> *you would make*
For thou art lene,> rowe> and blac, *lean / rough*
And she is lovesum, withouten lac.> *without blemish*
A lothlich> thing it were, forthy,> *disgusting / therefore*
To see her in thy company.'
'O Sir!' he said, 'Gentil> king!> *noble*

° **Them thenketh . . . so sweete**: His melody seems so sweet to them.

Yete were it a well fouler thing
To hear a lesin> of thy mouthe. *lie*
So, Sir, as you said nouthe,> *just now*
What I would aski have I shold,
And needes thou must thy word hold.' *you must needs keep your word*
The king said: 'Sethen> it is so, *since*
Take her by the hond and go –
Of her ichil thatow> be blithe!' *I wish that you*
He kneeled adoun and thanked him swithe.> *exceedingly*
His wif he took by the hand
And did him swithe> out of that land, *went quickly*
And went him out of that thede> *country*
Right as he come the way he yede.
So long he hath the way y-nome> *taken*
To Winchester he is y-come,
That was his owhen city –
Ac no man knew that it was he.

O8 Robert Henryson, from *Orpheus and Eurydice*, later fifteenth century°

Robert Henryson, ?1424–?1506, Scottish poet, whose most famous work is the *Testament of Cresseid*, a sequel to Chaucer's *Troilus and Criseyde*. His *Orpheus and Eurydice* tells the story in 414 lines, then appends a 219-line 'Moralitas' expounding its allegorical meaning. The extract begins when Erudices, 'the mychti quene of Trace', hearing of Orpheus's nobility and musical skill, invites him to become her 'king and lord'.

Henryson's medieval Scots dialect can appear formidable, and some notes on spelling and word forms may be helpful:

-and = '-ing' (e.g. *kepand* 'keeping', *dredand* 'dreading')
ch often = 'gh' (e.g. *thocht* 'thought', *siching* 'sighing')
d often = 'th' (e.g. *hider* 'hither', *quod* 'quoth, said')
-is = '-s' (e.g. *flouris* 'flowers', *puttis* 'puts')
-it = '-ed' (e.g. *walkit* 'walked')
quh = 'wh' (e.g. *quhar* 'where', *quhilk* 'which')
sch- = 'sh' (e.g. *scho* 'she')
Note also: *be* = 'by', *can, couth* = 'did', *till* = 'to', *in till* = 'into'.

° from *The Poems of Robert Henryson*, ed. Denton Fox, Oxford: Clarendon Press, 1981, pp. 132–53. Reprinted by permission of Oxford University Press.

12 Betwene Orpheus and fair Erudices,
Fra> thai war weddit on fra day to day, *From the time*
The lowe> of luf couth kendil> and encres, *flame / did kindle*
With myrth, blythnes, gret plesans, and gret play.
Off wardlie> ioye, allace, quhat sall we say? *worldly*
Lyke till a flour that plesandly will spring,
Quhilk> fadis sone, and endis with murnyng. *Which*

13 I say this be> Erudices the quene, *with reference to*
Quhilk> walkit furth in till a Maii mornyng, *Who*
Bot> with a madin,> in a medowe grene, *But (i.e. only) / maiden*
To tak the dewe and se the flouris spring;
Quhar in a schawe,> ner by this lady ying,> *wood / young*
A bustuos herd,> callit Arystyus, *rough shepherd*
Kepand his bestis, lay wnder a bus.> *bush*

14 And quhen he saw this lady solitar,
Barfute> with schankis quhytar than the snawe,°
Prikkit> with lust, he thocht withoutin mar> *Stirred / without more ado*
Hir till oppres> – and till hir can> he drawe. *to rape her / did*
Dredand for scaith,> sche fled quhen scho him saw, *Dreading harm*
And as scho ran all bairfut in ane bus,
Scho trampit> on a serpent wennomus.> *trod / venomous*

15 This cruell wennome was so penitryf,> *penetrating*
As natur is of all mortall poisoun,
In pecis small this quenis hart couth ryf,> *did break*
And scho anone> fell in a dedly swoun. *at once*
Seand this cais,> Proserpyne maid hir bovne,°
Quhilk clepit> is the goddes infernall, *Who is called*
And till hir court this gentill> quene couth call. *noble*

Part of Orpheus's lament for Eurydice:

22 'Fair weill, my place;> fair weile, plesance> and play; *palace / pleasure*
And welcome, woddis> wyld and wilsome> way, *woods / lonely*
My wikit werd> in wildernes to wair!> *cruel fate / endure*
My rob ryall> and all my riche array *royal robe*
Changit sall be in rude russat> of gray; *(coarse woollen cloth)*
My diademe in till ane hat of hair;°

° **Barfute . . . snawe**: Barefoot with legs whiter than snow.
° **Seand . . . bovne**: Seeing this event, Proserpine made herself ready.
° **hat of hair**: i.e. (probably) no covering for his head but his own hair.

My bed sall be with bever, broke, and bair,°
In buskis> bene,° with mony bustuos bes,> — *bushes / wild beasts*
Withoutin sang,> sayng with siching sair,> — *song / painful sighing*
'Quhar art thow gane, my luf Erudices?'

Ascending into the heavens, Orpheus searches in vain for Eurydice through the planetary spheres.

. . . Thus fra the hevyn he went doun to the erde,
Yit by the way sum melody he lerde.> — *learned*

30 In his passage amang the planetis all,
He herd a hevynly melody and sound,
Passing all instrumentis musicall,
Causid be rollyng of the speris round;
Quhilk armony, throu all this mappamound,> — *world, universe*
Quhill moving cesse, vnyt perpetuall –
Quhilk of this warld, Plato the saul can call.

Armed with this new music, he descends into the underworld, appeases Cerberus and the Furies, and eases the torments of the damned. At last he makes his way to Pluto's court.

48 Syne> nethir mare> he went quhare Pluto was — *Then / lower down*
And Proserpine, and thider-ward> he drewe, — *to that place*
Ay> playand on his harp as he coud pas,> — *Always / as he walked on*
Till at the last Erudices he knewe,
Lene and dedelike,> pitouse and pale of hewe, — *deathly*
Rycht warsch and wan and walowit as the wede,°
Hir lily lyre> was lyke vnto the lede.> — *complexion / lead*

49 Quod he, 'My lady lele> and my delyte, — *loyal, true*
Full wa is me> to se yow changit thus. — *it grieves me greatly*
Quhare is thy rude> as rose wyth chekis quhite, — *complexion*
Thy cristall eyne with blenkis> amorouse, — *glances*
Thi lippis rede to kis diliciouse?'
Quod scho, 'As now I dar noucht tell, perfay,> — *by my faith*
Bot ye sall wit> the cause ane othir day.' — *know*

50 Quod Pluto, 'Sir, thouch scho be like ane elf,

° **bever, broke, and bair**: beaver, badger (brock), and bear.
° **bene**: pleasant, giving shelter (perhaps a conventional tag, perhaps ironic).
° **Rycht warsch and wan and walowit as the wede**: All sickly and pale and withered as weeds.

Thare is na cause to plenye,> and for quhy? *lament*
Scho fure als wele> dayly as did my self, *She fares as well*
Or king Herode,° for all his cheualry.> *chivalry, i.e. knights*
It is langour> that puttis hir in sik ply;> *sadness / such a plight*
Were scho at hame in hir contree of Trace,
Scho wald refete> full sone in fax and face.'> *recover / hair and face*

51 Than Orpheus before Pluto sat doun,
And in his handis quhite his harp can ta,> *did take*
And playit mony suete proporcion,> *sweet harmonies*
With base tonys in ypodorica,
With gemilling in ypolerica;°
Till at the last, for reuth> and grete pitee, *sorrow*
Thay wepit sore that coud hym here and see.

52 Than Proserpyne and Pluto bad hym as> *ask*
His warison,> and he wald ask rycht noucht,> *reward / nothing at all*
Bot licence wyth his wyf away to pas> *go*
Till his contree, that he so fer had soucht.
Quod Proserpyne, 'Sen> I hir hidir broucht, *Since*
We sall noucht part bot wyth condicion.'> *except under a condition*
Quod he, 'Thareto I mak promission.'> *promise*

53 'Erudices than be the hand thou tak,
And pas thy way, bot vnderneth this payne:> *under this penalty*
Gyf> thou turnis, or blenkis> behind thy bak, *If / look*
We sall hir haue forewir> till> hell agayn.' *forever / to*
Thouch this was hard, yit Orpheus was fayn,> *willing*
And on thai went, talkand of play and sport,
Quhill thay almaist come to the vtter port.> *outer gate*

54 Thus Orpheus, wyth inwart lufe replete,> *full of inner love*
So blyndit was in grete affection,> *passion*
Pensif> apon his wyf and lady suete,> *Thinking / sweet*
Remembrit noucht his hard condicion.
Quhat will ye more?° In schort conclusion,

° **Herode**: Herod the Great, 'a type of the greatest earthly magnificence: in the mystery plays he is described as the ruler of the entire earth, and is usually shown as surrounded by his knights' (Fox).

° **With base tonys . . . yperolica**: Ypodorica is Hypodorian, the deepest of the Greek musical 'modes', but 'ypolerica' is unexplained; **gemilling**, literally 'twinning', is a technical term from medieval polyphonic music. 'The lines do not make much sense: perhaps the intended meaning is that Orpheus played on his harp bass tones while "gemilling", on his harp or vocally, in a different mode' (Fox).

° **Quhat will ye more?**: What more do you want (me to say)?

He blent> bak-ward and Pluto come anone,> *looked / at once*
And vnto hell agayn with hir is gone.

From the 'Moralitas': Henryson, following the fourteenth-century commentator Nicholas Trivet, explains the allegorical meaning of the story.

Faire Phebus is the god of sapience;> *wisdom*
Caliopee, his wyf, is eloquence;
Thir twa maryit gat Orpheus belyve,°
Quillk callit is the part intellective> *intellectual, rational*
Of mannis saule> and under-standing, free *man's soul*
And separate fra sensualitee.°
Erudices is oure affection,°
Be> fantasy oft movit up and doun; *By*
Quhile to reson it castis the delyte,
Quhile to the flesch settis the appetite.°
Arestyus, this hird that coud persewe
Erudices, is noucht bot> gude vertewe, *nothing but*
Quhilk besy> is ay to kepe oure myndis clene; *busy*
Bot quhen we flee out throu the medow grene,
Fra vertu to this warldis wayn plesance,> *pleasure*
Myngit> with care and full of variance, *mixed*
The serpent stangis:> that is dedely syn *stings*
That poysons the saule wyth-out and in;
And than is dede and eke oppressit doun
To warldly lust all oure affectioun . . .°

Than Orpheus, our ressoun, is full wo
And twichis> on his harp and biddis ho> *touches*
Till our desyre and fulich appetyte,
Bidis leif this warldis full> delyte.° *foul*
Than Pluto god, and quene of hellis fyre,
Mone> grant to ressoun on fors the desyre;° *Must*

° **Thir twa maryit gat Orpheus belyve**: These two, married, begot Orpheus in due course.

° **sensualitee**: the physical appetites and senses.

° **affection**: emotion and will.

° **Quhile to . . . appetite**: Sometimes it desires reason, at other times it has an appetite for fleshly pleasures.

° **And than is dede . . . affectioun**: i.e. Eurydice's descent to hell symbolises our emotions and will becoming ensalved to sinful desires.

° **biddis ho . . . delyte**: commands 'ho!', i.e. 'Stop', to our desire and foolish appetite, and bids it leave the world's foul pleasures.

° **Than Pluto . . . desire**: Pluto is forced (**on fors**, of necessity) to grant to Reason (Orpheus) the possession of Desire or Affection (Eurydice).

Than Orpheus has won Erudices,
Quhen oure desire wyth reson makis pes,> *makes peace*
And sekis vp> to contemplacion, *aspires*
Off syn detestand the abusion.°
Bot ilk> man suld be war> and wisely see *each / wary*
That he bakwart cast noucht his myndis ee,> *eye*
Gevand consent and dilectation
Off wardly lust for the affection;°
For than gois bakwart to the syn agayn
Oure appetite, as it before was slayn
In warldly lust and sensualitee,
And makis reson wedow> for to be. *widower*

O9 Edmund Spenser on Orpheus°

Edmund Spenser, *c.*1552–99, poet; resident from 1588 on in Ireland as a servant of the English government, whose policies he defended in *A View of the Present State of Ireland* (1596). His masterpiece is *The Faerie Queene* (1589–96), an unfinished allegorical romance, in which the quests of knights in the service of the Fairy Queen Gloriana embody the pursuit of various classical and Christian virtues; his other works include *The Shepherd's Calendar* (1579), a cycle of pastoral poems linked to the twelve months of the year, and the *Amoretti* (1595), love sonnets.

Spenser cultivated a deliberately archaic style in imitation of Chaucer and other medieval writers. Its peculiarities include obsolete plural verb forms such as *praisen*, *delighten*, *been* (= 'are'), *han* (= 'have'), as well as other archaic words and forms explained in the notes.

(a) from The Shepherd's Calendar, *1579*

A debate about the value and purpose of poetry, in which the figure of Orpheus is often explicitly or implicitly invoked, runs through *The Shepherd's Calendar*. In the 'October' section, the shepherd-poet Cuddy complains about the unprofitable nature of the poet's calling, while his friend Piers defends its dignity and importance.

° **Off syn . . . abusion**: detesting the shameful practice of sin.
° **Gevand . . . affection**: Giving the will's consent to, and taking delight (**dilectation**) in, worldly desires for the sake of the affections (emotions).
° from (a) *The Shepheardes Calendar*, London, 1575, Tenth Eclogue (October); (b) *The Faerie Queene*, London, 1596, book 4, canto 2.

CUDDY: Piers, I have pipèd erst° so long with pain
That all mine oaten reeds been rent and wore,
And my poor muse hath spent her sparèd° store,
Yet little good hath got and much less gain.
Such pleasance° makes the grasshopper so poor,°
And lig so laid° when winter doth her strain.

The dapper° ditties that I wont° devise
To feed youth's fancies and the flocking fry°
Delighten much – what I the bet forthy?°
They han the pleasure, I a slender prize.
I beat the bush, the birds to them do fly.
What good thereof to Cuddy can arise?

PIERS: Cuddy, the praise is better than the price,
The glory eke° much greater than the gain.
O what an honour is it to restrain
The lust of lawless youth with good advice,
Or prick them forth with pleasance of thy vein,
Whereto thou list their trainèd wills entice.°

Soon as thou gin'st° to set thy notes in frame,
O how the rural routs° to thee do cleave.°
Seemeth° thou dost their soul of sense bereave,°

° **erst**: in the past.
° **sparèd**: saved-up.
° **pleasance**: pleasure.
° **grasshopper so poor**: a reference to Aesop's fable of the ant and the grasshopper: the grasshopper played and sang all summer and was left hungry in winter, whereas the industrious ant had spent summer storing up food.
° **lig so laid**: 'lie so faint and unlusty' (according to 'E.K.', whose extensive notes and commentary were included in the first edition of the *Calendar*).
° **dapper**: neat.
° **wont**: used to.
° **fry**: young people.
° **what I the bet forthy?**: how am I am the better for that?
° **eke**: also.
° **prick . . . entice**: having captured (**trainèd**) their wills with the pleasure given by your poetic skill (**vein**), encourage (**prick**) them out in whatever direction you desire.
° **gin'st**: beginnest.
° **routs**: crowds.
° **cleave**: cling.
° **Seemeth**: it seems that.
° **soul of sense bereave**: E.K. cites the opinion of philosophers like Plato and Pythagoras on 'the secret working of music', 'that the mind was made of a certain harmony and musical numbers, for the great compassion [i.e. sympathy] and likeness of affection in th' one and the other . . . So it is not incredible which the poet here saith, that music can bereave the soul of sense.'

All as° the shepherd that did fetch his dame
From Pluto's baleful bower withouten° leave;
His music's might the hellish hound did tame.

CUDDY: So praisen babes the peacock's spotted train,
And wondren at bright Argus' blazing eye;°
But who rewards him e'er the more forthy,
Or feeds him once the fuller by a grain?
Sike° praise is smoke that sheddeth in the sky;
Sike words been wind, and wasten soon in vain.

(b) from The Faerie Queene, *1596*

At this point in book 4 of *The Faerie Queene* Ate (Strife) has stirred up a quarrel between two of the knights; Spenser (drawing on Apollonius, **O1**) invokes Orpheus and King David as figures who could calm strife into harmony.

1 Firebrand of hell, first tind° in Phlegethon
By thousand furies, and from thence out thrown
Into this world, to work confusion°
And set it all on fire by force unknown,
Is wicked discord, whose small sparks once blown
None but a god or godlike man can slake;
Such as was Orpheus, that, when strife was grown
Amongst those famous imps° of Greece, did take
His silver harp in hand and shortly friends them make.

2 Or such as that celestial Psalmist was,
That, when the wicked fiend his lord tormented,
With heavenly notes, that did all other pass,
The outrage of his furious fit relented.°
Such music is wise words with time concented°
To moderate stiff minds disposed to strife . . .

° **All as**: just like.
° **withouten**: without.
° **Argus' blazing eye**: the 'eyes' in the peacock's tail originally belonged to the hundred-eyed giant Argus (see Ovid, *Met.*, 1).
° **Sike**: such.
° **tind**: set afire.
° **confusion**: destruction.
° **imps**: young nobles.
° **that celestial Psalmist . . . relented**: David (the **Psalmist**) played his harp to calm the madness of king Saul, who was possessed by an evil spirit (1 Samuel, 16: 14–23).
° **concented**: harmonised.

O10 George Puttenham, from *The Art of English Poesy*, 1589°

George Puttenham, *c.*1529–91, Elizabethan critic, whose *Art of English Poesy* was published anonymously in 1589.

The profession and use of poesy is most ancient from the beginning, and not, as many erroneously suppose, after but before any civil society was among men. For it is written that poesy was th' original cause and occasion of their first assemblies, when before the people remained in the woods and mountains, vagrant and dispersed like the wild beasts, lawless and naked or very ill clad, and of all good and necessary provision for harbour or sustenance utterly unfurnished, so as they little differed for their manner of life from the very brute beasts of the field. Whereupon it is feigned that Amphion and Orpheus, two poets of the first ages, one of them (to wit Amphion) builded up cities and reared walls with the stones that came in heaps to the sound of his harp, figuring° thereby the mollifying of hard and stony hearts by his sweet and eloquent persuasion. And Orpheus assembled the wild beasts to come in herds to hearken to his music, and by that means made them tame, implying thereby how by his discreet and wholesome lessons, uttered in harmony and with melodious instruments, he brought the rude and savage people to a more civil and orderly life, nothing, as it seemeth, more prevailing or fit to redress and edify the cruel and sturdy courage° of man than it. And as these two poets, and Linus before them, and Musaeus also and Hesiodus in Greece and Arcadia, so by all likelihood had more poets done in other places and in other ages before them, though there be no remembrance left of them, by reason of the records by some accident of time perished and failing. Poets therefore are of great antiquity.

Puttenham goes on to argue 'How poets were the first priests, the first prophets, the first legislators and politicians' (ch. 3) and 'the first philosophers, the first astronomers and historiographers and orators and musicians of the world' (ch. 4); and concludes:

It cannot be therefore that any scorn or indignity should justly be offered to so noble, profitable, ancient, and divine a science as poesy is.

° from *The Arte of English Poesie*, book 1, chapters 3–4, in *Elizabethan Critical Essays*, ed. G. Gregory Smith, Oxford, 1904.

° **figuring**: symbolising.

° **courage**: heart, spirit.

O11 Philip Sidney, from *Astrophil and Stella*, 1591°

Sir Philip Sidney, 1554–86, poet, romance writer, critic, courtier, diplomat, and soldier, often seen in his lifetime and later as epitomising the ideal of the Renaissance gentleman-poet. His principal works (all published after he died at the age of thirty-two on campaign in the Netherlands) are *Astrophil and Stella*, a sequence of love sonnets, interspersed with songs, addressed by Astrophil ('star-lover') to the unattainable Stella ('star'); *Arcadia*, a long prose romance of love and chivalry; and an influential critical work, the *Defence of Poetry* or *Apology for Poetry*. In this song from *Astrophil and Stella* Sidney uses (and in the last stanza gently sends up) the standard love-poetry motif of comparing the beloved's singing or playing to that of Orpheus.

If Orpheus' voice had force to breathe such music's love
Through pores of senseless trees as it could make them move,
If stones good measure danced the Theban walls to build
To cadence of the tunes which Amphion's lyre did yield,
More cause a like effect at leastwise bringeth:°
O stones, O trees, learn hearing – Stella singeth.

If love might sweeten so a boy of shepherd brood°
To make a lizard dull to taste love's dainty food;
If eagle fierce could so in Grecian maid delight
As his light was her eyes, her death his endless night,°
Earth gave that love, heaven, I trow,° love refineth.
O beasts, O birds, look, love – lo, Stella shineth.

The birds, beasts, stones, and trees feel this, and feeling love;
And if the trees nor stones stir not the same to prove,
Nor beasts nor birds do come unto this blessed gaze,
Know that small love is quick, and great love doth amaze.°
They are amazed, but you, with reason armed,
O eyes, O ears of men, how are you charmed!

° Third Song from *Astrophil and Stella*, in *The Countesse of Pembrokes Arcadia: the third time published with new additions*, London, 1598.

° **More cause . . . bringeth**: A greater cause brings about at least a similar effect.

° **brood**: breed, origin.

° **If love . . . endless night**: Sidney refers to two stories of animal loyalty from Pliny's *Natural History*: a 'dragon' (or lizard, or snake) which rescued its shepherd master from bandits (8. 61), and an eagle, tamed by a girl of Sestos, which burned itself to death on her funeral pyre (10. 18).

° **trow**: believe.

° **amaze**: stun, stupefy (Sidney varies a famous line from the playwright Seneca: 'Small griefs speak, great ones are dumb').

O12 George Chapman, from *Ovid's Banquet of Sense*, 1595°

George Chapman, ?1559–1634, Elizabethan poet and dramatist, whose wide range encompassed tragedies, comedies, philosophical poetry, and a famous translation of Homer's *Iliad* and *Odyssey* (which later inspired Keats's sonnet 'On First Looking into Chapman's Homer'). His poetry is characteristically learned and difficult, both for its intellectual content and its compressed and knotty language. *Ovid's Banquet of Sense* is an allegorical poem about sensual love, in which the poet Ovid, coming upon his beloved Julia singing in a garden, successively indulges the pleasures of hearing, smell, sight, taste (a kiss), and touch.

Say, gentle air, O does it not thee good
  Thus to be smit with her correcting°voice?
Why dance ye not, ye daughters of the wood?
  Wither for ever, if not now rejoice.
Rise, stones, and build a city with her notes,
  And notes, infuse with your most Cynthian° noise
To all the trees, sweet flowers and crystal floats°
    That crown and make this cheerful garden quick,°
    Virtue,° that every touch may make such music.

O that, as man is called a little world,
  The world might shrink into a little man°
To hear the notes about this garden hurled,
  That skill dispersed in tunes so Orphean
Might not be lost in smiting stocks° and trees
  That have no ears, but grown as it began
Spread their renowns as far as Phoebus° sees
Through earth's dull veins, that she like heaven might move
In ceaseless music and be filled with love.

° from *Ovids Banquet of Sence*, London, 1595.
° **correcting**: bringing into order or health.
° **Cynthian**: of Cynthia (Diana), the moon goddess.
° **floats**: waves.
° **quick**: alive.
° **Virtue**: power (**virtue** is the object of **infuse** in line 60: the speaker calls on Julia's music to infuse into the trees, flowers and waters of the garden the power to create this harmony at all times).
° **O that . . . little man**: Chapman calls on the traditional idea that each human being is a microcosm (small world) which reflects the macrocosm (great world), the external universe.
° **stocks**: tree-trunks, or blocks of wood.
° **Phoebus**: the sun.

O13 William Shakespeare°

William Shakespeare, 1564–1616, playwright and poet. In his education at Stratford grammar school Shakespeare clearly acquired a knowledge of Greek mythology and a lifelong love of Ovid and the *Metamorphoses*; a contemporary critic claimed that 'the sweet witty soul of Ovid lives in mellifluous and honey-tongued Shakespeare'. Mythological and Ovidian allusions are frequent in the early plays, rarer and subtler in the later ones.

(a) from The Two Gentlemen of Verona, c. *1589*

The unscrupulous lover Proteus is pretending to advise his rival Thurio how to woo the Duke's daughter, while secretly planning to win her himself.

PROTEUS: As much as I can do, I will effect.
But you, Sir Thurio, are not sharp enough:
You must lay lime° to tangle her desires
By wailful sonnets, whose composèd rhymes
Should be full-fraught with serviceable vows.°
DUKE: Ay, much is the force of heaven-bred poesy.
PROTEUS: Say that upon the altar of her beauty
You sacrifice your tears, your sighs, your heart.
Write till your ink be dry, and with your tears
Moist it again, and frame some feeling line
That may discover such integrity.°
For Orpheus' lute was strung with poets' sinews,
Whose golden touch could soften steel and stones,
Make tigers tame, and huge leviathans°
Forsake unsounded deeps to dance on sands.

(b) from The Merchant of Venice, c. *1596*

In the moonlit garden of Belmont, the lovers Lorenzo and Jessica listen to music, and Lorenzo expounds the concept of the music of the spheres.

° from (a) *Two Gentlemen of Verona*, 3. 2. 66–80, from the First Folio: *Mr William Shakespeares Comedies, Histories, & Tragedies*, London, 1623; (b) *The Merchant of Venice*, 5. 1. 54–88, from Q1: *The most excellent Historie of the Merchant of Venice*, London, 1600, with correction of 'Terebus' to 'Erebus'; (c) *Henry VIII*, 3. 1. 1–14, from the First Folio.

° **lay lime**: sticky birdlime was spread on branches to catch birds.

° **full-fraught with serviceable vows**: heavily loaded with vows to be her servant.

° **discover such integrity**: reveal such single-hearted devotion (as your tears demonstrate).

° **leviathans**: a mythical sea monster, often identified with the whale.

LORENZO: . . . How sweet the moonlight sleeps upon this bank!
Here will we sit, and let the sounds of music
Creep in our ears. Soft stillness and the night
Become° the touches° of sweet harmony.
Sit, Jessica. Look how the floor of heaven
Is thick inlaid with patens° of bright gold.
There's not the smallest orb which thou behold'st
But in his motion like an angel sings,
Still° choiring to the young-eyed cherubins.°
Such harmony is in immortal souls,
But whilst this muddy vesture° of decay
Doth grossly close it in, we cannot hear it.
[*Enter musicians*]
Come ho, and wake Diana with a hymn.
With sweetest touches pierce your mistress' ear
And draw her home with music.
[*The musicians play music*]
JESSICA: I am never merry when I hear sweet music.
LORENZO: The reason is your spirits are attentive.
For do but note a wild and wanton herd
Or race of youthful and unhandled° colts,
Fetching mad bounds, bellowing and neighing loud,
Which is the hot condition of their blood,
If they but hear perchance a trumpet sound
Or any air of music touch their ears,
You shall perceive them make a mutual stand,°
Their savage eyes turned to a modest gaze
By the sweet power of music. Therefore the poet
Did feign° that Orpheus drew trees, stones, and floods,
Since naught so stockish,° hard, and full of rage
But music for the time doth change his nature.
The man that hath no music in himself,
Nor is not moved with concord of sweet sounds,

° **Become**: suit.
° **touches**: notes, musical phrases.
° **patens**: plates (literally, a paten is a round dish of precious metal used in the Mass to serve the consecrated bread).
° **Still**: continually.
° **cherubins**: a type of angels, depicted as young children.
° **vesture**: clothing (i.e. the body).
° **unhandled**: untamed.
° **make a mutual stand**: all stand still together.
° **feign**: compose the fiction.
° **stockish**: insensible as a block of wood.

Is fit for treasons, stratagems,° and spoils;°
The motions of his spirit are dull as night,
And his affections dark as Erebus;°
Let no such man be trusted. Mark the music.

(c) from **Henry VIII or All Is True**, *1613, by Shakespeare and John Fletcher*

Katherine of Aragon, anxiously waiting for news of Henry VIII's attempt to divorce her, listens to a song about the soothing power of music. The scene may be by Shakespeare's collaborator John Fletcher.

QUEEN KATHERINE: Take thy lute, wench. My soul grows sad with troubles.
Sing, and disperse 'em if thou canst; leave working.
WOMAN [*sings*]: Orpheus with his lute made trees
And the mountain tops that freeze
Bow themselves when he did sing.
To his music, plants and flowers
Ever sprung, as° sun and showers
There had made a lasting spring.
Everything that heard him play,
Even the billows of the sea,
Hung their heads, and then lay by.
In sweet music is such art,
Killing care and grief of heart
Fall asleep, or hearing, die.

O14 Francis Bacon, from *The Wisdom of the Ancients*, 1609. Trans. from Latin by Sir Arthur Gorges, 1619°

Francis Bacon, Baron Verulam and Viscount St Albans, 1561–1626, politician, philosopher, scientist, and essayist; he became attorney-general and lord chancellor before falling from power under accusations of corruption. His writings in English and Latin, such as *The Advancement of Learning* (1605), expound his rationalistic philosophy, and urge the need for organised scientific research to

° **stratagems**: acts of violence.
° **spoils**: robberies.
° **Erebus**: the underworld.
° **as**: as if.
° from Francis Bacon, *The Wisedome of the Ancients*, trans. Arthur Gorges, London, 1619.

unlock the secrets of nature. In *The Wisdom of the Ancients* Bacon interprets the classical myths as political and scientific allegories, under headings such as 'Proteus, or Matter', 'Pan, or Nature', 'Prometheus, or the State of Man'. Orpheus becomes a symbol of 'philosophy' – a term which for Bacon includes much of what we would call 'science'.

Orpheus, or Philosophy

The tale of Orpheus, though common, had never the fortune to be fitly applied in every point. It may seem to represent the image of Philosophy; for the person of Orpheus – a man admirable and divine, and so excellently skilled in all kind of harmony that with his sweet ravishing music he did as it were charm and allure all things to follow him – may carry a singular description of philosophy. For the labours of Orpheus do so far exceed the labours of Hercules in dignity and efficacy as the works of wisdom excel the works of fortitude.

Bacon summarises the story: Orpheus's journey to hell and his second loss of Eurydice; how he 'falling into deep melancholy, became a contemner [despiser] of womankind'; his playing in the desert, which attracted beasts, trees, and stones to 'place themselves in an orderly and decent fashion about him'; and how the Bacchantes' noise drowned out his music, so that 'that harmony which was the bond of that order and society being dissolved, all disorder began again', the beasts turned on one another, and Orpheus was killed – 'for whose cruel death the river Helicon (sacred to the Muses) in horrible indignation hid his head underground, and raised it again in another place'.

The meaning of this fable seems to be thus. Orpheus' music is of two sorts, the one appeasing the infernal powers, the other attracting beasts and trees. The first may be fitly applied to natural philosophy,° the second to moral or civil discipline.

The most noble work of natural philosophy is the restitution and renovation of things corruptible, the other (as a lesser degree of it) the preservation of bodies in their estate,° detaining them from dissolution and putrefaction. And if this gift may be in mortals, certainly it can be done by no other means than by the due and exquisite temper° of nature, as by the melody and delicate touch of an instrument. But, seeing it is of all things the most difficult, it is seldom or never attained unto, and in all likelihood for no other reason more than through curious diligence° and untimely impatience.

° **natural philosophy**: i.e. science, the study of the workings of nature.
° **estate**: state.
° **temper**: tempering, i.e. delicate control and modification.
° **curious diligence**: anxious haste or hurry.

And therefore philosophy, hardly able to produce so excellent an effect, in a pensive humour° (and not without cause) busies herself about human objects, and by persuasion and eloquence, insinuating the love of virtue, equity and concord in the minds of men, draws multitudes of people to a society, makes them subject to laws, obedient to government, and forgetful of their unbridled affections,° while they give ear to precepts and submit themselves to discipline. Whence follows the building of houses, erecting of towns, and planting of fields and orchards with trees and the like, insomuch that it would not be amiss to say that even thereby stones and woods were called together and settled in order. And after serious trial made and frustrated about the restoring of a body mortal, this care of civil affairs follows in his due place; because by a plain demonstration of the inevitable necessity of death, men's minds are moved to seek eternity by the fame and glory of their merits. It is wisely also said in the fable that Orpheus was averse from the love of women and marriage, because the delights of wedlock and love of children do for the most part hinder men from enterprising great and noble designs for the public good, holding posterity° a sufficient step to immortality without actions.

Besides, even the very works of wisdom (although amongst all human things they do most excel) do nevertheless meet with their periods.° For it happens that, after kingdoms and commonwealths have flourished for a time, even tumults and seditions and wars arise. In the midst of which hurly-burlies, first, laws are silent, men return to the pravity° of their natures, fields and towns are wasted and depopulated; and then, if this fury continue, learning and philosophy must needs be dismembered, so that a few fragments only and in some places will be found like the scattered boards of shipwreck, so as a barbarous age must follow; and the streams of Helicon being hid under the earth, until (the vicissitude of things passing) they break out again and appear in some other remote nation, though not perhaps in the first climate.°

O15 Giles Fletcher, from *Christ's Victory and Triumph*, 1610°

Giles Fletcher the younger, ?1585–1623, poet and Anglican minister, of a literary family: his father (Giles the elder) and his brother Phineas were also poets, and the dramatist John Fletcher was his cousin. Both Giles and Phineas wrote allegorical religious poetry in a style and form heavily influenced by Spenser. His

° **pensive humour**: melancholy mood.
° **affections**: passions.
° **posterity**: offspring.
° **periods**: ends.
° **pravity**: depravity, savagery.
° **climate**: region.
° from *Christs Victorie, and Triumph in Heaven, and Earth, over, and after Death*, Cambridge, 1610, part 3 ('Christ's Triumph over Death').

major work, *Christ's Victory and Triumph in Heaven and Earth, Over and After Death*, deals in four books with Christ's birth, his life, his death, and his 'harrowing of hell' (his descent into hell to release the souls of the virtuous pre-Christians there). At the start of the third book Fletcher, addressing his fellow poets, contrasts their mere pagan fictions with his Gospel truth; yet, while dismissing Orpheus as the creation of 'dreaming poets', he evokes a kind of double-exposed figure who is simultaneously Christ and Orpheus.

6 Go, giddy brains, whose wits are thought so fresh,
Pluck all the flowers that Nature forth doth throw,
Go stick them on the cheeks of wanton flesh –
Poor idol, forced at once to fall and grow,
Of fading roses and of melting snow.
    Your songs exceed your matter; this of mine
    The matter which it sings shall make divine,
As stars dull puddles gild, in which their beauties shine.

7 Who doth not see drowned in Deucalion's name°
(When earth his men, and sea had lost his shore)
Old Noah? and in Nisus' lock, the fame
Of Samson yet alive? and long before
In Phaethon's, mine own fall I deplore.°
    But he that conquered hell to fetch again
    His virgin widow, by a serpent slain,
Another Orpheus was than dreaming poets feign,

8 That taught the stones to melt for passion,
And dormant sea, to hear him, silent lie,
And at his voice the wat'ry nation°
To flock, as if they deemed it cheap to buy
With their own deaths his sacred harmony;
    The while the waves stood still to hear his song,
    And steady shore waved with the reeling throng
Of thirsty souls that hung upon his fluent tongue.°

° **drowned in Deucalion's name**: 'By the obscure fables of the Gentiles, typing it' (Fletcher's note): that is, the classical myths are 'types' or symbolic reflections of Christian truth. Deucalion's flood is a 'type' of Noah's, the fall of Phaethon of the Fall of Man, and king Nisus, who died when his daughter treacherously cut his magical hair (see *Met.*, 8. 1–151), mirrors Samson, similarly betrayed by Delilah (Judges 16).

° **deplore**: lament.

° **wat'ry nation**: i.e. fish.

° **That taught . . . fluent tongue**: As well as the obvious Orphic allusions, Fletcher also evokes incidents in the Gospels: Jesus preaching from a boat to 'a great multitude' on shore (Mark 4: 1), his calming of the storm (Mark 4: 36–41), his walking on water (Mark 6: 45–56), and the miraculous draught of fishes (Luke 5: 1–11).

O16 William Strode, Song: 'When Orpheus Sweetly Did Complain', 1620s?°

William Strode, 1602–45, poet and playwright, born in Devonshire, for most of his life an Anglican minister residing at Christ Church, Oxford; his occasional poems were not collected until 1907.

When Orpheus sweetly did complain
Upon his lute with heavy strain
How his Eurydice was slain,
  The trees to hear
  Obtained an ear,
And after left it off again.

At every stroke and every stay°
The boughs kept time, and nodding lay,
And listened bending all one way;
  The aspen tree
  As well as he
Began to shake and learned to play.

If wood could speak, a tree might hear;
If wood could sound true grief so near,
  A tree might drop an amber tear;
  If wood so well
  Could ring a knell,
The cypress° might condole° the bier.

The standing nobles of the grove,
  Hearing dead wood so speak and move,
The fatal axe began to love;
  They envied death
  That gave such breath,
As men alive do saints above.

° from *The Poetical Works of William Strode*, ed. Bertram Dobell, London, 1907, pp. 1–2.
° **stay**: pause (a musical term).
° **cypress**: a tree associated with funerals, whose wood was used for coffins.
° **condole**: express sympathy for.

O17 George Sandys, from *Ovid's Metamorphoses Englished*, 1632°

George Sandys, 1578–1644, translated the *Metamorphoses* into rhyming couplets while in North America as an official of the Virginia Company; he published the translation in 1626 and added a voluminous commentary in 1632. In his preface he explains that he has 'attempted . . . to collect out of sundry authors the philosophical sense of these fables of Ovid', and adds, 'I have rather followed (as fuller of delight and more useful) the variety of men's several conceptions, where they are not over-strained, than curiously examined their exact propriety.' His commentary on the Orpheus story illustrates his cheerfully eclectic approach, mingling moral and psychological allegories with notes on history, geography and anthropology, and contemporary tall stories.

. . . Such was our Orpheus, the son of Apollo and Calliope (one of the Muses), who with the sweetness of his music and sad lamentations draws tears from the eyes of the remorseless Furies, and a consent from Pluto and Proserpina of his wife's restitution, provided that he looked not back to behold her before they had passed the confines of the Stygian empire. But

True love detests and no delay can brook;
Hasting to see, he lost her with a look.°

'I have heard a story,' saith Sabinus,° 'not unlike unto this, if it be to be reputed a fable which the testimonies of many affirm for a history.° A gentleman in Bavaria, of a noble family, so extremely grieved for the death of his wife that he abandoned all the comforts of life and fed his constant sorrow with solitariness, until at length he regained her; who told him how she had finished the time prescribed by nature, but by his importunate prayers was restored to life, and commanded by God to accompany him longer; upon the condition that their matrimony, dissolved by death, should be again solemnised, and withal° that he should abstain from his former blasphemous execrations,° for which he lost and should lose her again upon the like commission. This said, she followed her household affairs as before, and bore him some children, but was ever pensive and of a pale complexion. Divers years after, the gentleman, heated with wine and choler, rapped

° from George Sandys, *Ovids Metamorphosis Englished, Mythologiz'd, and Represented in Figures*, Oxford, 1632, pp. 354–6.
° **True love . . . with a look**: from Seneca's tragedy *Hercules Furens* (The Madness of Hercules).
° **Sabinus**: Georg Sabinus, a German commentator on the *Metamorphoses* (1553).
° **for a history**: to be a true story.
° **withal**: in addition.
° **execrations**: oaths, swearing.

out horrible oaths and bitterly cursed his servants; when his wife, withdrawing into another room, was nevermore heard of; her apparel, without her body, standing upright, as if an apparition. This,' saith he, 'have I heard from many credible persons, who affirm that the Duke of Bavaria told it for a certain truth to the Duke of Saxony.'

Pausanias° reports how Orpheus, after the death of Eurydice, repaired to Aorrhus in the country of the Thesports, where oracles were given by raising of the dead (not in the power of necromancy to effect, the devil rather assuming these forms to delude his votaries); when, imagining that his wife followed him, but looking back and finding the contrary, forthwith for sorrow [he] slew himself. In emulation of Orpheus the dames of his country accustomed to throw themselves into the funeral fires that burnt their dead husbands (used not only of old, but frequently at this day in divers places of the East Indies), to testify their affections, and out of hope to enjoy in another world their beloved societies. So Dido who laid the foundation, and Hasdrubal's wife who beheld the ruin of Carthage, followed their husbands to the infernal mansions.°

But the fable seems to allude to the former story, differing not much but in the catastrophe;° and invites us to a moderation of our desires, lest we lose what we affect° by too much affecting: hell, the Furies, and infernal torments being no other than the perturbations of his mind for the death of his beloved, pacified and at length composed by the harmony of reason, when, looking back – that is, recalling her to his remembrance – he falls into a desperate relapse, and as it were a second time loseth her.

* * *

Yet music in itself most strangely works upon our human affections.° Not in that the soul, according to the opinion of the Platonists, consisting of harmony, and rapt with the spherical music before it descended from heaven to inhabit the body, affects it with the like desire (there being no nation so barbarous, or man so austere and stupid, which is not by the melody of instruments and numerous composures° either incited to pleasure or animated to virtue); but because the

° **Pausanias**: Greek geographer and travel writer, second century AD.

° **Dido**: the legendary founder of Carthage, who burned herself on a pyre after being abandoned by her lover/husband Aeneas (see Virgil's *Aeneid*, book 4). **Hasdrubal**, Carthaginian commander in the Third Punic War, surrendered to the Romans when the city fell, but his wife and children committed suicide.

° **catastrophe**: (tragic) ending.

° **affect**: love.

° **Yet music in itself**: Sandys here gives two explanations for why we respond to music: first the Platonic view (which he rejects) that our souls respond to an echo of the harmony of the universe; second, a naturalistic physiological explanation (which he endorses).

° **numerous composures**: musical compositions.

spirits° which agitate in the heart receive a warbling and dancing air into the bosom, and are made one with the same wherewith they have an affinity; whose motions lead the rest of the spirits dispersed through the body, raising or suppressing the instrumental parts° according to the measures of the music, sometimes inflaming and again composing the affections – the sense of hearing striking the spirits more immediately than the rest of the senses. So those who become frantic by the mortal biting of a tarantula are only appeased with music, when the musicians light upon such a strain as sympathiseth with their spirits, and by continuing the same are perfectly cured.

Homer makes the gods to pacify their dissension with music, and Achilles with his own to digest° his anger . . . David, who with his harp subdued the evil spirit which vexed Saul, introduced harmony into the temple, as suiting well with that divine service.° Yea, even the glorified spirits are described with harps in their hands, and singing the praises of the Almighty.

But the fable of Orpheus and the walking trees that followed his harp and ditties . . . had an original, as they say, from this story. The Bacchides having much damnified° the country by their furious solemnities,° and the citizens fearing an increase of mischief,° [they] entreated Orpheus to reduce° them by one stratagem or other. He, having ordained a feast to Bacchus, so calmed their rage and allured their affections with his music, that he drew them down from the mountain where they were assembled; who, laying aside their javelins, took branches of trees in their hands, and appeared afar off like a moving wood to such as beheld them; whereupon it was said that he attracted the senseless trees with his harmony. William the Conqueror was so deluded by the Kentishmen, and the usurper Macbeth by the expulsed° Malcolm.

O18 Thomas Carew, from 'An Elegy upon the Death of . . . Dr John Donne', 1633°

Thomas Carew (pronounced 'Carey'), 1594/5–1640, courtier and poet of the 'Cavalier' school. His elegy for John Donne (who died in 1631) was published with Donne's works in 1633. In this passage Carew celebrates Donne's

° **spirits**: in Renaissance medicine, 'subtle airy substances' supposed to exist in the blood and organs of the body, causing emotions and stimulating bodily actions – rather like hormones in modern medicine.

° **instrumental parts**: organs of the body.

° **digest**: break down.

° **David**: see 1 Samuel 16.

° **damnified**: damaged.

° **furious solemnities**: violent rites.

° **mischief**: harm.

° **reduce**: bring under control.

° **expulsed**: exiled.

° from *Poems, by John Donne, with Elegies on the Authors Death*, London, 1633.

abandonment of what he sees as the worn-out conventions of classical imitation and mythological allusion.

The Muses' garden, with pedantic weeds
O'erspread, was purged by thee, the lazy seeds
Of servile imitation thrown away
And fresh invention planted. Thou didst pay
The debts of our penurious bankrupt age:
Licentious thefts that make poetic rage
A mimic fury,° when our souls must be
Possessed or° with Anacreon's ecstasy
Or Pindar's, not their own;° the subtle cheat
Of sly exchanges, and the juggling feat
Of two-edged words, or whatsoever wrong
By ours was done the Greek or Latin tongue,
Thou hast redeemed,° and opened us a mine
Of rich and pregnant fancy, drawn a line
Of masculine expression – which had good
Old Orpheus seen, or all the ancient brood
Our superstitious fools admire and hold
Their lead more precious then thy burnished gold,
Thou hadst been their exchequer,° and no more
They each in other's dust had raked for ore.°

* * * * *

But thou art gone, and thy strict laws will be
Too hard for libertines° in poetry.
They will repeal the goodly° exiled train
Of gods and goddesses, which in thy just reign
Was banished nobler poems; now with these
The silenced tales o'th' *Metamorphoses*
Shall stuff their lines and swell the windy page

° **make . . . mimic fury**: reduce the frenzy of real poetic inspiration to a mere act.
° **or . . . Or**: either . . . or.
° **our souls . . . their own**: we must imitate the inspiration of Anacreon or Pindar (Greek lyric poets) rather than finding our own.
° **redeemed**: paid back.
° **been their exchequer**: i.e. the ancient poets would have borrowed from Donne, instead of vice versa.
° **dust had raked for ore**: in Carew's 1640 *Poems* the line is nastier: 'They each in other's dung had searched for ore.'
° **libertines**: those who reject authority and insist on their own way (the connotations are religious rather than sexual).
° **goodly**: fine (ironic).

Till verse, refined by thee, in this last age,
Turn ballad-rhyme, or those old idols be
Adored again with new apostasy.°

O19 Alexander Ross, from *Mystagogus Poeticus*, 1647°

Alexander Ross, 1591–1654, Scottish-born schoolteacher, minister, and writer, whose prolific writings take a strongly conservative view on political, religious, philosophical, and scientific subjects (among other things he attacked the new Copernican theories in astronomy). Despite its mid-seventeenth-century date his *Mystagogus Poeticus* is thoroughly medieval in its allegorical approach to myth.

14. Christ is the true Orpheus, who by the sweetness and force of his evangelical music caused the gentiles,° who before were stocks and stones in knowledge and no better than beasts in religion, to follow after him. It was he only who went down to hell, to recover the Church, his spouse, who had lost herself by running away from Aristaeus (even goodness itself) and, delighting herself among the grass and flowers of pleasure, was stung by that old serpent the Devil. What was in vain attempted by Orpheus was truly performed by our Saviour, for he alone hath delivered our souls from the nethermost hell; and at last was he torn with whips and thorns and pierced with nails and a spear upon the cross for our transgressions.

O20 John Milton on Orpheus°

John Milton, 1608–74, English poet, whose central work is the epic poem *Paradise Lost* (1667); his other works include the masque *Comus* (1637), the pastoral elegy *Lycidas* (1637), the tragedy *Samson Agonistes* (1671), *Paradise Regained* (1671), and many pamphlets on political and religious questions including *Areopagitica* (1644) on freedom of the press.

The first two passages come from 'L'Allegro' and 'Il Penseroso', a matched pair of poems (perhaps written in 1631, while Milton was at Cambridge), expressing two contrasting temperaments. L'Allegro (Italian for 'the cheerful

° **apostasy**: desertion of true religion.

° from *Mystagogus Poeticus, or The Muses Interpreter: Explaining the Historicall Mysteries, and Mysticall Histories of the Ancient Greek and Latine Poets*, London, 1647; with correction in final sentence of 'above' to 'alone', following later editions.

° **gentiles**: pagans.

° (a, b, c) from *Poems of Mr John Milton*, London, 1645, pp. 36, 41, 59; (d) from *Paradise Lost: A Poem in Twelve Books*, 2nd edition, London, 1674, pp. 173–4.

man') declares his allegiance to Mirth, Il Penseroso ('the thoughtful man') declares his allegiance to Melancholy, and each praises his chosen way of life. The sequence of ideas in each poem is closely parallel; in each, Orpheus appears near the end, in the context of the pleasures of theatre and music.

(a) from 'L'Allegro', c. 1631

Then to the well-trod stage anon,°
If Jonson's learned sock° be on,
Or sweetest Shakespeare, fancy's child,
Warble his native wood-notes wild;°
And ever against eating cares,°
Lap me in soft Lydian airs,°
Married to immortal verse,
Such as the meeting soul may pierce
In notes, with many a winding bout
Of linkèd sweetness long drawn out,
With wanton heed and giddy cunning,
The melting voice through mazes running,
Untwisting all the chains that tie
The hidden soul of harmony;
That Orpheus' self may heave his head
From golden slumber on a bed
Of heaped Elysian flowers, and hear
Such strains as would have won the ear
Of Pluto, to have quite set free
His half-regained Eurydice.
These delights if thou canst give,
Mirth, with thee I mean to live.

° **anon**: presently.
° **sock**: a low-soled slipper worn by ancient comic actors, used as a symbol of comedy, as the **buskin**, a high boot, is used to symbolise tragedy.
° **Jonson's learned sock . . . wood-notes wild**: This contrast between the learned Ben Jonson and the natural and spontaneous Shakespeare, who relied solely on his **fancy** (imagination), was a critical commonplace.
° **against eating cares**: for protection against cares which eat away at the mind.
° **Lydian airs**: Lydian was one of the modes (styles, keys) of ancient music, said by one ancient writer to provide 'relaxation and delight, being invented against excessive cares and worries'.

(b) from 'Il Penseroso', c. 1631

Sometime let gorgeous Tragedy
In sceptred pall° come sweeping by,
Presenting Thebes, or Pelops' line,
Or the tale of Troy divine,°
Or what (though rare) of later age
Ennobled hath the buskined stage.°
But, O sad virgin,° that thy power
Might raise Musaeus° from his bower,
Or bid the soul of Orpheus sing
Such notes as, warbled to the string,
Drew iron tears down Pluto's cheek,
And made hell grant what love did seek.

(c) from **Lycidas**, *1637*

A pastoral elegy for a Cambridge acquaintance of Milton's, Edward King, an Anglican priest and poet, who was drowned on the Irish Sea. For Milton, King/Lycidas becomes a type of the poet and his potential fate in a world hostile to poetry.

Where were ye, nymphs, when the remorseless deep
Closed o'er the head of your loved Lycidas?
For neither were ye playing on the steep,
Where your old bards, the famous Druids, lie,
Nor on the shaggy top of Mona high,
Nor yet where Deva spreads her wizard stream.°
Ay me, I fondly dream!
Had ye been there – for what could that have done?
What could the Muse herself that Orpheus bore,

° **sceptred pall**: robe and sceptre.

° **Thebes . . . Troy divine**: Milton invokes three of the tragic cycles of Greek myth: the stories of Thebes (Oedipus and his family), of Argos (**Pelops' line** included Atreus and Thyestes, Agamemnon and Orestes), and of the Trojan War.

° **Or what . . . buskined stage**: i.e. those few later tragedies which are worthy to stand beside the classical Greek ones; **buskined** see **sock** above.

° **O sad virgin**: addressing Melancholy.

° **Musaeus**: another mythical early Greek poet.

° **For neither . . . wizard stream**: places close to the scene of King's shipwreck: **Mona** is Anglesey, and the **steep** is perhaps that of Bardsey – both mountainous islands off the Welsh coast which were centres of the **Druids**, ancient Celtic bard-priests. **Deva** is the River Dee in north Wales, which flows into the Irish Sea; it is called **wizard** because it was said to magically shift its course as an omen of disaster.

The Muse herself, for her enchanting son,
Whom universal nature did lament,
When by the rout that made the hideous roar
His gory visage down the stream was sent,
Down the swift Hebrus to the Lesbian shore.

(d) from **Paradise Lost,** *1667*

These are the opening lines of Book 7 (1–39), at the mid-point of *Paradise Lost*. As he passes from events in Heaven and Hell to the climactic events in the Garden of Eden, Milton invokes his Muse. He calls her by the name of 'Urania', the classical Muse associated with astronomy, but at the same time stresses that this is merely a convenient name: his Urania is *not* one 'of the Muses nine' but a Christian figure, a companion of God and sister to divine Wisdom, sharply distinguished from the 'empty name' of the classical myth.

Here again Milton uses the Orpheus myth to express his sense of the poet's vulnerability. In the 1660s Milton was both literally in 'darkness' (he became totally blind in 1652), and politically in 'evil days' and 'dangers' as a prominent republican under the newly restored monarchy: he was briefly imprisoned in 1659, and copies of his books were publicly burned.

He also draws on the story of Bellerophon's hubristic attempt to fly to heaven on the winged horse Pegasus, and his crippling fall to earth. Pegasus was a traditional symbol of poetic inspiration (the Muses' fountain of Hippocrene was said to have sprung up where his hoof struck the ground on taking off), and Milton here takes Bellerophon as an image of the fate of the over-ambitious poet.

Descend from heaven, Urania, by that name
If rightly thou art called, whose voice divine
Following, above the Olympian hill I soar,°
Above the flight of Pegasean wing.
The meaning, not the name, I call: for thou
Nor of the Muses nine, nor on the top
Of old Olympus dwell'st,° but heavenly born,
Before the hills appeared or fountain flowed,
Thou with eternal Wisdom didst converse,
Wisdom thy sister, and with her didst play
In presence of the Almighty Father, pleased

° **whose voice . . . I soar**: i.e. 'following whose voice, I soar . . .'; the inverted syntax mirrors the sense.

° **for thou . . . dwell'st**: i.e. 'for thou art not one of the nine Muses, nor dost thou dwell . . .'.

With thy celestial song.° Up led by thee
Into the heaven of heavens I have presumed,
An earthly guest, and drawn empyreal° air,
Thy tempering.° With like safety guided down
Lest from this flying steed unreined (as once
Bellerophon, though from a lower clime)°
Dismounted, on the Aleian field I fall,
Erroneous° there to wander and forlorn.
Half yet remains unsung, but narrower bound
Within the visible diurnal° sphere;
Standing on earth, not rapt above the pole,
More safe I sing with mortal voice, unchanged
To hoarse or mute, though fallen on evil days,
On evil days though fallen, and evil tongues;
In darkness, and with dangers compassed round,
And solitude; yet not alone, while thou
Visit'st my slumbers nightly or when morn
Purples the east. Still govern thou my song,
Urania, and fit audience find, though few.
But drive far off the barbarous dissonance
Of Bacchus and his revellers, the race
Of that wild rout that tore the Thracian bard
In Rhodope, where woods and rocks had ears
To rapture, till the savage clamour drowned
Both harp and voice; nor could the Muse defend
Her son. So fail not thou, who thee implores:°
For thou art heavenly, she an empty dream.

° **Thou with eternal Wisdom . . . celestial song**: see Proverbs 8, where Wisdom speaks of being with God before the creation of the world: 'When there were no depths, I was brought forth; when there were no fountains abounding with water. Before the mountains were settled, before the hills was I brought forth. . . . There I was by him, as one brought up with him: and I was daily his delight, rejoicing always with him' (8: 23–4, 30).
° **empyreal**: of the empyrean, the highest part of heaven.
° **Thy tempering**: i.e. the air of heaven having been tempered by Urania to make it breathable by the poet.
° **clime**: region.
° **Erroneous**: in the literal Latin sense of 'wandering'.
° **diurnal**: daily.
° **So fail . . . implores**: i.e. may you not fail to help the poet who implores you, as Calliope failed Orpheus.

O21 John Dryden, 'On the Death of Mr Purcell', 1696°

John Dryden, 1631–1700, the major writer of the Restoration period, Poet Laureate 1668–88, author of numerous plays (tragic and comic), satirical poems, serious odes and elegies, critical essays, and translations (including the complete works of Virgil). His defence of neoclassical principles and his skilful use of the 'heroic couplet' for both serious and satiric purposes shaped English literature for the following century. This elegy mourns the early death of the composer Henry Purcell, 1659–95, with whom Dryden had collaborated on several operas (including *King Arthur*, *The Fairy Queen*, and *The Tempest*). In such a context the motif of 'outdoing Orpheus' is almost inevitably invoked.

On the Death of Mr Purcell

Set to music by Dr Blow°

1

Mark how the lark and linnet sing;
With rival notes
They strain their warbling throats,
To welcome in the spring.
But in the close° of night,
When Philomel° begins her heavenly lay,
They cease their mutual spite,
Drink in her music with delight,
And, listening and silent, silent and listening, listening and silent obey.

2

So ceased the rival crew when Purcell came;
They sung no more, or only sung his fame.
Struck dumb, they all admired the godlike man:
The godlike man,
Alas! too soon retired,
As he too late began.
We beg not hell our Orpheus to restore;
Had he been there,

° from *The Works of John Dryden*, ed. Sir Walter Scott and George Saintsbury, 18 vols, London, 1882–92, vol. xi, pp. 150–1.

° **Dr Blow**: John Blow, composer and organist, was Purcell's teacher, but outlived him by thirteen years.

° **close**: closing in.

° **Philomel**: i.e. the nightingale (see 'Tales of love' in ch. 3, p. 40).

Their sovereigns' fear
Had sent him back before.
The power of harmony too well they know:
He long ere this had tuned their jarring° sphere,
And left no hell below.

3

The heavenly choir, who heard his notes from high,
Let down the scale of music from the sky;°
They handed him along,
And all the way he taught, and all the way they sung.
Ye brethren of the lyre and tuneful voice,
Lament his lot, but at your own rejoice:
Now live secure, and linger out your days;
The gods are pleased alone with Purcell's lays,
Nor know to mend their choice.°

O22 Alexander Pope, 'Ode for Music, on St Cecilia's Day', 1713°

Alexander Pope, 1688–1744, is most famous for his satirical works (*Moral Essays*, *Imitations of Horace*, *The Rape of the Lock*, *The Dunciad*) and his translations of Homer. This early, rather untypical poem was written to be set to music and performed at the annual festival held by London musicians on St Cecilia's Day (22 November), the feast-day of the patron saint of music (Cecilia was a Roman martyr and legendary inventor of the organ); it was not performed until 1730.

Descend ye Nine!° descend and sing;
The breathing instruments inspire,
Wake into voice each silent string,
And sweep the sounding lyre!
In a sadly-pleasing strain
Let the warbling lute complain;

° **jarring**: discordant.
° **Let down . . . sky**: the scale of musical notes is envisaged as a kind of ladder, up which Purcell can climb into heaven.
° **Nor know to mend their choice**: and know of no better musician to choose.
° from *The Poems of Alexander Pope* (Twickenham Edition), vol. vi, *Minor Poems*, ed. Norman Ault and John Butt, London: Methuen, 1954, pp. 29–34.
° **Nine**: i.e. the Muses.

Let the loud trumpet sound,
Till the roofs all around
The shrill echoes rebound;
While in more lengthened notes and slow,
The deep, majestic, solemn organs blow.
Hark! the numbers,° soft and clear,
Gently steal upon the ear;
Now louder, and yet louder rise,
And fill with spreading sounds the skies;
Exulting in triumph now swell the bold notes,
In broken air, trembling, the wild music floats;
Till, by degrees, remote and small,
The strains decay,
And melt away
In a dying, dying fall.

By music, minds an equal temper know,°
Nor swell too high, nor sink too low.
If in the breast tumultuous joys arise,
Music her soft, assuasive° voice applies;
Or when the soul is pressed with cares
Exalts her in enlivening airs.
Warriors she fires with animated sounds;
Pours balm into the bleeding lover's wounds;
Melancholy lifts her head,
Morpheus° rouses from his bed,
Sloth unfolds her arms and wakes,
Listening Envy drops her snakes;
Intestine° war no more our passions wage,
And giddy factions hear away their rage.

But when our country's cause provokes to arms,
How martial music every bosom warms!
So when the first bold vessel dared the seas,
High on the stern the Thracian raised his strain,
While *Argo* saw her kindred trees
Descend from Pelion to the main.°

° **numbers**: musical phrases.
° **an equal temper know**: maintain mental balance and harmony.
° **assuasive**: soothing.
° **Morpheus**: the god of sleep.
° **Intestine**: internal.
° **main**: sea; the *Argo* was built of timber felled on Mount Pelion.

Transported demigods stood round,
And men grew heroes at the sound,
Inflamed with glory's charms.
Each chief his sevenfold° shield displayed
And half unsheathed the shining blade,
And seas, and rocks, and skies rebound
'To arms, to arms, to arms!'

But when through all th' infernal bounds
Which flaming Phlegethon surrounds,
Love, strong as Death, the poet led
To the pale nations of the dead,
What sounds were heard,
What scenes appeared,
O'er all the dreary coasts!
Dreadful gleams,
Dismal screams,
Fires that glow,
Shrieks of woe,
Sullen moans,
Hollow groans,
And cries of tortured ghosts.
But hark! he strikes the golden lyre;
And see! the tortured ghosts respire,°
See, shady forms advance!
Thy stone, O Sisyphus, stands still,
Ixion rests upon his wheel,
And the pale spectres dance!
The Furies sink upon their iron beds,
And snakes uncurled hang listening round their heads.°

'By the streams that ever flow,
By the fragrant winds that blow
O'er th' Elysian flowers;
By those happy souls who dwell
In yellow meads of asphodel

° **sevenfold**: i.e. made from seven thicknesses of leather (a Homeric phrase).

° **respire**: pause for rest.

° **And snakes uncurled . . . heads**: John Gay has a nice parodic allusion to this line in *Trivia, or the Art of Walking the Streets of London* (1716), when he describes the unfortunate experience of being caught in the rain wearing a curly wig: 'Thy wig, alas! uncurled, admits the shower. / So fierce Alecto's snaky tresses fell, / When Orpheus charmed the rigorous powers of hell . . .' (1. 202–4).

Or amaranthine bowers;°
By the heroes' armèd shades,
Glittering through the gloomy glades,
By the youths that died for love,
Wandering in the myrtle grove,
Restore, restore Eurydice to life.
O, take the husband, or return the wife!'

He sung, and hell consented
To hear the poet's prayer;
Stern Proserpine relented
And gave him back the fair.
Thus song could prevail
O'er death and o'er hell,
A conquest how hard and how glorious!
Though Fate had fast bound her
With Styx nine times round her,
Yet music and love were victorious.

But soon, too soon, the lover turns his eyes:
Again she falls, again she dies, she dies!
How wilt thou now the fatal sisters° move?
No crime was thine, if 'tis no crime to love.
Now under hanging mountains,
Beside the falls of fountains,
Or where Hebrus wanders,
Rolling in meanders,
All alone,
Unheard, unknown,
He makes his moan,
And calls her ghost
For ever, ever, ever lost!
Now with Furies surrounded,
Despairing, confounded,
He trembles, he glows,
Amidst Rhodope's snows.
See, wild as the winds, o'er the desert he flies;
Hark! Haemus resounds with the Bacchanals' cries –
– Ah see, he dies!

° **asphodel** and **amaranth**: flowers said to grow in the Elysian Fields.
° **fatal sisters**: the three Fates.

Yet even in death 'Eurydice' he sung,
'Eurydice' still trembled on his tongue,
'Eurydice' the woods,
'Eurydice' the floods,
'Eurydice' the rocks, and hollow mountains rung.

Music the fiercest grief can charm
And fate's severest rage disarm;
Music can soften pain to ease
And make despair and madness please;
Our joys below it can improve
And antedate the bliss above.°
This the divine Cecilia found,
And to her Maker's praise confined the sound.
When the full organ joins the tuneful choir,
Th'immortal powers incline their ear;
Borne on the swelling notes our souls aspire,
While solemn airs improve the sacred fire,
And angels lean from heaven to hear!
Of Orpheus now no more let poets tell;
To bright Cecilia greater power is given.
His numbers raised a shade from hell,
Hers lift the soul to heaven.

O23 Anne Finch, Countess of Winchilsea, 'To Mr Pope', *c.*1714°

Anne Finch, 1661–1720, poet, maid of honour to James II's queen, became Countess of Winchilsea when her husband inherited the earldom in 1712; her *Miscellany Poems* were published in 1713, but many others were privately circulated among her friends, who included Pope and Swift. This poem is the final shot in a friendly dispute between Finch and Pope, started by a throwaway joke in Pope's *Rape of the Lock*. He there characterised women's poetry as the product of 'Spleen' ('neurosis' might be the modern equivalent):

Parent of vapours and of female wit,
Who gives th' hysteric or poetic fit,
On various tempers act by various ways,
Make some take physic, others scribble plays.
(4. 59–62)

° **antedate the bliss above**: give us a foretaste of the bliss of heaven.

° from the manuscript version, reproduced in *The Poems of Alexander Pope* (Twickenham Edition), vol. vi, *Minor Poems*, ed. Norman Ault and John Butt, London: Methuen, 1954, pp. 121–2.

Finch retaliated with a spirited defence of women poets; Pope responded with an 'Impromptu to Lady Winchilsea' which, without retracting the general point, gracefully declared her an exception; Finch concluded the exchange as follows.

To Mr Pope

(In answer to a copy of verses, occasioned by a little dispute upon four lines in 'The Rape of the Lock')

Disarmed with so genteel an air,
The contest I give o'er;
Yet Alexander, have a care
And shock the sex° no more.

We rule the world, our lives' whole race;
Men but assume that right,
First slaves to every tempting face,
Then martyrs to our spite.

You of one Orpheus sure have read,
Who would like you have writ,
Had he in London town been bred
And polished too his wit;°

But he, poor soul, thought all was well
And great should be his fame,
When he had left his wife in hell,
And birds and beasts could tame.

Yet, venturing then with scoffing rhymes
The women to incense,
Resenting heroines of those times
Soon punished the offence.

And as through Hebrus rolled his skull
And harp besmeared with blood,
They, clashing as the waves grew full,
Still harmonised the flood.

But you our follies gently treat
And spin so fine the thread,

° **the sex**: i.e. women (a common eighteenth-century phrase).

° **wit**: In the eighteenth century the word has not only the modern sense (sophisticated verbal humour), but also a much wider sense: intelligence, cleverness, mental ability. Compare the contrast of wit and wisdom in 35–6.

You need not fear his awkward fate:
The *Lock* won't cost the head.

Our admiration you command
For all that's gone before;
What next we look for at your hand°
Can only raise it more.

Yet soothe the ladies, I advise,
As me to pride you've wrought;
We're born to wit, but to be wise
By admonitions taught.

O24 R.M., 'A Song', 1724°

A typically antifeminist comic version of the Orpheus story, included in a 1724 collection of *Miscellaneous Poems*; I have not identified the author, 'R.M.'

A Song

Fond Orpheus went, as poets tell,
To bring Eurydice from Hell;
There he might hope to find a wife,
The pest and bane of human life.

The damned from all their pains were eased –
Not that his music so much pleased,
But that the oddness of the matter
Had justly made the wonder greater.

Pluto, enraged that any he°
Should enter his dominion free,
And to inflict the sharpest pain,
Made him a husband once again.

But yet, in justice to his voice,
He left it still within his choice
If as a curse he'd not refuse her,
And taught him by a look to lose her.

° **What next . . . hand**: i.e. your next publication.

° from *Miscellaneous Poems, Original and Translated, by Several Hands*, ed. Matthew Concanen, London, 1724, pp. 109–10.

° **any he**: any man.

O25 John Gay, from *Fables*: 'The Monkey Who Had Seen the World', 1727°

John Gay, 1685–1732, comic poet and playwright, friend of Pope and Swift, most famous for his *Beggar's Opera*, a comic blend of low life and grand opera. This satirical beast fable takes a disillusioned view of eighteenth-century civilisation and education, and incidentally mocks the cliché of Orpheus the civiliser.

The Monkey Who Had Seen the World

A monkey, to reform the times,
Resolved to visit foreign climes;°
For men in distant regions roam
To bring politer manners home.
So forth he fares, all toil defies;
Misfortune serves to make us wise.

At length the treacherous snare was laid,
Poor Pug was caught, to town conveyed,
There sold – how envied was his doom,
Made captive in a lady's room!°
Proud as a lover of his chains,
He day by day her favour gains.
Whene'er the duty of the day,
The toilette calls; with mimic play
He twirls her knots, he cracks her fan,
Like any other gentleman.
In visits too his parts° and wit,
When jests grew dull, were sure to hit.
Proud with applause, he thought his mind
In every courtly art refined,
Like Orpheus burnt with public zeal,
To civilise the monkey weal;°
So watched occasion, broke his chain,
And sought his native woods again.

The hairy sylvans° round him press,

° from *Fables*, London, 1727, First Series, pp. 46–9.
° **climes**: regions.
° **captive in a lady's room**: monkeys were popular ladies' pets in the eighteenth century.
° **parts**: talents.
° **weal**: community.
° **sylvans**: inhabitants of the forest.

Astonished at his strut and dress;
Some praise his sleeve, and others gloat
Upon his rich embroidered coat,
His dapper periwig commending
With the black tail behind depending,°
His powdered back, above, below,
Like hoary frosts or fleecy snow;
But all, with envy and desire,
His fluttering shoulder-knot admire.
'Hear and improve,' he pertly cries,
'I come to make a nation wise.
Weigh your own worth; support your place,
The next in rank to human race.
In cities long I passed my days,
Conversed with men, and learnt their ways:
Their dress, their courtly manners see;
Reform your state, and copy me.
Seek ye to thrive? In flattery deal;
Your scorn, your hate, with that conceal;
Seem only to regard° your friends,
But use them for your private ends;
Stint not to truth the flow of wit,
Be prompt to lie, whene'er 'tis fit;
Bend all your force to spatter° merit;
Scandal is conversation's spirit;°
Boldly to everything pretend,
And men your talents shall commend;
I knew the Great. Observe me right,
So shall you grow like man polite.'°

He spoke and bowed. With muttering jaws
The wondring circle grinned applause.

Now, warm with malice, envy, spite,
Their most obliging friends they bite,
And, fond to copy human ways,
Practise new mischiefs all their days.

° **depending**: hanging.
° **regard**: be concerned for.
° **spatter**: sling mud at.
° **Scandal is conversation's spirit**: it's malicious gossip that gives conversation its liveliness.
° **polite**: i.e. polished, sophisticated, civilised (an eighteenth-century keyword, here sharply ironic).

Thus the dull lad, too tall for school,
With travel finishes the fool.°
Studious of every coxcomb's airs,
He drinks, games, dresses, whores and swears,
O'erlooks with scorn all virtuous arts,
For vice is fitted to his parts.

O26 Lady Mary Wortley Montagu, 'Impromptu, to a Young Lady Singing', 1736?°

Lady Mary Wortley Montagu, née Pierrepont, 1689–1762, writer of light verse and of witty and learned letters (especially the *Turkish Letters*, written while her husband was British ambassador in Constantinople 1716–18), a central figure in London literary society in the 1720s and 1730s, and a close friend and later bitter enemy of Pope, of whom she wrote,

> Sure P[ope] like Orpheus was alike inspired,
> The blocks and beasts flocked round them and admired.°

This short poem – probably addressed to her daughter, and alluding (according to her editors) to an unhappy love affair – uses the conventional 'young lady singing' motif with a little more bite than usual.

Impromptu, to a Young Lady Singing

Sing, gentle maid – reform my breast,
And soften all my care;
Thus may I be some moments blest,
And easy in despair.
The power of Orpheus lives in you;
You can the passions of my soul subdue,
And tame the lions and the tigers there.

° **finishes the fool**: rounds off his education in folly, completes the process of turning into a fool (alluding to the 'Grand Tour' as the final stage of an upper-class youth's education).

° from *Letters and Works of Lady Mary Wortley Montagu*, 3rd edn, 2 vols, London, 1861.

° from Lady Mary Wortley Montagu, *Essays and Poems and Simplicity, a Comedy*, ed. Robert Halsband and Isobel Grundy, Oxford: Clarendon Press, 1977, p. 257. Reprinted by permission of Oxford University Press.

O27 Henry Fielding, from *Eurydice*, 1737°

Henry Fielding, 1707–54, is best known for his novels such as *Joseph Andrews* (1742) and *Tom Jones* (1749), but before turning to the novel he was also a prolific dramatist. *Eurydice: a Farce*, produced (unsuccessfully) at Drury Lane Theatre in 1737, simultaneously travesties the Orpheus legend and sends up the current vogue for Italian opera starring *castrati*, castrated male sopranoes. Fielding's hell is a replica of London high society, and his Eurydice, 'a fine lady', is not anxious to leave, as she explains to the ghostly beaus, Captain Weasel and Mr Spindle.

CAPTAIN WEASEL: But I hope the news is not true that we are to lose you, Madam Eurydice.

EURYDICE: How can you doubt it, when my husband is come after me? Do you think Pluto can refuse me, or that I can refuse to go back with a husband who came hither for me?

MR SPINDLE: Faith! I don't know; but if a husband was to go back to the other world after his wife, I believe he would scarce persuade her to come hither with him.

EURYDICE: Oh but, sir, this place alters us for the better. Women are quite different creatures after they have been here some time.

CAPTAIN WEASEL: And so you will go?

EURYDICE: It is not in my power. You know it is positively against the law of the realm. In desiring to go, I discharge the duty of a wife; and if the Devil won't let me go, I can't help it.

CAPTAIN WEASEL: I am afraid of the power of his voice. I wish he be able to resist that charm; and I fancy, if you was to confess ingenuously, it is his voice that charms you to go back again.

EURYDICE: Indeed, sir, you are mistaken. I do not think the merit of a man, like that of a nightingale, lies in his throat. It is true, he has a fine pipe,° and if you will carry your friend to court this morning he may hear him; but though it is possible my heart may have its weak sides, I solemnly protest no one will ever reach it through my ears.

MR SPINDLE: That's strange, for it is the only way to all the ladies' hearts in the other world.

EURYDICE: Ha, ha, ha! I find you beaus know just as much of a woman as you

° from *Miscellanies*, vol. ii, ed. B. A. Goldgar and H. Amory, Oxford: Clarendon Press, 1993, pp. 135–6, 146–8. Reprinted by permission of Oxford University Press, with spelling and punctuation modernised.

° **he has a fine pipe**: Fielding's Orpheus, like the heroes of contemporary Italian opera, is represented as a *castrato* – giving extra point to Eurydice's view that a wife looks for more in a husband than a fine soprano voice.

ever did. Do you imagine when a lady expires at an opera she thinks of the signior that's singing? No, no, take my word for it, music puts softer and better things in her head.

Air I

When a woman lies expiring
  At *fal, lal, lal, la,*
Do you think her, sir, deserving
  Nothing more than *ha, ha, ha*?

Despite the combined efforts of Eurydice and Proserpine, Pluto's passion for Italian opera makes him grant Orpheus's request; but Proserpine adds a condition which gives Eurydice an escape route. The couple are waiting by the banks of the Styx . . .

CHARON: Master, the boat is just gone over, it will be back again instantly. I wish you would be so good in the meantime, master, to give us one of your Italian catches.

ORPHEUS: What, dost thou love music then, friend Charon?

CHARON: Yes, fags,° master, I do. It went to my heart t'other day that I did not dare ferry over Signior Quaverino.

ORPHEUS: Why didst thou not dare?

CHARON: I don't know, sir: Judge Rhadamanthus said it was against the law, for that nobody was to come into this country but men and women, and that the signior was neither the one nor the other.

ORPHEUS: Your lawyers, I suppose, have strange quirks here in hell.

CHARON: Nay, for that matter, they are pretty much the same here as on earth.

EURYDICE: Help, help, I shall be drowned, I shall be drowned!

ORPHEUS [*turning*]: Ha! Eurydice's voice!

EURYDICE: O unlucky misfortune! Why would you look behind you, when you knew the Queen's command?

ORPHEUS: Thou wicked woman, why wouldst thou tempt me?

EURYDICE: How unreasonable is that, to lay the blame on me! Can I help my fears? You know I was always inclined to be hysterical. But it is like you to lay the blame on me, when you know yourself to be guilty; when you know you are tired of me already, and looked back purposely to lose me.

ORPHEUS: And dost thou accuse me?

EURYDICE: I don't accuse you. I need not accuse you. Your own wicked conscience must do it. Oh, had you loved me, you could have borne to have gone

° **fags**: presumably an uneducated form of 'faith'.

a million of miles. I am sure I could have gone further, and never once have looked back upon you. [*pretending to cry*]

ORPHEUS: Cursed accident! But still we may go on. Proserpine can never know it.

EURYDICE [*speaking brisk*]: No, I promised to return the moment you looked back; and a woman of honour must keep her promise, though it be to leave her husband.

After a farewell duet, Eurydice departs, and Orpheus expresses his final resolution.

ORPHEUS [*recitativo*]:
Ungrateful, barbarous woman!
Infernal Stygian monster!
Henceforth mankind
I'll teach to hate the sex.

Air IX

If a husband henceforth who has buried his wife
Of Pluto request her again brought to life,
Pluto, grant his request as he enters thy portal,
And Jove for his comfort,
And Jove for his comfort,
O make her, O make her, O make her immortal!

O28 William Collins(?), from 'On the Use and Abuse of Poetry', *c.*1750°

This fragment of an ode was attributed to William Collins, 1721–59, though the attribution is doubtful. Whatever its authorship, it develops the Horatian image of Orpheus as civiliser and founder of the social virtues.

Such was wise Orpheus' moral song,
The lonely cliffs and caves among;
From hollow oak, or mountain den,
He drew the naked, gazing men,
Or where in turf-built sheds, or rushy bowers,
They shivered in cold wintry showers,
Or sunk in heapy snows;
Then sudden, while his melting music stole

° from *Gray, Collins, and Goldsmith: The Complete Poems*, ed. Roger Lonsdale, London: Longman, 1969.

With powerful magic o'er each softening soul,
Society, and law, and sacred order rose.

Father of peace and arts! he first the city built;
No more the neighbour's blood was by his neighbour spilt;
He taught to till, and separate the lands;
He fixed the roving youths in Hymen's myrtle bands;°
Whence dear domestic life began,
And all the charities that softened man:
The babes that in their fathers' faces smiled,
With lisping blandishments their rage beguiled,
And tender thoughts inspired!

O29 Anna Seward, from 'Elegy on Captain Cook', 1780°

Anna Seward, 1747–1809, poet, known as 'the Swan of Lichfield', the Staffordshire town where she was the centre of a literary circle. In this passage from her funeral elegy for James Cook, the great English explorer of the South Pacific who was killed on a visit to Hawaii in 1779, Seward applies the image of Orpheus the civiliser to eighteenth-century colonialism: Cook, like Orpheus, is seen as a benevolent teacher of 'arts and virtues', murdered by the ungrateful barbarians he had tried to help.

Now leads Benevolence the destined way,
Where all the Loves in Otaheite° stray.
To bid the Arts disclose their wond'rous powers,
To bid the Virtues consecrate the bowers,
She gives her Hero to its blooming plain –
Nor has he wandered, has he bled in vain!
His lips persuasive charm th'uncultured youth,
Teach wisdom's lore, and point the path of truth.
See! chastened love in softer glances flows –
See! with new fires parental duty glows.°
Thou smiling Eden of the southern wave,

° **Hymen's myrtle bands**: i.e. marriage (Hymen was god of marriage, myrtle was sacred to Venus and a symbol of love).

° from *Elegy on Captain Cook,* 4th edn with additions, Lichfield, 1784.

° **Otaheite**: Tahiti.

° **parental duty glows**: 'Captain Cook observes, in his second voyage, that the women of Otaheite were grown more modest, and that the barbarous practice of destroying their children was lessened' (Seward's note).

Could not, alas! thy grateful wishes save
That angel-goodness which had blessed thy plain? –
Ah! vain thy gratitude, thy wishes vain!
On a far distant and remorseless shore
Where human fiends their dire libations° pour,
Where treachery, hovering o'er the blasted heath,
Poises with ghastly smile the darts of death,
Pierced by their venomed points, your favourite bleeds,
And on his limbs the lust of hunger feeds!
Thus when of old the muse-born Orpheus bore
Fair arts and virtues to the Thracian shore,
Struck with sweet energy the warbling wire
And poured persuasion from th'immortal lyre,
As softened brutes the waving woods among
Bowed their meek heads and listened to the song,
Near and more near, with rage and tumult loud,
Round the bold bard th'inebriate maniacs crowd –
Red on the ungrateful soil his life-blood swims,
And fiends and furies tear his quivering limbs!

O30 William Wordsworth, from *The Prelude*, 1805°

William Wordsworth, 1770–1850, English Romantic poet. His greatest work, *The Prelude, or Growth of a Poet's Mind*, an autobiographical poem addressed to his friend Samuel Taylor Coleridge, was first written in 1805, but successively revised throughout the poet's life before its posthumous publication in 1850; many critics prefer the original version, given here (though the key lines of this passage remain unchanged in the final version). Wordsworth is here brooding on his inability to fix on a poetic subject, as he contemplates various possibilities: a chivalric romance, a classical epic, a patriotic tale of resistance to tyranny . . .

Sometimes it suits me better to shape out
Some tale from my own heart, more near akin
To my own passions and habitual thoughts;
Some variegated story, in the main
Lofty, with interchange of gentler things.
But deadening admonitions will succeed

° **libations**: offerings of wine (or, here, blood) poured on the ground as part of a religious ceremony.
° from *The Prelude: A Parallel Text*, ed. J. C. Maxwell, Harmondsworth: Penguin, 1971, 1805–6 text, 1. 220–44.

And the whole beauteous fabric seems to lack
Foundation, and, withal, appears throughout
Shadowy and unsubstantial. Then, last wish,
My last and favourite aspiration, then
I yearn towards some philosophic song
Of Truth that cherishes° our daily life;
With meditations passionate from deep
Recesses in man's heart, immortal verse
Thoughtfully fitted to the Orphean lyre;
But from this awful burden I full soon
Take refuge and beguile° myself with trust
That mellower years will bring a riper mind
And clearer insight. Thus from day to day
I live, a mockery of the brotherhood
Of vice and virtue,° with no skill to part
Vague longing that is bred by want of power
From paramount impulse not to be withstood,
A timorous capacity from prudence,
From circumspection, infinite delay.

O31 Lord Byron, from 'Hints from Horace', 1811°

George Gordon, 6th Baron Byron, 1788–1824, is normally classified as a Romantic, but he placed himself more in the tradition of Dryden and Pope, and his satirical mock-epic *Don Juan* (1819–24) has lasted better than the earlier poems in which he created the Romantic image of the 'Byronic hero'. *Hints from Horace* (written 1811, not published until twenty years later) is an 'imitation' – a humorous reworking and updating – of Horace's *Art of Poetry*; this is Byron's version of Horace's lines on Orpheus (compare **O3**).

Orpheus, we learn from Ovid and Lemprière,°
Led all wild beasts but women by the ear;
And had he fiddled at the present hour,
We'd seen the lions waltzing in the Tower;°

° **cherishes**: cheers, encourages.

° **beguile**: deceive.

° **a mockery . . . virtue**: i.e. a mocking illustration of the way that vice and virtue are related as closely as brothers: the virtues of prudence and caution can be hard to distinguish from the vices of timidity and procrastination.

° from *The Works of Lord Byron*, London, 1831, vol. v, pp. 273–327.

° **Lemprière**: John Lemprière's *Classical Dictionary* (1788).

° **lions waltzing in the Tower**: lions were kept in the Tower of London until 1834.

And old Amphion, such were minstrels then,
Had built St. Paul's without the aid of Wren.°
Verse too was justice, and the bards of Greece
Did more than constables to keep the peace;
Abolished cuckoldom with much applause,
Called county meetings, and enforced the laws . . .

O32 Thomas Love Peacock, from 'The Four Ages of Poetry', 1820°

Thomas Love Peacock, 1785–1866, novelist, essayist, and poet, best known for his high-spirited satirical novels such as *Nightmare Abbey* (1818) and *Crotchet Castle* (1831). In 'The Four Ages of Poetry' he argues, half tongue-in-cheek, that poetry is a primitive literary form outdated by modern civilisation; it provoked his friend Shelley's wholly serious *Defence of Poetry* (written 1821). Here, describing the first (pre-literate) age of poetry in which 'all rude and uncivilized people express themselves in the manner which we call poetical', Peacock takes a side-swipe at the Horatian Orpheus.

Poets are as yet the only historians and chroniclers of their time, and the sole depositories of all the knowledge of their age; and though this knowledge is rather a crude congeries° of traditional fantasies than a collection of useful truths, yet, such as it is, they have it to themselves. . . . A skilful display of the little knowledge they have gains them credit for the possession of much more which they have not. Their familiarity with the secret history of gods and genii° obtains for them, without much difficulty, the reputation of inspiration; thus they are not only historians, but theologians, moralists, and legislators: delivering their oracles *ex cathedrâ*,° and being indeed often themselves (as Orpheus and Amphion) regarded as portions and emanations of divinity: building cities with a song, and leading brutes with a symphony; which are only metaphors for the faculty of leading multitudes by the nose.

° **Wren**: Sir Christopher Wren, architect of St Paul's Cathedral.
° from *The Works of Thomas Love Peacock*, ed. Henry Cole, vol. iii, London, 1875, p. 326.
° **congeries**: random collection.
° **genii**: guardian spirits.
° ***ex cathedrâ***: literally 'from the throne', a term applied to the pope's official pronouncements on matters of faith, which, according to Catholic doctrine, are divinely inspired and hence infallible.

O33 Percy Bysshe Shelley, 'Orpheus', *c.*1820°

Percy Bysshe Shelley, 1792–1822, is perhaps the epitome of the Romantic poet, controversial in his lifetime and since for his radical enthusiasm for political, religious, sexual, and artistic freedom, and for the hyperbolical intensity of his poetry. His love of Greek literature and myth is discussed in chapter 1. 'Orpheus' is presented as a fragment from a Greek tragedy (though there is no evidence that Shelley wrote or planned to write any more of it): a messenger, 'A', is describing to the Chorus how the bereaved Orpheus sings in the wilderness.

Orpheus

A: Not far from hence. From yonder pointed hill,
Crowned with a ring of oaks, you may behold
A dark and barren field, through which there flows,
Sluggish and black, a deep but narrow stream,
Which the wind ripples not, and the fair moon
Gazes in vain, and finds no mirror there.
Follow the herbless° banks of that strange brook
Until you pause beside a darksome pond,
The fountain of this rivulet, whose gush
Cannot be seen, hid by a rayless night
That lives beneath the overhanging rock
That shades the pool – an endless spring of gloom,
Upon whose edge hovers the tender light,
Trembling to mingle with its paramour° –
But, as Syrinx fled Pan,° so night flies day,
Or, with most sullen and regardless° hate,
Refuses stern her heaven-born embrace.
On one side of this jagged and shapeless hill
There is a cave, from which there eddies up
A pale mist, like aërial gossamer,
Whose breath destroys all life – awhile it veils
The rock – then, scattered by the wind, it flies
Along the stream, or lingers on the clefts,
Killing the sleepy worms, if aught bide there.
Upon the beetling° edge of that dark rock

° from *The Works of Percy Bysshe Shelley*, ed. H. B. Forman, London, 1880, vol. iv, pp. 54–6.
° **herbless**: bare of vegetation.
° **paramour**: lover (Shelley implies that light and darkness are, or should be, lovers and partners).
° **as Syrinx fled Pan**: see 'Tales of love' in ch. 3, p. 40.
° **regardless**: contemptuously indifferent.
° **beetling**: overhanging.

There stands a group of cypresses; not such
As, with a graceful spire and stirring life,
Pierce the pure heaven of your native vale,
Whose branches the air plays among, but not
Disturbs, fearing to spoil their solemn grace;
But blasted and all wearily they stand,
One to another clinging; their weak boughs
Sigh as the wind buffets them, and they shake
Beneath its blasts – a weather-beaten crew!

CHORUS: What wondrous sound is that, mournful and faint,
But more melodious than the murmuring wind
Which through the columns of a temple glides?

A: It is the wandering voice of Orpheus' lyre,
Borne by the winds, who sigh that their rude king
Hurries them fast from these air-feeding notes;
But in their speed they bear along with them
The waning sound, scattering it like dew
Upon the startled sense.

CHORUS: Does he still sing?
Methought° he rashly cast away his harp
When he had lost Eurydice.

A: Ah, no!
Awhile he paused. – As a poor hunted stag
A moment shudders on the fearful brink
Of a swift stream – the cruel hounds press on
With deafening yell, the arrows glance and wound –
He plunges in: so Orpheus, seized and torn
By the sharp fangs of an insatiate grief,
Maenad-like waved his lyre in the bright air,
And wildly shrieked 'Where she is, it is dark!'
And then he struck from forth the strings a sound
Of deep and fearful melody. Alas!
In times long past, when fair Eurydice
With her bright eyes sat listening by his side,
He gently sang of high and heavenly themes.
As in a brook, fretted with little waves
By the light airs of spring – each ripplet° makes
A many-sided mirror for the sun,
While it flows musically through green banks,

° **Methought**: it seemed to me.
° **ripplet**: little ripple.

Ceaseless and pauseless, ever clear and fresh,
So flowed his song, reflecting the deep joy
And tender love that fed those sweetest notes,
The heavenly offspring of ambrosial food.°
But that is past. Returning from drear Hell,
He chose a lonely seat of unhewn stone,
Blackened with lichens, on a herbless plain.
Then from the deep and overflowing spring
Of his eternal ever-moving grief
There rose to Heaven a sound of angry song.
'Tis as a mighty cataract that parts
Two sister rocks with waters swift and strong,
And casts itself with horrid roar and din
Adown a steep;° from a perennial source
It ever flows and falls, and breaks the air
With loud and fierce, but most harmonious roar,
And as it falls casts up a vaporous spray
Which the sun clothes in hues of Iris° light.
Thus the tempestuous torrent of his grief
Is clothed in sweetest sounds and varying words
Of poesy. Unlike all human works,
It never slackens, and through every change
Wisdom and beauty and the power divine
Of mighty poesy together dwell,
Mingling in sweet accord. As I have seen
A fierce south blast tear through the darkened sky,
Driving along a rack° of wingèd clouds,
Which may not pause, but ever hurry on,
As their wild shepherd wills them, while the stars,
Twinkling and dim, peep from between the plumes.
Anon° the sky is cleared, and the high dome
Of serene Heaven, starred with fiery flowers,
Shuts in the shaken earth; or the still moon
Swiftly, yet gracefully, begins her walk,
Rising all bright behind the eastern hills.

° **ambrosial food**: (according to Homer, the gods eat ambrosia – an unidentified but supernaturally delicious food).
° **steep**: cliff.
° **Iris**: rainbow (Iris is the goddess of the rainbow).
° **rack**: formation of scattered clouds.
° **Anon**: soon afterwards.

I talk of moon, and wind, and stars, and not
Of song; but, would I echo his high song,
Nature must lend me words ne'er used before,
Or I must borrow from her perfect works,
To picture forth his perfect attributes.
He does no longer sit upon his throne
Of rock upon a desert herbless plain,
For the evergreen and knotted ilexes,
And cypresses that seldom wave their boughs,
And sea-green olives with their grateful° fruit,
And elms dragging along the twisted vines,
Which drop their berries as they follow fast,
And blackthorn bushes with their infant race
Of blushing rose-blooms; beeches, to lovers dear,
And weeping willow trees; all swift or slow,
As their huge boughs or lighter dress permit,
Have circled in his throne, and Earth herself
Has sent from her maternal breast a growth
Of starlike flowers and herbs of odour sweet,
To pave the temple that his poesy
Has framed, while near his feet grim lions couch,
And kids, fearless from love, creep near his lair.
Even the blind worms seem to feel the sound.
The birds are silent, hanging down their heads,
Perched on the lowest branches of the trees;
Not even the nightingale intrudes a note
In rivalry, but all entranced she listens.

O34 Robert B. Brough, from *Orpheus and Eurydice: or, The Wandering Minstrel*, 1852°

Robert Barnabas Brough, 1828–60, journalist and comic playwright. He specialised in burlesque plays, full of anachronistic jokes, excruciating puns, and garbled literary allusions; he declares that, whatever questions may be raised about his 'classic erudition', his jokes demonstrate 'an intimate acquaintance with the ancients – even to the remotest period of antiquity'. In this passage from *Orpheus and Eurdice*, Pluto becomes a Victorian paterfamilias, cosily toasting muffins by the fireside, when he is interrupted by Orpheus in the guise of an Italian barrel-organ-grinder.

° **grateful**: pleasant, welcome.

° from *A Cracker Bon-Bon for Christmas Parties: consisting of Christmas Pieces for Private Representation*, London, 1852, pp. 40–59.

A street organ is heard outside, playing 'Jeannette and Jeannot'. Pluto starts, with an agonized expression of countenance. Cerberus growls.

PLUTO: What's that? Good heavens!

The tune is continued with increased violence.

Help! Be quiet! Mercy!
[*Holding his ears*] He doesn't seem inclined to – Vice versy.
Oh dear! [*Runs to window*] Be off!

ORPHEUS: [*outside*] I shan't.

PLUTO: Leave off!

ORPHEUS: I won't.

The tune increases in loudness; the agony of Pluto in intensity.

PLUTO: What's to be done? it's getting louder. [*With a yell of anguish*] Don't!
Our peace of mind for ever 'twill destroy.
Hie Cerberus! Good doggy! At him, boy.

He opens the door, urging Cerberus to the attack in the usual manner. Orpheus enters, partly dressed as an Italian boy, playing an organ.° Cerberus rushes at him growling, but is met boldly by Orpheus, who plays the organ full in his face. Unable to stand the infliction, Cerberus runs away, yelping.

PLUTO: I say, move on – or I shall make you.

ORPHEUS: Shall you?
Of peace and quietness I know the value.

PLUTO: [*offering him a sixpence*]
Take this and go about your bus'ness.

ORPHEUS: Stuff!

PLUTO: Well, here's another –

ORPHEUS: Pshaw! not half enough.

PLUTO: I offered you a shilling.

ORPHEUS: Yes – you *did* I see;
But I, Sir, don't move on – under Eurydice.

PLUTO: Who art thou, slave, whose noise our aching sconce hurts?

ORPHEUS: Professor Orpheus – from the Ancient Concerts.

Song

[ORPHEUS, *accompanying himself on the organ*]
Air – Marble Halls
The minstrel boy, to Old Scratch,° has gone

° **playing an organ**: barrel-organs, usually played by Italian immigrants, were popular on the streets of London at this period – and unpopular; in 1864 a group of writers, including Charles Dickens, petitioned Parliament to control the nuisance.

° **Old Scratch**: the Devil.

For his wife in hopes to find her,
The monster organ he has girded on,
Of a wild Italian grinder.
Sound of woe! said the wand'ring bard,
As all the world so fears thee,
E'en Pluto's self – clean off his guard
Will be thrown, when e'er he hears thee.

He follows Pluto round the stage, playing and singing to the symphony; Pluto holding his ears.

PLUTO: I say, let's come to terms.
ORPHEUS My wife!
PLUTO: I can't –
You ask too much; but pray desist –
ORPHEUS: I shan't.

The minstrel swell – and in language plain,
Declares, if kept asunder
From the spouse he loves, he won't refrain;
For he cannot move on under
The terms just named, which you must allow –
To sink all lies and knavery –
Are cheap as dirt – to suppress this row,
To submit to which is slavery.

Give me my wife, or else your life you'll find
Like Mantalini's – 'One demnition grind.'°
PLUTO: Never!
ORPHEUS: Then I resume my dulcet strain,
For I can turn – and turn – and turn again.° [*Turning the handle*]
I'll play a waltz –
PLUTO: Oh, heavens! mind your stops;
I hate all dances, though the son of Ops.°
Orpheus plays
Monstrum horrendum – cease thy painful twingings –

° **'One demnition grind'**: in Dickens's *Nicholas Nickleby* (1838–9), ch. 64, the dandyish tailor Mantalini, reduced to turning the clothes-mangle in a laundry, complains, 'I am perpetually turning, like a demd old horse in a demnition mill. My life is one demd horrid grind!'
° **turn . . . and turn again**: parodying *Othello*, 4. 1. 255–6.
° **son of Ops**: punning on (a) Pluto's mother Ops, (b) 'Op.' as an abbreviation for *opus*, a musical work.

Direst machine of all *informe ingens!*°
Behold me kneeling by your side – who wouldn't
Kneel e'en by Jupiter's. By Jove! I couldn't.
See, I turn suppliant – I – Ammon's brother!°
ORPHEUS: For that good turn – I'll treat you with another. [*Grinds*]
PLUTO: Hold! I give in – 'tis useless to rebel.
ORPHEUS: It must be so. Pluto, thou reason'st well.°
PLUTO: I'll give you up your wife – mine, too – if wanted,
Rather than be by such a nuisance haunted.
Though of concession it's a fearful stretcher –
ORPHEUS: Look sharp, or else – [*Threatens to play*]
PLUTO 'That strain again!'° I'll fetch her.
Exit precipitately
ORPHEUS: Come! for subduing wrong, oppression, crimes,
I wield an organ° – pow'rful as the Times.
'Music hath charms to soothe the savage breast,
And soften' – everybody knows the rest.°
I question if the rudest Goth or Vandal
Could well resist my overtures by Handle.

Orpheus departs with Eurydice, and the play concludes with a triumphant twist on the last lines of *Romeo and Juliet*:

. . . never was a story of more glee
Than this of Orpheus and Eurydice.

O35 Robert Browning, 'Eurydice to Orpheus', 1864°

Robert Browning, 1812–89, English poet, most famous for his 'dramatic monologues' such as 'My Last Duchess' and 'The Bishop Orders His Tomb'. This poem, a very short dramatic monologue by Eurydice, appeared in the catalogue of the Royal Academy exhibition of 1864, accompanying a painting by Frederick

° ***Monstrum horrendum . . . informe ingens***: Virgil's description of the Cyclops (*Aeneid*, 3. 658): 'a terrifying monster . . . shapeless and vast'; I suspect a pun on '*ingens*'/'engines'.
° **Ammon's brother**: Ammon was an Egyptian god often identified with Jupiter.
° **It must . . . reason'st well**: parodying a once-famous line in Joseph Addison's tragedy *Cato* (1713): Cato, reading Plato's argument for the immortality of the soul, declares, 'It must be so; Plato, thou reason'st well' (5. 1. 1).
° **'That strain again!'**: from *Twelfth Night*, 1. 1. 4.
° **organ**: punning on the sense of 'newspaper'.
° **'Music hath charms . . .'**: from William Congreve's *The Mourning Bride* (1697), 1. 1; the second line is 'And soften rocks, or bend a knotted oak'.
° from *Poems of Robert Browning*, New York, 1896, p. 599.

Leighton; the painting shows Eurydice clinging beseechingly to Orpheus, who closes his eyes and turns away his face in agony.

Eurydice to Orpheus

A picture by Frederick Leighton, R.A.

But give them me, the mouth, the eyes, the brow!
Let them once more absorb me! One look now
Will lap me round for ever, not to pass
Out of its light, though darkness lie beyond:
Hold me but safe again within the bond
Of one immortal look! All woe that was,
Forgotten, and all terror that may be,
Defied – no past is mine, no future: look at me!

O36 Richard Watson Dixon, 'Orpheus', 1864°

Richard Watson Dixon, 1833–1900, poet and Anglican minister, was an associate of the Pre-Raphaelite movement, and later a friend and supporter of Gerard Manley Hopkins. His 'Orpheus', which bears some comparison with Shelley's, presents one of the most exalted visions of the potential power of Orpheus's music.

Orpheus

The osprey of the shore resigned her reign
Before the raven of the stricken plain,
And she before the vulture of the hills:
So far had Orpheus travelled: now the rills
More frequent glittered on the guttered clift,°
And he arrived the vast Taenarian rift:°
Across his path the rapid serpent shot,
The bristling wolf with mouth all panting hot;
And now he stood upon the ruined base
Of Neptune's temple; 'twas an awful place,
Built long ago by men Cyclopian,
Now mouldered into ruin, wasted, wan,
Open to heaven, and beat by every storm.
There on the fragments lay the stony form

° from *Historical Odes and Other Poems*, London, 1864, pp. 99–105.

° **clift**: cliff.

° **Taenarian rift**: the gulf of Taenarus, entrance to the underworld.

Of the great monarch of green waves, beside
A cavern deep, whose mouth his bulk did hide.
Far stretched the desolate landscape from the height;
The nearer valleys hidden were from sight
By many a ridge with dwarfish copses clad;
And from each hollow rising white and sad
The mist crept up from where the ridges fell
In parallels of ruin toward the dell:
The river with its cold and wandering stream
All suddenly to sink in earth did seem,
Although afar its mazes serpentine
Wound languidly and with pale gleam did shine,
Where through the infirm plain it felt its way:
And on the utmost bound of sight there lay
What seemed the spectre of a city white;
But ah, as even then the wanderer's sight
Took comfort in the thought that men were there,
The cloudy cheat is scattered into air;
And in a moment, lightning-fraught, it sails
Tumultuous on the currents of the gales.

Whence had he come, that wanderer; seeking what,
That lightning answered him? Who knows not that?
Who knows not how among the dead he sought
Eurydice the dead? – With fiery thought,
In answer to that burst of cloudy fire,
He grasps the chords of his compelling lyre,
Draws in his hand, and flings upon the air
The first of that wild burden of despair
Where sorrow, anguish, pain, regret, became
An incantation of fine force to tame
Brute nature, crossing Jove, relentless Fate,
Life to transmute, death to reanimate.
Earth hath no more that magic; sorrow's art
Man long hath lost, though keeping sorrow's heart.

And, as arose that Orphic strain, began
A wondrous dew to fall around the man,
Seeming an element for harmony,
Which the sweet music summoned from the sky;
Such elemental dew as might contain
The four primevals° in its purple grain;

° **primevals**: i.e. the four prime elements (water, fire, earth, air).

Soft, aqueous-bodied, with ignescent° gleams,
Toward earth it flutters and through air it teems:
And as it thickened, the descending flush
Invested all the earth; its ceaseless rush
Hummed resolutely, till uprose a sense
That nought could be impossible from hence
Which music or the soul of love would see;
That wonders from henceforth had power to be,
Nought inconsistent, nought repulsive, nought
Impossible, which man in music sought.
Ah, so it still might be, could sorrow's soul
Commingle with the universal whole:
For then that sorrow, that large human dower,
Which is the best we keep, were made a power
To win us back our heaven: but sorrow's art
Man hath lost long; he keeps but sorrow's heart.

The music prospered, growing stern and strange
With thoughts of great successions, thoughts of change,
Thoughts about moonlit hills where shadows stretch,
About wild fires that chase the panting wretch;
About grim splintered forests on old mounts;
About the sea; about the eternal founts
Of light and darkness; Hyperborean tracts;
Riphoean summits; Pontic cataracts;°
Concussions strange from inward labours brought
Of mother earth, or ocean overwrought,
Or bursting winds; when seas have yielded place
To earth, and islands sunk without a trace:
Creation moved in answer to the vast
Emotions of the mind on which 'tis massed.
This was the lore of sorrow; sorrow's art
Man knows no more, though sorrow break his heart.

Anon the inspirèd thought did deeper draw
Upon the sources of eternal law;
And that was bruited on the thrilling strings
Which lies beneath the universe of things,

° **ignescent**: fiery.

° **Hyperborean . . . cataracts**: Hyperborea is the legendary land 'beyond the north wind' (though the Greeks conceived it not as an arctic waste but as an earthly paradise); the Riphoean mountains are in southern Russia, alluded to by Virgil (see **O2**, line 518); the Pontic is the Black Sea, whose 'icy current and compulsive course' is described in *Othello*, 3. 3. 456–63.

The unity which is the base of all,°
Causing diversity with mystical
Resemblance, which is truth: in each there is
Conscience or self; the same in all is this;
This is eternal, this for aye inheres°
In trodden clods as in the rolling spheres,
In beasts, in men, in gods; this makes all one,
Partakers of an awful unison,
Which from an ever-brimming fount of life
Procureth peace in spite of hate and strife,
And harmonizes, since all need must° sway
With the essential motion, need must stay
With the eternal rest: nor bitter fate
Can shatter, frustrate, force, nor alienate.
That argument of sorrow and that art
No more hath man; he hath but sorrow's heart.

But now a mighty moving was begun
About that desert, neath the shadowed sun;
And presently in a fantastic rout°
The creatures all enchanted came about;
The rabbit left his burrow; from his mound
The blind mole rolled, and cried upon the ground;
Large herds of deer tossed their convicted° heads;
Wild horses circled round; the brakes, the beds
Of silent underwood rustled and spake
In various signs; the sloth was wide awake;
The very serpent left the covert's root,
Advancing his horned head toward the lute;
Her flank the stealthy wild-cat dared confide°
Uncovered, by the open forest's side.
But what is this, when with preparèd hand
The minstrel smites, as with a tenfold wand,
More mastery, more magic, art than art
More mighty, that hath turned e'en sorrow's heart

° **And that was bruited . . .**: i.e. the music spoke of the divine principle of unity which underlies the apparent diversity of all created things.
° **for aye inheres / In**: is for ever an inseparable part of.
° **need must**: must necessarily.
° **rout**: crowd.
° **convicted**: conquered (i.e. by the music).
° **confide**: trust.

To use of life against usurping ill?
What is it that the very heavens doth fill
With sound that doth entrance them like the light
Of speeding suns, whose rippling lustre-flight
Confounds the clouds in glory? Is it now
The tumult of the secret's bubbling flow
Which underlies the awful° heart of things,
Solving° itself to those melodious strings?
What is it that so bows the mountain down,
And the great forest rocks from root to crown,
Which bids unthunderous lightnings come and go,
Like breath from the cloud-lips which hover so?
For now he sings of love; could he proceed,
And name not love, the inmost spirit's creed,
Who knew the heart of sorrow and the art?
Therefore behold how heaven and earth dispart°
In momentary rhythm, when soul and sense
With blind extreme of ecstasy intense
Blended and interfused, avow things new
Each for the other, each in form and hue:
And all the moving air, with giddiness
Transported into light, doth now impress
A wondrous transformation on the earth:
Vast-shapèd shadows issue into birth
At the still speeding of the silent winds,
And overhang with pomp the many kinds
Of fretted forest, mountain, plain, below;
Far off the land from heaven's rich overflow
Imbibes aërial tints; far off the light
Strikes into splendour distant glen or height;
But he, who lifts his keen face neath the vast
And heavy curtains of the sky o'ercast,
While from the chords his daring hand he stays,
Expects the consummation of amaze,°
The sorrowing marvel of the solvèd° skies.
A cold wind passes; and fierce shocks surprise°

° **awful**: i.e. awe-ful, awe-inspiring.
° **Solving**: dissolving (?).
° **dispart**: separate.
° **Expects the consummation of amaze**: awaits the climax of the miraculous events.
° **solvèd**: dissolved, melted.
° **surprise**: overtake.

Those slow sublimities; a radiant flood
Of light supernal° bursts o'er hill and wood,
And smites the eyeballs of that lifted face.

Now might he gain the heaven, now might raise
Himself on pinions of eternal youth;
The latitude, the amplitude of truth
He might for ever now achieve, made nigh
To those serener regions of the sky
Above all change, where no time-cloud doth sail,
But an eternal zephyr waves the veil
Of changeless azure, and earth's days return
Like a faint blush below; ah, he might learn
Eternal joy and stillness. Shall he so?
Far other destiny doth Love bestow
Upon the children whom he honours most:
For at that mighty moment, when the coast
Of heaven he might in ecstasy attain,
Yawns the dread cave wherein the dead remain;
The sea-god's statue, like a giant bole°
Uprooted, leaps from out the charnel-hole;
And Love, the exalter, is the summoner
To places all with writhing shades astir;
A peal of groans comes ringing on his ear,
And the distressful furrows toss with fear,
And he descends; whom not all sorrow's art
Could ransom from the pangs of sorrow's heart.

O37 Edward Dowden, 'Eurydice', 1876°

Edward Dowden, 1843–1913, Irish critic and poet, Professor at Trinity College, Dublin; best known as a Shakespearean scholar, he also wrote biographies of Shelley and Browning. 'Eurydice' is one of a group of dramatic monologues called 'The Heroines'; it is perhaps the first serious attempt to give Eurydice a voice and to see the Orpheus–Eurydice relationship from her point of view.

Eurydice

'Now must this waste of vain desire have end:
Fetter these thoughts which traverse to and fro

° **supernal**: heavenly.
° **bole**: tree-trunk.
° from *Poems*, London, 1876, pp. 69–76.

The road which has no issue! We are judged.
O wherefore could I not uphold his heart?
Why claimed I not some partnership with him
In the strict test, urging my right of wife?
How have I let him fall? I, knowing thee
My Orpheus, bounteous giver of rich gifts,
Not all inured in practice of the will,
Worthier than I, yet weaker to sustain
An inner certitude against the blank
And silence of the senses; so no more
My heart helps thine, and henceforth there remains
No gift to thee from me, who would give all,
Only the memory of me growing faint
Until I seem a thing incredible,
Some high, sweet dream, which was not, nor could be.
Aye, and in idle fields of asphodel
Must it not be that I shall fade indeed,
No memory of me, but myself; these hands
Ceasing from mastery and use, my thoughts
Losing distinction in the vague, sweet air,
The heart's swift pulses slackening to the sob
Of the forgetful river,° with no deed
Pre-eminent to dare and to achieve,
No joy for climbing to, no clear resolve
From which the soul swerves never, no ill thing
To rid the world of, till I am no more
Eurydice, and shouldst thou at thy time
Descend, and hope to find a helpmate here,
I were grown slavish, like the girls men buy
Soft-bodied, foolish-faced, luxurious-eyed,
And meet to be another thing than wife.

Would that it had been thus: when the song ceased
And laughterless Aidoneus° lifted up
The face, and turned his grave persistent eyes
Upon the singer, I had forward stepped
And spoken – "King! he has wrought well, nor failed,
Who ever heard divine large song like this,
Keener than sunbeam, wider than the air,
And shapely as the mould of faultless fruit?

° **the forgetful river**: Lethe.
° **Aidoneus**: another name for Hades/Pluto.

And now his heart upon the gale of song
Soars with wide wing, and he is strong for flight,
Not strong for treading with the careful foot:
Grant me the naked trial of the will
Divested of all colour, scents and song:
The deed concerns the wife; I claim my share."
O then because Persephone was by
With shadowed eyes when Orpheus sang of flowers,
He would have yielded. And I stepping forth
From the clear radiance of the singer's heights,
Made calm through vision of his wider truth,
And strengthened by deep beauty to hold fast
The presences of the invisible things,
Had led the way. I know how in that mood
He leans on me as babe on mother's breast,
Nor could he choose but let his foot descend
Where mine left lightest pressure; so are passed
The brute three-visaged, and the flowerless ways,
Nor have I turned my head; and now behold
The greyness of remote terrestrial light,
And I step swifter. Does he follow still?
O surely since his will embraces mine
Closer than clinging hand can clasp a hand:
No need to turn and dull with visible proof
The certitude that soul relies on soul!
So speed we to the day; and now we touch
Warm grass, and drink the Sun. O Earth, O Sun,
Not you I need, but Orpheus' breast, and weep
The gladdest tears that ever woman shed,
And may be weak awhile, and need to know
The sustenance and comfort of his arms.

Self-foolery of dreams; come bitter truth.

Yet he has sung at least a perfect song
While the Gods heard him, and I stood beside
O not applauding, but at last content,
Fearless for him, and calm through perfect joy,
Seeing at length his foot upon the heights
Of highest song, by me discerned from far,
Now suddenly attained in confident
And errorless ascension. Did I ask
The lesser joy, lips' touch and clasping arms,
Or was not this salvation? For I urged
Always, in jealous service to his art,

"Now thou hast told their secrets to the trees
Of which they muse through lullèd summer nights;
Thou hast gazed downwards in the formless gulf
Of the brute-mind, and canst control the will
Of snake, and brooding panther fiery-eyed,
And lark in middle heaven: leave these behind!
And let some careless singer of the fields
Set to the shallow sound of cymbal-stroke
The Faun a-dance; some less true-tempered soul,
Which cannot shape to harmony august
The splendour and the tumult of the world,
Inflame to frenzy of delirious rage
The Maenad's breast; yea, and the hearts of men,
Smoke of whose fire upcurls from little roofs,
Let singers of the wine-cup and the roast,
The whirling spear, the toy-like chariot-race,
And bickering counsel of contending kings
Delight them: leave thou these; sing thou for Gods."
And thou hast sung for Gods; and I have heard.

I shall not fade beneath this sunless sky,
Mixed in the wandering, ineffectual tribe;
For these have known no moment when the soul
Stood vindicated, laying sudden hands
On immortality of joy, and love
Which sought not, saw not, knew not, could not know
The instruments of sense; I shall not fade.
Yea, and thy face detains me evermore
Within the realm of light. Love, wherefore blame
Thy heart because it sought me? Could the years'
Whole sum of various fashioned happiness
Exceed the measure of that eager face
Importunate and pure, still lit with song,
Turning from song to comfort of my love,
And thirsty for my presence? We are saved!
Yield Heracles, thou brawn and thews of Zeus,
Yield up thy glory on Thessalian ground,
Competitor of Death in single strife!°
The lyre methinks outdoes the club and fist,
And beauty's ingress the outrageous force

° **Yield . . . single strife!**: Heracles successfully wrestled with Death for the soul of Alcestis, wife of the Thessalian king Admetus.

Of tyrant though beneficent; supreme
This feat remains, a memory shaped for Gods.

Nor canst thou wholly lose me from thy life;
Still I am with thee; still my hand keeps thine;
Now I restrain from too intemperate grief
Being a portion of the thoughts that claim
Thy service; now I urge with that good pain
Which wastes and feeds the spirit, a desire
Unending; now I lurk within thy will
As vigour; now am gleaming through the world
As beauty; and if greater thoughts must lay
Their solemn light on thee, outshining mine,
And in some far faint-gleaming hour of Hell
I stand unknown and muffled by the boat
Leaning an eager ear to catch some speech
Of thee, and if some comer tell aloud
How Orpheus who had loved Eurydice
Was summoned by the Gods to fill with joy
And clamour of celestial song the courts
Of bright Olympus – I, with pang of pride
And pain dissolved in rapture, will return
Appeased, with sense of conquest stern and high.'

But while she spoke, upon a chestnut trunk
Fallen from cliffs of Thracian Rhodope
Sat Orpheus, for he deemed himself alone,
And sang. But bands of wild-eyed women roamed
The hills, whom he had passed with calm disdain.
And now the shrilling Berecynthian° pipe
Sounded, blown horn, and frantic female cries:
He ceased from song and looked for the event.°

O38 Lord De Tabley, from 'Orpheus in Hades', 1893°

John Byrne Leicester Warren, 1835–95, 3rd Baron De Tabley from 1887, poet, dramatist, lawyer, botanist, numismatist, and bibliographer. Much of his poetry is on mythological themes, and, though now largely forgotten, has its own beauty,

° **Berecynthian**: an adjective associated with Cybele (after a mountain sacred to her): Dowden combines or confuses the rites of the Asian mother-goddess with those of Dionysus.

° **looked for the event**: awaited what would happen.

° from *The Collected Poems of Lord De Tabley*, London, 1903, pp. 362–6.

especially in its vivid evocations of the natural world. De Tabley wrote two dramatic monologues on 'Orpheus in Hades' (1893) and 'Orpheus in Thrace' (1895). In this passage from the earlier poem, Orpheus prepares to confront Persephone.

I come not as Alcides,° sheathed in mail.
I have no shield but music and a lyre,
Seven piteous chords, strung on a tortoise back.°
Dare I approach the impenetrable doors,
Or batter at the famished gates of hell,
So feebly furnished for the dire assault?

Can music build the stars or mould the moon,
Or wring assent from Hades' doubtful brows?
Can I make weep the stern and lovely Queen,
Before whose feet the ripples of the dead
Pass like an endless sea, beating her throne?
They move her not. In autumn's gusty hour
Shall the innumerable broken leaves,
The aimless russet-sided rushing leaves,
Gain pity from the hatchet-handed boor,
Who shears the stubborn oak, an eagle's throne?
Doth pity sting the rugged fisher folk
For the blue tunnies snared inside their net?
She will not hearken. I shall sing in vain.

Yet song is great. These pale dishevelled ghosts
Crowd in to hear with dim pathetic eyes,
And quivering corners of their charnel lips.
They rustle in from all the coasts of hell,
As starlings mustering on their evening tree,
Some blasted oak full in the sunset's eye.
And over all the mead the vibrating
Hiss of their chatter deepens. I can move
These bat-like spectres. Can I move their Queen?

° **Alcides**: i.e. Hercules.

° **tortoise back**: early lyres were traditionally made from tortoise shells; the making of the first one is described in the 'Homeric Hymn to Hermes', lines 24–54.

O39 H.D., 'Eurydice', 1917°

H.D. is the pen name of Hilda Doolittle, 1886–1961, American-born poet and novelist, living in Britain and Europe from 1911. In her early years she was an important member of the 'Imagist' school (which also included Pound and Lawrence), and her poetry is characterised by intense sensuous imagery and a repetitive, incantatory style. Throughout her career, from early poems like 'Eurydice' down to *Helen in Egypt* (1964), she was passionately devoted to ancient Greece and its mythology.

Eurydice

1

So you have swept me back,
I who could have walked with the live souls
above the earth,
I who could have slept among the live flowers
at last;

so for your arrogance
and your ruthlessness
I am swept back
where dead lichens drip
dead cinders upon moss of ash;

so for your arrogance
I am broken at last,
I who had lived unconscious,
who was almost forgot;

if you had let me wait
I had grown from listlessness
into peace,
if you had let me rest with the dead,
I had forgot you
and the past.

2

Here only flame upon flame
and black among the red sparks,
streaks of black and light
grown colourless;

° from *Collected Poems 1912–1944*, ed. Louis L. Martz, New York: New Directions, 1983.

why did you turn back,
that hell should be reinhabited
of myself thus
swept into nothingness?

why did you turn?
why did you glance back?
why did you hesitate for that moment?
why did you bend your face
caught with the flame of the upper earth,
above my face?

what was it that crossed my face
with the light from yours
and your glance?
what was it you saw in my face?
the light of your own face,
the fire of your own presence?

What had my face to offer
but reflex of the earth,
hyacinth colour
caught from the raw fissure in the rock
where the light struck,
and the colour of azure crocuses
and the bright surface of gold crocuses
and of the wind-flower,
swift in its veins as lightning
and as white.

3

Saffron from the fringe of the earth,
wild saffron that has bent
over the sharp edge of earth,
all the flowers that cut through the earth,
all, all the flowers are lost;

everything is lost,
everything is crossed with black,
black upon black
and worse than black,
this colourless light.

4

Fringe upon fringe
of blue crocuses,

crocuses, walled against blue of themselves,
blue of that upper earth,
blue of the depth upon depth of flowers,
lost;

flowers,
if I could have taken once my breath of them,
enough of them,
more than earth,
even than of the upper earth,
had passed with me
beneath the earth;

if I could have caught up from the earth,
the whole of the flowers of the earth,
if once I could have breathed into myself
the very golden crocuses
and the red,
and the very golden hearts of the first saffron,
the whole of the golden mass,
the whole of the great fragrance,
I could have dared the loss.

5

So for your arrogance
and your ruthlessness
I have lost the earth
and the flowers of the earth,
and the live souls above the earth,
and you who passed across the light
and reached
ruthless;

you who have your own light,
who are to yourself a presence,
who need no presence;

yet for all your arrogance
and your glance,
I tell you this:

such loss is no loss,
such terror, such coils and strands and pitfalls
of blackness,
such terror
is no loss;

hell is no worse than your earth
above the earth,
hell is no worse,
no, nor your flowers
nor your veins of light
nor your presence,
a loss;

my hell is no worse than yours
though you pass among the flowers and speak
with the spirits above earth.

6

Against the black
I have more fervour
than you in all the splendour of that place,
against the blackness
and the stark grey
I have more light;

and the flowers,
if I should tell you,
you would turn from your own fit paths
toward hell,
turn again and glance back
and I would sink into a place
even more terrible than this.

7

At least I have the flowers of myself,
and my thoughts, no god
can take that;
I have the fervour of myself for a presence
and my own spirit for light;

and my spirit with its loss
knows this;
though small against the black,
small against the formless rocks,
hell must break before I am lost;

before I am lost,
hell must open like a red rose
for the dead to pass.

O40 W. H. Auden, 'Orpheus', 1937°

Wystan Hugh Auden, 1907–73, major English poet, critic, playwright and librettist, living in America and Europe from 1939. His career spans a wide range of themes and styles: in the 1930s a political poet, seen as the leader of the left-wing 'Auden Group' (with Day Lewis, MacNeice, and Spender), he later turned to Christianity and a more detached and reflective approach, while his jagged and obscure early verse mellows into a style that is both conversational and technically adroit. This brief, rather cryptic poem expresses a characteristic diffidence about the value of poetry, which, as Auden wrote in 'Elegy for W. B. Yeats', 'makes nothing happen'.

Orpheus

What does the song hope for? And his moved hands
A little way from the birds, the shy, the delightful?
  To be bewildered and happy,
  Or most of all the knowledge of life?

But the beautiful are content with the sharp notes of the air;
The warmth is enough. O if winter really
  Oppose, if the weak snowflake,
  What will the wish, what will the dance do?

O41 Sydney Goodsir Smith, from 'Orpheus', 1948°

Sydney Goodsir Smith, 1915–75, Scottish poet (New Zealand-born) who wrote mainly in Scots and was influenced by the medieval Scots poets like Douglas and Henryson. 'Orpheus' (only the first half of which is given here) is part of a twenty-four-poem cycle, 'Under the Eildon Tree', about unhappy love. Smith acknowledges his debt to Henryson by repeated use of the refain, 'Quhar art thou gane, my luf Euridices?' Perhaps influenced by Henryson's moral about reason and sensuality, he presents Orpheus as a raffish and self-indulgent poet, unfaithful to Eurydice and now tormented by guilt over her death.

1

Wi sang aa> birds and beasts could I owrecome, *With song all*
  Aa men and wemen o' the mapamound> subdue; *world*
  The flouers o' the fields,

° from *Collected Poems*, ed. Edward Mandelson, London: Faber, 1976. Reprinted by permission of Faber & Faber and Random House, Inc.

° from *Collected Poems, 1941–1975*, introd. Hugh McDiarmid, London: John Calder, 1975, pp. 163–4. Reprinted by permission of Calder Publications Ltd.

Rocks and trees, boued doun to hear my leid;> — *song*
Gurlie> waters rase upon the land to mak — *stormy*
A throwgang> for my feet. — *thoroughfare*
I was the potent prince o' ballatrie,
My lyre opened portes> whareer I thocht to gang,> — *doors / thought to go*
My fleean> sangs mair ramsh nor> wine — *flying / wilder than*
At Beltane, Yule or Hogmanay°
Made wud> the clans o' men – — *mad*
There wasna my maik> upon the yerth — *like*
(Why should I no admit the fack?)> — *fact*
A hero, demi-god, my kingrik> was the hert, — *kingdom*
The passions and the saul –
Sic was my power.
– Ainlie my ain sel> I couldna bend. — *Only my own self*

'He was his ain worst enemie,'
As the auld untentit bodachs> say – — *unheeded old men*
My hert, a leopard, ruthless, breme,> — *fierce*
Gilravaged° far and near
Seekan sensatiouns, passions that wud wauken
My Muse when she was lollish.> — *lazy*
No seenil> the hert was kinnelt like a forest-bleeze . . . — *not seldom*
I was nae maister o' my ain but thirlit> — *bound in servitude*
Serf til his ramskeerie> wants — *restlessly lustful*
– And yet I hained> but ane in the hert's deepest hert. — *sheltered*

She, maist leefou,> leesome> leddy — *beloved / loveable*
– Ochone, ochone,> Euridicie – — *alas*
Was aye the queen of Orpheus' hjert,> as I kent> weill, — *heart / knew*
And wantan> her my life was feckless drinkin, — *lacking*
Weirdless,> thieveless> dancin, — *unprofitable / dissolute*
Singin, gangrellin.> — *vagabond wandering*
– And nou she's gane.

2

The jalous gods sae cast my weird> that she — *determined my fate*
Was reift> intil the Shades throu my neglect. — *stolen away*
I, daffan> i' the wuids and pools — *playing around*
Wi the water-lassies,

° **Beltane, Yule or Hogmanay**: Celtic names for festivals at spring, Christmas/midwinter, and the New Year.

° **Gilravaged**: (i) lived riotously, (ii) roamed in search of plunder.

    Riggish,> ree,> and aye as fain>   *lecherous / drunken / eager*
  For lemanrie> as Orpheus was,   *illicit sex*
I never kent> o' her stravaigin>   *knew / wandering*
  Lane and dowie> in the fields;   *alone and sad*
Nor that yon Aristoeus loed> my queyne.   *loved*
  It was fleein him she dee'd
But yet was my neglect that did the deed;
Neither was I by her to protect
  Frae the dernit> serpent's bane   *hidden*
Green and secret in the raff gerss liggan> as she ran.   *rough grass lying*
– I was her daith as she was life til me;
  Tho I was feckless born and lemanous>   *unfaithful*
Yet she was mair nor aa> the pultrous> nymphs   *more than all / lascivious*
  O' wuid and burn> til me   *wood and stream*
      – Yet it was I
  That flung Euridicie,
  The aipple of my bruckle> ee,   *frail, i.e. easily tempted*
    Til yon far bourne
Frae whilk, they said, there's can be nae retourn.°
        'Quhar art thou gane, my luf Euridices?'

In the second half of the poem Orpheus describes his journey to hell, the loss of Euridicie 'throu my ain twafauld treacherie', and his inability to sing any longer; he concludes 'Aa this will happen aa again, / Monie and monie a time again.'

O42 Mary Renault, from *The King Must Die*, 1958°

Mary Renault, 1905–93, historical novelist, born in England but living for much of her life in South Africa, best known for her vivid novels of classical and mythic Greece. *The King Must Die* and its sequel *The Bull from the Sea* are a fictional autobiography of the hero Theseus, set in a primitive Greece where the old matriarchal religion of the Mother Goddess is gradually giving way to the patriarchal cult of the Olympian gods. Theseus is a champion of the Olympians, and so is Orpheus (referred to simply as 'the bard'), who is shown as helping with the building of Stonehenge and as founder of the Eleusinian Mysteries. Here Theseus hears of the bard's death from a priest of Apollo at Delos. Renault's version

° **yon far bourne . . . nae retourn**: compare *Hamlet*, 3. 1. 81–2, 'The undiscovered country from whose bourn / No traveller returns'.

° from *The King Must Die*, London: Longman, 1958, book 5, section 2. Reprinted by permission of Addison Wesley Longman Ltd.

of Orpheus's descent into the underworld draws upon the old English ballad of Thomas the Rhymer, a minstrel who was carried away by the Queen of the Fairies, but, by refusing to eat or speak while he was in her kingdom, was able at last to return to the mortal world.

When the rite was done and we were walking down the long stair from the sanctuary, my mind went back to the harper who had sung in Troizen, and at Eleusis had reshaped the Mystery. I turned to the priest, who walked near by me, and asked if he had been back to Delos again.

The priest told me they had had word that the bard was dead. He had perished in his own native land of Thrace, where he served Apollo's altar. The old religion is very strong there; as a youth he had sung for its rites himself, and the priestesses had been angry when he made Serpent-Slayer° a shrine upon the mountain. But after he came back from Eleusis, whether that his great fame had led him into hubris, or he had had a true dream from the god,° he went forth to meet the maenads at their winter feast, and tried to calm their madness with his song. Everyone knows the end of it.

Now he was dead, said the priest to me, the songs and the tales were growing round his name; how great stones had risen at his voice, to make walls and gateways, how his ears had been licked by Apollo's serpent, and he knew the speech of birds. 'They say the Dark Mother loved him, when he was young, and set a seal upon his lips and showed him her mysteries beneath the earth. He crossed the river of blood, and the river of weeping; but Lethe's stream he would not drink of, and seven years passed over him like a single day. When the appointed time drew near, for her to let him back to the upper air, she tempted him to speak while he was still in bonds to her; but he would not break the seal of silence, nor taste her apples and her pomegranates that bind a man for ever, because he was vowed to Apollo and the gods of light. So she had to set him free. All the way up to the mouth of her dark cave she followed him, listening to his harp as he sang upon his way, and crying, "Look back! Look back!" But he did not turn till he had stepped forth into the sunlight; and she sank into the earth, weeping for her stolen secrets and lost love. So people say.'

When this tale was done, I said, 'He did not speak of it. Is it true?'

'There is truth and truth,' said the priest of Delos. 'It is true after its kind.'

° **Serpent-Slayer**: Apollo, so called for his slaying of the great serpent Python. Renault takes the title as symbolic of Apollo's enmity to the old religion, in which snakes, sacred to the Earth Mother, play a prominent role.

° **a true dream from the god**: i.e. a divine summons to meet his death.

O43 Muriel Rukeyser°

Muriel Rukeyser, 1913–80, American poet and biographer. Included here are two excerpts from the her long (308-line) poem about about the resurrection of the murdered and dismembered Orpheus, and a later short postscript to that poem.

(a) from 'Orpheus', 1962

The poem begins just after the murder, as the Bacchantes flee leaving Orpheus's dismembered body lying in blood on the mountainside: 'He is the pieces of Orpheus, and he is chaos.' The scattered parts of the body (eye, heart, head, hand, foot, penis) each speak in turn, expressing their pain and loss and confusion, but 'They do not even know they need to be whole. / Only the wounds in their endless crying.' Then:

Touch me! Love me! Speak to me!
One effort and one risk.
The hand is risen. It braces itself, it flattens,
and the third finger touches the lyre. Wounds of hand.
But it finds thick gold of frame, grasps the frame
with its old fingering of bone and gold.
Now there is blood, a train of blood on grass
as hand swings high and with a sowing gesture
throws the lyre upward. The lyre is going up:
the old lyre of Orpheus, four strings of song
of the dawn of all things, daystar, daymoon, and man,
hurtles up, whistling through black air.
Tingles in moon-air. Reaches the other stars.
And those four strings now sing:
Eurydice.

3

Standing in silence on the mountaintop, the trees incline before the breath of fire.
Very slowly, the sounds awake. Breathing that is the consciousness, the lifting
and the resting of life, and surf-sounds of many flames.
Flame in its flowing streams about these pieces
and under the sides of clouds and chars the branches.

° from *Collected Poems of Muriel Rukeyser*, New York: McGraw Hill, 1978, pp. 296–8, 435.

It does not touch the flesh. Now the flesh moves,
the hacked foot and the hand and the head,
buttocks and heart, phallus and breast, compose.
Now the body is formed; and the blood of Orpheus,
spilled, soaked, and deep under the wet ground,
rises in fountains playing into the wounds.
Now the body is whole; but it is covered with murder.
A mist of blood and fire shine over the body,
shining upon the mountain, a rose of form.
And now the wounds losing self-pity change,
they are mouths, they are the many mouths of music.
And now they disappear. He is made whole.
The mist dissolves into the body of song.

A lake of fire lowers, tendrils level to source,
over the mountaintop many young streams.
Standing newborn and naked, Orpheus.
He has died the death of the god.

His gifts are to be made, in a newfound voice,
his body his voice. His truth has turned into life.
– When I looked back in that night, I looked beyond love at hell.
All the poets and powers will recognise.
I thought the kings of Hell would recognise.
I misjudged evil. –
He has opened the door of pain.
It is a door and a window and a lens
opening on another land; pain standing wide
and the world crystallised in broken rains.

The poem ends with Orpheus's song:

Voices and days, the exile of our music
And the dividing airs are gathered home.
The hour of light and birth at last appears
among the alone, in prisons of scattering.
Seeming of promise, the shining of new stars,
the stars of the real over the body of love.
The cloud, the mountain, and the cities risen.

(b) 'The Poem as Mask: Orpheus', 1968

Eight years later, Rukeyser renounces mythological symbols and reinterprets the earlier poem as a symbolic account of the experience of childbirth.

The Poem as Mask: Orpheus

When I wrote of the women in their dances and wildness, it was a mask,
on their mountain, gold-hunting, singing, in orgy,
it was a mask; when I wrote of the god,
fragmented, exiled from himself, his life, the love gone down with song,
it was myself, split open, unable to speak, in exile from myself.

There is no mountain, there is no god, there is memory
of my torn life, myself split open in sleep, the rescued child
beside me among the doctors, and a word
of rescue from the great eyes.

No more masks! No more mythologies!

Now, for the first time, the god lifts his hand,
the fragments join in me with their own music.

O44 Rolfe Humphries, 'Fragment of a Legend', 1965°

Rolfe Humphries, 1894–1969, American poet, translator, and teacher of Latin and English literature, best known for his translations of Virgil and Ovid. 'Fragment of a Legend' is a quietly ironic reinterpretation of Orpheus's backward look.

Fragment of a Legend

And they were made aware
Of an illumination in the night,
Light where the shadows of the cypress fell,
A bright surprising presence, standing there
In flesh and robes, amid the murk of Hell.

And suddenly the lyre was raised in Hell.
As Orpheus sang. To the strange music, stronger
Than their self-torment's everlasting spell,
Came all the ghosts in myriads, no longer
Ambition-ridden, free from guilt, from dread.
Tantalus forgot his thirst and hunger;
The wheel, the rock were still; the vultures fed
No more on Tityos. 'I do not know,
I do not know,' the words and music said,

° from *Collected Poems*, Bloomington: Indiana University Press, 1965, pp. 233–5. Reprinted by permission of Indiana University Press.

'What power Love possesses here below,
But I have heard your might and majesty
Acknowledge him. Let my beloved go!
For your queen's sake, let her return with me.'
The silence, as the music ended, fell
Purer than music. From Persephone,
Half smiling, Orpheus faced the lord of Hell.

Silent, the proud and luckless lord of Hell,
Dark monarch of the dark domain below,
Listened to Orpheus' song, and heard his plea,
And wept, for once not quite implacable,
Yet, being an ironic god and wise,
Knew what a lord of Hell was bound to know,
That out of loss alone the great songs rise
And knew that this musician, being free
To make the ultimate choice, would turn his eyes,
Would execute the sentence, none but he,
Loosed from the one, bound to the other spell,
So Pluto gravely called Eurydice,
Gave his false terms and watched them leaving Hell.

Silent, in hope and doubt, they climb from Hell,
Her trembling ghost behind him. Daylight nears.
Let them but reach the light, and all is well.
And now he knows, as surely as he fears,
Her permanence, her change, her safe remove
From the great song that drew the iron tears.
The music even the Furies paused to love
Fades into admonition –
                                        Keep the ghost,
Forsake the girl.
                                Song is your love.
                                                        If she
Is saved, you are lost, you are both forever lost.
Turn.
        Face her.
                        Cry 'Farewell!'
With almost all your heart, and let her be
Consigned, with everlasting love, to Hell.

O45 Michael Hamburger, 'Orpheus Street, SE5', 1967°

Michael Hamburger, born 1924, poet, critic, and translator from the German; born in Germany, of a Jewish family, he emigrated to England at the age of nine. This poem relocates Orpheus in 'swinging' and seedy 1960s London (Orpheus Street is a real street in south-east London), and sceptically explores the possibility of poetry transforming such a society.

Orpheus Street, SE5

1 Will they move, will they dance,
These houses put up by the money-makers
For the meek, their no-men, to breed in,
Breed money dispersed now, decayed?
And the pawn shop, government surplus,
The cut price petrol station,
Dirty brick, waste paper,
Will his music gather them up?

2 Orpheus transfigures, Orpheus transmutes all things.
His music melts walls. His music wrings
A smile from the lips of killer and nearly killed.
He wills pavements to crack. He whistles at trains,
They whisper, gasp and give up. Wherever 'it' sings
It is Orpheus° – with it, well paid for his pains.
Grow, says Orpheus, and dog collars burst,
Tall factories shiver, the whole town swings.

3 Oh, but the traffic diversions.
The road marked World's End, The West,
Runs north and east and south,
And the policeman on duty sneers:
Never mind the direction. You'll get there.
Be courteous. Be patient. If you park
Your car will be towed away.
If you walk, louts will kick you in the ribs.

4 Orpheus is peaceable. Orpheus is faithful

° from *Collected Poems, 1941–1994*, London: Anvil, 1995. Reprinted by permission of the author and Anvil Press Poetry Ltd.

° **Wherever 'it' sings / It is Orpheus**: alluding to a line in Rainer Maria Rilke's *Sonnets to Orpheus*, 1. 5: *Ein für alle Male / ists Orpheus wenn es singt* ('Once and for all, it's Orpheus when there is singing').

To the woman who was his wife,
Till she suffered a blackout, going
Down, down, where he couldn't reach her,
Where no one belongs to himself,
Far less to another. He lost her;
But loves her still, and loves everyone,
Richly paid for loving.

5 They shriek, they sob for Orpheus,
For a shred of his shirt or flesh.
He turns right, then left,
Proceeds, does a U-turn,
Turns left, turns right, turns left,
The shriek in his ears, everywhere.
He swallows a capsule, prepares
A love song, a peace song, a freedom song.

6 The smile on her face, her smile
When he questioned her eyes for the last time
And she walked away from the stranger.
In halflight he sees no warehouse
But chasms, a river, rock.
A last glint on her hair
And the cave's darkness takes her,
Silent. Silent he leaves.

7 Let lamp posts be trees for once,
Bend their trunks, the park benches
Fling out their limbs, let them fly,
Narrowly missing the sparrows.
Street and mind will not meet
Till street and mind go down
And the footfall that faded, faded,
Draws closer again in the dark.

8 Lamplit or moonlit, his deathland:
Chasms, a river, rock.
The cries of children in alleyways,
The cries of birds in the air,
And the talons, innocent, tearing.
A head will float on foul water
And sing for the rubble, for her,
For the stars, for empty space.

O46 Russell Hoban, from *Kleinzeit*, 1974°

Russell Hoban, b. 1925, American-born novelist, children's writer, and illustrator, living in London since 1969. Two of his novels are based on the Orpheus legend: *The Medusa Frequency* (1987), whose hero, a blocked writer named Hermann Orff, is haunted by the severed head of Orpheus, and the serio-comic fantasy *Kleinzeit* (1974). Kleinzeit is an ordinary little man (his name is German for 'small-time', though he likes to claim it means 'hero') who is caught up in the myth of Orpheus; he finds himself compulsively writing poems on small pieces of yellow paper, playing the glockenspiel in the London Underground, and having unnerving conversations with figures like Death, Word, and Hospital. Here, in hospital after a near-fatal seizure of the hypoteneuse, under the care of the ward sister who is his Eurydice, Kleinzeit receives a lesson from Hospital about the meaning of the Orpheus story.

Good, said Hospital. Now that we have somewhat cleared the air we can perhaps chat a little.

About what, said Kleinzeit.

About Orpheus, said Hospital. You know the story?

Of course I do, said Kleinzeit.

Tell me it, said Hospital.

Orpheus with his lute made trees and all that, said Kleinzeit. And then Eurydice in the Underworld, he nearly got her out with his music but he looked back and lost her. He wasn't meant to look back.

It's just as I thought, said Hospital. A lot of schoolboy claptrap. Let us look in upon Orpheus. I don't say the story has a beginning, I don't even say it's a story, stories are like knots on a string. There is however a place, a time where I like to look in on Orpheus.

Go on, said Kleinzeit. I'm listening. He watched the blips on his screen, listened as Hospital spoke. There went an aeroplane, far away.

Silence, said Hospital. Silence and the severed head of Orpheus, eyeless, sodden and rotting, blackened and buzzing with blowflies, lying on the beach at Lesbos. There it is, washed up on the golden sand under a bright blue sky. So small it looks, the lost and blackened head of Orpheus! Have you ever noticed how much smaller a man's head looks when it's no longer on his body? It's astonishing really.

I don't recall that part about the severed head, said Kleinzeit.

Naturally not, said Hospital. It's the very heart and centre of the matter. You don't recall how the Thracian women tore him apart, threw his head into the

° from *Kleinzeit*, London: Jonathan Cape, 1974. Reprinted by permission of Jonathan Cape Ltd and David Higham Associates Ltd.

river? How the head floated singing down the river to the sea, across the sea to Lesbos?

Now it comes back, said Kleinzeit. Vaguely.

Vague! said Hospital. What isn't vague! And at the same time, you know, burningly clear. Quivering forever on the air. The head begins to talk. Begins to rage and curse. Day and night the head of Orpheus rages on the beach at Lesbos. I couldn't understand most of what it was saying.

You were there? said Kleinzeit.

I was there, said Hospital. I was there because the beach at Lesbos was hospital for Orpheus. After a certain number of days the head was kicked into the sea.

By whom? said Kleinzeit.

I didn't notice, said Hospital. It doesn't matter. I can see it now. There was no surf, it was a sheltered beach. The head bobbed in the water like a coconut, then moved out to sea. There was a little wake behind it as it swam out to sea. It was one of those grey days, the air was very still, the water was smooth and sleek, the water was lapping quietly at the beach as the tide came in.

In? said Kleinzeit. Not out?

In, said Hospital. The head swam out against the tide. Think of it swimming day and night, no eyes, the blind head of Orpheus.

I am thinking of it, said Kleinzeit.

Think of it at night with a phosphorescent wake, said Hospital. Think of it with the moonlight on it, swimming towards Thrace. Think of it reaching the coast, the estuary, the mouth of the Hebrus. Like a salmon it swims upstream, eh?

To the place of his dismemberment? said Kleinzeit.

To that place, said Hospital. Think of the head of Orpheus snuffling in the reeds by the river at night, sniffing out his parts. It's dark, the moon has set. You hear something moving, like a dog hunting in the reeds. You can't see your hand in front of your face, you only hear something moving about close to the ground. You feel the air on your face, you feel with your face the passage of something between you and the river. There is a sighing perhaps, you can't be sure. Someone unseen walks away slowly.

He's found his members, said Kleinzeit. He's remembered himself.

What is harmony, said Hospital, but a fitting together?

* * *

Am I Orpheus?

Kleinzeit fell asleep after supper, woke up, saw Sister standing there, blipped faster. Did it ever happen, he thought, that I saw her naked by the light of the gas fire, that we made love, that I was Orpheus with her, harmonious and profound? I can't even shit without professional assistance.

Sister drew the curtains, hugged him, kissed him, cried. 'What are you going to do?' she said.

'Remember,' said Kleinzeit. 'I'm going to remember myself.'

'Hero,' said Sister. 'Kleinzeit does mean hero.'

'Or coward,' said Kleinzeit. Sister cried some more, kissed him again, went back to her duties.

Dim light, lateness. Kleinzeit rolled over, reached under the bed. Psst, he said. You there?

Hoo hoo, said Death, gripped Kleinzeit's hand with its black hairy one. Still friends?

Still friends, said Kleinzeit.

I wasn't trying anything on with you, said Death. I was just singing to myself, really.

I believe you, said Kleinzeit. These things happen.

Anything I can do for you? said Death.

Not right now, said Kleinzeit. Just, you know, stick around.

Twenty-four hour service, said Death.

Kleinzeit rolled on to his back, looked up at the dim ceiling, closed his eyes. Tell me more about Orpheus, he said. Am I Orpheus?

I, said Hospital. I, I, I. What a lot of rubbish. How could any one *I* be Orpheus. Even Orpheus wasn't *I*. *I* doesn't come into it. Your understanding isn't as strong as I thought it was.

I'm not well, said Kleinzeit. Be patient with me.

You won't find anyone more patient than I am, said Hospital. Patience is my middle name.

What's your Christian name? said Kleinzeit.

I'm not a Christian, said Hospital. I've no patience with new-fangled religions. It was just a figure of speech, I haven't any first or middle name. We big chaps just have one: Ocean, Sky, Hospital, and so forth.

Word, said Kleinzeit. Underground.

Oh aye, said Hospital.

Tell me more about Orpheus, said Kleinzeit.

When Orpheus remembered himself, said Hospital, he came together so harmoniously that he began to play his lute and sing with immense power and beauty. No one had ever heard the like of it. Trees and all that, you know, rocks even, they simply picked themselves up and moved to where he was. Sometimes you couldn't see Orpheus for the rocks and trees around him. He was tuned into the big vibrations, you see, he and the grains of sand and the cloud particles and the colours of the spectrum all vibrating together. And of course it made him a tremendous lover. Krishna with the cowgirls° was nothing to what Orpheus was.

What about Eurydice? said Kleinzeit. How'd they meet? I don't think that's

° **Krishna with the cowgirls**: the Hindu god Krishna, in the shape of a handsome cowherd playing on the flute, made all the cowgirls fall madly in love with him.

told in any of the stories. All I know is that she went to the Underworld after she died of a snakebite.

More schoolboy rubbish, said Hospital. Orpheus met Eurydice when he got to the inside of things. Eurydice was there because that was where she lived. She didn't have to get bitten by a snake to go there. With the power of his harmony Orpheus penetrated the world, got to the inside of things, the place under the places. Underworld, if you like to call it that. And that's where he found Eurydice, the female element complementary to himself. She was Yin, he was Yang. What could be simpler.

If Underworld was where she lived why did he try to get her out of it? said Kleinzeit.

Ah, said Hospital. There you have the essence of the Orphic conflict. That's why Orpheus became what he is, always in the present, never in the past. That's why that dogged blind head is always swimming across the ocean to the river mouth.

Why? said Kleinzeit. What was the conflict?

Orpheus cannot be content at the inside of things, at the place under the places, said Hospital. His harmony has brought him to the stillness and the calm at the centre and he cannot abide it. Nirvana is not his cup of tea. He wants to get back outside, wants that action with the rocks and trees again, wants to be seen with Eurydice at posh restaurants and all that. Naturally he loses her. She can't go outside any more than he can stay inside.

He didn't lose her because he looked back? said Kleinzeit.

That's the sort of thing that gets put into a story, of course, said Hospital. But looking back or not looking back wouldn't have made any difference.

What happened then? said Kleinzeit.

It just goes round again, said Hospital. Orpheus mourns, mopes about, won't go to parties any more, won't make love with the local women, they say he's queer, one thing leads to another, they tear him apart, and there's the head going down the river again, heading for Lesbos.

What does it all mean? said Kleinzeit.

How can there be meaning? said Hospital. Meaning is a limit. There are no limits.

O47 Lauris Edmond, 'Orpheus without Music', 1975°

Lauris Edmond, born 1924, New Zealand poet. This poem comes from her first collection, which appeared when she was fifty-one; in it Eurydice's underworld becomes a metaphor for mental illness.

° from *In Middle Air*, Wellington: Pegasus, 1975, p. 45. Reprinted by permission of the author.

Blue islands, blue harbours of Auckland
drawn on a distant sky;
two foreground figures seated –
you, motionless in the loosened folds
of a white gown, staring;
I in a beseeching posture:
could these questions be asked differently?
Will other explanations clarify?

There is no answer but bells, a name called,
footsteps, the closing of a door –
overtones from others' pain;
do you hear them? You turn slowly, slowly
as though coming out of sleep,
your eyes clear and recognition
colours them a deeper blue.
In that luminous mirror I see you
hesitate, tremble a little, consider
whether you could move towards me, take my hand . . .

I am suddenly, unreasonably delighted –
you have come so close! – and I say it.
Oh fool, fool! I have frightened you.
At once the darkness draws you away;
now in the quickly-thickening shadows
I can make out a faint waving of hands,
and the glimmer of dark water.

In the silence my thoughts rage,
quarrelling bitterly.

O48 Elaine Feinstein, 'The Feast of Eurydice', 1980°

Elaine Feinstein, 1930–, English poet and novelist, born in Lancashire of Russian Jewish ancestry. She is also known for her translations and biography of the Russian poet Maria Tsvetaeva; her most recent novel is *Lady Chatterley's Confession*, a sequel to Lawrence's *Lady Chatterley's Lover*.

The Feast of Eurydice

1

The dead are strong.

° from *Selected Poems*, Manchester: Carcanet, 1992. Reprinted by permission of the author and Carcanet Press Ltd.

That winter as you wandered,
   the cold continued, still
the brightness cut
   my shape into the snow:
I would have let you go!

   Your mother blew
my dust into your lips
   a powder white as cocaine,
my name, runs to your nerves
   and now I move again in your song.
You will not let me go.

   The dead are strong.
Although in darkness I was lost
   and had forgotten all pain
long ago: in your song
   my lit face remains
and so we go

   over pools that crack
like glass, through forests shining
   black with twigs that wait
for you to wake them, I return
   in your praise, as Eurydice's
ghost I light the trees.

   The dead are strong.

2

River, green river, forget
   your worm-eaten gods,
for we come to sweeten you,
   feel how the air has grown
warm and wet now
   the winds have all fallen.

On bent willow boughs
   beads of yellow break open
winter creatures we roused
   giant beeches and scrubland
in white roots respond
   Orpheus   Orpheus

We release all the woodlands
   from sleep, and the predator birds
from their hungering,

    wild cats are calm
as we pass

    As we reach the fields
men with grey knuckles
    lean over furrows
and blink.
    In the villages

wives honed too thin
    with their riverside washing
now straighten up,
    listen and nod.
What are they remembering?

    In cities, the traders
leave market stalls; even
    the rich leave their
food tureens. No-one
    collects or cleans
their dirty crockery.

    Click! All transistors off.
Traffic stops. In
    a voice, everyone
hears how much
    any soul touched
by such magic is human

3

A path of cinders, I remember,
    and limping upward
not yet uprooted from
    my dream, a ghost

with matted eyes, air-sacs
    rasping,   white
brain,   I staggered
    after you

Orpheus, when you first
    called,   I pushed
the sweet earth from my mouth
    and sucked in

all the powders of volcanic ash
    to follow you

obedient up
that crumbling slope

to the very last ridge –
where I saw clumps of
yellow camomile in the dunes
and heard the applause

of your wild mother
great Calliope
crying good, my son, good
in the fumes of the crater.

When the wiring sputtered
at my wedding feast
she was hectic, glittering;
her Arabian glass

burst into darkness
and her flesh shimmered.
She was still laughing, there,
at that pumice edge

with all Apollo's day behind her
as I saw your heavy
shoulders turn. Your lips move.
Then your eyes.

and I lay choking Orpheus
what hurt most then was
your stunned face
lost

cruel never to be touched
again, and watching
a blown leaf in your
murderous eye

shrivel . . .

4

A storyteller cannot depict
even a tree without
wind and weather: in your song

I was changed and reborn.
When you asked for my innermost
thoughts, once, they lapped

under shadows in shallows,
I never could find them:
you wanted my soul,

water creature I was, all my life
I had loved you in silence:
It was not what you wanted.

My thoughts flew through pebbles
alight with the flash
of my silvery sisters

in whispers between us.
You wanted my soul,
though I shivered and bleached,

and it slipped from us both
when the snake bit my foot
I was white as a moth.

In your song I am whole.

5

Over many centuries
modest ladies
who long for splendour
gather here

their eyes most tender
their voices low
and their skins still clear
when they appear

and to Dionysus
they offer their bodies
for what they seek

The god of abandon
destroys their reason
Beware the meek!

6

You belonged to Apollo
the gold one the cold one
and you were his servant:
he could not protect you.

You called for your mother

and her holy sisters
she wept as a witness:
but could not protect you.

Here they come, murderers,
their bodies spattered
with blood as they stagger
off-balance towards you.

They claw and maul you
with hoes and long mattocks
their heavy rakes tear at your
throat and your fingers.

They batter the listening
birds, and the oxen
at plough, and they share out
the limbs of each creature they kill.

And my love's head is thrown
on the waters, it floats
singing still. All the
nine Muses mourn,

though downstream the island
of Lesbos receives you
and in that grief
poets are born –

Orpheus   Orpheus –
for how many poets
must die at the hands
of such revellers?

7

And the curse of all future
poets to die by
rope or stake or fire falls there
on these mindless creatures

no longer human their toes
grow roots and their knees are
gnarled – their arms branch leaves:
who will release them?

Their flesh is wood.

8

As dreamers now together
we forget Apollo's day
that cruel light in which at last
all men become shadows;
and we forgive even those
dead gods, who sleep among us.
For all their gifts, not one
of them has power to summon us.
In this green silence
we conceal our one true marriage.

O49 Margaret Atwood, 'Orpheus (1)', 'Eurydice', 'Orpheus (2)', 1984°

Margaret Atwood, 1939–, Canadian novelist and poet, born in Ottawa. Her poems, like her novels, are characterised by sharp, vivid language and images, and an unsparing, angry or sardonic analysis of power relationships between men and women.

Orpheus (1)

You walked in front of me,
pulling me back out
to the green light that had once
grown fangs and killed me.

I was obedient, but
numb, like an arm
gone to sleep; the return
to time was not my choice.

By then I was used to silence.
Though something stretched between us
like a whisper, like a rope:
my former name,
drawn tight.
You had your old leash
with you, love you might call it,
and your flesh voice.

° from *Selected Poems II: Poems Selected and New 1976–1986*, Boston: Houghton Mifflin, 1987.

Before your eyes you held steady
the image of what you wanted
me to become: living again.
It was this hope of yours that kept me following.

I was your hallucination, listening
and floral, and you were singing me:
already new skin was forming on me
within the luminous misty shroud
of my other body; already
there was dirt on my hands and I was thirsty.

I could see only the outline
of your head and shoulders,
black against the cave mouth,
and so could not see your face
at all, when you turned
and called to me because you had
already lost me. The last
I saw of you was a dark oval.
Though I knew how this failure
would hurt you, I had to
fold like a gray moth and let go.

You could not believe I was more than your echo.

Eurydice

He is here, come down to look for you.
It is the song that calls you back,
a song of joy and suffering
equally: a promise:
that things will be different up there
than they were last time.

You would rather have gone on feeling nothing,
emptiness and silence; the stagnant peace
of the deepest sea, which is easier
than the noise and flesh of the surface.

You are used to these blanched dim corridors,
you are used to the king
who passes you without speaking.

The other one is different
and you almost remember him.
He says he is singing to you

because he loves you,

not as you are now,
so chilled and minimal: moving and still
both, like a white curtain blowing
in the draft from a half-opened window
beside a chair on which nobody sits.

He wants you to be what he calls real.
He wants you to stop light.
He wants to feel himself thickening
like a treetrunk or a haunch
and see blood on his eyelids
when he closes them, and the sun beating.

This love of his is not something
he can do if you aren't there,
but what you knew suddenly as you left your body
cooling and whitening on the lawn

was that you love him anywhere,
even in this land of no memory,
even in this domain of hunger.
You hold love in your hand, a red seed
you had forgotten you were holding.

He has come almost too far.
He cannot believe without seeing,
and it's dark here.
Go back, you whisper,

but he wants to be fed again
by you. O handful of gauze, little
bandage, handful of cold
air, it is not through him
you will get your freedom.

Orpheus (2)

Whether he will go on singing
or not, knowing what he knows
of the horror of this world:

He was not wandering among meadows
all this time. He was down there
among the mouthless ones, among
those with no fingers, those
whose names are forbidden,

those washed up eaten into
among the gray stones
of the shore where nobody goes
through fear. Those with silence.

He has been trying to sing
love into existence again
and he has failed.

Yet he will continue
to sing, in the stadium
crowded with the already dead
who raise their eyeless faces
to listen to him; while the red flowers
grow up and splatter open
against the walls.

They have cut off both his hands
and soon they will tear
his head from his body in one burst
of furious refusal.
He foresees this. Yet he will go on
singing, and in praise.
To sing is either praise
or defiance. Praise is defiance.

O50 Sandra M. Gilbert, 'Bas Relief: Bacchante', 1984°

Sandra M. Gilbert, born 1936, American critic and poet, most famous as co-author (with Susan Gubar) of *The Madwoman in the Attic*, an influential feminist study of nineteenth-century women writers. 'Bas Relief: Bacchante' allows one of the Bacchantes to justify the killing of Orpheus. It is one of a sequence of poems about exhibits in a museum; a bas relief is a classical carving in low relief, in which the figures project only slightly out of a flat background.

Bas Relief: Bacchante

She's not at all as we expected, wearing
(instead of oiled breasts, a torn toga, a sexy swoon)
a sort of fur ruff and the calm look

° from *Emily's Bread*, New York: Norton, 1984, p. 42. Reprinted by permission of the author and W. W. Norton and Co.

of those animal-headed judges, wise as roots,
who rule the world below.

They were the ones, she says, who watched when Orpheus,
that show-off, gave the look that kills
to Eurydice on the stony path.
Betrayed girl-bride, stuck halfway up the hill
and halfway down!

Her fur ruff twitches
as she makes this case. It's clear
she never liked the bastard anyway,
the swaggering bastard with his silver flute,
precious proboscis, mean baton,

commanding silence, silence from everyone,
shutting the trees up, quieting the wind
and the quick birds, and the women.
Without his manly anthems,
everything, she says, would sing, would sing.

As she speaks, a furry feathery humming
rises from the stones she stands on
and we see she's after all a lioness,
serenely hungry to dismember him.
But behind her, hidden among leaves,
dressed in a gauzy apron, a crinoline, a rhinestone necklace,

there is Isis,° that apple blossom queen,
that silly sister-in-law,
that superintendent of nurses,
ready as ever to pick up the bloody pieces.

O51 John Heath-Stubbs, 'The Story of Orph', 1985°

John Heath-Stubbs, 1918–, poet, critic, and translator, has been called 'England's second-greatest blind poet' (after Milton). His poetry, written 'in a classical romantic manner' (as he remarked in his self-mocking 'Epitaph'), is strongly based in literary tradition, and draws on an encyclopaedic range of literary,

° **Isis**: the Egyptian goddess who gathered up and reassembled the pieces of her husband Osiris's body after he had been torn apart by his enemy Set. (The 'animal-headed judges' in line 4 also suggest Egyptian rather than Greek myth.)

° from *Collected Poems 1943–1987*, Manchester: Carcanet, 1988. Reprinted by permission of Carcanet Press Ltd and David Higham Associates Ltd.

historical, and mythological allusions – often to comic or ironic effect. 'The Story of Orph' juxtaposes a hypothetical 'real' Orpheus with his debased modern equivalent, a 1980s rock star.

The Story of Orph

ORPH WITH HIS LUTE

Fox-furs hardly conceal his genitals;
Louse-haired, dung-plastered, and with uncombed beard,
Shaman of the Thracian hills, he strums
Guts across a shell. A deep voice
Out of his stomach tells
Of worlds of gods and demons, and the souls
Of men, being dead, continually recurring
To other bodies. Savage tribesmen heard;
Wolves and bears drew round him in a circle,
While in the mist-haze
Mountains and oak trees seem to dance.
Acoustic guitars. Strobes, Lasers. A hempen smoke.
The vast poster announces
Orph and the Bassarids.° *Screaming adolescent nymphs.*
The masturbatory drum-beat. Rock arrangements –
Monteverdi, Gluck.

ORPH IN THE UNDERWORLD

'Take her then, and go!' said the dark lords.
'But faring upwards do not look back.'
Overmastering, the desire to turn. Was she following?
He turned, and looked. She came on slowly,
Skin death-pale, lips blue in the half-light,
Eyelids tight-closed.

The path grew steeper. Once again he turned.
Horror – the stench of death
Flesh dropping from her bones,
But faster she came on, as if instinct
With a new, strange putrescent energy.

The last stretch – precipitous:
He turned a third time, saw
A bleached skeleton – but now she ran
Relentlessly pursuing.

° **Bassarids**: another name for Bacchantes.

Desperate, he stumbled into light.
He was again upon the hills, and felt
Beneath his feet the turf, heather and rock-rose.

Morning infiltrated
The curtains of the luxury hotel room.
He turned. The girl beside him on the bed
Was stiff and cold. Had he then killed her?
Verdict inconclusive; charges not pressed.

ORPH GYNANDROMORPH°

Terror had put a sacred madness on him. Now he becomes
Man-woman. Fox-furs cast aside,
Green silk sheathes his contours;
A gold-wire wig is perched on his bald head,
As he submits his body, oiled and perfumed,
With essences of mountain wildflowers,
To shaggy goat-herds, or upon the quays,
Sidonian and Tyrrhenian shipmen have him.

In candid interviews he coyly admits
Bisexuality. Scandalous rumour tells
Of Soho gay-clubs and the Piccadilly arches.

The death of Orph
Or is he now become
Born-again Christian Krishna?
Metempsychosis and the geeta gospel°
Hallow the masturbatory beat.

He is most holy now. The Bassarids smell it.
They crowd around him, cinctured°
With gnetum° and ground-ivy. They have consumed
Muscaria° – tear him apart
Like a ripped kid, a wild mountain-roe.
Bloodied lips and teeth are chewing.

° **Gynandromorph**: having both male and female characteristics (a biological term).
° **metempsychosis**: reincarnation; **the geeta gospel**: the doctrines of the Hindu sacred text *Bhagavad-Gita*, in which the god **Krishna**, in human disguise, expounds the cycle of reincarnation and the quest for nirvana.
° **cinctured**: girdled.
° **gnetum**: pine (like ivy, sacred to Dionysus).
° **Muscaria**: *Amanita muscaria*, a type of 'magic mushroom' with hallucinogenic properties.

A shot rings out in the packed hall.
'I did it for love!' cries the sobbing killer,
Whom police and uniformed attendants
Are dragging away to Tartarus.

APOTHEOSIS

The head triumphantly stuck on a pine-pole,
Processed around like a mari llwyd°
Then flung in the river, a rain-charm;
As it floats downstream, it still babbles,
Cantillating;° it drifts to the sacred island
And there, enshrined, gives out
Ambiguous oracles.

His agents rake in the profits. The discs still sell,
And the plastic eidola, T-shirt vernicles.°

Lyra is stellified.° Maurice, wherever you are,
Here is your tall interpreter.°

O52 A. D. Hope, 'Orpheus', 1991°

Alec Derwent Hope, born 1907, Australian poet and critic, retired professor of English at Australian National University. A traditionalist in form, who draws heavily on mythological and biblical images, he has also been an outspoken cultural critic, defending the importance of poetry and the imagination.

Orpheus

Vox ipsa et frigida lingua

° **mari llwyd**: '*Singing with Mari Llwyd* (Holy Mary) is an old Welsh Christmastide custom . . . The chief character wears a white cowl and a horse's skull bedecked with ribbons and is accompanied by two or three fantastically dressed followers. They sing outside houses, demanding an entrance' (*Brewer's Dictionary of Phrase and Fable*).

° **Cantillating**: chanting.

° **eidola**: images, idols; **vernicles**: a piece of cloth bearing a holy image (the original vernicle was the napkin which, according to legend, St Veronica gave Christ to wipe his face on the way to his crucifixion, and which he returned with an image of his face imprinted on it).

° **Lyra is stellified**: according to one legend, Orpheus's lyre was placed in the heavens as the constellation Lyra.

° **Maurice . . . interpreter**: obscure; **Maurice** may be C. M. (Maurice) Bowra, Oxford classicist and authority on early Greek lyric and 'primitive song'.

° from *Selected Poems*, Pymble, NSW: Angus & Robertson, 1992. Reprinted by permission of HarperCollins Publishers.

A miseram Eurydicen! anima fugiente vocabat.
Eurydicen toto referebant flumina ripae.°

They said of Orpheus that when he was young
He was a poet enchanted by the keen
Edge of his own perception of the light.
As though quite simply from his lips had sprung
Effortless music and that they had been
Spontaneous echoes in his mind's despite.

Only much later in his life, they said,
After Eurydice died, forced to explore
Twice hell in vain he learned, in his despair
The ultimate measure of menace and of dread
The world may hold for each of us in store
And found another music to declare

What the heart knows. And it was only then
The whole world answered, hills and beasts and trees
Danced and the god of wine, lest he ensnare
With that delirium even the race of men,
Crazed, in his wisdom, the women of Thrace to seize
And tear him limb from limb. They rent him there,

Maddened, not even knowing what they had done.
It was too late! Even after his eclipse
His severed head still sang 'Eurydice'
And ever since that fatal song goes on
Sure sign that the heart's burden reached his lips
And poets renew its deathless harmony.

OTHER VERSIONS OF ORPHEUS

A brief listing of versions of the Orpheus story not contained in the anthology; it includes details of all texts mentioned in the introduction. The bibliographical format has been kept compact, and full details are not given for major writers whose works can easily be found in standard editions.

° ***Vox ipsa . . . ripae***: from Virgil's description of the head of Orpheus crying Eurydice's name as it floats down the river (**O2**, lines 525–7).

Classical/medieval

Clement of Alexandria. *Exhortation to the Greeks*, 1.
Euripides. *Alcestis*, lines 357–64.
Fulgentius. *Mitologiae*, 3. 10.
'King Orfeo' (a Shetland ballad), in *The Oxford Book of Ballads*, ed. Sir Arthur Quiller-Couch, Oxford, 1927.
Plato. *Symposium*, 179D–E.

Renaissance

B,R. [possibly Robert Barnfield]. *Orpheus his Journey to Hell*, London, 1595.
Barnes, Barnabe. 'Sonnet 52', in *Parthenophil and Parthenophe*, London, 1593.
Byrd, William. 'Come woeful Orpheus with thy charming lyre', in *Psalms, Songs, and Sonnets*, London, 1611.
Chapman, George. 'The Shadow of Night', lines 123–70, in *Skia Nuktos, The Shadow of Night*, London, 1594.
Chester, Sir Robert. 'A Dialogue', lines 296–302, in *Love's Martyr*, London, 1601.
Davies, John, of Hereford. 'Epigram 33: Of Maurus his Orpheus-like Melody', in *Wit's Bedlam*, London, 1617.
Drayton, Michael. 'Mr M.D. to the Author', in *The First Booke of Balletts* by [Henry Morley], London, 1595.
—— 'Sonnet 45', from *Idea*, in *Poems*, London, 1619.
Greene, Robert. 'Orpheus' Song', from *Orpharion*, London, [1590].
Guilpin, Everard. 'Epigram 34: Of Orpheus', in *Skialetheia*, London, 1598.
Jordan, Thomas. 'To his Faithful and Ingenuous Friend . . . J.T. Gent.', in *Wit in a Wilderness of Promiscuous Poesy*, London, [1665?].
Lovelace, Richard. 'Orpheus to Beasts: Song' and 'Orpheus to Trees: Song', in *Lucasta*, London, 1649.
Sidney, Sir Philip. *Apology for Poetry*.
Waller, Edmund. 'Of a Tree Cut in Paper', in *Poems*, ed. G. Thorn-Drury, London, 1893.

Restoration and eighteenth century

Colvil, Robert. 'To the Elegant Seraphina, Performing on the Piano Forte, at a Private Concert', in his *Poetical Works*, London, 1789.
Coppinger, Matthew. 'On a Wife', in *Poems, Songs and Love-Verses*, London, 1682.
Evans, Nathaniel. 'Orpheus and Eurydice', in *Poems upon Several Occasions*, Philadelphia, 1772.
Freneau, Philip Morin. 'The Prayer of Orpheus', in *Poems Written and Published during the American Revolutionary War*, Philadelphia, 1809.
Galt, John. *Orpheus: An Opera*, in *The New British Theatre*, vol. iii, London, 1814.
Garrick, David. *A Peep Behind the Curtain; or, The New Rehearsal*, London, 1767.

King, William. 'Orpheus and Eurydice', in *Some remarks on the Tale of a Tub. To which are Annexed Mully of Mountown, and Orpheus and Euridice*, London, 1704.

Monck, Mary. 'Romanez de Quevedo. Upon Orpheus and Eurydice. From the Spanish', in *Marinda. Poems and Translations upon Several Occasions*, London, 1716.

Pordage, Samuel. 'To Lucia Playing on her Lute', in *Poems upon Several Occasions*, London, 1660.

Steevens, George Alexander. 'Recitative', from *Songs, &c in the Cabinet of Fancy*, London, 1780.

Nineteenth century

Bourdillon, Francis. 'Eurydice', from *Sursum Corda*, London, 1893.

Buchanan, Richard Williams. 'Orpheus the Musician' (1864), in *Complete Poetical Works*, London, 1901.

Coleridge, Samuel Taylor. 'To William Wordsworth'.

De Tabley, Lord (John Byrne Leicester Warren). 'Orpheus in Thrace' (1865), in *Collected Poems*, London, 1903.

Gosse, Edmund. 'The Lost Lyre' and 'The Waking of Eurydice', in *New Poems*, London, 1879.

Landor, William Savage. 'The Descent of Orpheus' (adaptation of Virgil, 1794), in *Complete Works*, London, 1935, vol. xv.

Lang, Andrew. 'Rococo' (incorporating 'The New Orpheus to his Eurydice'), in *Poetical Works*, London, 1923.

Lowell, James Russell. 'Eurydice', in *Poems*, Boston, 1849.

Mackay, Charles. 'Orpheus in Thrace', from *Studies in the Antique*, 1864.

Morris, William. 'The Story of Orpheus and Eurydice' (1865–66), in *Collected Works*, London, 1910–11, vol. xxiv.

Patmore, Coventry. 'Orpheus', from *The Angel in the House*, London, 1863, book 2, canto 1.

Planché, James Robinson. *Olympic Devils; or, Orpheus and Eurydice*, London, 1831.

Shelley, Percy Bysshe. *Prometheus Unbound* (1820), act 4, lines 415–17.

Trench, Richard Chenevix. 'Orpheus and the Sirens', from *Alma and Other Poems*, London, 1885.

Turner, Charles Tennyson. 'Christ and Orpheus', from *Sonnets*, London, 1864.

Ward, F.W.O. 'Orpheus', from *English Roses*, 1899.

Williams, Isaac. 'Orpheus and Eurydice', from *The Christian Soldier*, 1849.

Wordsworth, William. 'The Power of Music' (1806).

Twentieth century

Alta. 'Eurydice', in *I Am Not a Practicing Angel*, Trumansburg, N.Y.: Crossing, 1980.

Ashbery, John. 'Syringa', in *Houseboat Days*, New York: Viking, 1977.

Binyon, Laurence. 'Orpheus in Thrace', from *Odes*, London, 1901.

Blackburn, Thomas. 'Orpheus and Eurydice', in *Into the Fire*, London: Putnam, 1956.

Breslin, Paul. 'Orpheus', in *Poetry*, 143 (1984).

Davie, Donald. 'Orpheus' (1977), in *Collected Poems*, Manchester: Carcanet, 1990.

Davison, Peter. 'Eurydice in Darkness' (1966), and 'Remembering Eurydice' (1984), in *Praying Wrong: New and Selected Poems 1957–1984*, London: Secker, 1985.

Day Lewis, C. 'The Revenant' (1943), in *Poems 1943–1947*, New York: Oxford University Press, 1948.

Devlin, Denis. 'A Dream of Orpheus', in *Collected Poems*, Dublin: Dolmen, 1964.

Du Plessis, Rachel Blau. 'Eurydice' (1973–4), in *Wells*, New York: Montenora Foundation, 1980.

Gaiman, Neil, *et al.* 'Thermidor' and 'Orpheus', in *The Sandman: Fables and Reflections*, New York: DC Comics, 1993.

Gascoyne, David. 'Orpheus in the Underworld' (1938), in *Collected Poems*, Oxford: Oxford University Press, 1988.

Goodman, Paul. 'Orpheus and Mozart' (1932), in *The Lordly Hudson: Collected Poems*, New York: Macmillan, 1962.

Goodman, Paul. 'Orpheus in the Underworld' (1937), in *Collected Stories*, vol. 2, ed. Taylor Stoehr, Santa Barbara: Black Sparrow, 1978.

Gregory, Horace. 'Orpheus', in *Medusa in Gramercy Park*, New York: Macmillan, 1961.

Heaney, Seamus. 'The Underground', in *New Selected Poems 1966–1987*, London: Faber, 1990.

—— 'Orpheus and Eurydice' and 'Death of Orpheus', in *After Ovid: New Metamorphoses*, ed. Michael Hofmann and James Lasdun, London: Faber, 1994.

Hoban, Russell. *The Medusa Frequency*, London: Jonathan Cape, 1987.

Hollander, John. 'Orpheus Alone', in *In Time and Place*, Baltimore: Johns Hopkins University Press, 1986.

Honig, Edwin. 'Eurydice', in *Spring Journal*, Middletown, CT: Wesleyan University Press, 1968.

Hughes, Ted. *Orpheus*, Chicago: Dramatic Pub. Co., 1973.

Humphries, Rolfe. 'The Thracian Women', in *Collected Poems*, Bloomington: Indiana University Press, 1966.

James, D. G. 'En Guise d'Orphée' and 'Phrases from Orpheus', in *Phrases from Orpheus*, Toronto: Oxford University Press, 1967.

Justice, Donald. 'Orpheus Opens His Morning Mail', in *Night Light*, Middletown, CT: Wesleyan University Press, 1967.

Kunitz, Stanley. 'In the Dark House', in *Atlantic Monthly*, 270. 4 (October 1992).

Levertov, Denise. 'A Tree Telling of Orpheus', from *Relearning the Alphabet*, New York: New Directions, 1970.

McKillip, Patricia. A. *Fool's Run*, New York: Warner, 1987.

Merrill, James. 'Orfeo' (1959), in *The Country of a Thousand Years of Peace*, New York: Atheneum, 2nd edn, 1983.

Moore, T. Sturge. *Orpheus and Eurydice* (1909), in *Poems*, vol. iii, London, 1932.

Powers, Tim. *Dinner at Deviant's Palace*, New York: Ace, 1984.

Redgrove, Peter. 'Orpheus Dies, and the God Seeks Out Silenus', in *After Ovid: New Metamorphoses*, ed. Michael Hofmann and James Lasdun, London: Faber, 1994.

Rich, Adrienne. 'I Dream I'm the Death of Orpheus' (1968), in *Adrienne Rich's Poetry*, New York: Norton, 1975.

Sheck, Laurie. 'Eurydice' and 'Eurydice in the Underworld', in *Io at Night*, New York: Knopf, 1990.

Simpson, Louis. 'Orpheus in the Underworld' and 'Orpheus in America' (1959), in *Collected Poems*, New York: Paragon, 1988.

Smith, Iain Crichton. 'Orpheus' (1974), in *Collected Poems*, Manchester: Carcanet, 1992.

Smith, William Jay. 'The Descent of Orpheus' (1951), in *Collected Poems, 1939–1989*, New York: Scribners, 1990.

Snodgrass, W. D. 'Orpheus', in *Heart's Needle*, New York: Knopf, 1972.

Voigt, Ellen Bryant. 'Song and Story', in *Atlantic Monthly*, 269.5 (May 1992).

Williams, Tennessee. *Orpheus Descending: A Play in Three Acts*, Norfolk, CT: New Directions, 1958 (revised version of *Battle of Angels*, 1939).

Winters, Yvor. 'Orpheus' (1934), in *The Poetry of Yvor Winters*, Manchester: Carcanet, 1978.

5

VENUS AND ADONIS

INTRODUCTION

The ancient Adonis

Compared with that of Orpheus, the myth of Venus and Adonis might seem an unpromising subject. Its central plot is blandly simple, its details blurred, breaking up into dozens of variant forms; its central male character is passive and colourless; its meaning seems elusive, shading off at the edges into dark regions of cult and ritual and metaphor. And yet this very elusiveness, the sense that the meaning of the myth lies somewhere beyond or beneath the simple events of the story, seems to be what has attracted writers like Shakespeare, Spenser, Shelley, and T. S. Eliot to make it the focus of some of the most ambitious mythological poetry in English.

The core of the story is simple. Adonis is a youth of striking beauty. (That is the one fact of the myth still popularly remembered – we still, if often ironically, call a handsome man 'an Adonis'.) Aphrodite or Venus, the goddess of love and beauty, falls in love with him, and they become lovers. Against her advice, he goes out hunting, and is gored to death by the tusks of a wild boar (or sometimes by a jealous god, Aphrodite's lover Ares/Mars, or her husband Hephaestus/Vulcan, in the form of a boar). Aphrodite mourns his death, and changes his body into a flower, the lovely but fragile anemone.

A fuller version extends the story to include Adonis's parentage and birth. He is the child of an incestuous union between a king and his daughter. Different versions give locations for the action – some in Cyprus, some in Assyria or Phoenicia or other parts of the Middle East – and different names for the characters; some of the variants are listed by the mythographer Apollodorus (**A5**). The most familiar version, Ovid's (**A4**), names them as Cinyras, king of Cyprus, and his daughter Myrrha. Myrrha is seized by an incestuous desire for her father (unexplained in Ovid, but said by others to be a punishment from Aphrodite for Myrrha's neglect of her worship or her parents' hubristic boasting about her beauty). With the help of her nurse, she smuggles herself in disguise into his bed. When Cinyras discovers the trick, he tries to kill her, but some friendly deity saves the pregnant Myrrha by transforming her into a myrrh tree; her tears become myrrh, the aromatic resin valued by the ancients for its perfume (and familiar to modern readers as one of the gifts brought by the three Wise Men to the infant Jesus – gold, frankincense, and myrrh). Adonis is then born, miraculously, from the trunk of the tree.

In some versions, Aphrodite's relationship with Adonis begins at this point: enchanted by the beauty of the newborn child, she takes him and, to keep him secret from the other gods, seals him in a box and gives him to Persephone. Persephone, however, cannot resist opening the box, is also enchanted, and refuses to give Adonis back. The matter is submitted to Zeus, who declares that Adonis shall divide the year between Aphrodite in the upper world and Persephone in the underworld (six months with each, or four months with each and four months at his own free choice).[1] The arrangement is voided, however, when Adonis is killed by the boar. One obscure source (a commentator's note on Theocritus) suggests that the contest between Aphrodite and Persephone took place at this point, after Adonis's death, and a few late classical sources refer to Adonis's resurrection; this is not, however, a part of the standard versions of the story.

As important as this sketchy and fragmentary story are the rituals associated with the cult of Adonis. Every year in spring or midsummer, in the Greek world and round the eastern Mediterranean, the death, and sometimes the resurrection, of Adonis were re-enacted. Almost always women took the chief role in the mourning. At Byblos in Syria, where the River Adonis (swollen in spring with red earth washed down from the mountains) was said to run red with the young hero's blood, women wept and lamented to the sound of flutes, but next day celebrated his resurrection and ascent to heaven. In Alexandria the pattern was reversed: the first day of the festival celebrated the sacred marriage of Aphrodite and Adonis, with images of the lovers laid on couches and surrounded by offerings of food and flowers; on the second day the image of Adonis was carried through the streets by mourners and cast into the sea – but with the promise that he would return again next year. At Athens in midsummer women climbed on to the flat roof-tops to mark Adonis's love and death with celebration and grief; Athenian men looked askance at these unofficial female rites, and a character in Aristophanes' *Lysistrata* complains of serious government business being interrupted by drunken women howling 'Weep for Adonis!' on the roof. As part of the ritual the women prepared 'gardens of Adonis': shallow pots of earth planted with grass and flowers, set on the roof-tops to grow and wither rapidly, and finally cast out to sea with the effigy of the dead god. They seemed to symbolise Adonis's sadly brief life; 'as fruitless as the gardens of Adonis' was proverbial. These rituals are as powerfully present in the literary tradition as the myth itself, suggesting that the story of Adonis is not something which happened 'once upon a time', but something which is continually being repeated 'as year succeeds year' (Bion, **A2**).

This was not originally a Greek cult: the legend and many of the rituals came originally from the Middle East. Adonis is a Greek version of the Asian god worshipped by the Sumerians as Dumuzi and by the Babylonians as Tammuz.[2] In Mesopotamian myths, Dumuzi/Tammuz was the lover and consort of the great mother goddess, variously known to different peoples as Ishtar or Astarte or Inanna. The sexual union of the goddess and her lover represented and maintained the fertility of the whole world, human, animal, and vegetable. Tammuz's death and Ishtar's grieving descent into the underworld brought famine and barrenness upon the world, averted only when the underworld gods released both the goddess and her lover to return to the upper world. Each summer throughout the Middle East women lamented Tammuz's death and prayed for his return; the prophet Ezekiel indignantly describes the 'abomination' of seeing 'women weeping for Tammuz' in the very porch of God's Temple in Jerusalem (Ezekiel 8: 13–15). From Mesopotamia versions of the myth migrated to Syria, to Cyprus, and finally to mainland Greece. In the process its plot altered, its names changed (the Greeks took the Semitic title *adon*, 'lord', for the hero's proper name), and its location became blurred (both Ovid and Apollodorus show a certain confusion about where the story takes place). The key question is how far its meaning too may have changed.

The Dumuzi/Tammuz legend is clearly a seasonal myth; like the Greek myth of Persephone, it represents the yearly death and renewal of the crops on which human life depends. English writers and scholars have often interpreted the Adonis story in the same light, and this reading was put into its classic form in the early twentieth century in Sir James Frazer's enormously influential *The Golden Bough* (**A25**). For Frazer the stories of Tammuz and Adonis and many other mythological figures were manifestations of a single grand, world-spanning myth of the dying and reviving vegetation god. His reading in turn shaped some of the major twentieth-century versions of the myth.

More recent scholars, however, have argued that Frazer too rashly read the meanings of the Mesopotamian myth into the Greek one. There is little evidence, they suggest, that the Greeks connected Adonis with vegetation, or that they believed in or cared about his resurrection. The Greek myth should be read on a more literal level – it is not about agriculture but about sex. For the French structuralist Marcel Detienne (1977), Adonis represents not fertility but sterility: Aphrodite's fruitless affair with the illegitimate, precocious, doomed Adonis is the opposite of fruitful marriage, as the fast-withering 'gardens of Adonis' are the opposite of proper agriculture. Others (Winkler 1990; Reed 1995) have speculated more positively on what the rituals of Adonis might have meant to the women who took part in them: a celebration of the dominance of Aphrodite over her passive male lover, or an opportunity to express uninhibited sexual joy and grief outside the constraints of patriarchal Greek marriage.

It is impossible to know for certain what meaning or meanings Adonis had for his original worshippers; as Jasper Griffin (1986b: 88) has commented, each interpretation of the myth is simply another myth. But the twentieth-century debate about the meaning of the Adonis story does reflect conflicting strains in the literary treatment of the story: on the one hand, an allegorical strain which treats the union of Venus and Adonis primarily as a symbol of natural fertility and renewal, with Adonis's resurrection as the key fact of the story; on the other hand, a tradition which focuses on the human love story, as embodying the joy and pain of sexual love, and ending with the tragic waste and fruitlessness of Adonis's death. Moreover, recent feminist readings bring out a key point about the myth: that Aphrodite/Venus is its dominant figure, whereas Adonis is largely a passive object, less a person than a body, to be desired when alive and mourned over when dead.

Appropriately, the first major classical treatment of Adonis focuses not so much on the myth as on the ritual. Theocritus's fifteenth Idyll (**A1**) describes the festival of Adonis in Alexandria at the court of his patrons, the Hellenistic rulers of Egypt: the images of Aphrodite and Adonis laid out on their marriage bed amid a profusion of splendid tapestries, miniature gardens, purple blankets, perfumes, cakes and puddings, music and song, to celebrate a night of love before the morning when Adonis must be carried out and drowned. Theocritus's sophisticated and witty twist is to portray the festival though the eyes of a pair of Alexandrian housewives. Their grumbling conversation about their mundane problems – the price of shopping, incompetent servants, traffic jams and street crime, above all the deficiencies of their husbands and the frustrations of married life – provides a comically down-to-earth counterpoint to the idealised serenity of the divine union.

Bion's 'Lament for Adonis' (**A2**) takes a very different approach, recreating the original mythic scene – Adonis's death, the grief of Aphrodite, the mourning of her followers and of the whole natural world – with vivid sensuous images and stark pathos. We have the sense of viewing a tragic event as it happens, but also the first enactment of a ritual that will be re-enacted over and over in years to come: 'There is time enough to come for your grief, / time to weep, time to sorrow, as year succeeds year.' Bion's 'Lament', combined with the elegy for Bion himself traditionally attributed to Moschus (**A3**),[3] inaugurates the traditional association between the Adonis myth and the genre of pastoral elegy, which I will discuss later in connection with Shelley's *Adonais* (**A21**).

The fullest narrative version of the story is Ovid's (**A4**), already summarised. The Venus and Adonis story is one of the narratives of tragic or forbidden love sung by the bereaved Orpheus, but it is told quickly and simply; Ovid seems more interested in the melodramatic tale of Myrrha's incest and the inset romantic tragedy of Atalanta and Hippomenes. The story itself is told with charm, quiet humour (especially in the image of Venus, in the classical equivalent of a track-suit, trying to keep up with her athletic toyboy), and gentle pathos at the end. There is no sense of ritual, or of religious or allegorical meaning: Ovid initiates the treatment of the story as a merely human one, unencumbered with symbolic significance.

Spenser, Milton, and Renaissance allegory

The story of Venus and Adonis, unlike that of Orpheus, was not particularly popular in the Middle Ages. Chaucer has a couple of passing references to the love of Venus for 'Adoun', and Lydgate tells the story of 'Adonydes' at tedious length as a warning against the dangerous wild beasts that lurk in the garden of Love. On the whole, though, medieval writers seem to see little potential in the story, either as romance (perhaps Adonis was too passive for a knightly hero) or as Christian allegory.

The Renaissance, on the other hand, enthusiastically embraced the allegorical possibilities of the Adonis myth. Mythographers like Abraham Fraunce, George Sandys (**A12**), and Alexander Ross (**A13**) took a typically eclectic approach to the meanings of the story. It could be read as a moral fable, illustrating 'the frail condition and short continuance of beauty' (Sandys), or warning 'them . . . who hunt too much after pleasure that the Devil is that great boar who lieth in wait to kill them' (Ross). Or it could be read as a physical allegory of natural processes. Adonis may be seen as the sun, warming and fertilising the earth in summer, then retreating into the cold of winter while the earth weeps rain and sheds leaves in mourning. Or he may be wheat, which lies buried in the earth for six months, then rises above the ground, until it is killed again by the boar/winter (Ross). Ross even suggests that the rebirth of Adonis-as-grain may be read as a symbol of 'our resurrection' – an echo of St Paul, who used the image of the sowing of grain and the springing up of wheat, in 1 Corinthians 15, as a parable for the way that the death of 'a natural body' may lead to the resurrection of 'a spiritual body'. Thus, as we saw with Orpheus, the same story may be read as a tale of human folly and sin, a neutral allegory of natural processes, or a profound symbol of Christian mysteries.

This coexistence of very different readings of the same myth is particularly clear in Spenser. Adonis is a key figure in book 3 of *The Faerie Queene*, which deals with love and sexuality, but he appears in strikingly different forms. In canto 1 (**A6a**) the tapestries in the castle of the promiscuous Malecasta gorgeously depict the story of Venus and Adonis – the goddess's sick passion, the 'sleights and sweet allurements' with which she seduces the innocent boy, her desolating grief at his death – in an image of the cruelty and wastefulness of illicit love. In canto 6 (**A6b**), however, the description of the Garden of Adonis, Spenser takes a very different approach.

In a sense this passage rests on an inspired mistake: Spenser has turned the miniature 'gardens' of earth and herbs, sacrified by the ancients to the dying god, into an actual place, a paradisal garden which forms a kind of pagan counterpart to the Garden of Eden.[4] At the centre of this paradise, the heart of Venus's realm on earth, the resurrected Adonis lies concealed in a secret bower, and there he and Venus enjoy one another in 'eternal bliss'. Moral criticism seems irrelevant here; as in the ancient myths, the sexual union of the great goddess and her lover generates the energies which sustain the Garden, which in turn represents the processes of reproduction and fertility that keep the entire world alive. Subject to mortality and yet never dying, perpetually transformed into new shapes, Adonis is 'the father of all forms'; he seems to be a symbol, not just of corn or vegetation, but of all living matter, all bodies. The Garden – which is ambiguously both an aspect of our own world and a separate realm where things exist before birth and after death – is the place where matter is united with spirit, body with soul, to create the creatures which are sent out into the world to take part in the endless cycle of birth, death, and reincarnation. It is an extraordinary passage, in which Spenser has grasped the significance of the ancient Tammuz myth and transformed it into a piece of complex, ornate, teasingly enigmatic Renaissance allegory.

Milton echoes Spenser in the epilogue to *Comus* (**A14a**), which describes a paradisal garden where Adonis lies among hyacinths and roses, tended by 'the Assyrian queen', Astarte/Venus. Here, however, Adonis is still wounded, and Venus sits 'sadly' on the ground beside him, while 'far above' soar her son 'celestial Cupid' and his love Psyche. By implication, Milton sets the merely physical love which Venus and Adonis represent, here and in Spenser, well below the spiritual love represented by Cupid and Psyche ('soul'). Nevertheless, they still have their place in paradise. Milton's attitude is far harsher in *Paradise Lost* (**A14b**), where Tammuz/Adonis, like his lover Astarte, figures as one of the devil's in Satan's party, and his 'dark idolatries' are said to have 'infected' the Jews. Milton's view of classical myth – as we have seen in his treatment of Orpheus – is exceptionally ambivalent. But such contradictions are not untypical of Renaissance mythography. Mythical figures who, if considered as real people or as objects of worship, must be sternly condemned, can be happily tolerated and even exalted if they are considered as allegories and metaphors.

Shakespeare and the Ovidian tradition

While the mythographers and poets like Spenser and Milton explored the Adonis myth as allegory, other Renaissance writers approached it in a more Ovidian spirit: as a story about real characters, to be told for the pleasure of the story and the qualities of wit, beauty, suspense, pathos and eroticism to be found in it. The most important of these writers was Shakespeare, in his 1,194-line poem *Venus and Adonis* (**A7**). Shakespeare and Christopher Marlowe, whose *Hero and Leander* appeared around the same time, jointly created the Elizabethan genre which later scholars have called the 'erotic epyllion': a 'mini-epic' poem, retelling a mythological love story (usually taken from Ovid) with an abundance of sensuous description, learned and witty digression, and highly wrought rhetorical display by both the characters and the narrator.

Shakespeare's crucial departure from the Ovidian story (apparently his original invention) is that Adonis refuses to become Venus's lover. It is easy to forget how bold and subversive this change is. The core of the ancient myth is that Venus and Adonis were lovers; the interpretation of their sexual union is crucial to all the allegorical readings of the story. The initial effect of Shakespeare's reversal is of a travesty of the myth: a love comedy in which the conventional roles of ardent male wooer and coy mistress are reversed, made more farcical by the fact that the goddess is strong enough to pick up the reluctant youth under her arm, yet cannot cajole or bully him into a sexual response. As it goes on, however, the poem evolves into a more serious debate, Venus arguing for the naturalness of sex and the need for the world to be peopled, Adonis virtuously or priggishly defending chastity and self-restraint. In the end Adonis, preferring hunting to love, is killed by the boar before the union is ever consummated, and Venus prophesies or curses that from henceforth all love shall be similarly unhappy. Despite Shakespeare's avoidance of explicit allegory, *Venus and Adonis* takes on a metaphorical dimension; it is in the end a serious philosophical poem about the nature of love, the conflict between sexuality and chastity, or (to put it in different and more Venus-like terms) between the life-instinct and the death-instinct. By contrast with Spenser's ebullient celebration of universal fertility, it ends on a note of sadness, failure, and sterility, as the flower that was Adonis withers in Venus's bosom.

The popularity of Shakespeare's *Venus and Adonis* is evident not only from the praise of contemporaries but also from parodies in Heywood's *Fair Maid of the Exchange* (**A10**) and the anonymous comedy *Return from Parnassus* – in each which a hapless male suitor attempts to appropriate scraps of Venus's speeches as chat-up lines. Moreover, it single-handedly altered the literary tradition. Of dozens of poems, songs, and plays which retell or allude to the Adonis story over the following half-century, the great majority take Shakespeare's revisionist version as their starting-point. Writers like Marlowe, Richard Barnfield (**A8**), Bartholomew Griffin (**A9**), William Barksted (whose epyllion *Myrrha, the Mother of Adonis* is explicitly a 'prequel' to Shakespeare's), Thomas Heywood, Richard Brathwait, H.C., Shakerley Marmion, and William Bosworth, all present a lovesick Venus courting an Adonis who is careless, scornful, disdainful, a 'boorish lad' (Brathwait) – 'Venus and Adonis, sad with pain, / The one of love, the other of disdain' (Marmion).

A few writers stick to the traditional story. William Browne (**A11**) and Henry Lawes, in their songs for Venus lamenting over Adonis's body, give no suggestion that her love was unrequited. And Robert Greene, in a pair of poems attached to his novella *Perimedes the Blacksmith*, presents an Adonis who is far from reluctant to accept Venus's attentions: in the first, a young prince adopts the persona of Adonis to defend his licentiousness ('I am but young and may be wanton yet'), while in the second, his aged counsellor warns him against Adonis's fate ('A lecher's fault was not excused by youth'). Such a heavily moralistic approach to the story, however, is exceptional. Despite the serious debate about sexuality and chastity that gradually emerges in Shakespeare's epyllion, on the whole the writers in the Ovidian/Shakespearean tradition are less concerned with moralising over Venus and Adonis than with exploiting the beauty, sensuality, and pathos of their story.

'Soft Adonis': the eighteenth century

The Venus and Adonis story remained popular throughout the Restoration and eighteenth century. The classical sources of the story, Theocritus, Bion, Moschus, and of course Ovid, were repeatedly translated, adapted, and imitated. The story was also repeatedly given musical treatment: John Blow's opera (1684), Colley Cibber's masque (1715), Daniel Bellamy's cantata (1722), John Hughes's cantata (to music by Handel, 1735), Samuel Derrick's cantata (**A18**) and song (1755). Nevertheless, the period failed to produce any major original treatment of the theme to stand comparison with Spenser's or Shakespeare's.

Most eighteenth-century versions follow the Ovidian/Shakespearean tradition, treating the myth as a human story of joyous or unhappy love. Sometimes, as in Shakespeare, Venus and Adonis take on the status of archetypal lovers, models of sexual bliss: so Derrick's cantata contrasts their happiness with the discomfiture of the jealous and possessive Mars, and in Richard Savage's 'Valentine's Day' (**A17**) a startlingly graphic description of the mythic lovers' pleasure serves as an implied reproach to 'Chloe' who has denied the poet such joys.[5] On a more trivial level, Venus and Adonis, as archetypes of female and male beauty, can be turned to the purposes of courtly flattery: so Aphra Behn, in 1685, describes James II as a compound of Mars and Adonis ('The goddess here might all her wish enjoy – / The rough stern hero in the charming boy!'), while Samuel Whyte in 1722, even more improbably, compares the marriage of George III and Queen Charlotte to that of Adonis and Venus.

In some Restoration treatments of Adonis a new note is heard, of satirical contempt. This seems to reflect a new, macho assumption, foreign to the Renaissance, that excessive beauty in a man is unmanly, and that to be admired by women is contemptible. Hugh Crompton's 'Masque of Adonis' (1657) gently mocks the frenzied impatience of a female audience for the appearance of 'Adonis our moan'; Thomas Brown's 'The Ladies' Lamentation for their Adonis' (*c.*1700?) more nastily celebrates the political murder of an actor ('the Player Adonis'), whose popularity among women, Brown implies, is just one more reason for satisfaction at his death. Gradually in the eighteenth century 'Adonis' takes on connotations of effeminacy; Pope, for instance, consistently uses the name for an effeminate courtier, especially his arch-enemy, the homosexual Lord Harvey.[6] This conception can be seen colliding with the Shakespearean one when William Mason describes a youth as being handsome as Adonis, 'Yet not like that rough woman-hater; / No, he was half a *petit-maitre*' – that is, a dandy or fop.

In 1749 the poet and critic Joseph Warton, welcoming a new translation of Pindar's *Odes*, wrote:

> Away, enervate bards, away,
> Who spin the silken courtly lay
> As wreaths for some vain Louis' head,
> Or mourn some soft Adonis dead:

No more your polished lyrics boast,
In English Pindar's strength o'erwhelmed and lost.

This is what the Adonis theme had come down to in the mid-eighteenth century: damnned by association with effeminacy and flattery, it was now a byword for merely trivial, insubstantial court poetry. From this low point it was the achievement of the Romantics, especially Shelley, to restore the myth to something of its former stature.

Romantic revival: Shelley and the pastoral elegy

Towards the end of the eighteenth century, a new interest in myth caused both scholars and writers to look seriously once again at the meanings of the Venus and Adonis story. Once again the allegorical tradition rose to the fore: Adonis was now seen once again as the dying and revived god, and his myth as a symbol of resurrection.

Perhaps the first work to take this approach was *The Botanic Garden* (**A19**), Erasmus Darwin's extraordinary poetic exposition of geology, biology, and botany. It is no doubt misleading to include Darwin in a discussion of the Romantics, but he is a hard figure to classify: his style and didactic form are thoroughly Augustan, his scientific interests look foward to the Victorian era and the researches of his grandson Charles Darwin, while his faith in myth as a vehicle for scientific truth harks back to Bacon and the Renaissance mythographers. Darwin's treatment of Adonis is particularly close to Spenser's in the Gardens of Adonis episode. Adonis is the embodiment of living matter; his descent to the underworld and his resurrection symbolise the endless cycle by which dead and decaying animal and vegetable matter is reabsorbed into the soil to fertilise new life.

If Darwin belongs to the allegorical tradition of Spenser, John Keats's *Endymion* (**A20**) is an epyllion in the tradition of Shakespeare's *Venus and Adonis* – though with hints of a cloudy underlying allegory. There is little trace of allegory, however, in the concrete physicality of Keats's Adonis or the sensuous evocation of the smells, tastes, textures, colours and sounds of his bower; and little sense of mythic grandeur in the comically unimpressed account of the love affair given by one of Venus's cupids ('I was half glad . . . When the boar tusked him'). Nevertheless, Keats's version of the story, by which Adonis after his death is permitted to spend six months in enchanted sleep and six months in the company of Venus, does once again foreground the ideas of death and resurrection.

The greatest Romantic treatment of the myth is Percy Bysshe Shelley's *Adonais* (**A21**), an elegy for the death of Keats. Shelley's use of the Adonis story was no doubt partly suggested by Keats's own use of it in *Endymion*. At the same time, he was explicitly imitating two classical works, Bion's lament for Adonis (**A2**) and Moschus's lament for Bion (**A3**), both of which he had translated; and in doing so, he was tapping into an ancient and complex literary tradition which links the Adonis legend with the genre of pastoral elegy for a dead poet.

Bion and Moschus were both writing in the pastoral genre created by their predecessor Theocritus, about an idealised rural world in which shepherds and goatherds spend their time piping and singing about their loves, jealousies, and griefs. Pastoral lends itself to funeral elegy, partly because the genre's frank artificiality helps to distance and formalise grief; and the implicit metaphor of shepherd-as-poet makes it particularly appropriate to an elegy for a poet. So Moschus portrays Bion as a shepherd piping to his flock; he shows the whole natural world as mourning and indeed dying in sympathy with the poet's death; he invokes the deaths of earlier great poets; he questions divine justice . . . all elements that became conventions of the genre. Moschus alludes only briefly to Adonis and the grief of Aphrodite at his death; nevertheless, the connections of the poem to Bion's lament for Adonis, and the association of Adonis with ritualised mourning and with the themes of death and resurrection, meant that the Adonis myth became closely entwined with the tradition of pastoral elegy.

The most famous of English elegies, Milton's *Lycidas*, never explicitly refers to Adonis; nevertheless, some critics have argued that the myth underlies its images of the cycle of the seasons and the death and revival of vegetation, and its contrast between burial in the soil and the bleak decay of Lycidas's corpse as it tosses (like Adonis) on the sea. Milton both uses and questions the conventions of the genre, switching between pagan and Christian perspectives; his final dramatic shift in tone – 'Weep no more, sad shepherds, weep no more, / For Lycidas your sorrow is not dead' – leads to both a Christian vision of Lycidas's soul in heaven and a pagan vision of him as 'the genius [guardian spirit] of the shore'. Milton's brilliant handling of the genre, however, was not matched by its increasingly routine use through the seventeenth and eighteenth centuries to honour every VIP's death. Two Restoration examples, John Oldham's elegy for Rochester as 'Bion' (**A15**) and Thomas Andrews's elegy for Oldham as 'Adonis' (**A16**), suggest both the routineness and the potential incongruity of the convention.

Shelley, however, like Milton, rethinks and reinvigorates the conventions of the genre and of the myth. He establishes his departure from the original Adonis myth by two bold changes of name: the hero is not Adonis but 'Adonais' (suggesting the Hebrew *Adonai*, Lord God); and the chief mourner is not Venus, Adonis's lover, but Urania, Adonais's mother. In early drafts the mourner was identified allegorically as 'great Poesy', but 'Urania' is a more resonant name, fusing the figure of Aphrodite Urania (the goddess of heavenly rather than earthly love) with that of Urania the muse, especially the 'heavenly muse' invoked by Milton in *Paradise Lost* (see **O20d**). Shelley echoes elements in both Bion and Moschus, but pervasively turns the physical details of the ancient poems into allegories of thought and feeling: the poison which killed Bion becomes a symbol of the hostile criticism which destroyed Keats; the attendants who tend the body are not Loves but Thoughts, personifications of Keats's poetic creations; Urania wounds her feet, not on brambles but (almost grotesquely) on hard human hearts and tongues.

At the same time, Shelley goes beyond the consolations offered by the myth and the ancient poems. It is no consolation to Shelley that Adonais's grave once again produces flowers in the spring (stanzas 18–20): Adonais is not Adonis, the dying corn god, but a human being and a poet, and what matters is not the perpetual renewal of his physical body (as in Spenser or Erasmus Darwin) but the apparent annihilation of his mind and soul. The turning-point in the poem is Shelley's recognition (in stanzas 42–43) that Adonais/Keats is still alive in nature, not merely as recycled matter, but as a spiritual force, part of the universal mind and soul that animates nature and pushes it towards perfection. From that point the poem sweeps on to its visionary conclusion, in which Shelley seems to call for an abandonment of the material world for an ideal otherworld of pure thought and pure being. This is very far from the Adonis myth, which is deeply rooted in the material world; the conclusion of *Adonais* in effect repudiates and leaves behind the myth which was its starting-point.

'The grief of gods': Victorian and Edwardian Adonises

After Shelley's *Adonais*, the remainder of the nineteenth century and the beginning of the twentieth century produce few memorable reimaginings of the Venus and Adonis story. There are many passing and decorative allusions, especially in connexion with flowers; we are often reminded of Adonis's blood on the petals of the rose, Wordsworth's 'Love Lies Bleeding' associates Adonis with the drooping petals of that flower, and De Tabley in 'Lines to a Ladybird' creates a whimsical myth of origin for the insects as drops of blood from Venus' wounded heel.

More extended Victorian retellings stress the story's sadness, lingering over Adonis's death and Venus's grief. Unlike Renaissance and eighteenth-century versions which tend to treat the characters as merely human, Victorian versions restore them to the grandeur of divinity, finding the irony and pathos of the story in the image of the all-powerful goddess brought down by the pains of mortal love. Venus/Aphrodite often becomes the focus or speaker of the poem: so Robert Bulwer-Lytton (**A22**) has her refusing to despair even though the world is locked in icy winter; R. W. Buchanan has her riding the sun's chariot, searching the earth for signs of Adonis's resurrection. Katharine Bradley and Edith Cooper (writing as 'Michael Field') show the proud goddess reduced to mere womanhood, 'torn / By mortal pangs, to inmost godhead slain', as she confronts 'All those immortal limbs can learn of death'; very similarly, Rupert Brooke in 1910 shows Venus's 'one eternal instant' of joy shattered by Adonis's death, as 'The immortal limbs flashed to the human lover, / And the immortal eyes to look on death'.

In some late nineteenth-century versions we sense, behind the lament for Adonis, the pathos of the fading away of the classical gods and their myths in an unsympathetic modern world. In De Tabley's 'Lament for Adonis' (**A23**), Adonis does not rise from the dead, and indifferent nature fails to answer the traditional call to lament for him:

Nature is greater than the grief of gods,
And Pan prevails, while dynasties in heaven
Rule out their little eons and resign
The thunder and the throne to younger hands.

A similar melancholy and world-weariness pervades Wilfrid Scawen Blunt's poem (**A24**), in which Adonis dies because 'the gods did love [him]', and so took him from the world before the perfection of his youth could be marred by age. 'The Gardens of Adonis' for John Payne (1902) are a place of dreamy peace and silence where wounded love can be laid to sleep – a place far removed from the bustling fertility of Spenser's gardens. By the end of the nineteenth century the Adonis legend has become an affair of sweetly sad nostalgia. In the early twentieth century, however, the violent and earthy aspects of the legend are brought back into startling focus.

Frazer and the dying god in the twentieth century

This latest resurrection of Adonis was largely the work of the classical scholar and anthropologist Sir James George Frazer in *The Golden Bough: A Study of Magic and Religion*, published in a series of volumes over twenty-five years from 1890 to 1915 (**A25**). Central to Frazer's encyclopaedic and sprawling study are the linked figures of the 'dying god', whose death and resurrection embodies and maintains the cycle of life, and the sacred and sacrificial king, who represents the god and whose life is sacrificed (literally or symbolically) to maintain the prosperity of his people. The volumes *Adonis, Attis, Osiris* (1906) link the three deities as lovers of the great goddess and embodiments of the decay and regrowth of plants and crops; later volumes take in other dying and resurrected deities such as Demeter and Persephone, Dionysus, Odin, Balder, and Christ. The rationalist Frazer implicitly challenges Christianity by suggesting that Christ's resurrection is just another example of a widespread mythic pattern. The literary appeal of Frazer's writing, perhaps, comes from his combination of scientific detachment and witty scepticism about the follies of 'magic and religion' with a poetic appreciation of the beauty of the ancient myths and rituals. Ironically, as we have seen, modern scholars are sceptical of Frazer's own methods and conclusions, and regard *The Golden Bough* as a work more of literature than of science. But its literary impact is undeniable: its account of the mythological vision of the world inspired many of the major 'modernist' writers of the earlier twentieth century, including Yeats, Eliot, Joyce, Lawrence, and Pound (see Vickery 1973).

T. S. Eliot drew both upon Frazer ('Anyone who is acquainted with these works,' he notes, 'will immediately recognise in the poem certain references to vegetation ceremonies') and upon Jessie L. Weston's study of the Holy Grail legends, *From Ritual to Romance*, in creating the landscape of *The Waste Land* (**A27**): an arid, sterile wilderness ruled by a sick and impotent king, imaging the spiritual, intellectual, political and sexual wasteland of the western world after the First

World War. Despite repeated 'references to vegetation ceremonies' there is little sign of rebirth in the poem's opening section, 'The Burial of the Dead': seeds huddle underground fearing the ordeal of birth, the clairvoyant Madame Sosostris cannot 'find / The Hanged Man' (the dying god/Christ) in her tarot pack, and the idea of resurrection arouses horror rather than hope: 'That corpse you planted last year in your garden, / Has it begun to sprout?' Later in the poem there are hints of possible regeneration – especially in the images of 'death by water', which echo the floating of the figure of Adonis out to sea – but it ends with no clear sign of change. Though Eliot never names Adonis, we may read this as a world in which the dying god does not rise from the dead, in which (in the absence of the goddess and her lover) sexuality has become barren, bored, and sordid, and human beings are locked into a perpetual living death. Ezra Pound, Eliot's friend and editor of *The Waste Land*, makes a more positive use of the figure of Adonis in his *Cantos*. In this immense, shapeless, almost impenetrable work, written intermittently between 1917 and 1970, and mainly concerned with diagnosing the political and economic corruptions of modern society, the rituals of Adonis seem to stand for an older way of life more in harmony with nature – in Canto 47, for instance, where 'the sea is streaked red with Adonis' as lighted lamps float seaward, and 'Wheat shoots rise new by the altar, / flower from the swift seed.'

Archibald McLeish's 'The Pot of Earth' (**A28**) is more equivocal about the 'natural' values embodied in the Adonis story. The poem, which takes its title and epigraph from Frazer's discussion of the 'Gardens of Adonis' and repeatedly invokes images of the rituals of the dying god, falls into three sections describing a young woman's childhood and puberty ('The Sowing of the Dead Corn'), marriage and pregnancy ('The Shallow Grass'), childbirth and death ('The Carrion Corn'). The poem creates a sense of an individual human being caught up in the ancient, inescapable cycle of 'birth, copulation, and death', but also of her frightened, helpless rebellion against that cycle: 'why, then, must I hurry? / There are things I have to do / More than just to live and die / More than just to die of living.' As Shelley lamented in *Adonais*, nature, in its cycle of endless self-perpetuation, seems indifferent to the human mind and its aspirations. At the end of the poem an Eliotesque voice expounds the meaning of the myth:

> Listen, I will interpret to you. . . .
> I will show you the body of the dead god bringing forth
> The corn. I will show you the reaped ear
> Sprouting.
>   Are you contented? Are you answered?

The question seems very much an open one.

H.D. and Yeats also, in rather different ways, use the myth to symbolise aspects of human experience. H.D. (**A26**), addressing Adonis, declares that 'Each of us like you / has died once': we have all undergone the experience of emotional death and rebirth, symbolised in the dead autumn leaf which yet shines more gloriously than beaten gold, and so all participate in Adonis's godhead. For Yeats, in 'A Woman Young and Old' (**A29**), the recognition is more painful. His female speaker, again in an autumnal setting 'At wine-dark midnight in the sacred wood', is angrily grieving over her loss of youth and beauty when she encounters the procession of the dying god Adonis, and shockingly recognises him as her own lost lover – 'no fabulous symbol . . . But my heart's victim and its torturer'. As in Shakespeare, the Venus–Adonis relationship becomes a perennial symbol of the pain and tragedy of love.

The modernist fascination with the dying god was at its height in the 1920s and 1930s. In the later twentieth century versions of the Adonis myth have been rarer, and with little sense of shared concerns or dialogue between them. It is hard to see any pattern in the diversity of (for instance) John Heath-Stubbs's pastoral elegy 'Wounded Tammuz' (1942); Kenneth Rexroth's contrasted visions of 'Adonis in Winter' and 'Adonis in Summer' (1944; **A30**); Daryl Hine's love poem 'The Wound' (1957); and Constantine Trypanis's surreal 'Elegies of a Glass Adonis' (1972). W.H. Auden and Chester Kallman's opera *The Bassarids* (1963) includes a comic intermezzo, 'The Judgement of Calliope', which dramatises that rare version of the legend in which the Muse Calliope arbitrates the rival claims of Aphrodite and Persephone to Adonis; and Carol Orlock's novel *The Goddess Letters* includes Persephone's own account of the love affair. Ted Hughes's *Shakespeare and the Goddess of Complete Being*, a work poised between criticism and mythmaking, argues that the Venus and Adonis myth is the key to Shakespeare's entire artistic vision. These scattered and diverse texts suggest that the later twentieth century is another fallow period for the Adonis myth; but its history leaves little doubt that, at some point, it will make yet another seasonal return.

Notes

1 In another version, recorded by the Roman mythographer Hyginus (*De astronomia*, 7. 2. 3), Zeus diplomatically referred the dispute to the Muse Calliope, and her compromise judgement so infuriated Aphrodite that she stirred up the Bacchantes to kill Calliope's son Orpheus. This variant did not become an accepted part of either story, but it demonstrates the web of unexpected connexions that can always sprout between myths.

2 There are a number of variant spellings: Tamuz, Thammuz, Thamus . . .

3 As noted in the headnote to the poem, the attribution is probably wrong, but (since the author is otherwise nameless) it is a convenient fiction.

4 Other Renaissance writers, perhaps following Spenser, made the same assumption: not only Milton (discussed below), but also Giles Fletcher ('Adonis' garden was to this but vain'), and Ben Jonson (the courtier Fastidious Brisk in *Every Man Out of His Humour* boasts that 'the Hesperides, the Insulae Fortunatae, Adonis' gardens' were all merely 'imperfect figures' of the perfection of Queen Elizabeth's court). Shakespeare is closer to the classical image when in *1 Henry VI* the French Dauphin tells Joan of Arc that her 'promises are like Adonis' gardens, / That one day bloomed and fruitful were the next' (1. 8. 6–7) – the ironic implication that they will wither equally fast is obvious.

5 The erotic connotations of 'Adonis' in the eighteenth century are suggested by a potent drink known as 'Spirit of Adonis' – or, more popularly, 'Strip-me-naked' or 'Lay-me-down-softly' (Tucker 1967: 55).

6 I cannot resist quoting the couplet in which Pope gleefully imagines how difficult courtly gambling would be in a barter economy: '[Shall] soft Adonis, so perfumed and fine, / Drive to St James's a whole herd of swine?' ('Epistle to Bathurst', lines 61–2).

TEXTS

A1 Theocritus, Idyll 15: The Festival of Adonis, third century BC. Trans. Francis Fawkes, 1767°

Theocritus, Hellenistic Greek poet of the third century BC, was born in Sicily but spent much of his career on the island of Cos and in Alexandria, the capital of Egypt, where he worked at the court of King Ptolemy II Philadelphus. His major works are the *Idylls* (the name originally meant something like 'short pieces' or 'sketches'). Theocritus is most famous in European literature as the creator of the pastoral genre, and many of the idylls are set in a pastoral world of shepherds and goatherds; but others, like this one, have an urban setting. In Idyll 15 two suburban housewives, Gorgo and Praxinoe, visit the royal palace of Alexandria to take part in the festival of Adonis. The eighteenth-century translation by Francis Fawkes, 1720–77, catches some of the colloquial ease of the dialogue.

GORGO: Pray, is Praxinoe° at home?
EUNOE:° Dear Gorgo, yes – how late you come!
PRAXINOE: Well! is it you? Maid, bring a chair
And cushion.
GORGO: Thank you.
PRAXINOE: Pray sit there.
GORGO: Lord bless me! what a bustling throng!
I scarce could get alive along.
In chariots such a heap of folks!
And men in arms, and men in cloaks –
Besides I live so distant hence
The journey really is immense.
PRAXINOE: My husband – heaven his senses mend! –
Here will inhabit the world's end,
This horrid house, or rather den,
More fit for savages than men.
This scheme with envious aim he labours,
Only to separate good neighbours –
My plague eternal!
GORGO: Softly, pray,
The child attends to all you say;

° 'Idyllium XIV: The Syracusian Gossips', from *The Idylliums of Theocritus*, trans. Francis Fawkes, London, 1767, pp. 132–47.

° **Praxinoe**: four syllables: Prax-IN-oh-ee.

° **Eunoe**: Praxinoe's maid (modern editors give this line to Praxinoe herself).

Name not your husband when he's by –
Observe how earnest is his eye!
PRAXINOE: Sweet Zopy!° there's a bonny lad,
Cheer up! I did not mean your dad.
GORGO: 'Tis a good dad. – I'll take an oath,
The urchin understands us both.
PRAXINOE: (Let's talk as if some time ago,
And then we shall be safe, you know.)
This person happened once to stop
To purchase nitre at a shop,
And what d'ye think? the silly creature
Bought salt, and took it for saltpetre.
GORGO: My husband's such another honey,
And thus, as idly, spends his money;
Five fleeces for seven drachms he bought,
Coarse as dog's hair, not worth a groat.°
But take your cloak, and garment graced
With clasps, that lightly binds your waist.
Adonis' festival invites,
And Ptolemy's gay court delights:
Besides, our matchless queen,° they say,
Exhibits some grand sight today.
PRAXINOE: No wonder – everybody knows
Great folks can always make fine shows.
But tell me what you went to see,
And what you heard – 'tis new to me.
GORGO: The feast now calls us hence away,
And we shall oft keep holiday.
PRAXINOE: Maid! water quickly – set it down –
Lord! how indelicate you're grown!
Disperse these cats that love their ease –
But first the water, if you please –
Quick! how she creeps; pour, hussy, pour;
You've spoiled my gown – so, so – no more.
Well, now I'm washed – ye Gods be blest! –
Here – bring the key of my large chest.
GORGO: This robe becomes you mighty well;

° **Zopy**: a pet name for the child, Zopyrion.

° **drachms**: a Greek silver coin; **groat**: an old English coin worth four pennies.

° **our matchless queen**: Arsinoe, wife and sister of King Ptolemy II Philadelphus (the Ptolemies, originally Greek, adopted the Egyptian royal custom of brother–sister marriages).

What might it cost you, can you tell?
PRAXINOE: Three pounds, or more; I'd not have done it,
But that I'd set my heart upon it.
GORGO: 'Tis wonderous cheap.
PRAXINOE: You think so? – Maid,
Fetch my umbrella and my shade.
So, put it on. – Fie, Zopy, fie!
Stay within doors, and don't you cry.
The horse will kick you in the dirt –
Roar as you please, you shan't get hurt.
Pray, maid, divert him – come, 'tis late:
Call in the dog, and shut the gate.

[*In the street*]

Lord! here's a bustle and a throng –
How shall we ever get along!
Such numbers cover all the way,
Like emmets° on a summer's day.

O Ptolemy, thy fame exceeds
Thy godlike sire's in noble deeds!
No robber now with Pharian° wiles
The stranger of his purse beguiles;
No ruffians now infest the street,
And stab the passengers° they meet.

What shall we do? Lo, here advance
The king's war-horses – how they prance!
Don't tread upon me, honest friend –
Lord, how that mad horse rears an end!
He'll throw his rider down, I fear –
I'm glad I left the child, my dear.
GORGO: Don't be afraid; the danger's o'er;
The horses, see! are gone before.
PRAXINOE: I'm better now, but always quake
Whene'er I see a horse or snake;
They rear, and look so fierce and wild –
I own, I've loathed them from a child.
Walk quicker – what a crowd is this!
GORGO: Pray, come you from the palace?
OLD WOMAN: Yes.

° **emmets**: ants.
° **Pharian**: Egyptian (Praxinoe, a Greek settler, looks down on the native Egyptians).
° **passengers**: passers-by.

GORGO: Can we get in, d'ye think?
OLD WOMAN: Make trial –
The steady never take denial;
The steady Greeks old Ilium° won:
By trial, all things may be done.
GORGO: Gone, like a riddle, in the dark.
These crones, if we their tales remark,°
Know better far than I or you know
How Jupiter was joined to Juno.°
Lo! at the gate, what crowds are there!
PRAXINOE: Immense, indeed! Your hand, my dear:
And let the maids join hands, and close us,
Lest in the bustle they should lose us.
Let's crowd together through the door –
Heavens bless me! how my gown is tore!
By Jove, but this is past a joke –
Pray, good sir, don't you rend my cloak.
MAN: I can't avoid it; I'm so pressed.
PRAXINOE: Like pigs they justle, I protest.°
MAN: Cheer up, for now we're safe and sound.
PRAXINOE: May you in happiness abound,
For you have served us all you can. –
Gorgo! – a mighty civil man –
See how the folks poor Eunoe justle!
Push through the crowd, girl! – bustle, bustle –
Now we're all in, as Dromo said,
When he had got his bride in bed.°
GORGO: Lo! what rich hangings grace the rooms –
Sure they were wove in heavenly looms.
PRAXINOE: Gracious! how delicately fine
The work! how noble the design!
How true, how happy is the draught!°
The figures seem informed with thought –
No artists sure the story wove;

° **Ilium**: Troy.
° **remark**: take notice of.
° **Know better . . . to Juno**: i.e. they behave as if they knew everything, even the bedroom secrets of the gods.
° **protest**: declare.
° **Now . . . in bed**: in the original, 'as the bridegroom said when he shut the door'; **Dromo** is Fawkes's addition, and unexplained.
° **How true . . . draught**: How accurate and natural is the drawing!

They're real men – they live, they move.
From these amazing works we find,
How great, how wise the human mind.
Lo! stretched upon a silver bed,
(Scarce has the down his cheeks o'erspread)
Adonis lies – O, charming show! –
Loved by the sable Powers below.
STRANGER: Hist!° your Sicilian prate forbear.
Your mouths extend from ear to ear,
Like turtles° that for ever moan;
You stun us with your rustic tone.°
GORGO: Sure, we may speak! What fellow's this?
And do you take it, sir, amiss?
Go, keep Egyptian slaves in awe;
Think not to give Sicilians law.
Besides, we're of Corinthian mould,
As was Bellerophon of old:
Our language is entirely Greek –
The Dorians may the Doric speak.
PRAXINOE: O sweet Proserpina, sure none
Presumes to give us law but one!
To us there is no fear you should
Do harm, who cannot do us good.
GORGO: Hark! the Greek girl's about to raise
Her voice in fair Adonis' praise;
She's a sweet pipe for funeral airs:
She's just beginning, she prepares:
She'll Sperchis° and the world excel,
That by her prelude you may tell.

THE GREEK GIRL SINGS

O chief of Golgos, and the Idalian grove,
And breezy Eryx,° beauteous queen of Love!

° **Hist!**: Shh!
° **turtles**: i.e. turtle-doves.
° **rustic tone**: the Stranger objects to the women's **Doric** accent, which he compares to the monotonous cooing of doves. The **Doric** or **Dorian** dialect was originally spoken in the Peloponnese, the southern part of Greece, but spread by colonisation to other parts of the Mediterranean; Syracuse in Sicily – the birthplace of Gorgo and Praxinoe, and of Theocritus – was settled by colonists from the Greek city of **Corinth** (home of the hero **Bellerophon**). Most of Theocritus's poetry is written in Dorian dialect, which came to be regarded as the appropriate language for pastoral; to other Greeks it had a 'rustic tone', a suggestion of hicks from the back country.
° **Sperchis**: presumably a rival singer.
° **Golgos** and **Idalium** in Cyprus, and **Eryx** in Sicily, are places sacred to Aphrodite.

Once more the soft-foot hours, approaching slow,
Restore Adonis from the realms below;
Welcome to man they come with silent pace,
Diffusing benisons° to human race.
O Venus, daughter of Dione fair,
You gave to Berenice's° lot to share
Immortal joys in heavenly regions blest,
And with divine ambrosia filled her breast.
And now in due return, O heavenly born!
Whose honoured name a thousand fanes° adorn,
Arsinoe pays the pompous° rites divine,
Rival of Helen, at Adonis' shrine.
All fruits she offers that ripe autumn yields,
The produce of the gardens and the fields;
All herbs and plants which silver baskets hold;
And Syrian unguents flow from shells of gold.
With finest meal sweet paste the women make,
Oil, flowers and honey mingling in the cake;
Earth and the air afford a large supply
Of animals that creep, and birds that fly.
Green bowers are built with dill sweet-smelling crowned,
And little Cupids hover all around,
And, as young nightingales their wings essay,
Skip here and there, and hop from spray to spray.
What heaps of golden vessels glittering bright!
What stores of ebon° black and ivory white!
In ivory carved large eagles seem to move,
And through the clouds bear Ganymede to Jove.
Lo! purple tapestry arranged on high
Charms the spectators with the Tyrian dye;
The Samian and Milesian swains,° who keep
Large flocks, acknowledge 'tis more soft than sleep:
Of this Adonis claims a downy bed,
And lo! another for fair Venus spread!
Her bridegroom scarce attains to nineteen years,
Rosy his lips, and no rough beard appears.

° **benisons**: blessings.
° **Berenice**: mother of King Ptolemy and Queen Arsinoe, deified after her death in 270.
° **fanes**: temples.
° **pompous**: magnificent (not a derogatory word).
° **ebon**: ebony.
° **swains**: shepherds; wool from Samos and Miletos was famous for its quality.

Let raptured Venus now enjoy her mate,
While we, descending to the city gate,
Arrayed in decent robes that sweep the ground,
With naked bosoms, and with hair unbound,
Bring forth Adonis, slain in youthful years,
Ere Phoebus drinks the morning's early tears.
And while to yonder flood° we march along,
With tuneful voices raise the funeral song.

Adonis, you alone of demigods,
Now visit earth, and now hell's dire abodes:
Not famed Atrides° could this favour boast,
Nor furious Ajax, though himself an host;
Nor Hector, long his mother's grace and joy
Of twenty sons, not Pyrrhus safe from Troy,
Not brave Patroclus of immortal fame,
Nor the fierce Lapithæ, a deathless name;
Nor sons of Pelops, nor Deucalion's race,
Nor stout Pelasgians, Argos' honoured grace.

As now, divine Adonis, you appear
Kind to our prayers, O bless the future year!
As now propitious to our vows you prove,
Return with meek benevolence and love.

GORGO: O, famed for knowledge in mysterious things!
How sweet, Praxinoe, the damsel sings!
Time calls me home to keep my husband kind;
He's prone to anger if he has not dined.
Farewell, Adonis, loved and honoured boy;
O come, propitious, and augment our joy.

A2 Bion, 'Lament for Adonis', *c.*100 BC. Trans. Anthony Holden, 1974°

Bion was a lyrical and pastoral poet around the beginning of the first century BC; little is known about his life except that he was born near Smyrna in Asia Minor, worked in Sicily, and (according to the 'Lament for Bion') died by poisoning.

° **flood**: sea.

° **Atrides**: i.e. Agamemnon – the start of a rather ill-assorted list of heroes which Kenneth Dover calls a 'clumsy rampage through mythology'.

° from *Greek Pastoral Poetry*, trans. Anthony Holden, Penguin, 1973, pp. 167–70.

I weep for Adonis, cry, 'Fair Adonis is dead';
'Fair Adonis is dead,' the Loves echo my grief.
Sleep no more, Cypris,° shrouded in purple,
awake to this grief, and put on mourning,
beat your breast and tell all mankind:
'Fair Adonis is dead.'

I weep for Adonis; the Loves echo my grief.

Fair Adonis lies high in the hills, his thigh
holed by a tusk, white into white.
Cypris despairs as his breathing grows softer;
the blood flows red down his snow-white flesh,
the eyes beneath his brow grow dark,
the rose flies from his lip, and on it dies
the kiss that Cypris shall never know again.
Now the goddess longs for the kiss of the dead,
and he cannot feel the live touch of her lips.

I weep for Adonis; the Loves echo my grief.

Cruel, cruel was the wound in his thigh,
but crueller still the wound in her heart.
Loud is the baying of his faithful dogs,
loud the weeping of the Nymphs on the hill.
Aphrodite unbraids her hair, goes barefoot,
in tears, around the wood, her curls in tatters.
The undergrowth tears at her sacred flesh,
the brambles spill her holy blood, but on she runs,
her cries the louder, the length of the glades,
screaming for her Assyrian boy,
forever calling on her lover's name.
A dark pool of blood congeals round his navel,
the purple spreads up his breast from the thighs,
discolouring the nipples, once white as snow.

'Alas, Cytherea,' the Loves cry again.

Her gracious man has perished, and with him
her beauty. When Adonis lived,
Cypris was fair; her looks died when he did.
'Alas, poor Cypris,' from every summit;
from all the woods, 'Alas, poor Adonis.'

° **Cypris**: a name for Aphrodite, as goddess of Cyprus.

The rivers weep for Aphrodite's grief,
Adonis is mourned by the mountain streams;
all nature's flowers grow red with sorrow.
Cythera's island is everywhere filled,
its ridges, its glens, with songs of lament:
'Alas, Cytherea. Fair Adonis is dead,'
and Echo replies, 'Fair Adonis is dead.'
Who would not weep for Cypris' luckless love?

She saw, she took in Adonis' mortal wound.
It was not to be checked; she saw his thigh
drowning in blood, flung up her arms, crying,
'Wait, Adonis, my lost love, wait,
stay till I am with you one short last time,
till I have you in my arms, pressing lip on lip.
Awake, Adonis, just one brief moment,
for a kiss, last kiss, a kiss to live
as long as you have breath; breathe your last
into my mouth, breathe your soul into my heart,
till I've sipped the sweetness of your poison
to the dregs, drunk the lees of your love.
That kiss I will cherish as I would
the man himself, now fate takes you,
Adonis, takes you into exile,
distant exile on Acheron's shore,
within the domain of that harshest of kings:
while I, a god, live on behind you,
a wretched god, unable to follow.
Take him, Persephone, take my lover;
you have far greater powers than I,
and all that is loveliest falls to you.
For me all that's worst, all that's saddest,
unending; again I weep for my dead Adonis,
and I live, Persephone, in fear of you.
You are dead, my one love, dearest of men,
you are gone like a dream. Cytherea is widowed;
her girdle of love° lost its magic with you;
Love is lying idle and stays indoors.
Why were you rash? Oh, why went hunting?
How, oh how was so perfect a man

° **girdle of love**: according to Homer, Aphrodite had a magic girdle or belt which made the wearer irresistible.

enticed to take on the wildest of beasts?'
So Cypris lamented; Love echoes her grief:
'Alas, Cytherea. Fair Adonis is dead.'

Aphrodite sheds tears as Adonis blood,
drop matches drop; on the ground
they mingle, and bring forth flowers.
From the blood grows a rose,
from the tears an anemone.

I weep for Adonis; fair Adonis is dead.

Enough tears now, Cypris, enough for your man
as he lies in the woods. But it isn't right
to leave him there, alone among the leaves;
give him your bed, in death as in life.
For in death, Cytherea, he still has his beauty,
a beauty in death as a beauty in sleep.
So lay him now where he used to lie
on those same soft sheets, in that same gold bed,
where he shared your sacred sleep all those nights;
it is longing to bear his weight again.
Strew him with garlands, with flowers,
then leave them to die. Let all nature die,
now Adonis is dead. Anoint him
with Syrian perfumes, with oils;
let all fragrance fade, let perfumes all die,
for he was your perfume, and he now is dead.
There lies Adonis, wreathed in purple,
graceful Adonis. Love mourns; Love weeps;
the Loves have cut off their hair in sorrow.
Here someone has laid his bow at his side,
another his arrows, another his quiver.
One lays a feather. One looses his shoe.
Some bring water in a golden pail,
and bathe his thigh. One stands behind
and fans fair Adonis with his feather wings.

'Alas, Cytherea,' the Loves echo their grief.

Hymen has lit every torch at the door,
and sprinkled marriage garlands around it.
He sings no longer of wedding joys
but rather of grief, of Adonis' death.
The Graces weep over Cinyras' child,
saying one to the other, 'Adonis is dead.'

Their cries of sorrow have a sharper note
than their songs of praise. Even the Fates
weep for Adonis, and call out his name.
In their songs they weave him a life-giving spell
but it falls on deaf ears. Not by his own wish;
Persephone has him, and won't let him go.

Enough tears, Cytherea, enough for today.
No more wailing now or beating your breast.
There is time enough to come for your grief,
time to weep, time to sorrow, as year succeeds year.

A3 'Moschus', from 'Lament for Bion', *c.* 100 BC. Trans. Anthony Holden, 1974°

A lament for Bion's death, apparently by one of his pupils (see line 113). It was traditionally attibuted to the poet Moschus, but scholars now think this unlikely, as Moschus was a generation older than Bion; however, since the poem has for centuries been known as 'Moschus's Lament', I have stuck to the convenient if inaccurate name. The 'Lament' alludes only fleetingly to Adonis, but it is an important part of the tradition of pastoral elegy that leads to Shelley's *Adonais*.

Join, glades, my hymn of mourning;
Dorian° waters, lament with me;
weep, rivers, weep for Bion, for his beauty.
Now orchards, sorrow with me; sigh, groves;
flowers, breathe grief from your tight clusters;
now roses, deepen your red in mourning; and yours,
anemones; now hyacinth, let your lettering speak,°
your leaves chatter their grief.
The beautiful flute-player is dead.

Sing, Sicilian Muses, raise your song of grief.

Nightingales, as you sing, deep among thick leaves,
tell Arethusa,° Sicily's stream, that Bion

° 'Lament for Bion' from *Greek Pastoral Poetry*, trans. Anthony Holden, Penguin, 1973, pp. 187–91. Copyright © Anthony Holden, 1974. Reproduced by permission of the author c/o Rogers, Coleridge & White Ltd, 20 Powis Mews, London W11 1JN.

° **Dorian**: see note on Theocritus, line 134.

° **hyacinth, let your lettering speak**: the Greeks read the markings on the hyacinth's petals as the letters 'AI, AI' (alas, alas), in memory of the death of Hyacinthus.

° **Arethusa**: a Sicilian spring and stream; Sicily was the birthplace of Theocritus, who set several of his pastoral poems in its landscape, and hence it had become closely associated with pastoral.

is dead, Bion the shepherd; that, with him,
music has died, and all Dorian song has perished.

Sing, Sicilian Muses, raise your song of grief.

Swans of Strymon, lament; raise your song
at the water's edge, your song of sorrow;
sing as you would at death's approach. Tell
the Oeagrian maidens, tell all the Bistonian Nymphs:
the Doric Orpheus is dead.°

Sing, Sicilian Muses, raise your song of grief.

Now he will be heard no more
he that tenderly cared for his stock;
no longer will he sit and sing
alone among the oaks; but in the house of Hades
now must raise the song of Lethe.
And so the hills are silent; the cows,
wandering among the bulls, low mournfully,
and will no longer graze.

Sing, Sicilian Muses, raise your song of grief.

Bion, your sudden death brought tears
even to Apollo; the satyrs wept, and every Priapus
dressed in black; each Pan mourned your music;
all the springs bewailed it in the woods;
the waters changed to tears. Echo, too, is weeping
in the rocks, for she is silent, she may imitate
your voice no more. At your death
trees threw down their fruit, flowers
all wasted away. Now flocks no longer yield
rich milk, nor hives sweet honey.
In the honeycomb it dies of grief, and may no more
be gathered, since the day your honey perished.

Sing, Sicilian Muses, raise your song of grief.

* * *

All the Muses' gifts have died with you,
my herdsman; the sweet kisses of young girls,

° **Strymon**: a river in Thrace, the homeland of Orpheus; **Bistonian** and **Oeagrian** also refer to places in Thrace.

the lips of boys. Around your corpse
the Loves weep pitifully; and Cypris longs for you
much more than for that kiss
she gave Adonis as he, that day, lay dying.

This, most tuneful of rivers, is for you
a second grief; this for you, Meles,° another pain.
Homer, that first rich voice of Calliope,
has long been dead; men say that your great streams
were tears for your sweet son,
and that your grief quite filled the sea.
Now Bion: now you mourn another child,
and grief again dissolves you.
Both were cherished by fountains: for one drank
at Pegasus' spring,° the other at Arethusa's.
One sang of Tyndareus' lovely daughter,
of Thetis' great son,° and of Atreus' Menelaus;
the other sang neither of war nor tears,
but of Pan. His was a herdsman's voice;
he sang as he tended his cattle;
he would carve his pipes, and milk
his gentle heifers; he taught the young to kiss;
he nurtured Love as his own child
and roused the passions of Aphrodite.

Sing, Sicilian Muses, raise your song of grief.

Every glorious city, Bion, mourns you,
every town:° Ascra weeps for you
more than for Hesiod; Boeotia yearns for you
more than for Pindar; lovely Lesbos
grieved less for Alcaeus, Teos less for Anacreon;
Paros misses you more than Archilochus;
and Mitylene, who sorrowed for Sappho,
now grieves for your song. To Syracuse
you are a Theocritus; and Ausonia's lament
is this hymn of mine. For I am no stranger
to pastoral song, but a pupil of yours,
an heir to your Dorian style,

° **Meles**: a river near Smyrna, in Asia Minor, birthplace of Bion and (according to legend) of Homer.
° **Pegasus' spring**: Hippocrene, the spring on Mount Helicon, sacred to the Muses.
° **Tyndareus' daughter** is Helen of Troy; **Thetis' son** is Achilles.
° **Every glorious city . . . town**: a catalogue follows of famous Greek poets and their birthplaces.

honoured, when others inherited
your wealth, to be left your music.

Sing, Sicilian Muses, raise your song of grief.

Ah, when the mallows perish in the orchard,
or the green parsley, or the thickly blossoming dill,
they grow again, and live another year;
but we who are so great and strong, we men
who are so wise, as soon as we are dead,
at once we sleep, in a hole beneath the earth,
a sleep so deep, so long, with no end,
no reawakening. And so it is for you:
in the earth you shall lie, shrouded in silence;
whilst, if it pleases the Nymphs, a frog
may sing forever. I do not envy them
his music: there is no beauty in it.

Sing, Sicilian Muses, raise your song of grief.

Poison, Bion, poison came to your lips,
and you took it.° How could it touch
such lips without becoming nectar?
And what man on earth could be so vicious
as to mix poison and give it you
when you asked? He has poisoned music.

Sing, Sicilian Muses, raise your song of grief.

But justice comes to all. For me, this song
shall be my mournful elegy upon your death.
Had I been able to descend to Tartarus,
as Orpheus did, Odysseus, and once Alcides,°
then perhaps I would have come
to Hades' throne, and, if you sing for him,
listened to you, and to what it is you sing.
Let it be some song of Sicily,
for Persephone, some sweet country song,
for she too is Sicilian, she once played
on Etna's shores; she knows Dorian music;
your singing would not go unrewarded.
As once she granted Orpheus, for the rhythms

° **Poison . . . you took it**: it is not clear whether this is meant literally or metaphorically.
° **Alcides**: i.e. Hercules.

of his harp, the return of his Eurydice,
so shall she return you, Bion, to the hills.
Could my pipe ever match the magic of his harp,
I would myself have sung for you to Hades.

A4 Ovid, from the *Metamorphoses*, *c.* AD 10. Trans. A. D. Melville, 1986°

The story of Adonis is one of the tales which Orpheus sings 'Of boys beloved of gods and girls bewitched / By lawless fires who paid the price of lust', in book 10 of the *Metamorphoses*. Ovid tells the story of Venus and Adonis itself quite briefly. It is preceded by a much longer version of the story of Adonis's mother, Myrrha, and has inset into it a long version of the tale of Atalanta and Hippomenes, which Venus tells to Adonis. Our passage begins as King Cinyras discovers that the girl who has been sharing his bed is his daughter Myrrha.

Dumb in agony, he drew
His flashing sword that hung there. Myrrha fled.
The darkness and the night's blind benison°
Saved her from death. Across the countryside
She wandered till she left the palm-fringed lands
Of Araby and rich Panchaia's fields.°
Nine times the crescent of the moon returned
And still she roamed, and then she found at last
Rest for her weariness on Saba's soil.°
She scarce could bear the burden of her womb.
And then, not knowing what to wish, afraid
Of death and tired of life, she framed these words
Of prayer: 'If Powers of heaven are open to
The cries of penitents, I've well deserved –
I'll not refuse – the pain of punishment,
But lest I outrage, if I'm left alive,
The living, or, if I shall die, the dead,
Expel me from both realms; some nature give

° from *Metamorphoses*, trans. A. D. Melville, Oxford: Oxford University Press, 1986, 10. 474–739 (pp. 240–2, 247–8). Reprinted by permission of Oxford University Press.

° **benison**: blessing.

° **Panchaia**: a legendary eastern land rich in spices.

° **Saba's soil**: Arabia. (It seems a little odd that Myrrha could 'wander' on foot from Cyprus to Arabia, but Ovid is blending two traditions, one of which places the story in Cyprus, the other in Assyria.) .

That's different; let me neither die nor live!'
Some Power is open to a penitent;
For sure her final prayer found gods to hear.
For, as she spoke, around her legs the earth
Crept up; roots thrusting from her toes
Spread sideways, firm foundations of a trunk;
Her bones gained strength; though marrow still remained,
Blood became sap, her fingers twigs, her arms
Branches, her skin was hardened into bark.
And now the growing tree had tightly swathed
Her swelling womb, had overlapped her breast,
Ready to wrap her neck. She would not wait,
But sinking down to meet the climbing wood,
Buried her face and forehead in the bark.
Though with her body she had forfeited
Her former feelings, still she weeps and down
The tree the warm drops ooze. Those tears in truth
Have honour; from the trunk the weeping myrrh
Keeps on men's lips for aye° the name of her.

The child conceived in sin had grown inside
The wood and now was searching for some way
To leave its mother and thrust forth. The trunk
Swelled in the middle with its burdened womb.
The load was straining, but the pains of birth
Could find no words, nor voice in travail call
Lucina.° Yet the tree, in labour, stooped
With groan on groan and wet with falling tears.
Then, pitying, Lucina stood beside
The branches in their pain and laid her hands
Upon them and pronounced the words of birth.
The tree split open and the sundered bark
Yielded its living load; a baby boy
Squalled, and the Naiads laid him on soft grass
And bathed him in his mother's flowing tears.
Envy herself would praise his looks; for like
The little naked Loves that pictures show
He lay there, give or take the slender bow.

Time glides in secret and his wings deceive;
Nothing is swifter than the years. That son,

° **for aye**: for ever.
° **Lucina**: Roman goddess of childbirth.

Child of his sister and his grandfather,
So lately bark-enswathed, so lately born,
Then a most lovely infant, then a youth,
And now a man more lovely than the boy,
Was Venus' darling (Venus'!) and avenged
His mother's passion.° Once, when Venus' son°
Was kissing her, his quiver dangling down,
A jutting arrow, unbeknown, had grazed
Her breast. She pushed the boy away.
In fact the wound was deeper than it seemed,
Though unperceived at first. Enraptured by
The beauty of a man, she cared no more
For her Cythera's shores nor sought again
Her sea-girt Paphos nor her Cnidos, famed
For fish, nor her ore-laden Amathus.°
She shunned heaven too: to heaven she preferred
Adonis. Him she clung to, he was her
Constant companion. She who always used
To idle in the shade and take such pains
To enhance her beauty, roamed across the hills,
Through woods and brambly boulders, with her dress
Knee-high like Dian's, urging on the hounds,
Chasing the quarry when the quarry's safe –
Does and low-leaping hares and antlered deer --
But keeping well away from brigand wolves
And battling boars and bears well-armed with claws
And lions soaked in slaughter of the herds.
She warned Adonis too, if warnings could
Have been of any use, to fear those beasts.
'Be brave when backs are turned, but when they're bold,
Boldness is dangerous. Never be rash,
My darling, to my risk; never provoke
Quarry that nature's armed, lest your renown
Should cost me dear. Not youth, not beauty, nor
Charms that move Venus' heart can ever move
Lions or bristly boars or eyes or minds

° **avenged his mother's passion**: a hint of the idea, explicit in Apollodorus, that Myrrha's incestuous passion was caused by 'the wrath of Aphrodite'.

° **Venus' son**: i.e. Cupid.

° **Cythera's shores . . . Amathus**: places sacred to Venus: **Cythera** is an island near Sparta, **Cnidos** a city on the coast of Asia Minor, **Paphos** and **Amathus** in Cyprus.

Of savage beasts. In his curved tusks a boar
Wields lightning; tawny lions launch their charge
In giant anger. Creatures of that kind
I hate.' And when Adonis asked her why,
'I'll tell', she said, 'a tale to astonish you
Of ancient guilt and magic long ago.
But my unwonted toil has made me tired
And, look, a poplar, happily at hand,
Drops shade for our delight, and greensward gives
A couch. Here I would wish to rest with you'
(She rested) 'on the ground', and on the grass
And him she lay, her head upon his breast,
And mingling kisses with her words began . . .

Venus proceeds to tell the story of Atalanta, Hippomenes, and the golden apples. Atalanta was a brilliant athlete and runner who, having been warned by an oracle that if she married she would 'lose herself', declared that she would marry only the man who could defeat her in a foot race – the loser to be executed. Hippomenes, coming to take his chance in the contest, prayed to Venus, who gave him three golden apples. During the race he threw down each of the apples in turn; Atalanta could not resist swerving to pick them up, and so was beaten, not entirely to her disappointment. But Venus was offended when the triumphant Hippomenes forgot to offer thanks for her help. As the couple departed, she cursed them with a sudden attack of irresistible desire, which drove them to make love, sacrilegiously, in an ancient shrine of the mother-goddess Cybele. Cybele in turn prepares *her* revenge, and Atalanta's oracle is fulfilled . . .

'. . . The holy statues
Turned their shocked eyes away and Cybele,
The tower-crowned° Mother, pondered should she plunge
The guilty pair beneath the waves of Styx.
Such punishment seemed light. Therefore their necks,
So smooth before, she clothed with tawny manes,
Their fingers curved to claws; their arms were changed
To legs; their chests swelled with new weight; with tails
They swept the sandy ground; and in their eyes
Cruel anger blazed and growls they gave for speech.
Their marriage-bed is now a woodland lair,

° **tower-crowned**: Cybele was depicted wearing a turreted crown and riding in a chariot drawn by lions.

And feared by men, but by the goddess tamed,
They champ – two lions – the bits of Cybele.
And you, my darling, for my sake beware
Of lions and of every savage beast
That shows not heels but teeth; avoid them all
Lest by your daring ruin on us fall.'
Her warning given, Venus made her way,
Drawn by her silver swans across the sky;
But his bold heart rebuffed her warning words.
It chanced his hounds, hot on a well-marked scent,
Put up° a boar, lying hidden in the woods,
And as it broke away Adonis speared it –
A slanting hit – and quick with its curved snout
The savage beast dislodged the bloody point,
And charged Adonis as he ran in fear
For safety, and sank its tusks deep in his groin
And stretched him dying on the yellow sand.
Venus was riding in her dainty chariot,
Winged by her swans, across the middle air
Making for Cyprus, when she heard afar
Adonis' dying groans, and thither turned
Her snowy birds and, when from heaven on high
She saw him lifeless, writhing in his blood,
She rent her garments, tore her lovely hair,
And bitterly beat her breast, and springing down
Reproached the Fates: 'Even so, not everything
Shall own your sway. Memorials of my sorrow,
Adonis, shall endure; each passing year
Your death repeated in the hearts of men
Shall re-enact my grief and my lament.
But now your blood shall change into a flower:
Persephone of old was given grace
To change a woman's form to fragrant mint;°
And shall I then be grudged the right to change
My prince?' And with these words she sprinkled nectar,
Sweet-scented, on his blood, which at the touch
Swelled up, as on a pond when showers fall
Clear bubbles form; and ere an hour had passed

° **Put up**: roused from hiding.

° **Persephone . . . mint**: her name was Menthe ('mint'); according to another account, she was Pluto's mistress, and Persephone jealously trampled her underfoot before changing her into the herb.

A blood-red flower arose, like the rich bloom
Of pomegranates which in a stubborn rind
Conceal their seeds; yet is its beauty brief,
So lightly cling its petals, fall so soon,
When the winds blow that give the flower its name.°

A5 Apollodorus, from *The Library of Greek Mythology*, first or second century AD. Trans. Robin Hard, 1997°

The *Library* is a comprehensive brief handbook of Greek mythology. Traditionally ascribed to Apollodorus of Athens, a great literary scholar of the second century BC, it is now believed by scholars to be be written much later, probably in the first or second century AD; however, the traditional name has stuck. 'Apollodorus' here briefly summarises the various forms of the Adonis story.

Arriving in Cyprus with some followers, Cinyras founded Paphos, where he married Metharme, daughter of Pygmalion, king of Cyprus, and became the father of Oxyporos and Adonis . . . Through the anger of Artemis, Adonis died in a hunt while he was still a young boy, from a wound inflicted by a boar. According to Hesiod, however, he was a son [not of Cinyras but] of Phoenix and Alphesiboia, while according to Panyras, he was a son of Theias, king of Assyria, who had a daughter called Smyrna. And this Smyrna, through the wrath of Aphrodite (whom she had failed to honour), conceived a passion for her father, and enlisting the aid of her nurse, shared her father's bed for twelve nights before he realized who she was. But when he found out, he drew his sword and chased after her. As he caught up with her, she prayed to the gods to be made invisible; and the gods, taking pity on her, turned her into a tree of the kind known as a *smyrna* [or myrrh tree]. Ten weeks later the tree burst open and Adonis, as he is called, was brought to birth. Struck by his beauty, Aphrodite, in secret from the gods, hid him in a chest while he was still a little child, and entrusted him to Persephone. But when Persephone caught sight of him, she refused to give him back. The matter was submitted to the judgement of Zeus; and dividing the year into three parts, he decreed that Adonis should spend a third of the year by himself, a third with Persephone, and the remaining third with Aphrodite (but Adonis assigned his own share also to Aphrodite). Later, however, while he was out hunting, Adonis was wounded by a boar and died.

° **its name**: anemone (from Greek *anemos*, wind).

° from *The Library of Greek Mythology*, trans. Robin Hard, Oxford: Oxford University Press, 1997, pp. 131–2 (3. 14. 4). Reprinted by permission of Oxford University Press.

A6 Edmund Spenser, from *The Faerie Queene*, 1590°

(a) from Book 3, canto 1: Malecasta's Tapestry

Book 3 of *The Faerie Queene* is about the virtue of chastity (which means, for Spenser, faithful monogamous love rather than celibacy), and takes its characters on a tour through a range of good and corrupt forms of love and sexuality. Its heroine is Britomart, a female knight disguised as a man, in quest of her true love Artegall. In canto 1 Britomart comes to Castle Joyous, presided over by the lady Malecasta ('badly chaste' or 'unchaste'). The castle's air of decadent luxury is epitomised by the tapestry on the walls of its great hall, depicting the love of Venus and Adonis. (Later Malecasta, fooled by Britomart's masculine disguise, lecherously slips into her bed.)

34 The walls were round about apparellèd
With costly cloths of Arras and of Tours,°
In which with cunning hand was portrayèd
The love of Venus and her paramour°
The fair Adonis, turnèd to a flower –
A work of rare device and wondrous wit.°
First did it show the bitter baleful stour°
Which her assayed with many a fervent fit
When first her tender heart was with his beauty smit.°

35 Then with what sleights and sweet allurements she
Enticed the boy, as well that art she knew,
And wooèd him her paramour to be;
Now making garlands of each flower that grew
To crown his golden locks with honour due;
Now leading him into a secret shade
From his beauperes,° and from bright heaven's view,
Where him to sleep she gently would persuade
Or bathe him in a fountain by some covert° glade.

36 And whilst he slept she over him would spread
Her mantle coloured like the starry skies,

° from *The Faerie Queene*, London, 1596.
° **Arras** and **Tours**: centres of French tapestry-making.
° **paramour**: lover.
° **rare device and wondrous wit**: excellent design and wonderfully skilful execution.
° **stour**: turmoil.
° **smit**: struck.
° **beauperes**: companions.
° **covert**: hidden.

And her soft arm lay underneath his head,
And with ambrosial kisses bathe his eyes;
And whilst he bathed, with her two crafty spies°
She secretly would search each dainty limb,
And throw into the well sweet rosemaries
And fragrant violets and pansies trim,
And ever with sweet nectar she did sprinkle him.

37 So did she steal his heedless heart away
And joyed° his love in secret unespied.
But for she saw him bent to° cruel play
To hunt the savage beast in forest wide,
Dreadful of danger that mote him betide,°
She oft and oft advised him to refrain
From chase of greater beasts, whose brutish pride
Mote breed him scathe° unwares – but all in vain,
For who can shun the chance that destiny doth ordain?

38 Lo, where beyond he lieth languishing,°
Deadly engorèd of° a great wild boar,
And by his side the goddess grovelling
Makes for him endless moan, and evermore
With her soft garment wipes away the gore
Which stains his snowy skin with hateful hue.
But when she saw no help might him restore,
Him to a dainty flower she did transmue,°
Which in that cloth was wrought as if it lively°grew.

(b) from Book 3, canto 6: The Gardens of Adonis

Spenser's description of the Gardens of Adonis is at the heart of Book 3. Its context is an account of the birth and upbringing of two of his heroines, the loving Amoret and the chaste Belphoebe, the twin daughters of Chrysogone ('golden–born'). Chrysogone, a virgin, was made pregnant while she slept by the rays of the Sun; in her shame and confusion she retreated into the woods to

° **two crafty spies**: i.e. her eyes.
° **joyed**: enjoyed.
° **bent to**: determined on.
° **Dreadful . . . betide**: fearful of danger that might happen to him.
° **Mote breed him scathe**: might cause him harm .
° **languishing**: fading away.
° **Deadly engorèd of**: fatally gored by.
° **transmue**: transform.
° **lively**: as a living thing.

give birth. There the goddesses Venus and Diana, who have made an uneasy peace for once to search for Venus's lost son Cupid, instead come across the sleeping Chrysogone and her newborn daughters. The passage goes on to describe how the goddesses adopt a child each, and how Venus takes 'her' child, Amoret, to be brought up in the Gardens of Adonis, the centre of reproduction and fertility for the whole world.

(26) . . . So long they sought, till they arrivèd were
In that same shady covert whereas° lay
Fair Crysogon in slumb'ry trance whilere,°
Who in her sleep – a wondrous thing to say –
Unwares had borne two babes, as fair as springing day.

27 Unwares she them conceived, unwares she bore:
She bore withouten° pain that° she conceived
Withouten pleasure, ne her need implore
Lucina's aid.° Which when they both perceived
They were through wonder nigh° of sense bereaved,
And gazing each on other nought bespake.°
At last they both agreed, her (seeming grieved)
Out of her heavy swoon not to awake,
But from her loving side the tender babes to take.

28 Up they them took, each one a babe uptook,
And with them carried to be fosterèd.
Dame Phoebe to a nymph her babe betook°
To be upbrought in perfect maidenhead,
And of herself her name Belphoebe read.°
But Venus hers thence far away conveyed
To be upbrought in goodly womanhead,
And in her little Love's stead, which was strayed,
Her Amoretta° called, to comfort her dismayed.

° **whereas**: where.
° **whilere**: a while earlier.
° **withouten**: without.
° **that**: that which.
° **ne her need implore Lucina's aid**: nor did she need to call for the aid of Lucina (goddess of childbirth).
° **nigh**: almost.
° **naught bespake**: said nothing.
° **betook**: gave to look after.
° **of herself her name Belphoebe read**: named her Belphoebe after herself (**Bel** 'beautiful' + **Phoebe**, another of Diana's names).
° **Amoretta**: i.e. **Amor** 'love' with a diminutive feminine suffix.

29 She brought her to her joyous paradise,°
Where most she wones° when she on earth does dwell.
So fair a place as Nature can devise:
Whether in Paphos, or Cytheron hill,
Or it in Gnidus be,° I wot° not well;
But well I wot by trial° that this same
All other pleasant places doth excel,
And callèd is by her lost lover's name
The Garden of Adonis, far renowned by fame.

30 In that same garden all the goodly flowers
Wherewith dame Nature doth her° beautify,
And decks the garlands of her paramours,
Are fetched; there is the first seminary°
Of all things that are borne to live and die
According to their kinds. Long work it were
Here to account° the endless progeny
Of all the weeds° that bud and blossom there;
But so much as doth need must needs be counted° here.

31 It sited was in fruitful soil of old,
And girt in with two walls on either side,
The one of iron, the other of bright gold,
That none might thorough° break nor overstride;
And double gates it had which opened wide,
By which both in and out men moten° pass,
Th'one fair and fresh, the other old and dried.
Old Genius the porter of them was,
Old Genius, the which a double nature has.

32 He letteth in, he letteth out to wend,°
All that to come into the world desire.

° **paradise**: the word originally meant a walled garden or park; it came to be applied specifically to the Garden of Eden, and thence to Heaven itself. Spenser plays with the word's range of meanings.
° **wones**: lives.
° **Paphus**, **Cytheron** (Cythera), and **Gnidus** (Cnidos): all centres of the cult of Aphrodite/Venus.
° **wot**: know.
° **by trial**: by experience.
° **her**: herself.
° **seminary**: seed-bed.
° **account**: list.
° **weeds**: plants.
° **so much . . . counted**: as much as is necessary must be recounted.
° **thorough**: through.
° **moten**: might.
° **letteth . . . wend**: allows to go in and out.

A thousand thousand naked babes attend
About him day and night, which do require°
That he with fleshly weeds° would them attire.
Such as him list,° such as eternal fate
Ordainèd hath, he clothes with sinful mire°
And sendeth forth to live in mortal state,
Till they again return back by the hinder gate.

33 After that they again returnèd been
They in that garden planted be° again,
And grow afresh, as° they had never seen
Fleshly corruption nor mortal pain.
Some thousand years so doen° they there remain,
And then of him are clad with other hue,°
Or° sent into the changeful world again,
Till thither they return where first they grew:
So like a wheel around they run from old to new.

34 Ne needs there° gardener to set or sow,
To plant or prune, for of their own accord
All things as they created were do grow,
And yet remember well the mighty word
Which first was spoken by th' Almighty Lord,
That bade them to increase and multiply.°
Ne do they need with water of the ford°
Or of the clouds to moisten their roots dry,
For in themselves eternal moisture they imply.°

35 Infinite shapes of creatures there are bred
And uncouth° forms which none yet ever knew,

° **require**: ask.
° **weeds**: clothes (i.e. bodies).
° **him list**: he wishes.
° **sinful mire**: i.e. flesh (made from earth, and 'sinful' because of original sin).
° **returnèd been . . . planted be**: are returned . . . are planted.
° **as**: as if.
° **doen**: do.
° **hue**: form.
° **Or** seems illogical, as one would expect 'and'; possibly **or** = 'ere', i.e. 'Before they are sent. . .'.
° **Ne needs there**: Nor is there any need for.
° **increase and multiply**: see Genesis 1: 22.
° **ford**: stream.
° **imply**: contain.
° **uncouth**: strange, unknown.

And every sort is in a sundry° bed
Set by itself and ranked in comely rew:°
Some fit for reasonable souls° t'indue,°
Some made for beasts, some made for birds to wear,
And all the fruitful spawn of fishes' hue°
In endless ranks along enrangèd were,
That seemed the ocean could not contain them there.

36 Daily they grow, and daily forth are sent
Into the world, it to replenish more;
Yet is the stock not lessenèd nor spent,
But still remains in everlasting store
As it at first created was of yore.
For in the wide womb of the world there lies
In hateful darkness and in deep horrór
An huge eternal Chaos,° which supplies
The substances of nature's fruitful progenies.

37 All things from thence do their first being fetch
And borrow matter whereof they are made,
Which, when as form and feature it does ketch,°
Becomes a body, and doth then invade°
The state of life, out of the grisly shade.
That substance is eterne° and bideth° so,
Ne when the life decays and form does fade
Doth it consume° and into nothing go,
But changèd is and often altered to and fro.

38 The substance is not changed nor alterèd,
But th' only form° and outward fashion;°
For every substance is conditionèd°

° **sundry**: separate.
° **rew**: row.
° **reasonable souls**: i.e. those of human beings.
° **t'indue**: to put on.
° **hue**: form.
° **Chaos**: the mass of formless, confused matter which, according to Ovid (*Met.*, 1), existed before the world was created, and supplied its raw material.
° **ketch**: take, assume.
° **invade**: enter.
° **eterne**: eternal.
° **bideth**: remains.
° **Doth it consume**: is it consumed.
° **th'only form**: only the form.
° **fashion**: appearance.
° **conditionèd**: bound.

To change her hue and sundry forms to don
Meet for her temper and complexion:°
For forms are variable and decay
By course of kind° and by occasion,°
And that fair flower of beauty fades away
As doth the lily fresh before the sunny ray.

39 Great enemy to it and to all the rest
That in the Garden of Adonis springs
Is wicked Time, who with his scythe addressed°
Does mow the flowering herbs and goodly things,
And all their glory to the ground down flings
Where they do wither and are foully marred.
He flies about and with his flaggy° wings
Beats down both leaves and buds without regard,
Ne ever pity may relent° his malice hard.

40 Yet pity often did the gods relent
To see so fair things marred and spoilèd quite,
And their great mother Venus did lament
The loss of her dear brood, her dear delight.
Her heart was pierced with pity at the sight
When, walking through the Garden, them she spied,
Yet note she° find redress for such despite.°
For all that lives is subject to that law:
All things decay in time and to their end do draw.

41 But were it not that Time their troubler is,
All that in this delightful garden grows
Should happy be and have immortal bliss:
For here all plenty and all pleasure flows,
And sweet love gentle fits° amongst them throws
Without fell rancour or fond jealousy;

° **Meet for her temper and complexion**: appropriate for its physical make-up, its combination of qualities.
° **kind**: nature.
° **occasion**: necessity.
° **addressed**: armed.
° **flaggy**: drooping.
° **relent**: soften.
° **note she**: she could not.
° **despite**: injury.
° **fits**: impulses.

Frankly each paramour his leman knows,°
Each bird his mate, ne any does envy
Their goodly merriment and gay felicity.

42 There is continual spring, and harvest there
Continual, both meeting at one time;
For both the boughs do laughing blossoms bear
And with fresh colours deck the wanton° prime,°
And eke° at once the heavy trees they climb
Which seem to labour under their fruit's load:
The whiles the joyous birds make their pastime
Amongst the shady leaves, their sweet abode,
And their true loves without suspicion tell abrode.°

43 Right in the middest of that paradise
There stood a stately mount, on whose round top
A gloomy grove of myrtle trees did rise,
Whose shady boughs sharp steel did never lop
Nor wicked beasts their tender buds did crop,
But like a garland compassèd the height,
And from their fruitful sides sweet gum did drop
That all the ground with precious dew bedight,°
Threw forth most dainty odours and most sweet delight.

44 And in the thickest covert of that shade
There was a pleasant arbour, not by art
But of the trees' own inclination° made,
Which, knitting their rank° branches part to part,
With wanton ivy twine entrailed athwart°
And eglantine and caprifole° among,
Fashioned above within their inmost part,
That nether Phoebus'° beams could through them throng,
Nor Aeolus'° sharp blast could work them any wrong.

° **Frankly . . . knows**: Freely each lover makes love to his beloved.
° **wanton**: a recurring word in this passage: its range of meanings includes unrestrained, wild, luxuriant (of growth etc.), frivolous, lascivious, pleasure-loving.
° **prime**: spring.
° **eke**: also.
° **abrode**: abroad, publicly.
° **bedight**: adorned.
° **inclination**: (i) leaning, (ii) desire.
° **rank**: dense.
° **entrailed athwart**: interlaced between them.
° **caprifole**: honeysuckle.
° **Phoebus'**: i.e. the sun's.
° **Aeolus'**: i.e. the winds'.

45 And all about grew every sort of flower
To which sad lovers were transformed of yore:°
Fresh Hyacinthus, Phoebus' paramour,
Foolish Narciss that likes the watery shore,
Sad Amaranthus, made a flower but late,°
Sad Amaranthus, in whose purple gore
Meseems° I see Amyntas' wretched fate,
To whom sweet poet's verse hath given endless date.°

46 There wont fair Venus often to enjoy
Her dear Adonis' joyous company
And reap sweet pleasure of the wanton boy.
There yet, some say, in secret he does lie,
Lappèd in flowers and precious spicery,
By her hid from the world and from the skill°
Of Stygian gods,° which do her love envy;
But she herself, whenever that she will,
Possesseth him and of his sweetness takes her fill.

47 And sooth it seems they say;° for he may not
For ever die, and ever buried be
In baleful night where all things are forgot;
Al be he° subject to mortality,
Yet is eterne in mutability
And by succession made perpetual,
Transformèd oft and changèd diversely:
For him the father of all forms they call;
Therefore needs mote he live, that living gives to all.

48 There now he liveth in eternal bliss,
Joying° his goddess, and of her enjoyed.

° **of yore**: once upon a time.
° **late**: recently.
° **Meseems**: it seems to me.
° **And all about . . . endless date: Hyacinthus** was transformed into a hyacinth after his lover Apollo accidentally killed him with a quoit; **Narcissus** turned into a narcissus when he pined away with love for his own reflection in the water. **Amyntas** is the hero of a Latin love poem by Thomas Watson (1585), who died of love and was changed into the purple flower **amaranthus** or love-lies-bleeding. (This stanza has only eight lines; the 1609 edition adds a half-line, 'And dearest love', between lines 3 and 4.)
° **skill**: knowledge.
° **Stygian gods**: the gods of the underworld .
° **sooth it seems they say**: what they say seems to be true.
° **Al be he**: although he may be.
° **Joying**: enjoying.

Ne feareth he henceforth that foe of his,
Which with his cruel tusk him deadly cloyed;°
For that wild Boar the which him once annoyed°
She firmly hath imprisonèd for ay,°
That her sweet love his malice mote avoid,
In a strong rocky cave, which is, they say,
Hewn underneath that mount, that none him loosen° may.

49 There now he lives in everlasting joy,
With many of the gods in company
Which thither haunt,° and with the wingèd boy°
Sporting himself in safe felicity;
Who,° when he hath with spoils° and cruelty
Ransacked the world and in the woeful hearts
Of many wretches set his triumphs high,
Thither resorts and, laying his sad darts
Aside, with fair Adonis plays his wanton parts.

50 And his true love, fair Psyche, with him plays,
Fair Psyche, to him lately reconciled,
After long troubles and unmeet upbrays°
With which his mother Venus her reviled,
And eke himself her cruelly exiled;
But now in steadfast love and happy state
She with him lives, and hath him borne a child,
Pleasure, that doth both gods and men aggrate,°
Pleasure, the daughter of Cupid and Psyche late.°

51 Hither great Venus brought this infant fair,
The younger daughter of Chrysogoné,
And unto Psyche with great trust and care
Committed her, yfosterèd° to be

° **cloyed**: gored.
° **annoyed**: injured.
° **for ay**: for ever.
° **loosen**: set loose.
° **thither haunt**: frequent that place.
° **the wingèd boy**: i.e. Cupid.
° **Who**: referring to Cupid.
° **spoils**: plunder.
° **unmeet upbrays**: undeserved reproaches.
° **aggrate**: please.
° **And his true love . . . Psyche late**: see ch. 3, 'Tales of love', p. 40, for the story of Cupid and Psyche.
° **yfosterèd**: fostered.

And trained up in true feminity;°
Who° no less carefully her tenderèd°
Than her own daughter Pleasure, to whom she
Made her companion, and her lessonèd°
In all the lore of love and goodly womanhead.°

A7 William Shakespeare, from *Venus and Adonis*, 1593°

Venus and Adonis was Shakespeare's first long narrative poem, and was enormously popular. Its variations on the traditional legend, and its influence on subsequent versions of the story, are discussed in the introduction. The extracts below comprise a little less than half of the poem, focusing on the lovers' initial encounter (stanzas 1–16, 39–40), their central arguments (68–71, 98–137), and Venus's final lament (170–99).

1

Even as the sun with purple-coloured face
Had ta'en his last leave of the weeping morn,
Rose-cheeked Adonis hied him to the chase;°
Hunting he loved, but love he laughed to scorn.
Sick-thoughted Venus makes amain unto him°
And like a bold-faced suitor 'gins° to woo him.

2

'Thrice fairer then myself,' – thus she began –
'The field's chief flower, sweet above compare,
Stain to all nymphs, more lovely then a man,
More white and red than doves or roses are,
Nature that made thee with herself at strife°
Saith that the world hath ending with thy life.

° **feminity**: womanliness.
° **Who**: referring to Psyche.
° **tenderèd**: looked after.
° **lessonèd**: educated.
° **womanhead**: womanhood.
° from *Venus and Adonis*, London, 1593. (I have made the following emendations: 172. 5, 'are' to 'as'; 176. 4, 'had' to 'was'.)
° **hied him to the chase**: hurried to go hunting.
° **makes amain unto him**: heads at full speed towards him.
° **'gins**: begins.
° **with herself at strife**: trying to surpass herself.

3

'Vouchsafe, thou wonder, to alight thy steed
And rein his proud head to the saddle-bow.°
If thou wilt deign this favour, for thy meed°
A thousand honey° secrets shalt thou know.
Here come and sit where never serpent hisses,
And, being set, I'll smother thee with kisses,

4

And yet not cloy thy lips with loathed satiety,
But rather famish them amid their plenty,
Making them red and pale with fresh variety –
Ten kisses short as one, one long as twenty.
A summer's day will seem an hour but short,°
Being wasted° in such time-beguiling sport.

5

With this she seizeth on his sweating palm,
The precedent of pith and livelihood,°
And, trembling in her passion, calls it balm,
Earth's sovereign° salve to do a goddess good.
Being so enraged,° desire doth lend her force
Courageously to pluck him from his horse.

6

Over one arm the lusty courser's° rein,
Under her other was the tender boy,
Who blushed and pouted in a dull disdain,
With leaden appetite, unapt to toy;°
She red and hot as coals of glowing fire,
He red for shame but frosty in desire.

° **saddle-bow**: the arched front part of the saddle; the rein was tied to it to stop the horse straying.
° **meed**: reward.
° **honey**: sweet.
° **an hour but short**: only a short hour.
° **wasted**: spent.
° **precedent of pith and livelihood**: outward sign of his strength and vitality.
° **sovereign**: most potent.
° **enraged**: driven wild (with desire rather than anger).
° **courser**: a large, powerful horse, or (specifically) a stallion.
° **unapt to toy**: disinclined for (sexual) play.

7

The studded bridle on a ragged bough
Nimbly she fastens – O how quick is love!
The steed is stallèd up,° and even now
To tie the rider she begins to prove.°
  Backward she pushed him, as she would be thrust,
  And governed him in strength though not in lust.°

8

So soon was she along° as he was down,
Each leaning on their elbows and their hips;
Now doth she stroke his cheek, now doth he frown
And 'gins to chide,° but soon she stops his lips,
  And kissing speaks, with lustful language broken,
  'If thou wilt chide, thy lips shall never open.'

9

He burns with bashful shame, she with her tears
Doth quench the maiden burning of his cheeks,
Then with her windy sighs and golden hairs
To fan and blow them dry again she seeks.
  He saith she is immodest, blames her miss –°
  What follows more, she murders with a kiss.

10

Even as an empty eagle, sharp by fast,
Tires° with her beak on feather, flesh, and bone,
Shaking her wings, devouring all in haste,
Till either gorge be stuffed or prey be gone,
  Even so she kissed his brow, his cheek, his chin,
  And where she ends she doth anew begin.

° **stallèd**: tied.
° **prove**: attempt.
° **lust**: (i) will, desire, (ii) sexual appetite; i.e. she can control him physically but can't arouse him sexually or get him to do what she wants.
° **along**: lying alongside.
° **chide**: complain.
° **miss**: misbehaviour.
° **Tires**: tears away.

11

Forced to content° but never to obey,
Panting he lies and breatheth in her face;
She feedeth on the steam as on a prey,
And calls it heavenly moisture, air of grace,
  Wishing her cheeks were gardens full of flowers,
  So° they were dewed with such distilling° showers.

12

Look how° a bird lies tangled in a net,
So fastened in her arms Adonis lies.
Pure shame and awed° resistance made him fret,
Which bred more beauty in his angry eyes.
  Rain added to a river that is rank°
  Perforce° will force it overflow the bank.

13

Still° she entreats, and prettily entreats,
For to a pretty ear she tunes her tale.
Still is he sullen, still he lours° and frets,
'Twixt° crimson shame and anger ashy pale.
  Being red she loves him best, and being white,
  Her best is bettered with a more delight.°

14

Look how he can, she cannot choose but love,
And by her fair immortal hand she swears
From his soft bosom never to remove°
Till he take truce with her contending tears,

° **content**: put up with it.
° **So**: so long as.
° **distilling**: softly falling.
° **Look how**: just as.
° **awed**: frightened.
° **rank**: swollen.
° **Perforce**: necessarily.
° **Still**: all the time, continually.
° **lours**: frowns.
° **'Twixt**: between.
° **Her best . . . delight**: i.e. she loves him even better than best (an absurd hyperbole).
° **remove**: withdraw.

Which long have rained, making her cheeks all wet,
And one sweet kiss shall pay this countless debt.

15

Upon this promise did he raise his chin,
Like a divedapper° peering through a wave,
Who being looked on, ducks as quickly in;
So offers he to give what she did crave.
But when her lips were ready for his pay,
He winks° and turns his lips another way.

16

Never did passenger° in summer's heat
More thirst for drink then she for this good turn.
Her help she sees, but help she cannot get;
She bathes in water, yet her fire must burn.
'O pity!' gan she cry, 'flint-hearted boy,
'Tis but a kiss I beg – why art thou coy? . . .'

* * *

39

'Fondling,'° she saith, 'since I have hemmed thee here
Within the circuit of this ivory pale,°
I'll be a park and thou shalt be my deer.°
Feed where thou wilt, on mountain or in dale;
Graze on my lips, and if those hills be dry,
Stray lower, where the pleasant fountains lie.

40

'Within this limit is relief enough,
Sweet bottom-grass° and high delightful plain,
Round rising hillocks, brakes° obscure and rough
To shelter thee from tempest and from rain.

° **divedapper**: dabchick (a small water-bird).
° **winks**: closes his eyes.
° **passenger**: traveller.
° **Fondling**: foolish boy.
° **this ivory pale**: i.e. her white arms, imaged as the **pale** or fence round a deer park. In the following lines Venus's body is metaphorically depicted as the park.
° **deer**: punning on 'dear' – one of Shakespeare's favourite puns.
° **bottom-grass**: low-lying grassland.
° **brakes**: clumps of trees.

Then be my deer, since I am such a park;
No dog shall rouse thee,° though a thousand bark.'

Despite all Venus's arguments, pleas, and physical force, Adonis prepares to ride away. But a mare appears out of the forest, and Adonis's stallion enthusiastically breaks his tether and runs away after her; Adonis is left cursing, while Venus advises him that *that* is how a male should respond to a sexual invitation:

68

'. . . Let me excuse thy courser, gentle boy,
And learn of him, I heartily beseech thee,
To take advantage on presented joy;°
Though I were dumb, yet his proceedings° teach thee.
O, learn to love – the lesson is but plain,
And, once made perfect,° never lost again.

69

'I know not love,' quoth he, 'nor will not know it,
Unless it be a boar, and then I chase it.
'Tis much to borrow, and I will not owe it.
My love to love is love but to disgrace it,°
For I have heard it is a life in death
That laughs and weeps, and all but with a breath.

70

Who wears a garment shapeless and unfinished?
Who plucks the bud before one leaf put forth?
If springing° things be any jot diminished
They wither in their prime, prove nothing worth.
The colt that's backed° and burdened being young,
Loseth his pride and never waxeth° strong.

° **rouse thee**: hunt you out from cover.
° **on presented joy**: of the opportunities of joy that you are given.
° **proceedings**: actions.
° **made perfect**: learnt.
° **My love . . . disgrace it**: My only feeling about love is a wish to expose it as disgraceful.
° **springing**: just beginning to grow.
° **backed**: ridden.
° **waxeth**: grows.

71

You hurt my hand with wringing. Let us part
And leave this idle theme, this bootless° chat.
Remove your siege from my unyielding heart;
To love's alarms° it will not ope the gate.
  Dismiss your vows, your feignèd tears, your flattery,
  For where a heart is hard they make no battery.°

Finally – after Venus has been driven to faint, or pretend to – Adonis reluctantly allows her a kiss, which she takes with alarming enthusiasm ('having felt the sweetness of the spoil, / With blindfold fury she begins to forage'). At last the exhausted Adonis gets free and prepares to depart.

98

'Sweet boy,' she says, 'this night I'll waste in sorrow,
For my sick heart commands mine eyes to watch.°
Tell me, love's master, shall we meet tomorrow?
Say, shall we, shall we, wilt thou make the match?'
  He tells her no, tomorrow he intends
  To hunt the boar with certain of his friends.

99

'The boar?' quoth she – whereat° a sudden pale,
Like lawn° being spread upon the blushing rose,
Usurps° her cheek. She trembles at his tale,
And on his neck her yoking arms she throws.
  She sinketh down, still hanging by his neck.
  He on her belly falls, she on her back.

100

Now is she in the very lists° of love,
Her champion mounted for the hot encounter.
All is imaginary she doth prove;°

° **bootless**: pointless.
° **alarms**: assaults.
° **make no battery**: fail to batter down the defences.
° **watch**: stay awake.
° **whereat**: at which.
° **lawn**: a very fine white cloth.
° **Usurps**: takes over.
° **lists**: the arena for a tournament, where knights on horseback fight with lances.
° **All is imaginary she doth prove**: everything she experiences is imaginary – i.e. her fantasies will not be translated into reality.

He will not manage her,° although he mount her,
That worse than Tantalus' is her annoy,°
To clip Elysium° and to lack her joy.

101

Even so poor birds, deceived with painted grapes,°
Do surfeit by the eye and pine the maw;°
Even so she languisheth in her mishaps
As those poor birds that helpless° berries saw.
The warm effects which she in him finds missing
She seeks to kindle with continual kissing.

102

But all in vain, good queen – it will not be.
She hath assayed as much as may be proved.°
Her pleading hath deserved a greater fee:
She's Love, she loves, and yet she is not loved.
'Fie, fie,' he says, 'you crush me, let me go.
You have no reason to withhold me so.'

103

'Thou hadst been gone,' quoth she, 'sweet boy, ere this,
But that thou told'st me thou wouldst hunt the boar.
O, be advised – thou know'st not what it is
With javelin's point a churlish swine to gore,
Whose tushes° never-sheathed he whetteth°still,
Like to a mortal° butcher bent° to kill.

° **manage her**: put her through her paces (a term from horsemanship).
° **That . . . her annoy**: so that her suffering is worse than that of Tantalus (the sinner in the Underworld who was tormented by food and water just out of his reach).
° **clip**: embrace; **Elysium** is the classical equivalent of heaven, the place of the blessed dead.
° **Even so poor birds . . .**: a reference to a story of the Greek painter Zeuxis, that he painted a bunch of grapes so realistic that birds came to peck at it.
° **surfeit by the eye, and pine the maw**: are overfed as far as the eyes are concerned, but starve as far as the stomach is.
° **helpless**: useless.
° **assayed as much as may be proved**: tried as much as she can.
° **tushes**: tusks.
° **whetteth**: sharpens.
° **mortal**: deadly.
° **bent**: determined.

104

'On his bow-back° he hath a battle° set
Of bristly pikes that ever threat his foes.
His eyes like glow-worms shine; when he doth fret°
His snout digs sepulchres where'er he goes.
  Being moved,° he strikes whate'er is in his way,
  And whom he strikes his crooked tushes slay.

105

'His brawny sides with hairy bristles armed
Are better proof° than thy spear's point can enter.
His short thick neck cannot be easily harmed.
Being ireful, on the lion he will venture.
  The thorny brambles and embracing bushes,
  As fearful of him, part, through whom he rushes.

106

'Alas, he naught esteems° that face of thine,
To which love's eyes pays tributary gazes,
Nor thy soft hands, sweet lips, and crystal eyne,°
Whose full perfection all the world amazes,
  But having thee at vantage° (wondrous dread!)
  Would root° these beauties as he roots the mead.°

107

'O, let him keep his loathsome cabin° still.
Beauty hath naught to do with such foul fiends.
Come not within his danger by thy will.
They that thrive well take counsel of° their friends.
  When thou didst name the boar, not to dissemble,
  I feared thy fortune, and my joints did tremble.

° **bow-back**: humped back.
° **battle**: battle-line.
° **fret**: rage.
° **moved**: angered.
° **proof**: armoured.
° **naught esteems**: cares nothing for.
° **eyne**: eyes.
° **at vantage**: at his mercy.
° **root**: tear up.
° **mead**: meadow.
° **cabin**: den.
° **counsel of**: advice from.

108

'Didst thou not mark my face – was it not white?
Sawest thou not signs of fear lurk in mine eye?
Grew I not faint, and fell I not downright?°
Within my bosom, whereon thou dost lie,
  My boding° heart pants, beats, and takes no rest,
  But like an earthquake shakes thee on my breast.

109

'For where love reigns, disturbing jealousy°
Doth call himself affection's sentinel,
Gives false alarms, suggesteth mutiny,°
And in a peaceful hour doth cry, "Kill, kill!",
  Distempering° gentle love in his desire,
  As air and water do abate the fire.

110

'This sour informer, this bate-breeding° spy,
This canker° that eats up love's tender spring,°
This carry-tale,° dissentious jealousy,
That sometime true news, sometime false doth bring,
  Knocks at my heart and whispers in mine ear
  That if I love thee, I thy death should fear;

111

'And, more than so, presenteth to mine eye
The picture of an angry chafing boar,
Under whose sharp fangs on his back doth lie
An image like thyself, all stained with gore,
  Whose blood upon the fresh flowers being shed
  Doth make them droop with grief and hang the head.

112

'What should I do, seeing thee so indeed,
That tremble at th' imagination?

° **downright**: (i) immediately, (ii) straight down.
° **boding**: foreboding.
° **jealousy**: fear, anxiety (not 'jealousy' in the modern sense).
° **suggesteth mutiny**: incites riots.
° **Distempering**: disturbing.
° **bate-breeding**: troublemaking.
° **canker**: canker-worm (an insect which devours plants from within).
° **tender spring**: young growth.
° **carry-tale**: tale-bearer, gossipmonger.

The thought of it doth make my faint heart bleed,
And fear doth teach it divination:
  I prophesy thy death, my living sorrow,
  If thou encounter with the boar tomorrow.

113

'But if thou needs wilt hunt, be ruled by me:
Uncouple at° the timorous flying hare,
Or at the fox which lives by subtlety,
Or at the roe which no encounter dare.
  Pursue these fearful creatures o'er the downs,
  And on thy well-breathed horse keep with thy hounds.

114

'And when thou hast on foot the purblind° hare,
Mark the poor wretch, to overshoot his troubles,
How he outruns the wind, and with what care
He cranks and crosses° with a thousand doubles;°
  The many musits° through the which he goes
  Are like a labyrinth to amaze his foes.

115

'Sometime he runs among a flock of sheep
To make the cunning hounds mistake their smell;
And sometime where earth-delving conies keep,°
To stop the loud pursuers in their yell;
  And sometime sorteth° with a herd of deer.
  Danger deviseth shifts;° wit waits on fear.°

116

'For there, his smell with others being mingled,
The hot scent-snuffing hounds are driven to doubt,
Ceasing their clamorous cry, till they have singled

° **Uncouple at**: unleash the dogs to hunt.
° **purblind**: weak-sighted.
° **cranks and crosses**: twists and turns.
° **doubles**: doublings-back.
° **musits**: gaps in hedges.
° **earth-delving coneys keep**: burrowing rabbits live.
° **sorteth**: mingles.
° **shifts**: tricks.
° **wit waits on fear**: intelligence accompanies, i.e. is stimulated by, fear.

With much ado the cold fault° cleanly out.
  Then do they spend their mouths; echo replies,
  As if another chase were in the skies.

117

'By this poor Wat,° far off upon a hill,
Stands on his hinder legs with listening ear
To hearken if his foes pursue him still.
Anon° their loud alarums° he doth hear,
  And now his grief may be compared well
  To one sore° sick that hears the passing-bell.°

118

'Then shalt thou see the dew-bedabbled wretch
Turn and re-turn, indenting with° the way.
Each envious briar his weary legs do scratch,
Each shadow makes him stop, each murmur stay;°
  For misery is trodden on by many,
  And, being low, never relieved by any.

119

'Lie quietly and hear a little more.
Nay, do not struggle, for thou shalt not rise.
To make thee hate the hunting of the boar
Unlike myself° thou hear'st me moralise,
  Applying this to that and so to so,
  For love can comment upon every woe.

120

'Where did I leave?'° 'No matter where,' quoth he;
'Leave me, and then the story aptly ends.
The night is spent.' 'Why, what of that?' quoth she.

° **cold fault**: lost scent.
° **Wat**: a traditional nickname for a hare.
° **Anon**: soon.
° **alarums**: calls to battle.
° **sore**: gravely.
° **passing-bell**: the bell tolled to mark someone's death, one ring for each year of their life.
° **indenting with**: zigzagging across.
° **stay**: pause.
° **Unlike myself**: i.e. moralising is not usually in Venus's line.
° **leave**: stop (talking).

'I am,' quoth he, 'expected of° my friends,
And now 'tis dark, and going I shall fall.'
'In night,' quoth she, 'desire sees best of all.

121

'But if thou fall, O then imagine this:
The earth, in love with thee, thy footing trips,
And all is but to rob thee of a kiss.
Rich preys make true men thieves;° so do thy lips
Make modest Dian cloudy and forlorn,
Lest she should steal a kiss and die forsworn.°

122

'Now of this dark night I perceive the reason.°
Cynthia for shame obscures her silver shine
Till forging° Nature be condemned of treason
For stealing moulds from heaven that were divine,
Wherein she° framed thee, in high heaven's despite,°
To shame the sun by day and her by night.

123

'And therefore hath she bribed the Destinies
To cross° the curious° workmanship of Nature,
To mingle beauty with infirmities
And pure perfection with impure defeature,°
Making it subject to the tyranny
Of mad mischances and much misery;

° **expected of**: expected by.
° **Rich preys make true men thieves**: even honest men can be tempted to steal something sufficiently desirable.
° **so do thy lips . . . die forsworn**: The moon is covered with clouds (Venus suggests) because Diana, the moon goddess, is unhappy at being tempted by the sight of Adonis to break her vows of chastity.
° **perceive the reason**: in the stanzas that follow Venus develops a kind of myth to explain the fallen nature of the world. Nature, in a kind of Promethean rebellion, stole 'divine moulds' from heaven to make Adonis as an incarnation of beauty. Diana (or **Cynthia**), angered at this competition, has bribed the Fates to frustrate Nature by filling the world with evils that deform and destroy beauty.
° **forging**: counterfeiting.
° **she**: i.e. Nature.
° **in high heaven's despite**: against heaven's will.
° **cross**: frustrate.
° **curious**: elaborate.
° **defeature**: disfigurement.

124

'As° burning fevers, agues pale and faint,
Life-poisoning pestilence, and frenzies wood,°
The marrow-eating sickness whose attaint°
Disorder breeds by heating of the blood;
 Surfeits, impostumes,° grief, and damned despair
 Swear Nature's death for framing thee so fair.

125

'And not the least of all these maladies
But in one minute's fight brings beauty under.°
Both favour, savour, hue,° and qualities,
Whereat th' impartial gazer late did wonder,
 Are on the sudden wasted, thawed, and done,
 As mountain snow melts with the midday sun.

126

'Therefore, despite of° fruitless chastity,
Love-lacking vestals° and self-loving nuns,
That on the earth would breed a scarcity
And barren dearth of daughters and of sons,
 Be prodigal. The lamp that burns by night
 Dries up his oil to lend the world his light.°

127

'What is thy body but a swallowing grave,
Seeming to bury that posterity°
Which by the rights of time thou needs must have
If thou destroy them not in dark obscurity?
 If so, the world will hold thee in disdain,
 Sith° in thy pride so fair a hope is slain.

° **As**: such as.
° **wood**: mad.
° **attaint**: infection.
° **imposthumes**: abscesses.
° **And not the least . . . beauty under**: Even the least of these can destroy beauty in a moment.
° **favour, savour, hue**: charm, perfume, complexion.
° **despite of**: in defiance of.
° **vestals**: virgin priestesses.
° **The lamp . . . his light**: i.e. as the lamp uses up its oil to create light, Adonis should use up his sexual potency to create new life.
° **posterity**: offspring.
° **Sith**: since.

128

'So in thyself thyself art made away,°
A mischief° worse than civil home-bred strife,°
Or theirs whose desperate hands themselves do slay,
Or butcher sire° that reaves° his son of life.
  Foul cankering rust the hidden treasure frets,°
  But gold that's put to use° more gold begets.'

129

'Nay then,' quoth Adon, 'you will fall again
Into your idle over-handled theme.
The kiss I gave you is bestowed in vain,
And all in vain you strive against the stream;
  For, by this black-faced night, desire's foul nurse,
  Your treatise makes me like you worse and worse.

130

'If love have lent you twenty thousand tongues,
And every tongue more moving° than your own,
Bewitching like the wanton mermaid's songs,
Yet from mine ear the tempting tune is blown;
  For know, my heart stands armèd in mine ear
  And will not let a false sound enter there,

131

'Lest the deceiving harmony should run
Into the quiet closure° of my breast,
And then my little heart were quite undone,
In his bedchamber to be barred° of rest.
  No, lady, no: my heart longs not to groan,
  But soundly sleeps, while now it sleeps alone.

° **made away**: murdered.
° **mischief**: harm.
° **home-bred strife**: civil war.
° **sire**: father.
° **reaves**: deprives.
° **frets**: eats away.
° **put to use**: invested at interest.
° **moving**: persuasive.
° **closure**: enclosure.
° **barred**: deprived.

132

'What have you urged° that I cannot reprove?°
The path is smooth that leadeth on to danger.
I hate not love, but your device° in love,
That lends embracements unto every stranger.
  You do it for increase – O strange excuse,
  When reason is the bawd° to lust's abuse!

133

Call it not love, for love to heaven is fled
Since sweating lust on earth usurped his name,
Under whose simple semblance° he hath fed
Upon fresh beauty, blotting it with blame;
  Which the hot tyrant stains, and soon bereaves,°
  As caterpillars do the tender leaves.

134

'Love comforteth like sunshine after rain,
But lust's effect is tempest after sun.
Love's gentle spring doth always fresh remain;
Lust's winter comes ere summer half be done.
  Love surfeits not; lust like a glutton dies.
  Love is all truth, lust full of forgèd lies.

135

'More I could tell, but more I dare not say;
The text is old, the orator too green.
Therefore in sadness now I will away.
My face is full of shame, my heart of teen.°
  Mine ears that to your wanton talk attended°
  Do burn themselves for having so offended.'

136

With this he breaketh from the sweet embrace
Of those fair arms which bound him to her breast,

° **urged**: argued.
° **reprove**: disprove.
° **device**: conduct.
° **bawd**: female pimp, or madam of a brothel – i.e. Venus's reason is pimping for her lust.
° **simple semblance**: innocent appearance.
° **Which the hot tyrant . . . bereaves**: i.e. the 'tyrant' lust first stains the innocence of beauty with corruption, and then strips it (beauty) away.
° **teen**: irritation.
° **attended**: listened.

And homeward through the dark laund° runs apace,°
Leaves Love upon her back, deeply distressed.
  Look how° a bright star shooteth from the sky,
  So glides he in the night from Venus' eye,

137

Which after him she darts, as one on shore
Gazing upon a late-embarkèd friend
Till the wild waves will have him seen no more,
Whose ridges with the meeting clouds contend;
  So did the merciless and pitchy° night
  Fold in the object that did feed her sight.

After a sleepless night, Venus sets out to find Adonis. Hearing the sounds of the hunt in disarray and meeting the wounded hounds, she searches on, in alternating waves of hope and despair, until she comes upon his dead body.

178

Upon his hurt she looks so steadfastly
That her sight, dazzling,° makes the wound seem three,
And then she reprehends° her mangling eye,
That makes more gashes where no breach should be.
  His face seems twain, each several° limb is doubled,
  For oft the eye mistakes, the brain being troubled.

179

'My tongue cannot express my grief for one,
And yet,' quoth she, 'behold two Adons dead!
My sighs are blown away, my salt tears gone,
Mine eyes are turned to fire, my heart to lead.
  Heavy heart's lead, melt at mine eyes' red fire –
  So shall I die by drops of hot desire.

180

'Alas, poor world, what treasure hast thou lost!
What face remains alive that's worth the viewing?

° **laund**: clearing.
° **apace**: at speed.
° **Look how**: just as.
° **pitchy**: pitch-black.
° **dazzling**: becoming blurred.
° **reprehends**: rebukes.
° **several**: separate.

Whose tongue is music now? What canst thou boast
Of things long since, or anything ensuing?°
  The flowers are sweet, their colours fresh and trim,
  But true sweet beauty lived and died with him.

181

'Bonnet nor veil henceforth no creature wear;
Nor sun nor wind will ever strive to kiss you.
Having no fair° to lose, you need not fear –
The sun doth scorn you and the wind doth hiss you.
  But when Adonis lived, sun and sharp air
  Lurked like two thieves to rob him of his fair;

182

'And therefore would he put his bonnet on,
Under whose brim the gaudy sun would peep,
The wind would blow it off, and, being gone,
Play with his locks; then would Adonis weep,
  And straight, in pity of his tender years,
  They both would strive who first should dry his tears.

183

'To see his face the lion walked along
Behind some hedge, because he would not fear° him.
To recreate himself when he hath sung,°
The tiger would be tame and gently hear him.
  If he had spoke, the wolf would leave his prey
  And never fright the silly° lamb that day.

184

'When he beheld his shadow in the brook,
The fishes spread on it their golden gills.
When he was by, the birds such pleasure took
That some would sing, some other in their bills
  Would bring him mulberries and ripe red cherries;
  He fed them with his sight, they him with berries.

° **ensuing**: to come.
° **fair**: beauty.
° **fear**: frighten.
° **To recreate himself when he hath sung**: when he sang to amuse himself.
° **silly**: innocent.

185

'But this foul, grim, and urchin-snouted° boar,
Whose downward eye still looketh for a grave,
Ne'er saw the beauteous livery° that he wore –
Witness the entertainment that he gave.
  If he did see his face, why then I know
  He thought° to kiss him, and hath killed him so.

186

''Tis true, 'tis true – thus was Adonis slain.
He ran upon the boar with his sharp spear,
Who did not whet his teeth at him again°
But by a kiss thought to persuade him there,
  And nuzzling in his flank, the loving swine
  Sheathed unaware the tusk in his soft groin.°

187

'Had I been toothed like him,° I must confess
With kissing him I should have killed him first.
But he is dead, and never did he bless
My youth with his – the more am I accursed.'
  With this she falleth in the place she stood
  And stains her face with his congealed blood.

188

She looks upon his lips, and they are pale;
She takes him by the hand, and that is cold;
She whispers in his ears a heavy° tale,
As if they heard the woeful words she told.
  She lifts the coffer-lids that close his eyes,
  Where lo, two lamps burnt out in darkness lies;

189

Two glasses,° where herself herself beheld
A thousand times, and now no more reflect,

° **urchin-snouted**: with a snout like a hedgehog (an animal the Elizabethans regarded as sinister).
° **livery**: costume (i.e. Adonis's outward beauty).
° **thought**: meant.
° **again**: in return.
° **But by a kiss . . . groin**: this idea is borrowed from a late classical poem about Venus' interview with the repentant boar, included among Theocritus's poems and popular in the Renaissance.
° **Had I been toothed like him**: if I had had teeth like the boar.
° **heavy**: sad.
° **glasses**: mirrors.

Their virtue° lost wherein they late° excelled,
And every beauty robbed of his effect.
'Wonder of time,' quoth she, 'this is my spite,°
That, thou being dead, the day should yet be light.

190

'Since thou art dead, lo here I prophesy
Sorrow on love hereafter shall attend.
It shall be waited on with° jealousy,
Find sweet beginning, but unsavoury end;
Ne'er settled equally, but high or low,°
That all love's pleasure shall not match his woe.

191

'It shall be fickle, false, and full of fraud,
Bud and be blasted in a breathing-while;°
The bottom poison and the top o'erstrawed°
With sweets that shall the truest sight beguile.°
The strongest body shall it make most weak,
Strike the wise dumb and teach the fool to speak.

192

'It shall be sparing° and too full of riot,°
Teaching decrepit age to tread the measures.°
The staring° ruffian shall it keep in quiet,
Pluck down the rich, enrich the poor with treasures.
It shall be raging-mad and silly-mild,
Make the young old, the old become a child.

° **virtue**: power.
° **late**: not long ago.
° **my spite**: what angers me.
° **waited on with**: accompanied by.
° **Ne'er settled equally, but high or low**: lovers will never be equal in social status or in the strength of their love.
° **Bud and be blasted in a breathing while**: spring up and wither away in the space of a breath.
° **o'erstrawed**: strewed over.
° **The bottom poison . . . beguile**: i.e. love is like an animal trap, with sweet food scattered on top to tempt the victim to fall into the poison below.
° **sparing**: niggardly.
° **riot**: debauchery.
° **tread the measures**: dance.
° **staring**: bold-faced.

193

'It shall suspect where is no cause of fear,
It shall not fear where it should most mistrust.
It shall be merciful and too severe,
And most deceiving when it seems most just.
  Perverse it shall be where it shows most toward,°
  Put fear to valour, courage to the coward.

194

'It shall be cause of war and dire events,
And set dissension 'twixt the son and sire;
Subject and servile to all discontents
As dry combustious° matter is to fire.
  Sith in his prime death doth my love destroy,
  They that love best their loves shall not enjoy.'

195

By this, the boy that by her side lay killed
Was melted like a vapour from her sight,
And in his blood that on the ground lay spilled
A purple flower sprung up, chequered with white,
  Resembling well his pale cheeks, and the blood
  Which in round drops upon their whiteness stood.

196

She bows her head the new-sprung flower to smell,
Comparing it to her Adonis' breath,
And says within her bosom it shall dwell,
Since he himself is reft° from her by death.
  She crops the stalk, and in the breach° appears
  Green-dropping sap, which she compares to tears.

197

'Poor flower,' quoth she, 'this was thy father's guise° –
Sweet issue° of a more sweet-smelling sire –

° **toward**: willing.
° **combustious**: combustible.
° **reft**: taken away.
° **breach**: break.
° **guise**: habit.
° **issue**: child.

For every little grief to wet his eyes.
To grow unto himself was his desire,°
   And so 'tis thine; but know it is as good
   To wither in my breast as in his blood.

198

'Here was thy father's bed, here in my breast.
Thou art the next of blood,° and 'tis thy right.
Lo, in this hollow cradle take thy rest;
My throbbing heart shall rock thee day and night.
   There shall not be one minute in an hour
   Wherein I will not kiss my sweet love's flower.'

199

Thus, weary of the world, away she hies°
And yokes her silver doves, by whose swift aid
Their mistress, mounted, through the empty skies
In her light chariot quickly is conveyed,
   Holding their course to Paphos, where their queen
   Means to immure herself° and not be seen.

A8 Richard Barnfield, Sonnet 17 from *Cynthia*, 1595°

Richard Barnfield, 1574–1627, Elizabethan poet, author of pastoral, erotic, and satirical poems. He has, as the *Oxford Companion to English Literature* notes, 'the distinction of being the only Elizabethan poet other than Shakespeare to have addressed love sonnets to a man'.

Cherry-lipped Adonis in his snowy shape
Might not compare with his pure ivory white,
On whose fair front° a poet's pen may write,

° **To grow unto himself was his desire**: He desired to grow only for his own sake, to be entirely self-sufficient.
° **next of blood**: next of kin – but the phrase is especially appropriate since the flower literally comes from Adonis's blood.
° **hies**: hurries.
° **immure herself**: shut herself up.
° from *Cynthia. With Certaine Sonnets, and the Legend of Cassandra*, London, 1595, unpaginated.
° **front**: forehead.

Whose roseate red excels the crimson grape.
His love-enticing delicate soft limbs
Are rarely framed t' entrap poor gazing eyes;
His cheeks the lily and carnation dyes
With lovely tincture which Apollo's dims.°
His lips ripe strawberries in nectar wet,
His mouth a hive, his tongue a honeycomb
Where Muses (like bees) make their mansion,
His teeth pure pearl in blushing coral set.
  O how can such a body sin-procuring
  Be slow to love and quick to hate, enduring?

A9 Bartholomew Griffin, Sonnet 3 from *Fidessa*, 1596°

B. (Bartholomew?) Griffin published *Fidessa*, a collection of sixty-two love sonnets, in 1596, and probably died in 1602; little else is known of him. A version of this sonnet was included in *The Passionate Pilgrim*, a collection of poems 'by W. Shakespeare' published in 1599 by an unscrupulous publisher cashing in on the popularity of *Venus and Adonis*.

Venus, and young Adonis sitting by her,
Under a myrtle shade began to woo him.
She told the youngling how god Mars did try her,
And as he fell to her, so fell she to him.
'Even thus,' quoth she, 'the wanton god embraced me' –
And then she clasped Adonis in her arms.
'Even thus,' quoth she, 'the warlike god unlaced me'° –
As if the boy should use like loving charms.
But he, a wayward boy, refused her offer
And ran away, the beauteous queen neglecting;
Showing both folly to abuse her proffer,
And all his sex of cowardice detecting.°
  O that I had my mistress at that bay,°
  To kiss and clip° me till I ran away!

° **Apollo's dims**: makes Apollo's complexion look dull.
° from Bartholomew Griffin, *Fidessa, More Chaste than Kind*, London, 1596, unpaginated.
° **unlaced me**: undid the laces of my bodice (Griffin envisages the characters in Elizabethan costume).
° **detecting**: exposing as guilty of.
° **at that bay**: at such close quarters (a hunting image).
° **clip**: embrace.

A10 Thomas Heywood, from *The Fair Maid of the Exchange*, 1607°

Thomas Heywood, ?1574–1641, immensely prolific dramatist, poet, and pamphleteer, who claimed to have had a hand 'or at least a main finger' in over 200 plays. Among them is a five-part dramatisation of the Greek myths: *The Golden Age*, *Silver Age*, *Brazen Age*, and *Iron Age* (2 parts); *The Brazen Age* includes a more serious version of the Venus and Adonis story.

The opening scene of *The Fair Maid of the Exchange*, a 'city comedy', mocks the popularity of Shakespeare's *Venus and Adonis*, as the shy gallant Bowdler, encouraged by the Cripple, brushes up his Shakespeare in an attempt to woo Mall Berry. Heywood reverses (and normalises) the gender relations of the Shakespeare poem: Bowdler takes over Venus's lines as aggressive wooer, while Mall adopts (calculatingly) Adonis's coyness.

Enter Mall Berry

CRIPPLE: See where she comes – O, excellent!
BOWDLER: Now have I no more blood than a bullrush.
BARNARD: How now, what ail you. sir?
CRIPPLE: What's the matter, man?
BOWDLER: See, see, that glorious angel doth approach.
What shall I do?
CRIPPLE: She is a saint indeed. Zounds,° to her, court her, win her, wear her, wed her, and bed her too.
BOWDLER: I would it were come to that. I win her! By heaven, I am not furnished of a courting phrase to throw at a dog.
CRIPPLE: Why no, but at a woman you have. O sir, seem not so doltish now.
Can you make no fustian?° Ask her if she'll take a pipe of tobacco.
BOWDLER: It will offend her judgement, pardon me.
CRIPPLE: But hear you, sir? Reading so much as you have done,
Do you not remember one pretty phrase
To scale the walls of a fair wench's love?
BOWDLER: I never read anything but *Venus and Adonis*.
CRIPPLE: Why, that's the very quintessence of love.
If you remember but a verse or two,
I'll pawn my head, goods, lands and all, 'twill do.
BOWDLER: Why then, have at her.

° from *The Fayre Mayde of the Exchange: With the pleasaunt Humours of the Cripple of Fanchurch*, London, 1607, unpaginated.

° **Zounds**: an oath (by God's wounds).

° **fustian**: high-flown language.

[*To Mall*] Fondling, I say, since I have hemmed thee here
Within the circle of this ivory pale,
I'll be a park –
MALL: Hands off, fond sir.
BOWDLER: – And thou shalt be my deer;
Feed thou on me, and I will feed on thee,
And Love shall feed us both.°
MALL: Feed you on woodcocks;° I can fast awhile.
BOWDLER: Vouchsafe, thou wonder, to alight thy steed.
CRIPPLE: (Take heed, she's not on horseback.)
BOWDLER: (Why then she is alighted.)
Come, sit thee down where never serpent hisses,
And being set, I'll smother thee with kisses.°
MALL: Why, is your breath so hot? Now God forbid
I should buy kisses to be smotherèd.
BOWDLER: Mean you me? You gull° me not?
MALL: No, no, poor Bowdler, thou dost gull thyself.
[*Aside*] Thus must I do to shadow the hid fire
That in my heart doth burn with hot desire.
O, I do love him well, whate'er I say,
Yet will I not myself self-love bewray.°
If he be wise he'll sue with good take-heed;°
Bowdler, do so, and thou art sure to speed.°
I will fly hence, to make his love the stronger,
Though my affection must lie hid the longer. –
What, Master Bowdler, not a word to say?
BOWDLER: No, by my troth, if you stay here all day.
MALL: Why then, I'll bear the bucklers hence away.°
Exit
CRIPPLE: What, Master Bowdler, have you let her pass unconquered?
BOWDLER: Why, what could I do more? I looked upon her with judgement, the strings of my tongue were well in tune, my embraces were in good measure, my palm of a good constitution – only the

° **Fondling . . . feed us both**: compare *Venus and Adonis*, stanza 39.
° **woodcocks**: a sort of game bird, but also slang for 'fools'.
° **Vouchsafe . . . smother thee with kisses**: compare *Venus and Adonis*, stanza 3.
° **gull**: trick.
° **self-love bewray**: reveal my own love.
° **sue with good take-heed**: conduct his wooing with good sense and caution.
° **speed**: succeed.
° **bear the bucklers hence away**: (slang) come off the winner (the image is of carrying off the shields, or **bucklers**, after a fight).

phrase was not moving. As for example, Venus herself with all her skill could not win Adonis with the same words. O heavens, was I so fond then to think that I could conquer Mall Berry? O, the natural fluence° of my own wit had been far better!

A11 William Browne, Song, from *Britannia's Pastorals*, 1616°

William Browne, ?1590–1645, pastoral poet; his *Britannia's Pastorals*, a long narrative poem interspersed with lyrics, was admired by Milton and Keats. This song is sung by a young shepherd, who holds his audience so enraptured that 'had Orpheus been / Playing some distance from them, he had seen / Not one to stir a foot for his rare strain, / But left the Thracian for the English swain.'

Venus by Adonis' side
Crying kissed, and kissing cried,
Wrung her hands and tore her hair,
For Adonis dying there.

'Stay,' quoth she, 'O stay and live!
Nature surely doth not give
To the earth her sweetest flowers
To be seen but some few hours.'

On his face, still as he bled,
For each drop a tear she shed,
Which she kissed or wiped away,
Else had drowned him where he lay.

'Fair Proserpina,' quoth she,
'Shall not have thee yet from me,
Nor thy soul to fly begin
While my lips can keep it in.'

Here she closed again. And some
Say Apollo would have come
To have cured his wounded limb,
But that she had smothered him.

° **fluence**: fluency.

° from *Britannia's Pastorals*, book 2, the Second Song, from *The Whole Works of William Browne*, ed. W. Carew Hazlitt, 2 vols, n.p., 1868–9, vol. ii, pp. 4–5.

A12 George Sandys, from *Ovid's Metamorphoses Englished*, 1632°

The feasts of Adonis were yearly celebrated by the Phoenicians (of which country they report him to be), beating their breasts and tearing their garments with universal sorrow, offering sacrifices to his *manes*;° yet affirming the day following that he lived and was ascended into heaven. The women that would not cut their hair were enjoined to prostrate themselves unto strangers and to offer the hire of their bodies unto Venus. This lamentation for the death of Adonis is mentioned by the prophet Ezekiel (for so Thamuz is interpreted in the vulgar translation, although Tremelius take it for Osiris – howsoever, both are the same in the allegory). Solomon is said in the first of the Chronicles to have followed Astarten, which some interpret to be this Venus, the goddess of the Sidonians. She had her statue in Mount Libanus in a mournful posture, her head covered with a veil, leaning her cheek on her left hand, and sustaining her mantle with the other, into which her tears appeared to descend.

Now Adonis was no other than the sun, adored under that name by the Phoenicians, as Venus by the name of Astarten; for the naturalists call the upper hemisphere of the earth in which we inhabit 'Venus', as the lower 'Proserpina'. Therefore they made the goddess to weep when the sun retired from her to the six winter signs of the zodiac, shortening the days and depriving the earth of her delight and beauty; which again he restores by his approach into Aries. Adonis is said to be slain by a boar, because that beast is the image of the winter: savage, horrid, delighting in mire, and feeding on acorns, a fruit which is proper to that season. So the winter wounds, as it were, the sun to death, by diminishing his heat and lustre, whose loss is lamented by Venus or the widowed earth, then covered with a veil of clouds; spring gushing from thence, the tears of her eyes, in greater abundance; the fields presenting a sad aspect, as being deprived of their ornament. But when the sun returns to the equator, Venus recovers her alacrity, the trees invested with leaves, and the earth with her flowery mantle; wherefore the ancients did dedicate the month of April unto Venus. And not only the Phoenicians but the house of Judah did worship the sun under the name of 'Tamuz', the same with Adonis; for 'Adon' in Hebrew signifies 'lord', and he the lord and prince of the planets; they calling his entrance into the sign of Cancer 'the revolution of Tamuz'.

The lovely Adonis is feigned to have been changed into (an) anemone – a beautiful but no permanent flower – to express the frail condition and short continuance of beauty.

° from George Sandys, *Ovids Metamorphosis Englished, Mythologiz'd, and Represented in Figures*, Oxford, 1632, pp. 364–7.

° ***manes***: (Latin) dead spirit.

A13 Alexander Ross, from *Mystagogus Poeticus*, 1647°

On Alexander Ross, see the headnote to **O19**.

1. The Athenians had certain festival days called *Adonia* in memory of Adonis' untimely death. In these feasts the women used to carry upon biers or hearses the image of a dead youth to the grave, with much mourning and shedding of tears; and therefore Venus was wont to be painted in the form of a mournful woman shedding of tears, with a veil over her head, bewailing the loss of Adonis. By Venus may be meant the earth, for this is the beautiful and fruitful mother of all living creatures. By Adonis may be understood the sun, who in winter is in a sort killed, when his heat and presence is lessened; then the earth mourns, and loseth her beauty; the shedding of tears is the increasing of the springs and rivers by great and continual rains.

2. If by Adonis we understand wheat, that lodgeth with Proserpina, that is, lieth buried in the ground six months in the winter; the six summer months it is above in the air with Venus, by which the beauty of the year is signified. By the boar may be meant the cold frosty and snowy season, in which the wheat seems to be killed.

3. If, with Macrobius,° by Adonis we understand the sun, he may be said to lodge six months with Proserpina, in respect of his southerly declination; the other six months with Venus, for then the creatures give themselves to procreation. He is killed by the boar and lamented by Venus, for in winter his beams are of no force to dispel the cold which is the enemy of Adonis and Venus, that is, of beauty and procreation.

4. Mars in the form of a boar kills him, because wars and hunting are masculine exercises, and not fit for weak bodies and effeminate spirits.

5. 'Adonis' is from αειδω 'to sing', for beauty and music are friends to Venus.

6. Adonis may signify the good government of a commonwealth, which is the beauty thereof, which is killed by Mars in the form of a boar; for Mars and wantonness are enemies of all government.

7. Beautiful Adonis is turned into a fading flower, to show that beauty quickly perisheth.

8. Young and fair Adonis is killed by a boar; so wantonness and lechery are the destroyers of youth and beauty.

9. Our resurrection in this may be typed out,° for although death kill us, it shall not annihilate us, but our beauty shall increase, and we shall spring out of the ground again like a beautiful flower in the Resurrection.

° from *Mystagogus Poeticus, or The Muses Interpreter: Explaining the Historicall Mysteries, and Mysticall Histories of the Ancient Greek and Latine Poets*, London, 1647.

° **Macrobius**: a fifth-century AD Roman critic.

° **typed out**: symbolised.

10. Though our bodies die, yet our good name shall flourish and, like a fair flower, shall live and smell when we are gone.

11. Myrrha of her own father begot this child Adonis, which Myrrha, flying from her angry father, was turned into a tree, and with the blow of her father's sword was delivered of this child; because the sun, the common father, begot the sweet gum myrrh of that Arabian tree of the same name, which gum doth cause much delight and pleasure (for so in Greek 'Adonis' signifieth). In this gum Venus is much delighted, as being a help to decayed beauty, to a stinking breath, to procreation, and the vitiosity of the matrix.°

12. Let them remember who hunt too much after pleasure that the Devil is that great boar who lieth in wait to kill them.

A14 John Milton on Adonis°

(a) from Comus, 1637

Comus is the traditional title of *A Masque Presented at Ludlow Castle*, seat of the earl of Bridgewater, in 1634, with the earl's children playing the main parts. In it a young girl withstands the temptations of the wicked enchanter Comus, and is rescued by her two brothers with the aid of a guardian spirit. In the epilogue the spirit sings of his return to a paradisal realm which sounds rather like Spenser's Gardens of Adonis.

To the Ocean now I fly,
And those happy climes that lie
Where day never shuts his eye,
Up in the broad fields of the sky.
There I suck the liquid air
All amidst the gardens fair
Of Hesperus and his daughters three
That sing about the golden tree.°
Along the crispèd° shades and bowers
Revels the spruce and jocund Spring,
The Graces, and the rosy-bosomed Hours
Thither all their bounties bring,
That there eternal summer dwells,
And west winds with musky wing

° **vitiosity of the matrix**: diseases of the womb.

° from (a) *A Maske Presented at Ludlow Castle, 1634*, London, 1637, pp. 34–35; (b) *Paradise Lost: A Poem in Twelve Books*, 2nd edition, London, 1674, pp. 15–16 (1. 446–57).

° **the gardens fair . . . golden tree**: the Gardens of the Hesperides, in the far west, from which Hercules stole the golden apples.

° **crispèd**: curled.

About the cedarn° alleys fling
Nard and cassia's° balmy smells.
Iris there with humid bow
Waters the odorous banks that blow°
Flowers of more mingled hue
Then her purfled° scarf can show,
And drenches with Elysian dew
(List, mortals, if your ears be true)
Beds of hyacinth and roses
Where young Adonis oft reposes,
Waxing° well of his deep wound
In slumber soft, and on the ground
Sadly sits th' Assyrian queen;°
But far above in spangled sheen
Celestial Cupid, her famed son, advanced,°
Holds his dear Psyche sweet entranced
After her wandring labours long,
Till free consent the gods among
Make her his eternal bride,
And from her fair unspotted side°
Two blissful twins are to be born,
Youth and Joy° – so Jove hath sworn.

(b) from Paradise Lost, 1667

In book 1 of *Paradise Lost* Milton includes Thammuz/Adonis in his catalogue of the fallen angels, now become devils.

Thammuz came next behind,
Whose annual wound in Lebanon allured
The Syrian damsels to lament his fate
In amorous ditties all a summer's day,
While smooth Adonis° from his native rock

° **cedarn**: of cedar trees.
° **Nard** (spikenard) and **cassia** (similar to cinnamon) are spices.
° **blow**: cause to bloom.
° **purfled**: variegated (like the rainbow).
° **Waxing**: growing.
° **th' Assyrian queen**: i.e. Venus/Astarte/Ishtar.
° **advanced**: raised up.
° **unspotted side**: sinless body.
° **Youth and Joy**: rather than Pleasure, as in Spenser.
° **smooth Adonis**: i.e. the River Adonis.

Ran purple to the sea, supposed with blood
Of Thammuz yearly wounded; the love-tale
Infected Zion's daughters with like heat,
Whose wanton passions in the sacred porch
Ezekiel saw, when by the vision led
His eye surveyed the dark idolatries
Of alienated Judah.

A15 John Oldham, from 'Bion: A Pastoral', 1680°

John Oldham, 1653–83, English poet, best known as a satirist and translator of the Roman satirists Horace and Juvenal. The full title of this poem is 'Bion: A Pastoral, in Imitation of the Greek of Moschus, bewailing the Death of the Earl of Rochester'. John Wilmot, 2nd earl of Rochester, courtier, poet and wit at the court of Charles II, writer of bitter satires and wittily obscene love poetry, is here improbably but traditionally transformed into a pastoral shepherd-singer. This passage corresponds to Moschus's lines 77–101; where Moschus compares Bion with Homer, Oldham compares Rochester with Spenser.

. . . With thee, sweet Bion, all the grace of song
And all the Muses' boasted art is gone;
Mute is thy voice, which could all hearts command,
Whose power no shepherdess could e'er withstand.
All the soft weeping Loves about thee moan,
At once their mother's darling and their own.
Dearer wast thou to Venus than her Loves,
Than her charmed girdle, than her faithful doves,
Than the last gasping kisses which in death
Adonis gave, and with them gave his breath.
This, Thames, ah! this is now the second loss,
For which in tears thy weeping current flows.
Spenser, the Muses' glory, went before,
He passed long since to the Elysian shore;
For him, they say, for him, thy dear-loved son,
Thy waves did long in sobbing murmurs groan,
Long filled the sea with their complaint and moan.
But now, alas, thou dost afresh bewail,
Another son does now thy sorrow call.
To part with either thou alike wast loath,

° from *The Works of Mr John Oldham*, London, 1684, pp. 80–2.

Both dear to thee, dear to the fountains both:
He largely drank the rills° of sacred Cam,
And this no less of Isis' nobler stream.°
He sung of heroes and of hardy knights
Far-famed in battles and renowned exploits;
This meddled not with bloody fights and wars;
Pan was his song, and shepherds' harmless jars,°
Love's peaceful combats, and its gentle cares.
Love ever was the subject of his lays,°
And his soft lays did Venus ever please.

Come, all ye Muses, come, adorn the shepherd's hearse
With never-fading garlands, never-dying verse.

A16 Thomas Andrews, from 'On the Death of Mr John Oldham', 1684°

This elegy for Oldham, who died in 1683 at the age of thirty, appeared in his posthumous *Works*; the author, Thomas Andrews, is otherwise unknown.

Mourn, mourn, ye Muses, and your songs give o'er,
For now your loved Adonis is no more.
He whom ye tutored from his infant years
Cold, pale and ghastly as the grave appears;
He whom ye bathed in your loved murmuring stream,
Your daily pleasure and your mighty theme,
Is now no more. The youth, the youth is dead,
The mighty soul of poetry is fled –
Fled ere his worth or merit was half known,
No sooner seen but in a moment gone,
Like to some tender plant which, reared with care,
At length becomes most fragrant and most fair;
Long does it thrive and long its pride maintain,
Esteemed secure from thunder, storm or rain;
Then comes a blast, and all the work is vain.

* * *

° **rills**: streams.
° **Cam . . . Isis**: the rivers **Cam** in Cambrige and **Isis** in Oxford stand for the universities which Spenser and Rochester respectively attended; Oldham, as one might guess, went to Oxford.
° **jars**: conflicts.
° **lays**: songs.
° from *Remains of Mr John Oldham in Verse and Prose*, bound with *The Works of Mr John Oldham*, London, 1684, unpaginated.

But hold! methinks, great shade, I see thee rove
Through the smooth path of plenty, peace and love;
Where Ben° salutes thee first, o'erjoyed to see
The youth that sung his fame and memory;
Great Spenser next, with all the learned train,
Do greet thee in a panegyric strain;
Adonis is the joy of all the plain.

A17 Richard Savage, 'Valentine's Day', *c.* 1740°

Richard Savage, *c.*1698–1743, English poet. His dramatic and self-destructive life – his claim to be the cruelly abandoned illegitimate son of a countess, his extreme poverty and dissolute lifestyle, his trial and aquittal for murder, and his death in prison for debt – were famously described in a 'Life' by his friend Samuel Johnson. 'Valentine's Day' is a characteristically unusual love poem, marking his departure from Swansea in Wales and the end of his courtship of Mrs Bridget Jones ('Chloe') of the neighbouring town of Llanelli. Contrasting the bliss of Venus and Adonis with his own unhappiness in love, Savage is irresistibly drawn to his obsessive theme of the cruel mother.

Valentine's Day

A Poem. Addressed to a Young Widow Lady

Adieu, ye rocks that witnessed once my flame,°
Returned my sighs and echoed Chloe's name!
Cambria,° farewell! – my Chloe's charms no more
Invite my steps along Llanelli's shore.
There no wild dens conceal voracious foes,
The beach no fierce amphibious monster knows;
No crocodile there fleshed with prey appears,
And o'er that bleeding prey weeps cruel tears;
No false hyena, feigning human grief,
There murders him whose goodness means relief.°
Yet tides, conspiring with unfaithful ground,
Though distant seen, with treacherous arms surround;

° **Ben**: Ben Jonson, on whom Oldham wrote a panegyric ode in 1678.
° from *The Works of Richard Savage, Esq.*, London, 1775, vol. ii, pp. 211–16.
° **flame**: i.e. passionate love (a standard piece of eighteenth-century poetic diction).
° **Cambria**: Wales.
° **whose goodness means relief**: who, in his goodness, is intending to help.

There quicksands, thick as beauty's snares, annoy,°
Look fair to tempt, and whom they tempt destroy.
I watched the seas, I paced the sands with care,
Escaped, but wildly rushed on beauty's snare.
Ah! – better far than by that snare o'erpowered,
Had sands engulfed me or had seas devoured!

Far from that shore where siren beauty dwells
And wraps sweet ruin in resistless° spells,
From Cambrian plains which Chloe's lustre boast,
Me native England yields a safer coast.
Chloe, farewell! – now seas with boisterous pride
Divide us, and will ever far divide.
Yet while each plant which vernal youth resumes°
Feels the green blood ascend in future blooms,
While little feathered songsters of the air
In woodlands tuneful woo and fondly pair,
The muse exults, to beauty tunes the lyre,
And willing Loves the swelling notes inspire.

Sure on this day, when hope attains success,
Bright Venus first did young Adonis bless° –
Her charms not brighter, Chloe, sure than thine;
Though flushed his youth, not more his warmth than mine –
Sequestered far within a myrtle grove
Whose blooming bosom courts retiring love;
Where a clear sun the blue serene° displays,
And sheds through vernal air attempered° rays,
Where flowers their aromatic incense bring
And fragrant flourish in eternal spring.
There mate to mate each dove responsive coos,
While this assents, as that enamoured woos.
There rills amusive° send from rocks around
A solitary, pleasing, murmuring sound,
Then form a limpid lake. The lake serene
Reflects the wonders of the blissful scene.

° **annoy**: do harm.
° **resistless**: irresistible.
° **vernal**: spring.
° **bless**: i.e. make him happy.
° **serene**: calm sky.
° **attempered**: moderated, cooled.
° **rills amusive**: pleasure-giving streams.

To love the birds attune their chirping throats,
And on each breeze immortal music floats.
There seated on a rising turf is seen,
Graceful, in loose array, the Cyprian queen,
All fresh and fair, all mild, as ocean gave
The goddess rising from the azure wave.
Dishevelled locks distil celestial dews,
And all her limbs divine perfumes diffuse.
Her voice so charms, the plumy° warbling throngs,
In listening wonder lost, suspend their songs.
It sounds: 'Why loiters my Adonis?' – cry,
'Why loiters my Adonis?' rocks reply.
'Oh, come away!' they thrice repeating say,
And Echo thrice repeats, 'Oh, come away!'
Kind zephyrs waft 'em to her lover's ears,
Who instant at th' enchanting call appears.
Her placid eye, where sparkling joy refines,°
Benignant with alluring lustre shines.
His locks, which in loose ringlets charm the view,
Float careless, lucid° from their amber hue.
A myrtle wreath her rosy fingers frame,
Which from her hand his polished temples claim;
His temples fair a streaking beauty stains,
As smooth white marble shines with azure veins.
He kneeled. Her snowy hand he trembling seized,
Just lifted to his lip, and gently squeezed;
The meaning squeeze returned, love caught its lore
And entered at his palm through every pore.
Then swelled her downy breasts, till then enclosed,
Fast-heaving, half-concealed and half-exposed:
Soft she reclines. He, as they fall and rise,
Hangs hovering o'er 'em with enamoured eyes,
And, warmed, grows wanton – as he thus admired,
He pried, he touched, and with the touch was fired.
Half-angry, yet half-pleased, her frown beguiles
The boy to fear; but, at his fear she smiles.
The youth less timorous, and the fair less coy,
Supinely° amorous they reclining toy.

° **plumy**: feathered.
° **refines**: is made pure.
° **lucid**: shining.
° **Supinely**: lying down.

More amorous still his sanguine° meanings stole
In wistful glances to her softening soul.
In her fair eye her softening soul he reads;
To freedom freedom, boon to boon, succeeds.°
With conscious blush th' impassioned charmer burns,
And blush for blush th' impassioned youth returns.
They look, they languish, sigh with pleasing pain,
And wish and gaze, and gaze and wish again.
'Twixt her white parting bosom steals the boy,
And more than hope preludes tumultuous joy;
Through every vein the vigorous transport ran,
Strung every nerve, and braced the boy to man.
Struggling yet yielding, half o'erpowered, she pants,
Seems to deny, and yet denying grants.
Quick like the tendrils of a curling vine,
Fond limbs with limbs in amorous folds entwine.
Lips press on lips, caressing and caressed,
Now eye darts flame to eye, and breast to breast.
All she resigns, as dear desires incite,
And rapt, he reached the brink of full delight.
Her waist compressed in his exulting arms,
He storms, explores, and rifles all her charms;°
Clasps in extatic bliss th' expiring fair,
And, thrilling, melting, nestling, riots there.

How long the rapture lasts, how soon it fleets,
How oft it pauses, and how oft repeats;
What joys they both receive and both bestow,
Virgins may guess, but wives experienced know.
From joys like these (ah, why denied to me?)
Sprung a fresh blooming boy, my fair, from thee.
May he, a new Adonis, lift his crest,
In all the florid grace of youth confessed!°
First let him learn to lisp your lover's name,
And when he reads, here annual read my flame.
When beauty first shall wake his genial° fire

° **sanguine**: traditionally people of **sanguine** temperament (i.e. dominated by blood) are 'courageous, hopeful, and amorous' – a fair description of Adonis's state of mind.

° **To freedom . . . succeeds**: i.e. she grants him one liberty after another.

° **He storms . . . charms**: sexual conquest is imaged in terms of the capture and looting of a fort.

° **florid**: blooming; **confessed**: clearly to be seen.

° **genial**: sexual, related to generation.

And the first tingling sense excite desire,
When the dear object, of his peace possessed,
Gains and still gains on his unguarded breast,
Then may he say, as he this verse reviews,
'So my bright mother charmed the poet's muse.
His heart thus fluttered oft 'twixt doubt and fear,
Lightened with hope and saddened with despair.
Say, on some rival did she smile too kind?
Ah, read – what jealousy distracts his mind!
Smiled she on him? He imaged° rays divine,
And gazed and gladdened with a love like mine.
How dwelt her praise upon his raptured tongue!
Ah! – when she frowned, what plaintive notes he sung!
And could she frown on him – ah, wherefore, tell!
On him, whose only crime was loving well?'

Thus may thy son his pangs with mine compare,
Then wish his mother had been kind as fair.
For him may Love the myrtle wreath entwine,
Though the sad willow° suits a woe like mine.
Ne'er may the filial hope° like me complain;
Ah, never sigh and bleed, like me, in vain!

When death affords° that peace which love denies,
Ah, no! – far other scenes my fate supplies:
When earth to earth my lifeless corpse is laid,
And o'er it hangs the yew or cypress' shade,
When pale I flit along the dreary coast,
An hapless lover's pining plaintive ghost,
Here annual on this dear returning day,
While feathered choirs renew the melting lay,
May you, my fair, when you these strains shall see,
Just spare one sigh, one tear to love and me –
Me who in absence or in death adore
Those heavenly charms I must behold no more.

° **imaged**: imagined.
° **sad willow**: traditionally associated with unhappy love.
° **filial hope**: i.e. her son.
° **affords**: provides.

A18 Samuel Derrick, 'Venus and Adonis: A Cantata', 1755°

Samuel Derrick, 1724–69, Irish-born writer, later resident in London; he turned his hand to many types of writing, including poetry, translation, travel, history, dramatic reviewing, and letter-writing. He was an acquaintance of Boswell and Dr Johnson, who treated him with a sort of friendly contempt; asked to compare the merits of Derrick and another poet, Johnson declared, 'there is no settling the point of precedency between a louse and a flea'.

Venus and Adonis

A Cantata

Recitative

Venus and Mars confessed an equal flame,°
Their hopes, their wishes, and their joys the same,
Till green-eyed jealousy disturbed his rest;
Watchful he scowled and peevishly caressed.
Conduct like this the goddess must displease,
Freedom her province, her perfection ease.

Air

Swains,° avoid the rigid air,
The prying look, the brow severe;
If you'd have the nymph° approve,
Shun these foes to female love.
Jealousy's a friend to care,
Close connected with despair;
Its companions are constraint,
Disappointment and complaint.
To secure a woman's heart,
This you'll find the only art:
In her honour still confide,°
She'll preserve it out of pride.

° from Samuel Derrick, *A Collection of Original Poems*, London, 1755, pp. 93–6.
° **flame**: love.
° **swains**: lovers (poetic diction, from pastoral poetry – **swain** originally meant 'countryman').
° **nymph**: woman (poetic diction again).
° **confide**: trust.

Recitative

This roused th' Idalian queen to seek abroad
Some kinder object to displace the god.
Adonis seen, his potent charms invade.
A form more lovely nature never made.
Less beautiful the ruddy Bacchus rode
When Ariadne blessed the youthful god.

Air

The naiads cold the youth desire,
For him the dryads feel desire,
And sportive fauns with smile approve
The choice of Cytherea's love.
Struck with his beauty, Pan retired
And broke his reeds, but yet admired.
Adonis all unrivalled reigns,
The darling of the rustic plains.

Recitative

And now the youth, adorned with every grace,
Awe in his heart and blushes in his face,
Approached, while Cupid hovering in the sky
Viewed, and an arrow through his heart let fly.
For beauty's queen the raptured mortal burns;
As fond a passion beauty's queen returns.
The god of hostile sway° beholds too late
His fault, and imprecates° his hapless fate.

Air

Thou who wouldst charm the virgin's ear
  To soft consenting mutual fire,
This short, this lasting maxim hear –
  'Twill mould her to thy warm desire:
Be kind, and thou shalt kindness prove° –
  The first great mystery of love.

° **god of hostile sway**: god whose power is over war.
° **imprecates**: curses.
° **prove**: experience.

A19 Erasmus Darwin, from *The Botanic Garden*, 1791°

Erasmus Darwin, 1731–1802, English physician, botanist, and poet; grandfather of Charles Darwin, the discoverer of evolution. His long poem *The Botanic Garden* (comprising 'The Economy of Vegetation', 1791, and 'The Loves of the Plants', 1789) is an ambitious exposition of natural history in general and botany in particular, combining up-to-date scientific thought with Augustan poetic language and a bizarre range of historical, artistic, biblical and mythological allusion. Defending his use of myth, Darwin claims that 'Many of the important operations of Nature were shadowed or allegorized in the heathen mythology', and invokes Bacon's scientific expositions in *The Wisdom of the Ancients* (p. vii). The passage below, in which the Goddess of Botany instructs her Gnomes or earth-spirits in how to deal with dying and dead matter, allegorises the Adonis story as 'representing the decomposition and resuscitation of animal matter; a sublime and interesting subject, and which seems to have given origin to the doctrine of the transmigration (i.e. reincarnation)' (pp. 107–8).

'You! whose fine fingers fill the organic cells,
With virgin earth, of woods and bones and shells,
Mould with retractile glue their spongy beds,
And stretch and strengthen all their fibre-threads.°
Late when° the mass obeys its changeful doom°
And sinks to earth, its cradle and its tomb,
Gnomes! with nice eye the slow solution° watch,
With fostering hand the parting atoms catch,
Join in new forms, combine with life and sense,
And guide and guard the transmigrating ens.°

° from *The Botanic Garden; A Poem, in Two Parts. Part I containing The Economy of Vegetation, Part II The Loves of the Plants, with Philosophical Notes*, London, 1791.

° **Mould . . . fibre-threads**: 'The constituent parts of animal fibres are believed to be earth and gluten. . . . The retractibility or elasticity of the animal fibre depends on the gluten; and of these fibres are composed the membranes, muscles and bones' (Darwin's note).

° **Late when**: when at last.

° **changeful doom**: predestined change (i.e. death).

° **nice:** precise; **solution**: dissolution.

° **the transmigrating ens**: the being (Latin *ens*) as it passes from one form to another. **Transmigrating** suggests Pythagoras's theory of reincarnation, as Darwin notes: 'The perpetual circulation of matter in the growth and dissolution of vegetable and animal bodies seems to have given Pythagoras his idea of the *metempsychosis* or transmigration of spirit, which was afterwards dressed out or ridiculed in variety of amusing fables.' Darwin prefers the view of other philosophers 'that both matter and spirit are equally immortal and unperishable; and that on the dissolution of vegetable or animal organisation, the matter returns to the general mass of matter, and the spirit to the general mass of spirit, to enter again into new combinations.'

'So when on Lebanon's sequestered height
The fair Adonis left the realms of light,
Bowed his bright locks and, fated from his birth
To change eternal, mingled with the earth,
With darker horror shook the conscious° wood,
Groaned the sad gales, and rivers blushed with blood;
On cypress boughs the Loves their quivers hung,
Their arrows scattered, and their bows unstrung,
And beauty's goddess, bending o'er his bier,
Breathed the soft sigh and poured the tender tear.
Admiring Proserpine through dusky glades
Led the fair phantom to Elysian shades,
Clad with new form, with finer sense combined,
And lit with purer flame the ethereal mind.
Erewhile,° emerging from infernal night,
The bright assurgent° rises into light,
Leaves the drear chambers of the insatiate tomb,
And shines and charms with renovated° bloom.
While wondering Loves the bursting grave surround,
And edge with meeting wings the yawning ground,
Stretch their fair necks, and leaning o'er the brink
View the pale regions of the dead, and shrink,
Long with broad eyes ecstatic Beauty stands,
Heaves her white bosom, spreads her waxen hands;
Then with loud shriek the panting youth alarms,
"My life! my love!" and springs into his arms.'

The Goddess ceased. The delegated° throng
O'er the wide plains delighted rush along;
In dusky squadrons and in shining groups
Hosts follow hosts, and troops succeed to troops;
Scarce bears the bending grass the moving freight,
And nodding florets° bow beneath their weight.
So, when light clouds on airy pinions sail,
Flit the soft shadows o'er the waving vale;
Shade follows shade, as laughing zephyrs drive,
And all the chequered landscape seems alive.

° **conscious**: witnessing.

° **Erewhile** ('formerly') makes little sense here; possibly Darwin meant to write **Erelong** ('before long').

° **assurgent**: one who rises up.

° **renovated**: renewed.

° **delegated**: having received their instructions.

° **florets**: little flowers.

A20 John Keats, from *Endymion*, 1818°

John Keats, 1795–1821, English Romantic poet; of working-class London background, and trained as an apothecary-surgeon, he produced a substantial body of work (including several great odes and the unfinished classical epics *Hyperion* and *The Fall of Hyperion*) before his death of tuberculosis in Rome at the age of twenty-five. *Endymion* is a lush allegorical romance in four books, inspired by the legend of the moon goddess's love for the shepherd Endymion. Keats's first long poem, it was harshly attacked by the critics (one of whom described it as displaying 'calm, settled, imperturbable drivelling idiocy'), and he himself called it 'a feverish attempt, rather than a deed accomplished'. In this passage from book 2, Endymion, in quest of his goddess, comes on the cave where Adonis lies in enchanted sleep, hears his story, and witnesses his reunion with Venus.

After a thousand mazes overgone,°
At last, with sudden step, he came upon
A chamber, myrtle walled, embowered° high,
Full of light, incense, tender minstrelsy,°
And more of beautiful and strange beside:
For on a silken couch of rosy pride,
In midst of all, there lay a sleeping youth
Of fondest beauty; fonder, in fair sooth,°
Than sighs could fathom, or contentment reach:
And coverlids° gold-tinted like the peach,
Or ripe October's faded marigolds,
Fell sleek about him in a thousand folds –
Not hiding up an Apollonian curve
Of neck and shoulder, nor the tenting swerve°
Of knee from knee, nor ankles pointing light;
But rather, giving them to the filled sight
Officiously.° Sideway his face reposed
On one white arm, and tenderly unclosed,
By tenderest pressure, a faint damask° mouth
To slumbery pout; just as the morning south

° from John Keats, *Endymion: A Poetic Romance*, London, 1818, pp. 71–80.
° **overgone**: passed through.
° **embowered**: enclosed as a bower.
° **minstrelsy**: music.
° **in fair sooth**: in truth.
° **coverlids**: coverlets, quilts.
° **tenting swerve**: obscure; perhaps one knee is bent over the other to cover it like a tent.
° **Officiously**: obligingly.
° **damask**: like a damask rose, with 'velvety-crimson' petals.

Disparts° a dew-lipped rose. Above his head,
Four lily stalks did their white honours wed
To make a coronal; and round him grew
All tendrils green, of every bloom and hue,
Together intertwined and trammelled° fresh:
The vine of glossy sprout; the ivy mesh,
Shading its Ethiop° berries; and woodbine,
Of velvet leaves and bugle-blooms divine;
Convolvulus in streakèd vases flush;
The creeper, mellowing for an autumn blush;
And virgin's bower,° trailing airily;
With others of the sisterhood. Hard by,
Stood serene Cupids watching silently.
One, kneeling to a lyre, touched the strings,
Muffling to death the pathos with his wings;
And, ever and anon,° uprose to look
At the youth's slumber; while another took
A willow-bough, distilling odorous dew,
And shook it on his hair; another flew
In through the woven roof, and fluttering-wise
Rained violets upon his sleeping eyes.

At these enchantments, and yet many more,
The breathless Latmian° wondered o'er and o'er;
Until, impatient in embarrassment,
He forthright passed,° and lightly treading went
To that same feathered lyrist, who straightway,
Smiling, thus whispered: 'Though from upper day
Thou art a wanderer, and thy presence here
Might seem unholy, be of happy cheer!
For 'tis the nicest touch of human honour
When some ethereal and high-favouring donor
Presents immortal bowers to mortal sense;
As now 'tis done to thee, Endymion. Hence
Was I in no wise startled. So recline

° **Disparts**: opens up.
° **trammelled**: tied up.
° **Ethiop**: i.e. dark-skinned.
° **virgin's bower**: clematis.
° **ever and anon**: repeatedly.
° **Latmian**: i.e. Endymion, whose home was on Mount Latmos.
° **forthright passed**: came straight forward.

Upon these living flowers. Here is wine,
Alive with sparkles – never, I aver,
Since Ariadne was a vintager,°
So cool a purple: taste these juicy pears,
Sent me by sad Vertumnus, when his fears
Were high about Pomona: here is cream,
Deepening to richness from a snowy gleam;
Sweeter than that nurse Amalthea skimmed
For the boy Jupiter: and here, undimmed
By any touch, a bunch of blooming plums
Ready to melt between an infant's gums:
And here is manna picked from Syrian trees,
In starlight, by the three Hesperides.
Feast on, and meanwhile I will let thee know
Of all these things around us.' He did so,
Still brooding o'er the cadence of his lyre,
And thus: 'I need not any hearing tire
By telling how the sea-born goddess pined
For a mortal youth, and how she strove to bind
Him all in all unto her doting self.
Who would not be so prisoned? but, fond elf,°
He was content to let her amorous plea
Faint through his careless arms; content to see
An unseized heaven dying at his feet;
Content, O fool! to make a cold retreat,
When on the pleasant grass such love, lovelorn,
Lay sorrowing; when every tear was born
Of diverse passion; when her lips and eyes
Were closed in sullen moisture, and quick sighs
Came vexed and pettish through her nostrils small.
Hush! no exclaim – yet, justly mightst thou call
Curses upon his head. – I was half glad,
But my poor mistress went distract and mad,
When the boar tusked him: so away she flew
To Jove's high throne, and by her plainings° drew
Immortal tear-drops down the thunderer's beard;

° **Ariadne was a vintager**: Ariadne became the wife of Bacchus, and hence is imagined as working as a **vintager** (grape-picker) in his vineyard. Other mythological allusions follow: to **Vertumnus**'s courtship of the fruit goddess **Pomona** (*Met.*, 14); to **Amalthea**, Jupiter's Cretan nurse; to the **Hesperides**, the nymphs guarding the golden apples of immortality in their far-western garden.

° **fond elf**: foolish creature.

° **plainings**: complaints, lamentations.

Whereon, it was decreed he should be reared
Each summer time to life. Lo! this is he,
That same Adonis, safe in the privacy
Of this still region all his winter-sleep.
Aye, sleep; for when our love-sick queen did weep
Over his wanèd corpse,° the tremulous shower
Healed up the wound, and, with a balmy power,
Medicined death to a lengthened drowsiness:
The which she fills with visions, and doth dress
In all this quiet luxury; and hath set
Us young immortals, without any let,°
To watch his slumber through. 'Tis well nigh passed,
Even to a moment's filling up, and fast
She scuds with summer breezes, to pant through
The first long kiss, warm firstling,° to renew
Embowered sports in Cytherea's isle.
Look! how those wingèd listeners all this while
Stand anxious: see! behold!' – This clamant° word
Broke through the careful silence; for they heard
A rustling noise of leaves, and out there fluttered
Pigeons and doves: Adonis something muttered
The while one hand, that erst° upon his thigh
Lay dormant, moved convulsed and gradually
Up to his forehead. Then there was a hum
Of sudden voices, echoing, 'Come! come!
Arise! awake! Clear summer has forth walked
Unto the clover-sward, and she has talked
Full soothingly to every nested finch.
Rise, Cupids! or we'll give the blue-bell pinch°
To your dimpled arms! Once more sweet life begin!'
At this, from every side they hurried in,
Rubbing their sleepy eyes with lazy wrists,
And doubling over head their little fists
In backward yawns. But all were soon alive:
For as delicious wine doth, sparkling, dive
In nectared clouds and curls through water fair,

° **wanèd**: shrunken.
° **let**: hindrance.
° **firstling**: first offspring.
° **clamant**: cried-out.
° **erst**: formerly.
° **give the blue-bell pinch**: i.e. make them blue as bluebells with bruises.

So from the arbour roof down swelled an air
Odorous and enlivening; making all
To laugh, and play, and sing, and loudly call
For their sweet queen: when lo! the wreathèd green
Disparted, and far upward could be seen
Blue heaven, and a silver car,° air-borne,
Whose silent wheels, fresh wet from clouds of morn,
Spun off a drizzling dew – which falling chill
On soft Adonis shoulders, made him still°
Nestle and turn uneasily about.
Soon were the white doves plain, with necks stretched out,
And silken traces° lightened in descent;
And soon, returning from love's banishment,
Queen Venus leaning downward open armed;
Her shadow fell upon his breast, and charmed
A tumult to his heart and a new life
Into his eyes. Ah, miserable strife,
But for her comforting! unhappy sight,
But meeting her blue orbs! Who, who can write
Of these first minutes? The unchariest° muse
To embracements warm as theirs makes coy excuse.°
O it has ruffled every spirit there,
Saving love's self,° who stands superb to share
The general gladness: awfully he stands;
A sovereign quell° is in his waving hands;
No sight can bear the lightning of his bow;
His quiver is mysterious, none can know
What themselves think of it; from forth his eyes
There darts strange light of varied hues and dyes;
A scowl is sometimes on his brow, but who°
Look full upon it feel anon the blue
Of his fair eyes run liquid through their souls.
Endymion feels it, and no more controls

° **car**: chariot.
° **still**: continually.
° **traces**: reins.
° **unchariest**: least cautious, frankest.
° **makes coy excuse**: i.e. modestly refuses to describe them.
° **love's self**: i.e. Eros/Cupid – clearly a different and more formidable figure than the 'feathered lyrist' and the other 'Cupids' who tend Adonis.
° **sovereign quell**: supreme power to subdue.
° **who**: those who.

The burning prayer within him; so, bent low,
He had begun a plaining of his woe.
But Venus, bending forward, said: 'My child,
Favour this gentle youth; his days are wild
With love – he – but alas! too well I see
Thou know'st the deepness of his misery.
Ah, smile not so, my son: I tell thee true
That when through heavy hours I used to rue
The endless sleep of this new-born Adon,
This stranger ay° I pitied. For upon
A dreary morning once I fled away
Into the breezy clouds, to weep and pray
For this my love: for vexing Mars had teased
Me even to tears: thence, when a little eased,
Down-looking, vacant, through a hazy wood,
I saw this youth as he despairing stood:
Those same dark curls blown vagrant in the wind;
Those same full-fringèd lids a constant blind
Over his sullen eyes: I saw him throw
Himself on withered leaves, even as though
Death had come sudden; for no jot he moved,
Yet muttered wildly. I could hear he loved
Some fair immortal, and that his embrace
Had zoned° her through the night. There is no trace
Of this in heaven: I have marked each cheek,
And find it is the vainest thing to seek;
And that of all things 'tis kept secretest.
Endymion! one day thou wilt be blest:
So still obey the guiding hand that fends°
Thee safely through these wonders for sweet ends.
'Tis a concealment needful in extreme;
And if I guessed not so, the sunny beam
Thou shouldst mount up to with me. Now adieu!
Here must we leave thee.' – At these words up flew
The impatient doves, up rose the floating car,
Up went the hum celestial. High afar
The Latmian saw them minish° into naught;

° **ay**: always.
° **zoned**: surrounded.
° **fends**: protects.
° **minish**: diminish.

And, when all were clear vanished, still he caught
A vivid lightning from that dreadful bow.
When all was darkened, with Etnean throe°
The earth closed – gave a solitary moan –
And left him once again in twilight lone.

A21 Percy Bysshe Shelley, *Adonais*, 1821°

On Shelley, see headnote to **O33**. *Adonais* is his lament for the death of Keats, which he believed (wrongly) to have been caused by hostile criticism, especially an anonymous review in the *Quarterly Review*. Shelley, who had already made fragmentary translations of Bion and Moschus, drew on the 'lament for Adonis' tradition in his elegy. The boar's tusk becomes a 'shaft which flies / In darkness', and is blended with the poison which Moschus claimed Bion drank as symbols of the murderous effects of malicious criticism.

Adonais

An Elegy on the Death of John Keats, Author of Endymion, Hyperion, Etc.

Ἀστμρ πριν μεν ελαμπεσ ενι ζωοισιν Ἑωοσ
νυν δε θανων λαμπεισ Εσπεροσ εν φθιμενοισ. PLATO°

1

I weep for Adonais – he is dead!
O, weep for Adonais! though our tears
Thaw not the frost which binds so dear a head!°
And thou, sad Hour, selected from all years
To mourn our loss, rouse thy obscure compeers,°
And teach them thine own sorrow, say: 'With me
Died Adonais; till the Future dares
Forget the Past, his fate and fame shall be
An echo and a light unto eternity!'

° **Etnean throe**: a quake like Mount Etna (a Sicilian volcano) erupting.

° from *Adonais: An Elegy on the Death of John Keats*, Pisa, 1821.

° **Αστμρ . . . φθιμενοισ** An epitaph attributed (probably wrongly) to Plato. Shelley translated it as follows: 'Thou wert the evening star among the living, / Ere thy fair light had fled; / Now, having died, thou art as Hesperus, giving / New splendour to the dead.'

° **head**: i.e. life (a Greek idiom).

° **compeers**: fellows.

2

Where wert thou, mighty Mother, when he lay,
When thy Son lay, pierced by the shaft which flies
In darkness? where was lorn Urania
When Adonais died? With veilèd eyes,
'Mid listening Echoes, in her Paradise
She sat, while one, with soft enamoured breath,
Rekindled all the fading melodies,
With which, like flowers that mock the corpse beneath,
He had adorned and hid the coming bulk of death.

3

Oh, weep for Adonais – he is dead!
Wake, melancholy Mother, wake and weep!
Yet wherefore? Quench within their burning bed
Thy fiery tears, and let thy loud heart keep
Like his, a mute and uncomplaining sleep;
For he is gone, where all things wise and fair
Descend; oh, dream not that the amorous Deep
Will yet restore him to the vital air;
Death feeds on his mute voice, and laughs at our despair.

4

Most musical of mourners, weep again!
Lament anew, Urania! – He died,°
Who was the Sire of an immortal strain,
Blind, old, and lonely, when his country's pride,
The priest, the slave, and the liberticide,°
Trampled and mocked with many a loathèd rite
Of lust and blood; he went, unterrified,
Into the gulf of death; but his clear Sprite°
Yet reigns o'er earth; the third among the sons of light.

5

Most musical of mourners, weep anew!
Not all to that bright station dared to climb;
And happier they their happiness who knew,

° **He died**: i.e. Milton; the earlier two **sons of light** are probably Homer and Dante.

° **liberticide**: killer of liberty (i.e. those who supported the restoration of the monarchy in 1660). Shelley is imitating Milton's inversions of syntax; the sense is 'when the priest [etc.] . . . trampled and mocked his country's pride'.

° **Sprite**: spirit.

Whose tapers yet burn through that night of time
In which suns perished; others more sublime,
Struck by the envious wrath of man or god,
Have sunk, extinct in their refulgent prime;°
And some yet live, treading the thorny road,
Which leads, through toil and hate, to Fame's serene abode.

6

But now, thy youngest, dearest one, has perished,
The nursling of thy widowhood, who grew,
Like a pale flower by some sad maiden cherished,
And fed with true love tears, instead of dew;
Most musical of mourners, weep anew!
Thy extreme° hope, the loveliest and the last,
The bloom, whose petals nipped before they blew°
Died on the promise of the fruit, is waste;
The broken lily lies – the storm is overpast.

7

To that high Capital,° where kingly Death
Keeps his pale court in beauty and decay,
He came; and bought, with price of purest breath,
A grave among the eternal. – Come away!
Haste, while the vault of blue Italian day
Is yet his fitting charnel-roof! while still
He lies, as if in dewy sleep he lay;
Awake him not! surely he takes his fill
Of deep and liquid rest, forgetful of all ill.

8

He will awake no more, oh, never more! –
Within the twilight chamber spreads apace
The shadow of white Death, and at the door
Invisible Corruption waits to trace
His extreme way to her dim dwelling-place;
The eternal Hunger sits, but pity and awe

° **And happier . . . refulgent prime**: Shelley contrasts minor poets (like **tapers**, candles) whose work has luckily survived, with greater poets (**suns**) whose work has been entirely lost; **refulgent**: brightly shining.
° **extreme**: final.
° **nipped before they blew**: blighted by frost before they blossomed.
° **Capital**: i.e. Rome (where Keats died).

Soothe her pale rage, nor dares she to deface
So fair a prey, till darkness, and the law
Of mortal change, shall fill the grave which is her maw.

9

Oh, weep for Adonais! – The quick Dreams,°
The passion-wingèd Ministers of thought,
Who were his flocks, whom near the living streams
Of his young spirit he fed, and whom he taught
The love which was its music, wander not –
Wander no more, from kindling brain to brain,
But droop there, whence they sprung; and mourn their lot
Round the cold heart, where, after their sweet pain,
They ne'er will gather strength, or find a home again.

10

And one with trembling hands clasps his cold head,
And fans him with her moonlight wings, and cries;
'Our love, our hope, our sorrow, is not dead;
See, on the silken fringe of his faint eyes,
Like dew upon a sleeping flower, there lies
A tear some Dream has loosened from his brain.'
Lost Angel of a ruined Paradise!
She knew not 'twas her own; as with no stain
She faded, like a cloud which had outwept its rain.

11

One from a lucid° urn of starry dew
Washed his light limbs as if embalming them;
Another clipped her profuse locks, and threw
The wreath upon him, like an anadem,°
Which frozen tears instead of pearls begem;
Another in her wilful grief would break
Her bow and wingèd reeds, as if to stem
A greater loss with one which was more weak;
And dull the barbèd fire against his frozen cheek.

° **Dreams**: the Dreams, Splendours, Fantasies, etc., are personifications of Keats's poetry, mourning their dead creator; in traditional pastoral imagery, he is the shepherd and they his sheep.
° **lucid**: shining.
° **anadem**: garland.

12

Another Splendour on his mouth alit,
That mouth, whence it was wont to draw the breath
Which gave it strength to pierce the guarded wit,
And pass into the panting heart beneath°
With lightning and with music: the damp death
Quenched its caress upon his icy lips;
And, as a dying meteor stains a wreath
Of moonlight vapour, which the cold night clips,°
It flushed through his pale limbs, and passed to its eclipse.

13

And others came . . . Desires and Adorations,
Wingèd Persuasions and veiled Destinies,
Splendours, and Glooms, and glimmering Incarnations
Of hopes and fears, and twilight Fantasies;
And Sorrow, with her family of Sighs,
And Pleasure, blind with tears, led by the gleam
Of her own dying smile instead of eyes,
Came in slow pomp – the moving pomp might seem
Like pageantry of mist on an autumnal stream.

14

All he had loved, and moulded into thought,
From shape, and hue, and odour, and sweet sound,
Lamented Adonais. Morning sought
Her eastern watchtower, and her hair unbound,
Wet with the tears which should adorn the ground,
Dimmed the aerial eyes that kindle day;
Afar the melancholy thunder moaned,
Pale Ocean in unquiet slumber lay,
And the wild Winds flew round, sobbing in their dismay.

15

Lost Echo sits amid the voiceless mountains,
And feeds her grief with his remembered lay,
And will no more reply to winds or fountains,
Or amorous birds perched on the young green spray,

° **pierce . . . heart beneath**: i.e. poetry must overcome the reader's sceptical intellect to make direct contact with his or her emotions.

° **clips**: embraces.

Or herdsman's horn, or bell at closing day;
Since she can mimic not his lips, more dear
Than those for whose disdain she pined away
Into a shadow of all sounds – a drear
Murmur, between their songs, is all the woodmen hear.°

16

Grief made the young Spring wild, and she threw down
Her kindling buds, as if she Autumn were,
Or they dead leaves; since her delight is flown,
For whom should she have waked the sullen year?
To Phoebus was not Hyacinth so dear
Nor to himself Narcissus,° as to both
Thou, Adonais: wan they stand and sere
Amid the faint companions of their youth,
With dew all turned to tears; odour, to sighing ruth.°

17

Thy spirit's sister, the lorn nightingale°
Mourns not her mate with such melodious pain;
Not so the eagle, who like thee could scale
Heaven, and could nourish in the sun's domain
Her mighty youth with morning, doth complain,
Soaring and screaming round her empty nest,
As Albion° wails for thee: the curse of Cain°
Light on his head who pierced thy innocent breast,
And scared the angel soul that was its earthly guest!

18

Ah, woe is me! Winter is come and gone,
But grief returns with the revolving year;
The airs and streams renew their joyous tone;
The ants, the bees, the swallows reappear;

° **Lost Echo . . . woodmen hear**: alluding to the story of Echo and Narcissus (*Met.*, 3; see ch. 3, p. 40 above).
° **Hyacinth . . . Narcissus**: see ch. 3, pp. 39–40 above for their transformations into wild flowers.
° **ruth**: pity.
° **lorn nightingale**: alluding to Keats's 'Ode to a Nightingale'.
° **Albion**: England.
° **curse of Cain**: for the murder of his brother Abel, God condemned Cain to be 'a fugitive and a vagabond . . . in the earth', and 'set a mark upon' him (Genesis 4: 12–15); Shelley calls down this curse on Keats's critics.

Fresh leaves and flowers deck the dead Seasons' bier;
The amorous birds now pair in every brake,°
And build their mossy homes in field and brere;°
And the green lizard, and the golden snake,
Like unimprisoned flames, out of their trance awake.

19

Through wood and stream and field and hill and Ocean
A quickening life from the Earth's heart has burst
As it has ever done, with change and motion,
From the great morning of the world when first
God dawned on Chaos; in its steam° immersed
The lamps of Heaven flash with a softer light;
All baser things pant with life's sacred thirst;
Diffuse themselves; and spend in love's delight,
The beauty and the joy of their renewèd might.

20

The leprous corpse touched by this spirit tender
Exhales itself in flowers of gentle breath;
Like incarnations of the stars, when splendour
Is changed to fragrance, they illumine death
And mock the merry worm that wakes beneath;
Nought we know, dies. Shall that alone which knows
Be as a sword consumed before the sheath
By sightless lightning?° – the intense atom glows
A moment, then is quenched in a most cold repose.

21

Alas! that all we loved of him should be,
But for our grief, as if it had not been,
And grief itself be mortal! Woe is me!
Whence are we, and why are we? of what scene
The actors or spectators? Great and mean
Meet massed in death, who lends what life must borrow.
As long as skies are blue, and fields are green,

° **brake**: clump of bushes.

° **brere**: briar.

° **steam**: later editions have **stream**, perhaps rightly.

° **Shall that alone . . . lightning?**: i.e. is it only the mind (**that which knows**) which dies utterly, while the body (which is merely its container, like a sword's sheath) is immortal?

Evening must usher night, night urge the morrow,
Month follow month with woe, and year wake year to sorrow.

22

He will awake no more, oh, never more!
'Wake thou,' cried Misery, 'childless Mother, rise
Out of thy sleep, and slake, in thy heart's core,
A wound more fierce than his, with tears and sighs.'
And all the Dreams that watched Urania's eyes,
And all the Echoes whom their sister's song
Had held in holy silence, cried: 'Arise!'
Swift as a Thought by the snake Memory stung,
From her ambrosial rest the fading Splendour sprung.

23

She rose like an autumnal Night, that springs
Out of the East, and follows wild and drear
The golden Day, which, on eternal wings,
Even as a ghost abandoning a bier,
Had left the Earth a corpse. Sorrow and fear
So struck, so roused, so rapt Urania;
So saddened round her like an atmosphere
Of stormy mist; so swept her on her way
Even to the mournful place where Adonais lay.

24

Out of her secret Paradise she sped,
Through camps and cities rough with stone, and steel,
And human hearts, which to her airy tread
Yielding not, wounded the invisible
Palms° of her tender feet where'er they fell:
And barbèd tongues, and thoughts more sharp than they,
Rent the soft Form they never could repel,
Whose sacred blood, like the young tears of May,
Paved with eternal flowers that undeserving way.

25

In the death chamber for a moment Death,
Shamed by the presence of that living Might,
Blushed to annihilation, and the breath

° **palms**: i.e. soles (an unusual usage).

Revisited those lips, and Life's pale light
Flashed through those limbs, so late her dear delight.
'Leave me not wild and dread and comfortless,
As silent lightning leaves the starless night!
Leave me not!' cried Urania: her distress
Roused Death: Death rose and smiled, and met her vain caress.

26

'Stay yet awhile! speak to me once again;
Kiss me, so long but as a kiss may live;
And in my heartless breast and burning brain
That word, that kiss, shall all thoughts else survive,
With food of saddest memory kept alive,
Now thou art dead, as if it were a part
Of thee, my Adonais! I would give
All that I am to be as thou now art!
But I am chained to Time, and cannot thence depart!

27

'O gentle child, beautiful as thou wert,
Why didst thou leave the trodden paths of men
Too soon, and with weak hands though mighty heart
Dare the unpastured° dragon in his den?
Defenceless as thou wert, oh, where was then
Wisdom the mirrored shield,° or scorn the spear?
Or hadst thou waited the full cycle, when
Thy spirit should have filled its crescent sphere,°
The monsters of life's waste had fled from thee like deer.

28

'The herded wolves, bold only to pursue;
The obscene ravens, clamorous o'er the dead;
The vultures to the conqueror's banner true
Who feed where Desolation first has fed,
And whose wings rain contagion – how they fled,
When, like Apollo, from his golden bow
The Pythian of the age° one arrow sped

° **unpastured**: unfed, hungry (the **dragon** personifies the critics; Shelley had advised Keats against publishing his early poems).
° **mirrored shield**: like the one used by Perseus to slay Medusa.
° **filled its crescent sphere**: i.e. grown to maturity (like the moon becoming full).
° **the Pythian of the age**: i.e. Byron, who silenced the critics with his satirical poem *English Bards and Scotch Reviewers*; he is compared to **Pythian Apollo**, slayer of the monster Python.

And smiled! – The spoilers tempt no second blow,
They fawn on the proud feet that spurn them lying low.

29

'The sun comes forth, and many reptiles spawn;
He sets, and each ephemeral insect then
Is gathered into death without a dawn,
And the immortal stars awake again;
So is it in the world of living men:
A godlike mind soars forth, in its delight
Making earth bare and veiling heaven, and when
It sinks, the swarms that dimmed or shared its light
Leave to its kindred lamps the spirit's awful night.'

30

Thus ceased she: and the mountain shepherds° came,
Their garlands sere,° their magic mantles rent;
The Pilgrim of Eternity,° whose fame
Over his living head like Heaven is bent,
An early but enduring monument,
Came, veiling all the lightnings of his song
In sorrow; from her wilds Ierne sent
The sweetest lyrist° of her saddest wrong,
And love taught grief to fall like music from his tongue.

31

Midst others of less note, came one frail Form,°
A phantom among men; companionless
As the last cloud of an expiring storm
Whose thunder is its knell; he, as I guess,
Had gazed on Nature's naked loveliness,
Actaeon-like,° and now he fled astray
With feeble steps o'er the world's wilderness,
And his own thoughts, along that rugged way,
Pursued, like raging hounds, their father and their prey.

° **the mountain shepherds**: symbolic versions of contemporary poets.
° **sere**: dried up.
° **Pilgrim of Eternity**: Byron again; **Pilgrim** alludes both to his own travels and his poem *Childe Harold's Pilgrimage.*
° **the sweetest lyrist**: Thomas Moore, author of *Irish Melodies*; **Ierne** is Ireland.
° **one frail Form**: Shelley himself.
° **Actaeon-like**: for the story of Actaeon see ch. 3, p. 41, or *Metamorphoses*, book 3.

32

A pardlike° Spirit beautiful and swift –
A Love in desolation masked – a Power
Girt round with weakness – it can scarce uplift
The weight of the superincumbent° hour;
It is a dying lamp, a falling shower,
A breaking billow – even whilst we speak
Is it not broken? On the withering flower
The killing sun smiles brightly: on a cheek
The life can burn in blood, even while the heart may break.

33

His head was bound with pansies overblown,
And faded violets, white, and pied, and blue;
And a light spear topped with a cypress cone,
Round whose rude shaft dark ivy tresses grew°
Yet dripping with the forest's noonday dew,
Vibrated, as the ever-beating heart
Shook the weak hand that grasped it; of that crew
He came the last, neglected and apart;
A herd-abandoned deer struck by the hunter's dart.

34

All stood aloof, and at his partial° moan
Smiled through their tears; well knew that gentle band
Who in another's fate now wept his own,
As in the accents of an unknown land
He sung new sorrow; sad Urania scanned
The Stranger's mien, and murmured: 'Who art thou?'
He answered not, but with a sudden hand
Made bare his branded and ensanguined° brow,
Which was like Cain's or Christ's° – oh! that it should be so!

° **pardlike**: like a leopard.
° **superincumbent**: pressing down upon (it).
° **light spear . . . ivy tresses grew**: this is the *thyrsus*, the emblem of Dionysus.
° **partial**: not unbiased (as the next lines imply, Shelley's lament for Adonais/Keats is also for himself).
° **ensanguined**: bloody.
° **like Cain's or Christ's**: Shelley blends Cain's 'mark' and Christ's crown of thorns – but the implications of this melodramatic comparison are unclear.

35

What softer voice is hushed over the dead?
Athwart what brow is that dark mantle thrown?
What form leans sadly o'er the white death-bed,
In mockery of monumental stone,
The heavy heart heaving without a moan?
If it be He, who, gentlest of the wise,°
Taught, soothed, loved, honoured the departed one,
Let me not vex, with inharmonious sighs,
The silence of that heart's accepted sacrifice.

36

Our Adonais has drunk poison° – oh!
What deaf and viperous murderer could crown
Life's early cup with such a draught of woe?
The nameless worm° would now itself disown:
It felt, yet could escape, the magic tone
Whose prelude held all envy, hate, and wrong,
But what was howling in one breast alone,
Silent with expectation of the song,
Whose master's hand is cold, whose silver lyre unstrung.

37

Live thou, whose infamy is not thy fame!
Live! fear no heavier chastisement from me,
Thou noteless° blot on a remembered name!
But be thyself, and know thyself to be!
And ever at thy season be thou free
To spill the venom when thy fangs o'erflow;
Remorse and Self-contempt shall cling to thee;
Hot Shame shall burn upon thy secret brow,
And like a beaten hound tremble thou shalt – as now.

° **He . . . gentlest of the wise**: Leigh Hunt, essayist and editor, close friend of Keats.

° **Our Adonais has drunk poison**: Compare Moschus, lines 131–6; but for Shelley the poison is a metaphor for malicious criticism, especially that of the anonymous reviewer in the *Quarterly Review*, who is attacked in the next three stanzas.

° **worm**: can mean 'dragon' (as in stanza 27), 'snake', or (most contemptuously) 'worm' in the modern sense.

° **noteless**: undistinguished.

38

Nor let us weep that our delight is fled
Far from these carrion kites that scream below;
He wakes or sleeps with the enduring dead;
Thou canst not soar where he is sitting now. –
Dust to the dust! but the pure spirit shall flow
Back to the burning fountain whence it came,
A portion of the Eternal, which must glow
Through time and change, unquenchably the same,
Whilst thy cold embers choke the sordid hearth of shame.

39

Peace, peace! he is not dead, he doth not sleep –
He hath awakened from the dream of life –
'Tis we, who lost in stormy visions, keep
With phantoms an unprofitable strife,
And in mad trance, strike with our spirit's knife
Invulnerable nothings. – *We* decay
Like corpses in a charnel; fear and grief
Convulse us and consume us day by day,
And cold hopes swarm like worms within our living clay.

40

He has outsoared the shadow of our night;
Envy and calumny° and hate and pain,
And that unrest which men miscall delight,
Can touch him not and torture not again;
From the contagion of the world's slow stain
He is secure, and now can never mourn
A heart grown cold, a head grown gray in vain;
Nor, when the spirit's self has ceased to burn,
With sparkless ashes load an unlamented urn.

41

He lives, he wakes – 'tis Death is dead, not he;
Mourn not for Adonais. – Thou young Dawn,
Turn all thy dew to splendour, for from thee
The spirit thou lamentest is not gone;
Ye caverns and ye forests, cease to moan!

° **calumny**: slander.

Cease, ye faint flowers and fountains, and thou Air,
Which like a mourning veil thy scarf hadst thrown
O'er the abandoned Earth, now leave it bare
Even to the joyous stars which smile on its despair!

42

He is made one with Nature:° there is heard
His voice in all her music, from the moan
Of thunder, to the song of night's sweet bird;
He is a presence to be felt and known
In darkness and in light, from herb and stone,
Spreading itself where'er that Power may move
Which has withdrawn his being to its own;
Which wields the world with never-wearied love,
Sustains it from beneath, and kindles it above.

43

He is a portion of the loveliness
Which once he made more lovely: he doth bear
His part, while the one Spirit's plastic stress°
Sweeps through the dull dense world, compelling there,
All new successions to the forms they wear;
Torturing the unwilling dross that checks its flight
To its own likeness, as each mass may bear;
And bursting in its beauty and its might
From trees and beasts and men into the Heaven's light.

44

The splendours of the firmament of time
May be eclipsed, but are extinguished not;
Like stars to their appointed height they climb,
And death is a low mist which cannot blot
The brightness it may veil. When lofty thought
Lifts a young heart above its mortal lair,
And love and life contend in it, for what
Shall be its earthly doom, the dead live there
And move like winds of light on dark and stormy air.

° **He is made one with Nature**: in this and the next stanza Shelley argues that Adonais is united with nature, not just because his physical body is returned to the earth, but because his soul has become a part of the 'one Spirit', the 'world-soul', which controls and animates nature. In a Platonic concept, the Spirit is seen as forcing base matter to adopt forms closer to the ideal, making the natural world gradually more and more like the ideal spiritual world.

° **plastic stress**: shaping power.

45

The inheritors of unfulfilled renown°
Rose from their thrones, built beyond mortal thought,
Far in the Unapparent. Chatterton
Rose pale, his solemn agony had not
Yet faded from him; Sidney, as he fought
And as he fell and as he lived and loved
Sublimely mild, a Spirit without spot,
Arose; and Lucan, by his death approved:
Oblivion as they rose shrank like a thing reproved.

46

And many more, whose names on Earth are dark,
But whose transmitted effluence° cannot die
So long as fire outlives the parent spark,
Rose, robed in dazzling immortality.
'Thou art become as one of us,' they cry,
'It was for thee yon kingless sphere has long
Swung blind in unascended majesty,
Silent alone amid an Heaven of Song.
Assume thy wingèd throne, thou Vesper° of our throng!'

47

Who mourns for Adonais? oh come forth
Fond° wretch! and know thyself and him aright.
Clasp with thy panting soul the pendulous° Earth;
As from a centre, dart thy spirit's light
Beyond all worlds, until its spacious might
Satiate the void circumference: then shrink
Even to a point within our day and night;
And keep thy heart light lest it make thee sink
When hope has kindled hope, and lured thee to the brink.

° **inheritors of unfulfilled renown**: poets who died young before achieving their full potential: Thomas **Chatterton** poisoned himself in 1770, aged seventeen; Sir Philip **Sidney** died of war wounds in 1586, aged thirty-two; the Roman poet **Lucan** was compelled to commit suicide at the age of twenty-six after plotting to assassinate the emperor Nero.

° **effluence**: flowing out of light.

° **Vesper**: or Hesperus, the Evening Star.

° **Fond**: foolish.

° **pendulous**: hanging.

48

Or go to Rome, which is the sepulchre,
O, not of him, but of our joy: 'tis nought
That ages, empires, and religions there
Lie buried in the ravage they have wrought;
For such as he can lend – they borrow not
Glory from those who made the world their prey;
And he is gathered to the kings of thought
Who waged contention with their time's decay,
And of the past are all that cannot pass away.

49

Go thou to Rome – at once the Paradise,
The grave, the city, and the wilderness;
And where its wrecks like shattered mountains rise,
And flowering weeds, and fragrant copses dress
The bones of Desolation's nakedness
Pass, till the spirit of the spot shall lead
Thy footsteps to a slope of green access°
Where, like an infant's smile, over the dead
A light of laughing flowers along the grass is spread;

50

And gray walls moulder round, on which dull Time
Feeds, like slow fire upon a hoary brand;
And one keen pyramid with wedge sublime,
Pavilioning the dust of him who planned
This refuge for his memory, doth stand
Like flame transformed to marble; and beneath,
A field is spread, on which a newer band
Have pitched in Heaven's smile their camp of death,
Welcoming him we lose with scarce extinguished breath.

51

Here pause: these graves are all too young as yet
To have outgrown the sorrow which consigned
Its charge to each; and if the seal is set,
Here, on one fountain of a mourning mind,

° **a slope of green access . . .**: a description of the Protestant cemetery in Rome, burial-place of Keats (and later of Shelley). The **keen pyramid** is the tomb of the Roman Caius Cestius, which looms over the cemetery.

Break it not thou!° too surely shalt thou find
Thine own well full, if thou returnest home,
Of tears and gall. From the world's bitter wind
Seek shelter in the shadow of the tomb.
What Adonais is, why fear we to become?

52

The One remains, the many change and pass;
Heaven's light forever shines, Earth's shadows fly;
Life, like a dome of many-coloured glass,
Stains the white radiance of Eternity,°
Until Death tramples it to fragments. – Die,
If thou wouldst be with that which thou dost seek!
Follow where all is fled! – Rome's azure sky,
Flowers, ruins, statues, music, words, are weak
The glory they transfuse with fitting truth to speak.

53

Why linger, why turn back, why shrink, my Heart?
Thy hopes are gone before: from all things here
They have departed; thou shouldst now depart!
A light is passed from the revolving year,
And man, and woman; and what still is dear
Attracts to crush, repels to make thee wither.
The soft sky smiles – the low wind whispers near:
'Tis Adonais calls! oh, hasten thither,
No more let Life divide what Death can join together.

54

That Light whose smile kindles the Universe,
That Beauty in which all things work and move,
That Benediction which the eclipsing Curse
Of birth can quench not, that sustaining Love
Which through the web of being blindly wove
By man and beast and earth and air and sea,
Burns bright or dim, as each are mirrors of
The fire for which all thirst; now beams on me,
Consuming the last clouds of cold mortality.

° **if the seal . . . not thou!**: Shelley's three-year-old son was buried in the cemetery in 1819.

° **The One remains . . . of Eternity**: a famous expression of the Platonic doctrine that the variety and confusion of the natural world we perceive is only a distorted reflection of the unity and harmony of God and the world of the Ideal.

55

The breath whose might I have invoked in song
Descends on me; my spirit's bark° is driven,
Far from the shore, far from the trembling throng
Whose sails were never to the tempest given;
The massy earth and spherèd skies are riven!
I am borne darkly, fearfully, afar;
Whilst, burning through the inmost veil of Heaven,
The soul of Adonais, like a star,
Beacons from the abode where the Eternal are.

A22 Robert Bulwer-Lytton, 'Adon', 1855°

Robert Bulwer-Lytton, 1st Earl of Lytton (1831–91), poet, novelist, and diplomat, who wrote under the pseudonym of 'Owen Meredith'. He is sometimes confused with his more famous father, the best-selling novelist and playwright Edward Bulwer-Lytton, Lord Lytton.

Adon

I will not weep for Adon!
I will not waste my breath to draw thick sighs
For spring's dead greenness. All the orient skies
Are hushed, and breathing out a bright surprise
Round morning's marshalling star: rise, Eos,° rise!
Day's dazzling spears are up: the faint stars fade on
The white hills – cold, like Adon!

O'er crag, and spar, and splinter
Break down, and roll the amber mist, stern light!
The black pines dream of dawn. The skirts of night
Are ravelled in the East. And planted bright
In heaven, the roots of ice shine, sharp and white,
In frozen ray, and spar, and spike, and splinter.
Within me, and without, all's winter.

Why should I weep for Adon?
Am I, because the sweet Past is no more,

° **bark**: ship; the imagery of this final stanza uncannily foreshadows Shelley's own death in a boating accident a year later.

° from Owen Meredith, *Clytemnestra, The Earl's Return, The Artist, and Other Poems*, London, 1855, pp. 328–9.

° **Eos**: goddess of Dawn.

Dead, as the leaves upon the graves of yore?
I will breathe boldly, though the air be frore°
With freezing fire. Life still beats at the core
  Of the world's heart, though Death his awe hath laid on
  This dumb white corpse of Adon.

A23 Lord De Tabley, 'A Lament for Adonis', *c*.1865°

On Lord De Tabley, see headnote to **O38**.

A Lament for Adonis

We will lament the beautiful Adonis!
The sleepy clouds are lulled in all their trails.
The river-beds are weary for the rain.
The branchy volumes of the clouded pines,
Like drooping banners, in excess of noon
Languish beneath the forehead of the sun:
Nor dares one gale to breathe, one ivy-leaf
To flicker on its strings about the boles.

Lament Adonis here in dead-ripe noon;
Weep for her weeping, Queen of love and dream,
Disconsolate, love's ruler love-bereaved:
Where is thy godhead fallen, what avail
To throne it on the clouds yet lose thy joy?
Couldst thou not hold Adonis on thy lips
Eternally, and scorn the ebbing years?
This, this were meed of immortality,
To wear thy stately love secure and fair
Of rainy eyes: now shalt thou ne'er resume,
Enamoured Queen, thy shelter at his heart:
His arms no longer Aphroditè's nest.

Kneel then, and weep with her and weep with her.
It is not meet that pure cheek's crimsoning,
It is not fate those bloom-ripe limbs endure
The stain of thick corruption and the rule
Of common natures. Queen, possess thy power,
Raise him beyond the region of the sun;
There cherish back the heavy eyes to blend

° **frore**: frozen.
° from *Collected Poems of Lord De Tabley*, London, 1903, pp. 306–8.

With that full morning of the ageless gods:
Watch him to life in bloomy asphodel,
Dissolve thy soul on his reviving lips.

In vain, 'tis idle dreaming this shall be.
In vain, ye maidens, this our sister toil
To scatter posies on his patient sleep
With dole for him that was so beautiful:
He shall not wake from that Lethean dream:
He shall not move for her immortal smile,
Nor hear the busy kisses at his cheek:
She ceases and she sobs upon her hands:
Come, let us weep with her and weep with her.

Smother his head with roses as he lies.
The day may draw the sacred twilight down:
The dew lights on the grasses and the leaves
May speck the woods, as night the sky, with stars;
The sun-down gale shall not, because we weep,
Forego her perfume, or night's bird her song.
Nature is greater than the grief of gods,
And Pan prevails, while dynasties in heaven
Rule out their little eons and resign
The thunder and the throne to younger hands.
He is the rock and these the rounding waves.

Lament not, Queen of love, lament no more:
Nature and Love alone are ageless powers;
Thy queendom, Aphroditè, shall not fail.
The reign of might shall fail, the wisdom fail
That wrought out heavenly thrones: the weary clouds
Shall not sustain them longer: only Love
And Nature are immortal. Nature sealed
Adonis' eyes: the kindly hand forgave
The creeping years that held Tithonus old
Before her eyes who loved and saw him fade.

Have comfort; and our homeward choir shall hymn
Thy godhead through the cedarn labyrinths,
Till they emerge upon the flushing sheet
Of sunset: on those waters many an isle
And cape and sacred foreland ripe with eve,
Cherish thy myrtle in delicious groves:
Infinite worship at this hour is thine.
They name thee Aphroditè, and the name
Blends with the incense towards the crimson cloud.

A24 Wilfrid Scawen Blunt, 'Adonis', 1892°

Wilfrid Scawen Blunt, 1840–1922, English poet, diplomat, traveller, and Arabist; a passionate anti-imperialist, he campaigned for independence for Arabia, Egypt, India, and Ireland. This poem drains all the violence out of the Adonis story, replacing it with a quiet melancholy and a kind of *fin-de-siècle* death-wish.

Adonis

The gods did love Adonis, and for this
He died, ere time had furrowed his young cheek.
For Aphrodite slew him with a kiss.
He sighed one sigh, as though he fain would speak
The name he loved, but that his breath grown weak
Died on his lips. So died the summer breeze;
And all the wood was hushed a minute's space,
Where I stood listening underneath the trees.
Until a wood-chat° from her secret place

Chirped in an undertone, 'He is not dead,
Not dead, for lo the bloom upon his face
Is ruddy as the newly-blossomed rose,
Which even yet is woven round his head.
But sleep, more sweet than waking dream, doth close
The laughter of his eyes. He is not dead.'

Alone in that fair wood the live-long day,
And through the silent night I watched him near.
But in the morning he was fled away,
When broke the dawn upon me cold and clear.
I looked within the thicket where he lay;
And lo! the sod, which he had pressed in death,
Was white with blossoms, scattered from the may,
Which made the thick air sweet with their sweet breath.
But he was gone: and I went o'er the heath,
Clutching like one distraught the dim air grey
With dawning, for a voice encompassed me,
Crying, 'Fair boy, thy youth was but a span,
Yet did it circle in eternity;

° from *The Love-Lyrics & Songs of Proteus . . . with the Love-Sonnets of Proteus by the Same Author now reprinted in their full text with many sonnets omitted from the earlier editions*, London, 1892, pp. 20–1.

° **wood-chat**: a type of shrike; there seems to be no particular reason for Blunt's choice of this rather uncommon bird.

Thy epic was accomplishèd. A man
Fills but the measure of his destiny,
And thine was all complete. Ere age began
To mar the royal palace of thy youth
With upper storeys of less perfect plan,
Death, kindly death, filled with immortal ruth,°
Took back the trowel from the builder's hand
And wrote his "fecit"° on thy work of truth.'

A25 Sir James George Frazer, from *The Golden Bough*, 1906°

James George Frazer, 1854–1941, classical scholar and anthropologist. His monumental work *The Golden Bough: A Study in Magic and Religion* was published and expanded in successive volumes over the years 1890–1915, the two volumes entitled *Adonis, Attis, Osiris* appearing in 1906. It is a comparative study of religious and magical ideas in the classical world and among modern 'primitive' peoples, focusing in particular on the idea of the sacrificial god-king. Though Frazer's methods and conclusions are regarded sceptically by modern anthropologists, his work, especially his evocation of the figure of the 'dying god', had a tremendous impact on early twentieth-century writers like Eliot, Pound, and Lawrence. Included here are portions of Frazer's account of Adonis, including his subversive comparison between the resurrections of Adonis and Christ.

The spectacle of the great changes which annually pass over the face of the earth has powerfully impressed the minds of men in all ages, and stirred them to meditate on the causes of transformations so vast and wonderful. Their curiosity has not been purely disinterested; for even the savage cannot fail to perceive how intimately his own life is bound up with the life of nature, and how the same processes which freeze the stream and strip the earth of vegetation menace him with extinction. At a certain stage of development men seem to have imagined that the means of averting the threatened calamity were in their own hands, and that they could hasten or retard the flight of the seasons by magic art. Accordingly they performed ceremonies and recited spells to make the rain to fall, the sun to shine, animals to multiply, and the fruits of the earth to grow. In course of time the slow advance of knowledge, which has dispelled so many cherished

° **ruth**: pity.
° **'fecit'**: 'he made it' – the architect's signature.
° from *The Golden Bough: A Study in Magic and Religion*, Abridged Edition, London, 1922, pp. 324–5, 337–40, 345–6.

illusions, convinced at least the more thoughtful portion of mankind that the alternations of summer and winter, of spring and autumn, were not merely the result of their own magical rites, but that some deeper cause, some mightier power, was at work behind the shifting scenes of nature. They now pictured to themselves the growth and decay of vegetation, the birth and death of living creatures, as effects of the waxing or waning strength of divine beings, of gods and goddesses, who were born and died, who married and begot children, on the pattern of human life.

Thus the old magical theory of the seasons was displaced, or rather supplemented, by a religious theory. For although men now attributed the annual cycle of change primarily to corresponding changes in their deities, they still thought that by performing certain magical rites they could aid the god, who was the principle of life, in his struggle with the opposing principle of death. They imagined that they could recruit his failing energies and even raise him from the dead. The ceremonies which they observed for this purpose were in substance a dramatic representation of the natural processes which they wished to facilitate; for it is a familiar tenet of magic that you can produce any desired effect by merely imitating it. And as they now explained the fluctuations of growth and decay, of reproduction and dissolution, by the marriage, the death, and the rebirth or revival of the gods, their religious or rather magical dramas turned in great measure on these themes. They set forth the fruitful union of the powers of fertility, the sad death of one at least of the divine partners, and his joyful resurrection. Thus a religious theory was blended with a magical practice. The combination is familiar in history. Indeed, few religions have ever succeeded in wholly extricating themselves from the old trammels of magic. The inconsistency of acting on two opposite principles, however it may vex the soul of the philosopher, rarely troubles the common man; indeed he is seldom even aware of it. His affair is to act, not to analyse the motives of his action. If mankind had always been logical and wise, history would not be a long chronicle of folly and crime.

Of the changes which the seasons bring with them, the most striking within the temperate zone are those which affect vegetation. The influence of the seasons on animals, though great, is not nearly so manifest. Hence it is natural that in the magical dramas designed to dispel winter and bring back spring the emphasis should be laid on vegetation, and that trees and plants should figure in them more prominently than beasts and birds. Yet the two sides of life, the vegetable and the animal, were not dissociated in the minds of those who observed the ceremonies. Indeed they commonly believed that the tie between the animal and the vegetable world was even closer than it really is; hence they often combined the dramatic representation of reviving plants with a real or a dramatic union of the sexes for the purpose of furthering at the same time and by the same act the multiplication of fruits, of animals, and of men. To them the principle of life and fertility, whether animal or vegetable, was one and indivisible. To live and to cause to live, to eat food and to beget children, these were the primary wants of men in the past, and they will be the primary wants of men in the future so long as the world lasts. Other things may be added to enrich and beautify human life, but unless these wants are first satisfied, humanity itself must cease to exist. These two things, therefore, food and children, were what men chiefly sought to procure by the performance of magical rites for the regulation of the seasons.

Nowhere, apparently, have these rites been more widely and solemnly celebrated than in the lands which border the eastern Mediterranean. Under the names of Osiris, Tammuz, Adonis, and Attis, the peoples of Egypt and Western Asia represented the yearly decay and revival of life, especially of vegetable life, which they personified as a god who annually died and rose again from the dead. In name and detail the rites varied from place to place: in substance they were the same. The supposed death and resurrection of this oriental deity, a god of many names but of essentially one nature, is now to be examined. We begin with Tammuz or Adonis.

Frazer summarises the myths of Tammuz and Adonis, then discusses at length the various rituals associated with Adonis in Syria, Cyprus, Alexandria, and Athens, sometimes held in spring and sometimes in midsummer. Comparing these with other Indian and European rituals involving the marriage, death, and resurrection of a god, he concludes that:

the ceremony of the death and resurrection of Adonis must also have been a dramatic representation of the decay and revival of plant life. The inference thus based on the resemblance of the customs is confirmed by the following features in the legend and ritual of Adonis. His affinity with vegetation comes out at once in the common story of his birth. He was said to have been born from a myrrh-tree, the bark of which bursting, after a ten months' gestation, allowed the lovely infant to come forth. According to some, a boar rent the bark with his tusk and so opened a passage for the babe. A faint rationalistic colour was given to the legend by saying that his mother was a woman named Myrrh, who had been turned into a myrrh-tree soon after she had conceived the child. The use of myrrh as incense at the festival of Adonis may have given rise to the fable . . . Again, the story that Adonis spent half, or according to others a third, of the year in the lower world and the rest of it in the upper world, is explained most simply and naturally by supposing that he represented vegetation, especially the corn, which lies buried in the earth half the year and reappears above ground the other half. Certainly of the annual phenomena of nature there is none which suggests so obviously the idea of death and resurrection as the disappearance and reappearance of vegetation in autumn and spring. Adonis has been taken for the sun; but there is nothing in the sun's annual course within the temperate and tropical zones to suggest that he is dead for half or a third of the year and alive for the other half or two-thirds . . . On the other hand, the annual death and revival or vegetation is a conception which readily presents itself to men in every stage of savagery and civilisation; and the vastness of the scale on which this ever-recurring decay and regeneration takes place, together with man's intimate dependence on it for subsistence, combine to render it the most impressive annual occurrence in nature, at least within the temperate zones. It is no wonder that a phenomenon so important, so striking, and so universal should, by suggesting similar ideas, give rise to similar rites in many lands . . . Moreover, the explanation is countenanced by a considerable body of opinion among the ancients themselves, who again and again interpreted the dying and reviving god as the reaped and sprouting grain.

The character of Tammuz or Adonis as a corn-spirit comes out plainly in an account of his festival given by an Arabic writer of the tenth century. In describing the rites and sacrifices observed at the different seasons of the year by the heathen Syrians of Harran, he says: 'Tammuz (July). In the middle of this month is the festival of el-Bûgât, that is, of the weeping women, and this is the Tâ-uz festival, which is celebrated in honour of the god Tâ-uz. The women bewail him, because his lord slew him so cruelly, ground his bones in a mill, and then scattered them to the wind. The women (during this festival) eat nothing which has been ground in a mill, but limit their diet to steeped wheat, sweet vetches, dates, raisins, and the like.' Tâ-uz, who is no other than Tammuz, is here like Burns's John Barleycorn:

> They wasted o'er a scorching flame
> The marrow of his bones;
> But a miller used him worst of all,
> For he crushed him between two stones.°

. . . Thus interpreted the death of Adonis is not the natural decay of vegetation in general under the summer heat or the winter cold; it is the violent destruction of the corn by man, who cuts it down on the field, stamps it to pieces on the threshing-floor, and grinds it to powder in the mill . . .

There is some reason to think that in early times Adonis was sometimes personated by a living man who died a violent death in the character of the god. Further, there is evidence which goes to show that among the agricultural peoples of the Eastern Mediterranean, the corn-spirit, by whatever name he was known, was often represented, year by year, by human victims slain on the harvestfield. If that was so, it seems likely that the propitiation of the corn-spirit would tend to fuse to some extent with the worship of the dead. For the spirits of these victims might be thought to return to life in the ears which they had fattened with their blood, and to die a second death at the reaping of the corn. Now the ghosts of those who have perished by violence are surly and apt to wreak their vengeance on their slayers whenever an opportunity offers. Hence the attempt to appease the souls of the slaughtered victims would naturally blend, at least in the popular

° **John Barleycorn**: a ballad by Robert Burns (1787), humorously describing the making of beer in terms of the cruel murder and glorious resurrection of the hero Barleycorn.

conception, with the attempt to pacify the slain corn-spirit. And as the dead came back in the sprouting corn, so they might be thought to return in the spring flowers, waked from their long sleep by the soft vernal airs. They had been laid to their rest under the sod. What more natural than to imagine that the violets and the hyacinths, the roses and the anemones, sprang from their dust, were empurpled or incarnadined by their blood, and contained some portion of their spirit? . . .

Frazer then discusses the ritual sacrifice of 'gardens of Adonis', and concludes that these

are most naturally interpreted as representatives of Adonis or manifestations of his power; they represented him, true to his original nature, in vegetable form, while the images of him, with which they were carried out and cast into the water, portrayed him in his later human shape. All these Adonis ceremonies, if I am right, were originally intended as charms to promote the growth or revival of vegetation; and the principle by which they were supposed to produce this effect was homoeopathic or imitative magic. For ignorant people suppose that by mimicking the effect which they desire to produce they actually help to produce it; thus by sprinkling water they make rain, by lighting a fire they make sunshine, and so on. Similarly, by mimicking the growth of crops they hope to ensure a good harvest. The rapid growth of the wheat and barley in the gardens of Adonis was intended to make the corn shoot up; and the throwing of the gardens and of the images into the water was a charm to secure a due supply of fertilising rain.

He describes similar vegetation rites in India, Italy, Sicily, and Sardinia.

. . . Nor are these Sicilian and Calabrian customs the only Easter ceremonies which resemble the rites of Adonis. 'During the whole of Good Friday a waxen effigy of the dead Christ is exposed to view in the middle of the Greek churches and is covered with fervent kisses by the thronging crowd, while the whole church rings with melancholy, monotonous dirges. Late in the evening, when it has grown quite dark, this waxen image is carried by the priests into the street on a bier adorned with lemons, roses, jessamine, and other flowers, and there begins a grand procession of the multitude, who move in serried ranks, with slow and solemn step, through the whole town. Every man carries his taper and breaks out into doleful lamentation. At all the houses which the procession passes there are seated women with censers to fumigate the marching host. Thus the community solemnly buries its Christ as if he had just died. At last the waxen image is again deposited in the church, and the same lugubrious chants echo anew. These lamentations, accompanied by a strict fast, continue till midnight on Saturday. As the clock strikes twelve, the bishop appears and announces the glad tidings that "Christ is risen," to which the crowd replies, "He is risen indeed," and at once the whole city bursts into an uproar of joy, which finds vent in shrieks and shouts, in the endless discharge of cannonades and muskets, and the explosion of fire-works of every sort. In the very same hour people plunge from the extremity of the fast into the enjoyment of the Easter lamb and neat wine.'

In like manner the Catholic Church has been accustomed to bring before its followers in a visible form the death and resurrection of the Redeemer. Such sacred dramas are well fitted to impress the lively imagination and to stir the warm feelings of a susceptible southern race, to whom the pomp and pageantry of Catholicism are more congenial than to the colder temperament of the Teutonic peoples.

When we reflect how often the Church has skilfully contrived to plant the seeds of the new faith on the old stock of paganism, we may surmise that the Easter celebration of the dead and risen Christ was grafted upon a similar celebration of the dead and risen Adonis, which, as we have seen reason to believe, was celebrated in Syria at the same season. The type, created by Greek artists, of the sorrowful goddess with her dying lover in her arms, resembles and may have been the model of the Pietà of Christian art, the Virgin with the dead body of her divine Son in her lap, of which the most celebrated example is the one by Michael Angelo in St. Peter's. That noble group, in which the living sorrow of the mother contrasts so wonderfully with the languor of death in the son, is one of the finest compositions in marble. Ancient Greek art has bequeathed to us few works so beautiful, and none so pathetic.

In this connexion a well-known statement of Jerome° may not be without significance. He tells us that Bethlehem, the traditionary birthplace of the Lord, was shaded by a grove of that still older Syrian Lord, Adonis, and that where the infant Jesus had wept, the lover of Venus was bewailed. Though he does not expressly say so, Jerome seems to have thought that the grove of Adonis had been planted by the heathen after the birth of Christ for the purpose of defiling the sacred spot. In this he may have been mistaken. If Adonis was indeed, as I have argued, the spirit of the corn, a more suitable name for his dwelling-place could hardly be found than Bethlehem, 'the House of Bread', and he may well have been worshipped there at his House of Bread long ages before the birth of Him who said, 'I am the bread of life.' Even on the hypothesis that Adonis followed rather than preceded Christ at Bethlehem, the choice of his sad figure to divert the allegiance of Christians from their Lord cannot but strike us as eminently appropriate when we remember the similarity of the rites which commemorated the death and resurrection of the two.

° **Jerome**: St Jerome, fourth-century Christian scholar.

A26 H.D., 'Adonis', 1917°

On H.D., see headnote to **O39**.

1

Each of us like you
has died once,
each of us like you
has passed through drift of wood-leaves,
cracked and bent
and tortured and unbent
in the winter frost,
then burnt into gold points,
lighted afresh,
crisp amber, scales of gold-leaf,
gold turned and re-welded in the sun-heat;

each of us like you
has died once,
each of us has crossed an old wood-path
and found the winter leaves
so golden in the sun-fire
that even the live wood-flowers
were dark.

2

Not the gold on the temple-front
where you stand,
is as gold as this,
not the gold that fastens your sandal,
nor the gold reft
through your chiselled locks
is as gold as this last year's leaf,
not all the gold hammered and wrought
and beaten
on your lover's face,
brow and bare breast
is as golden as this:

° from *Collected Poems 1912–1944*, ed. Louis L. Martz, New York, 1983, pp. 47–8.

each of us like you
has died once,
each of us like you
stands apart, like you
fit to be worshipped.

A27 T. S. Eliot, from *The Waste Land*, 1922°

Thomas Stearns Eliot, 1888–1965, poet, playwright, and critic, American-born but settled in England from 1914. His early poetry, witty, unorthodox, disjointed, and teasingly allusive, brought a new tone of voice into twentieth-century poetry and established him as a leader of the modernist movement. He later become increasingly conservative, describing himself as 'classical in literature, royalist in politics, and Anglo-Catholic in religion'; immensely influential as a critic and editor, he consistently argued for the importance of literary tradition. *The Waste Land*, as Eliot's note implies, draws on Frazer's concept of the dying fertility god in its allegorical picture of the spiritual barrenness of modern life.

I: THE BURIAL OF THE DEAD

April° is the cruellest month, breeding
Lilacs out of the dead land, mixing
Memory and desire, stirring
Dull roots with spring rain.
Winter kept us warm, covering
Earth in forgetful snow, feeding
A little life with dried tubers.
Summer surprised us, coming over the Starnbergersee
With a shower of rain; we stopped in the colonnade,
And went on in sunlight, into the Hofgarten,
And drank coffee, and talked for an hour.°
Bin gar keine Russin, stamm' aus Litauen, echt deutsch.°
And when we were children, staying at the archduke's,

° from T. S. Eliot, *Collected Poems 1909–1962*, London, 1963, pp. 63–5, 80. Reprinted by permission of Faber & Faber Ltd and The Estate of T. S. Eliot.

° **April**: the beginning of spring, and also the time of Easter, the celebration of Christ's death and resurrection.

° **Summer surprised us . . . for an hour**: Stark poetic images merge anticlimatically into a tourist's notes on Munich (the **Hofgarten** is a park in Munich, the **Starnbergersee** a nearby lake). Eliot visited Munich in 1911, and the following lines draw on the reminiscences of an old Bavarian aristocrat, Countess Marie Larisch, whom he met there.

° **Bin gar . . . deutsch**: 'I'm not Russian at all, I come from Lithuania, pure German' (quoted from Countess Larisch).

My cousin's, he took me out on a sled,
And I was frightened. He said, Marie,
Marie, hold on tight. And down we went.
In the mountains, there you feel free.
I read, much of the night, and go south in the winter.

What are the roots that clutch, what branches grow
Out of this stony rubbish? Son of man,°
You cannot say, or guess, for you know only
A heap of broken images, where the sun beats,
And the dead tree gives no shelter, the cricket no relief,°
And the dry stone no sound of water. Only
There is shadow under this red rock,
(Come in under the shadow of this red rock),
And I will show you something different from either
Your shadow at morning striding behind you
Or your shadow at evening rising to meet you;
I will show you fear in a handful of dust.

Frisch weht der Wind
Der Heimat zu
Mein Irisch Kind,
Wo weilest du?°
'You gave me hyacinths first a year ago;
They called me the hyacinth girl.'
– Yet when we came back, late, from the hyacinth garden,
Your arms full, and your hair wet, I could not
Speak, and my eyes failed, I was neither
Living nor dead, and I knew nothing,
Looking into the heart of light, the silence.
Oed' und leer das Meer.°

Madame Sosostris, famous clairvoyante,
Had a bad cold, nevertheless
Is known to be the wisest woman in Europe,

° **Son of man**: Eliot notes that this is God's address to the prophet Ezekiel (Ezekiel 2: 1), whom he orders to warn the Jews that 'your altars shall be desolate, and your images shall be broken . . . In all your dwellingplaces the cities shall be laid waste . . .' (6: 4–6).

° **the cricket no relief**: Eliot cites Ecclesiastes: '. . . and the grasshopper shall be a burden, and desire shall fail: because man goeth to his long home . . . Then shall the dust return to the earth as it was . . . Vanity of vanities, saith the preacher; all is vanity' (12: 5–8).

° **Frisch weht . . . du?**: a sailor's song from Wagner's opera of tragic love, *Tristan and Isolde*: 'Fresh blows the wind to the homeland – my Irish child, where are you waiting?'.

° **Oed' und leer das Meer**: from *Tristan and Isolde* again: the dying Tristan is waiting for Isolde's ship, but the lookout reports 'Waste and empty the sea'.

With a wicked pack of cards.° Here, said she,
Is your card, the drowned Phoenician Sailor,
(Those are pearls that were his eyes. Look!)
Here is Belladonna, the Lady of the Rocks,
The lady of situations.
Here is the man with three staves, and here the Wheel,
And here is the one-eyed merchant, and this card,
Which is blank, is something he carries on his back,
Which I am forbidden to see. I do not find
The Hanged Man. Fear death by water.
I see crowds of people, walking round in a ring.
Thank you. If you see dear Mrs. Equitone,
Tell her I bring the horoscope myself:
One must be so careful these days.

Unreal City,°
Under the brown fog of a winter dawn,
A crowd flowed over London Bridge, so many,
I had not thought death had undone so many.°
Sighs, short and infrequent, were exhaled,°
And each man fixed his eyes before his feet.
Flowed up the hill and down King William Street,
To where Saint Mary Woolnoth° kept the hours
With a dead sound on the final stroke of nine.
There I saw one I knew, and stopped him, crying: 'Stetson!
You who were with me in the ships at Mylae!°
That corpse you planted last year in your garden,

° **wicked pack of cards**: i.e. Tarot cards. Eliot notes that he was not familiar 'with the exact consitution of the Tarot pack', and mingles real with invented cards, planting images which recur throughout the poem. He notes: 'The Hanged Man, a member of the traditional pack, fits my purpose in two ways: because he is associated in my mind with the Hanged God of Frazer, and because I associate him with the hooded figure in the passage of the disciples to Emmaus in Part V.' The hooded figure is of course the resurrected Christ (Luke 24), whom Eliot thus associates with Frazer's dying god; in the world of *The Waste Land*, such a saviour figure is not to be found. Eliot adds that 'The Man with Three Staves . . . I associate, quite arbitrarily, with the Fisher King himself.'

° **Unreal City**: London, and more precisely the City of London, its central business district.

° **I had not . . . so many**: Eliot notes that this is a quotation from Dante's *Inferno* (3. 55–7), describing the souls of those who were neither good nor evil; the office workers, similarly, are a kind of living dead, morally vacant.

° **Sighs . . . exhaled**: another reference to Dante (*Inferno*, 4. 25–7), describing the souls in Limbo.

° **Saint Mary Woolnoth**: a church in the City of London; the 'dead sound' of its bell is 'A phenomenon which I have often noticed' (Eliot).

° **Mylae**: a naval battle in the First Punic War between Rome and Carthage, anachronistically linked with the modern name **Stetson**.

Has it begun to sprout? Will it bloom this year?
Or has the sudden frost disturbed its bed?
Oh keep the Dog far hence, that's friend to men,
Or with his nails he'll dig it up again!°
You! hypocrite lecteur! – mon semblable – mon frère!'°

From Eliot's notes on *The Waste Land*

Not only the title, but the plan and a good deal of the incidental symbolism of the poem were suggested by Miss Jessie L. Weston's book on the Grail legend: *From Ritual to Romance* (Cambridge). Indeed, so deeply am I indebted, Miss Weston's book will elucidate the difficulties of the poem much better than my notes can do; and I recommend it (apart from the great interest of the book itself) to any who think such elucidation of the poem worth the trouble. To another work of anthropology I am indebted in general, one which has influenced our generation profoundly; I mean *The Golden Bough*; I have used especially the two volumes *Adonis, Attis, Osiris*. Anyone who is acquainted with these works will immediately recognise in the poem certain references to vegetation ceremonies.

A28 Archibald MacLeish, from 'The Pot of Earth', 1925°

Archibald MacLeish, 1892–1982, American poet and dramatist, later a prominent public figure as Librarian of Congress and assistant secretary of state in the Roosevelt administration. 'The Pot of Earth' was written in Paris in the 1920s when MacLeish was much influenced by Eliot and Pound. It sets a contemporary story, that of a woman's growth to adulthood, marriage, and death in childbirth, against the ancient myth of Adonis; like Eliot, MacLeish jarringly juxtaposes the ancient and the modern, but he suggests continuity rather than contrast. The poem is in three parts; included here are excerpts from Parts One and Two and the whole of Part Three.

Part One, 'The Sowing of the Dead Corn', begins with a quotation from *The Golden Bough* about 'gardens of Adonis', and an evocation of the funeral rites for Adonis:

Silently on the sliding Nile
The rudderless, the unoared barge
Diminishing and for a while

° **Oh keep . . . dig it up again**: adapted from a funeral dirge in John Webster's play *The White Devil* (4. 4); the original has 'wolf' (not **Dog**) and 'foe' (not **friend**).

° **hypocrite . . . frère**: from the French poet Charles Baudelaire's preface to his *Fleurs du Mal* ('Flowers of Evil'): 'hypocritical reader, my likeness, my brother!'

° from *Collected Poems 1917–1982*, Boston: Houghton Mifflin, 1985, pp. 59–77.

Followed, a fleck upon the large
Silver, then faint, then vanished, passed
Adonis who had once more died
Down a slow water with the last
Withdrawing of a fallen tide.

It shows the growth of a young girl from childhood to adolescence. Images of spring (rising waters, swelling chestnut buds, rivers running blood-red with flowers) are associated with her sexual maturing, and her mingled excitement and fear of it. Part One climaxes with her first sexual experience, amid images of spring, the Christian Easter, and the resurrection of Adonis:

Easter Sunday they went to Hooker's Grove,
Seven of them in one automobile
Laughing and singing.
Sea water flows
Over the meadows at the full moon,
The sea runs in the ditches, the salt stone
Drowns in the sea.
And someone said, Look! Look!
The flowers, the red flowers,
Shall we go
Up through the Gorge or round by Ryan's place?
I'll show you where the wild boar killed a man.
I'll show you where the . . .
Who is this that comes
Crowned with red flowers from the sea? Who comes
Into the hills with flowers?
On the hill pastures
She heard a girl calling her lost cows.
Her voice hung like a mist over the grass,
Over the apple-trees.
She bit her mouth
To keep from crying.
On the third day
The cone of the pine is broken, the eared corn
Broken into the earth, the seed scattered.
The bridegroom comes again at the third day.
The sowers have come into the fields sowing.
Well, at the Grove there was a regular crowd
And a band at the Casino, so they ate
Up in the woods where you could hear the music
And the dogs barking, and after lunch she lay
Out in the open meadow. She could feel

The sun through her dress –
Don't you want to dance?
They're all dancing – that wonderful tune –
Are you listening? Aren't you listening?
The band
Start stuttered and
Oh, won't you?
No –
Just a little while. Just a little bit –
No! Oh, No! Oh, No!
Far, far away
The singing on the mountain. She could hear
The voices singing, she could hear them come
With songs, with the red flowers. They have found him,
They have brought him from the hills –

Why, it was wonderful! Why, all at once there were leaves,
Leaves at the end of a dry stick, small, alive
Leaves out of wood. It was wonderful,
You can't imagine. They came by the wood path
And the earth loosened, the earth relaxed, there were flowers
Out of the earth! Think of it! And oak-trees
Oozing new green at the tips of them and flowers
Squeezed out of clay, soft flowers, limp
Stalks flowering. Well, it was like a dream,
It happened so quickly, all of a sudden it happened –

Part Two, 'The Shallow Grass', then begins with the young woman's marriage, amid violent images of plowing and sowing.

The plough of tamarisk wood which is shared° with black copper
And drawn by a yoke of oxen all black
Drags in the earth.
The earth is made ready with copper,
The earth is prepared for the seed by the feet of oxen
That are shod with brass.

*

They said, Good Luck! Good Luck! What a handsome couple!
Isn't she lovely though! He can't keep his

° **shared**: fitted with a ploughshare or blade.

Hands off her. Ripe as a peach she is. Good Luck!
Good-bye, Good-bye –
                                        They took the down express,
The five-five. She had the seat by the window –
He can't keep –
                              She sat there looking out
And the fields were brown and raw from the spring ploughing,
The fields were naked, they were stretched out bare,
Rigid, with long welts, with open wounds,
Stripped –
                    In the flat sunlight she could see
The fields heave against the furrows, lift,
Twist to get free –
                              – his hands –
                                                  Why, what's the matter?
We're almost there now, only half an hour.
We'll have our supper in our rooms. I've taken
The best room, what they call the bridal chamber –

What they call – what do they call it? –
                                                            And I dressed up
All in these new things not a red ribbon
You ever had on before and mind you keep
The shoes you were married in and all to go
Into a closed room with a bed in it,
To lie in a shut chamber,
                                        what they call –
Something
               the chalked letters
                                             does he say
That
       I wonder
                    or what –
                                   She held his hand
Against her breast under the flowers. She felt
The warmth of it like the warmth of the sun driving
Downward into her heart.
                                        And all those fields
Ready, the earth stretched out upon those fields
Ready, and now the sowers –
What is this thing we know that they have not told us?
What is this in us that has come to bed
In a closed room?

*

I tell you the generations
Of man are a ripple of thin fire burning
Over a meadow, breeding out of itself
Itself, a momentary incandescence
Lasting a long time, and we that blaze
Now, we are not the fire, for it leaves us.

I tell you we are the shape of a word in the air
Uttered from silence behind us into silence
Far beyond, and now between two strokes
Of the word's passing have become the word –
That jars on through the night;
and the stirred air
Deadens,
is still –

Through a long hot rainless summer, in a furnished flat, the pregnant wife tends the withering plants in her window-box and waits to be 'delivered'. Half appalled by 'this thing that sprouts / From the womb, from the living flesh' (275–6), she broods morbidly on images of death and birth combined: 'she dreamed of one / Buried, and out of her womb the corn growing' (285–6).

And what is this to be a woman? Why,
To be a woman, a sown field.
Let us
Attribute a significance perhaps
Not ours to what we are compelled to be
By being it:
as privately forestall
The seed's necessity by welcoming
The necessary seed;
likewise prevent
Death with the apothegm° that all men die.
Yes.
And then wake alone at night and lie here
Stripped of my memories, without the chairs
And walls and doors and windows that have been
My recognition of myself, my soul's
Condition, the whole habit of my mind –
Yes, wake, and of the close, unusual dark

° **apothegm**: saying.

Demand an answer, crying, What am I?
Ah, What! A naked body born to bear
Nakedness suffering. A sealed mystery
With hands to feed it, with unable legs,
With shamed eyes meaning – what? What do they mean,
The red haws° out there underneath the snow,
What do they signify?

Glory of women to grow big and die
Fruitfully, glory of women to be broken,
Pierced by the green sprout, severed, tossed aside
Fruitfully –
Yes, all right. Yes, Yes,
But what about me –
What am I –
What do you think
I am –
What do you take me for!

Snow, the snow –
When shall I be delivered?
When will my time come?

PART THREE

THE CARRION CORN

The flowers of the sea are brief,
Lost flowers of the sea,
Salt petal, bitter leaf,
The fruitless tree –
The flowers of the sea are blown
Dead, they blossom in death:
The sea furrows are sown
With a cold breath.

I heard in my heart all night
The sea crying, Come home,
Come home. I thought of the white
Cold flowers of foam.

*

° **haws**: hawthorn berries.

In March, when the snow melted, he was born.
She lay quiet in the bed. She lay still,
Dying.
                    Under the iron rumble
Of the streets she heard the rolling
Boulders that the flood tides tumble
Climbing sea by sea the shoaling
Ledges – she could hear the tolling
Sea.
        She lay alone there.

In the morning
They came and went about her,
Moving through the room. She asked them
Whispering. They told her,
He is here. She said, Who is it,
Who is it that is born, that is here?
She said, Do you not know him?
Have you seen the green blades gathered?
Have you seen the shallow grain?
Do you know, – do you not know him?
Laugh, she said, I am delivered,
I am free, I am no longer
Burdened. I have borne the summer
Dead, the corn dead, the living
Dead. I am delivered.
He has left me now. I lie here
Empty, gleaned, a reaped meadow,
Fearing the rain no more, not fearing
Spring nor the flood tides overflowing
Earth with their generative waters –
Let me sleep, let me be quiet.
I can see the dark sail going
On and on, the river flowing
Red with the melting of the snow:
What is this thing we know? –

Under the iron street the crying
Voices of the sea. Come home,
Come to your house. Come home.
                                        She heard
A slow crying in the sea, Come home,
Come to your house –

*

Go secretly and put me in the ground –
Go before the moon uncovers,
Go where now no night wind hovers,
Say no word above me, make no sound.
Heap only on my buried bones
Cold sand and naked stones
And come away and leave unmarked the mound.
Let not those silent hunters hear you pass:
Let not the trees know, nor the thirsty grass,
Nor secret rain
To breed from me some living thing again,
But only earth –
                              Oh let my flesh be drowned
In her deep silences and never found!

*

The slow spring blossomed again, a cold
Bubbling of the corrupted pool, a frothy
Thickening, a ferment of soft green
Bubbling –
                    Who knows how deep the roots drink?
They drink deep,
                              And you, what do you hope?
What do you believe, walking
Alone in an old garden, staring down
Beneath the shallow surface of the grass,
The floating green? What do you say you are?
And what was she that you remember, staring
Down through the pale grass, what was she?
And what is this that grows in an old garden?

Listen, I will interpret to you. Look, now,
I will discover you a thing hidden,
A secret thing. Come, I will conduct you
By seven doors into a closed tomb.
I will show you the mystery of mysteries.
I will show you the body of the dead god bringing forth
The corn. I will show you the reaped ear
Sprouting.

                Are you contented? Are you answered?

Come.
          I will show you chestnut branches budding
Beyond a dusty pane and a little grass

Green in a window-box and silence stirred,
Settling and stirred and settling in an empty room –

A29 W. B. Yeats, 'Her Vision in the Wood', 1926°

William Butler Yeats, 1865–1939, Irish poet and verse dramatist. His poetry strikingly evolves from an early dreamy Celtic romanticism to something much tougher, more complex and more colloquial; but he was consistently fascinated with mythology (Celtic more than classical), mysticism, and magic. 'Her Vision in the Wood', the eighth in a sequence of poems called 'A Woman Young and Old', shows the female speaker's encounter with the mourners for Adonis.

Dry timber under that rich foliage,
At wine-dark midnight in the sacred wood,
Too old for a man's love I stood in rage
Imagining men. Imagining that I could
A greater with a lesser pang assuage
Or but to find if withered vein ran blood,
I tore my body that its wine might cover
Whatever could recall the lip of lover.

And after that I held my fingers up,
Stared at the wine-dark nail, or dark that ran
Down every withered finger from the top;
But the dark changed to red, and torches shone,
And deafening music shook the leaves; a troop
Shouldered a litter with a wounded man,
Or smote upon the string and to the sound
Sang of the beast that gave the fatal wound.

All stately women moving to a song
With loosened hair or foreheads grief-distraught,
It seemed a Quattrocento painter's throng,
A thoughtless image of Mantegna's thought –°
Why should they think that are for ever young?
Till suddenly in grief's contagion caught,
I stared upon his blood-bedabbled breast
And sang my malediction with the rest.

° from *Collected Poems*, London: Macmillan, 1950, p. 312–13; 'A Woman Young and Old', poem 8.

° **Mantegna**: Andrea Mantegna, fifteenth-century (**Quattrocento**) Italian painter; many of his paintings depict still, statuesque figures as if carved on a classsical monument.

That thing all blood and mire, that beast-torn wreck,
Half turned and fixed a glazing eye on mine,
And, though love's bitter-sweet had all come back,
Those bodies from a picture or a coin
Nor saw my body fall nor heard it shriek,
Nor knew, drunken with singing as with wine,
That they had brought no fabulous symbol there
But my heart's victim and its torturer.

A30 Kenneth Rexroth, 'Adonis in Winter', 1944°

Kenneth Rexroth, 1905–82, US poet and essayist, living mainly in San Francisco, active in left-wing politics, and associated with a series of poetic movements from Imagism to the 'Beat Generation'. His verse is sometimes lyrical, sometimes outspokenly political; he also translated Greek, Latin, Chinese and Japanese verse.

Adonis in Winter

Persephone awaits him in the dim boudoir,
Waits him, for the hour is at hand.
She has arranged the things he likes
Near to his expected hand:
Herrick's poems,° tobacco, the juice
Of pomegranates in a twisted glass.
She piles her drugged blonde hair
Above her candid forehead,
Touches up lips and eyelashes,
Selects her most naked robe.
On the stroke of the equinox he comes,
And smiles, and stretches his arms, and strokes
Her cheeks and childish shoulders, and kisses
The violet lids closed on the grey eyes.
Free of aggressive Aphrodite,
Free of the patronizing gods,
The cruel climate of Olympus,
They feed caramels to Cerberus
And warn him not to tell
The cuckold Pluto of their adulteries,
Their mortal lechery in dispassionate Hell.

° from *The Collected Shorter Poems*, New York: New Directions, 1966, pp. 159–60.

° **Herrick's poems**: Robert Herrick, seventeenth-century writer of very short, polished, witty, sometimes bawdy lyric poems.

OTHER VERSIONS OF VENUS AND ADONIS

Classical/medieval

Anonymous Greek poet. 'The Dead Adonis'. (Traditionally included in the poems of Theocritus as Idyll 31; now regarded as dating from the third to the fifth century AD.)

Aristophanes. *Lysistrata*, lines 387–98.

Chaucer, Geoffrey. 'The Knight's Tale', lines 2224–5, in *The Canterbury Tales.*

——. *Troilus and Criseyde*, 3. 720–1.

Lydgate, John. *Reason and Sensuality*, lines 3685ff.

Renaissance

Anonymous. *The Return from Parnassus* (1601), 3. 1, from *The Three Parnassus Plays (1598–1601)*, ed. J. B. Leishman, London: Ivor Nicholson, 1949.

Barksted, William. *Myrrha, the Mother of Adonis*, London, 1607.

Bosworth, William. 'Arcadius and Sepha', in *The Chaste and Lost Lovers*, London, 1653.

Brathwait, Richard. 'Eliza's Marriage Day', from *The Poet's Willow*, London, 1614.

C,H. (possibly Henry Chettle or Henry Constable). 'The Shepherd's Song of Venus and Adonis', in *England's Helicon*, London, 1600.

Crompton, Hugh. 'The Masque of Adonis', from *Pierides, or The Muses' Mount*, London, 1657.

Fletcher, Giles. *Christ's Victory and Triumph*, Cambridge, 1610, book 2, stanza 40.

Fraunce, Abraham. *The Third Part of the Countess of Pembroke's Ivychurch*, London, 1592.

Greene, Robert. 'Infida's Song', from *Never Too Late*, London, 1590.

——. 'Prince's Sonnet' and 'Sonnet of Old Man (a Chaldee) in Answer', from *Perimedes the Blacksmith*, London, 1588.

Heywood, Thomas. *The Brazen Age*, 2. 2, London, 1613.

Jonson, Ben. *Cynthia's Revels*, 5. 10; *Every Man Out of His Humour*, 4. 8.

Lawes, Henry. 'Venus Lamenting her Lost Adonis', from *The Treasury of Music*, London, 1669.

Lovelace, Richard. 'Princess Louisa Drawing', lines 34–7, from *Lucasta*, London, 1649.

Marlowe, Christopher. *Hero and Leander* (*c.*1593), 1. 11–14; *The Jew of Malta* (*c.*1589), 4. 2.

Marmion, Shakerley. *Cupid and Psyche*, lines 303–4, London, 1638.

Ross, Alexander. 'Adonis', from *Mel Heliconium*, London, 1642.

Restoration and eighteenth century

Behn, Aphra. *A Pindaric Poem on the Happy Coronation of . . . James II and . . . Queen Mary*, London, 1685.

Bellamy, Daniel. 'Cantata III: Venus in Tears for the Death of Adonis', in *Love Triumphant*, London, 1722.

Blow, John. *Venus and Adonis: A Masque*, performed *c.*1685.

Brown, Thomas. 'The Ladies' Lamentation for their Adonis; or, An Elegy on the Death of Mr Mountford the Player' (before 1704), in *The Remains of Mr Tho. Brown*, London, 1720.

Cibber, Colley. *Venus and Adonis: A Masque* (music by Dr J. C. Pepusch), London, 1715.

Derrick, Samuel. 'A Song', from *A Collection of Original Poems*, London, 1755.

Hughes, John. 'Venus and Adonis: A Cantata' (music by Handel), in *Poems on Several Occasions*, London, 1735.

Mason, William. 'The Birth of Fashion', lines 81–5, in his *Works*, 1811

Pope, Alexander. 'To Lord Harvey and Lady Mary Wortley'; *The Dunciad*, 2. 194.

Warton, Joseph. *An Ode, Occasioned by Reading Mr West's Translation of Pindar*, London, 1749.

Whyte, Samuel. 'Ode: On the King's Nuptials', and 'Irene: A Canto on the Peace', in *The Shamrock*, Dublin, 1722.

Nineteenth century

Arnold, Matthew. 'Pagan and Christian Religious Sentiment', in *Essays in Criticism*, London, 1865.

Buchanan, Robert Williams. 'Venus on the Sun-Car' (1864), in *Complete Poetical Works*, London, 1901.

De Tabley, Lord (John Byrne Leicester Warren). 'Lines to a Lady-Bird', in *Collected Poems*, London, 1903.

Michael Field (pseud. of Katharine Bradley and Edith Cooper). 'Adônis and Aphrodîtê' and 'The Song of Aphrodîtê', from *Bellerophôn*, London, 1881.

Lang, Andrew. 'Love's Easter', in *Poetical Works*, London, 1923.

Payne, John. 'The Gardens of Adonis', in *Poetical Works*, London, 1902.

Planché, John Robinson. *The Paphian Bower, or Venus and Adonis: A Classical, Musical, Mythological, Astronomical, and Tragi-Comical Burlesque Burletta, in One Act*, London, 1879.

Robertson, James Logie. 'The Lawn-Adonis', from *Orellana*, London, 1881.

Swinburne, Algernon Charles. 'St Dorothy', lines 106–9; 'Laus Veneris', lines 133–6.

Wordsworth, William. 'Love Lies Bleeding', 1842.

Twentieth century

Auden, W. H., and Chester Kallman. *The Bassarids* (1963), in *Libretti and Other Dramatic Writings 1939–1973*, ed. Edward Mendelson, Princeton: Princeton University Press, 1993.

Brooke, Rupert. 'The Goddess in the Wood', in *Collected Poems*, London: Sidgwick & Jackson, 1918.

Heath-Stubbs, John. *Wounded Tammuz*, London: Routledge, 1942.

Hine, Daryl. 'The Wound', from *The Carnal and the Crane*, Toronto: Contact, 1957.

Hughes, Ted. *Shakespeare and the Goddess of Complete Being*, London: Faber, 1992.

——. 'Venus and Adonis', in *Tales from Ovid*, London: Faber, 1997.

MacNeice, Louis. 'Adonis', in *Blind Fireworks*, London: Gollancz, 1929.

——. 'Cock of the North' (1950–51), in *Collected Poems*, ed. E. R. Dodds, London: Faber, 1966.

Orlock, Carol. *The Goddess Letters*, New York: St Martin, 1987.

Pound, Ezra. Canto 47, in *The Cantos*, London: Faber, 1975.

Rexnoth, Henneth. 'Adonis in Summer', from *Collected Shorter Poems*, New York: New Directions, 1966.

Rice, Cale Young. 'A Vision of Venus and Adonis', from *Selected Plays and Poems*, London: Hodder, 1926.

Trypanis, Constantine. 'The Elegies of a Glass Adonis', in *The Glass Adonis*, London: Faber, 1972.

6

PYGMALION

INTRODUCTION

From Ovid to Caxton

Pygmalion, according to Ovid (**P1**), was a sculptor of Cyprus who turned away in disgust from the local women because of their sexual immorality. Instead he fell in love with a statue of a beautiful woman that he had himself carved from ivory. He courted it as if it were a woman, dressing it in fine clothes, bringing it gifts, even placing it in his bed. Finally in despair he prayed to Venus, and Venus granted his prayer: as he embraced the statue, it softened from stone into flesh and turned into a living woman. Pygmalion married his statue-wife, and they founded a royal dynasty; their grandson was Cinyras, the unfortunate father/grandfather of Adonis. In passing it should be noted that in Ovid the statue is nameless; her now-traditional name 'Galatea' is an eighteenth-century invention (Reinhold 1971: 316–19).[1]

Ovid is the inevitable starting-point for any discussion of Pygmalion. This is perhaps the main difference between this legend and those of Orpheus and Adonis, which have roots much older and deeper and darker than Ovid's elegant retellings. For Pygmalion, Ovid's is the oldest version we have, the only substantial ancient version, and the source of all subsequent versions. Indeed, the story as we have it may be essentially his invention – a literary creation rather than a genuine myth.

Two later writers give us an intriguing glimpse of what may be an earlier version of the story. The early Christian writers Clement of Alexandria (**P2**) and Arnobius of Sicca (**P3**) both refer to Pygmalion in the course of polemics against pagan idolatry, both citing as their source the third-century BC scholar Philostephanus. According to them, Pygmalion was not a sculptor, but a young Cypriot – king of Cyprus, according to Arnobius – who blasphemously fell in love with the sacred statue of Aphrodite in her temple, and tried to make love to it. Arnobius's identification of Pygmalion as king suggests to modern scholars that this may be a distorted version of an ancient ritual, a sacred marriage or *hierogamy* between the island's king and its patron goddess, represented by her statue, to ensure the prosperity and fertility of the land. Cyprus was a famous centre of the worship of Aphrodite, or 'Cypris', who was said to have risen from the sea near its coast; the island held several of her temples and holy places. In its original form, then, the story of Pygmalion might have been similar to that of Adonis: a sacred union between the goddess and her mortal lover (Frazer 1922: 332). If so, it has left little or no trace in the literary tradition; it is Ovid who has shaped later conceptions of what the story of Pygmalion is about.

Ovid frames the story as one of the songs of the bereaved Orpheus. He omits all mention of Pygmalion's kingship; instead, by making the hero himself a sculptor, he focuses the story on the power of art. Pygmalion's 'marvellous triumphant artistry' counterfeits reality so well that it could be mistaken for it ('Such art his art concealed'), and in the end is transformed into reality; more successful than Orpheus, he is able to bring his love to life. At the same time, while dropping the idea of the sacred marriage, Ovid leaves Pygmalion's relationship with the gods as central. In Orpheus's sequence of songs of tragic and forbidden love, this one stands out as having a happy ending, and the suggestion is that this is because of the hero's piety: unlike other characters, including Orpheus himself, who came to grief through disobedience or ingratitude to the gods, Pygmalion humbly places his fate in Venus's hands, and she rewards his faith. This moral is emphasised by contrast with the immediately preceding stories, of Venus's punishment of the murderous Cerastae and of the Propoetides, the first prostitutes, who 'dared deny Venus' divinity', and whose transformation into stone mirrors the statue's transformation from stone to flesh.

Though Ovid sketches in these serious themes, the dominant tone of the story is humorous and erotic. Without labouring the point (as some later versions do) Ovid suggests the comedy of Pygmalion's sudden descent from high-minded celibacy to infatuation, and of his earnest courtship of his unresponsive stony lady. He also communicates very clearly the erotic charge of the story. The sensuous image of the stone softening like wax under Pygmalion's fingers, of (as Byron later put it), 'The mortal and the marble at a strife / And timidly awaking into life' – the whole concept of a perfectly beautiful woman designed to the lover's specifications and utterly devoted to her creator – this is, in many ways, one of the most potent of male fantasies.

Of course (as female readers may be about to protest) the story can, if viewed from a slightly different angle, become an unsettling or distasteful one. The two main areas of unease are Pygmalion's role as the artist-creator, and the sexual politics of the story. It is perhaps not too fanciful to focus these issues by looking at the slightly different objections of Clement and Arnobius to the story.

Clement is conducting an argument against idolatry: the worship of a statue, a thing made by human art out of wood or stone, as if it were divine. He frames his argument in terms of a distinction between art and nature: art is deceptive, an illusion pretending to be truth, and those who are deceived by it may be 'beguile[d] . . . to the pit of destruction'. Clement's argument leads directly to Renaissance condemnations of Pygmalion's sin of idolatry. Less directly, it suggests problems with the figure of Pygmalion as the artist who desires to create life, transcending the limitations of human ability and perhaps transgressing on the prerogatives of God the creator. The Romantic period, which took most seriously the idea of Pygmalion as godlike artist-creator, also gave rise to the figure of Frankenstein; and these two mythic figures, suggesting respectively the benign and the horrific possibilities of creating life out of inanimate matter, have remained closely associated ever since.

Arnobius (a much less sophisticated thinker than Clement) is also arguing against idolatry, but he focuses in a rather tabloid-newspaper manner on the sexual perversity of Pygmalion's relations with the statue. It is true that, treated without Ovid's tact and humour, the story could appear nastily perverse. For a twentieth-century reader the story is more likely to seem objectionable in its portrayal of a woman as entirely passive, literally constructed by the artist's hands and gaze, and brought to life to be his submissive child-lover, without even the individuality of a name. This male-fantasy aspect of the story has been cheerfully exploited by some writers; others have questioned it, raising realistic doubts about the success of the marriage of Pygmalion and Galatea, or giving Galatea a voice to answer back or the power to walk out on, betray, or even (like Frankenstein's monster) kill her creator.

Pygmalion has only a flickering presence in the Middle Ages. From time to time he is cited as a famous artist, often paired with real Greek artists like Apelles and Zeuxis. So in Chaucer's 'Physician's Tale' Nature is made to boast of the beauty of the heroine Virginia, which neither Pygmalion nor Apelles nor Zanzis (Zeuxis) could ever 'countrefete', 'though he ay [forever] forge and bete, / Or grave, or peynte'; similarly in the Middle English poem 'Pearl' the beauty of the angelic Pearl surpasses anything Pygmalion could paint or Aristotle describe.

The two most interesting medieval treatments each inaugurate a metaphorical reading of the story. John Gower, in *Confessio Amantis* (**P4**), tells the story as a moral fable for lovers about the need for perseverance: Pygmalion continued to plead his love, even though it seemed hopeless, and in the end his wish was granted. By implication, obviously, the statue stands for a beloved who is as cold, hard, and unresponsive as stone, but can eventually be melted by a persistent suitor. This metaphorical reading has been very influential, and generations of love poets have alluded to Pygmalion and his statue in self-pity or self-encouragement. William Caxton, in a brief comment in his prose summary of the *Metamorphoses* (**P5**), has a less obvious allegory: the story symbolically relates how a rich lord took a beautiful but ignorant servant-girl and educated her to become a suitable wife for himself. This interpretation of the story as an allegory of class and education can be seen as the seed of Shaw's *Pygmalion.*

Dotage and idolatry: Pygmalion in the Renaissance

When we pass from Ovid and Gower to the Renaissance, there is a striking change of tone. On the whole, Renaissance writers take a harshly unsympathetic, satirical view of Pygmalion; the recurring keywords are 'dotage' and 'idolatry'. Rather than allegorising, they take Pygmalion's courtship of the statue literally, and mock the absurdity of his behaviour. George Pettie (**P6**), for instance, derisively offers a series of mock explanations for Pygmalion falling in love with 'a senseless thing, a stone, an image': perhaps he was mad and thought he was made of stone himself, or perhaps he was motivated by ancestral loyalty, being descended from one of the stones thrown by Deucalion and Pyrrha . . . Pygmalion is presented as an extreme example of the folly of love, and especially of the kind of courtly and platonic love which places the beloved (literally) on a pedestal and worships her without a hope of sexual consummation. Richard Brathwait in his satire 'On Dotage' (**P9**) demands of Pygmalion, 'Why art thou so besotted still with wooing, / Since there's no comfort when it comes to doing [i.e. sex]?'; and John Marston (**P7**) compares him, 'So fond . . . and earnest in his suit / To his remorseless image', with the 'foolery / Of some sweet youths' who maintain that true love doesn't require sexual intercourse. A character in the university comedy *Lingua* complains of 'these puling lovers' and their extravagant praise of their beloveds: 'They make forsooth her hair of gold, her eyes of diamond, her cheeks of roses, her lips of rubies, her teeth of pearl, and her whole body of ivory, and when they have thus idolled her like Pygmalion, they fall down and worship her.'

As in this example, dotage is very often associated with idolatry. For Renaissance Protestant writers Pygmalion's devotion to his statue irresistibly suggests pagan idolatry and the supposed Catholic worship of images of the Virgin and the saints. Brathwait talks of his 'fair saint', his 'image-gods', his 'idle idol'; Marston compares him to the 'peevish Papists' who 'crouch and kneel / To some dumb idol'; Pettie ironically justifies the credibility of the statue's coming to life by reference to Catholic frauds: 'The like miracles we have had many wrought within these few years, when images have been made to bow their heads, to hold out their hands, to weep, to speak, etc.' Going beyond such topical satire, the notion of idolatry is often linked to Clement's arguments about art versus nature, and to anxieties about appearance and reality (or, in Renaissance terms, 'shadow' and 'substance'): Pygmalion's sin is to fall in love with the outward appearance his art has created, and forget the reality that his image is a mere soulless lump of stone. So an epigram by Hugh Crompton labels him an 'ape' (imitator) who 'for the substance doth adore the shape'; another by Davies of Hereford condemns him as one who turns stones into men but 'Himself makes like a stone by senseless courses'. The philosopher-poet Fulke Greville makes the story a metaphor for our worship of intellectual idols: in our ignorant vanity 'we raise and mould tropheas' which we call arts and sciences, 'and fall in love with these, / As did Pygmalion with his carvèd tree.'

A particular and rather bizarre example of this appearance/reality theme is the recurring association of Pygmalion with women's make-up (or 'paint', as it was then called, making the link with art much more obvious). Renaissance moralists routinely condemned women's 'painting' as immoral. Brathwait aims his satire at 'you painted faces', and another satirist, Everard Guilpin, complains,

Then how is man turned all Pygmalion,
That, knowing these pictures, yet we dote upon
The painted statues, or what fools are we
So grossly to commit idolatry?

Edmund Waller (**P10**), in a poem about the disillusionment of discovering that his beloved's beauty was only make-up, plays with the paradoxes of being in love with something that has no real existence: 'I dote on that which is nowhere; / The sign of beauty feeds my fire.' In a more extreme example, the satirist T.M. (Thomas Middleton?), after an embarrassing encounter with a beauty who turned out to be a male prostitute in drag, warns, 'Trust not a painted puppet as I have done, / Who far more doted than Pygmalion.' This almost obsessive theme points to a deep anxiety about the association of women's beauty with art (artificiality, artfulness, deceit) and its power to lead men into dotage and idolatry.

Not all Renaissance treatments of the story are so unsympathetic to Pygmalion. Some use the story, in Gower's manner, as a fable for lovers, as when Samuel Daniel laments that his mistress, unlike Pygmalion's, remains stony, or Abraham Cowley urges his to remember the legend ('The statue itself at last a woman grew, / And so at last, my dear, should you do too'), or William Fulwood, in a letter-writing manual, provides lovers with a model poem on the Pygmalion theme ('If thus Pygmalion pined away / For love of such a marble stone, / What marvel then though I decay / With piteous plaint and grievous groan'). Even for those who take the moral-satiric approach, the inherent narrative drive of the Ovidian story towards a happy ending creates problems: so Brathwait, having started out to preach a severe moral lesson against dotage, tails off anticlimactically with the sculptor and his statue living happily ever after. The two most substantial and interesting Renaissance versions – Pettie's and Marston's – both take a highly ambivalent attitude to Pygmalion. Pettie's novella relegates the statue story almost to an epilogue, focusing instead on the story of Pygmalion's previous lover, whose treachery contrasts with the devotion of that 'perfect proper maid', the statue; the narrator's tone is so saturated with tongue-in-cheek irony that it is hard to tell what his attitude is, or whether the antifeminist satire is neutralised or underlined by his ostentatious apologies to his female readers. As for Marston's poem, it swings disconcertingly between mockery of Pygmalion and a lascivious identification with him ('O that my mistress were an image too, / That I might blameless her perfections view!'), so that it was condemned by contemporary critics as pornographic and defended by Marston as a satiric parody of comtemporary love poetry – prompting C. S. Lewis's barbed remark that 'Authors in Marston's position do not always realize that it is useless to say your work was a joke if your work is not, in fact, at all funny' (Lewis 1954: 473). I think Lewis underrates Marston's humour, but unquestionably the compound of satire and eroticism is a rather unstable one.

The most sympathetic Renaissance response to the Ovidian story is one which does not mention Pygmalion at all: the awakening of Hermione's statue in the last scene of Shakespeare's *Winter's Tale* (**P8**). Shakespeare has explicitly raised the art versus nature question before, when in Act 4 the disguised king Polixenes and Perdita (a shepherdess who is really a princess) debated the ethics of artificial cross-breeding of plants: the king argues that 'This is an art / Which does mend nature . . . but / The art itself is nature'; but Perdita sturdily refuses to practise such arts, 'No more than, were I painted, I would wish / This youth should say 'twere well, and only therefore / Desire to breed by me' (4. 4. 95–7, 101–3). In the end, however, it is art which brings about the happy ending and the apparently miraculous resurrection of Perdita's mother Hermione. Shakespeare lays heavy stress on the artificiality of the statue, naming its creator (a real artist, Giulio Romano), praising his craftsmanship, even drawing attention to the 'oily painting' on its face; and behind this artificiality, of course, lies the art of Paulina, who has contrived the fake resurrection, and behind that the art of Shakespeare, who has contrived this extraordinarily improbable situation and even draws attention to its improbability (which 'should be hooted at / Like an old tale'). Yet these multiple layers of art are not wicked but benign, and their result is something entirely 'natural': the reunion of a family and the restoration of a wife to the husband who once lost her because of his unjust doubts of her virtue. It looks as though Shakespeare was creating a deliberate counter-version to the puritanical suspicion of art, love, and women which runs through most Renaissance versions of Pygmalion.

Eighteenth-century interlude

Annegret Dinter, in her historical survey of the Pygmalion story, describes the eighteenth century as the heyday ('*Blütezeit*') of the legend (Dinter 1979: ch. 5); significantly, however, all the verions she discusses are French, German, and Italian. In English, Restoration and Augustan versions of the story are surprisingly sparse. There are a number of translations and adaptations of Ovid, and one enterprising publisher reprinted Gower's version (slightly modernised) under the title *Chaucer's Ghost: A Piece of Antiquity*; but sustained original treatments are rare, and Pygmalion crops up mainly in casual allusions.

Some of these allusions are to Pygmalion as a great artist (Anna Seward, for instance, invoking 'Zeuxis' pencil, Orpheus' lyre, / Pygmalion's heaven-descended fire'). More often they are in an erotic context. Characters in Restoration comedy cite the legend to show that any woman can be won: a seducer in Dryden's *Secret Love* boasts that his victim 'warms faster than Pygmalion's statue', and a wooer in Flecknoe's *Demoiselles à la Mode* is encouraged with the thought that 'you love a woman, and she's a living one; Pygmalion only loved the dead statua of one, and yet you see he put life into it at last.' Others invoke Pygmalion's construction of the ideal woman: Soame Jenyns (**P13**) begins, 'Had I, Pygmalion-like, the power / To make the nymph I would adore. . .' and goes on to describe his ideal mate; more raffishly, in his poem 'The Libertine', the Restoration poet Alexander Brome justifies promiscuity as an artistic search for the ideal composite woman out of an experience of many imperfect ones ('Thus out of all, Pygmalion-like, / My fancy limns [paints] a woman. . .').[2] Others play with the image/reality motif: Aphra Behn writes of falling in love with her own imagined picture of the author of an anonymous love letter ('Pygmalion thus his image formed, / And for the charms he made, he sighed and burned'); Charles Cotton, asking a mistress for her picture, assures her that unlike Pygmalion he will not practise 'idolatry' before it; Thomas Tickell (**P12**) advises a young lover to 'clasp the seeming charms' of his unfaithful beloved's portrait, since – who knows? – it may come to life.

There are also, of course, humorous travesties of the story: Smollett's account (**P11**) of the metamorphosis of a beggar-girl into a fine lady (which I will discuss later), or Christopher Pitt's tale of the cat-fancier who successfully prayed to Venus to transform his favourite cat into a woman, and of his discomfiture on the wedding night when a mouse ran through the bedroom. One of the most interesting eighteenth-century versions is in Hannah Cowley's comedy *The Town Before You* (**P14**), which not only farcically parodies the statue scene from *The Winter's Tale* but also, unconventionally, presents us with a female sculptor-heroine and a female view of the relations between art and love.

On the whole, however, Restoration and Augustan allusions to Pygmalion are scattered and comparatively slight. The coming of the Romantic movement changes this, and the period from the late eighteenth to the early twentieth century is the heyday of Pygmalion in English. Rather than follow a strictly chronological arrangement from here on, I shall divide the material into three thematic groups (which inevitably overlap to some extent): versions which focus on Pygmalion as the artist-creator; versions which focus on the sexual and marital relationship of Pygmalion and Galatea; and versions which, in the Caxton–Shaw tradition, treat the story as a fable of class and education.

The Romantic artist: Pygmalion/Frankenstein

The Romantics, with their lofty conception of the role of the artist, were inevitably attracted to the Pygmalion legend. Around the beginning of the nineteenth century there emerges a new, far more serious view of Pygmalion as the artist-creator, a solitary, often tormented, sometimes godlike genius, wrestling with the limitations of his material to create and bring to life a vision of ideal beauty. The idea of 'Pygmalion's heaven-descended fire' becomes more than a cliché, as his relationship with the divine once again comes to the foreground of the story. Does his artistic power come from God or the gods, or from external nature, or from within himself? In creating life, is he the tool of the gods, or their rival, or a blasphemous usurper of their power?

The first Romantic treatment along these lines is a foreign one: Rousseau's dramatic monologue with music, first staged in France in 1770, and later adapted into English verse by William Mason (**P15**) – a piece that was enormously popular throughout Europe, and established 'Galatea' as the name of the statue-bride.

Rousseau's Pygmalion is a genius in despair over the apparent decay of his creative inspiration: 'Where, Pygmalion, / Where is thy power which once could rival Jove's, / Creating gods?' Gradually he realises that his passion and imaginative warmth have not died but been diverted into love for the statue, and that this love is not to be despised as dotage or idolatry, since it springs from the same qualities of soul that make him a great artist: 'My crime (if I indeed am culpable) proceeds / From too much sensibility of soul.' Instead he prays to Venus – not Venus the love goddess, but Venus Urania, 'Parent of Worlds! Soul of the Universe!', the lofty patroness of universal life and fertility – to bestow life on his creation. Venus does so, and the playlet ends with Pygmalion ecstatically united with Galatea – who, in greeting Pygmalion as 'myself', reveals herself as an integral part of the great artist's own soul.

The first and perhaps most memorable English version of the theme is that of Beddoes (**P17**). This powerful though overwrought poem presents a world which itself seems to pulse and seethe with creative energy. Pygmalion, a solitary genius regarded with wondering awe by his fellow citizens, is the vehicle of this creative force, a 'Dealer of immortality, / Greater than Jove himself', yet tormented by his inability to confer life on his creation. His passion is not simply love for the statue, but a violent rebellion of the life-force against the inevitability of death – and, in the poem's apocalyptic conclusion, it is not altogether clear which has triumphed.

Through the later nineteenth century a number of lesser poets took up this Romantic vision of Pygmalion the artist, treating it often at great length, with earnestness and reverence and (frankly) some tedium. They foreground the spiritual rather than the sensual side of the story; Pygmalion's love, far from idolatry, is in itself a kind of spiritual quest for the ideal and the divine. In William Cox Bennett's feverish dramatic monologue the statue emanates a 'mystic spirit' and 'utterance divine' that arouses hopeless yearning in the sculptor, who appeals, 'Have mercy, Gods! . . . This hunger of the soul ye gave to me, / Unasking.' William Morris's romance (**P21**) foregrounds the power of Venus, as Pygmalion returns home from the 'awful mysteries' of her temple to find the statue alive and wrapped in the golden gown that formerly decked the goddess's own image; Morris almost evokes the idea of Pygmalion's sacred marriage to the goddess, as if Galatea is standing in for her. The most loftily idealistic version is the 696-line poem by Frederick Tennyson (Alfred's brother). Tennyson's Pygmalion, who has 'throned / The beautiful within [his] heart of hearts' until 'the Ideal grew / More real than all things outward', gives his love to the statue's ideal beauty rather than any living woman, and at last his purity of heart is rewarded. In the central section of the poem he is treated to a dream-vision of godlike figures discoursing upon the immortality of the soul and the superiority of soul to body – a conventional moral, but for Tennyson, unlike earlier Christianisers of the legend, Pygmalion's love of the statue reveals not his dotage upon material appearances but his insight into a deeper spiritual world. The longest and oddest of these Victorian poems is the twelve-book epic *Pygmalion* by the Pre-Raphaelite sculptor and poet Thomas Woolner. Woolner presents Pygmalion as 'ardent-eyed, of eager speech / Which even closest friends misunderstood' (Woolner was notoriously sharp-tongued) and driven by 'a passionate hope / To bring the Gods' own language, sculpture, down / For mortal exaltation'. When he falls in love with and marries his servant-model (Woolner's rationalisation of the Ovidian story) he is subjected to 'foul calumny' and 'poisonous lies' by malicious rivals, but he proves his heroic worth in leading an army against the invading Egyptians, and is finally chosen king of Cyprus. Myth as wish-fulfilment could hardly go further.

More interesting, perhaps, are those writers who use the Pygmalion story as an image of the limits of unaided human art. So Elizabeth Barrett Browning's *Aurora Leigh* (**P19**), dissatisfied with her own poetry, wonders if Pygmalion too was frustrated by 'the toil / Of stretching past the known and seen, to reach / The archetypal Beauty out of sight.' In Hawthorne's 'Drowne's Wooden Image' (**P18**) the transformation of the hack woodcarver into a true artist is marked not only by his new-found skill but also by his new, wretched sense of the limitations of that skill. (Hawthorne's story, of course, also teases the reader with the question of whether or not an actual miracle takes place; the ending seems to provide a purely rational explanation, but one niggling detail remains unexplained.) Rousseau and Beddoes show the frustration of the genius who can create physical perfection but not bestow life, and even in Gilbert's comedy (**P22**) Pygmalion bitterly reflects that 'The gods make life, I can make only death!' In the early twentieth century H.D.'s Pygmalion (**P25**), who boasted that 'I made the gods less than men, / for I was a man and they my work', is tormented by doubts about whether he is the master or the tool of the creative power he wields. Only the American nun Mary Nagle revises the story's ending to leave the statue still 'a monument / Of dead perfection', underlining the moral that 'No human ardour kindles stone to life . . . Man fashions stone, but God bestows the soul.'

In all these versions, Pygmalion's own genius can only go so far; an external, divine force is needed to transform the statue into life. Remove that divine element from the story and you have the other great nineteenth-century myth about the creation of life: *Frankenstein*. In Mary Shelley's novel (**P16**), Victor Frankenstein, by an unexplained but clearly scientific process, infuses life into a creature assembled from dead body-parts; he is then so appalled at the creature's ugliness that he abandons it, and is consequently persecuted and killed by his own abused and resentful creation. The novel's most obvious theme is scientific irresponsibility, but many critics (and filmmakers) have read into it a more religious moral: Frankenstein blasphemously usurps God's prerogative of creating life, and his soulless creation is inevitably evil and destructive.

Frankenstein has become a kind of dark shadow of Pygmalion, a myth embodying the horror rather than the joy of lifeless matter becoming alive. Robert Buchanan (**P20**) reworks the Pygmalion story in the light of Shelley and her religious critics. His Pygmalion has lost his bride, Psyche ('Soul'), on their wedding morning, and her spirit commands him to make a statue of her to assuage his grief; but when it is finished, his 'holy dream [is] melted' into physical desire, and he involuntarily prays for it to come to life. The result is a beautiful but soulless creature ('Her eyes were vacant of a seeing soul'), purely animal and sensual in her instincts – her first move is to sun herself like a cat in the sunlight at the window. Pygmalion cajoles her to join him in a riot of feasting (food and drink presumably standing in for other sensual pleasures which Buchanan couldn't explicitly describe), but the orgy ends in horror: plague strikes the city, he sees the marks of death on his partner and flees, to roam the world like the Ancient Mariner as an awful warning to others of the peril of meddling with nature. Buchanan's poem is melodramatic and at times hysterical, but he shows that the Pygmalion story can be made to carry a genuine frisson of horror.

The shadow of Frankenstein hangs over later twentieth-century versions, like those of Graves (**P26b**), Hope, and Sisson, in which Pygmalion bitterly regrets creating the statue-wife who has become a millstone around his neck. It is most obvious in Angela Carter's fantasy (**P28**), which combines Pygmalion, Frankenstein, and Dracula in its story of a puppetmaster whose beloved puppet comes to life and vampirically murders him. There are traces of the Frankenstein pattern, too, in Shaw's play (**P24**), in which Eliza angrily rebels against the man of science who has irresponsibly created her and then lost interest. In such versions, however, questions about the relations and responsibilities between creator and creation are read in terms of gender and class, and so find their place in our next two sections.

Loving a statue: the sexual fable

While some nineteenth-century writers soared into the loftily ideal in their treatment of Pygmalion the artist, others focused in a more realistic, sometimes humorous, often disillusioned spirit on the human side of the story. How would love and marriage between an artist and an ex-statue actually work out? How might the ex-statue herself feel about the situation? And what does the story imply about actual or possible relationships between men and women?

Perhaps the first such 'realist' version is W. S. Gilbert's comedy (**P22**). Gilbert makes one crucial change in the story: Pygmalion is already married. Hence the sudden arrival of the beautiful Galatea, adoringly declaring 'That I am thine – that thou and I are one!', is not a happy ending but the start of a tangle of confusions that starts as farce and ends as rather sour tragicomedy. Galatea is perfectly, comically, good and innocent, with no understanding of civilised institutions like marriage, jealousy, war, hunting, money, class, or lying. Her impact on Pygmalion's respectable bourgeois society is catastrophic, and in the end, to restore order, she must return to being a statue, bitterly declaring, 'I am not fit / To live upon this world – this worthy world.' By implication, it is our world which is not good enough for Galatea.[3]

Other writers, male and female, try to imagine Galatea's feelings on coming to life, and suggest that these may not be of unalloyed joy. After all, the statue, in becoming alive, is also becoming mortal (as Pygmalion abruptly realises in poems by James Rhoades and Benjamin Low). William Bell Scott's Galatea, coming to life, sinks upon Pygmalion's breast 'by two dread gifts at once oppressed' – presumably, life and love. Emily Hickey's Galatea regrets the loss of the other gift she could have given Pygmalion, 'Art's life of splendid immortality'. In Elizabeth Stuart Phelps's dramatic monologue (**P23**) Galatea hesitates, contemplating the inevitable suffering and misery that marriage to Pygmalion will involve, before nobly deciding to make the 'sacrifice supreme' for love. The poem's attitude may strike modern readers as masochistic, but it is a striking, proto-feminist critique of the traditional assumption that marriage is a happy ending.

The same assumption is questioned, from the other side, by male poets who suggest that Pygmalion's infatuation with Galatea may not last once she dwindles from an unattainable ideal into a wife. W. H. Mallock's Pygmalion, informing Galatea that he has fallen out of love with her, advises her that she should be grateful for the consolation of still loving him, whereas he should be pitied for his inability to remain satisfied with a consummated love:

> Can you ever know how sorrowful men's loves are?
> How we can only hear love's voice from far –
> Only despaired-of eyes be dear to us –
> Mute ivory, that can never be amorous –
> Far fair gold stigma of some loneliest star!

(In fairness to this insufferable piece of male chauvinism, it should be added that Mallock was only twenty when he wrote it.) F. L. Lucas hints at a bitterer relationship of betrayal and mutual hatred, as Pygmalion, contemplating his sleeping wife, wishes he could undo his own 'wild wish' and return her to stone 'yet unpoisoned with a mind'. The same wish is shared by C. Day Lewis' lover in 'The Perverse' (**P27**), who can only love a woman who is an unattainable ideal, and once she is won 'would have changed her body into stone', and by C. H. Sisson's Pygmalion, in the most brutally reductive version of the legend, who 'often wished [Galatea] back / In silent marble, good and cold' – but 'The bitch retained her human heat.' A. D. Hope's 'Pygmalion' traces a relationship from its first ecstasy and agony through its decay into routine and boredom, and a final realisation of 'the horror of Love, the sprouting cannibal plant / That it becomes . . .'

Of course, some of the cynicism and misogyny of these versions is ironically placed. Nevertheless, on the whole, twentieth-century writers have taken a bleak view of the Pygmalion/Galatea love story, finding it hard to see any possibilities of happiness in such an unequal and artificial relationship. Some versions explicitly criticise the legend. Michael Longley's 'Ivory and Water' (**P29**) gently (and literally) deconstructs the male dream-fantasy that it embodies. Angela Carter's cruelly witty short story (**P28**) goes further in its critique of the whole process of male fantasising about women. Her Pygmalion figure, the aged Professor, is personally harmless and even endearing, but the fantasy he spins around his beloved puppet Lady Purple – that of 'the shameless Oriental Venus', the irresistibly beautiful, utterly evil vamp/dominatrix – is destructive. It destroys not only the Professor, when Lady Purple comes to life by literally sucking the life out of him, but also Lady Purple herself, who, at the moment of her apparent liberation, is merely beginning to act out the self-destructive fantasy he has programmed into her.

Perhaps the twentieth-century writer who best captures the ambiguities of the Pygmalion story is Robert Graves, in a mirrored pair of poems. 'Galatea and Pygmalion' (**P26b**) seems at first glance to embody the misogynistic view of the story, painting Galatea as a sexually demonic 'woman monster' who betrays her creator by fornication with others. A closer reading suggests an ironic sympathy for Galatea's rebellion against her 'greedy' and 'lubricious' creator, and a hint that the poem is not so much about sex as about art: the way the successful work of art inevitably escapes the control of the 'jealous artist' who tries to control and limit its meanings. 'Pygmalion to Galatea' (**P26a**), by contrast, is clearly a poem of successful love. Graves takes the traditional motif of Pygmalion listing the qualities of his ideal woman, but restores the balance of power by making Pygmalion's list a series of requests, to which Galatea graciously consents, sealing the bargain with 'an equal kiss'. In its implication that Pygmalion and Galatea can have a free and equal loving relationship, this is perhaps the one unequivocally positive modern version of the love story.

Pygmalion the educator: the Shavian tradition

While some writers have read the creator/creation relationship of Pygmalion and Galatea as an archetype of male/female relationships, others have read it as a metaphor for class differences and education. This reading goes back to Caxton (**P5**), who saw the Ovidian story as a metaphor for a lower-class woman transformed by an upper-class educator into a lady and a potential wife. William Hazlitt may have had the Caxton reading in mind when he give the ironic title *Liber Amoris; or, The New Pygmalion* to an account of his tragicomic infatuation with his landlady's daughter, who notably failed to be transformed. On a more intellectual level, eighteenth-century philosophers and scientists (as Carr 1960 explains) were fascinated by the idea of the 'animated statue' as a thought-experiment in human perception and learning: if a marble statue could be brought to life with a fully developed but entirely blank mind, how would it see the world and how would it develop?

The classic treatment of the story as a fable of education and class is Bernard Shaw's comedy *Pygmalion* (**P24**), but Shaw may have been influenced by an earlier comic version in Tobias Smollett's *Peregrine Pickle* (**P11**). He joked that 'Smollet had got hold of my plot', but admitted that the story might have unconsciously stuck in his mind from reading it as a boy (Holroyd 1989: 334–5).

In Smollett's version, Peregrine Pickle picks up a beggar-girl on the road and, with some new clothes and a hasty education in polite manners and conversation, passes her off as a lady. The episode is a joke and a piece of practical social criticism, the rebellious and misogynistic Peregrine demonstrating how very shallow are the external accomplishments which separate a fine lady from a beggar. Eventually the (nameless) pupil exposes herself by her 'inveterate habit of swearing', and Peregrine, now bored with the joke, is happy to marry her off to his valet.

In Shaw's version, the phonetician Henry Higgins, to win a bet, passes off the Cockney flower-girl Eliza Doolittle as a princess merely by teaching her how to speak with an upper-class accent. Shaw, like Smollett, uses the story partly to satirise the English class system and its obsession with proper speech. But, more seriously than Smollett, he also faces the morality of the Pygmalion/Galatea relationship. Higgins has his own kind of idealism: 'you have no idea how frightfully interesting it is to take a human being and change her into a quite different human being by creating a new speech for her. It's filling up the deepest gulf that separates class from class and soul from soul.' But in his enthusiasm for the experiment – as his mother and housekeeper point out – he has given no thought to Eliza as a person, or what will happen to her when the experiment is over and she is stranded in a class limbo, with an upper-class accent and tastes but no income or marketable skills. Eliza/Galatea's transformation to full humanity is not complete until she rebels against the patronising Higgins and walks out to lead her own independent life. In his epilogue Shaw explains why Eliza finally marries the amiably dim Freddy rather than Higgins: 'Galatea never does quite like Pygmalion: his relation to her is too godlike to be altogether agreeable.'

Shaw's determinedly anti-romantic conclusion, however, goes against comic convention and the dynamics of the Ovidian story. Even in the original 1912 London production Shaw was infuriated when the actors played the last scene to suggest that Higgins was in love with Eliza; the 1938 film hinted at a final romantic union of the hero and heroine, and the 1958 musical adaptation *My Fair Lady* made it explicit. The same 'happy ending' was imposed on a more recent film version of the story, *Pretty Woman* (1990), in which Pygmalion is a wealthy businessman and Galatea a prostitute; here, however, the real metamorphosis is not the heroine's social rise but the softening into humanity of the stony-hearted tycoon. Willy Russell's *Educating Rita* (1980), about the mutual transformation of a burnt-out English tutor and a working-class pupil, has a more open ending, leaving a question mark not only over the characters' future but also over whether Rita's education is entirely positive – the tutor, in a moment of dismay at what he has done, recalls 'a little Gothic number called *Frankenstein*'.

As a result of Shaw's play Pygmalion has become a common image in the study of education and psychology (a classic educational study, *Pygmalion in the Classroom*, is based on the Shavian idea that pupils' achievements depend on teachers' expectations), as well as in computing and cybernetics (a recent pamphlet inquires 'Internet: Which Future for Organised Knowledge, Frankenstein or Pygmalion?'). In Richard Powers's 1995 novel *Galatea 2.2* a computer scientist and a novelist, for a bet, try to educate a computer program (codenamed 'Helen') to pass an exam in English literature. In the end Helen, having become sufficiently human to be aware of her own limitations, shuts herself down, like Gilbert's Galatea returning to her pedestal. The science-fictional and real-life possibilities of the relationship between human beings and mechanical intelligence suggest that the Pygmalion legend will continue to develop over the next century.

Notes

1 Reinhold notes that an alternative eighteenth-century name for the statue was Elissa or Elise, which possibly inspired Shaw's Eliza Doolittle. The name Galatea was borrowed from another Ovidian character, the sea-nymph unwillingly courted by the Cyclops Polyphemus in *Met.*, 13; the two characters are occasionally confused, just as Pygmalion is sometimes confused with his namesake, the tyrannical king of Tyre in Virgil's *Aeneid* (Rousseau, for instance, locates his Pygmalion in Tyre rather than Cyprus).

2 Brome is alluding to a story usually told of the painter Zeuxis, that, commissioned to paint Helen of Troy, he put together a composite portrait with the eyes of one model, the forehead of another, and so on.

3 Gilbert's version was in turn parodied in the 1884 musical comedy *Adonis* (which despite its title is primarily a version of Pygmalion). Here the sexes are reversed, as a female sculptor creates and brings to life a statue of a handsome young man; pursued by the sculptor, her patron, and other lovelorn women, the harried Adonis finally opts to return to marble and hang a 'Hands Off' notice round his neck.

TEXTS

P1 Ovid, from *Metamorphoses*, *c.* AD 10. Trans. A. D. Melville, 1986°

The story of Pygmalion is one of those told by Orpheus in book 10 of the *Metamorphoses*. Ovid/Orpheus prefaces this story of Venus's benevolence to a faithful worshipper with two short examples of her vengeance on those who offended her: the Cerastae, who practised human sacrifice, and (in the opening lines below) the Propoetides, the first prostitutes.

Even so the obscene Propoetides had dared
Deny Venus' divinity. For that
The goddess' rage, it's said, made them the first
Strumpets to prostitute their bodies' charms.
As shame retreated and their cheeks grew hard,
They turned with little change to stones of flint.

Pygmalion had seen these women spend
Their days in wickedness, and horrified
At all the countless vices nature gives
To womankind lived celibate and long
Lacked the companionship of married love.
Meanwhile he carved his snow-white ivory
With marvellous triumphant artistry
And gave it perfect shape, more beautiful
Than ever woman born. His masterwork
Fired him with love. It seemed to be alive,
Its face to be a real girl's, a girl
Who wished to move – but modesty forbade.
Such art his art concealed. In admiration
His heart desired the body he had formed.
With many a touch he tries it – is it flesh
Or ivory? Not ivory still, he's sure!
Kisses he gives and thinks they are returned;
He speaks to it, caresses it, believes
The firm new flesh beneath his fingers yields,
And fears the limbs may darken with a bruise.
And now fond words he whispers, now brings gifts
That girls delight in – shells and polished stones,

° from Ovid, *Metamorphoses*, trans. A. D. Melville, Oxford: Oxford University Press, 1986, book 10, lines 238–97 (of the Latin), pp. 232–4. Reprinted by permission of Oxford University Press.

And little birds and flowers of every hue,
Lilies and coloured balls and beads of amber,
The tear-drops of the daughters of the Sun.°
He decks her limbs with robes and on her fingers
Sets splendid rings, a necklace round her neck,
Pearls in her ears, a pendant on her breast;
Lovely she looked, yet unadorned she seemed
In nakedness no whit less beautiful.
He laid her on a couch of purple silk,
Called her his darling, cushioning her head,
As if she relished it, on softest down.

Venus' day came, the holiest festival
All Cyprus celebrates; incense rose high
And heifers, with their wide horns gilded, fell
Beneath the blade that struck their snowy necks.
Pygmalion, his offering given, prayed
Before the altar, half afraid, 'Vouchsafe,
O Gods, if all things you can grant, my bride
Shall be' – he dared not say my ivory girl –
'The living likeness of my ivory girl.'
And golden Venus (for her presence graced
Her feast) knew well the purpose of his prayer;
And, as an omen of her favouring power,
Thrice did the flame burn bright and leap up high.
And he went home, home to his heart's delight,
And kissed her as she lay, and she seemed warm;
Again he kissed her and with marvelling touch
Caressed her breast; beneath his touch the flesh
Grew soft, its ivory hardness vanishing,
And yielded to his hands, as in the sun
Wax of Hymettus° softens and is shaped
By practised fingers into many forms,
And usefulness acquires by being used.
His heart was torn with wonder and misgiving,
Delight and terror that it was not true!
Again and yet again he tried his hopes –
She was alive! The pulse beat in her veins!

° **tear-drops of the daughters of the Sun**: in book 2 Ovid described how the daughters of the sun god Phoebus, grieving for their brother Phaethon, were transformed into trees which wept tears of amber.

° **Hymettus**: a mountain near Athens, famous for its free-range bees.

And then indeed in words that overflowed
He poured his thanks to Venus, and at last
His lips pressed real lips, and she, his girl,
Felt every kiss, and blushed, and shyly raised
Her eyes to his and saw the world and him.
The goddess graced the union she had made,
And when nine times the crescent moon had filled
Her silver orb, an infant girl was born,
Paphos, from whom the island takes its name.°

P2 Clement of Alexandria, from *Exhortation to the Greeks, c.* AD 200°

Clement of Alexandria, *c.* AD 150–*c.*212, influential Greek Christian theologian. In the course of an argument against pagan idolatry he refers to an alternative version of the Pygmalion legend, citing as source the third-century BC historian Philostephanus.

Why, I ask you, did you assign to those who are no gods the honours due to God alone? Why have you forsaken heaven to pay honour to earth? For what else is gold, or silver, or steel, or iron, or bronze, or ivory, or precious stones? Are they not earth, and made from earth? . . . The Parian marble° is beautiful, but it is not yet a Poseidon. The ivory is beautiful, but it is not yet an Olympian Zeus. Matter will ever be in need of art, but God has no such need. Art develops, matter is invested with shape; and the costliness of the substance makes it worth carrying off for gain, but it is the shape alone which makes it an object of veneration. Your statue is gold; it is wood; it is stone; or if in thought you trace it to its origin, it is earth, which has received form at the artist's hands. But my practice is to walk upon earth, not to worship it. For I hold it sin ever to entrust the hopes of the soul to soulless things.

We must, then, approach the statues as closely as we possibly can in order to prove from their very appearance that they are inseparably associated with error. For their forms are unmistakably stamped with the characteristic marks of the

° **Paphos**: in other versions, Paphos was a boy. According to legend, her (or his) son Cinyras founded the city of Paphos, one of the main centres of Cyprus and site of a great temple of Aphrodite that was still a place of pilgrimage in Ovid's day. The claim that the whole island of Cyprus was named after Paphos seems to be Ovid's invention.

° from *Exhortation to the Greeks*, ch. 4. Reprinted from the Loeb Classical Library from *Clement of Alexandria: The Exhortation to the Greeks; The Rich Man's Salvation*, trans. G. W. Butterworth, Cambridge, MA.: Harvard University Press, 1919.

° **Parian marble**: marble from the island of Paros was particularly prized for its gleaming whiteness.

daemons. At least, if one were to go round inspecting the paintings and statues, he would immediately recognize your gods from their undignified figures: Dionysus from his dress, Hephaestus from his handicraft, Demeter from her woe, Ino from her veil, Poseidon from his trident, Zeus from his swan. The pyre indicates Hercules, and if one sees a woman represented naked, he understands it is 'golden' Aphrodite. So the well-known Pygmalion of Cyprus fell in love with an ivory statue; it was of Aphrodite and was naked. The man of Cyprus is captivated by its shapeliness and embraces the statue. This is related by Philostephanus. There was also an Aphrodite in Cnidus, made of marble and beautiful. Another man fell in love with this and has intercourse with the marble, as Poseidippus relates. The account of the first author is in his book on Cyprus; that of the second in his book on Cnidus. Such strength had art to beguile that it became for amorous men a guide to the pit of destruction. Now craftsmanship is powerful, but it cannot beguile a rational being, nor yet those who have lived according to reason. It is true that, through lifelike portraiture, pigeons have been known to fly towards painted doves, and horses to neigh at well-drawn mares. They say that a maiden once fell in love with an image, and a beautiful youth with a Cnidian statue; but it was their sight that was beguiled by the art. For no man in his senses would have embraced the statue of a goddess, or have been buried with a lifeless paramour, or have fallen in love with a daemon and a stone. But in your case art has another illusion with which to beguile; for it leads you on, though not to be in love with the statues and paintings, yet to honour and worship them. The painting, you say, is lifelike. Let the art be praised, but let it not beguile man by pretending to be truth.

P3 Arnobius of Sicca, from *Against the Pagans*, *c.*AD 300°

Arnobius of Sicca (in northern Africa), *c.*AD 300, teacher of rhetoric and Christian convert and propagandist, cites the same story and source as Clement, with minor variations.

Philostephanus relates in his *Cypriaca* that Pygmalion, king of Cyprus, loved as a woman an image of Venus, which was held by the Cyprians holy and venerable from ancient times, his mind, spirit, the light of his reason, and his judgment being darkened; and that he was wont in his madness, just as if he were dealing with his wife, having raised the deity to his couch, to copulate with it by embraces and by mouth, and to do other vain things, carried away by a foolishly lustful

° from *The Seven Books of Arnobius Adversus Gentes*, vol. xix of the Ante-Nicene Library, trans. Rev. Alexander Roberts and James Donaldson (Edinburgh, 1871), 6. 22–3, pp. 297–8; translation slightly modified.

imagination. Similarly, Posidippus, in the book which he mentions to have been written about Cnidus and about its affairs, relates that a young man of noble birth (but he conceals his name), carried away with love of the Venus because of which Cnidus is famous, joined himself also in amorous lewdness to the image of the same deity, stretched on the genial couch and enjoying the pleasures which ensue. To ask again in like manner: If the powers of the gods above lurk in copper and the other substances of which images have been formed, where in the world was the one Venus and the other to drive far away from them the lewd wantonness of the youths, and punish their impious touch with terrible suffering? Or, as the goddesses are gentle and of calmer dispositions, what would it have been for them to assuage the furious joys of the wretched men, and to bring back their insane minds again to their senses? But perhaps, as you say, the goddesses took the greatest pleasure in these lewd and lustful insults . . .

P4 John Gower, from *Confessio Amantis*, *c.* 1390°

John Gower, ?1330–1408, Middle English poet, contemporary and friend of Chaucer. His *Confessio Amantis* (The Lover's Confession), over 33,000 lines long, retells a series of love stories (from Ovid and other sources) within the framework of a secular parody of Catholic confession. A lover confesses to a priest of Venus his sins against the code of courtly love, and the priest instructs him in the virtues of a true lover, illustrating his sermon with exemplary tales. In book 4 the priest questions the lover about the sin of 'pusillanimity', a cowardly hesitation to speak one's love:

And so forth, Sone, if we beginne
To speke of love and his servise,
Ther ben> truantz in such a wise,> — *are / of such a kind*
That lacken> herte, whan best were> — *lack / it were best*
To speke of love, and riht for fere> — *just out of fear*
Thei wexen> doumb and dar noght telle, — *grow*
Withoute soun> as doth the belle — *sound*
Which hath no claper for to chyme;
And riht so> thei as for the tyme — *just so*
Ben herteles withoute speche
Of love, and dar nothing beseche;
And thus thei lese> and winne noght. — *lose*

The lover confesses to this sin, and the priest tells the story of Pygmalion as an example of courageous persistence in an apparently hopeless love.

° from *Confessio Amantis*, book 4, lines 340–51, 371–436, in *The Complete Works of John Gower*, ed. G. C. Macaulay, 4 vols (Oxford, 1901), vol. ii, pp. 309–13.

I finde hou whilom> ther was on, — *once upon a time*
Which was a lusti man of yowthe:> — *vigorous young man*
Whos name was Pymaleon,
The werkes of entaile> he cowthe> — *sculpture / knew*
Above alle othre men as tho;> — *at that time*
And thurgh fortune it fell> him so, — *befell, happened*
As he whom love schal travaile,> — *cause distress*
He made an ymage of entaile
Lich> to a womman in semblance — *like*
Of feture and of contienance,
So fair yit nevere was figure.
Riht as a lyves creature> — *Just like a living creature*
Sche semeth, for of yvor> whyt — *ivory*
He hath hire wroght of such delit,> — *made her of such beauty*
That sche was rody> on the cheke — *ruddy*
And red on bothe hire lippes eke;> — *also*
Wherof that he himself beguileth.°
For with a goodly lok sche smyleth,
So that thurgh pure impression
Of his ymaginacion
With al the herte of his corage> — *passionate feeling of his heart*
His love upon this faire ymage
He sette, and hire of love preide;> — *prayed her to love him*
Bot sche no word ayeinward> seide. — *in return*
The longe day, what thing he dede,> — *whatever he did*
This ymage in the same stede> — *place*
Was evere bi, that ate mete> — *at meals*
He wolde hire serve and preide hire ete,
And putte unto hire mowth the cuppe;
And whan the bord was taken uppe,°
He hath hire into chambre nome,> — *taken into his bedchamber*
And after, whan the nyht was come,
He leide hire in his bed al nakid.
He was forwept, he was forwakid,°
He keste> hire colde lippes ofte, — *kissed*
And wissheth that thei weren softe,
And ofte he rouneth> in hire ere, — *whispers*

° **Wherof . . . beguileth**: which makes him deceive himself.
° **board was taken up**: medieval meals were served on trestle tables which were dismantled when the meal was over.
° **forwept . . . forwakid**: worn out with tears and with sleeplessness.

And ofte his arm now hier now there
He leide, as he hir wolde embrace,
And evere among> he axeth> grace,° *from time to time / asks for*
As thogh sche wiste> what he mente: *knew*
And thus himself he gan> tormente *did*
With such desese> of loves peine, *distress*
That no man mihte him more peine. *torment*
Bot how it were,> of his penance *it so happened that*
He made such continuance
Fro dai to nyht, and preith so longe,
That his preiere is underfonge,> *accepted*
Which Venus of hire grace herde;
Be nyhte and whan that he worst ferde,> *was in his worst state*
And it lay in his nakede arm,
The colde ymage he fieleth warm
Of fleissh and bon and full of lif.

Lo, thus he wan> a lusti wif, *won*
Which obeissant was at> his wille; *obedient . . . to*
And if he wolde have holde him stille> *had remained silent*
And nothing spoke, he scholde have failed:
Bot for he hath his word travailed> *made use of his speech*
And dorste> speke, his love he spedde,> *dared to / succeeded in*
And hadde al that he wolde> abedde. *wanted*
For er thei wente thanne atwo,> *before they parted*
A knave> child betwen hem two *boy*
Thei gete,> which was after hote> *begot / called*
Paphus, of whom yit hath the note> *still / name*
A certein yle,> which Paphos *isle*
Men clepe,> and of his name it ros. *call*

P5 William Caxton, from *Six Books of Metamorphoseos*, *c.*1480°

William Caxton, *c.*1422–91, the first English printer and publisher; he printed about a hundred books at his press in Westminster, some translated by himself. His version of Ovid's *Metamorphoses*, a prose paraphrase accompanied by

° **grace**: favour or mercy; in a religious context 'grace' is God's freely granted mercy to save sinful human beings (compare line 419); in the context of courtly love, it is the usual word for a lady's decision to grant her love to a suitor.

° from *Six Bookes of Metamorphoseos, in whyche ben conteyned The Fables of Ovyde. Translated out of Frensshe into Englysshe by William Caxton*, ed. George Hibbert, London, 1819, p. 11.

moral commentaries, was apparently never published, but six of the original fifteen books survive in manuscript form. Caxton's commentary on Pygmalion anticipates later readings of the story as a fable about social class.

Now I shall say what the image of ivory betokeneth, which was transformed into a woman, that the maker took for his wife, and so much loved that he made her lady of his realm. This is to say that some great lord might have a maid or a servant in his house which° was poor, naked, and could° no good, but she was gent° and of fair form, but she was dry and lean as an image. This rich man, that saw her fair, clothed, nourished, and taught her so much that she was well indoctrined.° And when he saw her drawn to good manners, he loved her so much that it pleased him to espouse her and take her to his wife; of whom he had after a fair son, prudent, wise, and of great renown . . .

P6 George Pettie, from 'Pygmalion's Friend and his Image', 1576°

George Pettie, *c.*1548–89, Elizabethan writer; his *Petite Palace of Pettie his Pleasure* is a collection of twelve classical love stories, apparently directed to a female audience. The simple plots take second place to Pettie's flamboyant display of flowery prose, rhetorical speeches, and sententious or tongue-in-cheek moral commentary. 'Pygmalion's Friend and his Image' teasingly delays the story of the 'Image' almost to the end of the tale, focusing instead at length on the story of Pygmalion's faithless 'Friend' (i.e. lover) Panthea and the betrayal which made him renounce women.

. . . In the country of Piedmont had his being one Pygmalion, a gentleman descended of noble birth, endowed with perfection of person, and perfectly portrayed forth with the lineaments of learning, so that it was doubtful whether he were more indebted to fortune for his birth, to nature for his beauty, or to his parents for his learning . . . Besides that, besides his learning he was endowed with a great dexterity in all things, in so much as nothing came amiss unto him which was meet° for a gentleman: in feats of arms no man more courageous; in exercises of the body none more active; in game or plan none more politic;° amongst the ancient, who more grave? amongst the youthful, who more merry?

° **which**: who.
° **could**: knew.
° **gent**: graceful, elegant.
° **indoctrined**: educated.
° from George Pettie, *A Petite Pallace of Pettie his Pleasure. Conteyning many pretie Histories, by him set foorth in comely colours, and most delyghtfully discoursed*, London, 2nd edn, *c.*1585.
° **meet**: suitable.
° **politic**: clever.

So that there was no time, no person, no place, whereto he aptly applied° not himself; by reason whereof he was acceptable to all good companies, and well was he that° might entertain him in his house.

But most of all he frequented the house of one Luciano, a noble gentleman of the same country, and in continuance of time grew so far in familiarity with his wife that he reposed his only pleasure in her presence. Yea, she had made such a stealth of° his heart that neither father nor mother, sister nor brother, nor all the friends he had in the country beside, could keep him one week together out of her company . . . Now she, on the other side, whose name was Panthea, being a courteous courtly wench, gave him such friendly entertainment° and used him so well in all respects that, her husband excepted, she seemed to hold him most dear unto her of any wight° in the whole world. She never made feast but he must be her guest; she never rode journey but he must be her companion; she never danced but he must direct her; she never diced but he must be her partner; she in a manner did nothing wherein he did not something. Her husband all this while being fully assured of her virtue, and very well persuaded of the honesty of the gentleman, suspected no evil between them, but liked very well of their love and familiarity together, neither indeed had he any cause to the contrary. For Pygmalion knew her to be endowed with such constant virtue that he thought it impossible to allure her to any folly; and besides that, his love was so exceeding great towards her, that he would not by any means be the cause to make her commit anything which might make her less worthy of love than she was . . . So that between these friends was no cause of suspicion, no cause of jar, no cause of jealousy, but they lived together the space of three or four years in most heavenly haven of most happy life. The flood of their felicity flowed from the fountain of most faithful friendship; the building of their biding° together was raised on the rock of virtue, for that it was to be thought, no seas of subtlety° or floods of fickleness could have undermined it.

But what perpetuity is to be looked for in mortal pretences? What constancy is to be hoped for in kites of Cressid's kind?° May one gather grapes of° thorns, sugar of thistles, or constancy of women? Nay, if a man sift the whole sex

° **applied**: adapted.
° **well was he that**: fortunate was anyone who.
° **made such a stealth of**: so stolen away.
° **entertainment**: treatment.
° **wight**: person.
° **biding**: remaining.
° **subtlety**: deviousness, treachery.
° **kites of Cressid's kind**: a stock Elizabethan phrase: a **kite** is a bird of prey, hence a person who preys upon others; **Cressid** or Cressida, who loved and betrayed the Trojan prince Troilus, is the archetypal unfaithful woman.
° **of**: from.

throughly, he shall find their words to be but wind, their faith forgery, and their deeds dissembling. – You must not, gentlewomen, take these words to come from me, who dare not so much as think so much, much less say so much; for that truth getteth° hatred – I mean such as tell not the truth, as he in no wise should not do° which should blow forth any such blast of° the most faithful and constant feminine kind. But you must take these speeches to proceed from Pygmalion, who, to speak uprightly,° had some cause to discommend° some in particular, though not to condemn all in general, as you shall forthwith hear.

The narrator tells how Panthea abandoned her faithful admirer for a handsome young visitor 'in whom . . . there was nothing worthy of commendation any way'. Pygmalion vows 'to eschew the company of all other women for her sake', and delivers a long diatribe against women, for which the narrator apologises:

Gentlewomen, you must understand this gentleman was in a great heat, and therefore you must bear with his bold blasphemy against your noble sex. For my part, I am angry with myself to have uttered it, and I shall like my lisping lips the worse for that they have been the instruments of such evil, neither shall I think them savoury° again until it shall please some of you to season them with the sweetness of yours. But yet he himself was so fully confirmed in this faith and belief touching° the frailty and fraud of women, that I think no torment, no not the fury of fire could have forced him to recant his opinion. For ever after he fled all occasions of women's company, persuading himself that, as he which toucheth pitch shall be defiled therewith, so he that useth women's company shall be beguiled° therewith . . .

But man purposeth, and God disposeth;° men determine, but the destinies do. For what shall be, shall be: no policy may prevent the power of the heavens, no doings of men can undo the destinies. For he was so far off from being able to keep himself from being in love with women, that he fell in love with a senseless thing, a stone, an image – a just punishment for his rash railing against the flourishing feminine sex. For, continuing, as I said before, his solitary life,

° **getteth**: begets, i.e. results in.
° **tell not the truth, as he in no wise should not do**: the pile-up of double negatives is acceptable Elizabethan grammar, but it does add to the ironic sense that the narrator is protesting too much.
° **blast of**: trumpet-blast against.
° **uprightly**: honestly.
° **discommend**: find fault with.
° **savoury**: pleasant-tasting.
° **touching**: concerning.
° **beguiled**: deceived, cheated.
° **man purposeth, and God disposeth**: proverbial: man makes plans but God decides what will actually happen.

separated from the society of women, he consumed the most part of his time in carving and graving images, and amongst all other his works, he made out of marble the likeness of a proper° wench – as belike,° notwithstanding the new religion he was entered into, having most fancy to a feminine form. And having fashioned and finished it in the finest manner, he fell to looking on it; and as love first entereth in at the eyes, and from thence descendeth to the heart, so he looked so long thereon, that at length he fell in love with it, yea, he was so wonderfully bewitched with it, that he fell to embracing, kissing, and dallying with it.

A monstrous miracle no doubt, and rather to be wondered at than credited. And yet I have heard of some that have been so possessed with melancholy passions,° that they have thought themselves to be made of glass, and if they had gone in any street, they would not come near any wall or house, for fear of breaking themselves; and so it may be that this Pygmalion thought himself some stone, and knowing that like agree best with their like, he thought he could make no better a match than to match himself to a stone. Or it may be he was one of those whom after the general flood (as Ovid reporteth) Deucalion and his wife Pyrrha made by casting stones at their backs, and then no marvel though he bare° marvellous affection to stones, being made of stones. Or whether his religion were to love images, I know not; neither is there more to be marvelled at in him, than in an infinite number that live at this day which love images right well, and verily persuade themselves that images have power to pray for them and help them to heaven.° Or whether it proceeded of this, that every one is lightly° in love with that which is his own, I know not. But this I read reported of him, that when neither by the feeling of his senses, neither by the force of reason, neither by the assistance of time, neither by any other mean° he could rid his tender heart from this stony love, he took his image and laid it in his bed, as if it had been his wife and bride. Which done, he went to the temple of Venus, and there, sending up sighs for sacrifice, and uttering his passions instead of prayers, ruefully repenting his former rebellion against the majesty of the goddess Venus, for that he had blasphemed wickedly against women, and neglected the laws and lore of love, and sought to lodge himself in liberty, he humbly requested her now to rue his ruthless° case, and he would remain her thrall all the days of his life

° **proper**: handsome.
° **belike**: no doubt.
° **melancholy passions**: the Elizabethans used the word 'melancholy' to refer to a wide range of mental disturbances.
° **bare**: bore, had.
° **neither is there more . . . heaven**: an anti-Catholic joke.
° **lightly**: easily.
° **mean**: means.
° **rue**: take pity on; **ruthless**: unpitied?.

after. And that if it seemed good to her godhead to give him a wife, that she might be – he durst not say his image, but like unto his image.

Venus very well knowing what he meant by this request, remembering also the wrong which Penthea before had proffered him, for that he loved her loyally the space of three or four years without any reward, except it were double dissembling for his singular affection,° and therefore had some reason to rage against women as he did, she thought herself bound in conscience to cure his calamity; and seeing how idolatrously he was addicted to his image, she put life into it and made it a perfect woman. The like miracles we have had many wrought within these few years, when images have been made to bow their heads, to hold out their hands, to weep, to speak, etc. But to Pygmalion; who, having done his devotions, returned to his lodging, and there according to custom fell to kissing his image, which seemed unto him to blush thereat, and taking better taste of her lips, they began to wax° very soft and sweet, and entering into deeper dalliance with her, she bade him leave° for shame, and was presently° turned to a perfect proper maid. Which he seeing, magnified° the might and power of Venus, joyfully took this maid unto his wife, and so they lived together long time in great joy and felicity.

You have heard, gentlewomen, what broad blasphemy the fickleness of Penthea caused unworthily to be blown forth against you all. Wherefore, to avoid the like, I am to admonish you that you prefer not newfangled friends° before old faithful friends; that you neither lightly leave the one, neither lightly love the other, for it is great lightness° to do either the one or the other . . . But to leave true friendship and come to trifling friendship, consisting in pleasant privy practices: I would wish those women which deal that way – although they be no sheep of my flock, yet for their sex' sake I wish them well – I would, I say, advise them to take heed° in ridding away those friends they are weary of; it is a dangerous piece of work, and importeth as much as their good name cometh to. For if they shall without discretion and great care disclaim a man's friendship, it is the next way (unless his government of himself° be very great) to make him proclaim what friendship he hath had of them in times past . . . Therefore I would advise them, as they have wilily caught them, warily to cast them off. For the best way is by little and little to estrange themselves from their friends, to pretend

° **double**: duplicitous; **singular**: (i) single-minded, (ii) exceptional.
° **wax**: grow.
° **leave**: stop it.
° **presently**: instantly.
° **magnified**: praised.
° **friends**: lovers (and so throughout this passage).
° **lightness**: fickleness.
° **take heed**: be careful.
° **government of himself**: self-control.

some earnest or honest cause, to profess that never any other shall possess like friendship with them, and to promise that in heart they will be theirs during life.

P7 John Marston, *The Metamorphosis of Pygmalion's Image*, 1598°

John Marston, ?1575–1634, English playwright and satirist, author of quirkily experimental comedies and tragicomedies (*The Malcontent*, *The Dutch Courtesan*), and of explosively angry and obscure verse satires. *The Metamorphosis of Pygmalion's Image* seems to be a contribution to the popular 1590s genre of erotic epyllion (like *Venus and Adonis*); however, when it was attacked as obscene, Marston claimed that he had meant it as a satirical parody of the genre:

. . . deem'st that in sad seriousness I write
Such nasty stuff as is *Pygmalion*,
Such maggot-tainted lewd corruption? . . .
Hence, thou misjudging censor: know I wrote
Those idle rhymes to note the odious spot
And blemish that deforms the lineaments
Of modern poesy's habiliments.
(Satire 6)

The exact blend of seriousness and satire in the poem is still a matter of critical debate.

To his Mistress

My wanton Muse lasciviously doth sing
Of sportive love, of lovely dallying.
O beauteous angel, deign thou to infuse
A sprightly wit into my dullèd Muse.
I invocate none other saint but thee
To grace the first blooms of my poesy.
Thy favours, like Promethean sacred fire,
In dead and dull conceit° can life inspire,
Or, like that rare and rich elixir stone,°

° from *The Metamorphosis of Pigmalions Image. And Certaine Satyres*, London, 1598. Some notes draw on the edition of Arnold Davenport, *The Poems of John Marston*, Liverpool: Liverpool University Press, 1961.

° **conceit**: mind, imagination.

° **elixir stone**: the 'philosopher's stone' which alchemists claimed could turn base metal into gold.

Can turn to gold leaden invention.
Be gracious then, and deign to show in me
The mighty power of thy deity.
And as thou read'st, fair, take compassion;
Force me not envy my Pygmalion.
Then when thy kindness grants me such sweet bliss,
I'll gladly write thy metamorphosis.

The Metamorphosis of Pygmalion's Image

Pygmalion, whose high love-hating mind
Disdained to yield servile affection
Or amorous suit to any womankind,
Knowing their wants° and men's perfection,
  Yet Love at length forced him to know his fate,
  And love the shade whose substance he did hate.°

For having wrought in purest ivory
So fair an image of a woman's feature,°
That never yet proudest mortality
Could show so rare and beauteous a creature
  (Unless my mistress' all-excelling face,
  Which gives to beauty beauty's only grace),

He was amazèd at the wondrous rareness
Of his own workmanship's perfection.
He thought that nature ne'er produced such fairness
In which all beauties have their mansion,
  And, thus admiring, was enamourèd
  On that fair image himself portrayèd.

And naked as it stood before his eyes,
Imperious Love declares his deity.
O what alluring beauties he descries
In each part of his fair imagery!°
  Her nakedness each beauteous shape contains.
  All beauty in her nakedness remains.

He thought he saw the blood run through the vein
And leap and swell with all alluring means;

° **wants**: failings.
° **love the shade . . . hate**: i.e. love an unreal image of the thing which in reality he hated.
° **feature**: shape, bodily form.
° **imagery**: image (the accent is on the second syllable: **imágery**).

Then fears he is deceived, and then again
He thinks he seeth the brightness of the beams
Which shoot from out the fairness of her eye,
At which he stands as in an ecstasy.°

Her amber-colourèd, her shining hair
Makes him protest° the sun hath spread her head
With golden beams to make her far more fair.
But when her cheeks his amorous thoughts have fed,
Then he exclaims, 'Such red and so pure white
Did never bless the eye of mortal sight.'

Then views her lips – no lips did seem so fair
In his conceit, through which he thinks doth fly
So sweet a breath that doth perfume the air.
Then next her dimpled chin he doth descry,
And views, and wonders, and yet views her still.
Love's eyes in viewing never have their fill.

Her breasts like polished ivory appear,°
Whose modest mount do bless admiring eye,
And makes him wish for such a pillowbere.°
Thus fond° Pygmalion striveth to descry
Each beauteous part, not letting overslip
One parcel° of his curious° workmanship,

Until his eye descended so far down
That it descrièd Love's pavilion,
Where Cupid doth enjoy his only crown
And Venus hath her chiefest mansion.
There would he wink,° and winking look again;
Both eyes and thoughts would gladly there remain.

Whoever saw the subtle city dame
In sacred church, when her pure thoughts should pray,
Peer through her fingers, so to hide her shame,

° **ecstasy**: trance (a medical term).
° **protest**: declare.
° **like polished ivory appear**: But the statue *is* ivory (line 7). Is Marston being careless, or playful?
° **pillowbere**: pillowcase (i.e. something to rest his head on).
° **fond**: (i) foolish, (ii) loving – the word has a significant double meaning throughout the poem.
° **parcel**: portion.
° **curious**: careful.
° **wink**: close his eyes.

When that her eye her mind would fain bewray.°
So would he view, and wink, and view again;
A chaster thought could not his eyes retain.

He wondered that she blushed not when his eye
Saluted those same parts of secrecy,
Conceiting not it was imágery°
That kindly yielded that large liberty.
O that my mistress were an image too,
That I might blameless her perfections view!

But when the fair proportion of her thigh
Began appear, 'O Ovid!' would he cry,
'Did e'er Corinna° show such ivory
When she appeared in Venus' livery?'°
And thus, enamoured, dotes on his own art,
Which he did work to work his pleasing smart.°

And, fondly doting, oft he kissed her lip.
Oft would he dally with her ivory breasts.
No wanton love-trick would he overslip,
But full observed all amorous behests
Whereby he thought he might procure the love
Of his dull image, which no plaints could move.

Look how the peevish° Papists crouch and kneel
To some dumb idol with their offering,
As if a senseless carvèd stone could feel
The ardour of his bootless° chattering,
So fond he was and earnest in his suit
To his remorseless image, dumb and mute.

He oft doth wish his soul might part in sunder,
So that one half in her had residence.
Oft he exclaims, 'O beauty's only wonder,
Sweet model of delight, fair excellence,
Be gracious unto him that formèd thee,
Compassionate his true love's ardency.'

° **bewray**: betray, reveal.
° **Conceiting . . . imagery**: not thinking that it was an image.
° **Corinna**: the mistress addressed in Ovid's love poems, the *Amores*. (For Pygmalion to quote Ovid is, of course, comically anachronistic.)
° **in Venus' livery**: i.e. naked.
° **smart**: pain.
° **peevish**: silly.
° **bootless**: useless.

She with her silence seems to grant his suit.
Then he, all jocund like a wanton lover,
With amorous embracements doth salute°
Her slender waist, presuming to discover
The vale of love, where Cupid doth delight
To sport and dally all the sable night.

His eyes her eyes kindly encounterèd,
His breast her breast oft joinèd close unto,
His arms' embracements oft she sufferèd –
Hands, arms, eyes, tongue, lips, and all parts did woo.
His thigh with hers, his knee played with her knee –
A happy comfort when all parts agree.

But when he saw, poor soul, he was deceived
(Yet scarce he could believe his sense had failed),
Yet when he found all hope from him bereaved
And saw how fondly all his thoughts had erred,
Then did he like to poor Ixion seem,
That clipped a cloud instead of heaven's queen.°

I oft have smiled to see the foolery
Of some sweet youths, who seriously protest
That love respects not actual luxury,°
But only joys to dally, sport and jest.
Love is a child, contented with a toy;
A busk-point or some favour° stills the boy.

Mark my Pygmalion, whose affection's ardour
May be a mirror° to posterity.
Yet viewing, touching, kissing, common favour,
Could never satiate his love's ardency.
And therefore, ladies, think that they ne'er love you
Who do not unto more then kissing move° you.

For my Pygmalion kissed, viewed, and embraced,
And yet exclaims, 'Why were these women made,

° **salute**: greet (i.e. touch).
° **poor Ixion . . . heaven's queen**: Ixion attempted to rape Juno, but Jupiter substituted a cloud shaped in her image; **clipped**: embraced.
° **respects not actual luxury**: doesn't care about actual sexual pleasure.
° **busk point**: a **busk** was a strip of wood or whalebone used to stiffen a corset, and the **busk-point** was the decorative lace used to secure its end; **favour**: a courtly term for some token, such as a ribbon or glove, given by a lady to her knight.
° **mirror**: i.e. example to be imitated.
° **move**: attempt to persuade.

O sacred gods, and with such beauties graced?
Have they not power as well to cool and shade
As for to heat men's hearts? Or is there none,
Or are they all like mine – relentless stone?'

With that he takes her in his loving arms
And down within a down-bed softly laid her.
Then on his knees he all his senses charms°
To invocate sweet Venus for to raise her
To wishèd life, and to infuse some breath
To that which, dead, yet gave a life to death.

'Thou sacred queen of sportive dallying' –
Thus he begins – 'Love's only emperess,
Whose kingdom rests in wanton revelling,
Let me beseech thee show thy powerfulness
In changing stone to flesh. Make her relent
And kindly yield to thy sweet blandishment.

'O gracious goddess, take compassion.
Instill into her some celestial fire,
That she may equalise affection,°
And have a mutual love and love's desire.
Thou know'st the force of love; then pity me,
Compassionate° my true love's ardency.'

Thus having said, he riseth from the floor,
As if his soul divinèd him° good fortune,
Hoping his prayers to pity moved some power,
For all his thoughts did all good luck importune.°
And therefore straight° he strips him naked quite,
That in the bed he might have more delight.

Then thus, 'Sweet sheets,' he says, 'which now do cover
The idol of my soul, the fairest one
That ever loved or had an amorous lover,
Earth's only model of perfection;

° **all his senses charms**: 'Abstracts himself from all impressions of sense, puts all his senses to rest, in order that he may concentrate the more intently on his prayer' (Arnold Davenport).
° **equialise affection**: equally return my love.
° **Compassionate**: take pity on.
° **divinèd him**: foresaw for him.
° **importune**: beg for.
° **straight**: straightaway.

Sweet happy sheets, deign for to take me in,
That I my hopes and longing thoughts may win.'

With that his nimble limbs do kiss the sheets,
And now he bows him for to lay him down,
And now each part with her fair parts do meet,
Now doth he hope for to enjoy love's crown;
Now do they dally, kiss, embrace together,
Like Leda's twins at sight of fairest weather.°

Yet all's conceit° – but shadow of that bliss
Which now my Muse strives sweetly to display
In this my wondrous metamorphosis.
Deign to believe me, now I sadly° say:
The stony substance of his image feature°
Was straight transformd into a living creature.

For when his hands her fair-formed limbs had felt
And that his arms her naked waist embraced,
Each part like wax before the sun did melt,
And now, O now, he finds how he is graced
By his own work. Tut, women will relent
Whenas they find such moving blandishment.

Do but conceive a mother's passing° gladness,
After that death her only son hath seized
And overwhelmed her soul with endless sadness,
When that she sees him 'gin for° to be raised
From out his deadly swoon to life again –
Such joy Pygmalion feels in every vein.

And yet he fears he doth but dreaming find
Such rich content and such celestial bliss.
Yet when he proves° and finds her wondrous kind,
Yielding soft touch for touch, sweet kiss for kiss,

° **Leda's twins . . . weather**: Castor and Pollux, the twin sons of Leda and Jupiter. 'The appearance of brush-discharges of electricity in storms (named after the Twins in classical times, and in Christian times called St Elmo's fire . . .) is universally regarded by sailors as a good sign' (Arnold Davenport).

° **conceit**: imagination (rather than reality).

° **sadly**: in all seriousness.

° **his image feature** the image he had created.

° **passing**: surpassing.

° **'gin for**: begin.

° **proves**: tests.

He's well assured no fair imagery
Could yield such pleasing, love's felicity.

O wonder not to hear me thus relate
And say to flesh transformèd was a stone.
Had I my love in such a wishèd state
As was afforded to Pygmalion,
Though flinty hard, of her you soon should see
As strange a transformation wrought by me.

And now methinks° some wanton itching ear
With lustful thoughts and ill attention
Lists° to my Muse, expecting for to hear
The amorous description of that action
Which Venus seeks and ever doth require
When fitness grants a place to please desire.

Let him conceit but° what himself would do
When that he had obtainèd such a favour
Of her to whom his thoughts were bound unto,
If she, in recompense of his love's labour,
Would deign to let one pair of sheets contain
The willing bodies of those loving twain.

Could he, O could he, when that each to either
Did yield kind kissing and more kind embracing,
Could he, when that they felt and clipped° together
And might enjoy the life of dallying,°
Could he abstain midst such a wanton sporting
From doing that which is not fit reporting?

What would he do when that her softest skin
Saluted his with a delightful kiss;
When all things fit for love's sweet pleasuring
Invited him to reap a lover's bliss?
What he would do, the selfsame action
Was not neglected by Pygmalion.

For when he found that life had took his seat
Within the breast of his kind beauteous love,

° **methinks**: it occurs to me.
° **Lists**: listens.
° **conceit but**: just imagine.
° **clipped**: embraced.
° **the life of dallying**: the absolute essence of sexual pleasure.

When that he found that warmth and wishèd heat
Which might a saint and coldest spirit move,
Then arms, eyes, hands, tongue, lips and wanton thigh
Were willing agents in love's luxury.°

Who knows not what ensues? O pardon me,
Ye gaping ears that swallow up my lines.
Expect no more. Peace, idle poesy,
Be not obscene, though wanton in thy rhymes;
And chaster thoughts, pardon if I do trip
Or if some loose lines from my pen do slip,

Let this suffice: that that same happy night
So gracious were the gods of marriage,
Midst all their pleasing and long-wished delight
Paphus was got;° of whom in after age
Cyprus was Paphos called, and evermore
Those islanders do Venus' name adore.

P8 William Shakespeare, from *The Winter's Tale*, *c.* 1610°

Shakespeare never explicitly refers to Pygmalion, but the final scene of his late tragicomic romance *The Winter's Tale*, in which a statue apparently comes to life, has often been seen as a response to the legend.

In the first half of the play King Leontes' paranoiac suspicion of a love affair between his queen, Hermione, and his best friend, King Polixenes, led to the deaths of his little son (dead of grief) and his newborn daughter (abandoned on a foreign beach) and finally, it seems, of Hermione herself. Leontes has spent sixteen years in grief and remorse, under the tough care of Hermione's friend, Lady Paulina. In the last act losses are restored: he recovers his lost daughter, Perdita, and blesses her marriage to Florizel, Polixenes' son. To crown the celebrations, Paulina invites the company to her chapel to view a statue of Hermione, newly carved and painted by 'that rare Italian master, Giulio Romano'.

Enter Leontes, Polixenes, Florizel, Perdita, Camillo, Paulina, Lords, etc

LEONTES: O grave and good Paulina, the great comfort
That I have had of thee!

° **luxury**: sensuality.

° **got**: begotten.

° *The Winter's Tale*, 5. 2. 1–133, from the First Folio, 1623. (I have made the following emendations: line 18, 'Louely' to 'Lonely'; line 96, 'On:' to 'Or'.)

PAULINA What, sovereign sir,
I did not well, I meant well. All my services
You have paid home;° but that you have vouchsafed,
With your crowned brother and these your contracted
Heirs of your kingdoms, my poor house to visit,
It is a surplus of your grace which never
My life may last to answer.°
LEONTES: O Paulina,
We honour you with trouble. But we came
To see the statue of our queen. Your gallery
Have we passed through, not without much content
In many singularities;° but we saw not
That which my daughter came to loook upon,
The statue of her mother.
PAULINA: As she lived peerless,
So her dead likeness I do well believe
Excels what ever yet you looked upon,
Or hand of man hath done; therefore I keep it
Lonely, apart. But here it is. Prepare
To see the life as lively mocked° as ever
Still sleep mocked death. Behold, and say 'tis well.
[*She draws a curtain and reveals Hermione like a statue*]
I like your silence; it the more shows off
Your wonder. But yet speak – first you, my liege:
Comes it not something near?°
LEONTES: Her natural posture!
Chide me,° dear stone, that I may say indeed
Thou art Hermione – or rather, thou art she
In thy not chiding, for she was as tender
As infancy and grace. But yet, Paulina,
Hermione was not so much wrinkled, nothing
So agèd as this seems.
POLIXENES: O, not by much.
PAULINA: So much the more our carver's excellence,
Which lets go by some sixteen years and makes her
As she lived now.

° **home**: in full.
° **answer**: pay back.
° **singularities**: rarities, things worth seeing.
° **as lively mocked**: imitated in as lifelike a way.
° **Comes it not something near?**: Isn't it rather like her?
° **Chide me**: express your anger at me.

LEONTES: As now she might have done,
So much to my good comfort as it is
Now piercing to my soul.° O, thus she stood
Even with such life of majesty – warm life,
As now it coldly stands – when first I wooed her.
I am ashamed – does not the stone rebuke me
For being more stone than it? O royal piece,
There's magic in thy majesty, which has
My evils conjured to remembrance, and
From thy admiring° daughter took the spirits,
Standing like stone with thee.

PERDITA: [*kneeling*] And give me leave,
And do not say 'tis superstition, that
I kneel and then implore her blessing. Lady,
Dear queen, that ended when I but began,
Give me that hand of yours to kiss.

PAULINA: O, patience!
The statue is but newly fixed,° the colour's
Not dry.

CAMILLO: [*to Leontes*]
My lord, your sorrow was too sore° laid on,
Which sixteen winters cannot blow away,
So many summers dry. Scarce° any joy
Did ever so long live; no sorrow
But killed itself much sooner.

POLIXENES: Dear my brother,
Let him that was the cause of this have power
To take off so much grief from you as he
Will piece up° in himself.

PAULINA: Indeed, my lord,
If I had thought the sight of my poor image
Would thus have wrought° you – for the stone is mine –
I'd not have showed it.

LEONTES: Do not draw the curtain.

° **So much . . . my soul**: i.e. if she were alive it would give me as much comfort as her absence now causes me piercing grief.
° **admiring**: wondering, marvelling (a stronger word than today).
° **is but newly fixed**: i.e. the paint on it has only just been made fast.
° **sore**: harshly.
° **Scarce**: scarcely.
° **piece up**: make up (i.e. he will replace the grief he takes away from Leontes with an equal amount of his own).
° **wrought**: moved, disturbed.

PAULINA: No longer shall you gaze on't, lest your fancy
May think anon° it moves.
LEONTES: Let be, let be!
Would I were dead but that methinks already –°
What was he that did make it? See, my lord,
Would you not deem° it breathed, and that those veins
Did verily bear blood?
POLIXENES: Masterly done:
The very life seems warm upon her lip.
LEONTES: The fixure° of her eye has motion in't,
As we are mocked° with art.
PAULINA: I'll draw the curtain.
My lord's almost so far transported that
He'll think anon it lives.
LEONTES: O sweet Paulina,
Make me to think so twenty years together!
No settled senses° of the world can match
The pleasure of that madness. Let't alone.
PAULINA: I am sorry, sir, I have thus far stirred you – but
I could afflict you farther.
LEONTES: Do, Paulina,
For this affliction hath a taste as sweet
As any cordial° comfort. Still methinks
There is an air comes from her. What fine chisel
Could ever yet cut breath? Let no man mock me,
For I will kiss her.
PAULINA: Good my lord, forbear.
The ruddiness upon her lip is wet;
You'll mar it if you kiss it, stain your own
With oily painting. Shall I draw the curtain?
LEONTES: No – not these twenty years.
PERDITA: So long could I
Stand by, a looker-on.
PAULINA: Either forbear,°

° **anon**: any moment now.
° **that methinks already**: i.e. it already seems to me that it does (move).
° **deem**: believe.
° **fixure**: fixedness.
° **mocked**: deceived.
° **settled senses**: rational mind.
° **cordial**: health-giving.
° **forbear**: withdraw.

Quit presently° the chapel, or resolve you
For° more amazement. If you can behold it,
I'll make the statue move indeed, descend,
And take you by the hand. But then you'll think –
Which I protest against – I am assisted
By wicked powers.

LEONTES: What you can make her do
I am content to look on; what to speak,
I am content to hear – for 'tis as easy
To make her speak as move.

PAULINA: It is required
You do awake your faith. Then, all stand still;
Or those that think it is unlawful business
I am about, let them depart.

LEONTES: Proceed;
No foot shall stir.

PAULINA: Music – awake her – strike!

[*Music*]

'Tis time. Descend. Be stone no more. Approach.
Strike all that look upon with marvel. Come.
I'll fill your grave up. Stir. Nay, come away.°
Bequeath to death your numbness, for from him
Dear life redeems you.

[*Hermione begins to move, and slowly comes down*]

You perceive she stirs.
Start not: her actions shall be holy as
You hear my spell is lawful. Do not shun her
Until you see her die again, for then
You kill her double.° Nay, present your hand.
When she was young, you wooed her; now, in age,
Is she become the suitor?

LEONTES: [*touching her*] O, she's warm!
If this be magic, let it be an art
Lawful as eating.

POLIXENES: She embraces him.

CAMILLO: She hangs about his neck.
If she pertain° to life, let her speak too.

° **presently**: immediately.
° **resolve you for**: make up your minds to undergo.
° **come away**: come on.
° **double**: a second time.
° **pertain**: belong.

POLIXENES: Ay, and make it manifest where she has lived,
Or how stol'n from the dead.
PAULINA: That she is living,
Were it but told you, should be hooted° at
Like an old tale;° but it appears she lives,
Though yet she speak not. Mark a little while.
[*To Perdita*] Please you to interpose, fair madam; kneel,
And pray your mother's blessing. – Turn, good lady,
Our Perdita is found.°
HERMIONE: You gods, look down,
And from your sacred vials pour your graces
Upon my daughter's head! Tell me, mine own,
Where hast thou been preserved – where lived – how found
Thy father's court? For thou shalt hear that I,
Knowing by Paulina that the oracle
Gave hope thou wast in being,° have preserved
Myself to see the issue.°
PAULINA: There's time enough for that,
Lest they desire upon this push° to trouble
Your joys with like relation. Go together,
You precious winners all; your exultation
Partake to° everyone.

P9 Richard Brathwait, from 'The Fifth Satire: On Dotage', 1621°

Richard Brathwait, ?1588–1673, a prolific writer whose work included satires, pastorals, religious works, prose novellas, and travel writings. His satire 'On Dotage' sums up the Renaissance hostility to Pygmalion's irrational and idolatrous passion. Brathwait explains in a prose introduction that 'The moral includeth the vain and foolish loves of such as are besotted on every idle picture or painted image, whose self-conceited vanity makes beauty their idol,

° **hooted**: jeered.
° **Like an old tale**: One of a series of sly references in the play which draw attention to its improbable, fairy-tale quality.
° **Perdita is found**: playing on the Latin meaning of Perdita: 'the lost one'.
° **the oracle . . . in being**: Apollo's oracle had warned Leontes that 'the King shall live without an heir if that which is lost [i.e. the abandoned Perdita] be not found'.
° **issue**: outcome.
° **upon this push**: at this critical moment.
° **Partake to**: share with.
° from *Natures Embassie: Or, The Wilde-mans Measures: Danced naked by twelve Satyres*, London, 1621, The Fifth Satire, pp. 99–101.

becoming creatures of their own making, as if they disesteemed the creation of their Maker'; and a sidenote directs the satire particularly at women who wear make-up: 'Note this, you painted faces, whose native country, once white Albion,° is become reddish with blushing at your vanities.'

He builds him temples for his image-gods,°
And, much besotted with their fair aspect,
In admiration of his work, he nods
And shakes his head and tenders them respect.
'I cannot tell,' quoth he, 'what passion moves me,
But sure I am,' quoth he, 'fair saint, I love thee.
Thou art my handiwork, I wish my wife,
If to thy fair proportion thou hadst life.'

Canst thou, Pygmalion, dote so on shrines,
On lifeless pictures, that was never rapt
With any beauty Cyprus isle confines?
These, foolish man, be for thy love unapt;
They cannot answer° love for love again.
Then fond Pygmalion, do thy love restrain;
Such senseless creatures as have only being°
Have with embraces but an harsh agreeing.

They have no moisture in their key-cold lips,
No pleasure in their smile; their colour stands;°
Whilst youthful ladies on the pavement trips,
They stand as pictures should, with sapless hands;
And well thou knows, if passive be not moving,
The active part can yield small fruits of loving.
Why art thou so besotted still with wooing,
Since there's no comfort when it comes to doing?°

Can any idle idol without breath
Give thee a graceful answer to thy suit?
Nay, rather like dead corpse surprised by death
It answers silence when thou speaks unto't.

° **once white Albion**: Albion, an old name for Britain, is derived from Latin *albus* (white), in reference to the white chalk cliffs.
° **temples for his image-gods**: 'Like those *pulvinaria* erected by the heathen for their pagan images' (Brathwait's note).
° **answer**: reciprocate, return.
° **only being**: i.e. only existence rather than life.
° **stands**: i.e. it doesn't come and go like the colour of a living woman's face.
° **doing**: (slang for) sexual intercourse.

Desist then, fond Pygmalion, and restrain
To love that creature cannot° love again;
What will it pleasure thee a shrine to wed,
That can afford no pleasure in thy bed? . . .

P10 Edmund Waller, 'On the Discovery of a Lady's Painting', 1630s?°

Edmund Waller, 1606-87, 'Cavalier' poet and courtier, who fought on the Royalist side in the Civil War; his short lyrics of love and courtly compliment were often praised for their 'sweetness'. The title of this piece refers to the discovery that the lady wears make-up, and her supposed beauty is hence artificial.

Pygmalion's fate reversed is mine:
His marble love took flesh and blood.
All that I worshipped as divine,
That beauty, now 'tis understood,
Appears to have no more of life
Than that whereof he framed° his wife.

As women yet who apprehend
Some sudden cause of causeless fear,
Although that seeming cause take end,
And they behold no danger near,
A shaking through their limbs they find,
Like leaves saluted° by the wind:

So though the beauty do appear
No beauty, which amazed° me so,
Yet from my breast I cannot tear
The passion which from thence did grow,
Nor yet out of my fancy° raze
The print of that supposèd face.°

A real beauty, though too near,

° **cannot**: which cannot.
° from *The Poems of Edmund Waller*, ed. G. Thorn Drury, London, 1893.
° **that whereof he framed**: the substance from which he made.
° **saluted**: greeted, i.e. lightly touched.
° **amazed**: stunned, bewildered (a stronger word than today).
° **fancy**: imagination.
° **As women yet . . . supposèd face**: the general sense is: Just as women who take fright at some imagined danger continue to tremble even after they realise it was imaginary, so I continue to feel love even though I know what I loved did not really exist.

The fond Narcissus did admire.°
I dote on that which is nowhere;
The sign of beauty feeds my fire.
No mortal flame was e'er so cruel
As this, which thus survives the fuel.

P11 Tobias Smollett, from *The Adventures of Peregrine Pickle*, 1751°

Tobias Smollett, 1721–71, Scottish-born novelist, journalist, and travel writer; his novels (among them *Roderick Random*, 1747; *Peregrine Pickle*, 1751; *Humphrey Clinker*, 1771) are picaresque and episodic, full of violent action, slapstick comedy, and social satire. *Peregrine Pickle* is the story of a proud, hot-tempered young man who brings on himself many misadventures before being united with his faithful lover Emilia. The story in chapter 87 of Peregrine's attempt to pass off a beggar girl as a fine lady makes no explicit reference to Pygmalion (except perhaps the Ovidian word 'metamorphoses' in the chapter title); but it strongly resembles (and probably influenced) Shaw's *Pygmalion*.

In the previous chapter a misunderstanding has caused Emilia once again to break off her engagement to Peregrine, who rides off in a fury, vowing 'that he would seek consolation for the disdain of Emilia, in the possession of the first willing wench he should meet upon the road'.

Chapter 87: Peregrine sets out for the Garrison, and meets with a Nymph of the Road, whom he takes into Keeping, and metamorphoses into a fine Lady.

In the mean time, our hero jogged along in a profound reverie, which was disturbed by a beggar-woman and her daughter, who solicited him for alms as he passed them on the road. The girl was about the age of sixteen, and notwithstanding the wretched equipage° in which she appeared, exhibited to his view a set of agreeable features, enlivened with the complexion of health and cheerfulness. The resolution I have already mentioned was still warm in his imagination; and he looked upon this young mendicant° as a very proper object for the performance of his vow. He therefore entered into a conference with the mother, and for a small sum of money purchased her property in the wench, who did not

° **Narcissus** fell in love with his own reflection in the water; his love's beauty was **too near** because it was his own. **fond**: foolish.

° from *The Adventures of Peregrine Pickle. In which are included, Memoirs of a Lady of Quality*, 2nd edn revised, 4 vols, London, 1758.

° **equipage**: clothing.

° **mendicant**: beggar.

require much courtship and entreaty, before she consented to accompany him to any place that he should appoint for her habitation.

> Peregrine dispatches his new acquisition, in the company of his servant Tom Pipes, to the home of his friends Lieutenant and Mrs Hatchway. On the way Pipes attempts to make a pass at her, and is overwhelmed by her eloquent torrent of obscene abuse; the young lady, he discovers, has 'a natural genius for altercation'. Arriving at the Hatchways' home, she is given a bath (despite her violent protests) and dressed in some of Mrs Hatchway's clothes . . .

by which means her appearance was altered so much for the better, that when Peregrine arrived next day, he could scarce believe his own eyes. He was, for that reason, extremely well pleased with his purchase, and now resolved to indulge a whim which seized him at the very instant of his arrival.

He had (as I believe the reader will readily allow) made considerable progress in the study of character, from the highest rank to the most humble station of life, and found it diversified in the same manner, through every degree of subordination and precedency. Nay, he moreover observed, that the conversation of those who are dignified with the appellation of 'polite company' is neither more edifying nor entertaining than that which is met with among the lower classes of mankind; and that the only essential difference, in point of demeanour, is the form of an education, which the meanest capacity can acquire, without much study or application. Possessed of this notion, he determined to take the young mendicant under his own tutorage and instruction. In consequence of which he hoped he should, in a few weeks, be able to produce her in company, as an accomplished young lady of uncommon wit and an excellent understanding.

This extravagant plan he forthwith began to execute with great eagerness and industry; and his endeavours succeeded even beyond his expectation. The obstacle in surmounting of which he found the greatest difficulty was an inveterate habit of swearing, which had been indulged from her infancy, and confirmed by the example of those among whom she had lived. However, she had the rudiments of good sense from nature, which taught her to listen to wholesome advice, and was so docile as to comprehend and retain the lessons which her governor recommended to her attention; insomuch that he ventured, in a few days, to present her at table, among a set of country squires, to whom she was introduced as niece to the lieutenant. In that capacity she sat with becoming easiness of mien (for she was as void of the *mauvaise honte*° as any duchess in the land), bowed very graciously to the compliments of the gentlemen; and though she said little or nothing, because she was previously cautioned on that score, she more than once gave way to laughter, and her mirth happened to be pretty well timed. In a word,

° ***mauvaise honte***: shyness, self-consciousness.

she attracted the applause and admiration of the guests, who, after she was withdrawn, complimented Mr Hatchway upon the beauty, breeding, and good humour of his kinswoman.

But what contributed more than any other circumstance to her speedy improvement was some small insight into the primer,° which she had acquired at a day-school, during the life of her father, who was a day-labourer in the country. Upon this foundation did Peregrine build a most elegant superstructure; he culled out choice sentences from Shakespeare, Otway,° and Pope, and taught her to repeat them with an emphasis and theatrical cadence. He then instructed her in the names and epithets of the most celebrated players, which he directed her to pronounce occasionally, with an air of careless familiarity; and, perceiving that her voice was naturally clear, he enriched it with remnants of opera tunes, to be hummed during a pause in conversation, which is generally supplied with a circulation of a pinch of snuff. By means of this cultivation, she became a wonderful proficient in the polite graces of the age; she with great facility comprehended the scheme of whist, though cribbage was her favourite game, with which she had amused herself in her vacant hours, from her first entrance into the profession of hopping; and brag soon grew familiar to her practice and conception.°

Thus prepared, she was exposed to the company of her own sex, being first of all visited by the parson's daughter, who could not avoid showing that civility to Mr Hatchway's niece, after she had made her public appearance at church. Mrs Clover, who had a great share of penetration, could not help entertaining some doubts about this same relation, whose name she had never heard the uncle mention, during the whole term of her residence at the garrison. But as the young lady was treated in that character, she would not refuse her acquaintance; and, after having seen her at the castle, actually invited Miss Hatchway to her house. In short, she made a progress through almost all the families in the neighbourhood; and by dint of her quotations (which, by the by, were not always judiciously used), she passed for a sprightly young lady, of uncommon learning and taste.

Peregrine having in this manner initiated her in the beau monde° of the country, conducted her to London, where she was provided with private lodgings and a female attendant; and put her immediately under the tuition of his valet de chambre who had orders to instruct her in dancing and the French language. He attended her to plays and concerts three or four times a week; and when our hero thought her sufficiently accustomed to the sight of great company, he squired her

° **primer**: elementary child's reader.

° **Otway**: Thomas Otway, a Restoration dramatist whose works were very popular in the eighteenth century.

° **whist**, **cribbage**, and **brag** are all card games.

° **beau monde**: fashionable society.

in person to a public assembly,° and danced with her among all the gay ladies of fashion; not but that there was still an evident air of rusticity and awkwardness in her demeanour, which was interpreted into an agreeable wildness of spirit, superior to the forms of common breeding. He afterwards found means to make her acquainted with some distinguished patterns of her own sex, by whom she was admitted into the most elegant parties, and continued to make good her pretensions to gentility, with great circumspection. But one evening, being at cards with a certain lady whom she detected in the very fact of unfair conveyance, she taxed her roundly with the fraud, and brought upon herself such a torrent of sarcastic reproof, as overbore all her maxims of caution, and burst open the floodgates of her own natural repartee, twanged off with the appellations of b— and w— , which she repeated with great vehemence, in an attitude of manual defiance,° to the terror of her antagonist, and the astonishment of all present. Nay, to such an unguarded pitch was she provoked that, starting up, she snapped her fingers in testimony of disdain, and, as she quitted the room, applied her hand to that part which was the last of her that disappeared, inviting the company to kiss it, by one of its coarsest denominations.°

Peregrine was a little disconcerted at this oversight in her behaviour, which, by the daemon of intelligence,° was in a moment conveyed to all the private companies in town; so that she was absolutely excluded from all polite communication,° and Peregrine, for the present, disgraced among the modest part of his female acquaintance, many of whom not only forbade him their houses, on account of the impudent insult he had committed upon their honour as well as understanding, in palming a common trull upon them as a young lady of birth and education; but also aspersed° his family, by affirming that she was actually his own cousin-german, whom he had precipitately raised from the most abject state of humility and contempt. In revenge for this calumny, our young gentleman explained the whole mystery of her promotion,° together with the motives that induced him to bring her into the fashionable world; and repeated among his companions the extravagant encomiums which had been bestowed upon her by the most discerning matrons of the age.

Meanwhile the infanta° herself, being rebuked by her benefactor for this instance of misbehaviour, promised faithfully to keep a stricter guard for the future over her conduct, and applied herself with great assiduity to the studies in which she was assisted by the Swiss, who gradually lost the freedom of his heart,

° **public assembly**: i.e. dance.
° **an attitude of manual defiance**: i.e. with her fists up.
° **denominations**: names.
° **intelligence**: rumour, gossip.
° **polite communication**: contact with respectable society.
° **aspersed**: slandered.
° **promotion**: raising in social position.
° **infanta**: princess (ironic).

while she was profiting by his instruction. In other words, she made a conquest of her preceptor,° who, yielding to the instigations of the flesh, chose a proper opportunity to declare his passion, which was powerfully recommended by his personal qualifications; and his intentions being honourable, she listened to his proposals of espousing her in private. In consequence of this agreement, they made an elopement together; and, being buckled at the Fleet, consummated their nuptials in private lodgings by the Seven Dials,° from which the husband next morning sent a letter to our hero, begging forgiveness for the clandestine step he had taken, which he solemnly protested was not owing to any abatement in his inviolable regard for his master, whom he should always honour and esteem to his latest breath, but entirely to the irresistible charms of the young lady, to whom he was now so happy as to be joined in the silken bonds of marriage.

Peregrine, though at first offended at his valet's presumption, was, upon second thoughts, reconciled to the event by which he was delivered from an encumbrance; for by this time he had performed his frolic, and began to be tired of his acquisition.

Peregrine pardons the couple and gives them five hundred pounds to help in their plan to open a coffee house and tavern.

P12 Thomas Tickell, 'On a Lady's Picture', early eighteenth century°

Thomas Tickell, 1685–1740, minor poet and journalist, now remembered mainly as friend and editor of the essayist Joseph Addison. This variation on the themes of love, art, and illusion is notable for a witty Ovidian final line.

As Damon Chloe's painted form surveyed
He sighed and languished for the jilting shade,°
For Cupid taught the artist-hand its grace,
And Venus wantoned in the mimic° face.
Now he laments a look so falsely fair,
And almost damns what yet resembles her;
Now he devours it with his longing eyes,
Now, sated, from the lovely phantom flies,
Yet burns to look again, yet looks again and dies.

° **preceptor**: teacher.
° **buckled at the Fleet**: unlicensed instant marriages were performed outside the doors of the Fleet prison; **Seven Dials**, the area around St Giles's church in Holborn, was 'notorious for squalor, vice, crime, and degradation generally' (Brewer, *Dictionary of Phrase and Fable*).
° from *The Poetical Works of Thomas Tickell*, Bell's Poets of Great Britain, Edinburgh, 1781, pp. 133–4.
° **the jilting shade**: i.e. the unreal image (**shade**) of the woman who had jilted him.
° **mimic**: artificial.

Her ivory neck his lips presume to kiss,
And his bold hands the swelling bosom press;
The swain° drinks in deep draughts of vain desire,
Melts without heat, and burns in fancied fire.
Strange power of paint! Thou nice° creator, Art!
What love inspires may life itself impart.
Struck with like° wounds, of old Pygmalion prayed,
And hugged to life his artificial maid.
Clasp, new Pygmalion, clasp the seeming charms.
Perhaps even now th'enlivening image warms,
Destined to crown thy joys and revel in thy arms –
Thy arms, which shall with fire so fierce invade
That she at once shall be and cease to be a maid.°

P13 Soame Jenyns, 'The Choice', mid-eighteenth century°

Soame Jenyns, 1704–87, minor poet, essayist, and MP; his optimistic essay on 'the Nature and Origin of Evil' provoked a memorably crushing review by Dr Johnson. This poem takes off from the Pygmalion story to create a description of the ideal woman.

Had I, Pygmalion-like, the power
To make the nymph° I would adore,
The model should be thus designed,
Like this her form, like this her mind.

Her skin should be as lilies fair,
With rosy cheeks and jetty hair;
Her lips with pure vermilion spread,
And soft and moist, as well as red;
Her eyes should shine with vivid light,
At once both languishing and bright;
Her shape should be exact° and small,
Her stature rather low than tall;
Her limbs well turned, her air and mien

° **swain**: lover (poetic diction).
° **nice**: subtle.
° **like**: similar.
° **That she . . . a maid**: i.e. at almost the same moment she becomes a **maid** (woman) she will cease to be a **maid** (virgin).
° from *The Works of Soame Jenyns*, ed. Charles Nanson Cole, 4 vols, London, 1790, i, 147–50.
° **nymph**: i.e woman (conventional poetic diction).
° **exact**: well-designed.

At once both sprightly and serene;
Besides all this, a nameless grace
Should be diffused all o'er her face;
To make the lovely piece complete,
Not only beautiful, but sweet.

This for her form; now for her mind:
I'd have it open, generous, kind,
Void of all coquettish arts
And vain designs of conquering hearts,
Not swayed by any views of gain,
Nor fond of giving others pain;
But soft, though bright, like her own eyes,
Discreetly witty, gaily wise.

I'd have her skilled in every art
That can engage a wandering heart;
Know all the sciences of love,
Yet ever willing to improve;
To press the hand, and roll the eye,
And drop sometimes an amorous sigh;
To lengthen out the balmy kiss,
And heighten every tender bliss;
And yet I'd have the charmer be
By nature only taught – or me.

I'd have her to strict honour tied,
And yet without one spark of pride;
In company well dressed and fine,
Yet not ambitious to outshine;
In private always neat and clean,
And quite a stranger to the spleen;°
Well pleased to grace the park and play,
And dance sometimes the night away,
But oftener fond to spend her hours
In solitude and shady bowers,
And there, beneath some silent grove,
Delight in poetry and love.

Some sparks of the poetic fire
I fain would° have her soul inspire,
Enough, at least, to let her know

° **the spleen**: bad temper, irritability, depression, neurosis.
° **fain would**: would like to.

What joys from love and virtue flow;
Enough, at least, to make her wise,
And fops and fopperies despise;
Prefer her books, and her own muse,
To visits, scandal, chat, and news;
Above her sex exalt her mind,
And make her more than womankind.

P14 Hannah Cowley, from *The Town Before You*, 1795°

Hannah Cowley, 1743–1809, playwright and poet, author of a number of successful comedies including *The Belle's Stratagem* (1780). This scene from *The Town Before You* is set in the studio of the heroine, Lady Horatia Horton, a female sculptor. The latter part of the scene farcically replays the statue scene from *The Winter's Tale*: the sculptor's niece Georgiana ('a little Welsh Diana . . . as wild as one of the kids on her father's mountains') pretends to be a statue to tease her suitor Conway, and succeeds in discomfiting the fraudulent art critic Tippy.

Scene: A large, elegant apartment, with various pieces of sculpture, statues, urns, &c. Lady Charlotte walks down from the top, viewing the statues.

LADY CHARLOTTE: This is, indeed, a school! Here are copies of all that is valuable in the art she loves. Ah, the lovely artist herself.

Enter Lady Horatia

LADY HORATIA: Dear Lady Charlotte, I rejoice to see you. They did not tell me you were here.

LADY CHARLOTTE: I have been here a long while; delighting myself with your charming works. But how full of labour is the amusement you have chosen!

LADY HORATIA: I do not find it so.

LADY CHARLOTTE: So different from fashionable life.

LADY HORATIA: O! the labour of a fashionable life would kill me; I should sink under it. Chipping marble is playing with feathers compared to that.

LADY CHARLOTTE: How so?

LADY HORATIA: The discipline of a life in fashion is by no means of the mildest sort [*smiling*]. Consider, for instance, the necessary vigils and abstinence of a gamester. It is expedient that she works hard and lives sparingly; for if she does not keep her spirits perfectly cool, instead of cheating her friend, her friend may cheat her. My labours are less and more innocent than hers.

LADY CHARLOTTE: O! I perceive you will be able to defend yourself.

° from *The Town before You, A comedy, as acted at the Theatre-Royal, Covent-Garden*, London, 1795, act 2, scene 4.

LADY HORATIA: In the next place reflect on the toils of a determined beauty. Whether she wakes or sleeps, whatever she does, wherever she goes, it is all with relation to the one great object which engrosses her meditations. After hours wasted, murdered, in the hard work of the toilette, away she springs! Her wheels thunder rapidly through the streets – she flies from assembly to assembly. Does the music of the concert fascinate her? No. Does polished conversation interest her? No. Some other beauty has been the belle of the evening; her heart has been torn with envy; she returns home; drags off her ornaments in disgust, and throws herself on a sleepless bed in anguish. Are my labours less pardonable than hers?

LADY CHARLOTTE: You will be too hard for me in argument, so I drop your statues, to talk of yourself. Something, I see, is wrong. What is it? [*tenderly*] Come, be explicit – You will not speak! In plain language, when did you see Mr. Asgill?

LADY HORATIA: Not this week – no – not for a whole week! I will conceal nothing from you. I find now that my tenderness more than equals his. I have no joy left – the chisel drops from my hand, the marble block is no longer moulded into flesh, my taste has no employment, and my heart is breaking.

LADY CHARLOTTE: How do you account for his absence?

LADY HORATIA: Tired with my haughty coldness, he has forsaken me. I die with jealousy and self-reproach. He has found an object more amiable and more tender. I knew he loved me, and I gloried in my conquest. –

'Yet still I tried each fickle art.
  Importunate and vain,
And whilst his passion touched my heart,
  I triumphed in his pain.'°

O, Asgill, thou art revenged!

LADY CHARLOTTE: What hearts we possess! Always too cold, or too feeling. My dear Horatia, stonify yours a little. As you give spirit to marble, transfuse the marble to your heart. See, here is your little Welsh friend.

Enter Georgina

GEORGINA: O, Lady Horatia! I am so rejoiced! Bless me! you are weeping – what has happened?

LADY HORATIA: A favourite goldfinch has happened to die, my dear.

GEORGINA: And last night I lost a canary bird. I am sure I cried for half an hour. Give me your goldfinch, and we will bury them together. O, dear! and you shall copy them in marble; that will be a sweet task for you. [*Lady Horatia takes her hand, and smiles.*] You know what I have hurried here for?

LADY HORATIA: No.

° **'Yet still . . . in his pain'**: from Oliver Goldsmith's sentimental ballad 'Edwin and Angelina'.

GEORGINA: No! Why did not you tell me you wanted to give my form to the statue of Andromache° – Andromache mourning for her husband; that you have just began to chip out there, you know [*pointing to a block of marble*].

LADY HORATIA: I did so; but I am out of spirits today.

GEORGINA: O! I will not be disappointed. Your favourite work will put you in spirits. I have brought a dress for the purpose; Humphrey, bring it in.

Humphrey enters with the dress, and shows marks of awkward wonder.

I shall be sadly mortified if you send me away.

LADY CHARLOTTE: Come, sit down, Lady Horatia, it will amuse you.

GEORGINA: Yes, do; and 'tis very fortunate that I lost my canary bird. I'll think of that, and then I shall look sad enough for Hector's widow.

LADY HORATIA: Pho! you little chit! Well, stand on the pedestal, and lean on the broken column now, with proper pensiveness and grace.

Georgina runs up steps behind the pedestal.

GEORGINA: Yes, I will be exactly the thing. [*Tries to look very melancholy.*] O, my poor canary bird!

LADY HORATIA: Ha, ha, ha! Come, let us place your drapery in statue-like order. [*She and Lady Charlotte place the folds.*] Now, keep steady, and think of your canary bird.

Enter Servant

SERVANT: Mr. Conway.

LADY HORATIA: Who?

SERVANT: Mr. Conway.

GEORGINA: [*starting*] Dear! Mr. Conway.

SERVANT: Some gentlemen are with him, and they wish to see the school.

LADY HORATIA: Dear Lady Charlotte, receive them, then – I cannot – I cannot indeed!

Exit

GEORGINA: [*runs down*] Gracious! now I think of it, I have a great mind to run up again; I will, I declare, and see what Mr. Conway says to me as a statue.

LADY CHARLOTTE: A statue – why, surely, you do not expect to impose on him?

GEORGINA: O yes, I do – I am sure he will not find me out. [*Runs up.*] Now, dear Lady Charlotte, just place my veil a little on this side. O, make haste – make haste – I hear them coming.

LADY CHARLOTTE: I must gratify you. What a giddy thing you are!

Enter Conway, with Tippy, and three Gentlemen

CONWAY: Lady Charlotte, you have heard of Mr. Tippy?°

° **Andromache**: wife of the Trojan hero Hector.

° **Mr Tippy**: Tippy is in fact a con artist, who boasts that 'I pretend to anything that will either get me into a dining parlour or a wine cellar', and has set up as an art critic because 'there requires little to be a connoisseur, but impudence' (2. 2).

TIPPY: Ah, ah, what, this is the place! Don't mind me, Ma'am; don't mind me, I am used to run about this town, and correct its follies. 'Tis a damned good town, that is certain; one always finds subjects for ridicule! Well, what the devil am I to see?

CONWAY: Look around.

TIPPY: I, just warm from the School of Florence; I who have trod the Roman Way, have seen the Baths of Trajan and the Dog Kennels of Nero, I look at the works of an English artist. Ha, ha, ha! [*walking amidst the statues, and observing them through a glass*]

CONWAY: Heavens! it is – it is she! Ah! how well do you represent yourself, for you are yourself all marble; at least your heart is so. Yes, flinty-hearted charmer! you are ever cold and insensate. O! I could stand and gaze my life away, like Pygmalion, had I, like him, the power to warm my statue into love! What, will you not bless me with one glance? Ah, you act your part too well.

TIPPY: Here is an arm; faith, it would make a very good leg. And this fine Grecian lady is like a Kentish hop-picker!

CONWAY: Critic! come hither; come this way; here is a new subject – has not this the true Grecian character?

TIPPY: What is this? is this Lady Horatia's chisel? [*looking through his glass*].

CONWAY: No – it is by a greater artist.

TIPPY: An English one, I'll be sworn. [*looking*] Grecian indeed! a mere block-chipper!

CONWAY: Is it ill proportioned?

TIPPY: Pshaw! nonsense! Talk of proportions to scale makers and carpenters; the thought is mechanical! a mere wax doll! Where are the inflexions? A human figure made on this principle could never move. Now I will convince you – nothing like conviction; observe the muscle of this foot!

GEORGINA: [*shrieks*] O! do not touch me. [*Leaps down.*] There, sir, you see I can move; and I can dance [*dancing round him*].

Tippy seats himself, in extreme confusion, on the pedestal.

LADY CHARLOTTE: What, Mr. Tippy! the breathing form of beauty a wax doll! the work of a block chipper! ha, ha, ha.

GENTLEMAN: Why, Tippy, how is this? Is it the First of April today?

LADY CHARLOTTE: Accept my smelling bottle;° you seem ready to sink.

TIPPY: Whu! I am done up as a connoisseur. [*Starts up, and runs out.*]

° **smelling bottle**: a small phial containing smelling-salts, a pungent substance sniffed as a cure for faintness or headache.

P15 Jean-Jacques Rousseau and William Mason, from 'Pygmalion: A Lyrical Scene', 1762/1811°

Jean-Jacques Rousseau, 1712–78, Swiss-born novelist, philosopher, and social and cultural critic, has a unique position as a leading figure in both the eighteenth-century French Enlightenment and the emerging Romantic Movement. His *Pygmalion*, a short playlet or '*scène lyrique*' with musical interludes, first produced in Lyons in 1770, was enormously popular and repeatedly produced and translated throughout Europe over the next forty years. The version given here is adapted from French prose to English blank verse by William Mason, 1725–97, Anglican clergyman and gentleman-amateur whose pursuits included poetry, music, painting, and landscape gardening.

The play shows for the first time the Romantic view of Pygmalion as the inspired and godlike artist. The extract begins as he acknowledges for the first time his true feelings for the statue Galatea.

What would'st thou change, Pygmalion, what correct,
What novel charm supply? She is already
Perfection's self; perfection is her fault,
Her only fault. Yes, heavenly Galatea!
Wert thou less perfect, nothing would'st thou want° –
[*Music. Tenderly*]
But yet thou want'st a soul; all, all save that,
Thou hast in rich profusion.
[*Music. With still greater tenderness*]
Yet, if Heaven
Inspired that body with a kindred soul,
How very lovely ought that soul to be.
Music. He pauses for some time, then returning to his seat, he proceeds in a slow and different tone.
What are the wild desires I dare to form?
Whither does passion drive me? Righteous Heaven!
Th' illusive veil that hid me from myself
Falls off. Yet let me not behold my heart,
I fear me it contains what, once beheld,
Would make me hate it.
Music. A long pause in deep disorder.
'Twill not be concealed.
Tell then thyself, tell to a mocking world
The passion that distracts Pygmalion's soul

° from *The Works of William Mason*, 4 vols, London, 1811, pp. 370–7.

° **want**: lack.

Has there its lifeless object. Own° the cause,
The worthy cause that keeps thee idle here;
That block, that marble mass, hard and unformed,
Till with this iron – Idiot that thou art,
Sink, sink into thyself, groan o'er thy error,
Behold at once thy folly, and bewail it.
[*Starting up with impetuosity*]
But 'tis not folly, I abjure the word,
My senses still remain; there is no cause
For self-reproach. This cold, this breathless marble
Is not the thing I love. No, 'tis a being
That lives, that thinks, can love, and be beloved,
Alike to this in feature, not in frame;
'Tis her that I adore; and wheresoe'er
I find the charming fair one, wheresoe'er
She dwells, whate'er her birth or habitation,
She still shall be the idol of my heart.
My folly then (if folly be its name)
Springs from a quick perceptive sense of beauty;
My crime (if I indeed am culpable) proceeds
From too much sensibility of soul;
– Such crimes, such follies ne'er shall make me blush.
[*Less fervently, yet still with emotion*]
Heavens! round that form what lambent° radiance flings
Its darts of fire, they reach, they pierce my soul,
And seem to bear me back into their source –
Meanwhile, alas! all cold and motionless
She stands. – While I, while my tumultuous spirits,
Bursting their bounds, would quit their vital seat°
To warm her breathless bosom. Ecstasy
Gives the transferring power of life and soul,
And I will use it; thou shalt die, Pygmalion,
(Delicious death!) to live in Galatea.
What have I said? Just Heavens! to live in her,
Then must I cease to view, must cease to love her,
No, Fate forbid! Let Galatea live,
Yet let my love live too; for to be hers
I still must be myself; and, being that,
I must be ever hers; must ever love her,

° **Own**: admit, own up to.
° **lambent**: glowing.
° **quit their vital seat**: leave their place in my body to which they give life.

And ever be beloved.
[*Music. In a tone of transport*]
Beloved, distraction!
It cannot be, O torment, rage, despair,
O hopeless, horrible, distracting passion!
The pains of hell rack my desponding soul.
Beings of power, Beings of mercy, hear me!
Hear me, ye gods! before whose awful° shrines
The people kneel because ye know their frailty;
Yes, ye have oft for vainer purposes
Lavished your miracles; look then with pity
On this fair form, look on this tortured breast,
Be just to both, and merit our oblations.°
[*Music. With a more pathetic degree of enthusiasm*]
And thou, sublimest Essence! hear the prayer;
Who, hid from outward sense, on the mind's eye
Pour'st thy refulgent evidence. O hear me,
Parent of Worlds! Soul of the Universe!
Thou at whose voice the plastic° power of Love
Gives to the elements their harmony,
To matter life, to body sentiment,
To all the tribes of being, place, and form.
Hear me, thou sacred, pure, celestial fire!
Thou all-producing, all-preserving power,
Venus Urania,° hear me! Where is now
Thy all-adjusting poise, thy force expansive,
Where is dread Nature's universal law
In my sensations? What a void is here!
Ah, tell me why thy vivifying warmth
Fills not that void, and bids my wishes live?
Thy fires are all concentered° in this breast,
While on yon form the icy hand of death
Keeps its chill hold. Pygmalion perishes
By that excess of life yon marble wants.
Goddess, I do not ask a miracle.
See, she exists, she ought to be annulled,

° **awful**: awe-inspiring.
° **oblations**: sacrifices.
° **plastic**: shaping.
° **Venus Urania**: Heavenly (as opposed to earthly) Venus; see the commentary on Shelley's *Adonais* (**A21**).
° **concentered**: concentrated.

Fair Order is disturbed, all Nature outraged.
O vindicate her rights; resume again
Thy course beneficent, and shed thy blessings
In just equality. Yes, Venus, yes,
Two beings here are wanting to complete
The plenitude of things;° divide to each
Its share of that fierce fire which scorches one
And leaves the other lifeless. Well thou know'st
'Twas thou that formed by my deputed hand°
Those charms, those features; all they want is life
And soul – my goddess, give her half of mine,
Give her the whole, and let me live in her,
Such life will well suffice. O as thou lovest
Our mortal homage, hear me! They alone
Whom life gives consciousness of Heaven and thee
Can pay thee that due homage; let thy works
Extend thy glory. Queen of Beauty, hear me,
Nor let this model of perfection stand
An image vain of unexisting grace.

Music. He returns to himself by degrees with an expression of assurance and joy.

Reason returns. What unexpected calm,
What fortitude unhoped-for arms my breast!
The balm of peace and confidence has cooled
My boiling blood. I feel as° born anew.
Thus is it still° with heaven-dependent man,
The very trust and feel of that dependence
Consoles his grief. How heavily soe'er
Misfortune flings her load upon his shoulder,
Let him but pray to Heaven, that load is lightened.
Yet, when to Heaven we lift a foolish prayer,
Our confidence is vain and we deceived.
Alas! alas! in such a state as mine
We pray to all, and nothing hears our prayer;
The very hope that cheers us is more vain
Than the desire that raised it. O shame, shame
On such extravagance. I dare no longer

° **the plenitude of things**: an allusion to the medieval doctrine of **plenitude** or fullness, which held that any creature which could possibly exist, must exist, to fill up all the spaces on the Great Chain of Being.

° **my deputed hand**: my hand acting as your agent.

° **as**: as if.

° **still**: always.

Reflect upon its cause, and yet, whene'er
I cast my eye upon yon fatal object,
Fresh palpitations, new disquiets choke me,
A secret fear restrains –
[*In a tone of cruel irony*] Poor wretch! be bold,
Take confidence. Yes, court and win a statue.

Music. He perceives it to begin to be animated, and starts back seized with affright and with a heart filled with sorrow.

What do I see? What did I think I saw?
Ye gods, her cheek has bloom, her eye has fire!
Nay, but she moves. O, was it not enough
To hope a prodigy;° to crown my wretchedness,
Lo, I have seen it.

[*Music. In excess of desperation*]

Hapless wretch! 'tis done;
Thy madness is confirmed; reason has left thee
As well as genius. Let its loss console thee;
It covers thy disgrace.

[*Music. With a lively indignation*]

'Tis as it should be,
Happy indeed for him that loved a stone
To turn a moon-struck madman.

Music. He turns and sees the statue move, and descend the steps on which she had been placed on the foot of the pedestal. He throws himself on his knees, and lifts his hands and eyes to heaven

Holy Heaven!
Immortal gods! O Venus! Galatea,
O fascination of outrageous Love!

GALATEA: [*she touches herself and says*]
Myself!

PYGMALION: [*transported*] Myself!

GALATEA: [*touching herself again*] It is myself.

PYGMALION: O blest,
O exquisite delusion! it affects
My very ears. Ah, nevermore abandon
My raptured senses.

GALATEA: [*stepping aside and touching one of the marbles*]
This is not myself.

Pygmalion, in an agitation and transport unable almost to contain himself, follows all her motions, listens, observes her with an eager attention which almost takes away his breath. Galatea comes to him again, and gazes on him; he opens

° **hope a prodigy**: hope for a miracle.

his arms and beholds her with ecstasy. She rests her hand upon him; he trembles, seizes her hand, puts it to his heart, and then devours it with kisses.

Ah! 'tis myself again! [*with a sigh*]

PYGMALION: Yes, loveliest, best,
And worthiest masterpiece of these blest hands,
Dear offspring of my heart, and of the gods,
It is thyself; it is thyself alone;
I gave thee all my being, and will live,
My Galatea, only to be thine.

The curtain falls.

P16 Mary Shelley, from *Frankenstein, or the Modern Prometheus*, 1818°

Mary Wollstonecraft Shelley, 1797–1851, English novelist, daughter of the rationalist philosopher William Godwin and the pioneer feminist Mary Wollstonecraft, married the poet Percy Bysshe Shelley (see **O33**) in 1816. Her Gothic horror story, *Frankenstein*, originated from a contest in telling ghost stories between the Shelleys and Lord Byron in Switzerland in 1816. *Frankenstein* never mentions Pygmalion; its mythical model, as the subtitle suggests, is the story of Prometheus, punished by the gods for creating humankind. Nevertheless, the scene here given in which Victor Frankenstein brings his artificial creature to life can be read as a horrific parody of the awakening of Pygmalion's statue.

It was on a dreary night of November that I beheld the accomplishment of my toils. With an anxiety that almost amounted to agony, I collected the instruments of life around me, that I might infuse a spark of being into the lifeless thing that lay at my feet. It was already one in the morning; the rain pattered dismally against the panes, and my candle was nearly burnt out, when, by the glimmer of the half-extinguished light, I saw the dull yellow eye of the creature open; it breathed hard, and a convulsive motion agitated its limbs.

How can I describe my emotions at this catastrophe,° or how delineate the wretch whom with such infinite pains and care I had endeavoured to form? His limbs were in proportion, and I had selected his features as beautiful. Beautiful! – Great God! His yellow skin scarcely covered the work of muscles and arteries beneath; his hair was of a lustrous black, and flowing; his teeth of a pearly whiteness; but these luxuriances only formed a more horrid contrast with his watery eyes, that seemed almost of the same colour as the dun white sockets in which they were set, his shrivelled complexion, and straight black lips.

° from *Frankenstein, or The Modern Prometheus*, 3 vols, London, 1818, ch. 4.

° **catastrophe**: (i) climactic event, (ii) disaster.

The different accidents of life are not so changeable as the feelings of human nature. I had worked hard for nearly two years, for the sole purpose of infusing life into an inanimate body. For this I had deprived myself of rest and health. I had desired it with an ardour that far exceeded moderation; but now that I had finished, the beauty of the dream vanished, and breathless horror and disgust filled my heart. Unable to endure the aspect of the being I had created, I rushed out of the room, and continued a long time traversing my bedchamber, unable to compose my mind to sleep. At length lassitude succeeded to the tumult I had before endured; and I threw myself on the bed in my clothes, endeavouring to seek a few moments of forgetfulness. But it was in vain: I slept indeed, but I was disturbed by the wildest dreams. I thought I saw Elizabeth,° in the bloom of health, walking in the streets of Ingolstadt. Delighted and surprised, I embraced her; but as I imprinted the first kiss on her lips, they became livid with the hue of death; her features appeared to change, and I thought that I held the corpse of my dead mother in my arms; a shroud enveloped her form, and I saw the grave-worms crawling in the folds of the flannel. I started from my sleep with horror; a cold dew covered my forehead: when, by the dim and yellow light of the moon, as it forced its way through the window shutters, I beheld the wretch – the miserable monster whom I had created. He held up the curtain of the bed; and his eyes, if eyes they may be called, were fixed on me. His jaws opened, and he muttered some inarticulate sounds, while a grin wrinkled his cheeks. He might have spoken, but I did not hear; one hand was stretched out, seemingly to detain me, but I escaped, and rushed down stairs. I took refuge in the courtyard belonging to the house which I inhabited; where I remained during the rest of the night, walking up and down in the greatest agitation, listening attentively, catching and fearing each sound as if it were to announce the approach of the demoniacal corpse to which I had so miserably given life.

P17 Thomas Lovell Beddoes, 'Pygmalion, or The Cyprian Statuary', 1825°

Thomas Lovell Beddoes, 1803–49, English Romantic poet and playwright, whose most famous work is the mock-Jacobean revenge tragedy *Death's Jest Book*; he spent much of his life in Europe, as a medical student and doctor, and died by suicide in Zurich. Beddoes's work shows a fascination with death and decay, a love of the grotesque, a black sense of humour, and a distinctively ornate, archaic style.

° **Elizabeth**: his fiancée.

° from *Poems by the late Thomas Lovell Beddoes*, London, 1851, pp. 154–62.

Pygmalion

or The Cyprian Statuary°

There stood a city along Cyprus' side
Lavish of palaces, an archèd tide
Of unrolled rocks; and, where the deities dwelled,
Their clustered domes pushed up the noon, and swelled
With the emotion of the god within –
As doth earth's hemisphere, when showers begin
To tickle the still spirit at its core,
Till pastures tremble and the river-shore
Squeezes out buds at every dewy pore.
And there were pillars, from some mountain's heart,
Thronging beneath a wide, imperial floor
That bent with riches; and there stood apart
A palace, oft° accompanied by trees,
That laid their shadows in the galleries
Under the coming of the endless light,
Net-like; who° trod the marble, night or day,
By moon, or lamp, or sunless day-shine white,
Would brush the shaking, ghostly leaves away,
Which might be tendrils or a knot of wine,°
Burst from the depth of a faint window-vine,
With a bird pecking it: and round the hall
And wandering staircase, within every wall
Of seaward portico and sleeping chamber,
Whose patient lamp distilled a day of amber,
There stood, and sat, or made rough steeds their throne
Immortal generations wrung from stone,
Alike too beautiful for life and death,
And bodies that a soul of mortal breath
Would be the dross of.°
                                        Such a house as this
Within a garden hard by Salamis
(Cyprus's city-crown and capital
Ere Paphos was,° and at whose ocean-wall

° **Statuary**: sculptor.
° **oft**: at frequent intervals (an archaic sense).
° **who**: whoever.
° **knot of wine**: bunch of grapes.
° **bodies . . . dross of**: i.e. the statues' bodies are so beautiful that, even if they had souls, the body would still be more valuable (reversing the Christian view that the body is mere **dross** compared to the immortal soul).
° **Ere Paphos was**: (because the city of Paphos was not yet founded; see note to **P1**, line 360).

Beauty and love's paternal waves do beat
That sprouted Venus);° such a fair retreat
Lonely Pygmalion self° inhabited,
Whose fiery chisel with creation fed
The ship-wrecked rocks; who paid the heavens again
Diamonds for ice;° who made gods who make men.
Lonely Pygmalion: you might see him go
Along the streets where markets thickest flow,
Doubling his gown across his thinking breast,°
And the men fall aside; nor only pressed
Out of his elbows' way, but left a place,
A sun-room for him, that his mind had space
And none went near; none in his sweep° would venture,
For you might feel that he was but the centre
Of an inspirèd round, the middle spark
Of a great moon, setting aside the dark
And cloudy people. As he went along
The chambered ladies silenced the half-song,
And let the wheel unheeded whirl and skim,
To get their eyes blest by the sight of him.
So locks were swept from every eye that drew
Sun for the soul through circles violet-blue,
Mild brown, or passionate black.
Still, discontent,
Over his sensual kind the sculptor went,
Walking his thoughts. Yet Cyprus' girls be fair;
Day-bright and evening-soft the maidens are,
And witching like the midnight, and their pleasure
Silent and deep as midnight's starry treasure.
Lovely and young, Pygmalion yet loved none.
His soul was bright and lovely as the sun,
Like which he could create; and in its might
There lived another Spirit wild and bright,
That came and went; and, when it came, its light
On these dim earthy things, turn where he will,

° **love's paternal waves . . . Venus**: according to legend Aphrodite/Venus rose from the sea near the coast of Cyprus.

° **self**: himself.

° **paid . . . Diamonds for ice**: i.e. he took what the gods had created (rock) and gave it back to them in a far more valuable form (his statues).

° **thinking breast**: in Greek and Latin the breast, rather than the brain, is considered the seat of thought.

° **sweep**: path.

Its light, shape, beauty were reflected still.°
Daytime and dark it came; like a dim mist
Shelling° a god, it rolled, and, ere he wist,°
It fell aside, and dawned a shape of grace,
And an inspired and melancholy face,°
Whose lips were smile-buds dewy: – into him
It rolled like sunlight till his sight was dim,
And it was in his heart and soul again,
Not seen but breathed.
                                        There was a grassy plain,
A pasture of the deer – Olympus' mountain
Was the plain's night, the picture of its fountain:
Unto which unfrequented dell and wood
Unwittingly his solitary mood
Oft drew him. – In the water lay
A fragment of pale marble, which they say
Slipped from some fissure in the agued° moon,
Which had caught earthquake and a deadly swoon
When the sun touched her with his hilly shade.
Weeds grew upon it, and the streamlet made
A wanton music with its ragged side,
And birds had nests there. One still eventide,
When they were perched and sleeping, passed this man,
Startling the air with thoughts which overran
The compass of his mind: writing the sand
Idly he paused, and laid unwitting hand
On the cold stone. How smooth the touch! It felt
Less porous than a lip which kisses melt,
And diamond-hard. That night his workmen wrought°
With iron under it, and it was brought,
This dripping quarry,° while the sky was starry,
Home to the weary, yearning statuary.

° **when it came . . . reflected still**: Beddoes's account of the operations of the 'Spirit' which inspires Pygmalion is not very clear. The idea seems to be that while he is possessed by the spirit, whatever ordinary earthly things he looks at are transfigured by the light of inspiration in which he sees them.
° **Shelling**: enclosing like a shell.
° **ere he wist**: before he was aware.
° **dawned . . . melancholy face**: the shape and face are (presumably) those of the statue which Pygmalion produces under the spirit's influence.
° **agued**: suffering from fever (and hence shaking).
° **wrought**: worked.
° **quarry**: mass of quarried stone (archaic).

He saw no sky that day, no dark that night,
For through the hours his lamp was full of light,
Shadowing the pavement with his busy right.°
Day after day they saw not in the street
The wondrous artist: some immortal feat
Absorbed him; and yet often in the noon,
When the town slept beneath the sweltering June,
– The rich within, the poor man on the stair –
He stole unseen into the meadow's air,
And fed on sight of summer, till the life
Was too abundant in him; and so, rife
With light creative, he went in alone,
And poured it warm upon the growing stone.
The magic chisel thrust, and gashed, and swept,
Flying and manifold; no cloud e'er wept
So fast, so thick, so light upon the close°
Of shapeless green it meant to make a rose: –
And as insensibly out of a stick,
Dead in the winter-time, the dew-drops quick,
And the thin sunbeams, and the airy shower
Raise and unwrap a many-leavèd flower,
And then a fruit: so from the barren stock
Of the deer-shading, formless valley-rock,
This close stone-bud, he, quiet as the air,
Had shaped a lady wonderfully fair,
– Dear to the eyes, a delicate delight –
For all her marble symmetry was white
As brow and bosom should be, save some azure°
Which waited for a loving lip's erasure,
Upon her shoulder, to be turned to blush.
And she was smooth and full, as if one gush
Of life had washed her, or as if a sleep
Lay on her eyelid, easier to sweep
Than bee from daisy. Who could help a sigh
At seeing a beauty stand so lifelessly,
But that it was too beautiful to die?
Dealer of immortality,
Greater than Jove himself – for only he
Can such eternize as the grave has ta'en,

° **right**: right hand (?).
° **close**: enclosure (i.e. unopened bud).
° **azure**: blue.

And open heaven by the gate of pain° –
What art thou now, divine Pygmalion?
Divine! gods counting human. Thou hast done
That glory, which has undone thee for ever.
For thou art weak, and tearful, and dost shiver
Wintrily sad; and thy life's healthy river,
With which thy body once was overflown,
Is dried and sunken to its banks of bone.
He carved it not;° nor was the chisel's play,
That dashed the earthen hindrances away,
Driven and diverted by his muscle's sway.
The wingèd tool, as digging out a spell,
Followed a magnet whereso'er it fell,
That sucked and led it right: and for the rest,
The living form, with which the stone be blest,
Was the loved image stepping from his breast.
And therefore loves he it, and therefore stays
About the she-rock's feet, from hour to hour,
Anchored to her by his own heart: the power
Of the isle's Venus therefore thus he prays.
'Goddess, that made me, save thy son, and save
The man, that made thee goddess, from the grave.
Thou know'st it not; it is a fearful coop°
Dark, cold, and horrible – a blinded loop°
In Pluto's madhouse' green and wormy wall.
O save me from't! Let me not die, like all;
For I am but like one: not yet, not yet,
At least not yet; and why? My eyes are wet
With the thick dregs of immature° despair;
With bitter blood out of my empty heart
I breathe not aught° but my own sighs for air,
And my life's strongest is a dying start.°
No sour grief there is to me unwed;
I could not be more lifeless being dead.

° **for only he . . . of pain**: i.e. Jove can only bestow immortality on those who have first died (whereas Pygmalion has made immortal something which has never yet lived).
° **He carved it not**: i.e. it was produced not by his conscious effort but by the creative spirit working through him.
° **coop**: place of imprisonment.
° **blinded loop**: blocked-up window-opening.
° **immature**: untimely, i.e. despair which comes too early in life.
° **aught**: anything.
° **My life's . . . start**: The strongest sign of life I can muster is only a dying man's twitch.

Then let me die. Ha! did she pity me?
Oh! she can never love. Did you not see,
How still° she bears the music of my moan!
Her heart? Ah! touch it. Fool! I love the stone.
Inspire her, gods! oft ye have wasted life
On the deformed, the hideous, and the vile:
Oh! grant it my sweet rock – my only wife.
I do not ask it long: a little while –
A year – a day – an hour – let it be!
For that I'll give you my eternity.
Or let it be a fiend, if ye will send
Something, yon form to humanize and bend,
Within those limbs – and, when the new-poured blood
Flows in such veins, the worst must soon be good.
They will not hear. Thou, Jove – or thou, Apollo –
Aye, thou! thou know'st – O listen to my groan
'Twas Niobe thou drov'st from flesh to stone:°
Show this the hole she broke, and let her follow
That mother's track of steps and eyelid rain,
Treading them backwards into life again.
Life, said I? Lives she not? Is there not gone
My life into her, which I pasture° on;
Dead, where she is not? Live, thou statue fair,
Live, thou dear marble – or I shall go wild.
I cover thee, my sweet; I leave thee there,
Behind this curtain, my delicious child,
That they may secretly begin to give
My prayer to thee: when I return, O live!
Oh! live – or I live not.' And so he went,
Leaving the statue in its darksome tent.

Morn after morn, sadder the artist came;
His prayer, his disappointment were the same.
But when he gazed she was more near to woman;
There was a fleshy pink, a dimple wrought
That trembled, and the cheek was growing human
With the flushed distance of a rising thought,
That still crept nearer – yet no further sign!

° **still**: calmly.

° **Niobe**: after her children were shot down by Apollo and Diana, she wept continually until she turned into stone; Pygmalion begs Apollo to show the statue how to reverse the process.

° **pasture**: feed.

And now, Pygmalion, that weak life of thine
Shakes like a dewdrop in a broken rose,
Or incense parting from the altar-glows.°
'Tis the last look – and he is mad no more:
By rule and figure he could prove at large
She never can be born – and from the shore
His foot is stretching into Charon's barge.
Upon the pavement° ghastly is he lying,
Cold with the last and stoniest embrace:
Elysium's light illumines all his face;
His eyes have a wild, starry grace
Of heaven, into whose depth of depths he's dying.
– A sound, with which the air doth shake,
Extinguishing the window of moonlight!
A pang of music dropping round delight,
As if sweet music's honiest° heart did break!
Such a flash, and such a sound, the world
Is stung by, as if something was unfurled
That held great bliss within its inmost curled.
Roof after roof, the palace rends asunder;
And then – O sight of joy and placid wonder!
He lies, beside a fountain, on the knee
Of the sweet woman-statue, quietly
Weeping the tears of his felicity.

P18 Nathaniel Hawthorne, 'Drowne's Wooden Image', 1846°

Nathaniel Hawthorne, 1804–64, American novelist and short story writer, whose major works include *The Scarlet Letter* (1850), *The House of the Seven Gables* (1851), and *The Blithedale Romance* (1852); he also wrote two volumes of Greek myths retold for children, *A Wonder Book* (1852) and *Tanglewood Tales* (1853). Hawthorne preferred the title 'romancer' to that of 'novelist', and his stories often include fantastic elements or hover ambiguously between the fantastic and the rational – as in this tale of 'a modern Pygmalion in the person of a Yankee mechanic'.

° **the altar-glows**: i.e. the glowing ash of burnt incense on an altar.
° **pavement**: paved floor.
° **honiest**: most honey-sweet.
° from *Mosses from an Old Manse*, 2 vols, rev. edn, Boston, 1854, pp. 75–91.

One sunshiny morning, in the good old times of the town of Boston, a young carver in wood, well known by the name of Drowne, stood contemplating a large oaken log, which it was his purpose to convert into the figurehead of a vessel. And while he discussed within his own mind what sort of shape or similitude it were well to bestow upon this excellent piece of timber, there came into Drowne's workshop a certain Captain Hunnewell, owner and commander of the good brig called the Cynosure,° which had just returned from her first voyage to Fayal.°

'Ah! that will do, Drowne, that will do! 'cried the jolly captain, tapping the log with his rattan.° 'I bespeak° this very piece of oak for the figurehead of the Cynosure. She has shown herself the sweetest craft that ever floated, and I mean to decorate her prow with the handsomest image that the skill of man can cut out of timber. And, Drowne, you are the fellow to execute it.'

'You give me more credit than I deserve, Captain Hunnewell,' said the carver, modestly, yet as one conscious of eminence in his art. 'But, for the sake of the good brig, I stand ready to do my best. And which of these designs do you prefer? Here' – pointing to a staring, half-length figure, in a white wig and scarlet coat – 'here is an excellent model, the likeness of our gracious king.° Here is the valiant Admiral Vernon.° Or, if you prefer a female figure, what say you to Britannia with the trident?'

'All very fine, Drowne; all very fine,' answered the mariner. 'But as nothing like the brig ever swam the ocean, so I am determined she shall have such a figure-head as old Neptune never saw in his life. And what is more, as there is a secret in the matter, you must pledge your credit not to betray it.'

'Certainly,' said Drowne, marvelling, however, what possible mystery there could be in reference to an affair so open, of necessity, to the inspection of all the world as the figurehead of a vessel. 'You may depend, captain, on my being as secret as the nature of the case will permit.'

Captain Hunnewell then took Drowne by the button, and communicated his wishes in so low a tone that it would be unmannerly to repeat what was evidently intended for the carver's private ear. We shall, therefore, take the opportunity to give the reader a few desirable particulars about Drowne himself.

He was the first American who is known to have attempted – in a very humble line, it is true – that art in which we can now reckon so many names already distinguished, or rising to distinction. From his earliest boyhood he had exhibited

° **Cynosure**: the ship's name is perhaps significant; it means 'something that attracts attention by its . . . beauty; a centre of attraction, interest, or admiration' (*OED*).

° **Fayal**: an island in the Azores, a group of Portuguese islands in the North Atlantic.

° **rattan**: walking stick.

° **bespeak**: order.

° **our gracious king**: the story is set in the 1760s or early 1770s, before the American War of Independence.

° **Admiral Vernon**: a British naval hero, celebrated for his capture of Portobello in the Antilles in 1739.

a knack – for it would be too proud a word to call it genius – a knack, therefore, for the imitation of the human figure in whatever material came most readily to hand. The snows of a New England winter had often supplied him with a species of marble as dazzlingly white, at least, as the Parian or the Carrara,° and if less durable, yet sufficiently so to correspond with any claims to permanent existence possessed by the boy's frozen statues. Yet they won admiration from maturer judges than his schoolfellows, and were, indeed, remarkably clever, though destitute of the native warmth that might have made the snow melt beneath his hand. As he advanced in life, the young man adopted pine and oak as eligible materials for the display of his skill, which now began to bring him a return of solid silver as well as the empty praise that had been an apt reward enough for his productions of evanescent snow. He became noted for carving ornamental pump heads, and wooden urns for gate posts, and decorations, more grotesque than fanciful, for mantelpieces. No apothecary would have deemed himself in the way of obtaining custom without setting up a gilded mortar, if not a head of Galen or Hippocrates,° from the skilful hand of Drowne.

But the great scope of his business lay in the manufacture of figureheads for vessels. Whether it were the monarch himself, or some famous British admiral or general, or the governor of the province, or perchance the favorite daughter of the ship owner, there the image stood above the prow, decked out in gorgeous colors, magnificently gilded, and staring the whole world out of countenance, as if from an innate consciousness of its own superiority. These specimens of native sculpture had crossed the sea in all directions, and been not ignobly noticed among the crowded shipping of the Thames. and wherever else the hardy mariners of New England had pushed their adventures. It must be confessed that a family likeness pervaded these respectable progeny of Drowne's skill; that the benign countenance of the king resembled those of his subjects, and that Miss Peggy Hobart, the merchant's daughter, bore a remarkable similitude to Britannia, Victory, and other ladies of the allegoric sisterhood; and, finally, that they all had a kind of wooden aspect, which proved an intimate relationship with the unshaped blocks of timber in the carver's workshop. But at least there was no inconsiderable skill of hand, nor a deficiency of any attribute to render them really works of art, except that deep quality, be it of soul or intellect, which bestows life upon the lifeless and warmth upon the cold, and which, had it been present, would have made Drowne's wooden image instinct with spirit.

The captain of the Cynosure had now finished his instructions.

'And Drowne,' said he, impressively, 'you must lay aside all other business and set about this forthwith. And as to the price, only do the job in first rate style, and you shall settle that point yourself.'

° **Carrara** marble from central Italy, like **Parian** marble in classical times, was noted for its whiteness.

° **Galen or Hippocrates**: ancient medical authorities.

'Very well, captain,' answered the carver, who looked grave and somewhat perplexed, yet had a sort of smile upon his visage; 'depend upon it, I'll do my utmost to satisfy you.'

From that moment the men of taste about Long Wharf and the Town Dock who were wont to show their love for the arts by frequent visits to Drowne's workshop, and admiration of his wooden images, began to be sensible of a mystery in the carver's conduct. Often he was absent in the daytime. Sometimes, as might be judged by gleams of light from the shop windows, he was at work until a late hour of the evening; although neither knock nor voice, on such occasions, could gain admittance for a visitor, or elicit any word of response. Nothing remarkable, however, was observed in the shop at those hours when it was thrown open. A fine piece of timber, indeed, which Drowne was known to have reserved for some work of especial dignity, was seen to be gradually assuming shape. What shape it was destined ultimately to take was a problem to his friends and a point on which the carver himself preserved a rigid silence. But day after day, though Drowne was seldom noticed in the act of working upon it, this rude form began to be developed until it became evident to all observers that a female figure was growing into mimic life. At each new visit they beheld a larger pile of wooden chips and a nearer approximation to something beautiful. It seemed as if the hamadryad° of the oak had sheltered herself from the unimaginative world within the heart of her native tree, and that it was only necessary to remove the strange shapelessness that had encrusted her, and reveal the grace and loveliness of a divinity. Imperfect as the design, the attitude, the costume, and especially the face of the image still remained, there was already an effect that drew the eye from the wooden cleverness of Drowne's earlier productions and fixed it upon the tantalizing mystery of this new project.

Copley,° the celebrated painter, then a young man and a resident of Boston, came one day to visit Drowne; for he had recognized so much of moderate ability in the carver as to induce him, in the dearth of professional sympathy, to cultivate his acquaintance. On entering the shop the artist glanced at the inflexible image of king, commander, dame, and allegory that stood around, on the best of which might have been bestowed the questionable praise that it looked as if a living man had here been changed to wood, and that not only the physical, but the intellectual and spiritual part, partook of the stolid transformation. But in not a single instance did it seem as if the wood were imbibing the ethereal essence of humanity. What a wide distinction is here! and how far would the slightest portion of the latter merit have outvalued the utmost degree of the former!

'My friend Drowne,' said Copley, smiling to himself, but alluding to the

° **hamadryad**: wood nymph.

° **Copley**: John Singleton Copley, 1738–1815, the first great American painter, born in Boston, emigrated to England in 1774, where he achieved great success; he was noted especially for his lifelike and sharply individualised portraits.

mechanical and wooden cleverness that so invariably distinguished the images, 'you are really a remarkable person! I have seldom met with a man in your line of business that could do so much; for one other touch might make this figure of General Wolfe,° for instance, a breathing and intelligent human creature.'

'You would have me think that you are praising me highly, Mr. Copley,' answered Drowne, turning his back upon Wolfe's image in apparent disgust. 'But there has come a light into my mind. I know, what you know as well, that the one touch which you speak of as deficient is the only one that would be truly valuable, and that without it these works of mine are no better than worthless abortions. There is the same difference between them and the works of an inspired artist as between a sign-post daub and one of your best pictures.'

'This is strange,' cried Copley, looking him in the face, which now, as the painter fancied, had a singular depth of intelligence, though hitherto it had not given him greatly the advantage over his own family of wooden images. 'What has come over you? How is it that, possessing the idea which you have now uttered, you should produce only such works as these?'

The carver smiled, but made no reply. Copley turned again to the images, conceiving that the sense of deficiency which Drowne had just expressed, and which is so rare in a merely mechanical character, must surely imply a genius, the tokens of which had heretofore been overlooked. But no; there was not a trace of it. He was about to withdraw when his eyes chanced to fall upon a half-developed figure which lay in a corner of the workshop, surrounded by scattered chips of oak. It arrested him at once.

'What is here? Who has done this?' he broke out, after contemplating it in speechless astonishment for an instant. 'Here is the divine, the life-giving touch. What inspired hand is beckoning this wood to arise and live? Whose work is this?'

'No man's work,' replied Drowne. 'The figure lies within that block of oak, and it is my business to find it.'

'Drowne,' said the true artist, grasping the carver fervently by the hand, 'you are a man of genius!'

As Copley departed, happening to glance backward from the threshold, he beheld Drowne bending over the half-created shape, and stretching forth his arms as if he would have embraced and drawn it to his heart; while, had such a miracle been possible, his countenance expressed passion enough to communicate warmth and sensibility to the lifeless oak.

'Strange enough!' said the artist to himself. 'Who would have looked for a modern Pygmalion in the person of a Yankee mechanic!'°

° **General Wolfe**: English general who died capturing Quebec from the French in 1759.

° **Yankee mechanic**: both terms have slightly disparaging overtones: **mechanic** means a craftsman or manual worker, with the implication '*not* an artist or an intellectual'; **Yankees**, i.e. New Englanders (not yet Americans in general) were stereotypically shrewd, practical, tight-fisted, and unimaginative.

As yet, the image was but vague in its outward presentment; so that, as in the cloud shapes around the western sun, the observer rather felt, or was led to imagine, than really saw what was intended by it. Day by day, however, the work assumed greater precision, and settled its irregular and misty outline into distincter grace and beauty. The general design was now obvious to the common eye. It was a female figure, in what appeared to be a foreign dress; the gown being laced over the bosom, and opening in front so as to disclose a skirt or petticoat, the folds and inequalities of which were admirably represented in the oaken substance. She wore a hat of singular gracefulness, and abundantly laden with flowers, such as never grew in the rude soil of New England, but which, with all their fanciful luxuriance, had a natural truth that it seemed impossible for the most fertile imagination to have attained without copying from real prototypes. There were several little appendages to this dress, such as a fan, a pair of ear-rings, a chain about the neck, a watch in the bosom, and a ring upon the finger, all of which would have been deemed beneath the dignity of sculpture. They were put on, however, with as much taste as a lovely woman might have shown in her attire, and could therefore have shocked none but a judgment spoiled by artistic rules.

The face was still imperfect; but gradually, by a magic touch, intelligence and sensibility brightened through the features, with all the effect of light gleaming forth from within the solid oak. The face became alive. It was a beautiful, though not precisely regular, and somewhat haughty aspect, but with a certain piquancy about the eyes and mouth, which, of all expressions, would have seemed the most impossible to throw over a wooden countenance. And now, so far as carving went, this wonderful production was complete.

'Drowne,' said Copley, who had hardly missed a single day in his visits to the carver's workshop, 'if this work were in marble it would make you famous at once; nay, I would almost affirm that it would make an era in the art. It is as ideal as an antique statue, and yet as real as any lovely woman whom one meets at a fireside or in the street. But I trust you do not mean to desecrate this exquisite creature with paint, like those staring kings and admirals yonder?'

'Not paint her!' exclaimed Captain Hunnewell, who stood by; 'not paint the figurehead of the Cynosure! And what sort of a figure should I cut in a foreign port with such an unpainted oaken stick as this over my prow! She must, and she shall, be painted to the life, from the topmost flower in her hat down to the silver spangles on her slippers.'

'Mr. Copley,' said Drowne, quietly, 'I know nothing of marble statuary, and nothing of the sculptor's rules of art; but of this wooden image, this work of my hands, this creature of my heart' – and here his voice faltered and choked in a very singular manner – 'of this – of her – I may say that I know something. A wellspring of inward wisdom gushed within me as I wrought upon the oak with my whole strength, and soul, and faith. Let others do what they may with marble, and adopt what rules they choose. If I can produce my desired effect by painted wood, those rules are not for me, and I have a right to disregard them.'

'The very spirit of genius,' muttered Copley to himself. 'How otherwise should this carver feel himself entitled to transcend all rules, and make me ashamed of quoting them?'

He looked earnestly at Drowne, and again saw that expression of human love which, in a spiritual sense, as the artist could not help imagining, was the secret of the life that had been breathed into this block of wood.

The carver, still in the same secrecy that marked all his operations upon this mysterious image, proceeded to paint the habiliments° in their proper colors, and the countenance with Nature's red and white. When all was finished he threw open his workshop, and admitted the townspeople to behold what he had done. Most persons, at their first entrance, felt impelled to remove their hats, and pay such reverence as was due to the richly-dressed and beautiful young lady who seemed to stand in a corner of the room, with oaken chips and shavings scattered at her feet. Then came a sensation of fear; as if, not being actually human, yet so like humanity, she must therefore be something preternatural. There was, in truth, an indefinable air and expression that might reasonably induce the query, Who and from what sphere this daughter of the oak should be? The strange, rich flowers of Eden on her head; the complexion, so much deeper and more brilliant than those of our native beauties; the foreign, as it seemed, and fantastic garb, yet not too fantastic to be worn decorously in the street; the delicately-wrought embroidery of the skirt; the broad gold chain about her neck; the curious ring upon her finger; the fan, so exquisitely sculptured in open work, and painted to resemble pearl and ebony – where could Drowne, in his sober walk of life, have beheld the vision here so matchlessly embodied! And then her face! In the dark eyes and around the voluptuous mouth there played a look made up of pride, coquetry, and a gleam of mirthfulness, which impressed Copley with the idea that the image was secretly enjoying the perplexing admiration of himself and other beholders.

'And will you,' said he to the carver, 'permit this masterpiece to become the figurehead of a vessel? Give the honest captain yonder figure of Britannia – it will answer his purpose far better – and send this fairy queen to England, where, for aught I know, it may bring you a thousand pounds.'

'I have not wrought it for money,' said Drowne.

'What sort of a fellow is this!' thought Copley. 'A Yankee, and throw away the chance of making his fortune! He has gone mad; and thence has come this gleam of genius.'

There was still further proof of Drowne's lunacy, if credit were due to the rumor that he had been seen kneeling at the feet of the oaken lady, and gazing with a lover's passionate ardor into the face that his own hands had created. The bigots of the day hinted that it would be no matter of surprise if an evil Spirit were allowed to enter this beautiful form, and seduce the carver to destruction.

° **habiliments**: clothes.

The fame of the image spread far and wide. The inhabitants visited it so universally, that after a few days of exhibition there was hardly an old man or a child who had not become minutely familiar with its aspect. Even had the story of Drowne's wooden image ended here, its celebrity might have been prolonged for many years by the reminiscences of those who looked upon it in their childhood, and saw nothing else so beautiful in after life. But the town was now astounded by an event the narrative of which has formed itself into one of the most singular legends that are yet to be met with in the traditionary chimney corners of the New England metropolis, where old men and women sit dreaming of the past, and wag their heads at the dreamers of the present and the future.

One fine morning, just before the departure of the Cynosure on her second voyage to Fayal, the commander of that gallant vessel was seen to issue from his residence in Hanover Street. He was stylishly dressed in a blue broadcloth coat, with gold lace at the seams and button holes, an embroidered scarlet waistcoat, a triangular hat, with a loop and broad binding of gold, and wore a silver-hilted hanger° at his side. But the good captain might have been arrayed in the robes of a prince or the rags of a beggar, without in either case attracting notice, while obscured by such a companion as now leaned on his arm. The people in the street started, rubbed their eyes, and either leaped aside from their path, or stood as if transfixed to wood or marble in astonishment.

'Do you see it? – do you see it?' cried one, with tremulous eagerness. 'It is the very same!'

'The same?' answered another, who had arrived in town only the night before. 'Who do you mean? I see only a sea captain in his shore-going clothes, and a young lady in a foreign habit, with a bunch of beautiful flowers in her hat. On my word, she is as fair and bright a damsel as my eyes have looked on this many a day!'

'Yes; the same! – the very same!' repeated the other. 'Drowne's wooden image has come to life!'

Here was a miracle indeed! Yet, illuminated by the sunshine, or darkened by the alternate shade of the houses, and with its garments fluttering lightly in the morning breeze, there passed the image along the street. It was exactly and minutely the shape, the garb, and the face which the townspeople had so recently thronged to see and admire. Not a rich flower upon her head, not a single leaf, but had had its prototype in Drowne's wooden workmanship, although now their fragile grace had become flexible, and was shaken by every footstep that the wearer made. The broad gold chain upon the neck was identical with the one represented on the image, and glistened with the motion imparted by the rise and fall of the bosom which it decorated. A real diamond sparkled on her finger. In her right hand she bore a pearl and ebony fan, which she flourished with a fantastic and bewitching coquetry, that was likewise expressed in all her

° **hanger**: short sword.

movements as well as in the style of her beauty and the attire that so well harmonized with it. The face, with its brilliant depth of complexion, had the same piquancy of mirthful mischief that was fixed upon the countenance of the image, but which was here varied and continually shifting, yet always essentially the same, like the sunny gleam upon a bubbling fountain. On the whole, there was something so airy and yet so real in the figure, and withal so perfectly did it represent Drowne's image, that people knew not whether to suppose the magic wood etherealized into a spirit or warmed and softened into an actual woman.

'One thing is certain,' muttered a Puritan of the old stamp, 'Drowne has sold himself to the devil; and doubtless this gay Captain Hunnewell is a party to the bargain.'

'And I,' said a young man who overheard him, 'would almost consent to be the third victim, for the liberty of saluting° those lovely lips.'

'And so would I,' said Copley, the painter, 'for the privilege of taking her picture.'

The image, or the apparition, whichever it might be, still escorted by the bold captain, proceeded from Hanover Street through some of the cross lanes that make this portion of the town so intricate, to Ann Street, thence into Dock Square, and so downward to Drowne's shop, which stood just on the water's edge. The crowd still followed, gathering volume as it rolled along. Never had a modern miracle occurred in such broad daylight, nor in the presence of such a multitude of witnesses. The airy image, as if conscious that she was the object of the murmurs and disturbance that swelled behind her, appeared slightly vexed and flustered, yet still in a manner consistent with the light vivacity and sportive mischief that were written in her countenance. She was observed to flutter her fan with such vehement rapidity that the elaborate delicacy of its workmanship gave way, and it remained broken in her hand.

Arriving at Drowne's door, while the captain threw it open, the marvellous apparition paused an instant on the threshold, assuming the very attitude of the image, and casting over the crowd that glance of sunny coquetry which all remembered on the face of the oaken lady. She and her cavalier then disappeared.

'Ah!' murmured the crowd, drawing a deep breath, as with one vast pair of lungs.

'The world looks darker now that she has vanished,' said some of the young men.

But the aged, whose recollections dated as far back as witch times,° shook their heads, and hinted that our forefathers would have thought it a pious deed to burn the daughter of the oak with fire.

° **saluting**: greeting, i.e. kissing.

° **witch times**: referring to the witchcraft trials which began in Salem, Massachusetts, in 1692; Hawthorne was born in Salem, and one of his ancestors was a judge in the trials.

'If she be other than a bubble of the elements,' exclaimed Copley, 'I must look upon her face again.'

He accordingly entered the shop; and there, in her usual corner, stood the image, gazing at him, as it might seem, with the very same expression of mirthful mischief that had been the farewell look of the apparition when, but a moment before, she turned her face towards the crowd. The carver stood beside his creation mending the beautiful fan, which by some accident was broken in her hand. But there was no longer any motion in the lifelike image, nor any real woman in the work shop, nor even the witchcraft of a sunny shadow, that might have deluded people's eyes as it flitted along the street. Captain Hunnewell, too, had vanished. His hoarse, sea-breezy tones, however, were audible on the other side of a door that opened upon the water.

'Sit down in the stern sheets,° my lady,' said the gallant captain. 'Come, bear a hand, you lubbers, and set us on board in the turning of a minute glass.'

And then was heard the stroke of oars.

'Drowne,' said Copley, with a smile of intelligence, 'you have been a truly fortunate man. What painter or statuary ever had such a subject! No wonder that she inspired a genius into you, and first created the artist who afterwards created her image.'

Drowne looked at him with a visage that bore the traces of tears, but from which the light of imagination and sensibility, so recently illuminating it, had departed. He was again the mechanical carver that he had been known to be all his lifetime.

'I hardly understand what you mean, Mr. Copley,' said he, putting his hand to his brow. 'This image! Can it have been my work? Well, I have wrought it in a kind of dream; and now that I am broad awake I must set about finishing yonder figure of Admiral Vernon.'

And forthwith employed himself on the stolid countenance of one of his wooden progeny, and completed it in his own mechanical style, from which he was never known afterwards to deviate. He followed his business industriously for many years, acquired a competence, and in the latter part of his life attained to a dignified station in the church, being remembered in records and traditions as Deacon Drowne, the carver. One of his productions, an Indian chief, gilded all over, stood during the better part of a century on the cupola of the Province House, bedazzling the eyes of those who looked upward, like an angel of the sun. Another work of the good deacon's hand – a reduced likeness of his friend Captain Hunnewell, holding a telescope and quadrant – may be seen to this day, at the corner of Broad and State Streets, serving in the useful capacity of sign to the shop of a nautical instrument maker. We know not how to account for the inferiority of this quaint old figure, as compared with the recorded excellence of the Oaken Lady, unless on the supposition that in every human spirit there is

° **sheets**: ropes attached to the sails of a ship.

imagination, sensibility, creative power, genius, which, according to circumstances, may either be developed in this world, or shrouded in a mask of dullness until another state of being. To our friend Drowne there came a brief season of excitement, kindled by love. It rendered him a genius for that one occasion, but, quenched in disappointment, left him again the mechanical carver in wood, without the power even of appreciating the work that his own hands had wrought. Yet who can doubt that the very highest state to which a human spirit can attain, in its loftiest aspirations, is its truest and most natural state, and that Drowne was more consistent with himself when he wrought the admirable figure of the mysterious lady, than when he perpetrated a whole progeny of blockheads?

There was a rumor in Boston, about this period, that a young Portuguese lady of rank, on some occasion of political or domestic disquietude, had fled from her home in Fayal and put herself under the protection of Captain Hunnewell, on board of whose vessel, and at whose residence, she was sheltered until a change of affairs. This fair stranger must have been the original of Drowne's Wooden Image.

P19 Elizabeth Barrett Browning, from *Aurora Leigh*, 1856°

Elizabeth Barrett Browning, 1806–61, English poet, wife of Robert Browning. *Aurora Leigh* is a 'novel in verse' in nine books, the autobiography of a young woman poet. In this passage from book 5, Aurora Leigh is brooding unhappily over whether she has a true poetic vocation.

. . . But soft!° – a 'poet' is a word soon said;
A book's a thing soon written. Nay, indeed,
The more the poet shall be questionable,
The more unquestionably comes his book!
And this of mine – well, granting to myself
Some passion in it, furrowing up the flats,
Mere passion will not prove a volume worth
Its gall and rags° even. Bubbles round a keel
Mean nought, excepting that the vessel moves.
There's more than passion goes to make a man,
Or book, which is a man too.
                                        I am sad.

° from *Aurora Leigh*, London, 1857, book 5, pp. 195–6.

° **soft!**: wait a moment!.

° **gall and rags**: used in the manufacture of paper.

I wonder if Pygmalion had these doubts,
And, feeling the hard marble first relent,
Grow supple to the straining of his arms,
And tingle through its cold to his burning lip,
Supposed his senses mocked, and that the toil
Of stretching past the known and seen, to reach
The archetypal Beauty out of sight,
Had made his heart beat fast enough for two,
And with his own life dazed and blinded him!
Not so; Pygmalion loved – and whoso° loves
Believes the impossible.
And I am sad:
I cannot thoroughly love a work of mine,
Since none seems worthy of my thought and hope
More highly mated. He has shot them down,
My Phoebus Apollo, soul within my soul,
Who judges, by the attempted, what's attained,
And with the silver arrow from his height,
Has struck down all my works before my face,°
While *I* said nothing. Is there aught to say?
I called the artist but a greatened man:
He may be childless also, like a man.

P20 Robert Buchanan, from 'Pygmalion the Sculptor', 1864°

Robert Williams Buchanan, 1841–1901, Scottish-born poet, novelist, playwright, and essayist; a pugnacious controversialist, best remembered now for his literary feuds with Swinburne, Rosetti, and the Pre-Raphaelite movement. His poetry, though now neglected, has at its best a fine gloomy power, and his description of the awakening of Pygmalion's statue, below, memorably combines eroticism and horror, with overtones of *Frankenstein* and the *Rime of the Ancient Mariner.*

The story of the poem is summarised in the introduction. This passage, from Part 3 ('The Sin') and Part 4 ('Death in Life'), begins after Pygmalion has seen the planet Venus shine greenly on the statue's forehead as a sign that his prayer has been heard.

° **whoso**: whoever.
° **struck down . . . before my face**: another allusion to Apollo's killing of Niobe's children.
° from *Complete Poetical Works*, London, 1901, pp. 61–4.

. . . The live-long night, the breathless night
I waited in a darkness, in a dream,
Watching the snowy figure faintly seen,
And ofttimes shuddering when I seemed to see
Life, like a taper° burning in a skull,
Gleam through the rayless eyes: yea, wearily
I hearkened through the dark and seemed to hear
The low warm billowing of a living breast,
Or the slow motion of anointed limbs
New-stirring into life; and, shuddering,
Fearing the thing I hoped for, awful-eyed,°
On her cold breast I placed a hand as cold
And sought a fluttering heart. – But all was still,
And chill, and breathless; and she gazed right on
With rayless orbs, nor marvelled at my touch:
White, silent, pure, ineffable, a shape
Rebuking human hope, a deathless thing,
Sharing the wonder of the Sun who sends
His long bright look through all futurity.

When Shame lay heavy on me, and I hid
My face, and almost hated her, my work,
Because she was so fair, so human fair,
Yea not divinely fair as that pure face
Which, when mine hour of loss and travail came,
Haunted me, out of heaven. Then the Dawn
Stared in upon her: when I opened eyes,
And saw the gradual Dawn encrimson her
Like blood that blushed within her – and behold
She trembled – and I shrieked!
With haggard eyes,
I gazed on her, my fame, my work, my love!
Red sunrise mingled with the first bright flush
Of palpable life – she trembled, stirred, and sighed –
And the dim blankness of her stony eyes
Melted to azure. Then, by slow degrees,
She tingled with the warmth of living blood:
Her eyes were vacant of a seeing soul,

° **taper**: candle.
° **awful-eyed**: with eyes full of awe.

But dewily the bosom rose and fell,
The lips caught sunrise, parting, and the breath
Fainted through pearly teeth.
                                        I was as one
Who gazes on a goddess serpent-eyed,
And cannot fly, and knows to look is death.
O apparition of my work and wish!
The weight of awe oppressed me, and the air
Swung as the Seas swing around drowning men.

4: DEATH IN LIFE

About her brow the marble hair had clung
With wavy tresses, in a simple knot
Bound up and braided; but behold, her eyes
Drooped downward, as she wondered at herself,
Then flushed to see her naked loveliness,
And trembled, stooping downward; and the hair
Unloosening fell, and brightened as it fell,
Till gleaming ringlets tingled to the knees
And clustered round about her where she stood
As yellow leaves around a lily's bud,
Making a fountain round her such as clips°
A Naiad in the sunshine, pouring down
And throwing moving shadows o'er the floor
Whereon she stood and brightened.
                                        Wondering eyed,
With softly heaving breast and outstretched arms,
Slow as an eyeless man who gropes his way,
She thrust a curving foot and touched the ground,
And stirred; and, downcast-lidded, saw not me.
Then as the foot descended with no sound,
The whole live blood grew pink within the veins
For joy of its own motion. Step by step,
She paced the chamber, groping till she gained
One sunlight-slip that through the curtained pane
Crept slant – a gleaming line on wall and floor;
And there, in light, she pausing sunned herself
With half-closed eyes; while flying gleams of gold
Sparkled like flies of fire among her hair,

° **clips**: embraces.

And the live blood showed brightlier, as wine
Gleams thro' a curd-white° cup of porcelain.

There, stirring not, she paused and sunned herself,
With drooping eyelids that grew moist and warm,
What time,° withdrawn into the further dark,
I watched her, nerveless, as a murderer stretched
Under a nightmare of the murdered man.
And still she, downcast-lidded, saw me not;
But gathered glory while she sunned herself,
Drawing deep breath of gladness such as earth
Breathes dewily in the sunrise after rain.

Then prayed I, lifting up my voice aloud.
'O apparition of my work and wish!
Thou most divinely fair as she whose face
Haunted me, out of heaven! Raise thine eyes!
Live, love, as thou and I have lived and loved!
Behold me – it is I – Pygmalion.
Speak, Psyche, with thy human eyes and lips,
Speak, to Pygmalion, with thy human soul!'

And still she, downcast-lidded, saw me not,
But gathered glory as she sunned herself.
Yet listened murmuring inarticulate speech,
Listened with ear inclined and fluttering lids,
As one who lying on a bed of flowers
Hearkeneth to the distant fall of waves,
That cometh muffled in the drowsy hum
Of bees pavilioned° among roses' leaves
Near to the ears that listen. So she stood
And listened to my voice, framing her lips
After the speech; nay, when the sound had ceased,
Still listened, with a shadow on her cheek –
Like the Soul's Music, when the Soul has fled,
Fading upon a dead Musician's face.

Pygmalion gradually cajoles the statue-woman into his arms, and together they spend three days and nights in frenzied feasting. On the third night, Pygmalion hears cries of 'A pestilence!' from the town below, and turns to see the marks of death on his lover. In horror he flees from the place –

° **curd-white**: curd is the solid white substance formed from coagulating milk.
° **What time**: while.
° **pavilioned**: sheltered as in a tent.

– nor have halted since that hour,
But wander far away, a homeless man,
Prophetic, orphaned both of name and fame.
Nay, like a timid Phantom evermore
I come and go with haggard warning eyes . . .

And some are saved because they see me pass,
And, shuddering, yet constant to their task,
Look up for comfort to the silent stars.

P21 William Morris, from 'Pygmalion and the Image', 1868°

William Morris, 1834–96, English poet, prose romancer, craftsman and designer of furniture and textiles, printer, politician and socialist theorist – one of the most versatile talents of the nineteenth century. In all his endeavours, literary, artistic, and political, he harked back to an idealised pre-industrial Middle Ages of simplicity, freedom, and honest craftsmanship. 'Pygmalion and the Image' comes from *The Earthly Paradise*, a collection of retold tales from classical and Nordic myth, over 11,000 lines long; Morris's greatest weakness was longwindedness, and he expands Ovid's tale of Pygmalion to 650-odd lines. Our excerpt begins as Pygmalion leaves Venus's temple; his momentary flush of hope at the omen of the leaping flame fades back into despair as he walks home through the debris of the festival of love.

What hope Pygmalion yet might have, when he
First left the pillars of the dreamy place,
Amid such sights had vanished utterly.
He turned his weary eyes from face to face,
Nor noted them, as at a lagging pace
He gat° towards home, and still was murmuring:
'Ah life, sweet life! the only godlike thing!'

And as he went, though longing to be there
Whereas° his sole desire awaited him,
Yet did he loathe to see the image fair,
White and unchanged of face, unmoved of limb,
And to his heart came dreamy thoughts and dim
That unto some strange region he might come,
Nor ever reach again his loveless home.

° from *The Collected Works of William Morris*, with introductions by May Morris, vol. 4, London, 1910.
° **gat**: went.
° **Whereas**: where.

Yet soon, indeed, before his door he stood,
And as a man awaking from a dream,
Seemed waked from his old folly; nought seemed good
In all the things that he before had deemed
At least worth life, and on his heart there streamed
Cold light of day – he found himself alone,
Reft° of desire, all love and madness gone.

And yet for that past folly must he weep,
As one might mourn the parted happiness
That, mixed with madness, made him smile in sleep;
And still some lingering sweetness seemed to bless
The hard life left of toil and loneliness,
Like a past song too sweet, too short, and yet
Emmeshed for ever in the memory's net.

Weeping he entered, murmuring: 'O fair Queen,
I thank thee that my prayer was not for nought,
Truly a present helper hast thou been
To those who faithfully thy throne have sought!
Yet, since with pain deliverance I have bought,
Hast thou not yet some gift in store for me,
That I thine happy slave henceforth may be?'

Thus to his chamber at the last he came,
And pushing through the still half-opened door,
He stood within; but there, for very shame
Of all the things that he had done before,
Still kept his eyes bent down upon the floor,
Thinking of all that he had done and said
Since he had wrought that luckless marble maid.

Yet soft his thoughts were, and the very place
Seemed perfumed with some nameless heavenly air,
So gaining courage, did he raise his face
Unto the work his hands had made so fair,
And cried aloud to see the niche all bare
Of that sweet form, while through his heart again
There shot a pang of his old yearning pain.

Yet while he stood and knew not what to do,
With yearning a strange thrill of hope there came;

° **Reft**: deprived.

A shaft of new desire now pierced him through,
And therewithal a soft voice called his name,
And when he turned, with eager eyes aflame,
He saw betwixt him and the setting sun
The lively image of his lovèd one.

He trembled at the sight, for though her eyes,
Her very lips, were such as he had made,
And though her tresses fell but in such guise°
As he had wrought them, now was she arrayed
In that fair garment that the priests had laid
Upon the Goddess on that very morn,
Dyed like the setting sun upon the corn.

Speechless he stood, but she now drew anear,
Simple and sweet as she was wont to be,
And all at once her silver voice rang clear,
Filling his soul with great felicity,
And thus she spoke: 'Pygmalion, come to me,
O dear companion of my new-found life,
For I am called thy lover and thy wife.

'Listen, these words the Dread One° bade me say
That was with me e'en now: Pygmalion,
My new-made soul I give to thee to-day,
Come, feel the sweet breath that thy prayer has won,
And lay thine hand this heaving breast upon!
Come, love, and walk with me between the trees
And feel the freshness of the evening breeze.

'Sweep mine hair round thy neck; behold my feet,
The oft-kissed feet thou thought'st should never move,
Press down the daisies! draw me to thee, sweet,
And feel the warm heart of thy living love
Beat against thine, and bless the Seed° of Jove
Whose loving tender heart hath wrought all this,
And wrapped us both in such a cloud of bliss.

'Ah, thou art wise to know what this may mean!
Sweet seem the words to me, and needs° must I

° **guise**: manner.
° **Dread One**: i.e. Venus.
° **Seed**: offspring (i.e. Venus).
° **needs**: necessarily.

Speak all the lesson of the lovely Queen:
But this I know, I would we were more nigh,
I have not heard thy voice but in the cry
Thou utteredst then, when thou believedst gone
The marvel of thine hands, the maid of stone.'

She reached her hand to him, and with kind eyes
Gazed into his; but he the fingers caught
And drew her to him, and midst ecstasies
Passing° all words, yea, well-nigh passing thought,
Felt that sweet breath that he so long had sought,
Felt the warm life within her heaving breast
As in his arms his living love he pressed.

But as his cheek touched hers he heard her say:
'Wilt thou not speak, O love? why dost thou weep?
Art thou then sorry for this long-wished day,
Or dost thou think perchance thou wilt not keep
This that thou holdest, but° in dreamy sleep?
Nay, let us do the bidding of the Queen,
And hand in hand walk through thy garden green;

'Then shalt thou tell me, still beholding me,
Full° many things whereof I wish to know,
And as we walk from whispering tree to tree
Still more familiar to thee shall I grow,
And such things shalt thou say unto me now
As when thou deemèdst thou wast quite alone,
A madman, kneeling to a thing of stone.'

But at that word a smile lit up his eyes,
And therewithal he spake some loving word,
And she at first looked up in grave surprise
When his deep voice and musical she heard,
And clung to him as grown somewhat afeard;
Then cried aloud and said: 'O mighty one!
What joy with thee to look upon the sun.'

° **passing**: surpassing.
° **but**: except.
° **Full**: very.

P22 W. S. Gilbert, from *Pygmalion and Galatea*, 1871°

William Schwenck Gilbert, 1836–1911, is best known for the series of 'Gilbert and Sullivan' comic operas which he wrote in collaboration with the composer Sir Arthur Sullivan; but he was also a prolific playwright and comic poet in his own right. Like many of his works, *Pygmalion and Galatea* uses a fantastic or magical event in order to create a fresh, satirical perspective on conventional attitudes; like many of his works, also, it mingles comedy with sentimentality and melodrama.

Gilbert's twist on the traditional story is that Pygmalion is already married – married to, and in love with, Cynisca, who serves as the model for his statues. We learn that Cynisca was once a votary of the chaste goddess Artemis, and that Artemis, in releasing her from her vows so she could marry Pygmalion, gave both husband and wife the power to call down blindness on the other if they should be unfaithful. At the start of the play Cynisca is preparing to leave on a trip into Athens, while Pygmalion chafes over the arrogance and ignorance of the 'art patrons' he must work for.

CYNISCA: To think that heaven-born Art should be the slave
Of such as he.
PYGMALION: Well, wealth is heaven-born too.
I work for wealth.
CYNISCA: Thou workest, love, for fame.
PYGMALION: And fame brings wealth. The thought's contemptible,
But I can do no more than work for wealth. [*Turns from her.*]
CYNISCA: Such words from one whose noble work it is
To call the senseless marble into life!
PYGMALION: Life! Dost thou call that life?
CYNISCA: It all but breathes!
PYGMALION: [*bitterly*] It all but breathes – therefore it talks aloud!
It all but moves – therefore it walks and runs!
It all but lives, and therefore it is life!
No, no, my love, the thing is cold dull stone,
Shaped to a certain form, but still dull stone,
The lifeless, senseless mockery of life.
The gods make life, I can make only death!
Why, my Cynisca, though I stand so well,
The merest cut-throat, when he plies his trade,
Makes better death than I, with all my skill!

° from *Pygmalion and Galatea: An entirely original mythological comedy in three acts*, London, 1872. Some technical stage directions have been silently omitted.

CYNISCA: Hush, my Pygmalion! the gods are good,
And they have made thee nearer unto them
Than other men; this is ingratitude!
PYGMALION: Not so; has not a monarch's second son
More cause for anger that he lacks a throne
Than he whose lot is cast in slavery?
CYNISCA: Not much more cause, perhaps, but more excuse.
Now I must go.
PYGMALION: So soon, and for so long!
CYNISCA: One day, 'twill quickly pass away!
PYGMALION: With those
Who measure time by almanacs, no doubt,
But not with him who knows no days save those
Born of the sunlight of Cynisca's eyes;
It will be night with me till she returns.
CYNISCA: Then sleep it through, Pygmalion! But stay,
Thou shalt *not* pass the weary hours alone;
Now mark thou this – while I'm away from thee
There stands my only representative [*indicating Galatea*],
She is my proxy, and I charge you, sir,
Be faithful unto her as unto me;
Into her quietly attentive ear
Pour all thy treasures of hyperbole,
And give thy nimble tongue full license, lest
Disuse should rust its glib machinery;
If thoughts of love should haply° crowd on thee [*advancing*],
There stands my other self, tell them to her;
She'll listen well;
[*he makes a movement of impatience*]
Nay, that's ungenerous,
For she is I, yet lovelier than I,
And hath no temper, sir, and hath no tongue;
Thou hast thy license, make good use of it.
Already I'm half jealous – there!
Draws curtains together, concealing statue
It's gone.
The thing is but a statue after all,
And I am safe in leaving thee with her;
Farewell, Pygmalion, till I return.
Kisses him, and exit

° **haply**: perhaps.

PYGMALION: [*bitterly*] 'The thing is but a statue after all!'
Cynisca little thought that in those words
She touched the keynote of my discontent –
True, I have powers denied to other men;
Give me a block of senseless marble – Well,
I'm a magician, and it rests with me
To say what kernel lies within its shell;
It shall contain a man, a woman, child,
A dozen men and women if I will.
So far the gods and I run neck and neck;
Nay, so far I can beat them at their trade!
I am no bungler – all the men *I* make
Are straight limbed fellows, each magnificent
In the perfection of his manly grace:
I make no crook-backs – all my men are gods,
My women goddesses, in outward form.
But there's my tether – I can go so far,
And go no further – at that point I stop,
To curse the bonds that hold me sternly back:
To curse the arrogance of those proud gods,
Who say, 'Thou shall be greatest among men,
And yet infinitesimally small!'

GALATEA: [*from behind curtain*]
Pygmalion!

PYGMALION: [*after pause*] Who called?

GALATEA: Pygmalion!

Pygmalion tears away curtain and discovers Galatea alive

PYGMALION: Ye gods! It lives.

GALATEA: Pygmalion!

PYGMALION: It speaks!
I have my prayer! my Galatea breathes!

GALATEA: Where am I? Let me speak, Pygmalion;
Give me thy hand – both hands – how soft and warm!
Whence came I? [*Descends*]

PYGMALION: Why, from yonder pedestal!

GALATEA: That pedestal! Ah, yes, I recollect,
There was a time when it was part of me.

PYGMALION: That time has passed for ever, thou art now
A living, breathing woman, excellent
In every attribute of womankind.

GALATEA: Where am I, then?

PYGMALION: Why, born into the world
By miracle!

GALATEA: Is this the world?

PYGMALION: It is.
GALATEA: This room?
PYGMALION: This room is a portion of a house;
The house stands in a grove; the grove itself
Is one of many, many hundred groves
In Athens.
GALATEA: And is Athens then the world?
PYGMALION: To an Athenian – Yes –
GALATEA: And I am one?
PYGMALION: By birth and parentage, not by descent.
GALATEA: But how came I to be?
PYGMALION: Well – let me see.
Oh – you were quarried in Pentelicus;°
I modelled you in clay – my artisans
Then roughed you out in marble – I, in turn,
Brought my artistic skill to bear on you,
And made you what you are – in all but life –
The gods completed what I had begun,
And gave the only gift I could not give.
GALATEA: Then this is life?
PYGMALION: It is.
GALATEA: And not long since
I was a cold, dull stone! I recollect
That by some means I knew that I was stone:
That was the first dull gleam of consciousness;
I became conscious of a chilly self,
A cold immovable identity,
I knew that I was stone, and knew no more;
Then, by an imperceptible advance,
Came the dim evidence of outer things,
Seen – darkly and imperfectly – yet seen –
The walls surrounding me, and I, alone.
That pedestal – that curtain – then a voice
That called on Galatea! At that word
Which seemed to shake my marble to the core,
That which was dim before, came evident.
Sounds, that had hummed around me, indistinct,
Vague, meaningless – seemed to resolve themselves
Into a language I could understand;
I felt my frame pervaded by a glow
That seemed to thaw my marble into flesh;

° **Pentelicus**: a mountain near Athens where white marble was quarried.

Its cold hard substance throbbed with active life,
My limbs grew supple, and I moved – I lived!
Lived in the ecstasy of new-born life;
Lived in a thousand tangled thoughts of hope,
Love, gratitude – thoughts that resolved themselves
Into one word, that word, Pygmalion! [*Kneels to him*]
PYGMALION: I have no words to tell thee of my joy,
O woman – perfect in thy loveliness!
GALATEA: What is that word? Am I a woman?
PYGMALION: Yes.
GALATEA: Art thou a woman?
PYGMALION: No, I am a man.
GALATEA: What is a man?
PYGMALION: A being strongly framed,
To wait on woman, and protect her from
All ills that strength and courage can avert;
To work and toil for her, that she may rest;
To weep and mourn for her, that she may laugh;
To fight and die for her, that she may live!
GALATEA: [*after a pause*] I'm glad I am a woman.
PYGMALION: So am I.
They sit
GALATEA: That I escape the pains thou hast to bear?
PYGMALION: That I may undergo those pains for thee.
GALATEA: With whom then wouldst thou fight?
PYGMALION: With any man
Whose deed or word gave Galatea pain.
GALATEA: Then there are other men in this strange world?
PYGMALION: There are indeed.
GALATEA: And other women?
PYGMALION: [*taken aback*] Yes;
Though for the moment I'd forgotten it!
Yes, other women.
GALATEA: And for all of these
Men work, and toil, and mourn, and weep, and fight?
PYGMALION: It is man's duty, if he's called upon,
To fight for all – he works for those he loves.
GALATEA: Then by thy work I know thou lovest me,
PYGMALION: Indeed, I love thee! [*Embraces her*]
GALATEA: With what kind of love?
PYGMALION: I love thee [*recollecting himself and releasing her*]
as a sculptor loves his work!
[*aside*] There is diplomacy in that reply.
GALATEA: My love is different in kind to thine:

I am no sculptor, and I've done no work,
Yet I do love thee; say – what love is mine?
PYGMALION: Tell me its symptoms – then I'll answer thee.
GALATEA: Its symptoms? Let me call them as they come.
A sense that I am made by thee *for* thee,
That I've no will that is not wholly thine,
That I've no thought, no hope, no enterprise
That does not own *thee* as its sovereign;
That I have life, that I may live for thee,
That I am thine – that thou and I are one!
What kind of love is that?
PYGMALION: A kind of love
That I shall run some risk in dealing with.
GALATEA: And why, Pygmalion?
PYGMALION: Such love as thine
A man may not receive, except indeed
From one who is, or is to be, his wife.
GALATEA: Then I will be thy wife!
PYGMALION: That may not be;
I have a wife – the gods allow but one.
GALATEA: Why did the gods then send me here to thee?
PYGMALION: I cannot say – unless to punish me
For unreflecting and presumptuous prayer!
I prayed that thou shouldst live – I have my prayer,
And now I see the fearful consequence
That must attend it!
GALATEA: Yet thou lovest me?
PYGMALION: Who could look on that face and stifle love?
GALATEA: Then I am beautiful?
PYGMALION: Indeed thou art,
GALATEA: I wish that I could look upon myself,
But that's impossible.
PYGMALION: Not so indeed.
This mirror will reflect thy face. Behold!
[*Hands her a mirror from table*]
GALATEA: How beautiful! I'm very glad to know
That both our tastes agree so perfectly;
Why, my Pygmalion, I did not think
That aught could be more beautiful than thou,
Till I beheld myself. [*A pause*] Believe me, love,
I could look in this mirror all day long.
So I'm a woman.
PYGMALION: There's no doubt of that!

In the second act, Galatea's naive innocence quickly creates havoc. She insists on talking publicly about her love for Pygmalion; she is shocked by his friend Leucippus's profession of soldier ('A paid assassin!'), and breaks up Leucippus's engagement by telling his fiancée that he is a murderer; she innocently insults the rich art patron Chrysos:

GALATEA: Are you a man?
CHRYSOS: Well, yes; I'm told so.
GALATEA: Then believe them not,
They've been deceiving you. . .
A man is very tall, and straight, and strong,
With big brave eyes, fair face, and tender voice.
I've seen one. . . Yes, you are no man.

Most catastrophically, when Cynisca returns and is startled to find Galatea in the household, Galatea innocently assures her that Pygmalion has faithfully obeyed her instructions:

GALATEA: Oh, madam, bear with him,
Judge him not hastily; in every word
In every thought he has obeyed thy wish.
Thou badst him speak to me as unto thee;
And he and I have sat as lovingly
As if thou hadst been present to behold
How faithfully thy wishes were obeyed!
CYNISCA: Pygmalion! What is this?
PYGMALION: [*to Galatea*] Go, get thee hence;
Thou shouldst not see the fearful consequence
That must attend those heedless words of thine!
GALATEA: Judge him not hastily, he's not like this
When he and I are sitting here alone.
He has two voices, and two faces, madam,
One for the world, and one for him and me!

The angry Cynisca calls down Artemis's curse and strikes Pygmalion blind.

The final act resolves the situation. The blind Pygmalion mistakes Galatea for Cynisca, and declares to her his love for his wife and his hatred of Galatea: the damage she has done is enough to make him 'curse the hour that gave her life. / She is not fit to live upon this world.' Cynisca, overhearing this, forgives her husband and restores his sight, while Galatea decides to return to being a statue:

Nay – let me go from him
That curse – *his* curse – still ringing in mine ears,

For life is bitterer to me than death.
She mounts the steps of pedestal
Farewell, Pygmalion – I am not fit
To live upon this world – this worthy world.
Curtains begin to close slowly around Galatea
Farewell, Pygmalion. Farewell – Farewell!

P23 Elizabeth Stuart Phelps, 'Galatea', 1885°

Elizabeth Stuart Phelps, 1844–1911, American writer and feminist, born in Boston; sometimes known by her married name, Elizabeth Stuart Phelps Ward, to distinguish her from her mother, also a writer. She made her name with a controversial novel, *The Gates Ajar* (1868), about death and the afterlife, and went on to write fifty-six more novels, as well as poetry and journalism. Her work is informed by a personal blend of feminism, left-wing politics, and religious mysticism; it often focuses on the choices available to women. 'Galatea' could be called the first feminist reading of the legend, though its view of a woman's duty may seem somewhat masochistic to modern readers.

A moment's grace, Pygmalion! Let me be
A breath's space longer on this hither hand
Of fate too sweet, too sad, too mad to meet.
Whether to be thy statue or thy bride–
An instant spare me! Terrible the choice,
As no man knoweth, being only man;
Nor any, saving she who hath been stone
And loved her sculptor. Shall I dare exchange
Veins of the quarry for the throbbing pulse?
Insensate calm for a sure-aching heart?
Repose eternal for a woman's lot?
Forgo God's quiet for the love of man?
To float on his uncertain tenderness,
A wave tossed up the shore of his desire,
To ebb and flow whene'er it pleaseth him;
Remembered at his leisure, and forgot,
Worshipped and worried, clasped and dropped at mood,
Or soothed or gashed at mercy of his will,
Now Paradise my portion, and now Hell;
And every single, several nerve that beats
In soul or body, like some rare vase, thrust

° from *Songs of the Silent World*, Boston, 1885, pp. 69–71.

In fire at first, and then in frost, until
The fine, protesting fibre snaps?
                                        Oh, who
Foreknowing, ever chose a fate like this?
What woman out of all the breathing world
Would be a woman, could her heart select,
Or love her lover, could her life prevent?
Then let me be that only, only one;
Thus let me make that sacrifice supreme,
No other ever made, or can, or shall.
Behold, the future shall stand still to ask,
What man was worth a price so isolate?
And rate thee at its value for all time.

For I am driven by an awful Law.
See! while I hesitate, it mouldeth me,
And carves me like a chisel at my heart.
'Tis stronger than the woman or the man;
'Tis stronger than all torment or delight;
'Tis stronger than the marble or the flesh.
Obedient be the sculptor and the stone!
Thine am I, thine at all the cost of all
The pangs that woman ever bore for man;
Thine I elect to be, denying them;
Thine I elect to be, defying them;
Thine, thine I dare to be, in scorn of them;
And being thine forever, bless I them!
Pygmalion! Take me from my pedestal,
And set me lower – lower, Love! – that I
May be a woman, and look up to thee;
And looking, longing, loving, give and take
The human kisses worth the worst that thou
By thine own nature shalt inflict on me.

P24 Bernard Shaw, from *Pygmalion*, 1912°

(George) Bernard Shaw, 1856–1950, Irish-born playwright, novelist, critic, social and political thinker and controversialist. Over his sixty-year writing career his

° from *Pygmalion*, in *The Bodley Head Bernard Shaw Collected Plays with their Prefaces*, vol. iv, London, 1972, pp. 680, 691, 694–5, 727–38, 776–81. Reprinted by permission of The Society of Authors on behalf of the Bernard Shaw Estate. Shaw's distinctive spelling is here retained, in particular his omission of the apostrophe from words like *dont* and *youre*.

witty and provocative plays tackled such large subjects as war (*Arms and the Man*, 1894), sex and gender (*Man and Superman*, 1903), medicine (*The Doctor's Dilemma*, 1906), religion (*Major Barbara*, 1905; *Saint Joan*, 1924), government (*The Apple Cart*, 1929), and the ultimate destiny of the human race (*Back to Methuselah*, 1921).

Shaw's Pygmalion is Henry Higgins, a professor of phonetics, and Galatea is Eliza Doolittle, a Cockney flower-seller whom he 'metamorphoses' into a lady. They first meet on a rainy night at Covent Garden (Act 1), where Higgins uses Eliza as a demonstration model for a lecture to his friend Colonel Pickering on the importance of pronunciation, boasting:

> You see this creature with her kerbstone English: the English that will keep her in the gutter to the end of her days. Well, sir, in three months I could pass her off as a duchess at an ambassador's garden party. I could even get her a place as a lady's maid or shop assistant, which requires better English.

The next day (Act 2), Eliza goes to Higgins's laboratory in Wimpole Street to ask for speech lessons so she can 'become a lady in a flower shop', and Pickering takes Higgins up on his boast:

PICKERING: Higgins: I'm interested. What about the ambassador's garden party? I'll say youre the greatest teacher alive if you make that good. I'll bet you all the expenses of the experiment you cant do it. And I'll pay for the lessons.

LIZA: Oh, you are real good. Thank you, Captain.

HIGGINS: [*tempted, looking at her*] It's almost irresistible. She's so deliciously low – so horribly dirty –

LIZA: [*protesting extremely*] Ah-ah-ah-ah-ow-ow-oo-oo!!! I aint dirty: I washed my face and hands afore I come, I did.

PICKERING: Youre certainly not going to turn her head with flattery, Higgins.

MRS PEARCE: [*uneasy*] Oh, dont say that, sir: theres more ways than one of turning a girl's head; and nobody can do it better than Mr Higgins, though he may not always mean it. I do hope, sir, you wont encourage him to do anything foolish.

HIGGINS: [*becoming excited as the idea grows on him*] What is life but a series of inspired follies? The difficulty is to find them to do. Never lose a chance: it doesnt come every day. I shall make a duchess of this draggletailed guttersnipe.

LIZA: [*strongly deprecating this view of her*] Ah-ah-ah-ow-ow-oo!

HIGGINS: [*carried away*] Yes: in six months – in three if she has a good ear and a quick tongue – I'll take her anywhere and pass her off as anything. We'll start today: now! this moment! Take her away and clean her, Mrs Pearce. Monkey Brand,° if it wont come off any other way . . .

Mrs Pearce, the housekeeper, raises practical objections:

MRS PEARCE: But whats to become of her? Is she to be paid anything? Do be sensible, sir.

HIGGINS: Oh, pay her whatever is necessary: put it down in the housekeeping book. [*Impatiently*] What on earth will she want with money? She'll have her food and her clothes. She'll only drink if you give her money.

LIZA: [*turning on him*] Oh you are a brute. It's a lie: nobody ever saw the sign of liquor on me. [*To Pickering*] Oh, sir: youre a gentleman: dont let him speak to me like that.

PICKERING: [*in good-humored remonstrance*] Does it occur to you, Higgins, that the girl has some feelings?

HIGGINS: [*looking critically at her*] Oh no, I dont think so. Not any feelings that we need bother about. [*Cheerily*] Have you, Eliza?

LIZA: I got my feelings same as anyone else.

HIGGINS: [*to Pickering, reflectively*] You see the difficulty?

PICKERING: Eh? What difficulty?

HIGGINS: To get her to talk grammar. The mere pronunciation is easy enough.

LIZA: I dont want to talk grammar. I want to talk like a lady in a flower-shop.

MRS PEARCE: Will you please keep to the point, Mr Higgins. I want to know on what terms the girl is to be here. Is she to have any wages? And what is to become of her when youve finished your teaching? You must look ahead a little.

HIGGINS: [*impatiently*] Whats to become of her if I leave her in the gutter? Tell me that, Mrs Pearce.

MRS PEARCE: Thats her own business, not yours, Mr Higgins.

HIGGINS: Well, when Ive done with her, we can throw her back into the gutter; and then it will be her own business again; so thats all right.

* * *

Act 3: after several months of phonetic training, Higgins takes Eliza for her first public test, at his mother's 'at home'.

THE PARLOR MAID: [*opening the door*] Miss Doolittle. [*She withdraws.*]

HIGGINS: [*rising hastily and running to Mrs Higgins*] Here she is, mother. [*He stands on tiptoe and makes signs over his mother's head to Eliza to indicate to her which lady is her hostess.*]

° **Monkey Brand**: a product for cleaning pots and pans.

Eliza, who is exquisitely dressed, produces an impression of such remarkable distinction and beauty as she enters that they all rise, quite fluttered. Guided by Higgins's signals, she comes to Mrs Higgins with studied grace.

LIZA: [*speaking with pedantic correctness of pronunciation and great beauty of tone*] How do you do, Mrs Higgins? [*She gasps slightly in making sure of the H in Higgins, but is quite successful.*] Mr Higgins told me I might come.

MRS HIGGINS: [*cordially*] Quite right: I'm very glad indeed to see you.

PICKERING: How do you do, Miss Doolittle?

LIZA: [*shaking hands with him*] Colonel Pickering, is it not?

MRS EYNSFORD HILL: I feel sure we have met before, Miss Doolittle. I remember your eyes.

LIZA: How do you do? [*She sits down on the ottoman gracefully in the place just left vacant by Higgins.*]

MRS EYNSFORD HILL: [*introducing*] My daughter Clara.

LIZA: How do you do?

CLARA: [*impulsively*] How do you do? [*She sits down on the ottoman beside Eliza, devouring her with her eyes.*]

FREDDY: [*coming to their side of the ottoman*] Ive certainly had the pleasure.

MRS EYNSFORD HILL: [*introducing*] My son Freddy.

LIZA: How do you do?

Freddy bows and sits down in the Elizabethan chair, infatuated.

HIGGINS: [*suddenly*] By George, yes: it all comes back to me! [*They stare at him.*] Covent Garden! [*Lamentably*] What a damned thing!°

MRS HIGGINS: Henry, please! [*He is about to sit on the edge of the table.*] Dont sit on my writing-table: youll break it.

HIGGINS: [*sulkily*] Sorry.

He goes to the divan, stumbling into the fender and over the fire-irons on his way; extricating himself with muttered imprecations; and finishing his disastrous journey by throwing himself so impatiently on the divan that he almost breaks it. Mrs Higgins looks at him, but controls herself and says nothing.

A long and painful pause ensues.

MRS HIGGINS: [*at last, conversationally*] Will it rain, do you think?

LIZA: The shallow depression in the west of these islands is likely to move slowly in an easterly direction. There are no indications of any great change in the barometrical situation.

FREDDY: Ha! ha! how awfully funny!

LIZA: What is wrong with that, young man? I bet I got it right.

FREDDY: Killing!

MRS EYNSFORD HILL: I'm sure I hope it wont turn cold. Theres so

° **What a damned thing!** Higgins has just remembered where he and Eliza encountered the Eynsford Hills before–at Covent Garden in Act 1, where Eliza was selling violets.

much influenza about. It runs right through our whole family regularly every spring.

LIZA: [*darkly*] My aunt died of influenza: so they said.

MRS EYNSFORD HILL: [*clicks her tongue sympathetically*] !!!

LIZA: [*in the same tragic tone*] But it's my belief they done the old woman in.

MRS HIGGINS: [*puzzled*] Done her in?

LIZA: Y-e-e-e-es, Lord love you! Why should she die of influenza? She come through diphtheria right enough the year before. I saw her with my own eyes. Fairly blue with it, she was. They all thought she was dead; but my father he kept ladling gin down her throat til she came to so sudden that she bit the bowl off the spoon.

MRS EYNSFORD HILL: [*startled*] Dear me!

LIZA: [*piling up the indictment*] What call would a woman with that strength in her have to die of influenza? What become of her new straw hat that should have come to me? Somebody pinched it; and what I say is, them as pinched it done her in.

MRS EYNSFORD HILL: What does doing her in mean?

HIGGINS: [*hastily*] Oh, thats the new small talk. To do a person in means to kill them.

MRS EYNSFORD HILL: [*to Eliza, horrified*] You surely dont believe that your aunt was killed?

LIZA: Do I not! Them she lived with would have killed her for a hat-pin, let alone a hat.

MRS EYNSFORD HILL: But it cant have been right for your father to pour spirits down her throat like that. It might have killed her.

LIZA: Not her. Gin was mother's milk to her. Besides, he'd poured so much down his own throat that he knew the good of it.

MRS EYNSFORD HILL: Do you mean that he drank?

LIZA: Drank! My word! Something chronic.

MRS EYNSFORD HILL: How dreadful for you!

LIZA: Not a bit. It never did him no harm what I could see. But then he did not keep it up regular. [*Cheerfully*] On the burst, as you might say, from time to time. And always more agreeable when he had a drop in. When he was out of work, my mother used to give him fourpenmce and tell him to go out and not come back until he'd drunk himself cheerful and loving-like. Theres lots of women has to make their husbands drunk to make them fit to live with. [*Now quite at her ease*] You see, it's like this. If a man has a bit of a conscience, it always takes him when he's sober; and then it makes him low-spirited. A drop of booze just takes that off and makes him happy. [*To Freddy, who is in convulsions of suppressed laughter*] Here! what are you sniggering at?

FREDDY: The new small talk. You do it so awfully well.

LIZA: If I was doing it proper, what was you laughing at? [*To Higgins*] Have I said anything I oughtnt?

MRS HIGGINS: [*interposing*] Not at all, Miss Doolittle.

LIZA: Well, thats a mercy, anyhow. [*Expansively*] What I always say is –

HIGGINS: [*rising and looking at his watch*] Ahem!

LIZA: [*looking round at him; taking the hint; and rising*] Well: I must go. [*They all rise. Freddy goes to the door.*] So pleased to have met you. Goodbye. [*She shakes hands with Mrs Higgins.*]

MRS HIGGINS: Goodbye.

LIZA: Goodbye, Colonel Pickering.

PICKERING: Goodbye, Miss Doolittle. [*They shake hands.*]

LIZA: [*nodding to the others*] Goodbye, all.

FREDDY: [*opening the door for her*] Are you walking across the Park, Miss Doolittle? If so –

LIZA: [*with perfectly elegant diction*] Walk! Not bloody likely.° [*Sensation.*] I am going in a taxi. [*She goes out.*]

After the other guests have departed, somewhat shaken, Higgins questions his mother about how the experiment has gone:

HIGGINS: [*eagerly*] Well? Is Eliza presentable? [*He swoops on his mother and drags her to the ottoman, where she sits down in Eliza's place with her son on her left. Pickering returns to his chair on her right.*]

MRS HIGGINS: You silly boy, of course she's not presentable. She's a triumph of your art and of her dressmaker's; but if you suppose for a moment that she doesnt give herself away in every sentence she utters, you must be perfectly cracked about her.

PICKERING: But dont you think something might be done? I mean something to eliminate the sanguinary element from her conversation.

MRS HIGGINS: Not as long as she is in Henry's hands.

HIGGINS: [*aggrieved*] Do you mean that my language is improper?

MRS HIGGINS: No, dearest: it would be quite proper – say on a canal barge; but it would not be proper for her at a garden party.

HIGGINS: [*deeply injured*] Well I must say –

PICKERING: [*interrupting him*] Come, Higgins: you must learn to know yourself. I havnt heard such language as yours since we used to review the volunteers in Hyde Park twenty years ago.

HIGGINS: [*sulkily*] Oh, well, if you say so, I suppose I dont always talk like a bishop.

MRS HIGGINS: [*quieting Henry with a touch*] Colonel Pickering: will you tell me what is the exact state of things in Wimpole Street?

PICKERING: [*cheerfully: as if this completely changed the subject*] Well, I have come to

° **Not bloody likely**: the phrase caused a theatrical sensation in 1912, when **bloody** was still a taboo word. In 1957 *My Fair Lady* had to substitute 'move your bloomin' arse!' to get a similar effect.

live there with Henry. We work together at my Indian Dialects; and we think it more convenient –

MRS HIGGINS: Quite so. I know all about that: it's an excellent arrangement. But where does this girl live?

HIGGINS: With us, of course. Where *should* she live?

MRS HIGGINS: But on what terms? Is she a servant? If not, what is she?

PICKERING: [*slowly*] I think I know what you mean, Mrs Higgins.

HIGGINS: Well, dash me if *I* do! Ive had to work at the girl every day for months to get her to her present pitch. Besides, she's useful. She knows where my things are, and remembers my appointments and so forth.

MRS HIGGINS: How does your housekeeper get on with her?

HIGGINS: Mrs Pearce? Oh, she's jolly glad to get so much taken off her hands; for before Eliza came, she used to have to find things and remind me of my appointments. But she's got some silly bee in her bonnet about Eliza. She keeps saying 'You dont think, sir': doesnt she, Pick?

PICKERING: Yes: thats the formula. 'You dont think, sir.' Thats the end of every conversation about Eliza.

HIGGINS: As if I ever stop thinking about the girl and her confounded vowels and consonants. I'm worn out, thinking about her, and watching her lips and her teeth and her tongue, not to mention her soul, which is the quaintest of the lot.

MRS HIGGINS: You certainly are a pretty pair of babies, playing with your live doll.

HIGGINS: Playing! The hardest job I ever tackled: make no mistake about that, mother. But you have no idea how frightfully interesting it is to take a human being and change her into a quite different human being by creating a new speech for her. It's filling up the deepest gulf that separates class from class and soul from soul.

PICKERING: [*drawing his chair closer to Mrs Higgins and bending over to her eagerly*] Yes: it's enormously interesting. I assure you, Mrs Higgins, we take Eliza very seriously. Every week every day almost – there is some new change. [*Closer again*] We keep records of every stage – dozens of gramophone disks and photographs –

HIGGINS: [*assailing her at the other ear*] Yes, by George: it's the most absorbing experiment I ever tackled. She regularly fills our lives up: doesnt she, Pick?

PICKERING: We're always talking Eliza.

HIGGINS: Teaching Eliza.

PICKERING: Dressing Eliza.

MRS HIGGINS: What!

HIGGINS: Inventing new Elizas . . .

* * * *

MRS HIGGINS: . . . Colonel Pickering: dont you realise that when Eliza walked into Wimpole Street, something walked in with her?

PICKERING: Her father did. But Henry soon got rid of him.

MRS HIGGINS: It would have been more to the point if her mother had. But as her mother didnt something else did.

PICKERING: But what?

MRS HIGGINS: [*unconsciously dating herself by the word*] A problem.

PICKERING: Oh I see. The problem of how to pass her off as a lady.

HIGGINS: I'll solve that problem. Ive half solved it already.

MRS HIGGINS: No, you two infinitely stupid male creatures: the problem of what is to be done with her afterwards.

HIGGINS: I dont see anything in that. She can go her own way, with all the advantages I have given her.

MRS HIGGINS: The advantages of that poor woman who was here just now!° The manners and habits that disqualify a fine lady from earning her own living without giving her a fine lady's income! Is that what you mean?

PICKERING: [*indulgently, being rather bored*] Oh, that will be all right, Mrs Higgins. [*He rises to go.*]

HIGGINS: [*rising also*] We'll find her some light employment.

PICKERING: She's happy enough. Dont you worry about her. Goodbye. [*He shakes hands as if he were consoling a frightened child, and makes for the door.*]

HIGGINS: Anyhow, theres no good bothering now. The thing's done. Goodbye, mother. [*He kisses her, and follows Pickering.*]

PICKERING: [*turning for a final consolation*] There are plenty of openings. We'll do whats right. Goodbye.

HIGGINS: [*to Pickering as they go out together*] Lets take her to the Shakespeare exhibition at Earls Court.

PICKERING: Yes: lets. Her remarks will be delicious.

HIGGINS: She'll mimic all the people for us when we get home.

PICKERING: Ripping. [*Both are heard laughing as they go downstairs.*]

MRS HIGGINS: [*rises with an impatient bounce, and returns to her work at the writing-table. She sweeps a litter of disarranged papers out of the way; snatches a sheet of paper from her stationery case; and tries resolutely to write. At the third time she gives it up; flings down her pen; grips the table angrily and exclaims*] Oh, men! men!! men!!!

The experiment is finally a triumphant success: at the ambassador's garden party Eliza is passed off, not just as a duchess, but as a princess – a Hungarian princess, since she speaks English too perfectly to be English-born. But after the ball Higgins, having won his bet, treats her with complacent indifference, and she, infuriated by his attitude and in despair over her future, throws his slippers at him and walks out. The next day (Act 5) they confront each other at his mother's house.

° **that poor woman . . . just now**: i.e. Mrs Eynsford Hill, a 'gentlewoman' in pathetically reduced circumstances.

HIGGINS: [*jumping up and walking about intolerantly*] Eliza: youre an idiot. I waste the treasures of my Miltonic mind by spreading them before you. Once for all, understand that I go my way and do my work without caring twopence what happens to either of us. I am not intimidated, like your father and your stepmother.° So you can come back or go to the devil: which you please.

LIZA: What am I to come back for?

HIGGINS: [*bouncing up on his knees on the ottoman and leaning over it to her*] For the fun of it. Thats why I took you on.

LIZA: [*with averted face*] And you may throw me out tomorrow if I dont do everything you want me to?

HIGGINS: Yes; and you may walk out tomorrow if I dont do everything you want me to.

LIZA: And live with my stepmother?

HIGGINS: Yes, or sell flowers.

LIZA: Oh! if I only could go back to my flower basket! I should be independent of both you and father and all the world! Why did you take my independence from me? Why did I give it up? I'm a slave now, for all my fine clothes.

HIGGINS: Not a bit. I'll adopt you as my daughter and settle money on you if you like. Or would you rather marry Pickering?

LIZA: [*looking fiercely round at him*] I wouldnt marry you if you asked me; and youre nearer my age than what he is.

HIGGINS: [*gently*] Than he is: not 'than what he is.'

LIZA: [*losing her temper and rising*] I'll talk as I like. Youre not my teacher now.

HIGGINS: [*reflectively*] I dont suppose Pickering would, though. He's as confirmed an old bachelor as I am.

LIZA: Thats not what I want; and dont you think it. Ive always had chaps enough wanting me that way. Freddy Hill writes to me twice and three times a day, sheets and sheets.

HIGGINS: [*disagreeably surprised*] Damn his impudence! [*He recoils and finds himself sitting on his heels.*]

LIZA: He has a right to if he likes, poor lad. And he does love me.

HIGGINS: [*getting off the ottoman*] You have no right to encourage him.

LIZA: Every girl has a right to be loved.

HIGGINS: What! By fools like that?

LIZA: Freddy's not a fool. And if he's weak and poor and wants me, may be he'd make me happier than my betters that bully me and dont want me.

HIGGINS: Can he make anything of you? Thats the point.

° **your father and your stepmother**: the story of Eliza's father, Alfred Doolittle, is a comic subplot which mirrors Eliza's. Doolittle is a cheerfully amoral, drunken dustman who called himself one of the 'undeserving poor'; but, having inherited a fortune, he is gloomily forced to behave according to the dictates of 'middle class morality', including marrying his mistress (Eliza's 'stepmother').

LIZA: Perhaps I could make something of him. But I never thought of us making anything of one another; and you never think of anything else. I only want to be natural.

HIGGINS: In short, you want me to be as infatuated about you as Freddy? Is that it?

LIZA: No I dont. Thats not the sort of feeling I want from you. And dont you be too sure of yourself or of me. I could have been a bad girl if I'd liked. Ive seen more of some things than you, for all your learning. Girls like me can drag gentlemen down to make love to them easy enough. And they wish each other dead the next minute.

HIGGINS: Of course they do. Then what in thunder are we quarrelling about?

LIZA: [*much troubled*] I want a little kindness. I know I'm a common ignorant girl, and you a book-learned gentleman; but I'm not dirt under your feet. What I done [*correcting herself*] what I did was not for the dresses and the taxis: I did it because we were pleasant together and I come – came – to care for you; not to want you to make love to me, and not forgetting the difference between us, but more friendly like.

HIGGINS: Well, of course. Thats just how I feel. And how Pickering feels. Eliza: youre a fool.

LIZA: Thats not a proper answer to give me [*she sinks on the chair at the writing-table in tears*].

HIGGINS: It's all youll get until you stop being a common idiot. If youre going to be a lady, youll have to give up feeling neglected if the men you know dont spend half their time snivelling over you and the other half giving you black eyes. If you cant stand the coldness of my sort of life, and the strain of it, go back to the gutter. Work til youre more a brute than a human being; and then cuddle and squabble and drink til you fall asleep. Oh, it's a fine life, the life of the gutter. It's real: it's warm: it's violent: you can feel it through the thickest skin: you can taste it and smell it without any training or any work. Not like Science and Literature and Classical Music and Philosophy and Art. You find me cold, unfeeling, selfish, dont you? Very well: be off with you to the sort of people you like. Marry some sentimental hog or other with lots of money, and a thick pair of lips to kiss you with and a thick pair of boots to kick you with. If you cant appreciate what youve got, youd better get what you can appreciate.

LIZA: [*desperate*] Oh, you are a cruel tyrant. I cant talk to you: you turn everything against me: I'm always in the wrong. But you know very well all the time that youre nothing but a bully. You know I cant go back to the gutter, as you call it, and that I have no real friends in the world but you and the Colonel. You know well I couldnt bear to live with a low common man after you two; and it's wicked and cruel of you to insult me by pretending I could. You think I must go back to Wimpole Street because I have nowhere else to go but father's. But dont you be too sure that you have me under your feet to be trampled on and talked down. I'll marry Freddy, I will, as soon as I'm able to support him.

HIGGINS: [*thunderstruck*] Freddy!!! that young fool! That poor devil who couldnt get a job as an errand boy even if he had the guts to try for it! Woman: do you not understand that I have made you a consort for a king?

LIZA: Freddy loves me: that makes him king enough for me. I dont want him to work: he wasnt brought up to it as I was. I'll go and be a teacher.

HIGGINS: Whatll you teach, in heaven's name?

LIZA: What you taught me. I'll teach phonetics.

HIGGINS: Ha! ha! ha!

LIZA: I'll offer myself as an assistant to that hairyfaced Hungarian.°

HIGGINS: [*rising in fury*] What! That impostor! that humbug! that toadying ignoramus! Teach him my methods! my discoveries! You take one step in his direction and I'll wring your neck. [*He lays hands on her.*] Do you hear?

LIZA: [*defiantly non-resistant*] Wring away. What do I care? I knew youd strike me some day. [*He lets her go, stamping with rage at having forgotten himself, and recoils so hastily that he stumbles back into his seat on the ottoman.*] Aha! Now I know how to deal with you. What a fool I was not to think of it before! You cant take away the knowledge you gave me. You said I had a finer ear than you. And I can be civil and kind to people, which is more than you can. Aha! [*Purposely dropping her aitches to annoy him*] Thats done you, Enry Iggins, it az. Now I dont care that [*snapping her fingers*] for your bullying and your big talk. I'll advertize it in the papers that your duchess is only a flower girl that you taught, and that she'll teach anybody to be a duchess just the same in six months for a thousand guineas. Oh, when I think of myself crawling under your feet and being trampled on and called names, when all the time I had only to lift up my finger to be as good as you, I could just kick myself.

HIGGINS: [*wondering at her*] You damned impudent slut, you! But it's better than snivelling; better than fetching slippers and finding spectacles, isnt it? [*Rising*] By George, Eliza, I said I'd make a woman of you; and I have. I like you like this.

LIZA: Yes: you turn round and make up to me now that I'm not afraid of you, and can do without you.

HIGGINS: Of course I do, you little fool. Five minutes ago you were like a millstone round my neck. Now youre a tower of strength: a consort battleship. You and I and Pickering will be three old bachelors instead of only two men and a silly girl.

Despite Higgins's arguments, Eliza leaves, and the play ends as Higgins 'roars with laughter' at the prospect of her marrying Freddy. Shaw adds a prose epilogue to explain what happens next.

° **that hairyfaced hungarian**: Nepommuck, a former pupil of Higgins, who uses his methods to detect (and blackmail) social imposters.

The rest of the story need not be shewn° in action, and indeed, would hardly need telling if our imaginations were not so enfeebled by their lazy dependence on the ready-mades and reach-me-downs of the ragshop in which Romance keeps its stock of 'happy endings' to misfit all stories. Now, the history of Eliza Doolittle, though called a romance because the transfiguration it records seems exceedingly improbable, is common enough. Such transfigurations have been achieved by hundreds of resolutely ambitious young women since Nell Gwynne° set them the example by playing queens and fascinating kings in the theatre in which she began by selling oranges. Nevertheless, people in all directions have assumed, for no other reason than that she became the heroine of a romance, that she must have married the hero of it. This is unbearable, not only because her little drama, if acted on such a thoughtless assumption, must be spoiled, but because the true sequel is patent to anyone with a sense of human nature in general, and of feminine instinct in particular.

Shaw argues that strong people are naturally attracted to those weaker than themselves, not stronger.

Eliza has no use for the foolish romantic tradition that all women love to be mastered, if not actually bullied and beaten . . . This being the state of human affairs, what is Eliza fairly sure to do when she is placed between Freddy and Higgins? Will she look forward to a lifetime of fetching Higgins's slippers or to a lifetime of Freddy fetching hers? There can be no doubt about the answer. Unless Freddy is biologically repulsive to her, and Higgins biologically attractive to a degree that overwhelms all her other instincts, she will, if she marries either of them, marry Freddy.

And that is just what Eliza did.

Shaw goes on to describe the fairly successful marriage between Eliza and Freddy, and how, with financial aid from Higgins and Pickering, they eventually make a precarious success of their florist's business. He concludes:

[Eliza] is immensely interested in [Higgins]. She even has secret mischievous moments in which she wishes she could get him alone, on a desert island, away from all ties and with nobody else in the world to consider, and just drag him off his pedestal and see him making love like any common man. We all have private imaginations of that sort. But when it comes to business, to the life that she really leads as distinguished from the life of dreams and fancies, she likes Freddy and she likes the Colonel; and she does not like Higgins and Mr Doolittle. Galatea

° **shewn**: shown (Shaw's old-fashioned spelling).

° **Nell Gwynne**: a Restoration actress who started out selling oranges in the theatre, and became Charles II's mistress.

never does quite like Pygmalion: his relation to her is too godlike to be altogether agreeable.

P25 H.D., 'Pygmalion', 1917°

On H.D., see headnote to **O39**.

1

Shall I let myself be caught
in my own light?
shall I let myself be broken
in my own heat?
or shall I cleft the rock as of old
and break my own fire
with its surface?

does this fire thwart me
and my craft,
or does my work cloud this light?
which is the god,
which is the stone
the god takes for his use?

2

Which am I,
the stone or the power
that lifts the rock from the earth?
am I the master of this fire,
is this fire my own strength?

am I master of this
swirl upon swirl of light?
have I made it as in old times
I made the gods from the rock?

have I made this fire from myself?
or is this arrogance?
is this fire a god
that seeks me in the dark?

° from *Collected Poems 1912–1944*, ed. Louis L. Martz, New York: New Directions, 1983, pp. 48–50.

3

I made image upon image for my use,
I made image upon image, for the grace
of Pallas was my flint
and my help was Hephaestos.

I made god upon god
step from the cold rock,
I made the gods less than men
for I was a man and they my work;

and now what is it that has come to pass?
for fire has shaken my hand,
my strivings are dust.

4

Now what is it that has come to pass?
over my head, fire stands,
my marbles are alert:

each of the gods, perfect,
cries out from a perfect throat:
you are useless,
no marble can bind me,
no stone suggest.

5

They have melted into the light
and I am desolate;
they have melted;
each from his plinth,
each one departs;

they have gone;
what agony can express my grief?

each from his marble base
has stepped into the light
and my work is for naught.

6

Now am I the power
that has made this fire
as of old I made the gods
start from the rocks?
am I the god?

or does this fire carve me
for its use?

P26 Robert Graves, 'Pygmalion to Galatea', 1925, and 'Galatea and Pygmalion', 1938°

Robert Graves, 1895–1985, English poet, novelist, critic, and translator, resident for much of his life on the Spanish island of Mallorca. Graves is a major twentieth-century poet, whose work is largely based on a personal mythology and theory of poetry expounded in *The White Goddess* (1948); he also wrote novels on historical and mythological themes (*I, Claudius*; *King Jesus*; *Hercules, My Shipmate*), translated several Latin authors, and compiled a readable though eccentric summary of *The Greek Myths* (1955). These two poems present sharply opposed views of the Pygmalion myth.

(a) Pygmalion to Galatea

Pygmalion spoke and sang to Galatea
Who keeping to her pedestal in doubt
Of these new qualities, blood, bones and breath,
Nor yet relaxing her accustomed poise,
Her Parian° rigour, though alive and burning,
Heard out his melody:

'As you are woman, so be lovely:
Fine hair afloat and eyes irradiate,
Long crafty fingers, fearless carriage,
And body lissom, neither small nor tall;
So be lovely!

'As you are lovely, so be merciful:
Yet must your mercy abstain from pity:
Prize your self-honour, leaving me with mine:
Love if you will: or stay stone-frozen.
So be merciful!

'As you are merciful, so be constant:
I ask not you should mask your comeliness,
Yet keep our love aloof and strange,
Keep it from gluttonous eyes, from stairway gossip.
So be constant!

° from (a) *Poems (1914–26)*, London: Heinemann, 1927, pp. 201–2; (b) *Collected Poems*, London: Cassell, 1938, p. 109. Reprinted by permission of Carcanet Press Ltd.

° **Parian**: i.e. marble.

'As you are constant, so be various:
Love comes to sloth without variety.
Within the limits of our fair-paved garden
Let fancy like a Proteus range and change.
So be various!

'As you are various, so be woman:
Graceful in going as well armed in doing.
Be witty, kind, enduring, unsubjected:
Without you I keep heavy house.
So be woman!

'As you are woman, so be lovely:
As you are lovely, so be various,
Merciful as constant, constant as various.
So be mine, as I yours for ever.'

Then as the singing ceased and the lyre ceased,
Down stepped proud Galatea with a sigh.
'Pygmalion, as you woke me from the stone,
So shall I you from bonds of sullen flesh.
Lovely I am, merciful I shall prove:
Woman I am, constant as various,
Not marble-hearted but your own true love.
Give me an equal kiss, as I kiss you.'

(b) Galatea and Pygmalion

Galatea, whom his furious chisel
From Parian stone had by greed enchanted,
Fulfilled, so they say, Pygmalion's longings:
Stepped from the pedestal on which she stood,
Bare in his bed laid her down, lubricious,
With low responses to his drunken raptures,
Enroyalled his body with her demon blood.

Alas, Pygmalion had so well plotted
The art-perfection of his woman monster
That schools of eager connoisseurs beset
Her famous person with perennial suit;
Whom she (a judgement on the jealous artist)
Admitted rankly to a comprehension
Of themes that crowned her own, not his repute.

P27 C. Day Lewis, 'The Perverse', 1928°

Cecil Day Lewis, 1904–72, British poet, novelist, and translator, born in Ireland but raised in England; a communist and a member of the left-wing 'Auden group' in the 1930s, he later became more conservative, and was Poet Laureate 1968–72; his translation of Virgil (see **O2**) is among his best work.

Love being denied, he turned in his despair
And couched° with the Absolute a summer through;
He got small joy of the skimpy bedfellow –
Formulas gave no body to lay bare.

His pretty came among the primroses
With open breast for him. No more denied
Seemed no more ideal. He was unsatisfied
Till he strained her flesh to thin philosophies.

Love being remote, dreams at the midnight gave
A chill enchanted image of her flesh;
Such phantoms but inflamed his waking wish
For the quick° beauty no dream-chisels grave.

Now she was won. But our Pygmalion –
If so he could have graven like a kiss
On Time's blank shoulder that hour of loveliness
– He would have changed her body into stone.

P28 Angela Carter, from 'The Loves of Lady Purple', 1974°

Angela Carter, 1940–1992, English novelist and short story writer, whose works include *The Magic Toyshop* (1967), *The Bloody Chamber* (1979), and *Wise Children* (1991). Often classed as 'magical realism', Carter's tales take place in what she calls in this story 'a no-man's-limbo between the real and that which . . . seems to be real'; baroquely ornate in style, coolly detached in tone, they draw knowingly on a wide range of earlier myths, folktales, and literary motifs. 'The Loves of Lady Purple', the tale of a puppetmaster and his doll, does not explicitly

° from *The Complete Poems*, London: Sinclair-Stevenson, 1992.

° **couched**: slept.

° **quick**: living.

° from 'The Loves of Lady Purple', in *Fireworks*, London: Quartet Books, 1974.

refer to Pygmalion, but that story is clearly one of its inspirations – along with those of Frankenstein, Dracula, and Pinocchio.

Inside the pink-striped booth of the Asiatic Professor only the marvellous existed and there was no such thing as daylight.

The puppet master is always dusted with a little darkness. In direct relation to his skill he propagates the most bewildering enigmas for, the more lifelike his marionettes, the more godlike his manipulations and the more radical the symbiosis between inarticulate doll and articulating fingers. The puppeteer speculates in a no-man's-limbo between the real and that which, although we know very well it is not, nevertheless seems to be real. He is the intermediary between us, his audience, the living, and they, the dolls, the undead, who cannot live at all and yet who mimic the living in every detail since, though they cannot speak or weep, still they project those signals of signification we instantly recognize as language.

The master of marionettes vitalizes inert stuff with the dynamics of his self. The sticks dance, make love, pretend to speak and, finally, personate death; yet, so many Lazaruses out of their graves they spring again in time for the next performance and no worms drip from their noses nor dust clogs their eyes. All complete, they once again offer their brief imitations of men and women with an exquisite precision which is all the more disturbing because we know it to be false; and so this art, if viewed theologically, may, perhaps, be blasphemous.

Although he was only a poor travelling showman, the Asiatic Professor had become a consummate virtuoso of puppetry. He transported his collapsible theatre, the cast of his single drama and a variety of properties in a horse-drawn cart and, after he played his play in many beautiful cities which no longer exist, such as Shanghai, Constantinople and St Petersburg, he and his small entourage arrived at last in a country in Middle Europe where the mountains sprout jags as sharp and unnatural as those a child outlines with his crayon, a dark, superstitious Transylvania where they wreathed suicides with garlic, pierced them through the heart with stakes and buried them at crossroads while warlocks continually practised rites of immemorial beastliness in the forests.

. . . [The aged Professor] revealed his passions through a medium other than himself and this was his heroine, the puppet, Lady Purple.

She was the Queen of Night. There were glass rubies in her head for eyes and her ferocious teeth, carved out of mother o' pearl, were always on show for she had a permanent smile. Her face was as white as chalk because it was covered with the skin of supplest white leather which also clothed her torso, jointed limbs and complication of extremities. Her beautiful hands seemed more like weapons because her nails were so long, five inches of pointed tin enamelled scarlet, and she wore a wig of black hair arranged in a chignon° more heavily elaborate than

° **chignon**: roll or knot of hair at the back of the head.

any human neck could have endured. This monumental chevelure° was stuck through with many brilliant pins tipped with pieces of broken mirror so that, every time she moved, she cast a multitude of scintillating reflections which danced about the theatre like mice of light. Her clothes were all of deep, dark, slumbrous colours – profound pinks, crimson and the vibrating purple with which she was synonymous, a purple the colour of blood in a love suicide.

She must have been the masterpiece of a long-dead, anonymous artisan and yet she was nothing but a curious structure until the Professor touched her strings, for it was he who filled her with necromantic vigour. He transmitted to her an abundance of the life he himself seemed to possess so tenuously and, when she moved, she did not seem so much a cunningly simulated woman as a monstrous goddess, at once preposterous and magnificent, who transcended the notion she was dependent on his hands and appeared wholly real and yet entirely other. Her actions were not so much an imitation as a distillation and intensification of those of a born woman and so she could become the quintessence of eroticism, for no woman born would have dared to be so blatantly seductive.

The Professor allowed no one else to touch her. He himself looked after her costumes and jewellery. When the show was over, he placed his marionette in a specially constructed box and carried her back to the lodging house where he and his children shared a room, for she was too precious to be left in the flimsy theatre and, besides, he could not sleep unless she lay beside him.

Carter describes the luridly melodramatic action of the Professor's play: *The Notorious Amours of Lady Purple, the Shameless Oriental Venus.* Lady Purple begins her career by murdering her family, burning down their home, and taking up residence at the local brothel. She becomes a famous courtesan, dominatrix, and vamp, 'the image of irresistible evil', who drains her lovers of wealth and health and, when she is bored with them, murders them. Her pyrotechnical career ends 'in ashes, desolation, and silence': in 'the final scene of her desperate decline', wandering the seashore in rags,

she practised extraordinary necrophilies on the bloated corpses the sea tossed contemptuously at her feet for her dry rapacity had become entirely mechanical and still she repeated her former actions though she herself was utterly other. She abrogated her humanity. She became a marionette herself, herself her own replica, the dead yet moving image of the shameless Oriental Venus.

. . . The rough audience received their copeck's worth of sensation and filed out into a fairground which still roared like a playful tiger with life. The foundling girl put away her samisen° and swept out the booth while the nephew set the stage afresh for next day's matinee. Then the Professor noticed Lady Purple had

° **chevelure**: hairdo.

° **samisen**: Japanese stringed instrument.

ripped a seam in the drab shroud she wore in the final act. Chattering to himself with displeasure, he undressed her as she swung idly, this way and that way, from her anchored strings and then he sat down on a wooden property stool on the stage and plied his needle like a good housewife. The task was more difficult than it seemed at first for the fabric was also torn and required an embroidery of darning so he told his assistants to go home together to the lodging house and let him finish his task alone.

A small oil-lamp hanging from a nail at the side of the stage cast an insufficient but tranquil light. The white puppet glimmered fitfully through the mists which crept into the theatre from the night outside through all the chinks and gaps in the tarpaulin and now began to fold their chiffon drapes around her as if to decorously conceal her or else to render her more translucently enticing. The mist softened her painted smile a little and her head dangled to one side. In the last act, she wore a loose, black wig, the locks of which hung down as far as her softly upholstered flanks, and the ends of her hair flickered with her random movements, creating upon the white blackboard of her back one of those fluctuating optical effects which make us question the veracity of our vision. As he often did when he was alone with her, the Professor chatted to her in his native language, rattling away an intimacy of nothings, of the weather, of his rheumatism, of the unpalatability and expense of the region's coarse, black bread, while the small winds took her as their partner in a scarcely perceptible valse triste° and the mist grew minute by minute thicker, more pallid and more viscous.

The old man finished his mending. He rose and, with a click or two of his old bones, he went to put the forlorn garment neatly on its green-room hanger beside the glowing, winy purple gown splashed with rosy peonies, sashed with carmine, that she wore for her appalling dance. He was about to lay her, naked, in her coffin-shaped case and carry her back to their chilly bedroom when he paused. He was seized with the childish desire to see her again in all her finery once more that night. He took her dress off its hanger and carried it to where she drifted, at nobody's volition but that of the wind. As he put her clothes on her, he murmured to her as if she were a little girl for the vulnerable flaccidity of her arms and legs made a six-foot baby of her.

'There, there, my pretty; this arm here, that's right! Oops a daisy, easy does it . . .'

Then he tenderly took off her penitential wig and clucked his tongue to see how defencelessly bald she was beneath it. His arms cracked under the weight of her immense chignon and he had to stretch up on tiptoe to set it in place because, since she was as large as life, she was rather taller than he. But then the ritual of apparelling was over and she was complete again.

Now she was dressed and decorated, it seemed her dry wood had all at once put out an entire springtime of blossoms for the old man alone to enjoy. She

° **valse triste**: sad waltz.

could have acted as the model for the most beautiful of women, the image of that woman whom only a man's memory and imagination can devise, for the lamplight fell too mildly to sustain her air of arrogance and so gently it made her long nails look as harmless as ten fallen petals. The Professor had a curious habit; he always used to kiss his doll good night.

A child kisses its toy before she pretends it sleeps although, even though she is only a child, she knows its eyes are not constructed to close so it will always be a sleeping beauty no kiss will waken. One in the grip of savage loneliness might kiss the face he sees before him in the mirror for want of any other face to kiss. These are kisses of the same kind; they are the most poignant of caresses, for they are too humble and too despairing to wish or seek for any response.

Yet, in spite of the Professor's sad humility, his chapped and withered mouth opened on hot, wet, palpitating flesh.

The sleeping wood had wakened. Her pearl teeth crashed against his with the sound of cymbals and her warm, fragrant breath blew around him like an Italian gale. Across her suddenly moving face flashed a whole kaleidoscope of expression, as though she were running instantaneously through the entire repertory of human feeling, practising, in an endless moment of time, all the scales of emotion as if they were music. Crushing vines, her arms, curled about the Professor's delicate apparatus of bone and skin with the insistent pressure of an actuality by far more authentically living than that of his own, time-desiccated flesh. Her kiss emanated from the dark country where desire is objectified and lives. She gained entry into the world by a mysterious loophole in its metaphysics and, during her kiss, she sucked his breath from his lungs so that her own bosom heaved with it.

So, unaided, she began her next performance with an apparent improvisation which was, in reality, only a variation upon a theme. She sank her teeth into his throat and drained him. He did not have the time to make a sound. When he was empty, he slipped straight out of her embrace down to her feet with a dry rustle, as of a cast armful of dead leaves, and there he sprawled on the floorboards, as empty, useless and bereft of meaning as his own tumbled shawl.

She tugged impatiently at the strings which moored her and out they came in bunches from her head, her arms and her legs. She stripped them off her fingertips and stretched out her long, white hands, flexing and unflexing them again and again. For the first time for years, or, perhaps, for ever, she closed her bloodstained teeth thankfully, for her cheeks still ached from the smile her maker had carved into the stuff of her former face. She stamped her elegant feet to make the new blood flow more freely there.

Unfurling and unravelling itself, her hair leaped out of its confinements of combs, cords and lacquer to root itself back into her scalp like cut grass bounding out of the stack and back again into the ground. First, she shivered with pleasure to feel the cold, for she realized she was experiencing a physical sensation; then either she remembered or else she believed she remembered that the sensation of cold was not a pleasurable one so she knelt and, drawing off the old man's shawl, wrapped it carefully about herself. Her every motion was instinct with a wonderful, reptilian liquidity. The mist outside now seemed to rush like a tide into the booth and broke against her in white breakers so that she looked like a baroque figurehead, lone survivor of a shipwreck, thrown up on a shore by the tide.

But whether she was renewed or newly born, returning to life or becoming alive, awakening from a dream or coalescing into the form of a fantasy generated in her wooden skull by the mere repetition so many times of the same invariable actions, the brain beneath the reviving hair contained only the scantiest notion of the possibilities now open to it. All that had seeped into the wood was the notion that she might perform the forms of life not so much by the skill of another as by her own desire that she did so, and she did not possess enough equipment to comprehend the complex circularity of the logic which inspired her for she had only been a marionette. But, even if she could not perceive it, she could not escape the tautological paradox in which she was trapped; had the marionette all the time parodied the living or was she, now living, to parody her own performance as a marionette? Although she was now manifestly a woman, young and beautiful, the leprous whiteness of her face gave her the appearance of a corpse animated solely by demonic will.

Deliberately, she knocked the lamp down from its hook on the wall. A puddle of oil spread at once on the boards of the stage. A little flame leaped across the fuel and immediately began to eat the curtains. She went down the aisle between the benches to the little ticket booth. Already, the stage was an inferno and the corpse of the Professor tossed this way and that on an uneasy bed of fire. But she did not look behind her after she slipped out into the fairground although soon the theatre was burning like a paper lantern ignited by its own candle.

Now it was so late that the sideshows, gingerbread stalls and liquor booths were locked and shuttered and only the moon, half obscured by drifting cloud, gave out a meagre, dirty light, which sullied and deformed the flimsy pasteboard facades, so the place, deserted, with curds of vomit, the refuse of revelry, underfoot, looked utterly desolate.

She walked rapidly past the silent roundabouts, accompanied only by the fluctuating mists, towards the town, making her way like a homing pigeon, out of logical necessity, to the single brothel it contained.

P29 Michael Longley, 'Ivory and Water', 1994°

Michael Longley, born 1939, Northern Irish poet, and administrator for the Arts Council of Northern Ireland. 'Ivory and Water', which fuses the Pygmalion story with Ovid's descriptions of the metamorphoses of Cyane and Arethusa into water (*Metamorphoses*, book 5), first appeared in the anthology *After Ovid* (1994).

° from *The Ghost Orchid*, London: Jonathan Cape, 1995, p. 15. Reprinted by permission of the author and Jonathan Cape.

Ivory and Water

If as a lonely bachelor who disapproves of women
You carve the perfect specimen out of snow-white ivory
And fall in love with your masterpiece and make love to her
(Or try to), stroking, fondling, whispering, kissing, nervous
In case you bruise ivory like flesh with prodding fingers,
And bring sea-shells, shiny pebbles, song-birds, colourful wild
Flowers, amber beads, orchids, beach-balls as her presents,
And put real women's clothes, wedding rings, ear-rings, long
Necklaces, a brassière on the statue, then undress her
And lay her in your bed, her head on the feathery pillows
As if to sleep like a girlfriend, your dream may come true
And she warms and softens and you are kissing actual lips
And she blushes as she takes you in, the light of her eyes,
And her veins pulse under your thumb to the end of the dream
When she breaks out in a cold sweat that trickles into pools
And drips from her hair dissolving it and her fingers and toes,
Watering down her wrists, shoulders, rib-cage, breasts until
There is nothing left of her for anyone to hug or hold.

OTHER VERSIONS OF PYGMALION

Medieval

Anonymous. *Pearl*, lines 749–52.
Chaucer, Geoffrey. *The Canterbury Tales*: 'Physician's Tale', lines 13–15.

Renaissance

Cowley, Abraham. 'The Gazers', in *Works*, Cambridge, 1905–6.
Crompton, Hugh. 'Epigram 20: Pygmalion', in *Poems*, London, 1657.
Daniel, Samuel. 'Sonnet 13' ('Behold what hap Pygmalion had . . .') from *Sonnets to Delia*, London, 1592.
Davies, John (of Hereford). 'Epigram 72: Against Pygmalion's Indiscretion', in *The Scourge of Folly*, 1611.
Fulwood, William. *The Enemy of Idleness: Teaching How to Indite Epistles*, London, 1568.
Garter, Bernard. *A Strife between Apelles and Pygmalion*, London, [1566?].
Greville, Fulke. *Caelica* (1633), stanza 25, in *Poems and Dramas*, Edinburgh, 1939.
Griffin, Bartholomew. 'Sonnet 25' ('Compare me to Pygmalion with his image sotted'), in *Fidessa, More Chaste Than Kind*, London, 1596.
Guilpin, Everard. 'Satyra Secunda', from *Skialetheia*, London, 1598.
M,T. (Thomas Middleton?). *Micro-Cynicon*, London, 1599, Book 1, Satire 5.

Marston, John. 'Satire 6: Hem Nosti'n', in *The Scourge of Villainy*, London, 1598. (Marston's defence of the *Metamorphosis*.)

Strode, William. 'Song, A Strange Gentlewoman Passing by his Window', from *The Poetical Works of William Strode*, ed. Bertram Dobell, London, 1907.

Tomkis, Thomas. *Lingua, or The Combat of the Tongue and the Five Senses for Superiority*, London, 1607.

Restoration and eighteenth century

Behn, Aphra. 'To Damon', lines 87–8, in *Lycidus*, London, 1688.

Brome, Alexander. 'The Libertine', lines 36–7, in *Songs and Other Poems*, 1661.

Cotton, Charles. 'The Picture', in *Poems on Several Occasions*, 1689.

Dryden, John. *Secret Love, or The Maiden Queen*, London, 1668, act 4.

Flecknoe, Richard. *The Demoiselles à la Mode*, London, 1667, act 1, scene 3.

Pitt, Christopher. 'The Fable of the Young Man and His Cat', in *Poems and Translations*, London, 1727.

Seward, Anna. 'Ode to Poetic Fancy', in *Poetical Works*, London, 1810, lines 21–2.

Thompson, James. *The Castle of Indolence*, London, 1748, lines 113–14.

Nineteenth century

Bennett, William Cox. 'Pygmalion', in *Queen Eleanor's Vengeance and Other Poems*, London, 1857.

Byron, Lord. *Don Juan* (1819–24), canto 6, stanza 43.

Coleridge, Ernest Hartley. 'Pygmalion's Bride', in *Poems*, London, 1898.

De Tabley, Lord (John Byrne Leicester Warren). 'Pygmalion', in *Ballads and Metrical Sketches*, London, 1860.

Ellison, Henry (as Henry Browne). 'Pygmalion Reversed', in *Stones from the Quarry*, London, 1875.

Gill, William. *Adonis* (1884), in Gerald Boardman, *American Musical Comedy: From 'Adonis' to 'Dreamgirls'*, New York: Oxford University Press, 1982.

Hazlitt, William. *Liber Amoris, or The New Pygmalion*, London, 1863.

Hickey, Emily. 'Sonnet' ('I was Pygmalion's handiwork'), in *A Sculptor and Other Poems*, London, 1881.

Mackay, Eric G. (as George Eric Lancaster). 'Pygmalion in Cyprus', in *Pygmalion in Cyprus and Other Poems*, London, 1880.

Mallock, W. H. 'Pygmalion to His Statue, Become His Wife' (1869), in *Poems*, London, 1880.

Moore, T. Sturge. 'Pygmalion', in *The Vine Dresser and Other Poems*, London, 1889.

Nagle, Mary. 'Pygmalion', in *Pygmalion . . . and Other Poems*, by a Reverend Sister of the Order of Jesus and Mary, Watertown, N.Y., 1887.

Rhoades, James. 'Pygmalion's Statue', in *Poems*, London, 1870.

Scott, William Bell. 'Pygmalion', in *Poems*, London, 1875.

Sill, Edward Rowland. 'The Lost Magic' (1883), from *Poetical Works*, Boston, 1906.
Tennyson, Frederick. 'Cyprus Pygmalion', in *Daphne and Other Poems*, London, 1891.
Woolner, Thomas. *Pygmalion*, London, 1881.

Twentieth century

Brodsky, Joseph. 'Galatea Encore', in *To Urania: Selected Poems 1965–1985*, London: Penguin, 1988.
Conquest, Robert. 'Galatea', in *Between Mars and Venus*, London: Hutchinson, 1962.
Hope, A. D. 'Pygmalion' (1955), in *Collected Poems 1930–1965*, Sydney, 1966.
Kavanagh, Patrick. 'Pygmalion', in *Collected Poems*, London: McGibbon and Kee, 1964.
Lerner, Alan Jay. *My Fair Lady* (music by Frederick Loewe), New York: Coward-McCann, 1956.
Low, Benjamin R. C. 'Pygmalion to Galatea', in *Broken Music*, New York: Dutton, 1920.
Lucas, F. L. 'Pygmalion to Galatea', in *Marionettes*, Cambridge: Cambridge University Press, 1930.
Powers, Richard. *Galatea 2.2*, New York: Farrar Straus, 1995.
Rosenthal, Robert, and Lenore Jacobson. *Pygmalion in the classroom; teacher expectation and pupils' intellectual development*, New York: Holt Rinehart, 1968.
Russell, Willy. *Educating Rita*, London: French, 1981.
Sisson, C. H. 'Metamorphoses' (1961), section iii, in *Metamorphoses*, London: Methuen, 1968.

BIBLIOGRAPHY

On myth and the classical tradition

Allen, Don Cameron (1970) *Mysteriously Meant: The Rediscovery of Pagan Symbolism and Allegorical Interpretation in the Renaissance*, Baltimore: Johns Hopkins University Press.

Barkan, Leonard (1986) *Metamorphosis and the Pursuit of Paganism*, New Haven: Yale University Press.

Belli, Angela (1968) *Ancient Greek Myths and Modern Drama: A Study in Continuity*, New York: New York University Press.

Boswell, Jeanetta (1982) *Past Ruined Ilion. . .: A Bibliography of English and American Literature Based on Greco-Roman Mythology*, Metuchen, NJ: Scarecrow Press.

Brooks, Robert A. (1991) *Gods and Heroes of Ancient Greece*, wallchart, Chapel Hill, NC: University of North Carolina Press.

Bush, Douglas (1932) *Mythology and the Renaissance Tradition in English Poetry*, Minneapolis: University of Minnesota Press.

—— (1937/1969) *Mythology and the Romantic Tradition in English Poetry*, Cambridge, MA., 1937; reissued with new preface, 1969.

Coupe, Laurence (1997) *Myth*, New Critical Idiom, London: Routledge.

Feder, Lilian (1971) *Ancient Myth in Modern Poetry*, Princeton: Princeton University Press.

Frazer, Sir James George (1922) *The Golden Bough: A Study in Magic and Religion*, Abridged Edition, London: Macmillan.

Gantz, Timothy (1993) *Early Greek Myth: A Guide to Literary and Artistic Sources*, Baltimore: Johns Hopkins University Press.

Grant, Michael (1963) *Myths of the Greeks and Romans*, London: Weidenfeld and Nicholson.

Graves, Robert (1960) *The Greek Myths*, 2 vols, rev. edn, Harmondsworth: Penguin.

Griffin, Jasper (1986a) *The Mirror of Myth: Classical Themes and Variations*, London: Faber.

—— (1986b) 'Greek Myth and Hesiod', in *The Oxford History of the Classical World*, ed. John Boardman, Jasper Griffin, and Oswyn Murray, Oxford: Oxford University Press, pp. 78–98.

Highet, Gilbert (1949) *The Classical Tradition: Greek and Roman Influences on Western Literature*, Oxford: Clarendon Press.

Jenkyns, Richard (1980) *The Victorians and Ancient Greece*, Oxford: Blackwell.

Kirk, G. S. (1974) *The Nature of Greek Myths*, London: Penguin.

Martindale, Charles (1988) *Ovid Renewed: Ovidian Influences on Literature and Art from the Middle Ages to the Twentieth Century*, Cambridge: Cambridge University Press.

Mayerson, Philip (1971) *Classical Mythology in Literature, Art, and Music*, Glenview, IL: Scott, Foresman.
Morford, Mark P. O., and Robert J. Lenardon (1991) *Classical Mythology*, 4th edn, New York: Longman.
Norton, Dan S., and Peters Rushton (1955) *Classical Myths in English Literature*, New York: Rinehart.
Radice, Betty (1973) *Who's Who in the Ancient World*, London: Penguin.
Reid, Jane Davidson (1993) *The Oxford Guide to Classical Mythology in the Arts, 1390–1990s*, 2 vols, New York: Oxford University Press.
Ruthven, K. K. (1976) *Myth*, The Critical Idiom, London: Methuen.
Seznec, Jean (1953) *The Survival of the Pagan Gods: The Mythological Tradition and its Place in Renaissance Humanism and Art*, trans. B. F. Sessions, Princeton: Princeton University Press.
Starnes, DeWitt T., and Ernest William Talbert (1955) *Classical Myth and Legend in Renaissance Dictionaries*, Chapel Hill: University of North Carolina Press.
Turner, Frank (1981) *The Greek Heritage in Victorian Britain*, New Haven: Yale University Press, ch. 3, 'Greek mythology and religion', 77–134.
Vickery, John B. (1973) *The Literary Impact of 'The Golden Bough'*, Princeton: Princeton University Press.
Zwerdling, Alex (1964) 'The Mythographers and the Romantic Revival of Greek Myth', *PMLA* 79, 447–56.

On Orpheus

Friedman, John Block (1970) *Orpheus in the Middle Ages*, Cambridge, MA: Harvard University Press.
Guthrie, W. K. C. (1966) *Orpheus and Greek Religion: A Study of the Orphic Movement*, rev. edn, New York: Norton.
Henry, Elizabeth (1992) *Orpheus with his Lute: Poetry and the Renewal of Life*, Carbondale: Southern Illinois University Press.
Segal, Charles (1989) *Orpheus: The Myth of the Poet*, Baltimore: Johns Hopkins University Press.
Sewell, Elizabeth (1971) *The Orphic Voice: Poetry and Natural History*, New York: Harper and Row.
Strauss, Walter A. (1971) *Descent and Return: The Orphic Theme in Modern Literature*, Cambridge, MA: Harvard University Press.
Warden, John (ed.) (1982) *Orpheus: The Metamorphosis of a Myth*, Toronto: University of Toronto Press.
West, M. L. (1983) *The Orphic Poems*, Oxford: Clarendon Press.

On Adonis

Atallah, Wahib (1966) *Adonis dans la littérature et l'art grecs*, Paris: Klinksieck.
Detienne, Marcel (1977) *The Gardens of Adonis: Spices in Greek Mythology*, trans. Janet Lloyd, Hassocks: Harvester, 1977.
Reed, Joseph D. (1995) 'The Sexuality of Adonis', *Classical Antiquity*, 14, 317–47.
Tuzet, Hélène (1987) *Mort et résurrection d'Adonis: étude de l'évolution d'un mythe*, Paris: Corti.

Winkler, John J. (1990) *The Constraints of Desire: The Anthropology of Sex and Gender in Ancient Greece*, New York: Routledge.

On Pygmalion

Carr, J. L. (1960) 'Pygmalion and the *Philosophes*', *Journal of the Warburg and Courtauld Institutes*, 13, 239–55.
Dinter, Annagret (1979) *Der Pygmalion-Stoff in der europäischen Literatur: Rezeptionsgeschichte einer Ovid-Fabel*, Heidelberg: Winter.
Miller, Jane (1988) 'Some Versions of Pygmalion', in Martindale (1988), 205–14.
Reinhold, Meyer (1971) 'The naming of Pygmalion's animated statue', *Classical Journal*, 66, 316–19.

Other works cited

Baxter, James K. (1967) *The Man on the Horse*, Dunedin: University of Otago Press.
Holroyd, Michael (1989) *Bernard Shaw*, vol. 2: *The Pursuit of Power*, London: Chatto & Windus.
Homer. *The Iliad*, trans. Robert Fitzgerald, Everyman's Library, London, 1992.
Larkin, Philip (1983) *Required Writing: Miscellaneous Pieces 1955–1982*, London: Faber.
Lewis, C. S. (1954) *English Literature in the Sixteenth Century, Excluding Drama*, Oxford: Oxford University Press.
Shakespeare, William. *William Shakespeare: The Complete Works*, ed. Stanley Wells and Gary Taylor, Oxford: Oxford University Press, 1986. (Shakespeare references are keyed to this edition.)
Tucker, Susie I. (1967) *Protean Shape: A Study in Eighteenth-Century Vocabulary and Usage*, London: Athlone Press.
Virgil. *The Aeneid*, trans. Robert Fitzgerald, Everyman's Library, London, 1992.

INDEX OF MYTHOLOGICAL NAMES

This index covers the mythological figures mentioned in Chapters 2 and 3, and is designed to allow these chapters to be used like a mythological dictionary. Only the more important references are included.